Footprint Handbook
Peru
ROBERT & DAISY KUNSTAETTER
BEN BOX

This is
Peru

Ever since Hiram Bingham first described Machu Picchu as a "wonderland", the fabled Inca city has become one of the most recognized images in the world, so much so that it virtually represents Peru, acting as a magnet for every visitor. But it's not even half the story. Peru has more ancient archaeological sites than any other country in South America, and more are being found all the time. Many are still off the beaten path and offer the more intrepid visitor the thrill of genuine exploration. Trekking to such sites, be it with an organized group or on your own, is one of the finest experiences the country has to offer.

There is also much more to Peru than old stones. Of the 117 recognized life zones on the planet, Peru has 84, from mangroves to cloudforest, mist-fuelled oases in the desert to glacial lakes. It also has 28 out of 32 climate types. Amazingly, 60% of the country is jungle, even though less than 6% of its population lives there. Despite ongoing development, much of the Peruvian Amazon remains intact, and this vast green carpet is home to some of the greatest diversity of plants and wildlife on the planet. Not a year goes by without the recording of plants and animals previously unknown to science.

Peru is also a country of fiestas, and it would be an unusual visit to Peru that did not encounter at least one. Masks and costumes tell centuries-old stories and reveal an intense spirituality which enriches daily life. Christian saints are carried through the streets as if they were the Inca emperors' sacred remains. Pachamama – Mother Earth – is offered a drop of every drink, and animal spirits and old combats come alive in masquerades.

Peru is a wonderland, indeed, with the uncanny knack of springing new surprises at every turn.

Robert and Daisy Kunstaetter
Ben Box

Best of
Peru

❶ Lima

Peru's vibrant, sprawling and grimy capital is a world unto itself and the obligatory point of arrival for most visitors. The city's fine museums, colonial buildings, vibrant nightlife and world famous dining will entertain, excite and inform. Page 32.

❷ Cordillera Blanca

A region of jewelled lakes and sparkling white mountain peaks, the Cordillera Blanca attracts mountaineers, hikers, cyclists and rafters in their thousands. Here stand some of the highest mountains in South America, with 30 snow-crested peaks over 6000 m. Page 86.

❸ Chavín de Huantar

This archaeological site belonged to one of the earliest and most influential cultures in pre-Inca Peru, and it has some extraordinary carvings and stonework. In the lee of the Cordillera Blanca, it is also one of the most spectacularly situated sites in the country. Page 101.

❹ Huaca de la Luna

The remains of the once-mighty Moche Empire are located near Trujillo on the north coast. They have revealed fabulous multicoloured friezes of gods from the first millennium AD and even the mummy of a tattooed woman. Page 138.

❺ North coast beaches

Peru's northern seaboard enjoys a rain-free climate all year, and boasts the country's finest beaches for bathing and surfing. When not riding the breakers, you can visit nature reserves or party into the small hours of the star-lit night. Page 152.

❼ Nazca Lines

The enigmatic Nazca Lines, whose origin and function continue to puzzle scientists, are etched into miles of barren southern desert. Their sheer scale and wonder can only be appreciated from the air. Page 249.

❻ Chachapoyas

Home to the mysterious 'Cloud People', Kuélap is an enigmatic site located in the northern highland Chachapoyas region. The area is also home to mysterious cities and inaccessible cliff-side burial sites, as well as the outstanding Leymebamba museum and the spectacular 771-m Gocta waterfall. Page 203.

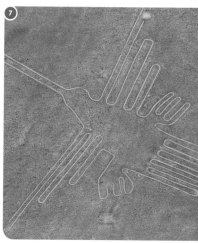

❽ Arequipa

Elegant Arequipa is known as the 'White City'. Spanish colonial churches, mansions and the Plaza de Armas all shine with pearly volcanic stonework. In contrast, the city's most famous jewel, the Santa Catalina Convent, is painted in bright colours, a gorgeous little city within a city. Page 262.

❾ Colca and Cotahuasi canyons

Come face to face with the majestic Andean condor, rising on morning thermals from the depths of the Colca or Cotahuasi canyons, two of the deepest in the world. Both offer world-class kayaking for those with a taste for profound adventure. Page 282.

❿ Lake Titicaca

The sapphire-blue waters of Lake Titicaca are bathed in a unique high-altitude light that no photograph can convey. Inhabiting its islands and the surrounding *puna* are Aymara, Quechua and Uros communities, many of whom remain faithful to their traditional cultures. Page 304.

⓫ Cuzco

Cuzco, navel of the ancient Inca world, is Peru's tourism central, and for good reason. Colonial churches, convents and extensive pre-Columbian ruins are interspersed with countless hotels, bars and restaurants that cater to the over one million tourists who visit every year from all over the world. Page 340.

⓬ Q'eswachaka

Every year in June, over 400 Quechua families from four communities join forces for four days to reconstruct the Inca rope bridge at Q'eswachaka using ancestral tools and materials. Witnessing this impressive feat of ancient civil and social engineering is an unforgettable experience. Page 383.

⓭ Machu Picchu

No amount of hype can dilute the tremendous feeling of awe on first arriving at Machu Picchu. A complete Inca city, for centuries it was buried in jungle until Hiram Bingham stumbled upon it in 1911. Page 409.

⓮ Tambopata

The steamy southern jungles are home to a huge diversity of habitats and bird species. Large mammals, including tapirs, giant anteaters, otters and primates, are fairly easy to spot due to lack of hunting pressure. Page 512.

COLOMBIA

ECUADOR

Tumbes

5

Sullana
Piura

Jaén

Chachapoyas
Moyobamba
Tarapoto

6

Chiclayo

Cajamarca

Iquitos

Pucallpa

Huanchaco
Trujillo **4**
*Huaca de
la Luna* **2**

Cordillera Blanca

Chimbote

*Chavín de
Huantar*

Huaraz **3**
Huánuco

Cerro De Pasco

Manu
National
Park

Las Piedras

Madre Dios

Puerto
Maldonado

La Oroya

*Tambopata
National
Reserve* **14**

LIMA **1**

Huancayo

Huancavelica

*Machu
Picchu* **13**

11

Ayacucho

Choquequirao

Cuzco

Abancay

*Paracas
Peninsula*

Pisco

12

Q'eswachaka

Ica

Pacific Ocean

Nazca **7**

*Colca &
Cotahuasi
canyons* **9**

10

Puno

*Lake
Titicaca*

8

Arequipa

Moquegua

Ilo

CHILE

N

100 km
100 miles

BRAZIL

BOLIVIA

Route planner

The variety that Peru offers the visitor is enormous. The problem, if you're on a tight schedule, is how to fit it all in. Above all, don't attempt to do too much. Take it easy and give yourself time to appreciate one of the most beautiful and fascinating countries on earth. Peru is larger than most visitors realize and has a great many different regions. The capital, Lima, is a world unto itself. On either side of this oversized metropolis, the north and south of the country are each divided into coast, highlands and jungle. Every region has its own special atmosphere and its own long list of attractions. From among them you can select the elements that suit you best and, depending on transport links, you can tailor your own itinerary.

For the following routes, all travel is by road unless indicated otherwise. However, if you're short of time, flying will give you greater flexibility.

One to two weeks

a whistle-stop tour of the country's highlights

Southern highlights This circuit covers some of the most popular destinations in the country. Spend a couple of days in Lima, visiting the city's fascinating museums to gain an overview of the country's exceptionally rich history and culture. If your budget allows, you can also make the most of the capital's great gastronomy and vibrant nightlife. Then fly to Cuzco for a taste of its Inca and colonial heritage. On a short visit, you can catch the train from Cuzco directly to Machu Picchu, but if you prefer to hike the Inca Trail or any of the worthwhile alternatives, you need to consider additional time in the region. From Cuzco, travel to Puno to visit the shores and islands of beautiful Titicaca, the highest navigable lake in the world. Continue to the white city of Arequipa to take-in its fine colonial architecture and more great dining opportunities. You can head out from the city to visit the awe-inspiring Colca Canyon, before flying back to Lima.

Right: Plaza de Armas, Lima
Opposite page: Ukukus at Q'Olloriti

Northern highlights Alternatively, you might prefer to avoid the tourist honeypot of Cuzco and explore a different part of the country. Start, once again, in Lima, before travelling to Huaraz in the Cordillera Blanca. Only seven hours by road from the capital, it's one of the world's premier high-altitude recreation areas, with unparalleled ease of access. A few days hiking or climbing could easily be combined with the coastal archaeological sites and fine museums near the colonial city of Trujillo and further north around Chiclayo and Lambayeque. From here, continue to the Chachapoyas region, which also contains a bewildering number of pre-Hispanic archaeological sites and the spectacular Gocta waterfall. For the final stage of your trip, either travel down the beautiful road that descends from the mountains to the subtropical city of Tarapoto, or take an even more spectacular ride to Cajamarca, surrounded by thermal baths, archaeological and historical sites and lovely countryside. From both Tarapoto and Cajamarca, you can catch a flight back to Lima.

Three to four weeks

there's so much more to see

Adding an extra two weeks to your trip would allow you to combine the two itineraries above into a more comprehensive tour. Alternatively, try one of the following routes:

Extended southern route A trip to the central Andes from Lima will take you off the beaten path, calling at Huancayo, Huancavelica and Ayacucho in a week to 10 days. Obviously the more time you allow, the more variety you'll see, especially in the Mantaro Valley near

Top: Gotca waterfall
Above: Virgen del Carmen parade, Pisac
Opposite page: Amazon river house, Iquitos

Huancayo, and the places of historical interest around Ayacucho. These are also two of the best places to experience festivals and buy handicrafts. From Ayacucho, you can travel to Cuzco via Andahuaylas and Abancay. As an alternative to the highlands, head south from Lima on the Pan-American Highway for a week or so on the southern coast, taking in the Paracas Peninsula, with its marine birdlife, and the incredible Nazca Lines. A paved road runs from Nazca, via Abancay, to Cuzco.

On this extended itinerary you should have time to see much more of Cuzco and its surroundings, especially the Sacred Valley of the Incas. Instead of the trek to Machu Picchu, you could try the more demanding and rewarding hike to the Inca city of Choquequirao. From Cuzco, make a trip to the southern jungle, either by flying or travelling overland to Puerto Maldonado. Manu National Park and the Tambopata National Reserve provide wonderful opportunities for nature enthusiasts to enjoy the highest levels of biodiversity in the world. Fly back to Lima, either from Puerto Maldonado or Cuzco.

Extended northern route Travel overland from Lima to Huaraz for trekking in the Cordilleras Blanca or Huayhuash. Both the Huayhuash and Alpamayo circuits are excellent long-distance high-altitude treks in this area. Head to Trujillo to visit the archaeological sites but break up a surfeit of sightseeing at the popular seaside resort of Huanchaco, before continuing to Chiclayo and Chachapoyas as above. Then descend from the mountains to Tarapoto and Yurimaguas, and travel by riverboat to Iquitos. The Amazonian city is the jumping-off point for the northern jungle, where there is a good network of jungle lodges. From Iquitos, catch a flight back to Lima.

Best
trekking
destinations

Huayhuash Circuit

The Cordillera Huayhuash was made famous by Joe Simpson's mountaineering classic, *Touching the Void*. The Huayhuash trekking circuit from Chiquián to Cojitambo has eight passes over 4700 m and requires plenty of stamina. You will be rewarded with views of massive ice faces rising out of the *puna*, azure lakes, deep gorges and high pastures. Page 120.

Cordillera Blanca

North of Lima, the Cordillera Blanca is the trekking heart of Peru. The most popular multi-day trek in this area takes three to five days from the **Santa Cruz Valley to Llanganuco** or vice versa. Less travelled and more demanding, but well worth the additional effort, is the **Alpamayo Circuit**, a seven- to 12-day trek around one of the most perfect peaks in the world. Both of these trekking routes are offered by many tour operators or they can be undertaken independently by those with sufficient experience. Pages 113 and 115.

Above: Cordillera Blanca
Right: Huayhuash Circuit

Ausangate Circuit

Visible from Cuzco, the strikingly beautiful summit of Ausangate stands at 6384 m. The four- to six-day circuit of the mountain includes spectacular vistas of the heavily glaciated Cordillera Vilcanota, two passes over 5000 m, hot springs and beautiful turquoise lakes. The circuit rarely drops below 4000 m, so trekkers need to be fit and well acclimatized before attempting it. Page 384.

Choquequirao

This Inca city is as spectacularly sited as Machu Picchu but far less visited. The four- to five-day hike starts at the village of Cachora (accessed from Cuzco) at 2875 m, descends into the seemingly bottomless Apurímac canyon at 1500 m and climbs back up to Choquequirao at 3000 m, so you can figure out just how much climbing up and down is involved. Do this trek now, before the cable car arrives. Page 386.

Capaq Ñan – the Great Inca Road

The world-famous trekking routes to Machu Picchu follow but a tiny fraction of the 25,000-km Inca road network. Vestiges of the Capaq Ñan can be found the length of the Andes and in Peru there are many well-preserved sections which make exceptional off-the-beaten-path trekking routes. The ancient road and stairway to Pariacaca in the Central Highlands and the 200-km stretch from Huari to Huánuco Viejo are but two examples. Pages 435 and 468.

The classic Inca Trail

Peru's most famous trek is a four- or five-day organized hike through magnificent scenery, varied ecology and Inca ruins to Machu Picchu. For all its popularity, this is no easy stroll: it starts at 2600 m, climbs up to 4200 m, descends 1000 m on an Inca stairway, and, depending on the time of year, includes freezing nights and/or deep mud. Page 419.

Top: Ausangate Circuit
Above left: Choquequirao
Above middle: Classic Inca Trail
Above right: Capaq Ñan near Huarautambo

Paracas National Reserve, Paracas, Ica Region

When to go

Peru's high season in the highlands is from May to September, when the weather is most stable for hiking and climbing. At this time the days are generally clear and sunny, though nights can be very cold at high altitude. During the wettest months in the highlands, November to April, some roads become impassable and hiking trails can be very muddy. April and May, at the end of the highland rainy season, is a beautiful time to see the Peruvian Andes, but the rain may linger, so be prepared.

On the coast, high season is September, and Christmas to February. The summer months are from December to April, but from approximately May to October much of this area is covered with *garúa*, a blanket of cloud and mist. At this time only the northern beaches near Tumbes are warm and pleasant enough for swimming.

The best time to visit the jungle is during the dry season, from April to October. During the wet season (November to April), it is oppressively hot (40°C and above) and while it only rains for a few hours at a time, which is not enough to spoil your trip, it is enough to make some roads virtually impassable, making travel more difficult.

The high season for foreign tourism is from June to September (but year-round in Cuzco and Machu Picchu) while domestic tourism peaks on certain holidays, Christmas, Semana Santa and Fiestas Patrias. Prices rise and accommodation and bus tickets are harder to come by. If you know when you will be travelling, buy your tickets in advance.

Festivals

Every bit as important as knowing where to go and what the weather will be like is Peru's festival calendar. At any given time of the year there'll be a festival somewhere in the country, drawing people from miles around. Check the website of iPerú ⓘ *www.peru.travel*, and see the Festivals listings under each relevant town. ➤ *For more information on the historic roots behind Peru's festivals, see page 553.*

Jan **Marinera** festival, Trujillo. An opportunity to see Marinera dancers.

1st week of Feb **Fiesta of the Virgen de la Candelaria**, takes place along the shores of Lake Titicaca near the Bolivian border and features dance groups from around the region.

Feb/Mar/Apr **Carnaval** is held over the weekend before Ash Wed, and **Semana Santa** (Holy Week), ends on Easter Sun. Carnaval is celebrated in most of the Andes, and Semana Santa throughout Peru. Accommodation and transport is heavily booked and prices rise considerably. Book tickets and make hotel bookings early.

1 May **Fiesta de la Cruz** is held over much of the central and southern highlands and on the coast.

Jun **Andinismo**, Huaraz, a week-long festival held at the beginning of the month. In Cuzco, the entire month is one huge fiesta, culminating in **Inti Raymi**, on 24th, one of Peru's prime tourist attractions. This date is also celebrated for **San Juan** in the jungle lowlands.

29 Jun Many places on the coast celebrate **San Pedro y San Pablo**.

30 Aug **Santa Rosa de Lima**, in Lima.

Sep **Spring festival**, in Trujillo. An opportunity to see Marinera dancers.

Oct **Señor de los Milagros**, Lima, held on several dates throughout the month.

1 Nov **Todos los Santos** (All Saints).

8 Dec **Festividad de la Inmaculada Concepción**.

What to do

Birdwatching

Peru is the number one country in the world for birdwatching. Its varied geography and topography, and its wildernesses of so many different life zones have endowed it with the greatest biodiversity and variety of birds on Earth. Some 18.5% of all the world's bird species and 45% of all neotropical birds occur in Peru. Birds breed all year round, but there's a definite peak in breeding activity – and consequently birdsong – just before the rains come in Oct, and this makes it rather easier to locate many birds between Sep and Christmas. See www.peru.travel or www.perubirdingroutes.com for further details.

Details of the following key sites are given in the main travelling text: Paracas National Reserve; Loma de Lachay; Huascarán Biosphere Reserve; Chiclayo and the route via Abra Patricia to Moyobamba; Iquitos; Manu Biosphere Reserve; and Tambopata National Reserve. A great 3- to 4-week combination trip would be to spend 16 days in Manu, then 2-3 days in the highlands at Abra Málaga and 2-3 days in the Huascarán Biosphere Reserve. A trip into the Marañón Valley and Abra Patricia (Chiclayo-Moyobamba) can be substituted for Manu; this allows access to some of the most sought-after endemics, but would produce far fewer species. More information on the birds of Peru is given in the Flora and fauna section on page 568.

Climbing

The Cordillera Blanca is an ice climber's paradise. It takes just 1 or 2 days to reach the snowline on most mountains in the most intensive grouping of glaciated peaks in South America. The statistics are impressive: more than 50 summits between 5000 m and 6000 m (with over 20 surpassing 6000 m); and 663 glaciers. It is not unusual for climbers to reach 3 or more 6000-m summits, climbed Alpine-style, during a 3-week trip. The degree of difficulty ranges from Pisco (5752 m), an excellent acclimatizer or novice's mountain (still demanding), to Copa (6173 m), of moderate difficulty, and the tremendous challenges of Alpamayo (5947 m), Artesonraju (6025 m), Quitaraju (6036 m) and Ranrapalca (6162 m). Huaraz is the main climbing centre in the Cordillera Blanca and has a growing infrastructure. It is also home to the **Peruvian Mountain Guide Association**

(**Asociación de Guías de Montaña del Perú**) or **AGMP**, Casa de Guías, Plaza Ginebra 28-g, T043-421811.

The Huayhuash is a little more remote; Chiquián, northwest of the range, and Cajatambo to the south have few facilities for climbers. It is possible to contact guides, *arrieros*, porters and cooks in Chiquián, although it is best to enquire in Huaraz first. The Huayhuash has some of the most spectacular ice walls in Peru. The Jirishancas and Yerupajas (Grande and Chico) are the most popular and demanding.

The cordilleras Vilcabamba and Vilcanota have the enticing peaks of Salkantay (6271 m) and Ausangate (6398 m), but Cuzco is not as developed for climbing as other locations. This is one of the genuine attractions of Peruvian *andinismo* – there is always another mountain more remote to feed the appetite. Huagurunchu (5730 m), for instance, in the central Andes, is barely known, and Coropuna, Peru's third highest at 6425 m, is hardly ever climbed.

Rock climbing is great in the *quebradas*, where the rock is most solid (frost-shattered higher up). This is becoming more popular, particularly in the Quebrada de Llaca, near Huaraz, and for beginners at Monterrey. Other rock climbs in the Huaraz area are the boulders of Huanchac, the 'Sphinx', or Torre de Parón and routes in the Rurec Valley.

Cultural tourism

This covers more esoteric pursuits, such as archaeology and mystical tourism. Several of the tour operators listed in this guide offer customized packages for special-interest groups. Under the umbrella heading *turismo vivencial* are a variety of interesting community-based tourism projects in archaeology, agro-tourism, education, llama trekking, nature tourism and traditional medicine. Private operators and some language schools also offer the opportunity to get involved in community projects.

The **Ministerio de Cultura** (www.mcultura.gob.pe) should be contacted by archaeologists for permits and information. The **Museo Nacional de Antropología y Arqueología** in Pueblo Libre, is the centre for archaeological investigation, and the **Museo de la Nación** holds interesting exhibitions.

Diving

Diving off the Paracas Peninsula is rewarding, as is the warmer tropical ocean with larger fish off Tumbes. It is also practised in the Bahía de Pucusana. The best season for visibility is Mar to Nov because the rivers from the mountains don't deposit silt into the sea at this time. Operators are listed in the What to do sections throughout the book; the website www.perudivers.com is a good place to start. If you plan to dive make sure that you are fit to do so. The **British Sub-Aqua Club (BSAC)**, Telford's Quay, South Pier Rd, Ellesmere Port, Cheshire CH65 4FL, UK, T01513-506200, www.bsac.com, can put you in touch with doctors who will carry out medical examinations. Check that any dive companies you use are reputable and have the appropriate certification from the **Professional**

Association of Diving Instructors (PADI), www.padi.com, which has offices and centres worldwide.

Kayaking

Peru offers outstanding whitewater kayaking for all standards of paddlers from novice to expert. Some 1st descents remain untested owing to logistical difficulties, though they are slowly being ticked off by a dedicated crew of local and internationally renowned kayakers. For the holiday paddler, it's probably best to join up with a rafting company (listed in the What to do sections throughout the book), who will gladly carry all your gear (plus any non-paddling companions) and provide you with superb food while you enjoy the river from an unladen kayak. There is a small selection of kayaks available in Peru for hire from about US$25-35 a day. For complete novices, some companies offer 2- to 3-day kayak courses on the Urubamba and Apurímac that can be booked locally. Kayaking is also offered on Lake Titicaca. For expedition paddlers, bringing your own kayak is the best option, though it is becoming increasingly expensive to fly with your boats around Peru. A knowledge of Spanish is indispensable.

Mountain biking

With its amazing diversity of trails, tracks and rough roads, Peru is surely one of the last great mountain-bike destinations yet to be fully discovered. Whether you are interested in a 2-day downhill blast from the Andes to the Amazon jungle or an extended off-road journey, then Peru has some of the world's best biking opportunities. The problem is finding the routes, as trail maps are virtually non-existent and the few main roads are often congested with traffic and far from fun to travel along. A few specialist agencies run by dedicated mountain bikers offer single tracks and dirt roads that criss-cross the Andes, putting together exciting routes to suit every type of cyclist. Useful contacts include **Amazonas Explorer** in Cuzco (www.amazonas-explorer. com); **Mountain Bike Adventures** in Huaraz (www.chakinaniperu.com) and **Perú Bike** in Lima (www.perubike.com). When signing up for a mountain-bike trip, remember that you are in the Andes so if you are worried about your fitness and the altitude, make sure you do a predominantly downhill trip.

Some companies offer imported high-quality, full-suspension mountain bikes with hydraulic disc brakes; others are less flash. Whatever the original quality of the bike, check that it has been properly and regularly maintained and that the guide gives you a full explanation of how to ride it properly. Poorly maintained bikes can be dangerous, and you may have very little come back after an accident, especially if booking and paying from overseas. Trips should have a support vehicle for the duration, not just to drop you off and meet you at the end. Guides should carry a first aid kit and a puncture repair kit at the very least (a comprehensive tool kit is preferable);

they should also be knowledgeable about bike mechanics. Bikes do go wrong, punctures are frequent and people do fall off, so it is essential that your guide provides this minimum cover. Also try to check that the company is operating legally in Peru; a website booking facility is not enough.

Parapenting and hang-gliding

Vuelo libre is its name in Peru. Flying from the coastal cliffs is easy and the thermals are good. The Callejón de Huaylas is more risky owing to variable thermals, crosswinds and a lack of good landing sites, but there is a strong allure to flying at 6000 m in front of the glaciers of Huascarán. The area with the greatest potential is the Sacred Valley of Cuzco, which has excellent launch sites, thermals and reasonable landing sites. The season in the sierra is May to Oct, with the best months being Aug and Sep. Some flights in Peru have exceeded 6500 m.

While the attraction of parapenting or hang-gliding in the sierras is very great, with mountains on all sides and steep valleys below, most pilots are to be found in Lima. Arranging a tandem jump or a course is easy: just go to Parque del Amor in Miraflores in the afternoon and see who is hanging around waiting for the thermals and the breeze. Jumping off the cliff gives a completely different perspective on the city as you fly above the Pacific breakers and the traffic on the coastal boulevard, with a pelican's view of the blocks of flats and offices. There are other launch sites on the coast

south of Lima, in the Callejón de Huaylas, Arequipa, the Central Highlands and in the Cuzco region.

Operators in Lima include **Aeroxtreme** (www.aeroxtreme.com), **Andean Trail Perú** (www.andeantrailperu.com), **Fly Adventure** (www.flyadventure.net), **Infinity** (www.infinitycross.com) and **Peru Fly** (www.perufly.com). Make sure your chosen operator has the backing of the **Asociación Peruana de Vuelo Libre** (**APVL**), http://apvl.pe/. Also see What to do on page 74.

Rafting

Peru is rapidly becoming one of the world's premier destinations for whitewater rafting. Several of its rivers are rated in the world's top 10 and a rafting trip, be it for one or 10 days, is now high on any adventurer's 'must-do' list of activities while travelling in Peru. It is not just the adrenalin rush of big rapids that attract, it is the whole experience of accessing areas beyond the reach of motor vehicles that few if any have ever visited. This may be tackling sheer-sided, mile-deep canyons, travelling silently through pristine rainforest, or canoeing across the stark altiplano, high in the Andes.

If you are looking to join a rafting expedition of some length, then it is definitely worth signing up before you set foot in Peru. Some long expeditions have fewer than 2 or 3 scheduled departures a year and the companies that offer them only accept bookings well in advance as they are logistically extremely difficult to organize. For the popular day trips and expeditions on the Apurímac there are regular departures (the latter in the dry season only). If you can spare a couple of days to wait for a departure then it is fine to book in Cuzco. It also gives you the chance to talk to the company that will be operating your tour. There are day-trip departures all year and frequent multi-day departures in the high season. Note that the difficulty of the sections changes between the dry and rainy season; some become extremely difficult or impassable in the rainy season (Dec-Mar). The dry season is Apr/May to Sep (but can be as late as Nov).

In 2015 a regulatory body for rafting operators was being set up to ensure that companies are able to run professional trips, that they employ international-standard safety techniques, that guides are adequately qualified and legally allowed to work in Peru and that equipment is regularly checked. It is hoped that, once fully in place, this body will weed out the poor practices, equipment and guides that have undermined this fun and exciting sport. Until then the rule of thumb is if companies are not legally registered in Peru, then don't book with them. For more information on staying safe when rafting, see box, page 376.

Surfing

Peru is a top, internationally renowned surfing destination. Its main draws are the variety of waves and the year-round action. Point breaks, left and right reef breaks and waves of up to 6 m can all be found from Sep to Feb in the north and from Mar to Dec in the south, though May is often ideal south of Lima.

Ocean swells are affected by 2 currents: the warm El Niño in the north and the cold Humboldt current in the south arriving from Antarctica. Pimentel, near Chiclayo, is the dividing point between these 2 effects, but a wet suit is normally required anywhere south of Piura.

The biggest wave is at Pico Alto (sometimes 6 m in May), south of Lima, and the largest break is 800 m at Chicama, near Trujillo. There are more than 30 top surfing beaches. North of Lima these include: Chicama, Pacasmayo, Punta Tur, Punta Nonura, El Golf, Cabo Blanco, Los Organos and Máncora (all left break). South of Lima the best beaches are: Punta Hermosa, Punta Rocas (right break) and Pico Alto (right break, best in May), the pick of the bunch. Huaico/Santa Rosa (left break), Cabo Negro (left break), Sangallán (right break); El Olón and Piedras Negras (left breaks) and Caleta La Cruz (right break), are all near Ilo.

International competitions are held at Pico Alto (Balin Open in May) and Punta Rocas (during the summer months). For further information, contact **Eco-Innovation Tours** (www.eco-innovationtours.com); **Federación Deportiva Nacional de Tabla (Fenta;** www.surfingperu.com.pe); **Olas Peru Surf Travel** (www.olasperusurftravel.com and www.olasperu.com) and **Peru Surf Guides** (www.perusurfguides.com). A surfing magazine, *Tablista*, is published bimonthly. Also look out for the free

X3Mag and consult Footprint's *Surfing the World*.

Trekking

Peru has some of the finest trekking opportunities in all of South America. The best known routes around the *nevados* are the Llanganuco to Santa Cruz loop; the Ausangate circuit; and a strenuous trek around the Huayhuash. Other good areas include the Colca Canyon, the Chincheros area and the upper Cañete Valley.

The other type of trekking for which Peru is justifiably renowned is walking among ruins and, above all, for the Inca Trail. However, there are very many other walks of this type in a country rich in archaeological heritage. Indeed, it is difficult to go hiking in Peru without stumbling on something of archaeological interest. Some of the best are: the valley of the Río Atuen near Leymebamba and the entire Chachapoyas region; the Tantamayo ruins above the Marañón; the Cotahuasi Canyon; and beyond Machu Picchu to Vilcabamba and Choquequirao. People tend to think of the Inca Trail to Machu Picchu as the only stretch of Inca roadway that can be walked. It is, however, just a tiny fraction of the vast Inca road network; see box, Stairway to heaven, page 435.

Most walking is on clear trails, well-trodden by the *campesinos* who populate most parts of the Peruvian Andes. If you camp on their land, ask permission first and, of course, do not leave any litter. Tents, sleeping bags, mats and stoves can easily be hired in Huaraz and Cuzco, but check carefully for quality. If you have your own trusted gear, it is best to bring it with you.

Some trekking and climbing companies show very little concern for their clients regarding acute mountain sickness, AMS, which is a considerable risk in the Andes. Many commercial treks are unfortunately scheduled faster than the recommended 300 m per day, even the very popular Santa Cruz trek near Huaraz. You should be wary of agencies wanting to sell you trips with fast ascents. Of course, if you trek independently, then you are free to go at your own pace.

For advice and information, contact the **Asociación de Guías de Montaña del Perú** (see Climbing, above). Also look out for *Trekking Peru (*www.trekkingperu. org), a specialist guidebook scheduled for publication in 2016. See the colour section for more detailed descriptions of some of the treks listed above.

Shopping tips

Almost everyone who visits Peru will end up buying a souvenir of some sort from the vast array of arts and crafts (*artesanía*) on offer. The best and cheapest place to shop for souvenirs, and pretty much anything else in Peru, is in the street markets that can be found absolutely everywhere. The country also has its share of shiny, modern shopping centres, especially in the capital, but remember that the high overheads are reflected in the prices.

What to buy and where to find it

It is possible to find all kinds of **handicraft** in Lima. The prices are often the same as in the highlands, and the quality is good. Recommended buys are: silver and gold handicrafts; hand-spun and hand-woven textiles; manufactured textiles in indigenous designs; llama and alpaca wool products such as ponchos, rugs, hats, blankets, slippers, coats and sweaters; *arpilleras* (appliqué pictures of Peruvian life), which are made with great skill and originality by women in the shanty towns; and fine leather products that are mostly handmade. Another good buy is **clothing** made from high-quality Pima cotton, grown in Peru.

The *mate burilado*, or engraved gourd found in every tourist shop, is cheap and one of the most genuine expressions of folk art in Peru. These are cheaper if bought in the villages of Cochas Grande or Cochas Chico near Huancayo in the Central Highlands. The Mantaro Valley is generally renowned for its folk culture, including all manner of *artesanía*.

Alpaca clothing, such as sweaters, hats and gloves, is cheaper in the sierra, especially in Puno. Another good source is Arequipa, where alpaca cloth for suits, coats, etc (mixed with 40% sheep's wool) can be bought cheaply from factories. Lima is more expensive, but may be the best bet in terms of quality. Note that if you want to make sure you're buying genuine alpaca, check that it is odourless when wet or dry; wet llama, in contrast, stinks.

One of the best places in Peru to look for *artesanía* is Ayacucho in the Central Highlands. Here you'll find excellent woven textiles, as well as the beautifully intricate **retablos**, or Saint Mark's boxes. Cuzco is one of the main weaving centres and a good place to shop for textiles, as well as excellent woodcarvings. Also recommended for textiles is Cajamarca. The island of Taquile on Lake Titicaca is a good place to buy *ch'uspas* (bags for coca leaves), *chumpis* (belts) and *chullos* (knitted hats with traditional ear flaps). For a more detailed look at Peruvian arts and crafts, see page 546. For tips on bargaining, see page 585.

Where to stay

from luxury hotels to wild camping and everything in between

Accommodation is plentiful throughout the price ranges and finding a hotel room to suit your budget should not present any problems, especially in the main tourist areas and larger towns and cities. The exception to this is during the Christmas and Easter holiday periods, during Carnival, Cuzco in June and for the Independence celebrations at the end of July, when all hotels are crowded and prices rise. It's advisable to book in advance at these times and also during school holidays and local festivals, see page 597. All accommodation registered with **iPeru** is listed on their website, www.peru.travel.

Hotels, hostales, pensiones and hospedajes

There are many top-class hotels in Lima and Cuzco and in the main tourist centres, such as Arequipa, Iquitos and Trujillo. In less-visited places the choice of better-class hotels is more limited. Accommodation is more expensive in Lima and in jungle towns such as Iquitos and Puerto Maldonado. It also tends to be pricier in the north compared with the south, especially on the coast. If you want a room with air conditioning, expect to pay around 30% extra.

All hotels in the upper price brackets charge 18% sales tax (IGV) and 10% service on top of prices (foreigners should not have to pay the sales tax on hotel rooms; neither tax is included in prices given in the accommodation listings, unless specified). The more expensive hotels charge in dollars.

Price codes

Where to stay	
$$$$	over US$150
$$$	US$66-150
$$	US$30-65
$	under US$30

Price of a double room in high season, including taxes.

Restaurants	
$$$	over US$12
$$	US$7-12
$	US$6 and under

Prices for a two-course meal for one person, excluding drinks or service charge.

Places that offer accommodation should (but may not) have a plaque outside bearing the letters **H** (Hotel), **Hs** (Hostal), **HR** (Hotel Residencial) or **P** (Pensión) according to type. A hotel has 51 rooms or more, a *hostal* 50 or fewer. The categories do not describe quality or facilities, although, generally speaking, a *pensión* or *hospedaje* will be cheaper than a hotel or *hostal*. Most mid-range hotels have their own restaurants serving lunch and dinner, as well as breakfast. Many budget places serve continental breakfast. Most places are friendly and helpful, irrespective of the price, particularly smaller *pensiones* and *hospedajes*, which are often family-run and will treat you as another member of the family.

The cheapest (and often the nastiest) hotels can be found around bus and train stations. If you're just passing through and need a bed for the night, then they may be acceptable. The better-value accommodation is generally found on and around the main plaza (though not always).

Youth hostels

The office of the Youth Hostel Association of Peru, **Asociación Peruana de Albergues Turísticos Juveniles** and **Administradora Peruana Hostelling International** ⓘ *Av Casimiro Ulloa 328, Miraflores, Lima T01-446 5488, www. hostellingperu.com.pe*, has information about youth hostels.

Camping

Camping on trekking routes and in wilderness areas is delightful, but there can be problems with robbery when camping near towns or villages, so ask permission to camp in a backyard or *chacra* (farmland). Most Peruvians are used to campers, but in some remote places people may never have seen a tent. Be casual about it; do not unpack all your gear, rather leave it inside your tent (especially at night), and never leave a tent unattended. Camping gas in screw-top containers is available in the main cities. Those with stoves designed for white-gas should use *bencina*, available from hardware stores (*ferreterías*) in larger towns.

Food
& drink

seafood, guinea pig and high-end gastronomy

Food

Coastal cuisine

The best coastal dishes are seafood-based, the most popular being *ceviche*. This is a dish of raw white fish marinated in lemon juice, onion and hot peppers. Traditionally, *ceviche* is served with corn-on-the-cob, *cancha* (toasted corn), yucca and sweet potatoes. *Tiradito* is *ceviche* without onions made with plaice. Another mouth-watering fish dish is *escabeche* – fish with onions, hot green pepper, red peppers, prawns (*langostinos*), cumin, hard-boiled eggs, olives, and sprinkled with cheese (it can also be made with chicken). For fish on its own, don't miss the excellent *corvina*, or white sea bass. You should also try *chupe de camarones*, which is a shrimp stew made with varying ingredients. Other fish dishes include *parihuela*, a popular bouillabaisse which includes *yuyo de mar*, a tangy seaweed, and *aguadito*, a thick rice and fish soup said to have rejuvenating powers.

A favourite northern coastal dish is *seco de cabrito*, roasted kid (baby goat) served with beans and rice, or *seco de cordero* which uses lamb instead. Also good is *aji de gallina*, a rich and spicy creamed chicken, and duck is excellent. *Humitas* are small, stuffed dumplings made with maize.

The *criollo* cooking of the coast has a strong tradition and can be found throughout the country. A dish almost guaranteed to appear on every restaurant menu is *lomo saltado*, a kind of stir-fried beef with onions, vinegar, ginger, chilli, tomatoes and fried potatoes, served with rice. Other popular examples are *cau cau*, made with tripe, potatoes, peppers and parsley and served with rice, and *anticuchos*, which are shish kebabs of beef heart with garlic, peppers, cumin seeds and vinegar. *Rocoto relleno* is a very spicy hot pepper stuffed with beef and vegetables, often served with *pastel de papas*, potato slices baked with eggs and cheese, to cool the fire. *Palta rellena* is avocado filled with chicken or Russian salad. *Estofado de carne* is a stew that often contains wine and *carne en adobo* is a cut and seasoned steak.

ON THE ROAD

Inca Kola

The high international profile currently enjoyed by upscale Peruvian gastronomy has tended to overshadow some of the country's less sophisticated tastes. Among the latter shines a fluorescent yellow, syrupy sweet soft drink, so brightly coloured that you might think it glows in the dark.

Invented by a British immigrant named Isaac Lindley, who arrived in Callao in 1910, it is said to be made from *hierba luisa* (lemon verbena), although sceptics would say it more closely resembles boiled lollipops. Be that as it may, the beverage has captured the national imagination and palate since its launch in 1935. The Lindley family business thrived for many decades, thanks to the Peruvian population's impressively sweet tooth. Even Coca Cola is reported to have added extra sugar to its formula in Peru in order to try to keep up with Inca Kola. Peru's 'golden kola' has been part-owned by its arch international rival since 1999, but it continues to be a hugely popular drink and an important icon of Peruvian national identity.

Two good dishes that use potatoes are *causa* and *carapulca*. Causa is made from mashed potatoes with lemon juice, layered with a filling of crabmeat, tuna or sardine, or, on other occasions, a vegetable salad which might include peppers, egg, olives, cheese, corn and sweet potato; it is served with marinated onions.

Highland cuisine

The staples of highland cooking, corn and potatoes, come in a variety of shapes, sizes and colours. A popular potato dish is *papa a la huancaína*, which is topped with a spicy sauce made with *Leche Glória* (the ubiquitous tinned evaporated milk) and cheese. The most commonly eaten corn dishes are *choclo con queso,* corn on the cob with cheese, and *tamales*, boiled corn dumplings filled with meat and wrapped in a banana leaf. Most typical of highland food is *pachamanca*, a combination of meats (beef, lamb, pork, chicken), potatoes, sweet potatoes, corn, beans, cheese and corn humitas, all slow-cooked in the ground, dating back to Inca times.

Meat dishes are many and varied. *Ollucos con charqui* is a kind of potato with dried meat, *sancochado* is meat and all kinds of vegetables stewed together and seasoned with ground garlic, and *lomo a la huancaína* is beef with egg and cheese sauce. Others include *fritos*, fried pork, usually eaten in the morning; *chicharrones*, deep fried chunks of pork ribs and chicken or fish, and *lechón*, baked pork. A delicacy in the highlands is *cuy*, guinea pig. Very filling and good value are the many soups and broths (*caldos*) on offer, such

Lima

Peru's much-maligned capital deserves a second look

It is a well-established cliché to call Lima a city of contradictions. In this sprawling metropolis you'll encounter grinding poverty and conspicuous wealth in abundance. The hardships of the poor are all too evident in the rubbish-strewn shanty towns you pass on the traffic-clogged drive from the airport.

Lima's image as a place to avoid or quickly pass through is enhanced by the thick grey blanket of chilly fog that descends in May and hangs around for the next seven months. Wait until the blanket is pulled aside in November to reveal bright blue skies, and, suddenly, Limeños descend on the city's beaches for a raucous mix of sun, sea, salsa and ceviche.

Lima can entertain, excite and inform. It boasts some of the finest historical monuments and museums in the country, and its colonial centre is one of Peru's UNESCO World Heritage Sites. Strenuous efforts are now being made to refurbish the historical districts. Most visitors choose to stay in Miraflores, San Isidro or Barranco, where plush hotels and shiny shopping centres rub shoulders with pre-Inca pyramids. Here, restaurants serve the city's famed cuisine, and bars keep the party going into the small hours. Scratch beneath that coating of grime and traffic fumes and you'll find that Lima is one of the most vibrant and hospitable cities anywhere.

Best for
Cuisine ▪ Museums ▪ Nightlife

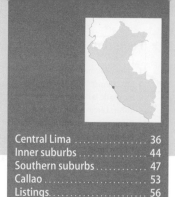

Footprint picks

⭐ **Plaza de Armas**, page 37

Explore this square at the heart of colonial Lima.

⭐ **San Francisco**, page 39

Visit the catacombs and admire the lavish interior of this baroque church.

⭐ **Museo de la Nación**, page 45

Learn about the art and history of the aboriginal peoples of Peru at this unmissable museum.

⭐ **Museo Larco de Lima**, page 46

Gain an excellent overview of Peru's cultures through their pottery.

⭐ **Parque del Amor and Parque Maria Reiche**, page 47

Escape the big city buzz for a stroll in these urban parks.

⭐ **Barranco**, page 50

Discover Lima's contemporary art scene and then party the night away.

⭐ **Pachacámac**, page 52

Re-imagine the archaeological site as it was in its heyday, as the largest city and ceremonial centre on the coast of Peru.

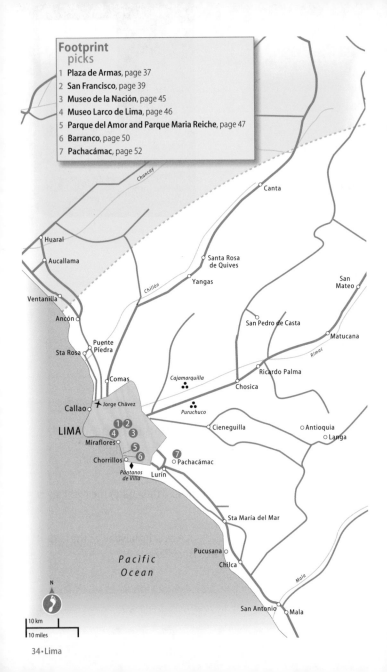

Chancay

Canta

Huaral

Aucallama

Santa Rosa
de Quives

San
Mateo

Chillón

Yangas

Ventanilla

Ancón

San Pedro de Casta

Matucana

Puente
Piedra

Rímac

Sta Rosa

Comas

Cajamarquilla

Ricardo Palma

Callao

Jorge Chávez

Chosica

LIMA

Puruchuco

Miraflores

Cieneguilla

Antioquia

Langa

Chorrillos

Pachacámac

Pántanos
de Villa

Lurín

Sta María del Mar

Pacific
Ocean

Pucusana

Chilca

Mala

N

San Antonio

Mala

10 km
10 miles

Essential Lima

Finding your feet

All international flights land at Jorge Chávez airport in Callao, 16 km northwest of the centre; take a taxi. If arriving by bus, most of the terminals are just south of the historic centre on Avenida Carlos Zavala. This is not a safe area so you should take a taxi to and from there. Miraflores is 15 km south of the centre. It has a good mix of places to stay, parks, great ocean views, bookstores, restaurants and cinemas. Neighbouring San Isidro is the poshest district, while Barranco, a little further out, is a centre for nightlife. Callao, Peru's major port, merges with Lima but is a city in its own right, with over one million inhabitants.

Getting around

Downtown Lima can be explored on foot by day; at night a radio taxi is safest. Buses, combis and colectivos provide an extensive public transport system but are not entirely safe. Termini are posted above the windscreens, with the route written on the side; all vehicles stop when flagged down. There is also the Metropolitano rapid transit bus system and a limited metro service, neither of which is particularly useful for visitors.

In most cases, taxis are the best way to travel between different districts. Bear in mind that Lima's roads are horribly congested at all times of day, so allow plenty of time to get from A to B.

Addresses

Several blocks, each with its own name, make up a *jirón* (often abbreviated to Jr). Street corner signs bear the names of both the *jirón* and the block. New and old names of streets are used interchangeably: remember that Colmena is also Nicolás de Piérola; Wilson is Inca Garcilaso de la Vega, and Carabaya is also Augusto N Wiese.

When to go

Lima two distinct seasons. The winter is May to November, when a *garúa* (mist) hangs over the city, making everything grey, damp and cold. The sun breaks through around November and temperatures rise. The temperature in the coastal suburbs is lower than the centre because of the sea's influence.

Time required

A few days are enough to see the highlights; a full week will allow more in-depth exploration.

Weather Lima

January	February	March	April	May	June
26°C 20°C 2mm	26°C 20°C 1mm	26°C 20°C 0.5mm	24°C 17°C 0mm	22°C 15°C 0mm	20°C 15°C 4mm

July	August	September	October	November	December
19°C 15°C 3mm	18°C 13°C 9mm	19°C 13°C 1mm	20°C 14°C 1mm	22°C 16°C 0.5mm	24°C 18°C 0mm

Sights
in Lima

Central Lima

the traditional heart of the city retains its colonial core

An increasing number of buildings in the centre are being restored and the whole area is being given a new lease of life as the architectural beauty and importance of the Cercado (as it is known) is recognized. Most of the tourist attractions are in this area. Some museums are only open 0900-1300 from January to March, and some are closed entirely in January.

1 Lima

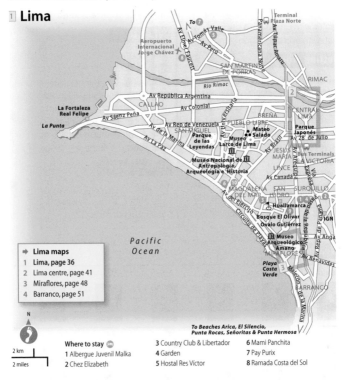

Pacific Ocean

To Beaches Arica, El Silencio,
Punta Rocas, Señoritas & Punta Hermosa

2 km
2 miles

Where to stay
1 Albergue Juvenil Malka
2 Chez Elizabeth
3 Country Club & Libertador
4 Garden
5 Hostal Res Víctor
6 Mami Panchita
7 Pay Purix
8 Ramada Costa del Sol

★ Plaza de Armas (Plaza Mayor) and around

One block south of the Río Rímac lies the Plaza de Armas, or Plaza Mayor, which has been declared a World Heritage Site by UNESCO. Running along two sides are arcades with shops: Portal de Escribanos and Portal de Botoneros. In the centre of the plaza is a bronze fountain dating from 1650.

The **Palacio de Gobierno** ⓘ *Mon-Fri 0830-1300, 1400-1730*, on the north side of the Plaza, stands on the site of the original palace built by Pizarro. The changing of the guard is at 1145-1200. The palace can be visited on a free 45-minute tour (Spanish and English); register two days in advance at the palace's tourist office (ask guard for directions).

The **Cathedral** ⓘ *T01-427 9647, Mon-Fri 0900-1700, Sat 1000-1300; entry to cathedral US$3.65, ticket also including Museo Arzobispado US$11,* was reduced to rubble in the earthquake of 1746. The reconstruction, on the lines of the original, was completed 1755. Note the splendidly carved stalls (mid-17th century), the silver-covered altars surrounded by fine woodwork, mosaic-covered walls bearing the coats of arms of Lima and Pizarro and an allegory of Pizarro's commanders, the 'Thirteen Men of Isla del Gallo'. The remains of Francisco Pizarro, found in the crypt, lie in a small chapel, the first on the right of the entrance. The cathedral's **Museo de Arte Religioso** has sacred paintings, portraits, altar pieces and other items, as well as a café and toilets. Next to the cathedral is the **Archbishop's Palace and museum** ⓘ *T01-427 5790, Mon-Sat 0900-1700,* rebuilt in 1924, with a superb wooden balcony. Permanent and temporary exhibitions are open to the public.

Just behind the Municipalidad de Lima is **Pasaje Ribera el Viejo**, which has been restored and is now a pleasant place, with several good cafés with outdoor seating. Nearby is the **Casa Solariega de Aliaga** ⓘ *Unión 224, T01-427 7736, Mon-Fri 0930-1300, 1430-1745, US$11, knock on the door and wait to see if anyone will let you in, or contact in advance for tour operators who offer guided visits.* It is still occupied by the Aliaga family and is open to the public and for functions. The house contains what is said to be the oldest ceiling in Lima and is furnished entirely in the colonial style. The **Casa de la**

9 Sonesta El Olivar
10 Tambopacaya

El Tren Eléctrico ▬▬▬
Metropolitano bus line ▬▬▬

BACKGROUND

Lima

Lima, capital of Peru, is built on both sides of the Río Rímac, at the foot of Cerro San Cristóbal. It was originally named *La Ciudad de Los Reyes*, in honour of the Magi, at its founding by conquistador Francisco Pizarro in 1535. From then until the independence of the South American republics in the early 19th century, it was the chief city of Spanish South America. The name Lima, a corruption of the Quechua name *Rimac* (speaker), was not adopted until the end of the 16th century.

The Universidad de San Marcos was founded in 1551 and a printing press in 1595, both among the earliest of their kind in South America. Lima's first theatre opened in 1563, and the Inquisition was introduced in 1569 (it was not abolished until 1820). For some time the Viceroyalty of Peru embraced Colombia, Ecuador, Bolivia, Chile and Argentina. There were few cities in the Old World that could rival Lima's power, wealth and luxury, which was at its height during the 17th and early 18th centuries. The city's wealth attracted many freebooters and in 1670 a protecting wall 11 km long was built round it, then destroyed in 1869. The earthquake of 1746 destroyed all but 20 houses, killed 4000 inhabitants and ended the city's pre-eminence. It was only comparatively recently, with the coming of industry, that Lima began to change into what it is today.

Over the years the city has changed out of all recognition. The metropolitan area contains 8.6 million people, which equates to half the urban population of Peru and nearly one-third of the country's total population. Two-thirds of Peru's industries are located in the capital. Many of the hotels and larger businesses have relocated to the fashionable suburbs of Miraflores and San Isidro, thus moving the commercial heart of the city away from the Plaza de Armas. Modern Lima is seriously affected by smog for much of the year and is surrounded by poor grimy neighbourhoods. Many of these former squatters' camps of shacks in the desert have evolved into bustling working-class districts, home to millions of inhabitants and much of the city's commercial activity. They are generally not safe to visit on your own, but going accompanied by a local friend or guide can provide an eye-opening insight into the reality of life in Lima. See also page 55.

Gastronomía Nacional Peruana ① *Conde de Superunda 170, T01-426 7264, www. limacultura.pe, US$1, behind the Correo Central,* has an extensive permanent collection of objects and displays on Peruvian food, historic and regional. It also has temporary exhibitions on the same theme. All signs are in Spanish.

East of Plaza de Armas

The first two blocks of Calle Ancash, from Calle Carabaya (on the east side of the Palacio de Gobierno) to San Francisco church, have been designated the 'tourist circuit of the Calles El Rastro y Pescadería'. (These are the colonial names of these two blocks.) The circuit starts from Desamparados railway station, which now houses fascinating exhibitions on Peruvian themes, and includes the open-air **Museo de Sitio Bodega y Quadra** ⓘ *Ancash 213, Tue-Sun 0900-1700, free,* which displays the foundations of an old building, the Casa de la Literatura and several historic houses. The area is due to be pedestrianized.

At the end of the circuit is the baroque church of ★**San Francisco** ⓘ *1st block of Jr Lampa, corner of Ancash, T01-426 7377 ext 111, www.museocatacumbas.com, daily 0930-1645, guided tours only, US$2.75, students half price, US$0.40 children,* which was finished in 1674 and withstood the 1746 earthquake. The nave and aisles are lavishly decorated in Mudéjar style. The monastery is famous for the Sevillian tilework and panelled ceiling in the cloisters (1620). The catacombs under the church and part of the monastery are well worth seeing. The late 16th-century **Casa de Jarava** or **Pilatos** ⓘ *Jr Ancash 390,* is opposite. Close by, **Casa de las Trece Monedas** ⓘ *Jr Ancash 536,* still has the original doors and window grills. **Parque de la Muralla** ⓘ *daily 0900-2000,* on the south bank of the Rímac, incorporates a section of the old city wall, fountains, stalls and street performers. There is a cycle track, toilets and places to eat both inside and near the entrance on Calle de la Soledad.

The **Palacio Torre Tagle** (1735) ⓘ *Jr Ucayali 363, Mon-Fri during working hours,* is the city's best surviving example of secular colonial architecture. Today, it is used by the Foreign Ministry, but visitors are allowed to enter courtyards to inspect the fine Moorish-influenced wood-carving in balconies and wrought ironwork. At Ucayali 391 and also part of the Foreign Ministry is the Centro Cultural Inca Garcilaso, which holds cultural events. **Casa de la Rada**, or **Goyeneche** ⓘ *Jr Ucayali 358,* opposite, is a fine mid 18th-century French-style town house which now belongs to a bank. The patio and first reception room are open occasionally to the public. **Museo Banco Central de Reserva** ⓘ *Jr Ucayali at Jr Lampa, T01-613 2000 ext 2655, Tue-Fri 1000-1630, Wed 1000-1900, Sat-Sun 1000-1300, free, photography prohibited,* houses a large collection of pottery from the Vicus or Piura culture (AD 500-600) and gold objects from Lambayeque, as well as 19th- and 20th-century paintings: both sections are highly recommended. **San Pedro** ⓘ *3rd block of Jr Ucayali, Mon-Sat 0930-1145, 1700-1800,* finished by Jesuits in 1638, has marvellous altars with Moorish-style balconies, rich gilded wood carvings in choir and vestry, and tiled throughout. Several Viceroys are buried here; the bell called La Abuelita, first rung in 1590, sounded the Declaration of Independence in 1821.

Between Avenida Abancay and Jr Ayacucho is **Plaza Bolívar**, where General José de San Martín proclaimed Peru's independence. The plaza is dominated by the equestrian statue of the Liberator. Behind lies the Congress building which occupies the former site of the Universidad de San Marcos and is now the **Museo del Congreso y de la Inquisición** ⓘ *Plaza Bolívar, C Junín 548, near the corner of Av Abancay, T01-311 7777, ext 5160, www.congreso.gob.pe/museo.htm, daily 0900-1700, free.* The main hall, with a splendidly carved mahogany ceiling, remains untouched. The Court of Inquisition was held here from 1584; between 1829 and 1938 it was used by the Senate. In the basement there is a recreation *in situ* of the

BACKGROUND

Court of Inquisition

Established by Royal Decree in 1569, the Court of Inquisition in Lima soon proved to be a particularly cruel form of justice, even by the standards of the day.

During its existence, the court meted out many horrific tortures on innocent people. Among the most fashionable methods of making the accused confess their 'sins' were burning, dismemberment and asphyxiation, to name but a few. The most common form of punishment was public flogging, followed by exile and death by burning. Up until 1776, 86 people were recorded as having been burned alive and 458 excommunicated.

Given that no witnesses were called except the informer and that the accused was not allowed to know the identity of the accuser, this may have been less a test of religious conviction than a means of settling old scores. This Kafkaesque nightmare was then carried into the realms of surreal absurdity during the process of judgement. A statue of Christ was the final arbiter of guilt or innocence but had to express its belief in the prisoner's innocence with a shake of the head. Needless to say, not too many walked free.

The Inquisition was abolished by the Viceroy in 1813 but was later reinstated before finally being proscribed in 1820.

gruesome tortures (see The Court of Inquisition, above). A description in English is available at the desk and students will offer to show round for a tip.

East of the historic centre, next to the Mercado Central in Barrios Altos, is Lima's **Chinatown** (Barrio Chino). Chinese people born in Peru are referred to as 'Tu-San' and number more than one million, making them the largest population of first-generation Chinese in all of Latin America. Some of the first immigrants arrived at the port of Callao in 1849 to work the coastal fields, replacing the black slaves who were given their freedom by the President Ramón Castilla in 1851. More Chinese settled in Chiclayo, Trujillo and the jungle city of Iquitos. On the seventh block of Jr Ucayali (also known as Calle Capón) is the Portada China, the gateway to Chinatown. It was a gift from the Taiwanese government in 1971.

West of Plaza de Armas

The 16th-century **Santo Domingo church and monastery** ⓘ *T01-427 6793, monastery and tombs Mon-Sat 0900-1230, 1500-1800; Sun and holidays morning only, US$1.65*, is on the first block of Jr Camaná. The attractive first cloister dates from 1603. Beneath the sacristy are the tombs of San Martín de Porres, one of Peru's most revered saints, and Santa Rosa de Lima (see below). In 1669, Pope Clement presented the alabaster statue of Santa Rosa in front of the altar. Behind Santo Domingo is **Alameda Chabuca Granda**, named after one of Peru's greatest singers. In the evening there are free art and music shows and you can sample foods from all over Peru. A couple of blocks beyond Santo Domingo is **Casa de Osambela** or **Oquendo** ⓘ *Conde de Superunda 298, T01-427*

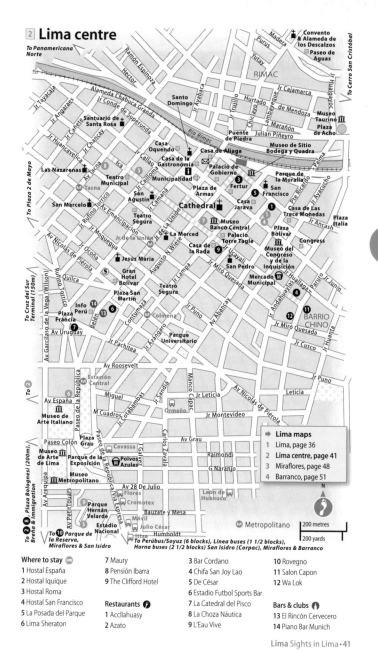

2 Lima centre

To Panamericana
Norte

RIMAC

Convento
& Alameda de
los Descalzos

Paseo de
Aguas

To Cerro San Cristóbal

Madera
Purus
Yutay

Ramón Espinoza
Hector

Jr Cajamarca

Alameda Chabuca Granda

Jr Conde de Superunda

Jr Tayacaja

Jr Angaraes

Santo
Domingo

Jr Cañete

Jr Huancavelica

Santuario de
Santa Rosa

Hurtado
de Mendoza

Museo
Taurino

Jr Chancay

Jr Chancay

Marañón

Plaza
de Acho

Las Nazarenas

Casa
Oquendo

Casa de la
Gastronomía

Puente
de Piedra

Julian Piñeyro

Museo de Sitio
Bodega y Quadra

Casa de Aliaga

To Plaza 2 de Mayo

Jr Tacna

Ica

Teatro
Municipal

Jr Callloma

Municipalidad

Palacio de
Gobierno

Parque de
la Muralla

San Marcelo

San Agustín

San
Agustín

Plaza de
Armas

Fertur

San
Francisco

Casa de Las
Trece Monedas

Camaná

Cathedral

Casa
Jarava

Plaza
Italia

Teatro
Segura

Jr Moquegua

Jr de la Unión

La Merced

Museo
Banco Central

Palacio
Torre Tagle

Plaza
Bolívar

Jr Ancash

Congress

To Plaza 2 de Mayo

Av Emancipación

Jesús María

Casa de
la Rada

Ucayali

San Pedro

Museo del
Congreso
y de la
Inquisición

Av Nicolás de Piérola

Jr Ocoña

Gran
Hotel
Bolívar

Augusto N Wiese

Jr Lampa

Jr Miró Quesada

Mercado
Municipal

To Cruz del Sur
Terminal (150m)

Quilca

Rufino Torrico

Plaza San
Martín

Teatro
Segura

Jr Abancay

BARRIO
CHINO

Info
Perú

Plaza
Francia

Belén

Coptemaza

Jr Puno

Jr Miró Quesada

Av Uruguay

Jr Azángaro

Colmena

Jr Cusco

Jr Pachitea

Parque
Universitario

Av Roosevelt

Estación
Central

Av España

Miguel

M Cuadros

M Corabambas

Jr Sandia

Jr Leticia

Leticia

Av Nicolás de Piérola

Jr Puno

To 2

Museo de
Arte Italiano

Paseo de la República

Ormeño

Jr Montevideo

Manco Cápac

Carlos Zavala

Paseo Colón

Plaza
Grau

Cavassa

Av Grau

Museo
de Arte
de Lima

Museo
Metropolitano

Polvos
Azules

Galvez

Raimondi

G Naranjo

To Plaza Bolognesi (200m)

Paseo de la República

Av 28 De Julio

León de
Huanuco

To 8

Plaza Bolognesi
Breña & Immigration

Parque
Hernán
Velarde

Flores

Cromotex

Bauzate y Mesa

Móvil

To 10 Parque de
la Reserva,
Miraflores & San Isidro

Estadio
Nacional

Av Petit Touars

Julio César

Iztsa

Humboldt

Metropolitano

To Perúbus/Soyuz (6 blocks), Línea buses (1 1/2 blocks),
Horna buses (2 1/2 blocks) San Isidro (Corpac), Miraflores & Barranco

Lima maps
1 Lima, page 36
2 Lima centre, page 41
3 Miraflores, page 48
4 Barranco, page 51

N

200 metres
200 yards

Where to stay
1 Hostal España
2 Hostal Iquique
3 Hostal Roma
4 Hostal San Francisco
5 La Posada del Parque
6 Lima Sheraton
7 Maury
8 Pensión Ibarra
9 The Clifford Hotel

Restaurants
1 Acllahuasy
2 Azato
3 Bar Cordano
4 Chifa San Joy Lao
5 De César
6 Estadio Futbol Sports Bar
7 La Catedral del Pisco
8 La Choza Náutica
9 L'Eau Vive
10 Rovegno
11 Salon Capon
12 Wa Lok

Bars & clubs
13 El Rincón Cervecero
14 Piano Bar Munich

BACKGROUND
Impressions of Lima

Ever since the earthquake of 1746 all but razed the city to the ground, descriptions of Lima have tended towards the unfavourable. Take the German naturalist and traveller Alexander Von Humboldt, for instance, who considered life in the city to be tedious with its lack of diversions, and described touring round the capital in 1802 thus: "The filthyness of the streets, strewn with dead dogs and donkeys, and the unevenness of the ground make it impossible to enjoy." Charles Darwin, who made a short visit in 1839 during his historic research trip on the *Beagle*, was no less graphic in his appraisal. He found it "in a wretched state of decay; the streets are nearly unpaved and heaps of filth are piled up in all directions where black vultures pick up bits of carrion."

Rather more complimentary was Jean Jacques Tschudi, the Swiss naturalist. He wrote: "The impression produced at first sight of Lima is by no means favourable, for the periphery, the quarter which the stranger first enters, contains none but old, dilapidated and dirty homes; but on approaching the vicinity of the principal square, the place improves so greatly that the miserable appearance it presents at first sight is easily forgotten."

The French feminist, Flora Tristan, who was Paul Gauguin's grandmother, came to Peru in 1834. She travelled extensively in the country and wrote a fascinating account of her experience, *Peregrinaciones de una Paria*, in which she painted Lima in a most favourable light: "The city has many beautiful monuments", she wrote: "The homes are neatly constructed, the streets well marked out, are long and wide." Paul Gauguin himself spent his formative years in Lima, where he was brought by his parents who were fleeing Napoleon Bonaparte's France. Towards the end of his life Gauguin wrote a collection of memoirs in which he included his impressions of Lima.

7987 (ask the caretaker if you can visit). It is said that José de San Martín stayed here after proclaiming independence from Spain. The house is typical of Lima secular architecture with two patios, a broad staircase leading from the lower to the upper floor, fine balconies and an observation tower. It is now the Centro Cultural Inca Garcilaso de la Vega and headquarters of various academies. A few blocks west is **Santuario de Santa Rosa** ⓘ *Av Tacna, 1st block, T01-425 1279, daily 0930-1300, 1500-1800, free to the grounds*, a small but graceful church and a pilgrimage centre, consisting of the hermitage built by Santa Rosa herself, the house in which she was born, a section of the house in which she attended to the sick, her well and other relics.

Due west of the Plaza de Armas is **San Agustín** ⓘ *Jr Ica 251, T01-427 7548, daily 0830-1130, 1630-1900, ring for entry*, whose façade (1720) is a splendid example of churrigueresque architecture. There are carved choir stalls and effigies, and a sculpture of Death, said to have frightened its maker into an early grave. The church has been restored since the last earthquake, but the sculpture of Death is in storage. Further west, **Las Nazarenas church** ⓘ *Av Tacna, 4th block, T01-423 5718, daily 0700-1200, 1600-2000,* is built around an image of Christ Crucified painted by a liberated slave in 1655. This is the most venerated image in Lima and is carried through the streets on a silver litter, along with an oil copy of El Señor de los Milagros (Lord of Miracles) encased in a gold frame (the whole weighing nearly a ton), on 18, 19 and 28 October and again on 1 November (All Saints' Day). *El Comercio* newspaper and local pamphlets give details of times and routes.

San Marcelo ⓘ *Rufino Torrico y Emancipación, daily for Mass,* is another church worth seeing for its two beautiful colonial doors, religious paintings and attractive Sevillian tiles. It was first built in the 16th century but has been modified over the centuries. The gold-leaf high altar and pulpit date from the 18th century.

Plaza Dos de Mayo is just over a kilometre west of the Plaza de Armas. Just to the south, on Avenida Alfonso Uguarte, is the **Museo Nacional de la Cultura Peruana** ⓘ *Av Alfonso Uguarte 650, T01-423 5892, www.facebook.com/MuseoNacionaldelaCulturaPeruana, Tue-Sat 1000-1700, US$1.70, students US$0.70.* The museum has an extraordinary mock Tiahuanaco façade and houses a rather disjointed collection of pre-Colombian and modern artefacts, including *mate burilado* (carved gourds), retablos, textiles, keros and *huacos* (pottery finds). There are examples of ceramics and cloth from Amazonian tribes and a set of watercolours by Panco Fierro, the 19th century costumbrista artist. The museum holds regular cultural events.

South of Plaza de Armas

The Jr de La Unión, the main shopping street, runs southwest from the Plaza de Armas. It has been converted into a pedestrian precinct which teems with life in the evening. In the two blocks south of Jr Unión, known as Calle Belén, several shops sell souvenirs and curios. **La Merced** ⓘ *Unión y Miró Quesada, T01-427 8199, Mon-Sat 0800-1245, 1600-2000, Sun 0700-1300, 1600-2000; monastery daily 0800-1200 and 1500-1730,* is in Plazuela de la Merced. The first Mass in Lima was said here on the site of the first church to be built. The restored façade is a fine example of colonial Baroque. Inside are some magnificent altars and the tilework on some of the walls is noteworthy. A door from the right of the nave leads into the Monastery. The cloister dates from 1546.

Jr de la Unión leads to **Plaza San Martín**, which has a statue of San Martín in the centre. The plaza has been restored with colourful flower beds and is now a nice place to sit and relax. On its west side is the refurbished **Gran Hotel Bolívar** ⓘ *Jr de la Unión 958, T01-619 7171, www.granhotelbolivar.com.pe,* which has a huge stained-glass dome over the entrance lobby. Its **El Bolivarcito** bar calls itself 'La Catedral del Pisco Sour'.

Further south, the **Museo de Arte Italiano** ⓘ *Paseo de la República 250, T01-423 9932, Tue-Fri 0900-1900, Sat-Sun 1100-1700, US$1,* is in a wonderful neoclassical building, given to Peru on the centenary of its independence. Note the remarkable mosaic murals on the outside. It consists of a large collection of Italian and other European works of art and houses the **Instituto de Arte Contemporáneo**, which has many exhibitions.

Across Avenida 9 de Diciembre from here is the **Parque de la Exposición**, inaugurated for the Lima International Exhibition in 1872. The **Palacio de la Exposición**, built in 1868, now houses the **Museo de Arte de Lima** ⓘ *Paseo Colón 125, T01-204 0000, www.mali.pe, Tue-Sun 1000-2000, Sat 1000-1700, US$2 minimum, US$4 suggested, children, students and over-65s US$1.35, guides US$1, bilingual guides available 1030-1600, signs in English*. There are more than 7000 exhibits, giving a chronological history of Peruvian cultures and art from the Paracas civilization up to today. It includes excellent examples of 17th- and 18th-century Cuzco paintings, a beautiful display of carved furniture, heavy silver and jewelled stirrups and also pre-Columbian pottery. The Filmoteca (movie club) is on the premises and shows films just about every night; see the local paper for details, or look in the museum itself.

The grounds now incorporate the **Gran Parque Cultural de Lima**. Inaugurated in January 2000, this large park has an amphitheatre, Japanese garden, food court and children's activities. Relaxing strolls through this green, peaceful and safe oasis in the centre of Lima are recommended. In the south of the park is the **Museo Metropolitano** ⓘ *Av 28 de Julio, T01-433 7122, www.limacultura.pe, Tue-Sat 1000-2000, Sun from 1100, US$1.35, which* has audiovisual displays and temporary exhibitions about the history of Lima; it also hosts lectures and has a library.

In **Parque de la Reserva** ⓘ *block 6 of Av Arequipa and Jr Madre de Dios opposite Estadio Nacional, Santa Beatriz, www.parquedelareserva.com.pe, Mon, Tue 0600-1300, Wed-Sun and holidays 0600-1300, 1500-2230*, is the **Circuito Mágico del Agua** ⓘ *displays at 1915, 2015, 2130, US$1.50*, a display of 13 fountains, the highest reaching 80 m, enhanced by impressive light and music shows three times a night. It's great fun and very popular.

Inner suburbs

visit the major museums for an overview of Peru's history and culture

Rímac and Cerro San Cristóbal

The **Puente de Piedra**, behind the Palacio de Gobierno, is a Roman-style stone bridge built in 1610, crossing the Río Rímac to the district of the same name. On Jr Hualgayoc is the bullring in the **Plaza de Acho**, inaugurated on 20 January 1766, with the **Museo Taurino** ⓘ *Hualgayoc 332, T01-482 3360, Mon-Sat 0800-1600, US$1, students US$0.50, photography US$2*. Apart from matador's relics, the museum contains good collections of paintings and engravings, some of the latter by Goya. There are two bullfight seasons: October to first week in December and during July.

The **Convento de Los Descalzos** ⓘ *Alameda de Los Descalzos,Rímac, T01-481 0441, Wed-Sun 1000-1300, 1500-1800, US$1, guided tour only, 45 mins in Spanish (worth it)*, was founded in 1592. It contains over 300 paintings of the Cuzco, Quito and Lima schools which line the four main cloisters and two ornate chapels. The chapel of El Carmen was constructed in 1730 and is notable for its baroque gold leaf altar. The museum shows the life of the Franciscan friars during colonial and early republican periods. The cellar, infirmary, pharmacy and a typical cell have been restored.

Cerro San Cristóbal dominates downtown Lima. It can be visited on a one-hour minibus tour ⓘ *Camaná y Conde Superunda, every 15 mins daily 1000-2100, US$3*, departing from in front of Santo Domingo. The tour includes a look at the rundown Rímac district, passes the Convento de los Descalzos (see above), ascends the hill through one of the city's oldest shanties with its brightly painted houses and spends about 20 minutes at the summit, where there is a small museum and café. There are excellent views on a clear day. The second half of the trip is a historical tour. **Urbanito buses** ⓘ *T01-424 3650, www.urbanito.com.pe*, also include Cerro San Cristóbal on their three-hour tour of central Lima, departing from the Plaza de Armas (weekends and holidays only).

San Borja
★**Museo de la Nación** ⓘ *Javier Prado Este 2465, T01-613 9393 ext 2484, www.cultura.gob.pe, Tue-Sun 0900-1700, closed major public holidays, US$2.50, 50% discount with ISIC card*. Located in the huge **Banco de la Nación** building is the museum for the exhibition and study of the art and history of the aboriginal races of Peru. There are good explanations in Spanish and English on Peruvian history, with ceramics, textiles and displays of many ruins in Peru. It is arranged so that you can follow the development of Peruvian precolonial history through to the time of the Incas. A visit is recommended before you go to see the archaeological sites themselves. There are displays of the tomb of the Señor de Sipán, artefacts from Batán Grande near Chiclayo (Sicán culture), reconstructions of the friezes found at Huaca La Luna and Huaca El Brujo, near Trujillo, and of Sechín and other sites. 'Yuyanapaq' is a photographic record of the events of 1980-2000. Temporary exhibitions are held in the basement, where there is also a Ministerio de Cultura bookshop. The museum has a cafetería.

To get there, take a taxi from downtown Lima or Miraflores US$3.20. From Avenida Garcilaso de la Vega in downtown Lima take a combi with a 'Javier Prado/Aviación' window sticker. Get off at the 21st block of Javier Prado at Avenida Aviación. From Miraflores take a bus down Avenida Arequipa to Avenida Javier Prado (27th block), then take a bus with a 'Todo Javier Prado' or 'Aviación' window sticker.

Surco
Museo de Oro del Perú ⓘ *Alonso de Molina 1100, Monterrico, Surco (between blocks 18 and 19 of Av Primavera), Lima 33, T01-345 1292, www.museoroperu.com. pe. Daily 1030-1800, closed 1 Jan, 1 May, 28 Jul, 25 Dec.US$11.55, children under 11 US$5.60; multilingual audioguides available*. This museum houses an enormous collection of Peruvian gold, silver and bronze objects, together with an impressive international array of arms and military uniforms from Spanish colonial times to the present day and textiles from Peru and elsewhere. Allow plenty of time to appreciate all that is on view. More than one hundred of its pieces can be seen in the **Sala Museo Oro del Perú**, in Larcomar (see below).

Breña and Pueblo Libre

West of the centre, adjacent to Plaza de la Bandera, is the archaeological site **Huaca Mateo Salado** ⓘ *corner of Avs Tingo María (Breña) and M H Cornejo (Pueblo Libre), T01-476 9887, tours Thu-Sun 0900-1600, US$3.35,* a large administrative and ceremonial centre from the Ychma culture (AD 1100-1450). It was also occupied by the Incas. It has five terraced pyramids made of rammed earth, now designated with the letters A, B, C, D and E. A second section of the complex can be seen by block 16 of Avenida Tingo María. South of here, in the Pueblo Libre district is a trio of important museums, including the unmissable Museo Larco de Lima.

Museo Nacional de Antropología, Arqueología e Historia ⓘ *Plaza Bolívar, Pueblo Libre (not to be confused with Plaza Bolívar in the centre), T01-463 5070, Tue-Sat 0900-1700, Sun and holidays 0900-1600, US$4, students US$1.20, guides available for groups; taxi from downtown US$3; from Miraflores US$4.* The original museum of anthropology and archaeology has ceramics from the Chimú, Nazca, Mochica and Pachacámac cultures, a display on the Paracas culture, various Inca curiosities and works of art, and interesting textiles. **Museo Nacional de Historia** ⓘ *T01-463 2009, Tue-Sat 0900-1700, Sun and holidays 0900-1600, US$3.65,* in a mansion occupied by San Martín (1821-1822) and Bolívar (1823-1826) is next door. It exhibits colonial and early republican paintings, manuscripts and uniforms.

To get there, take any public transport on Avenida Brasil with a window sticker saying 'Todo Brasil'. Get off at the 21st block called Avenida Vivanco. Walk about five blocks down Vivanco. The museum will be on your left. From Miraflores take bus SM 18 Carabayllo-Chorrillos, marked 'Bolívar, Arequipa, Larcomar', get out at block 8 of Bolívar by the Hospital Santa Rosa and walk down Avenida San Martín five blocks until you see a faded blue line marked on the pavement; turn left. The blue line is a pedestrian route (15 minutes) linking the Museo Nacional de Antropología, Arqueología e Historia to the **Museo Larco de Lima.**

★**Museo Larco de Lima** ⓘ *Av Bolívar 1515, T01-461 1312, www.museolarco. org, 0900-2200, 0900-1800 24 Dec-1 Jan, US$10.55 (half price for students, seniors US$8.75); texts in Spanish, English and French, disabled access, photography not permitted; taxi from downtown, Miraflores or San Isidro 15 mins, US$4.* Located in an 18th-century mansion, itself built on a seventh-century pre-Columbian pyramid, this museum has a collection which gives an excellent overview on the development of Peruvian cultures through their pottery. It has the world's largest collection of Moche, Sicán and Chimú pieces. There is a Gold and Silver of Ancient Peru exhibition, a magnificent textile collection and a fascinating erotica section. Don't miss the storeroom with its vast array of pottery, unlike anything you'll see elsewhere. There is a library and computer room for your own research and a good café open during museum hours, see below. It is surrounded by beautiful gardens, has a new entrance and park outside.

To get there, take any bus to the 15th block of Avenida Brasil. Then take a bus down Avenida Bolívar. From Miraflores, take the SM 18 Carabayllo-Chorrillos (see above), to block 15 of Bolívar.

San Isidro, Miraflores and Barranco are the hub of the capital's social life, with numerous hotels, restaurants and night spots (see pages 58, 64 and 69). There are also beaches further south and a number of sights worth seeing. Avenida Arequipa runs south for 52 blocks from downtown Lima to Parque Kennedy in Miraflores. Alternatively, the Vía Expresa, a six-lane urban freeway locally known as 'El Zanjón' (the Ditch) is the fastest route across the city.

San Isidro

To the east of Avenida La República, down Calle Pancho Fierro, is **El Olivar**, an olive grove planted by the first Spaniards which has been turned into a park. Some 32 species of birds have been recorded there. Between San Isidro and Miraflores is **Huallamarca** ⓘ *C Nicolás de Rivera 201 and Av Rosario, T01-222 4124, Tue-Sun 0900-1700, US$1.75*. An adobe pyramid of the Maranga (Lima) culture, it dates from about AD 100-500, but has later Wari and Inca remains. There is a small site museum. To get there, take bus 1 from Av Tacna, or minibus 13 or 73 to Choquechaca, then walk.

★Miraflores

Parque Kennedy and the adjoining **Parque Central de Miraflores** are located between Avenida Larco and Avenida Mcal Oscar Benavides (locally known as Avenida Diagonal). The extremely well-kept park area has a small open-air theatre with performances Thursday to Sunday and an arts and crafts market most evenings of the week. To the north is the former house and now museum of the author **Ricardo Palma** ⓘ *Gral Suárez 189, T01-445 5836, http://ricardopalma.miraflores.gob.pe, Mon-Fri 0915-1245, 1430-1700, US$2.20, includes video and guided tour*.

At the southern end of Avenida Larco and running along the Malecón de la Reserva is the renovated **Parque Salazar** and the modern shopping centre called **Centro Comercial Larcomar**. Here you will find expensive shops, hip cafés and discos and a wide range of restaurants, all with a beautiful ocean view. The 12-screen cinema is one of the best in Lima and even has a 'cine-bar' in the 12th theatre. Don't forget to check out the Cosmic Bowling Alley with its black lights and fluorescent balls.

A few hundred metres to the north is the famous ★**Parque del Amor**, a great place for a stroll where, on just about any night, you'll see at least one wedding party taking photos. North of Parque del Amor is **Parque María Reiche**, where the Nazca Lines are portrayed with living

> **Tip...**
>
> There is no shortage of buses along Av Arequipa; windscreens display 'Todo Arequipa' heading south and 'Wilson/Tacna' heading north. To get directly to Parque Kennedy from downtown, look for 'Larco/Schell/Miraflores', 'Chorrillos/Huaylas' or 'Barranco/Ayacucho'. Buses to Barranco can be caught on Av Tacna, Av Wilson (also called Garcilaso de la Vega), Av Bolivia and Av Alfonso Ugarte.

Tip...
Do not be tempted to walk down the path from Miraflores near Larcomar to the road along the Costa Verde below. Neither the path nor the road are safe – robberies have occurred.

plants. It's an interesting way to see these famous designs if you don't have time to visit Nazca itself.

Museo Arqueológico Amano ⓘ *Retiro 160, 11th block of Av Angamos Oeste, Miraflores, T01-441 2909, www.fundacionmuseoamano.org.pe, by appointment only Mon-Fri 1500-1630, donations (photography prohibited),* has artefacts from the Chancay, Chimú and Nazca periods, which were owned by the late Mr Yoshitaro Amano. It has one of the most complete exhibits of Chancay weaving and is particularly interesting for pottery and pre-Columbian textiles, all superbly displayed and lit. To get there,

3 **Miraflores**

take a bus or colectivo to the corner of Avenida Arequipa y Avenida Angamos and another one to the 11th block of Avenida Angamos Oeste. Taxi from downtown costs US$3.20; from Parque Kennedy, US$2.25.

The **Museo Poli** ⓘ *Almte Cochrane 466, T01-422 2437, tours US$15 pp, allow 2 hrs; call in advance,* is one of the best private collections of colonial and pre-Columbian artefacts in Peru, including material from Sipán.

Turn off Avenida Arequipa at 45th block to reach **Huaca Pucllana** ⓘ *General Borgoño, 8th block s/n, T01-445 8695, www.mirafloresperu.com/huacapucllana/, Wed-Mon 0900-1600, US$4.25, students US$2, includes 45-min tour in Spanish or English,* a pre-Inca site which is under excavation. Originally a Lima culture temple to the goddesses of sea and moon (AD 200-700), it became a Wari burial site (AD 700-900) before being abandoned. Ychsma occupation (AD 1000-1470) and

100 metres
100 yards

➡ **Lima maps**
1 Lima, page 36
2 Lima centre, page 41
3 **Miraflores, page 48**
4 Barranco, page 51

subsequent looting followed. It has a small site museum with some objects from the site itself, a garden of traditional plants and animals and a souvenir shop (see Restaurants, below).

★Barranco

The 45-minute walk south from Miraflores to Barranco along the Malecón is recommended in summer. This suburb was already a seaside resort by the end of the 17th century. There are many old mansions in the district, in a variety of styles, several of which are now being renovated, particularly on Calle Cajamarca and around San Francisco church. Barranco is quiet by day but comes alive at night (see Restaurants and Bars pages 68 and 69).

The attractive public library, formerly the town hall, stands on the plaza. It contains the helpful **municipal tourist office** ⓘ *T01-719 2046*. Nearby is the interesting *bajada*, a steep path leading down to the beach. The **Puente de los Suspiros** (Bridge of Sighs) crosses the *bajada* to the earthquake-damaged La Ermita church (only the façade has been restored) and leads towards the Malecón, with fine views of the bay. A number of artists have their workshops in Barranco and there are several chic galleries, such as **Galería San Francisco** ⓘ *Pl San Francisco 208, T01-477 0537*; **Lucía de la Puente** ⓘ *Sáenz Peña 206, T01-477 9740, www.gluciadelapuente.com (next to Hotel B, see below)*; and **Wu** ⓘ *Sáenz Peña 206, T01-247 4685, www.wugaleria.com*.

The **Museo de Arte Contemporáneo de Lima (MAC Lima)** ⓘ *Av Miguel Grau 1511, beside the municipal stadium, near Miraflores, T01-514 6800, www.maclima. pe, US$2, Sun US$0.35, Tue-Sun 1000-1800, with guided tour*, has permanent Latin American and European collections and holds temporary exhibitions. **MATE (Asociación Mario Testino)** ⓘ *Av Pedro de Osma 409, T01-251 7755, www.mate.pe, US$5.55, Tue-Sat 1100-2000, Sun 1100-1800, with audio tour (no other explanations)*, is the world-renowned fashion photographer's vision of modern art, with a shop and excellent café/restaurant. Next door, by contrast, and equally important is the **Museo de Arte Colonial Pedro de Osma** ⓘ *Av Pedro de Osma 423, T01-467 0141, www.museopedrodeosma.org, Tue-Sun 1000-1800, US$6.75, students half price, guided tours in English or Spanish*, a private collection of colonial art of the Cuzco, Ayacucho and Arequipa schools. On the same avenue, but close to the plaza is the **Museo de la Electricidad** ⓘ *Av Pedro de Osma 105, T01-477 6577, http:// museodelaelectricidad.blogspot.co.uk, daily 0900-1700, free*, which has exhibits on electricity generation and its history in Peru.

Chorrillos and around

The district of Chorrillos, beyond Barranco, has a redesigned Malecón and fashionable beachfront with mosaics and parks. It has always been a popular resort and is a good place to go to find fish restaurants. Playa Herradura is a little further on and is well-known for surfing. From Chorrillos there is access to two worthwhile sights.

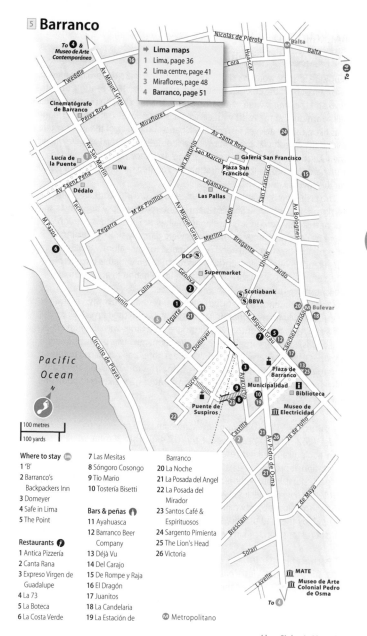

⑤ Barranco

➡ **Lima maps**
1 Lima, page 36
2 Lima centre, page 41
3 Miraflores, page 48
4 Barranco, page 51

To ④ &
Museo de Arte
Contemporáneo

Cinematógrafo
de Barranco

Lucía de
la Puente

Wu

Dédalo

Galería San Francisco

Plaza San
Francisco

Las Pallas

BCP Ⓢ

Supermarket

Scotiabank Ⓢ
BBVA Ⓢ

Ⓜ Bulevar

Pacific
Ocean

Plaza de
Barranco

Municipalidad ℹ

Biblioteca

Museo de
Electricidad

Puente
de Suspiros

MATE

Museo de Arte
Colonial Pedro
de Osma

To ④

100 metres
100 yards

BACKGROUND

A fashion for passion

A unique form of women's clothing was worn by Lima's upper-class *mestizas* (women born in the colonies of Spanish origin) in the 18th century. Both the *saya* and the *manto* were of Moorish origin. The *saya* was an overskirt of dark silk, worn tight at the waist with either a narrow or wide bottom. The *manto* was like a thick black veil fastened by a band at the back of the waist where it joined the *saya*. It was brought over the shoulders and head and drawn over the face so closely that only a small, triangular space was left uncovered, sufficient for one eye to peep through. This earned them the title '*las tapadas*', or 'the covered ones'.

The fashion was created by Lima's *mestizas* in order to compete in the flirting stakes with their Spanish-born counterparts, whose tiny waists and coquettish fan-waving was turning men's heads. The *tapadas*, though veiled, were by no means modest. Their skirts were daringly short, revealing their appealingly tiny feet, and necklines plunged to scandalously low levels. The French feminist, Flora Tristan, was much taken with this brazen show. She commented: "I am sure it needs little imagination to appreciate the consequences of this time-honoured practice."

One consequence of this fashion, which ensured anonymity, was that Lima's *mestizas* could freely indulge in romantic trysts with their lovers. Often, however, they were content with flirting – sometimes with their unwitting husbands. Another consequence of their anonymity was political. Many *tapadas* used their afternoon strolls to pass notes and messages to the organizers of the independence movement. This romantic and political intrigue usually took place on the Paseo de Aguas, a walkway of pools and gardens built by the viceroy.

Pántanos de Villa ① *www.prohvilla.munlima.gob.pe, daily 0830-1630, US$2.75, guides US$7 (max 20 people), boat trip US$4.10.* This 396-ha wildlife sanctuary is an ecological wetland reserve with brackish water and abundant emergent vegetation. It provides the habitat for waterfowl typical of coastal Peru, including 17 species of migratory shorebirds. There are several species of fish, four types of reptile and over 50 species of waterplants. The visitor centre has lots of information in Spanish. Allow up to two hours for a visit and take binoculars if you have them. Access is by the road that goes to the seaside district of La Villa; the nearest public transport stops about 1 km away, so it's best to take a taxi from Barranco, US$5.

★**Pachacámac** ① *T01-430 0168, http://pachacamac.cultura.pe, Tue-Sat 0900-1700, Sun 0900-1600; closed public holidays except by appointment, US$3.50, students US$1.75, guide US$7.* When the Spaniards arrived, Pachacámac in the Lurín valley was the largest city and ceremonial centre on the coast. A wooden statue of the creator-god, after whom the site is named, is in the site museum. Hernando Pizarro was sent here by his brother in 1533 in search of gold for Inca emperor Atahualpa's ransom. In their fruitless quest, the Spaniards destroyed images and killed the priests. The ruins encircle the top of a low hill, whose crest was crowned with a **Temple of the Sun**, now partially restored. Slightly apart is the reconstructed **House of the Mamaconas**, where the 'chosen women' spun fine cloth for the Inca and his court. An impression of the scale of the site can be gained from the top of the Temple of the Sun, or from walking or driving the 3-km circuit, which is covered by an unmade road for cars and tour buses.

The site is large and it is expected that tourists will be visiting by vehicle (there are six parking areas). However, there are also combis from the Pan-American Highway (southbound) to Pachacámac for US$0.85 (the window sticker reads 'Pachacámac/Lurín'; let the driver know you want to get off at the ruins. A taxi from downtown will cost approximately US$5.50; pay extra for the driver to wait as you'll struggle to find a taxi back into the city.

Lima's beaches

Even though the water of the whole bay has been declared unsuitable for swimming, Limeños see the beach more as part of their culture than as a health risk. On summer weekends (December-April) the city's beaches get very crowded and lots of activities are organized. The beaches of **Miraflores**, **Barranco** and **Chorrillos** are popular, but the sand and sea here are dirty. It's much better to take a safe taxi south along the *Circuito de Playas* to Playa Arica (30 km south of Lima). There are many great beaches for all tastes between here and San Bartolo (45 km south). If you really want the height of fashion head to **Asia**, Km 92-104, where there are some 20 beaches with boutiques, hotels, restaurants and condos.

> **Tip...**
> Robbery is a serious threat on the beaches. Don't take any belongings of value with you; take care on the walkways down, and don't camp on the beach overnight.

Callao

it may not be pretty, but the port area is worth a look

There is no separation between Lima and Callao; the two cities run into each other and the road between the two is lined with factories. But Callao is a city in its own right, the second largest in Peru with over one million inhabitants (many more if you include shanty town dwellers). Callao (not Lima) is the location of Jorge Chávez International Airport and is the most important Peruvian port. Shipyards far from the sea load newly built fishing vessels on to huge lorries to be launched into the ocean here. Most parts of the city are ugly, unkempt, poor and dangerous. However, if you are willing to use some imagination and you like ports, Callao is worth visiting. Some attempts have been made to restore the historic centre and port area. See www.regioncallao.gob.pe and www.municallao.gob.pe for local information.

BACKGROUND
Callao

Founded in 1537, Callao used to be one of the most important cities in South America, the only seaport on the continent authorized to trade with Spain during the 16th and 17th centuries. During much of the 16th century Spanish merchants were plagued by threats from English privateers, such as Sir Francis Drake, who were all too willing to relieve the Spanish armada of its colonial spoils. The harbour was fortified in 1639 in order to prevent such attacks. In 1746, the port was completely destroyed by a massive wave, triggered by the terrible earthquake of that year. According to some sources, all 6000 of Callao's inhabitants were drowned. The watermark is still visible on the outside of the 18th-century church of Nuestra Señora del Carmen de la Legua, which stands near the corner of Avenida Oscar Benavides and the airport road, Avenida Elmer Faucett. In 1850, the first railway in South America was opened between Lima and Callao. It was used not only as a passenger service but also, more importantly, for the growing import-export trade, transporting ore from the mines in the Central Highlands and manufactured goods from incoming ships.

Sights

The most elegant area of Callao proper is **Plaza Grau**. It is well maintained and from here you can see a large part of the port and the Palomino Islands (inhabited by birds, seals and other marine species), including Isla San Lorenzo. This island has an underwater military bunker, where two famous prisoners were incarcerated: Abimael Guzmán, founder of Sendero Luminoso, and Víctor Polay, leader of MRTA.

Bright pleasure boats, complete with life jackets, make trips to the end of La Punta beach from the pier next to Plaza Grau, about 25 minutes, and agencies arrange cruises to the islands (eg Viento Sur, Ecocruceros, page 75, and others); ask around, as departures are mostly unscheduled. Several houses surrounding the Iglesia Matriz have been restored, but generally the centre is in a state of permanent decay. **Museo Naval del Perú** ① *Av Jorge Chávez 123, T01-429 4793, Tue-Sun 0900-1600, US$1*, has models of Peruvian and foreign ships, weapons, uniforms, torpedoes and other relics. There are also interesting photographs. It's recommended if you are in the area. **La Fortaleza Real Felipe** and **Museo del Ejército** ① *T01-429 0532, daily 0900-1400, US$4, no cameras allowed*, is an enormous Spanish castle in the heart of the city. It is still used by the Peruvian armed forces, but some areas are open to the public. These include buildings within the fort, a museum, the fortifications and plenty of cannons. In the Chucuito district, between the Fortaleza and La Punta, the houses are all strikingly painted in bright colours.

La Punta

Founded in 1555, La Punta is a green peninsula next to Callao. It has only 6800 permanent residents and enjoys the relaxed, nostalgic atmosphere of a beach

Lima's shanty towns

If you take a bus out of Lima, you will see many shanty towns along the highway. Variously known as *invasiones*, *asentamientos humanos* or *pueblos jóvenes*, the shanty towns of Lima are monumental reminders of racial division and social inequality, and of the poverty in which more than half of the capital's population lives. Millions of people have no access to clean drinking water. Most of the Peruvians living in these settlements came from the provinces, escaping misery and the civil war of the 1980s and 1990s. They simply squatted on the hills surrounding Lima, only trying later to legalize their property.

There are old, 'established' shanty towns, like **Villa El Salvador**, with officially over 445,000 inhabitants in 2013 (probably more than that), as well as newer, rapidly expanding ones, like **Mi Perú** in Ventanilla, 20 km behind Jorge Chávez airport, which has about 60,000 inhabitants and was due to become the seventh district of Callao in 2014. Some shanty towns, such as **Lurigancho** and **Canto Grande**, were controlled by Shining Path during the civil war. Others (around the Central Highway that leads towards the Andes) became infamous for sheltering delinquents and drug addicts. There is even one shanty town housing Cuban exiles who escaped from the island looking for 'freedom' and a better life (now they wish they had stayed at home). Some settlements consist of reed and bamboo shacks without roofs; others have developed an infrastructure, including markets, shops, restaurants and cafés.

Divisions in Peruvian society run very deep. Early on, many of the shanty town dwellers did not even know of the existence of posh neighbourhoods like San Isidro and Miraflores. Needless to say, most inhabitants of the rich parts of Lima never visit shanty towns. With time and the pervasive influence of the media, however, this has begun to change.

Some visitors feel a voyeuristic fascination for Lima's poorest districts. Villa El Salvador, one of the oldest and biggest shanty towns, is now a municipality in its own right (www.munives.gob.pe) and is the only one that can be visited without much danger. It is at the southern end of the Tren eléctrico, so you can take a train there even if you don't feel the urge to wander around. The station is above street level, giving a general view of the place. Travel only by day, wear modest clothes and, if you venture out of the station, stick to the main street. Under no circumstances should you travel by public transport to other shanty towns. Almost without exception, they are dangerous, especially after dark. Every week, there are countless cases of robbery, stabbing, burglary and rape. Murder is not uncommon.

resort, with good local seafood restaurants, pleasant walks, friendly people and great views. It's an interesting place to come for lunch, but the ride back to Lima, even in a taxi, can be dangerous at night, as you have to drive through

Callao proper. La Punta's main artery, **Avenida Coronel Bolognesi**, is lined with impressive old villas. There is a well-maintained Malecón, parallel to Bolognesi, that affords a lovely walk with great views of the islands, sailing boats and Callao port. On the corner of El Malecón and Jirón García y García is the **Club de Regatas Lima**, with a nice café and view from the second floor (open sporadically). Nearby is the Club de Regatas Unión. Along El Malecón is a pebble beach, Cantolao, but the water is not very clean, due to the proximity of Callao port.

Listings Lima *maps p36, p41, p48, p51*

Tourist information

iPerú
Has offices at Jorge Chávez **international airport** (T01-574 8000, daily 24 hrs); **Casa Basadre** (Av Jorge Basadre 610, San Isidro, T01-421 1627/1227, Mon-Fri 0900-1800); and **Larcomar shopping centre** (La Rotonda nivel 2, stand 211-212, Miraflores, T01-445 9400, daily 1100-2100).

Municipal tourist kiosk
Pasaje Escribanos, behind the Municipalidad, near the Plaza de Armas, T01-632 1542, www.visitalima.pe and www.munlima.gob.pe. Daily 0900-1700.
Ask about guided walks in the city centre. There are 8 kiosks in Miraflores: Parque Central; Parque Salazar; Parque del Amor; González Prada y Av Petit Thouars; Av R Palma y Av Petit Thouars; Av Larco y Av Benavides; Huaca Pucllana (closed Sat afternoon); and Ovalo Gutiérrez.

South American Explorers
Enrique Palacios 956, Miraflores, T01-445 3306/447 7731, dial 011-51-1 from USA, www.saexplorers.org. Mon-Fri 0930-1700, Sat 0930-1300.
Offers various services for its members.

Tourist Police
Jr Moore 268, Magdalena at the 38th block of Av Brasil, T01-460 1060/ T0800-22221. Daily 24 hrs.
Are friendly and very helpful if you have your property stolen, English spoken. Also at Av España y Av Alfonso Ugarte; Colón 246, Miraflores, T01-243 2190, and at the airport. For an English website, see www.limaeasy.com and for an upmarket city guide see www.limainside.net.

Where to stay

If you are only staying a short time and want to see the main sites, Central Lima is the most convenient place to stay. However, it is not as safe at night as the more upmarket areas of Miraflores, San Isidro and Barranco. All hotels in the upper price brackets charge 18% state tax and service on top of prices. In hotels foreigners pay no tax and the amount of service charge is up to the hotel. Neither is included in the prices below, unless otherwise stated. All those listed below have received good recommendations.
Lima has several international, high-class chain hotels: **JW Marriott**, www.marriott.com; **Lima Sheraton**, www.sheraton.com; **Sofitel Royal Park**, www.sofitel.com; **Swissôtel Lima**, www.lima.swissotel.com; **Westin**, www.starwoodhotels.com. All are recommended.

There are dozens of hostels in Lima offering dormitory accommodation and charging US$10-17 pp, usually including a simple breakfast, hot water in shared bathrooms, kitchen facilities, bar and living room. Double rooms with private bathrooms start at about US$30. Some hostels are linked to travel agents or adventure tour companies.

Central Lima

$$$ The Clifford Hotel
Parque Hernán Velarde 27, near 1st block of Av Petit Thouars, Sta Beatriz, T01-433 4249, www.thecliffordhotel.com.pe.
Nicely converted, republican town house in a quiet and leafy park. Rooms and suites, has a bar, café and conference room.

$$$ Maury
Jr Ucayali 201, T01-428 8188, hotmaury@rcp.net.pe.
The most upmarket hotel in the historical centre, but past its heyday, secure. The bar is reputed to be the home of the first-ever pisco sour (this is, of course, disputed!).

$$ Hostal Iquique
Jr Iquique 758, Breña (discount for SAE members), T01-433 4724, www.hostal-iquique-lima.com.
Rooms on top floor at the back are best, from singles with shared bath to triples with private bath, well-kept if a bit noisy and draughty, use of kitchen, warm water, safe, airport pick up.

$$ La Posada del Parque
Parque Hernán Velarde 60, near 1st block of Av Petit Thouars, Sta Beatriz, T01-433 2412, www.incacountry.com.
A charmingly refurbished old house with a collection of fine handicrafts, in a safe area, comfortable rooms, breakfast

0800-0930, airport transfer 24 hrs for US$18 for 1-3 passengers (US$8 pp for larger groups), no credit cards, cash only. Always check the website for special offers and gifts. The owners speak good English. Excellent value. Gay friendly. Has an agreement with the nearby Lawn Tennis Club (Arenales 200 block) for guests to eat at the good-value **Set Point** restaurant and use the gym.

$$-$ Hostal España
Jr Azángaro 105, T01-427 9196, www.hotelespanaperu.com.
A long-standing travellers' haunt, rooms or dormitories, fine old building, motorcycle parking, laundry service, roof garden, good café, can be very busy.

$ Hostal Roma
Jr Ica 326, T01-427 7576, www.hostalroma.8m.com.
Over 35 years in the business, rooms sleep 1-4, private or shared bath, hot water, often full, luggage deposit and safe box, motorcycle parking, airport transfers (**Roma Tours** arranges city tours – but shop around if you want to, flight reservations). Next door is **Café Carrara**.

$ Hostal San Francisco
Jr Azángaro 127, T01-426 2735.
Dormitories with and without bathrooms, safe, Italian/Peruvian owners, good service, café.

$ Pensión Ibarra
Av Tacna 359, 1402 y 1502 (elevator to 14th/15th floors doesn't run all hours), no sign, T01-427 8603/1035, pensionibarra@gmail.com.
Breakfast US$4, discount for longer stay, basic, noisy, use of kitchen, balcony with views of the city, helpful owners (2 sisters), hot water, full board available (good small café almost next door). Reserve in advance; taxis can't

stop outside so book airport pick-up (US$18.50) for safe arrival.

Inner suburbs

San Miguel and Magdalena del Mar are on the seaward side of Pueblo Libre.

$$ Mami Panchita

Av Federico Gallessi 198 (ex-Av San Miguel), San Miguel, T01-263 7203, www.mamipanchita.com.
Dutch/Peruvian-owned, English, Dutch and Spanish spoken, includes breakfast and welcome drink, comfortable rooms with bath, hot water, living room and bar, patio, email service, book exchange, airport transfers, 15 mins from airport, 15 mins from Miraflores, 20 mins from historical centre. Frequently recommended.

$ Tambopacaya

Jr Manco Capac 212 (block 31 of Av Brasil), Magdalena del Mar, T01-261 6122, www. tambopacaya.com.
All rooms and dorms have private bath, hot water, use of kitchen, laundry, guided tours, airport transfers, convenient for airport and centre.

San Isidro

$$$$ Country Club

Los Eucaliptos 590, T01-611 9000, www.hotelcountry.com.
Excellent, fine service, luxurious rooms, good bar and restaurant, classically stylish with a fine art collection.

$$$$ Libertador Hotels Peru

Los Eucaliptos 550, T01-518 6300, www.libertador.com.pe.
Overlooking the golf course, full facilities for the business traveller, large comfortable rooms in this relatively small hotel, fine service, good restaurant.

$$$$ Sonesta El Olivar

Pancho Fierro 194, T01-712 6000, www.sonesta.com/Lima.
Excellent, one of the top 5-star hotels in Lima overlooking El Olivar park, modern, good restaurant and bar, terrace, gym, pool, quiet, very attentive, popular.

$$$ Garden

Rivera Navarrete 450, T01-200 9800, www.gardenhotel.com.pe.
Good beds, small restaurant, ideal for business visitors, convenient, good value.

$$ Chez Elizabeth

Av del Parque Norte 265, San Isidro, T9980 07557, http://chezelizabeth.typepad.fr.
Family house in residential area 7 mins' walk from Cruz del Sur bus station. Shared or private bathrooms, TV room, laundry, airport transfers.

$ Albergue Juvenil Malka

Los Lirios 165 (near 4th block of Av Javier Prado Este), San Isidro, T01-442 0162, www.youthhostelperu.com.
Dormitory style, 4-8 beds per room, also private doubles ($$), English spoken, laundry, climbing wall, nice café, airport transfer.

Miraflores

$$$$ Casa Andina Private Collection

Av La Paz 463, T01-213 4300, www.casa-andina.com.
Top of the range hotel in this recommended Peruvian chain (see below), modern, well-appointed large rooms with safe, cable TV, Wi-Fi, good bathrooms. Fine food in **Alma** restaurant and good value café, **Sama**, 1st class service, bar, pool and gym.

$$$$ Belmond Miraflores Park

Av Malecón de la Reserva 1035, T01-610 4000, www.miraflorespark.com.

An Orient Express hotel, excellent service and facilities, beautiful views over the ocean, top class. Rooftop, open-air, heated pool and spa which looks out over the ocean, open to the public when you buy a spa treatment.

$$$$ Sonesta Posadas del Inca
Alcanfores 329, T01-241 7688,
www.sonesta.com/Miraflores/.
Part of renowned chain of hotels, convenient location, cable TV, a/c, restaurant.

$ $$ Alemán
Arequipa 4704, T01-445 6999,
www.hotelaleman.com.pe.
No sign, comfortable, quiet, garden, excellent breakfast, smiling staff.

$$$ Antigua Miraflores
Av Grau 350 at C Francia, T01-201 2060,
www.antiguamiraflores.com.
A small, elegant hotel in a quiet but central location, excellent service, tastefully furnished and decorated, gym, good restaurant. Recommended.

$$$ Casa Andina
Av 28 de Julio 1088, T01-241 4050,
www.casa-andina.com.
Also at Av Petit Thouars 5444, T01-447 0263, in Miraflores. The 'Classic' hotels in this chain have similar facilities and decor. Very neat, with many useful touches, comfortable beds, fridge, safe, laundry service, buffet breakfast, other meals available. Check website for discounts and for the more upmarket **Casa Andina Select** at Schell 452, T01-416 7500 ($$$$-$$$), with disabled facilities.

$$$ Casa de Baraybar
Toribio Pacheco 216, T01-652 2262,
www.casadebaraybar.com.
1 block from the ocean, extra long beds, a/c or fan, colourful decor, high

ceilings, 24-hr room service, laundry, airport transfers free for stays of 3 nights. Bilingual staff. Recommended.

$$$ La Castellana
Grimaldo del Solar 222, T01-444 4662,
www.castellanahotel.com.
Pleasant, good value, nice garden, safe, expensive restaurant, laundry, English spoken.

$$$ José Antonio
28 de Julio 398 y C Colón, T01-445 7743,
www.hotelesjoseantonio.com.
Good in all respects, including the restaurant, large modern rooms, jacuzzis, swimming pool, business facilities, helpful staff speak some English.

$$$ San Antonio Abad
Ramón Ribeyro 301, T01-447 6766,
www.hotelsanantonioabad.com.
Secure, quiet, helpful, tasty breakfasts, 1 free airport transfer with reservation, justifiably popular, good value.

$$$ Señorial
José González 567, T01-445 0139,
www.senorial.com.
100 rooms, with restaurant, room service, comfortable, nice garden, parking, good services.

$$$-$$ Hostal El Patio
Diez Canseco 341, T01-444 2107,
www.hostalelpatio.net.
Very nice suites and rooms, comfortable, English and French spoken, convenient, *comedor*, gay friendly. Very popular, reservations are essential.

$$$-$$ Inka Frog
Gral Iglesias 271, T01-445 8979,
www.inkafrog.com.
Self-styled "Exclusive B&B", comfortable, nice decor, lounge with huge TV, rooftop terrace, good value.

$$ Casa Rodas
*Av Petit Thouars 4712, T01-447 5761,
and Tarapacá 250, T01-242 4872,
www.casarodas.com.*
Both houses have rooms for 2, 3 or 4,
good beds ($$$ with private bath),
hot water, helpful staff.

$$ El Carmelo
*Bolognesi 749, T01-446 0575,
www.hostalelcarmelo.com.pe.*
Great location a couple of blocks from
the Parque del Amor, small restaurant
downstairs serving *criolla* food and
ceviche, good value, comfortable,
breakfast extra.

$$ La Casa Nostra
Av Grimaldo del Solar 265, T01-241 1718.
Variety of rooms (from singles to quad),
all with private bath, good service,
convenient, safe, money exchange,
laundry, tourist information. Popular.

$$ Sipán
*Paseo de la República 6171, T01-241 3758,
www.hotelsipan.com.*
Very pleasant, on the edge of a
residential area next to the Vía Expresa
(which can be heard from front rooms).
Economical meals available in restaurant,
24-hr room service, security box, secure
parking. Airport transfers available.

$$-$ Albergue Turístico Juvenil Internacional
*Av Casimiro Ulloa 328, San Antonio,
T01-446 5488, www.limahostell.com.pe.*
Dormitory accommodation or a
double private room, basic cafeteria,
travel information, laundry facilities,
swimming pool often empty, extra
charge for breakfast, safe, situated in a
nice villa; 20 mins' walk from the beach.
Bus No 2 or colectivos pass Av Benavides
to the centre.

$$-$ Condor's House
*Martín Napanga 137, T01-446 7267,
www.condorshouse.com.*
Award-winning, quiet hostel, 2 categories
of dorm rooms with lockers, good
bathrooms, also doubles, good meeting
place, TV room with films, book
exchange, *parrillada* prepared once
a week, bar. Helpful staff.

$$-$ Explorer's House
*Av Alfredo León 158, by 10th block of
Av José Pardo, T01-241 5002, http://
explorershouselima.com.*
No sign, but plenty of indications of the
house number, dorm with shared bath,
or double rooms with bath, hot water,
laundry service, Spanish classes, English
spoken, very welcoming.

$$-$ Flying Dog
*Diez Canseco 117, T01-212 7145,
www.flyingdogperu.com.*
Also at Lima 457 and Olaya 280, all
with dorms, doubles, triples, quads.
All are on or near Parque Kennedy,
with kitchen, lockers, but all have
different features. There are others
in Cuzco, Iquitos and Arequipa.

$$-$ HosteLima
*Cnel Inclán 399, T01-242 7034,
www.hostelima.com.*
Private double rooms and brightly-
painted dorms, close to Parque Kennedy,
helpful staff, safe, bar/restaurant and
snack shop, movie room, Play Station 3,
travel information.

$$-$ The Lighthouse
*Cesareo Chacaltana 162, T01-446 8397,
www.thelighthouseperu.com.*
Near Plaza Morales Barros, British/
Peruvian-run, relaxed, small dorm or
private rooms with private or shared
bath. Good services, small indoor patio.

$$-$ Loki Backpackers

José Galvez 576, T01-651 2966,
www.lokihostel.com.
In a quiet area, the capital's sister to
the party hostel of the same name in
Cuzco, doubles or dorms, good showers,
cooked breakfast extra, Fri barbecues,
lockers, airport transfers.

$$-$ Pariwana

Av Larco 189, T01-242 4350,
www.pariwana-hostel.com.
Party hostel with doubles and dorms in
the heart of Miraflores, individual lockers
with power outlets so you can leave your
gadgets charging in a safe place. Always
lots going on here.

$$-$ Pirwa

González Prada 179, T01-444 1266 and
Coronel Inclán 494 (B&B), T01-242 4059,
www.pirwahostelsperu.com.
Members of a chain of hostels in Peru
(Cuzco, Arequipa, Puno, Nazca); González
Prada is a bit cheaper but both have
choice of dorms and double rooms,
lockers, transfers arranged, bike rental.

$$-$ Albergue Verde

Grimaldo del Solar 459, T01-657 4948,
www.albergueverde.com.
Nice small hostal with private and shared
rooms for 3-5 people, comfortable beds,
helpful owner and staff, airport and bus
terminal pick up.

$ Blue House

José González 475, T01-445 0476,
www.bluehouse.com.pe.
A true backpacker hostel, most rooms
with bath including a double, basic but
good value for the location, terraza with
parrilla, films to watch.

$ Casa del Mochilero

Cesareo Chacaltana 130A, T01-444
9089, pilaryv@hotmail.com (casa-del-
mochilero on Facebook).
Ask for Pilar or Juan, dorms or double
room on terrace, all with shared bath,
breakfast and internet extra, hot water,
lots of information.

$ Friend's House

Jr Manco Cápac 368, T01-446 6248,
Friends.House.Miraflores.Lima.Peru
on Facebook.
Very popular, reserve in advance.
Near Larcomar shopping centre, with
dormitory accommodation with
shared bath and hot water, plenty of
good information and help, family
atmosphere. Highly recommended. They
have another branch at José González
427, T01-446 3521. Neither branch is
signed, except on the bell at No 427.

$ Hitchhikers B&B Backpackers

Bolognesi 400, T01-242 3008,
www.hhikersperu.com.
Located close to the ocean, mixture of
dorms and private rooms with shared
or private bath ($$), nice patio, plenty
of parking, bicycles to borrow, airport
transfers. Also has a hostel in Cuzco.

Barranco

$$$$ B

San Martín 301, T01-700 5106,
www.hotelb.pe.
Boutique hotel in an early 20th-century
mansion. Beautifully redesigned as a
luxury hotel in the original building
and a contemporary wing, eclectic
design features and a large collection
of mostly modern art, next to Lucía de
la Puente gallery and convenient for
others, blog and Facebook give cultural
recommendations, highly regarded

Mediterranean/Peruvian restaurant, cocktail bar, plunge pool, excellent service. In Relais y Châteaux group.

$$-$ Barranco's Backpackers Inn
Mcal Castilla 260, T01-247 1326.
Ocean view, colourful rooms, all en suite, shared and private rooms, tourist information.

$$-$ Domeyer
C Domeyer 296, T01-247 1413, www.domeyerhostel.net.
Private or shared rooms sleeping 1-3 people in a historic house. Hot water 24 hrs, laundry service, secure, gay friendly.

$$-$ Safe in Lima
Alfredo Silva 150, T01-252 7330, www.safeinperu.com.
Quiet, Belgian-run hostal with family atmosphere, single, double and triple rooms, very helpful, airport pick-up US$28, good value, reserve in advance, lots of information for travellers.

$ The Point
Malecón Junín 300, T01-247 7997, www.thepointhostels.com.
Rooms range from doubles to large dormitories, all with shared bath, very popular with backpackers (book in advance at weekends), laundry, gay friendly, restaurant, bar, party atmosphere most of the time, but also space for relaxing, weekly barbecues, travel centre.

Callao (near the airport)

$$$$ Ramada Costa del Sol
Av Elmer Faucett s/n, T01-711 2000, www.ramada.com.
Within the airport perimeter. Offers day rates as well as overnights if you can't get into the city. Good service, buffet breakfast, but high-priced because of lack of competition and expensive extras.

$$ Hostal Residencial Víctor
Manuel Mattos 325, Urb San Amadeo de Garagay, Lima 31, T569 4662, www.hostalvictor.com.
5 mins from the airport by taxi, or phone or email in advance for free pick-up, large comfortable rooms, hot water, 10% discount for Footprint book owners, American breakfast (or packed breakfast for early departure), evening meals can be ordered locally, 2 malls with restaurants, shops, cinemas, etc nearby, very helpful.

$$-$ Pay Purix
Av Japón (formerly Bertello Bolatti), Mz F, Lote 5, Urb Los Jazmines, 1a Etapa, Callao, T01-484 9118, www.paypurix.com.
3 mins from airport, can arrange pick-up (taxi US$6, US$2 from outside airport). Hostel with doubles and dorms, convenient, washing machine, English spoken, CDs, DVDs, games and use of kitchen.

Restaurants

18% state tax and 10% service will be added to your bill in middle- and upper-class restaurants. Chinese is often the cheapest at around US$5 including a drink. For the rise of Peruvian cuisine, see Gastronomic Lima, page 64.

Central Lima

$$$ Wa Lok
Jr Paruro 864 and 878, Barrio Chino, T01-427 2656.
Good dim sum, cakes and fortune cookies (when you pay the bill). English spoken, very friendly.

Also at Av Angamos Oeste 700,
Miraflores, T01-447 1329.

$$ Chifa San Joy Lao
Ucayali 779.
A *chifa* with a good reputation, one of
several on the pedestrianized part of the
Barrio Chino.

$$ L'Eau Vive
*Ucayali 370, also opposite the Torre Tagle
Palace, T01-427 5612. Mon-Sat, 1230-1500
and 1930-2130.*
Run by nuns, fixed-price lunch menu,
Peruvian-style in interior dining room,
or à la carte in either of dining rooms
that open on to patio, excellent, profits
go to the poor, Ave María is sung nightly
at 2100.

$$ Salon Capon
Jr Paruro 819.
Good dim sum, at this recommended
chifa. Also has a branch at Larcomar
shopping centre, which is $$, elegant
and equally recommended.

$$-$ Bar Cordano
*Ancash 202 y Carabaya (in Calles El Rastro
y Pescadería zone).*
Historic tavern serving Peruvian food
and drinks, great atmosphere, favoured
by politicians.

$$-$ De César
*Ancash 300, T01-428 8740.
Open 0700-2300.*
Old-fashioned atmosphere, apart from
the 3 TVs, breakfasts, snacks, seafood,
meat dishes, pastas, pizza, juices, coffees
and teas. Good food.

$$-$ Rovegno
*Arenales 456 (near block 3 of Arequipa),
T01-424 8465.*
Italian and Peruvian dishes, home-made
pasta, also serves snacks and sandwiches
and has a bakery. Good value.

$ Accllahuasy
*Jr Ancash 400. Around the corner from
Hostal España. Daily 0700-2300.*
Good Peruvian dishes.

$ La Catedral del Pisco
*Jr de la Unión 1100 esq Av Uruguay 114,
T01-330 0079. Daily 0800-2200.*
Comida criolla and drinks, including free
Peruvian coffee (excellent) or pisco sour
for Footprint Handbook owners! Live
music at night, Wi-Fi.

Breña and Pueblo Libre

$$$-$$ Café del Museo
*At the Museo Larco, Av Bolívar 1515,
T01-462 4757. Daily 0900-2200, seating
inside and on the terrace.*
Specially designed interior, selection
of salads, fine Peruvian dishes, pastas
and seafood, a tapas bar of traditional
Peruvian foods, as well as snacks,
desserts and cocktails. Highly regarded.

$$ La Choza Náutica
*Jr Breña 204 and 211 behind
Plaza Bolognesi, T01-423 8087,
www.chozanautica.com.*
Good *ceviche* and friendly service;
has 3 other branches.

$$-$ Antigua Taberna Quierolo
*Av San Martín 1090, 1 block from
Plaza Bolívar, T01-460 0441, http://
antiguatabernaqueirolo.com.*
Atmospheric old bar with glass-fronted
shelves of bottles, marble bar and old
photos, owns bodega next door. Serves
simple lunches, sandwiches and snacks,
good for wine, does not serve dinner.

$ Azato
*Av Arica 298, 3 blocks from Plaza
Bolognesi, T01-423 0278.*
Excellent and cheap Peruvian dishes.

In recent years Lima has become known as the 'gastronomic capital of South America', thanks to a revolution in Peruvian cuisine. The city's culinary prestige is reflected in the fact that the Mistura festival (www.mistura.pe) in September 2014 attracted over 300,000 visitors. At the heart of much of today's Peruvian gastronomy are traditional ingredients, from the coast, the Andes and the jungle. The star chefs all recognize the debt they owe to the cooks of the different regions. Their skill is in combining the local heritage with the flavours and techniques that they have learnt elsewhere, without overwhelming what is truly Peruvian.

There are several restaurants in the city that are championed as having achieved the height of culinary excellence. They are often priced beyond the average traveller's budget, but a meal at one of these could be the ideal way to celebrate a special occasion. Most serve à la carte and a tasting menu. Beyond Lima there are also many excellent innovative restaurants in Arequipa (see www.festisabores.com), Cuzco, Ayacucho and elsewhere. Don't forget that the regional cooking that provided inspiration for Peru's growing international fame is still very much alive and well, often in much more modest surroundings than the fine dining settings of the capital.

Gastón Acurio is usually credited with being the forerunner of the evolution of Peruvian cuisine. He is also recognized for his community work. In 2014 Acurio and his wife, Astrid, moved their flagship restaurant, Astrid y Gastón Casa Moreyra (www.astridygaston.com), from Miraflores to a historic building in San Isidro at Avenida Paz Soldán 290. Other ventures include *ceviche* at La Mar (Av Lar 770, Miraflores, T01-421 3365), *anticuchos* at Panchita (Av 2 de Mayo 298, Miraflores, T01-242 5957, see Facebook page) and his chain of T'anta cafés; there are branches behind the Municipalidad in the city centre, at Pancho Fierro 115 in San Isidro and in Larcomar.

Central (Santa Isabel 376, Miraflores, T01-446 9301, www.centralrestaurante. com.pe) presents Virgilio Martínez award-winning, sophisticated recipes fusing Peruvian ingredients and molecular cuisine.

San Isidro

$$$ Antica Pizzería
Av Dos de Mayo 732, T01-222 8437.
Very popular, great ambience, excellent food, Italian owner. Also in Barranco at Alfonso Ugarte 242, www.anticapizzeria.com.pe.

$$$ Chifa Titi
Av Javier Prado Este 1212, Córpac, T01-224 8189, www.chifatiti.com.
Regarded by many as the best Chinese restaurant in Lima with over 60 years in operation.

$$$-$$ Segundo Muelle
Av Conquistadores 490, T01-717 9998, www.segundomuelle.com.

Manifiesto (Independencia 130, Miraflores, T01-249 5533, www.manifiesto.pe) is billed as 'Tacna meets Italy', bringing together the birthplace and family roots of chef Giacomo Bocchio.

Rafael Osterling has two restaurants in the city: Rafael (San Martín 300, Miraflores, T01-242 4149, www.rafaelosterling.com), celebrated for its classic Peruvian dishes incorporating flavours from around the globe, especially the Mediterranean, and El Mercado (H Unanue 203, Miraflores, T01-221 1322), which concentrates on seafood, reflecting all the influences on Peruvian cooking.

At IK (Elias Aguirre 179, Miraflores, T01-652 1692, reservas@ivankisic.pe, see Facebook page), molecular gastronomy meets Peruvian ingredients at the late Ivan Kisic's restaurant.

Lima 27 (Santa Lucía 295 no sign, T01-221 5822, www.lima27.com) is a modern restaurant behind whose black exterior you will find contemporary Peruvian cuisine. It's in the same group as Alfresco (Malecón Balta 790, T01-242 8960), Cala on Costa Verde (http://calarestaurante.com), and a new sandwich bar, Manduca, in Jockey Plaza.

Pedro Miguel Schiaffino's Malabar (Camino Real 101, San Isidro, T01-440 5200, http://malabar.com.pe) takes the Amazon and its produce as the starting point for its dishes, as does Schiaffino's Amaz (Av La Paz 1079, Miraflores, T01-221 9393). This eatery is in a group of four places under the Hilton Hotel. Also here is Ache (Av La Paz 1055, T01-221 9315, achecocinanikkei on Facebook) which specializes in Japanese fusion cuisine.

La Picantería (Moreno 388 y González Prada, Surquillo, T01-241 6676, www.picanteriasdelperu.com) serves excellent seafood, first-class *ceviche*, has a fish-of-the-day lunch menu and a good bar.

Fiesta Gourmet (Av Reducto 1278, T01-242 9009, www.restaurantfiesta gourmet.com) specializes in superb food from Chiclayo and the north coast, served in fancy surroundings.

At AlmaZen (Federico Recavarrén 298 y Galvez, T01-243 0474) you will find one of the best organic slow-food restaurants in Latin America.

Ceviches and other very good seafood dishes, including Japanese, popular.

$$ Chez Philippe
Av 2 de Mayo 748, T01-222 4953, www.chez-philippe.net.
Pizza, pasta and crêpes, wood oven, rustic decor (same owners as Pizza B&B in Huaraz) and a huge choice of beers.

$$ Como Agua para Chocolate
Pancho Fierro 108, T01-222 0297.
Dutch/Mexican-owned restaurant, specializing in Mexican food as the name suggests, also has a very amusing Dutch night once a month. SAE members get a discount.

Cafés

Havanna
Miguel Dasso 165, www.havanna.pe.
Branch of the Argentine coffee and
alfajores chain, others in the city
include **Larcomar**.

News Café
*Av Santa Luisa 110. Mon-Fri 1000-2300,
Sat 1200-2300, Sun 1200-1700.*
Great salads and desserts, popular and
expensive. With another branch at
Av Larco 657, Miraflores.

Miraflores
Calle San Ramón, known as 'Pizza Street'
(across from Parque Kennedy), is a
pedestrian walkway lined with popular
outdoor restaurants/bars/discos that are
open until the wee small hours. Good-
natured touts try to entice diners and
drinkers inside with free offers.

$$$ El Kapallaq
*Av Petit Thouars 4844, T01-444 4149.
Mon-Fri 1200-1700 only.*
Prize-winning Peruvian restaurant
specializing in seafood and fish,
excellent *ceviches*.

$$$ El Rincón Gaucho
Av Armendáriz 580, T01-447 4778.
Good grill, renowned for its steaks.

$$$ Huaca Pucllana
*Gral Borgoño cuadra 8 s/n, alt cuadra
45 Av Arequipa, T01-445 4042, www.
resthuacapucllana.com.*
Facing the archaeological site of the
same name, contemporary Peruvian
fusion cooking, very good food in an
unusual setting, popular with groups.

$$$ La Gloria
*Atahualpa 201, T01-445 5705, www.
lagloriarestaurant.com. Mon-Sat
from 1300 and again from 2000.*

Popular upmarket restaurant serving
Peruvian food, classic and contemporary
styles, good service.

$$$ La Preferida
*Arias Araguez 698, T01-445 5180,
http://restaurantelapreferida.com.
Daily 0800-1700.*
Seafood restaurant and tapas bar, with
delicious *ceviches*, also has a branch in
Monterrico.

$$$ La Trattoria
*Manuel Bonilla 106, T01-446 7002,
www.latrattoriadimambrino.com,
1 block from Parque Kennedy.*
Italian cuisine, popular, good desserts.
Has another branch, **La Bodega**,
opposite entrance to Huaca Pucllana.

$$$ Las Brujas de Cachiche
*Av Bolognesi 472, T01-447 1883,
www.brujasdecachiche.com.pe.
Mon-Sat 1200-2400, Sun 1230-1630.*
An old mansion converted into bars
and dining rooms, fine traditional food
(menu in Spanish and English), live
criollo music.

$$$ Rosa Náutica
*T01-445 0149, www.larosanautica.com.
Daily 1230-0200.*
Built on old British-style pier (Espigón
No 4), in Lima Bay. Delightful opulence,
fine fish cuisine, experience the
atmosphere by buying a beer in the bar
at sunset.

$$$ Saqra
*Av La Paz 646, T01-650 88 84, www.
saqra.pe. Mon-Thu 1200-2400,
Fri-Sat 1200-0100.*
Colourful and casual, indoor or outdoor
seating, interesting use of ingredients
from all over Peru, classic flavours with a
fun, innovative twist, inspired by street
food and humble dishes, vegetarian

options, many organic products. Also good cocktail bar. Go with a group to sample as many dishes as possible.

$$$ Sí Señor
Jr Bolognesi 706, T01-445 3789.
Mexican food, cheerful, interesting decor, huge portions.

$$$-$$ Chifa Internacional
Av República de Panamá 5915, T01-445 3997, www.chifainternacional.com. Mon-Fri 1230-1530, then from 1900, Sat 1230-1600, then from 1900, Sun 1200-2315.
Great *chifa* in San Antonio district of Miraflores.

$$$-$$ Las Tejas
Diez Canseco 340, T01-444 4360. Daily 1100-2300.
Good, typical Peruvian food, especially *ceviche*.

$$$-$$ Punto Azul
San Martín 595, Benavides 2711, with other branches in San Isidro, Surco and San Borja, http://puntoazulrestaurante. com. Tue-Sun 1100-1600 (San Martín 595 also open Mon-Sat 1900-2400).
Popular, well-regarded chain of seafood and *ceviche* restaurants.

$$ Café Tarata
Pasaje Tarata 260, T01-446 6330.
Good atmosphere, family-run, good varied menu.

$$ El Huarike
Enrique Palacios 140, T01-241 6086.
Fashionable, interesting combinations of *ceviche* and sushi, also cooked seafood dishes.

$$ El Parquetito
Lima 373 y Diez Canseco, T01-444 0490.
Peruvian food from all regions, good menu, serves breakfast, eat inside or out.

$$ Lobo del Mar – Octavio Otani
Colón 587, T01-242 1871.
Basic exterior hides one of the oldest *cevicherías* in Miraflores, excellent, a good selection of other seafood dishes.

$$ Mama Olla
Pasaje Tarata 248.
Charming café on a pedestrian walkway, huge menu, big portions.

$ Govinda
Schell 630.
Vegetarian, from Hare Krishna foundation, lunch *menú* US$3.

$ Madre Natura
Chiclayo 815, T01-445 2522, www.madrenaturaperu.com. Mon-Sat 0800-2100.
Natural foods shop and eating place, very good.

Cafés

Café Café
Martin Olaya 250, at the corner of Av Diagonal.
Very popular, good atmosphere, over 100 different blends of coffee, good salads and sandwiches, very popular with 'well-to-do' Limeños. Also in Larcomar.

Café de la Paz
Lima 351, middle of Parque Kennedy.
Good outdoor café right on the park, expensive, great cocktails, with another branch on Pasaje Tarata.

Café La Máquina
Alcanfores 323.
Friendly small café and bar with good cocktails, lunch menu, interesting sandwiches and great cakes.

C'est si bon
Av Cdte Espinar 663.
Excellent cakes by the slice or whole,
best in Lima.

Chef's Café
Av Larco 375 and 763.
Nice places for a sandwich or coffee.

Haiti
Av Diagonal 160, Parque Kennedy.
Open almost round the clock daily.
Great for people watching, good
ice cream.

La Lucha
Av Benavides y Olaya (under Flying Dog),
on Parque Kennedy, with a small branch
nearby between Olaya and Benavides
and another on Ovalo Gutiérrez.
Excellent hot sandwiches, limited range,
choice of sauces, great juices, *chicha*
morada and *café pasado*. Good for a
wholesome snack.

La Tiendecita Blanca
Av Larco 111 on Parque Kennedy.
One of Miraflores' oldest, expensive,
good people-watching, very good cakes,
European-style food and delicatessen.

Pan de la Chola
Av La Mar 918, El-Pan-de-la-Chola
on Facebook.
Café and bakery specializing in
sourdough bread, Peruvian cheeses,
teas, juices and sweets.

San Antonio
Av 28 de Julio y Reducto (many other
eating places at this junction).
Fashionable *pastelería* chain with hot
and cold lunch dishes, good salads,
inexpensive, busy. Other branches at
Av Angamos Oeste 1494, Rocca de
Vergallo 201, Magdalena del Mar,
and Av Primavera 373, San Borja.

Barranco

$$$ Canta Rana
Génova 101, T01-247 7274. Sun-Mon
1200-1800, Tue-Sat 1200-2300.
Good *ceviche*, expensive, small portions,
but the most popular local place on Sun.

$$$ La 73
Av Sol Oeste 176, casi San Martín, at the
edge of Barranco.
Mostly meat dishes, has a lunch menu,
look for the Chinese lanterns outside,
good reputation.

$$$ La Costa Verde
On Barranquito beach, T01-247 1244,
www.restaurantecostaverde.com.
Daily 1200-2400, Sun buffet.
Excellent fish and wine, expensive
but considered one of the best.

$$$ La Pescadería
Grau 689, T01-477 0966,
www.lapescaderia.pe.
A recommended *cevichería* and
tienda for formal and informal eating.

$$$-$$ Tío Mario
Jr Zepita 214, on the steps to the Puente
de Suspiros.
Excellent *anticuchería*, serving delicious
Peruvian kebabs, always busy, fantastic
service, varied menu and good prices.

$$ Las Mesitas
Av Grau 341, T01-477 4199.
Open 1200-0200.
Traditional tea rooms-cum-restaurant,
serving Creole food and traditional
desserts which you won't find anywhere
else, lunch *menú* served till 1400 US$3.

$$-$ Sóngoro Cosongo
Ayacucho 281, T01-247 4730, at the top
of the steps down to Puente de Suspiros,
www.songorocosongo.com.

Good-value *comida criolla*, "un poco de todo".

Cafés

La Boteca
Grau 310-312.
Smart-looking café-bar.

Expreso Virgen de Guadalupe
San Martín y Ayacucho.
Café and vegetarian buffet in an old tram, also seating in the garden, more expensive at weekends.

Tostería Bisetti
Pedro de Osma 116, www.cafebisetti.com.
Coffee, cakes and a small selection of lunchtime dishes, service a bit slow but a nice place.

Bars and clubs

See also Entertainment (below) for a list of peñas offering live music and dancing.

Central Lima
The centre of town, specifically Jr de la Unión, has numerous nightclubs, but it's best to avoid the nightspots around the intersection of Av Tacna, Av Piérola and Av de la Vega, as these places are rough and foreigners will receive much unwanted attention. For the latest gay and lesbian nightspots, check out www.gayperu.com.

El Rincón Cervecero
Jr de la Unión (Belén) 1045, www.rinconcervecero.com.pe.
German-style pub, fun.

Estadio Futbol Sports Bar
Av Nicolás de Piérola 926 on the Plaza San Martín, T01-428 8866. Mon-Wed 1215-2300, Thu 1215-2400, Fri-Sat 1215-0300, Sun 1215-1800.

Beautiful bar with a disco, international football theme, good international and creole food.

Piano Bar Munich
Jr de la Unión 1044 (basement).
Small and fun.

Miraflores

La Tasca
Av Diez Canseco 117, very near Parque Kennedy, part of the Flying Dog group and under one of the hostels (see Where to stay, above).
Spanish-style bar with cheap beer (for Miraflores). An eclectic crowd including ex-pats, travellers and locals. Gay-friendly. Small and crowded.

Media Naranja
Schell 130, at bottom of Parque Kennedy.
Brazilian bar with drinks and food.

Murphy's
Schell 619, T01-447 1082.
Mon-Sat from 1600.
Happy hours every day with different offers, lots of entertainment, very popular.

The Old Pub
San Ramón 295 (Pizza St), www.oldpub.com.pe.
Cosy, with live music most days.

Treff Pub Alemán
Av Benavides 571-104, T01-444 0148 (hidden from the main road behind a cluster of tiny houses signed 'Los Duendes').
A wide range of German beers, plus cocktails, good atmosphere, darts and other games.

Barranco
Barranco is the capital of Lima nightlife. The following is a short list of some of the better bars and clubs. The pedestrian

walkway Pasaje Sánchez Carrión, right off the main plaza, has watering holes and discos on both sides. Av Grau, just across the street from the plaza, is also lined with bars, including the **Lion's Head Pub** (Av Grau 268, p 2) and **Déjà Vu** at No 294. Many of the bars in this area turn into discos later on.

Ayahuasca
San Martín 130.
In the stunning Berninzon House, which dates from the Republican era, a chilled out lounge bar with several areas for eating, drinking and dancing. Food is expensive and portions are small, but go for the atmosphere.

Barranco Beer Company
Grau 308, T01-247 6211, www.barranco beer.com. Closed Mon, open from 1900 on Tue, 1200 on Wed-Sun, closes 1700 on Sun.
Artisanal brewhouse.

El Dragón
N de Piérola 168, T01-715 5043.
Popular bar and venue for music, theatre and painting.

Juanitos
Av Grau, opposite the park. Daily 1600-0400.
Barranco's oldest bar, where writers and artists congregate, a perfect spot to start the evening.

La Noche
Bolognesi 307, at Pasaje Sánchez Carrión, www.lanoche.com.pe.
A Lima institution. High standard live music, Mon is jazz night, all kicks off at around 2200.

La Posada del Angel
3 branches, Pedro de Osma 164 and 214, T01-247 0341, see Facebook.

These are popular bars serving snacks and meals.

La Posada del Mirador
Ermita 104, near the Puente de los Suspiros (Bridge of Sighs), see Facebook.
Beautiful view of the ocean, but you pay for the privilege.

Santos Café & Espirituosos
Jr Zepita 203, just above the Puente de Suspiros, T01-247 4609, also on Facebook. Mon-Sat 1700-0100.
Favourite spot for trendy young professionals who want to drop a few hundred soles, relaxed, informal but pricey.

Sargento Pimienta
Bolognesi 757, www.sargentopimienta. com.pe. Tue-Sat from 2200.
Live music, always a favourite with Limeños.

Victoria
Av Pedro de Osma 135.
New upmarket pub in the beautiful Casa Cillóniz, serving up a selection of beers, cocktails, snacks and live music.

Entertainment

Theatre and concert tickets can be booked through **Teleticket**, T01-613 8888, Mon-Fri 0900-1900, www. teleticket.com.pe. For cultural events, see *Lima Cultural*, www.limacultura.pe, the city's monthly arts programme.

Cinemas
The newspaper *El Comercio* lists cinema information in the section called *Luces*. Mon-Wed reduced price at most cinemas. Most films are in English with subtitles and cost from US$7-8.75 in Miraflores and malls, US$3-4 in the centre. The best cinema chains in the city are **Cinemark**, **Cineplanet** and **UVK Multicines**.

Cinematógrafo de Barranco, *Pérez Roca 196, Barranco, T01-264 4374.* Small independent cinema showing a good choice of classic and new international films.
Filmoteca de Lima, *Centro Cultural PUCP, Camino Real 1075, San Isidro, T01-616 1616, http://cultural.pucp.edu.pe.*

Peñas

Del Carajo, *Catalino Miranda 158, Barranco, T01-247 7977, www.delcarajo. com.pe.* All types of traditional music.
De Rompe y Raja, *Manuel Segura 127, T01-636 1518, www.derompeyraja.pe. Thu, Fri, Sat.* Popular for music, dancing and *criolla* food.
La Candelaria, *Av Bolognesi 292, Barranco, T01-247 1314, www. lacandelariaperu.com. Fri-Sat 2130 onwards.* A good Barranco *peña*.
La Estación de Barranco, *Pedro de Osma 112, T01-477 5030, www. laestaciondebarranco.com.* Good, family atmosphere, varied shows.
Las Brisas de Titicaca, *Héroes de Tarapacá 168, at 1st block of Av Brasil near Plaza Bolognesi, T01-715 6960, www. brisasdeltiticaca.com.* A Lima institution.
Sachun, *Av del Ejército 657, Miraflores, T01-441 0123, www.sachunperu.com.* Great shows on weekdays as well.

Theatre

El Gran Teatro Nacional, *corner of Avs Javier Prado and Aviación, San Borja.* Capable of seating 1500 people, it hosts concerts, opera, ballet and other dance as well as other events.
Teatro Municipal, *Jr Ica 377, T01-315 1300 ext 1767, see Facebook.* Completely restored after a fire, with full programmes and a theatre museum on Huancavelica.
Teatro Segura, *Jr Huancavelica*

265, T01-427 9491. Stages professional performances.

There are many other theatres in the city, some of which are related to cultural centres. All have various cultural activities; the press gives details of performances: **CCPUCP** (see Cinemas, above); **Instituto Cultural Peruano-Norteamericano** (Jr Cusco 446, Lima Centre, T01-706 7000, central office at Av Angamos Oeste 160, Miraflores, www.icpna.edu.pe); **Centro Cultural Peruano Japonés** (Av Gregorio Escobedo 803, Jesús María, T01-518 7450, www.apj.org.pe).

Festivals

18 Jan Founding of Lima.
Mar/Apr Semana Santa, or Holy Week, is a colourful spectacle with processions.
28-29 Jul Independence, with music and fireworks in the Plaza de Armas on the evening before.
30 Aug Santa Rosa de Lima.
Mid-Sep Mistura, www.mistura. pe, a huge gastronomy fair in Parque Exposición, with Peruvian foods, celebrity chefs, workshops and more.
Oct The month of **Our Lord of the Miracles**; see Las Nazarenas church, page 354.

Shopping

Bookshops

Crisol, *Ovalo Gutiérrez, Av Santa Cruz 816, San Isidro, T01-221 1010, below Cine Planet.* Large bookshop with café, titles in English, French and Spanish. Also in Jockey Plaza Shopping Center, Av Javier Prado Este 4200, Surco, T01-436 0004, and other branches, www.crisol.com.pe.
Epoca, *Av Cdte Espinar 864, Miraflores, T01-241 2951.* Great selection of books, mostly in Spanish.

Ibero Librerías, *Av Diagonal 500,*
T01-242 2798, Larco 199, T01-445 5520, in
Larcomar, Miraflores, and other branches,
www.iberolibros.com. Stocks Footprint
Handbooks as well as a wide range of
other titles.

Camping equipment

It's better to bring all camping and
hiking gear from home. Camping gas
(the most popular brand is **Doite**,
which comes in small blue bottles)
is available from any large hardware
store or bigger supermarket.
Alpamayo, *Av Larco 345, Miraflores at*
Parque Kennedy, T01-445 1671. Mon-Fri
1000-1330, 1430-2000, Sat 1000-1400.
Sleeping mats, boots, rock shoes,
climbing gear, water filters, tents,
backpacks etc, very expensive but top
quality equipment. Owner speaks fluent
English and offers good information.
Altamira, *Arica 880, Parque Damert,*
behind Wong on Ovalo Gutiérrez,
Miraflores, T01-445 1286. Sleeping bags,
climbing gear, hiking gear and tents.
Camping Center, *Av Benavides*
1620, Miraflores, T01-445 5981, www.
campingperu.com. Mon-Fri 1000-2000,
Sat 1000-1400. Selection of tents,
backpacks, stoves, camping and
climbing gear.
El Mundo de las Maletas, *Preciados 308,*
Higuereta-Surco, T01-449 7850. Daily 0900-
2200. For suitcase repairs.
Tatoo, *CC Larcomar, locs 123-125B,*
T01-242 1938, www.tatoo.ws. For top-
quality imported ranges and own
brands of equipment.
Todo Camping, *Av Angamos Oeste 350,*
Miraflores, near Av Arequipa, T01-242
1318. Sells 100% deet, blue gas canisters,
lots of accessories, tents, crampons
and backpacks.

Handicrafts

Miraflores is a good place for high quality,
expensive handicrafts; there are many
shops on and around the top end of
Av La Paz (starting at Av Ricardo Palma).
Agua y Tierra, *Diez Canseco 298 y*
Alcanfores, Miraflores, T01-444 6980.
Fine crafts and indigenous art.
Alpaca 859, *Av Larco 859, Miraflores.* Good
quality alpaca and baby alpaca products.
Arte XXI, *Av La Paz 678, Miraflores, T01-*
447 9777, www.artemania-21.com. Gallery
and store for contemporary and colonial
Peruvian paintings.
Artesanía Santo Domingo, *Plazuela*
Santo Domingo, by the church of that
name, in Lima centre, T01-428 9860.
Good Peruvian crafts.
Centro Comercial El Alamo, *corner of*
La Paz y Diez Canseco, Miraflores. Artesanía
shops with good choice.
Dédalo, *Paseo Sáenz Peña 295, Barranco,*
T01-652 5400, http://dedaloarte.blogspot.
co.uk. A labyrinthine shop selling furniture,
jewellery and other items, as good as a
gallery. It also has a nice coffee shop and
has cinema shows. Other branches on
Parque Kennedy and at Larcomar.
Kuna by Alpaca 111, *Av Larco 671,*
Miraflores, T01-447 1623, www.kuna.
com.pe. High-quality alpaca, baby alpaca
and vicuña items. Also in Larcomar
(loc 1-07), Museo Larco, the airport,
Jockey Plaza, at hotels and in San Isidro.
Kuntur Wasi, *Ocharán 182, Miraflores,*
opposite Sol de Oro hotel, look for the sign
above the wall, T01-447 7173, kunturh@
speedy.com.pe. English-speaking owners
are very knowledgeable about Peruvian
textiles; often have exhibitions of fine
folk art and crafts.
La Casa de la Mujer Artesana, *Juan*
Pablo Ferandini 1550 (Av Brasil cuadra
15), Pueblo Libre, T01-423 8840, www.
casadelamujerartesana.com. Mon-Fri

0900-1300, 1400-1700. A cooperative run by the Movimiento Manuela Ramos, excellent quality work mostly from *pueblos jóvenes*.

Las Pallas, *Cajamarca 212, Barranco, T01-477 4629, www.laspallas.com.pe. Mon-Sat 0900-1900.* Very high quality handicrafts, English, French and German spoken.

Luz Hecho a Mano, *Berlín 399, Miraflores, T01-446 7098.* Lovely handmade handbags, wallets and other leather goods including clothing which last for years and can be custom made.

Museo de la Nación *(see page 45),* often hosts specialist handicrafts markets presenting individual work from across Peru during national festivals. There are bargains in high-quality Pima cotton.

Jewellery
On Cs La Esperanza and La Paz, Miraflores, dozens of shops offer gold and silverware at reasonable prices.

Ilaria, *Av 2 de Mayo 308, San Isidro, T01-512 3530, www.ilariainternational.com.* Jewellery and silverware with interesting designs. There are other branches in Lima, Cuzco, Arequipa and Trujillo.

Maps
Instituto Geográfico Nacional, *Av Aramburú 1190, Surquillo, T01-475 9960, www.ign.gob.pe. Mon-Fri 0830-1645.* It has topographical maps of the whole country, mostly at 1:100,000, political and physical maps of all departments and satellite and aerial photographs. You may be asked to show your passport when buying these maps.

Lima 2000, *Av Arequipa 2625 (near the intersection with Av Javier Prado), T01-440 3486, www.lima2000.com.pe. Mon-Fri 0900-1300, 1400-1800.* Has excellent street maps of Lima, from tourist maps, US$5.55, to comprehensive books US$18.

Also has country maps (US$5.55-9.25), maps of Cuzco, Arequipa, Trujillo and Chiclayo and tourist maps of the Inca Trail, Colca and Cordillera Blanca. **South American Explorers** (see page 56) also stocks these and IGN maps.

Markets
All are open 7 days a week until late(ish).

Feria Nacional de Artesanía de los Deseos y Misterios, *Av 28 de Julio 747, near junction with Av Arequipa and Museo Metropolitano.* Small market specializing in charms, remedies, fortune-telling and trinkets from Peru and Bolivia.

Mercado 1, *Surquillo, cross Paseo de le República from Ricardo Palma, Miraflores and go north 1 block.* Food market with a huge variety of local produce. C Narciso de la Colina outside has various places to eat, including Heladería La Fiorentina, No 580, for excellent ice creams.

Mercado Inca, *Av Petit Thouars, blocks 51-54 (near Parque Kennedy, parallel to Av Arequipa), Miraflores.* An unnamed crafts market area, with a large courtyard and lots of small flags. This is the largest crafts arcade in Miraflores. From here to C Ricardo Palma the street is lined with crafts markets.

Parque Kennedy, *the main park of Miraflores.* Hosts a daily crafts market from 1700-2300.

Polvos Azules, *on García Naranjo, La Victoria, just off Av Grau in the centre of town.* The 'official' black market, sells just about anything; it is generally cheap and very interesting; beware pickpockets.

What to do

Cycling
Bike Tours of Lima, *Bolívar 150, Miraflores, T01-445 3172, www.biketours oflima.com.* Offer a variety of day tours

through the city of Lima by bike, also bicycle rentals.

BikeMavil, *Av Aviación 4023, Surco, T01-449 8435, see Facebook page. Mon-Sat 1030-2000.* Rental service, repairs, tours, selection of mountain and racing bikes.

Buenas Biclas, *Domingo Elías 164, Miraflores, T01-241 9712, www. buenasbiclas.com. Mon-Fri 1000-2000, Sat 1000-1400.* Mountain bike specialists, knowledgeable staff, good selection of bikes, repairs and accessories.

Casa Okuyama, *Manco Cápac 590, La Victoria, T01-330 9131. Mon-Fri 0900-1300, 1415-1800, Sat 0900-1300.* Repairs, parts, try here for 28-in tyres, excellent service.

Cycloturismo Peru, *T99-9012 8105, www. cicloturismoperu.com.* Offers good value cycling trips around Lima and beyond, as well as bike rental. The owner, Aníbal Paredes, speaks good English, is very knowledgeable and is the owner of **Mont Blanc Gran Hotel**.

Mirabici, *Parque Salazar, T01-673 3903. Daily 0800-1900.* Bicycle hire, US$7.50 per hr (tandems available); they also run bike tours 1000-1500, in English, Spanish and Portuguese. Bikes to ride up and down Av Arequipa can be rented on Sun 0800-1300, US$3 per hr, leave passport as deposit, www.jafibike.com.

Perú Bike, *T01-260 8225, www.perubike. com.* Experienced agency leading tours, professional guiding, mountain bike school and workshop.

Diving

Peru Divers, *Av Defensores del Morro 175, Chorrillos, T01-251 6231, www. perudivers.com.* Owner Lucho Rodríguez is a certified PADI instructor who offers certification courses, tours and a wealth of good information.

Hiking

Trekking and Backpacking Club, *Jr Huáscar 1152, Jesús María, Lima 11, T01-423 2515, T94-3866 794, www. angelfire.com/mi2/tebac.* Sr Miguel Chiri Valle, treks arranged, including in the Cordillera Blanca.

Paragliding

Aeroxtreme, *Trípoli 345, dpto 503, T01-242 5125, www.aeroxtreme.com.* One of several outfits offering parapenting in Lima, 20 years' experience.

Andean Trail Perú, *T99-836 3436, www. andeantrailperu.com.* For parapenting tandem flights, US$53, and courses, US$600 for 10 days. They also have a funday for US$120 to learn the basics. Trekking, kayaking and other adventure sports arranged.

Textiles/cultural tours

Puchka Perú, *www.puchkaperu.com.* Web-based operator specializing in textiles, folk art and markets. Fixed-date tours involve meeting artisans, workshops, visit to markets and more. In association with Maestro Máximo Laura, world-famous weaver, http:// maximolauratapestries.com, whose studio in Urb Brisas de Santa Rosa III Etapa, Lima can be visited by appointment, T01-577 0952. See also Museo Máximo Laura in Cuzco.

Tour operators

Do not conduct business anywhere other than in the agency's office and insist on a written contract.

The Andean Experience Co, *Sáenz Peña 214, Barranco, T01-700 5100, www. andean-experience.com.* Offers tailor-made itineraries designed to match each traveller's personal interests, style and preferences to create ideal Peru trips.

Aracari Travel Consulting, *Schell 237, of 602, Miraflores, T01-651 2424, www.aracari. com*. Regional tours throughout Peru, also 'themed' and activity tours, has a very good reputation.

Coltur, *Av Reducto 1255, Miraflores, T01-615 5555, www.colturperu.com*. Very helpful, experienced and well-organized tours throughout Peru.

Condor Travel, *Armando Blondet 249, San Isidro, T01-615 3000, www.condortravel. com*. Highly regarded operator with tailor-made programmes, special interest tours, luxury journeys, adventure travel and conventional tourism. One-stop shopping with own regional network.

Dasatariq, *Av Reducto 1255, Miraflores, T01-447 2741, www.dasatariq.com*. Also in Cuzco. Well-organized, helpful, with a good reputation.

Domiruth Travel Service S.A.C, *Av Petit Thouars 4305, Miraflores, T01-610 6000, www.domiruth.com*. Tours throughout Peru, from the mystical to adventure travel. See also **Peru 4x4 Adventures**, part of Domiruth, Jr Rio de Janeiro 216-218, www. peru4x4adventures.com, for exclusive 4WD tours with German, English, Spanish, Italian and Portuguese-speaking drivers.

Ecocruceros, *Av Arequipa 4964, of 202, Miraflores, T01-226 8530, www. islaspalomino.com*. Daily departures from Plaza Grau in Callao (see page 54) to see the sea lions at Islas Palomino, 4 hrs with 30-40 mins wetsuit swimming with guide, snack lunch, US$48 (take ID), reserve a day in advance.

Excursiones MYG, *T01-241 8091*. Offers a variety of tours in Lima and surroundings, including historic centre, nighttime, culinary tours, Caral, and further afield.

Explorandes, *C San Fernando 287, Miraflores, T01-200 6100, www. explorandes.com*. Award-winning company. Offers a wide range of adventure and cultural tours throughout the country. Also offices in Huaraz and Cuzco (see pages 95 and 373).

Fertur Peru Travel, *C Schell 485, Miraflores, T01-242 1900; and Jr Junín 211, Plaza de Armas, T01-427 2626; USA/ Canada T1-877 247 0055 toll free, UK T020-3002 3811, www.fertur-travel.com. Mon-Fri 0900-1900, Sat 0900-1600*. Siduith Ferrer de Vecchio, CEO of this agency, is highly recommended; she offers tour packages and up-to-date tourist information on a national level, and also great prices on national and international flights, discounts for those with ISIC and youth cards and for South American Explorers members. Other services include flight reconfirmations, hotel reservations and transfers to and from the airport or bus or train stations. Also in Cuzco at Simón Bolívar F23, T084-221304.

Il Tucano Peru, *Elías Aguirre 633, Miraflores, T01-444 9361, 24-hr number T01-975 0537S, www.iltucanoperu.com*. Personalized tours for groups or individuals throughout Peru, also 4WD overland trips, 1st-class drivers and guides, outstanding service and reliability.

Info Perú, *Jr de la Unión (Belén) 1066, of 102, T01-425 0414, www.infoperu.com.pe. Mon-Fri 0900-1800, Sat 0930-1400*. Run by a group of women, ask for Laura Gómez, offering personalized programmes, hotel bookings, transport, free tourist information, sale of maps, books and souvenirs, English and French spoken.

InkaNatura Travel, *Manuel Bañon 461, San Isidro, T01-203 5000, www.inkanatura. com*. Also in Cuzco and Chiclayo, experienced company with special emphasis on both sustainable tourism and conservation, especially in Manu and Tambopata, also birdwatching, and on the archaeology of all of Peru.

Lima Mentor, *T01-243 2697, www. limamentor.com*. Contact through web, phone or through hotels. An agency offering cultural tours of Lima using freelance guides in specialist areas (eg gastronomy, art, archaeology, Lima at night), entertaining, finding different angles from regular tours. Half-day or full day tours.

Lima Tours, *N de Piérola 589 p 18, T01-619 6900, www.limatours.com.pe*. Very good for tours in the capital and around the country; programmes include health and wellness tours.

Peru For Less, *ASTA Travel Agent, Luis García Rojas 240, Urb Humboldt, T01-273 2486, US office: T1-877-269 0309, UK office: T+44-203-002 0571, Cuzco office: T084-254800, www.peruforless.com*. Will meet or beat any published rates on the internet from outside Peru. Good reports.

Peru Hop, *Av Larco 812, p 3, corner with San Martín, T01-242 2140, www.peruhop. com*. A hop-on, hop-off bus service from Lima to Cuzco via Paracas, Nazca, Arequipa, daily departures, tours of places of interest, a variety of passes with different prices.

Peru Rooms, *Av Dos de Mayo 1545 of 205, San Isidro, T01-422 3434, www. perurooms.com*. Internet-based travel service offering 3- to 5-star packages throughout Peru, cultural, adventure and nature tourism.

Rutas del Peru SAC, *Av Enrique Palacios 1110, Miraflores, T01-445 7249, www. rutasdelperu.com*. Bespoke trips and overland expeditions in trucks.

Viajes Pacífico (Gray Line), *Av Paseo de la República 6010, p 7, T01-610 1911, www. graylineperu.com*. Tours throughout Peru and South America.

Viracocha, *Av Vasco Núñez de Balboa 191, Miraflores, T01-445 3986, peruviantours@ viracocha.com.pe*. Very helpful, especially for flights, adventure, cultural, mystical and birdwatching tours.

Open-top bus tours Mirabús (T01-242 6699, www.mirabusperu.com), runs many tours of the city and Callao (from US$3.50 to US$30) – eg Lima half day by day, Lima by night, Costa Verde, Callao, Gold Museum, Miraflores, Pachacámac with Paso horses display and dance show, Caral. Similar services concentrating on the city are offered by **Turibus** (T01-230 0909, www. turibusperu.com) from Larcomar.

Private guides The **MITINCI** (Ministry of Industry Tourism, Integration and International Business) certifies guides and can provide a list. Most are members of **AGOTUR** (Asociación de Guías Oficiales de Turismo) (Av La Paz 678, Miraflores (for correspondence only), www.agotur.com). Book in advance. Most guides speak a foreign language.

Transport

Air

For details of flights and general airport information, see Getting there, page 575. **Jorge Chávez Airport** (flight information T01-511 6055, www.lap.com.pe) is 16 km from the centre of Lima in Callao. It has all the facilities one would expect of an international airport. Information desks can be found in both domestic and international Arrivals. There is also a hotel and transport booking desk in international Arrivals. The airport has car hire offices, Global Net ATMs, *casas de cambio* and a bank (note that exchange rates are marginally poorer than outside), public telephones and a **Telefónica** *locutorio* (daily 0700-2300). Internet facilities are more expensive than in the city, but most of the airport has free Wi-Fi. Mobile phones can be hired in international Arrivals. Smart shops, restaurants and cafés are plentiful.

Transport from the airport

Remise taxis have desks outside both international and domestic Arrivals: **Taxi Green** (T01-484 4001, www.taxigreen. com.pe); **Mitsu** (T01-261 7788, www. mitsoo.net); and **CMV** (T01-219 0266, http://cmvtaxi.pe). As a rough guide, these companies charge US$20-30 to the centre, US$22-32 to Miraflores and San Isidro, a bit more to Barranco. In the same place is the desk of **Peruvian Shuttle** (T01-373 5049, www.peruvian-shuttle.com), which runs private, shared and group transfers to the city: from US$6 pp shared, US$23-40 private. If you do not opt for one of these companies, taxi drivers await passengers in the entrance hall. Their fares vary little from

Tip...
Do not go to the airport's car park exit to find a taxi without an airport permit outside the perimeter. Although these are much cheaper, they are not safe even by day, far less so at night. See Arriving at night, page 78.

the transport companies, although they will charge more at night.

Travelling by bus to/from the airport is not recommended, especially with luggage. Certainly, do not take the cheapest, stopping buses to the centre along Av Faucett as they are frequently robbed. If you must travel by public transport, pay more for a non-stop service. Combis to the centre (the junction of Alfonso Ugarte and Av Venezuela) charge US$0.50. Combis to Miraflores are marked 'Callao-Ate' with a big red 'S' ('La S') and can be caught outside the airport on Av Faucett, US$0.55. Note that luggage is not allowed on public buses except very late at night or early in the morning.

Bus

Local Bus routes are shared by buses, combis (mid-size) and colectivos (mini-vans or cars). None is particularly safe; it is better to take a taxi (see below for recommendations). Colectivos run 24 hrs, although less frequently 0100-0600; they are quicker than buses and stop wherever requested. Buses and combis charge about US$0.40-0.45, colectivos a little more. On public holidays, Sun and from 2400 to 0500 every night, a small charge is added to the fare.

The **Metropolitano** (T01-203 9000, www.metropolitano.com.pe) is a system of articulated buses running on

ON THE ROAD
Arriving at night

A number of international flights arrive at Lima airport in the small hours of the morning. The iPerú tourist information office (upstairs in the departures area and very helpful), money changing facilities and most other airport services operate around the clock. Don't change more money than you need though, as rates at the airport are very poor.

There is one expensive hotel (Ramada Costa del Sol, see page 62) with a walkway connecting it directly to the airport terminal; if you don't want to stay there, the airport has ample seating areas and is safe. Most hotels can arrange for airport pickup for between US$14 and US$30. Smaller hotels do not have their own vehicles and will usually just send a taxi driver to meet you. With any transport service, always confirm the price in advance. Taxi Green (www. taxigreen.com.pe) is a popular choice, providing safe service at posted prices. Independent taxi drivers who hang around outside the terminal building may be more expensive. Under no circumstances should you leave the airport perimeter to look for a taxi in the street. This is not safe even by day, far less so at night. It is worth noting that the ride to your hotel may be quicker in the middle of the night, as this is the only time when the streets of Lima are not completely clogged with traffic. See also Transport from the airport, page 77.

dedicated lanes north–south across the city from Naranjal in Comas to Estación Central (in front of the **Sheraton** hotel; estimated journey time 32 mins) and then south along the Vía Expresa/Paseo de la República to Matellini in Chorrillos (estimated journey time 32 mins); there are purpose-built stations along the route. The **Metropolitano** tends to be very crowded and is of limited use to visitors, but can be handy for reaching Miraflores (use stations between Angamos and 28 de Julio) and Barranco (Bulevar is 170 m from the Plaza). There are two branches through downtown Lima, either via Av Alfonso Ugarte and Plaza 2 de Mayo, or via Jr Lampa and Av Emancipación. Fares are paid using a prepaid and rechargeable card (minimum S/.5, US$1.75), available from every station; each journey costs S/.2.50 (US$0.80). Services run Mon-Sat 0500-

2300 with shorter hours on Sun and on some sections. There are express services Mon-Fri 0600-0900 and 1635-2115 between certain stations.

Long distance There are many different bus companies, but the larger ones are better organized, leave on time and do not wait until the bus is full. Leaving or arriving in Lima by bus in the rush hour can add an extra hour to the journey. All bus companies have their own offices and terminals in the centre of the city, many around Carlos Zavala, but this is not a safe area. Many north-bound buses also have an office and stop at the Terminal Plaza Norte (http://granterminalterrestre.com, Metropolitano Tomás Valle), not far from the airport, which is handy for those who need to make a quick bus connection after landing in Lima. Many south-bound buses are at the Terminal Terrestre Lima

Sur, at Km 11-12 on the Panamericana Sur by Puente Atocongo (Metro Atocongo).

Cruz del Sur (T01-311 5050, www.cruzdelsur.com.pe) has its main terminal at Av Javier Prado 1109, La Victoria, with *Cruzero* and *Cruzero Suite* services (luxury buses) and *Imperial* service (quite comfortable buses and periodic stops for food and bathroom breaks, a cheap option with a quality company) to most parts of Peru. Another terminal is at Jr Quilca 531, Lima centre, for *Imperial* services to Arequipa, Ayacucho, Chiclayo, Cuzco, Huancayo, Huaraz, and Trujillo. There are sales offices throughout the city, including at Terminal Plaza Norte.

Ormeño (www.grupo-ormeno.com.pe) and its affiliated bus companies depart from and arrive at Av Javier Prado Este 1057, Santa Catalina, T01-472 1710, but the terminal at Av Carlos Zavala 177, Lima centre, T01-427 5679, is the best place to get information and buy any Ormeño ticket. **Ormeño** offers *Royal Class* and *Business Class* service to certain destinations. These buses are very comfortable with bathrooms and hostess, etc.

Cial, República de Panamá 2460, T01-207 6900 ext 119, and Paseo de la República 646, T01-207 6900 ext 170, has national coverage.

Flores (T01-332 1212, www.floreshnos.net) has departures to many parts of the country, especially the south from terminals at Av Paseo de le República 683, Av Paseo de le República 627 and Jr Montevideo 523. Some of its services are good quality.

Other companies include:

Cavassa, Raimondi 129, Lima centre, T01-431 3200, www.turismocavassa.com.pe. Also at Terminal Plaza Norte. Services to **Huaraz**.

Cromotex, Av Nicolás Arriola 898, Santa Catalina; Av Paseo de La República 659, T01-424 7575, www.cromotex.com.pe. To **Cuzco** and **Arequipa**.

Ittsa, Paseo de la República 809, T01-423 5232, www.ittsabus.com. Also at Terminal Plaza Norte. Good service to the north, **Chiclayo**, **Piura**, **Tumbes**.

Julio César, José Gálvez 562, La Victoria, T01-424 8060, www.transportesjuliocesar.com.pe. Also at Terminal Plaza Norte. Good service to **Huaraz**; recommended to arrive in Huaraz and then use local transport to points beyond.

Línea, Paseo de la República 941-959, Lima centre, T01-424 0836, www.transporteslinea.com.pe. Also at Terminal Plaza Norte (T01-533 0739). Among the best services to destinations in the **north**.

Móvil, Av Paseo de La República 749, Lima centre (near the national stadium); Av Alfredo Mendiola 3883, Los Olivos, and Terminal Terrestre Lima Sur, T01-716 8000, www.moviltours.com.pe. To **Huaraz** and **Chiclayo** by *bus cama*, and **Chachapoyas**.

Oltursa, Aramburú 1160, San Isidro, T01-708 5000, www.oltursa.pe. A reputable company offering top-end services to **Nazca**, **Arequipa** and destinations in **northern Peru**, mainly at night.

Soyuz, Av México 333, T01-205 2370, www.soyuz.com.pe. To **Ica** every 7 mins,

Tip...
In the weeks either side of 28/29 July (Independence), and of the Christmas/New Year holiday, it is practically impossible to get bus tickets out of Lima, unless you book in advance. Bus prices double at these times.

well organized. As **PerúBus**, www.perubus.com.pe, the same company runs north to **Huacho** and **Barranca**.

Tepsa, Javier Prado Este 1091, La Victoria; Av Gerardo Unger 6917, T01-617 9000, www.tepsa.com.pe. Also at Terminal Plaza Norte (T01-533 1524). Services to the north as far as **Tumbes** and the south to **Tacna**.

Transportes Chanchamayo, Av Nicolás Arriola 535, La Victoria, T01-265 6850, www.transportes chanchamayo.com. To **Tarma**, **San Ramón** and **La Merced**.

Transportes León de Huánuco, Av 28 de Julio 1520, La Victoria, T01-424 3893. Daily to **Huánuco**, **Tingo María**, **La Merced** and **Pucallpa**.

International Ormeño (see above) to **Guayaquil** (29 hrs with a change of bus at the border, US$56), **Quito** (38 hrs, US$75), **Cali** (56 hrs, US$131), **Bogotá** (70 hrs, US$141), **Caracas** (100 hrs, US$150), **Santiago** (54 hrs, US$102), **Mendoza** (78 hrs, US$159), **Buenos Aires** (90 hrs, US$148), **São Paulo** (90 hrs); a maximum of 20 kg is allowed pp. **Cruz del Sur** to **Guayaquil** (3 a week, US$85), **Buenos Aires** (US$201) and **Santiago**

(US$130). **El Rápido** (Abtao 1279, La Victoria, T01-432 6380, www.elrapidoint.com.ar) to **Buenos Aires**, Mon, Wed, Fri; connections in Mendoza to other cities in Argentina and Uruguay.

Car hire

Most companies have an office at the airport, where you can arrange everything and pick up and leave the car. It is recommended to test drive before signing the contract as quality varies. It can be much cheaper to rent a car in a town in the Sierra for a few days than to drive from Lima; also companies don't have a collection service. Cars can be hired from: **Paz Rent A Car**, Av Diez Canseco 319, of 15, Miraflores, T01-446 4395, T99-993 9853, www.perupazconsortium.com.pe. **Budget**, T01-204 4400, www.budgetperu.com. Prices range from US$35 to US$85 depending on type of car. Make sure that your car is in a locked garage at night.

Metro

The 1st line of the Tren Eléctrico (www.lineauno.pe) runs from Villa El Salvador in the southeast of the city to Bayóvar in the northeast, daily 0600-2230. Each journey costs S/.1.50 (US$0.55); pay by swipe card S/.5 (US$1.75). Metro stations Miguel Grau, El Ángel and Presbítero Maestro lie on the eastern edge of the downtown area. Construction work has started on the next section.

Taxi

Taxis do not use meters although some have rate sheets (eg **Satelital**, T01-355 5555, http://3555555satelital.com). Agree the price of the journey beforehand and insist on being taken to the destination of your choice. At night, on Sun and holidays expect a surcharge of 35-50%.

The following are taxi fares for some of the more common routes, give or take a sol. From downtown Lima to: Parque Kennedy (Miraflores), US$4; Museo de la Nación, US$3.75; San Isidro, US$3.75; Barranco, US$4.75. From Miraflores (Parque Kennedy) to: Museo de la Nación, US$2.75; Archaeology Museum, US$3.75; Barranco, US$4.80. By law, all taxis must have the vehicle's registration number painted on the side. They are often white or yellow, but can come in any colour, size or make. Licensed and phone taxis are safest, but if hailing a taxi on the street, local advice is to look for an older driver rather than a youngster.

There are several reliable phone taxi companies, which can be called for immediate service, or booked in advance; prices are 2-3 times more than ordinary taxis: to the airport, US$15; to suburbs, US$10. Try **Taxi Real**, T01-215 1414, www.taxireal.com; **Taxi Seguro**, T01-536 6956, www.taxisegurolima. com; **Taxi Tata**, T01-274 5151, www. tata-taxis.com. If hiring a taxi by the hour, agree on price beforehand, US$7-9. **Note** Drivers don't expect tips; give them small change from the fare.

Train
Details of the service on the Central Railway to Huancayo are given under Huancayo, page 433.

Huaraz & the Cordilleras

trek among some of South America's loftiest peaks

The Cordillera Blanca is a region of lakes and mountain peaks that attracts mountaineers, hikers, cyclists and rafters in their thousands. Here stand some of the highest mountains in South America, with 30 snow-crested peaks over 6000 m, including Huascarán, the highest mountain in Peru at 6768 m.

This area contains the largest concentration of glaciers found in the world's tropical zone: a source of both beauty and danger. The turquoise lakes that form in the terminal moraines are the jewels of the Andes, and you should hike up to at least one during your stay, but their tranquility masks a frightening history, when dykes have broken, sending tons of water hurtling down the canyons. Earthquakes, too, have scarred the high valleys; the mass grave that was once the old town of Yungay is a very humbling place.

Southeast of Huaraz, the Cordillera Huayhuash equals the Cordillera Blanca in beauty and majesty and is also a very popular destination for trekkers and climbers, offering the best-known long-distance trek in northern Peru. There are also various archaeological sites in the region, the most famous of which is the fortress-temple of Chavín de Huantar, on the east side of the Cordillera Blanca.

Best for
Scenery ▪ Solitude ▪ Trekking

Footprint picks

★ **Chavín de Huantar**, page 101

This is one of Peru's most important pre-Inca archaeological sites.

★ **The bus ride through Punta Olímpica**, page 102

A spectacular tunnel at 4700 m connects Chacas with Carhuaz in the Callejón de Huaylas.

★ **Yungay**, page 105

The old village is a haunting reminder of the sometimes merciless power of nature.

★ **Laguna Parón**, page 106

A day trek (or taxi) from Caraz will take you to this exquisite lake surrounded by majestic peaks.

★ *Puyas raimondii*, page 107

Witness the flowering of these remarkable Andean plants.

★ **Llanganuco–Santa Cruz, Alpamayo North or Huayhuash**, pages 113-121

Don't miss the chance to tackle one of these classic treks.

Mollepata

Buldibuyo

Tayabamba

Pallasca

Cabana

Huancaspata

San Pedro de Chonta

Huacrachuco

Corongo Tarica Sihuas

Pasacancha

Tres Cruces

Yuramarca

Cordillera

Pomabamba

Piscobamba

6 Alpamayo (5947m) Yaino

Huallanca

Cañón del Pato Rio Santa Cruz **4 6** Laguna Parón

Puente Llacma

Cashapampa Vaquería Yanama

San Luis

Llamellín

Portachuelo de Llanganuco (4767m)

Caraz **3** Yungay Lagunas de Llanganuco Punta Olímpica (4890m) Huascarán (6768m) Chacas

Pamparomas **5**

Pueblo Libre Mancos

Blanca Huari

Sechín Carhuaz

Tantamayo

Rio Santo Marcará Parque Nacional Huascarán Huántar Chavín de Pariarca

Cordillera Negra Anta Collón

Monterrey Willkawain San Marcos

Llata Quivilla

Pariacoto Huaraz Chavín **1** Chavín de Huantar

Callejón de Conchucos

Yaután Casma Punta Callan (4200m) Olleros Cahuish Tunnel (4550m)

Chavinillo

Recuay La Unión Chavinillo

Catac

Culebras Huansala

La Merced Pachacato Huallanca Huánuco Viejo

Aija Carpa

Huayán Baños

Huarmey Huayllapampa Chiquián

Marca Laguna Conococha Aquia **6** Cordillera Huayhuash

Conococha (4100m) Yerupajá (6634m)

Cajatambo

Raura

Oyón

Footprint picks

1 **Chavín de Huantar**, page 101
2 **The bus ride through Punta Olímpica**, page 102
3 **Yungay**, page 105
4 **Laguna Parón**, page 106
5 *Puyas raimondii*, page 107
6 **Llanganuco–Santa Cruz, Alpamayo North or Huayhuash**, pages 113-121

Essential Huaraz and the Cordilleras

Finding your feet

Established in July 1975, **Parque Nacional Huascarán** includes the entire Cordillera Blanca above 4000 m, with an area of 3400 sq km. It is a UNESCO World Biosphere Reserve and part of the World Heritage Trust. The park's objectives are to protect the flora, fauna, geology, archaeological sites and scenic beauty of the Cordillera. Park fees are US$8 for three daytime visits (no overnight stays). Permits for 21 to 30 days (for trekking and climbing) cost US$25 (70 soles) and must be bought at the park office in Huaraz (Jr Federico Sal y Rosas 555, by Plazuela Belén, T043-422086, pnhuascaran@sernanp.gob.pe, Monday-Friday 0830-1300, 1430-1700), or at rangers posts at Llanganuco and Huascarán (for the Llanganuco–Santa Cruz trek), or at Collón for the Quebrada Ishinca. Current regulations state that local guides are mandatory everywhere in the park except designated 'Recreation Zones' (areas accessible by car). Tourists must hire a licensed tour operator for all activities and those operators may only employ licensed guides, cooks, *arrieros* and porters. Fees, regulations and their implementation change frequently; always confirm details in Huaraz.

Getting around

The best way to explore the Cordilleras is, of course, on foot. However, there are also numerous buses and minivans daily between Huaraz and Caraz in the Callejón de Huaylas, and more limited services to settlements on the eastern side of the Cordillera Blanca. The bus journey through the Punta Olímpica tunnel is an extraordinary experience that shouldn't be missed. For information on trekking in the cordilleras, see page 113.

When to go

The months of May to September are the dry season and best for trekking, although conditions vary from year to year. From November to April the weather is usually wet, views may be restricted by cloud, and paths are likely to be muddy.

Time required

You could spend anything from one to four weeks in this region, depending on how much trekking you want to do. Most circuits can be hiked in five days, but there are also worthwhile day hikes and longer routes, such as the Alpamayo Circuit.

Weather Huaraz

January	February	March	April	May	June
13°C	14°C	14°C	12°C	11°C	10°C
1°C	1°C	0°C	-1°C	-1°C	-3°C
122mm	131mm	126mm	93mm	55mm	69mm

July	August	September	October	November	December
9°C	9°C	9°C	10°C	11°C	12°C
-3°C	-3°C	-3°C	-2°C	-2°C	-1°C
61mm	47mm	62mm	85mm	96mm	112mm

Cordillera
Blanca

Apart from the range running along the Chile-Argentina border, the highest mountains in South America lie along the Cordillera Blanca and are perfectly visible from many spots. From Huaraz alone, you can see more than 23 peaks of over 5000 m, of which the most notable is Huascarán (6768 m), the highest mountain in Peru. Although the snowline is receding, the Cordillera Blanca still contains the largest concentration of glaciers found in the world's tropical zone; these are matched in splendour by the turquoise-coloured lakes that form in the terminal moraines. Here also is one of Peru's most important pre-Inca sites, at Chavín de Huantar.

Towards Huaraz and the cordilleras

North from Lima the Pan-American Highway parallels the coast and a series of roads branch off east for the climb up to Huaraz in the Callejón de Huaylas, gateway to **Parque Nacional Huascarán** (see page 85). Probably the easiest route to Huaraz is the paved road that branches off the highway north of Pativilca, 203 km from Lima. The road climbs increasingly steeply to the chilly pass at 4080 m (Km 120). Shortly after, **Laguna Conococha** comes into view, where the Río Santa rises. A road branches off from Conococha to **Chiquián** (see page 119) and the **Cordilleras Huayhuash** and **Raura** to the southeast. After crossing a high plateau the main road descends gradually for 47 km until **Catac**, where another road branches east to Chavín and on to the **Callejón de Conchucos** on the eastern side of the Cordillera Blanca. Huaraz is 36 km further on. From Huaraz the road continues north between the towering Cordillera Negra, snowless and rising to 4600 m, and the snow-covered Cordillera Blanca.

The alternative routes to the Callejón de Huaylas are via the Callán pass from Casma to Huaraz (fully paved, see page 131), and from Chimbote to Caraz via the Cañón del Pato (partly paved, rough and spectacular; page 130).

Located 420 km from Lima, Huaraz is the capital of Ancash department and the main town in the Cordillera Blanca, with a population of 115,000. It is expanding rapidly as a major tourist centre but is also a busy commercial hub, especially on market days. At 3091 m, it is a prime destination for hikers and a Mecca for international climbers.

Sights in Huaraz

Huaraz's setting, at the foot of the Cordillera Blanca, is spectacular. The town was almost completely destroyed in the earthquake of May 1970. The Plaza de Armas has since been rebuilt, but the new **Cathedral** is still under construction. **Museo Arqueológico de Ancash** ⓘ *Ministerio de Cultura, Plaza de Armas, Mon-Sat 0900-1700, Sun 0900-1400,* contains stone monoliths and *huacos* from the Recuay culture, well labelled. The main thoroughfare, Avenida Luzuriaga, is bursting at the seams with travel agencies, climbing equipment hire shops, restaurants, cafés and bars. A good district for those seeking peace and quiet is La Soledad, six blocks uphill from the Plaza de Armas on Avenida Sucre. Here, along Sucre and Jr Amadeo Figueroa, are many hotels and rooms for rent in private homes. The **Sala de Cultura SUNARP** ⓘ *Av Centenario 530, Independencia, T043-421301, Mon-Fri 1700-2000, Sat 0900-1300, free,* often has interesting art and photography exhibitions by local artists.

Around Huaraz

About 8 km to the northeast is **Willkawain** ⓘ *Tue-Fri 0830-1600, Sat-Sun 0900-1330, US$1.75, take a combi from 13 de Diciembre and Jr Cajamarca, US$0.50, 20 min, direct to Willkawain.* The ruins (AD 700-1100, Huari Empire) consist of one large three-storey structure with intact stone roof slabs and several small structures. About 500 m past Willkawain is Ichicwillkawain with several similar but smaller structures. A well-signed trail climbs from Wilkawain to Laguna Ahuac (Aguak Cocha, 4580 m); it's a demanding acclimatization hike (12 km return), with no services along the way.

North of Huaraz, 6 km along the road to Caraz at 2780 m, are the **Termas de Monterrey** ⓘ *lower pool, US$0.85; upper pool (closed Mon for cleaning), US$1.35; tubs US$1.35 per person for 20 mins. City buses run along Av Luzuriaga to Monterrey until 1900, US$0.22, taxi US$2-3.* There are two pools here (the upper one is nicer), plus individual and family tubs, restaurants and hotels. Monterrey gets crowded at weekends and holidays.

> **Tip...**
>
> Huaraz has its share of crime, especially since the arrival of mining and during the high tourist season. Women should not go to surrounding districts and sites alone. Muggings have taken place on the way to Laguna Churup, on the way to the Mirador Rataquenua, and also between the Monterrey thermal baths and Wilcawain ruins; do not walk this way.

Tourist information

iPerú

*Pasaje Atusparia, of 1, Plaza de Armas,
T043-428812, iperuhuaraz@promperu.
gob.pe, Mon-Sat 0900-1800, Sun 0900-*
*1300. Also at Jr San Martín cuadra 6 s/n,
daily 0800-1100, and at Anta airport
when flights arrive.*

1 Huaraz

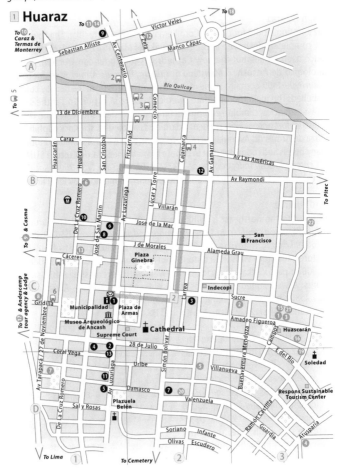

Policía de Turismo
Av Luzuriaga on Plaza de Armas,
around the corner from iPerú, T043-
421351, divtueco_huaraz@yahoo.com.
Mon-Sat 0730-2100.
The place to report crimes and resolve
issues with tour operators, hotels, etc. All
female officers, limited English spoken.

Indecopi
Av Gamarra 671, T043-423899,
www.indecopi.gob.pe.
Government consumer protection
office. Very effective but not always
quick. Spanish only.

Where to stay

Hotels fill up rapidly in high season
(May-Sep), especially during public
holidays and special events when
prices rise (beware overcharging).
Touts meet buses and aggressively
"suggest" places to stay. Do not
be put off your choice of lodging;
phone ahead to confirm.

N

200 metres

200 yards

Where to stay ◎
1 Albergue Churup *C3*
2 Alojamiento El Jacal *C3*
3 Alojamiento Soledad *C3*
4 Andino Club *D3*
5 Angeles Inn *D2*
6 Backpackers *B1*
7 Benkawasi *D1*
8 Casa Jaimes *C1*
9 Edward's Inn *B1*
10 El Patio *A1*
11 Hatun Wasi *A1*
12 Hostal Colomba *A2*
13 Hostal Quintana *C1*
14 Jo's Place *A2*
15 La Cabaña *C3*
16 La Casa de Zarela *C3*
17 Lodging Caroline *C1*
18 Lodging House Ezama *A3*
19 Olaza's B&B *D3*
20 Res NG *D2*
21 Res Sucre *C3*
22 San Sebastián *B3*

Restaurants ●
1 Bistro de los Andes *C2*
2 Café El Centro *C1*
3 Cafetería y Juguería *C2*
4 California Café *C1*
5 Chifa Jim Hua *D1*
6 Fuente de Salud *B1*
7 Huaraz Querido *D2*
8 Las Puyas *B1*
9 Mi Comedia *A1*
10 Panadería La Alameda *B1*
11 Panadería Montserrat *D1*
12 Papa Loca *B2*
13 Pizza Bruno *D1*

Transport ◻
1 Sandoval/Chavín
   Express *C1*
2 Combis to Caraz *A1, A2*
3 Combis to Wilcawain *A2*
4 Julio César *B2*
5 Móvil Tours *A1*
6 Terminal de
   Transportistas
   Zona Sur *C1*
7 Trans Huandoy *A2*

$$$$-$$$ Andino Club
Pedro Cochachín 357, some way
southeast of the centre (take a
taxi after dark), T043-421662,
www.hotelandino.com.
Swiss-run hotel with very high standards,
excellent restaurant, variety of rooms
including panoramic views, balcony,
fireplace, jacuzzi and sauna.

$$$ El Patio
Av Monterrey, 250 m downhill from
the Monterrey baths, T043-424965,
www.elpatio.com.pe.
Very colonial-style with lovely gardens,
comfortable rooms, singles, doubles
and triples, some with balconies, also
4 lodges with fireplaces. Meals on
request, bar.

$$$ Hostal Colomba
Francisco de Zela 210, just off
Centenario across the river, T043-
421501, www.huarazhotel.com.
Lovely old hacienda, family-run,
garden with playground and
sports, safe parking, gym and
well-equipped rooms sleeping 1-6,
comfortable beds, restaurant.

➡ **Huaraz maps**
1 Huaraz, page 88
2 Huaraz centre,
   page 90

➡ **Huaraz maps**
1 Huaraz, page 88
2 **Huaraz centre,**
   page 90

Where to stay ⬤
1 Oscar's Hostal

Restaurants 🍴
1 Café Andino &
  Familia Meza Lodging
2 Chilli Heaven
3 Créperie Patrick
4 El Horno Pizzería Grill
5 Encuentro
6 Maialino
7 Pizza B&B

8 Pizzería Landauro
9 Rinconcito Minero
10 Rossanero
11 Sabor Salud
12 Trivio

Bars & clubs 🎵
13 '13 Buhos'
14 Amadeus
15 Extreme &
   Monttrek Agency
16 Taberna Tambo

$$$ The Lazy Dog Inn

30 mins' drive from Huaraz (US$10 by taxi), close to the boundary of Huascarán National Park, 3.1 km past the town of Marian, close to the Quebrada Cojup, T943-789330, www.thelazydoginn.com.
Eco-tourism lodge actively involved in community projects (see www.andeanalliance.org), water recycling systems and composting toilets. Beautifully designed in warm colours, great location gives access to several mountain valleys. Organizes horse riding and hiking trips. Excellent home-cooked breakfast and dinner included. Canadian owned, English spoken. Recommended.

$$$-$$ San Sebastián

Jr Italia 1124, T043-426960, www.sansebastianhuaraz.com.
Elegant, modern hotel, comfortable beds with duvets, parking available, helpful, good views.

$$-$ Albergue Churup

Jr Amadeo Figueroa 1257, T043-424200, www.churup.com.
13 rooms with private bath or 2 dorms with shared bath, hot water, fire in sitting room on 4th floor, cafeteria, use of kitchen 1800-2200, lots of information, laundry, book exchange, English spoken, Spanish classes, adventure travel tours, extremely helpful. Airport transfers and free pick-up from bus.

$$-$ Edward's Inn

Bolognesi 121, T043-422692, www.huaraz.com/edwards.
With or without bath, nice garden, laundry, breakfast extra, insist on proper rates in low season, popular. Edward speaks English and has 30 years' experience trekking, climbing and guiding in the area. He also rents gear.

$$-$ Hatun Wasi
Jr Daniel Villayzán 268, T043-425055.
Family-run hotel next to Jo's Place. Spacious rooms, with hot water, pleasant roof terrace, ideal for breakfasts, with great views of the Cordillera.

$$-$ La Casa de Zarela
J Arguedas 1263, T043-421694, www.lacasadezarela.hostel.com.
Hot water, use of kitchen, laundry facilities, popular with climbers and trekkers, owner Zarela who speaks English organizes groups and is very knowledgeable.

$$-$ Residencial NG
Pasaje Valenzuela 837, T043-421831, www.residencialng.com.
Breakfast, hot water, good value, helpful, has restaurant.

$ Alojamiento El Jacal
Jr Sucre 1044, T043-424612.
With or without shower, hot water, helpful family, garden, laundry facilities.

$ Alojamiento Soledad
Jr Amadeo Figueroa 1267, T043-421196, www.lodgingsoledad.com.
Simple breakfast, private and shared bath, abundant hot water, use of kitchen, family home and atmosphere, secure, trekking information and tours. Warmly recommended.

$ Andescamp Hostel
Jr Huáscar 615, T043-423842, www.andescamphostel.com.
Hostel with dorms and private rooms, some with bath, and snack bar.

$ Angeles Inn
Av Gamarra 815, T043-422205, solandperu@yahoo.com.
No sign, look for Sol Andino travel agency in same building (www.

solandino.com), laundry facilities, garden, hot water, owners Max and Saul Angeles are official guides, helpful with trekking and climbing, rent equipment.

$ Backpackers
Av Raimondi 510, T043-421773, www.huaraz.com/backpackers.
Breakfast not included. Dorms or private room with bathroom. Spacious, hot showers, good views, energetic staff, a real bargain, but heavy traffic outside.

$ Benkawasi
Parque Santa Rosa 928, 10 mins from centre, T043-423150, http://huarazbenkawasi.com.
Doubles, also rooms for 3, 4 and dorm, hot water, breakfast US$5, laundry, games room, pick-up from bus station. Owner Benjamín Morales also has **Xtreme Bar**, **Infinite Tours**, for mountain bike hire and tours of the National Park, and a lodge at Playa Tortugas, near Casma (arranges downhill biking from Huaraz).

$ Casa Jaimes
Alberto Gridilla 267, T043-422281, 2 blocks from the main plaza, www.casajaimes.com.
Dormitory with hot showers, laundry facilities, has maps and books of the region. Noisy but otherwise good.

$ Familia Meza
Lúcar y Torre 538, behind Café Andino (enquire here), T043-421203.
Shared bath, hot water, laundry facilities, popular with trekkers, mountaineers and bikers.

$ Hostal Quintana
Mcal Cáceres 411, T043-426060, www.hostal-quintana.com.
English, French, Italian and Spanish spoken, mountain gear rental, 2 of the owner's sons are certified guides and can

arrange itineraries, laundry facilities, café popular with trekkers.

$ Jo's Place
Jr Daniel Villayzan 276, T043-425505, www.huaraz.com/josplace.
Safe, hot water at night, nice mountain views, garden, terrace, English owner, warm atmosphere, popular.

$ La Cabaña
Jr Sucre 1224, T043-423428.
Shared and double rooms, hot showers, laundry, popular, safe for parking, bikes and luggage, English and French spoken, good value.

$ Lodging Caroline
Urb Avitentel Mz D-Lt 1, T043-422588, http://carolinelodging.com.
Colourful dorms in main building or private rooms in newer annex. Gay friendly. 10-min walk from centre, free pickup from bus station (phone ahead), hot water, tourist information, laundry, helpful. Compare tours offered here with those of established operators.

$ Lodging House Ezama
Mariano Melgar 623, Independencia, T043-423490, 15 mins' walk from Plaza de Armas (US$0.50 by taxi), www.huaraz.com/ezama.
Light, spacious rooms, hot water, safe, helpful.

$ Oscar's Hostal
La Mar 624, T043-422720, cvmonical@hotmail.com.
Hot water, cheap breakfast next door, good beds, cheaper in low season, helpful.

$ Residencial Sucre
Sucre 1240, T043-422264, filibertor@terra.com.pe.

Private house, kitchen, laundry facilities, hot water, English, German and French spoken, mountaineering guide, Filiberto Rurush, can be contacted here.

Restaurants

$$$ Créperie Patrick
Luzuriaga 422.
Excellent crepes, fish, quiche, spaghetti and good wine.

$$$ Pizza Bruno
Luzuriaga 834. Open from 1600-2300.
Best pizza, excellent crêpes and pastries, good service, French owner Bruno Reviron also has a 4WD with driver for hire.

$$$-$$ Mi Comedia
Av Centenario 351, T043-587954. Open 1700-2300.
Wood-oven pizzas, rustic European style, very good service.

$$$-$$ Trivio
Parque del Periodista. Open for lunch and dinner.
Creative food, good coffee, nice view.

$$ Bistro de los Andes
Plaza de Armas 2nd floor, T043-426249.
Great food, owner speaks English, French and German. Plaza branch has a nice view of the plaza. Wide range of dishes including breakfasts.

$$ Chilli Heaven
Parque Ginebra, T043-396085.
Run by a British biker, specializing in spicy food (Mexican, Indian, Thai), book exchange.

$$ El Horno Pizzería Grill
Parque del Periodista, T043-424617.
Good atmosphere, fine grilled meats and nice location.

$$ Fuente de Salud
J de la Mar 562.
Vegetarian, also meat and pasta dishes,
serves good soups and breakfast.

$$ Huaraz Querido
Bolívar 981. Open for lunch only.
Very popular place for great ceviche
and other fish dishes.

$$ Maialino
Parque Ginebra, T940-241660.
Popular for Italian and local dishes, cosy,
welcoming, set meal for lunch
and dinner costs US$2.50.

$$ Papa Loca
*Av Raimondi 903, T978-495271,
papalocarestaurant on Facebook.
Tue-Sun 1700-2300.*
Varied menu from Peruvian to British
and Irish, good quality and value.
Recommended.

$$ Pizza B&B
La Mar 674, beside laundry of same name.
Excellent traditional sauces for pizza and
pasta, and desserts.

$$ Pizzería Landauro
*Sucre, on corner of Plaza de Armas.
Closed 1200-1800 and Sun.*
Very good for pizzas, Italian dishes,
sandwiches, breakfasts, nice atmosphere.

$$ Rinconcito Minero
J de Morales 757.
Breakfast, lunch, vegetarian options,
coffee and snacks

$$ Sabor Salud
Luzuriaga 672, upstairs.
Pizzeria with vegetarian and Italian food.

$$-$ Chifa Jim Hua
*Luzuriaga y Damasco. Mon-Sat 0900-
1500, 1800-2400, Sun 1800-2200.*
Large, tasty portions, economical *menú*.

$$-$ Encuentro
*Parque del Periodista and Julian de
Morales 650, www.restaurantencuentro.
com. Opens 0700.*
Breakfast, lunch and dinners,
very busy, good.

$ Las Puyas
Morales 535.
Popular with gringos, good *sopa criolla*
and trout, also serves breakfast.

Cafés

Café Andino
*Lúcar y Torre 538, 3rd floor, T043-421203,
www.cafeandino.com.*
Peruvian/American-owned café-
restaurant-bar with book exchange
and extensive lending library in
many languages. A great place to
relax and meet other travellers, nice
atmosphere, warmly recommended.
Owner Chris Benway also runs **La Cima
Logistics** (www.lacimalogistics.com),
for custom outfitting in Cordilleras
Blanca and Huayhuash.

Café El Centro
28 de Julio 592.
Good breakfast for US$1.30-2, great
chocolate cake and apple pie.

Cafetería y Juguería
Sucre 806.
Cheap café just above the Plaza. Serves
excellent yogurt and honey drinks,
among other treats.

California Café
*28 de Julio 562, T043-428354,
http://huaylas.com/californiacafe/
california.htm.*
Excellent breakfast, great coffee
and chocolate cake, book exchange.
Californian owner is a good source of

information on trekking in the Cordillera Huayhuash and security issues.

Panadería La Alameda
Juan de La Cruz Romero 523 near market.
Excellent bread and sweets.

Panadería Montserrat
Av Luzuriaga 928.
Good bakery and café, cheap, pleasant atmosphere, good for a snack.

Rossanero
Luzuriaga entre Sucre y J de Morales, 2nd floor.
'Sofa-cafe' with extensive menu, ice cream, reasonable prices.

Bars and clubs

13 Buhos Bar
José de la Mar 2nd floor, above Makondo's.
Afternoon, evening and nightspot, very popular, owner makes his own craft beer. Good music, games, nice ambience.

Amadeus
Parque Ginebra.
Bar-disco.

Taberna Tambo
José de la Mar 776. Open 1000-1600, 2000-early hours.
Folk music daily, disco, full on, non-stop dance mecca. Very popular with both locals and gringos.

Vagamundo
J de Morales 753.
Popular bar with snacks and football tables.

Xtreme
Luzuriaga 646. Open 1900-0200.
Very popular with *gringos*, soft music.

Festivals

3 May Patron saints' day, **El Señor de la Soledad**, celebrations last a week.
Jun Semana del Andinismo, international climbing week.
Jun San Juan and **San Pedro** are celebrated throughout the region during the last week of Jun.
Aug Inkafest, mountain film festival, dates change each year.

Shopping

Clothing
For local sweaters, hats, gloves and wall hangings at good value, try Pasaje Mcal Cáceres, off Luzuriaga; the stalls off Luzuriaga between Morales and Sucre; Bolívar cuadra 6, and elsewhere. **Last Minute Gifts** (Lucar Y Torre 530, 2nd floor), and **Peru Magico** (Sucre ½ block from Plaza), both sell hats, clothing, souvenirs and jewellery.

Markets
The central market offers various canned and dry goods, as well as fresh fruit and vegetables. Beware pickpockets in this area. There are also several supermarkets in town (see Huaraz centre map), do not leave valuables in your bags while shopping.

What to do

Try to get a recommendation from someone who has recently returned from a tour or trek, or see South American Explorers' recommendations in the Lima office. All agencies run conventional tours to Llanganuco (US$12 per person, very long day) and Chavín (8-10 hrs, US$14 per person), entry tickets not included. Many hire equipment.

Horse riding

Posada de Yungar, *Yungar (about 20 km from Huaraz on the Carhuaz road), T043-421267/967-9836.* Swiss-run. Ask for José Flores or Gustavo Soto. US$4.50 per hr on nice horses; good 4-hr trip in the Cordillera Negra.

Sr Robinson Ayala Gride, *T043-423813.* Contact him well in advance for half-day trips; enquire at El Cortijo restaurant, on Huaraz-Caraz road, Km 6.5. He is a master paso rider.

Mountain biking

Mountain Bike Adventures, *Lúcar y Torre 530, T043-424259, www. chakinaniperu.com.* Contact Julio Olaza. US$60 pp for day trip, all inclusive, various routes, excellent standard of equipment. Julio speaks excellent English and also runs a book exchange, sells topo maps and climbing books.

Trekking and climbing

Trekking tours cost US$50-70 pp per day, climbing US$100-140 pp per day. Many companies close in low season.

Active Peru, *Gamarra 699 y Sucre, T043-423339, www.activeperu.com.* Offers classic treks, climbing, plus standard tours to Chavín and Llanganuco, among others, good in all respects, Belgian owner speaks Dutch, German and English.

Alpa-K, *Parque Ginebra 30-B, above Montañero, www.alpa-k.org.* Owner Bertrand offers tours throughout Peru and has a B&B ($) on the premises. French, Spanish and some English spoken.

Andean Footsteps, *Carretera Huaraz-Caraz Km 14, Paltay, and Jr José Olaya 103, Huaraz, T943-318820, www. andeanfootsteps.com.* British/Peruvian operation (Yvonne Danson and David Maguiña), specializing in treks, climbs

and tours with a commitment to using local personnel and resources. Local projects are sponsored.

Andean Kingdom, *Parque Ginebra next to Casa de Guías, T043-425555, www. andeankingdom.com.* Free information, maps, climbing wall, rock and ice climbing, including multi-day courses, treks, equipment rental, English and some Hebrew spoken, can be very busy. The company has a Refugio de Montaña, **Hatun Machay** ($), near the excellent rock-climbing site of Hatun Machay in the Cordillera Negra, with kitchen facilities and heating, transport arranged.

Andescamp, *Jr Huáscar 615, T043-423842, or T943-563424, www.andescamphostel. com.* Popular agency and hostel (see above), especially with budget travellers. Only qualified guides used for climbing trips. Variety of treks, mountaineering expeditions and courses, rafting, paragliding and other adventure sports.

Cordillera Blanca Adventures, *run by the Mejía Romero family, Los Nogales 108, T043-421934, www.cordillerablanca.org.* Experienced, quality climbing/trekking trips, good guides/equipment.

Explorandes, *Gamarra 835, T043-421960, www.explorandes.com.*

Galaxia Expeditions, *Parque del Periodista, T043-425355, www.galaxia-expeditions.com.* Usual range of tours, climbing, hiking, biking, equipment hire, etc. Go to the office to buy tours direct, do not buy from unscrupulous sub-contractors.

Huascarán, *Jr Pedro Campos 711, Soledad, T043-424504, www.huascaran-peru.com.* Contact Pablo Tinoco Depaz, one of the brothers who run the company. Good 4-day Santa Cruz trip. Good food and equipment, professional service, free loan of waterproofs and pisco sour on last evening.

ON THE ROAD
Trekking and climbing in the Cordilleras

The Cordillera Blanca offers popular backpacking and trekking, with a network of trails used by the local people and some less well-defined mountaineers' routes. Most circuits can be hiked in five days. Although the trails are easily followed, they are rugged with high passes, between 4000 m and 5000 m, so backpackers should be fit, acclimatized to the altitude and able to carry all equipment. Essential items are a tent, warm sleeping bag, stove, and protection against wind and rain (the weather is unreliable and you cannot rule out rain and hail storms even in the dry season). Less stamina is required if you hire mules to carry equipment.

Safety The height of the Cordillera Blanca and the Callejón de Huaylas ranges and their location in the tropics create conditions different from the Alps or even the Himalayas. Fierce sun makes the mountain snow porous and glaciers move more rapidly. Deglaciation is rapidly changing the face of the Cordillera. Older maps do not provide a reliable indication of the extent of glaciers and snow fields (according to some studies 15% of the range's glaciers have disappeared since the 1970s), so local experience is important. If the national park rules prohibiting independent treks or climbs have been lifted, move in groups of four or more, reporting to the Casa de Guías (see opposite) or the office of the guide before departing, giving the date at which a search should begin, and leaving your embassy's telephone number, with money for the call. International recommendations are for a 300 m per day maximum altitude gain. Be wary of agencies wanting to sell you trips with very fast ascents (but ask around if this is what you want).

It is imperative that all climbers carry adequate insurance (it cannot be purchased locally). Be well prepared before setting out on a climb. Wait or cancel your trip when the weather is bad. Every year climbers are killed through failing to take weather conditions seriously. Climb only when and where you have sufficient experience.

Rescue services, while better than in the past, may not be up to international standards. In the event of an emergency try calling the Casa de Guías,

Kallpa, *José de la Mar y Luzuriaga, p 2, T043-427868*. Organizes treks, rents gear, arranges arrieros and mules, very helpful.
Montañero, *Parque Ginebra 30-B, T043-426386, www.trekkingperu.com*. Run by veteran mountain guide Selio Villón. German, French and English spoken.
Monttrek, *Luzuriaga 646, upstairs, T043-421124, monttrek@terra.com.pe*. Good trekking/climbing information,

advice and maps, ice and rock climbing courses (at Monterrey), tours to Laguna Churup and the 'spectacular' Luna Llena tour; also hire mountain bikes, run ski instruction and trips, and river rafting. Helpful, conscientious guides. Next door in the Pizzería is a climbing wall, good maps, videos and slide shows. For new routes/maps contact Porfirio

T043-427545 or 421811; Edson Ramírez at the national park office, T944-627946 or T943-626627; or the Police, T105. Satellite phones can be rented through the Casa de Guías and there is cell-phone coverage in some (but not all) parts of the Cordillera Blanca.

Personal security and responsibility Before heading out on any trekking route, always enquire locally about crime levels. The Cordillera Blanca is generally safe, but muggings are not unknown. On all treks in this area, respect the locals' property, leave no rubbish behind, do not give sweets or money to children who beg and remember your cooking utensils and tent would be very expensive for a *campesino*, so be sensitive and responsible. Along the most popular routes, campers have complained that campsites are dirty, toilet pits foul and that rubbish is not taken away by groups. Do your share to make things better.

Information Casa de Guías, Plaza Ginebra 28-g in Huaraz, T043-421811. Monday-Saturday 0900-1300, 1600-1800. This is the climbers' and hikers' meeting place. It has a full list of all members of the Asociación de Guías de Montaña del Perú (AGMP) throughout the country and has useful information, books, maps, arrangements for guides, *arrieros*, mules, etc. It also operates as an agency and sells tours. Notice board, postcards and posters for sale, and there's a good restaurant (daily 0700-1100, 1700-2300).

Guides, arrieros and porters The Dirección de Turismo issues qualified guides and *arrieros* (muleteers) with a photo ID. Note down the name and card number in case you should have any complaints. Most guides are hired in Huaraz or, to a lesser extent, in Caraz. Prices apply across the region, with some minor variations in the smaller towns: *arriero*, US$18 per day; donkey or mule, US$8 per day; trekking guides US$40-70 per day (more for foreign guides); climbing guides US$90-200 per day (more for foreign guides), depending on the difficulty of the peak; cooks US$30-40 per day; all subject to change. You are required to provide or pay for food and shelter for all *arrieros*, porters, cooks and guides. Associations of *arrieros*: Humacchuco-Llanganuco (for porters and cooks), T943-786497, victorcautivo@hotmail.com. Pashpa Arrieros, T043-830540/83319. Musho Arrieros, T043-230003/814416. Collon Arrieros (for llama trekking), T043-833417/824146.

Cacha Macedo, 'Pocho', at Monttrek or at Jr Corongo 307, T043-423930.
Peruvian Andes Adventures, *José Olaya 532, T043-421864, www.peruvianandes. com*. Run by Hisao and Eli Morales, professional, registered mountain and trekking guides. All equipment and services for treks of 3-15 days, climbing technical and non-technical peaks, or just day walks. Vegetarians catered for.

Quechua Explorer, *Sucre 705 of 4, T043-422886, www.quechuaexplorer. com*. Hiking, mountaineering, rock and ice climbing, rafting, biking, cultural and ecological tourism, experienced and friendly guides.
Quechuandes, *Av Luzuriaga 522, T943-562339, www.quechuandes.com*. Trekking, mountaineering, rock climbing, ice climbing, skiing, mountain biking and

other adventure sports, guides speak Spanish, Quechua, English and/or French. Animal welfare taken seriously with weight limits of 40kg per donkey.

Respons Sustainable Tourism Center, *Jr Eulogio del Rio 1364, Soledad, T956-125568, www.respons.org.* Sustainable tourism initiatives, community based, with trekking, homestays, tours, volunteering and other responsible travel ideas.

Guides For details of the Casa de Guías, see box, page 96.

Aritza Monasterio, *through Casa de Guías.* Speaks English, Spanish and Euskerra.

Augusto Ortega, *Jr San Martín 1004, T043-424888.* Is the only Peruvian to have climbed Everest.

Christopher Benway, *La Cima Logistics, cafeandino@hotmail.com.* Makes custom arrangements for climbing and trekking trips.

Filiberto Rurush Paucar, *Sucre 1240, T043-422264 (Lodging Casa Sucre).* Speaks English, Spanish and Quechua.

Genaro Yanac Olivera, *T043-422825.* Speaks good English and some German, also a climbing guide.

Hugo Sifuentes Maguiña, *Siex (Sifuentes Expeditions), Jr Huaylas 139, T043-426529, www.siexperu.com.* Trekking, rock climbing and less adventurous tours.

Koky Castañeda, *T043-427213, or through Skyline Adventures, or Café Andino.* Speaks English and French, UIAGM Alpine certified.

Max, Misael and Saul Angeles, *T043-456891/422205 (Sol Andino agency).* Speak some English, know Huayhuash well.

Máximo Henostrosa, *T043-426040.* Trekking guide with knowledge of the entire region.

Ted Alexander, *Skyline Adventures, Pasaje Industrial 137, Cascapampa, Huaraz, T043-427097, www.skyline-adventures. com.* US outward bound instructor, very knowledgeable.

Tjen Verheye, *Jr Carlos Valenzuela 911, T043-422569.* Is Belgian and speaks Dutch, French, German and reasonable English, runs trekking and conventional tours and is knowledgeable about the Chavín culture.

Camping gear The following agencies are recommended for hiring gear: **Andean Kingdom, Galaxia Expeditions, Monttrek, Kallpa** and **Montañero**. Also

Skyline, **Andean Sport Tours** (Luzuriaga 571, T043-421612), and **MountClimb** (Jr Mcal Cáceres 421, T043-426060, mountclimb@yahoo.com). Casa de Guías rents equipment and sells dried food. Check all camping and climbing equipment very carefully before taking it. Quality varies and some items may not be available, so it's best to bring your own. All prices are standard, but not cheap, throughout town. All require payment in advance, passport or air ticket as deposit and rarely give any money back if you return gear early. Many trekking agencies sell screw-on camping gas cartridges. White gas (*bencina*) is available from *ferreterías* on Raymondi below Luzuriaga and by Parque Ginebra.

Tour operators

Chavín Tours, *José de la Mar, T043-421578, www.chavintours.com.pe*. All local tours, long-standing agency with its head office in Lima.
Pablo Tours, *Luzuriaga 501, T043-421145, www.pablotours.com*. For all local tours, also with many years of operation.

Air
LC Peru flies twice daily to/from **Lima**, 1 hr.

Bus
Many of the companies have their offices along Av Raymondi and on Jr Lúcar y Torre. Some recommended companies are: **Cavassa**, Jr Lúcar y Torre 446, T043-425767; **Rodríguez**, J de Morales 650, T043-429253; **Cruz del Sur**, Bolívar Mz C Lote 12, T043-728726; **Empresa 14**, Fitzcarrald 216, T043-421282, terminal at Bolívar 407;

Julio César, Prol Cajamarca s/n, cuadra 1, T043-396443; **Móvil**, Av Confraternidad Internacional Oeste 451, T043-422555; **Oltursa**, Av Raymondi 825, T043-423717; **Z-Buss**, Av Raymondi, T043-428327.

Long distance To **Lima**, 7-8 hrs, US$17-30 (**Móvil** prices), large selection of ordinary service and luxury coaches throughout the day. To **Casma** via the Callán pass and Pariacoto (150 km, fully paved), 4 hrs, US$9, best to travel by day and sit on the left for views. **Transportes Huandoy**, Fitzcarrald 261, T043-427507 (terminal at Caraz 820), daily at 0800, 1000 and 1300. **Yungay Express**, Raymondi 930, T043-424377, 3 a day; they continue to Chimbote, 185 km. To **Chimbote**, Yungay Express, daily, US$12, 7 hrs via Caraz and the Cañon del Pato (sit on the right for the most exciting views). **Línea** (Simón Bolívar 450, T043-726666), **Móvil** and **Empresa 14** (see above) go via Pativilca (160 km, 4 hrs; total journey, 7 hrs); most continue to **Trujillo**, 8-9 hrs at night, US$17-30.

Within the Cordillera Blanca Several buses and frequent minivans run daily, 0500-2000, between Huaraz and **Caraz**, 1¼ hrs, US$2, from the parking area by the bridge on Fitzcarrald, no luggage racks, you might have to pay an extra seat for your bag. To **Chavín**, 110 km, 2 hrs (sit on left side for best views), US$6: **Sandoval/Chavín Express**, Mcal Cáceres 338, 3 a day. Also **Trans Río Mosna**, Mcal Cáceres 265, T043-426632, 3 a day; buses go on to **Huari**, 4 hrs, US$7.50.
  To **Chacas**, US$7, and **San Luis**, an unforgettable ride via the 4700-m-high Punta Olímpica tunnel, US$8, at 0700 with **Virgen de Guadalupe**, Caraz 607. **Renzo**, Raymondi 821, T043-425371, runs to Chacas daily (0615, 1400), **Piscobamba** and **Pomabamba** (0630,

best, and 1900). **Los Andes**, same office as Yungay Express, T043-427362, daily 0630 to Yungay, US$1, Lagunas de Llanganuco, US$7, Yanama, US$7, Piscobamba, US$8 and Pomabamba, US$9, 8 hrs. This route is also served by **La Perla de Alta Mayo**, daily 0630, 8 hrs to Pomabamba, US$9. To **Sihuas**, also **Sandoval/Chavín Express**, Tue/Fri 0800; **Perú Andino**, 1 a week, 8 hrs, US$11.

Colectivos to **Recuay**, US$0.75, and **Catac**, US$0.85, daily at 0500-2100, from Gridilla, just off Tarapacá (Terminal de Transportistas Zona Sur). To **Chiquián** for the Cordillera Huayhuash, 120 km, 3½ hrs, with **Trans El Rápido**, Bolognesi 216, T043-422887, at 1345, or **Chiquián Tours**, on Tarapacá behind the market. To **Huallanca** (Huánuco) on the paved road through Conococha, Chiquián, Aquia to Huansala, then by good dirt road to Laguna Pachacoto and Huallanca to **La Unión** (paving under way). Departs Huaraz twice a day, 1st at 1300, with **Trans El Rápido**, as before, US$8. Frequent daily service from Huallanca to **Huánuco**.

Taxi
Standard fare in town is about US$1, more at night; radio taxis T043-421482 or 422512.

Chavín and the Callejón de Conchucos
don't miss this pre-Inca fortress-temple

From Huaraz it is possible to make a circuit by road, visiting Chavín de Huantar, Huari, San Luis, Yanama and Yungay but bear in mind that the road north of Chavín is gravel and rough in parts and the bus service is infrequent.

South of Huaraz
South of Huaraz is **Olleros**, from where the spectacular and relatively easy three- to four-day hike to Chavín, along a pre-Columbian trail, starts. Some basic meals and food supplies are available; for guides and prices, see Huaraz listings, page 95. Alternatively, if you're travelling by road to Chavín, head south from Huaraz on the main road for 38 km to **Catac** (two basic hotels and a restaurant), where a paved road branches east for Chavín.

Further south, the Pumapampa valley is a good place to see the impressive *Puya raimondii* plants (see A blooming century, page 108). A 14-km gravel road leads from Pachacoto to a park office at 4200 m, where you can spend the night. Walking up the road from this point, you will see the gigantic plants, whose flower spike can reach 12 m in height and takes 100 years to develop. The final flowering (usually in May) is a spectacular sight. Another good spot, and less visited, is the **Queshque Gorge**, which is easy to find by following the Río Queshque from Catac.

From Catac to Chavín is a magnificent journey. The road passes Lago Querococha, and there are good views of the Yanamarey peaks. At the top of the route the road cuts through a huge rock face, entering the Cahuish tunnel at 4516 m. The tunnel has no light and is single lane with a small stream running through it. Cyclists must have powerful lights so that trucks and buses can see them. On the other side of the tunnel, the road descends into the Tambillo valley, then the Río Mosna gorge before Chavín.

BACKGROUND
The stone gods of Chavín

Based on physical evidence from the study of this 17-acre site, the temple of Chavín de Huantar is thought to have been a major ceremonial centre. Its architecture and sculpture had a strong impact on the artistic and cultural development of a large part of the coast and central highlands of Peru.

What first strikes visitors is the quality of the stonework. The sculptures have three functions: architectural, ornamental and cultist. Examples include the Lanzón, the Tello obelisk and the Raimondi stela; the latter two are currently held at the Museo Nacional de Antropología, Arqueología e Historia in Lima (see page 46).

At 5 m high, the **Lanzón** is the crowning glory of the Chavín religion and stands at the heart of the underground complex. Its Spanish name comes from the lance-, or dagger-like shape of the monolith which appears to be stuck in the ground. Carved into the top of the head are thin, grooved channels; some speculate that animals, or even humans, may have been sacrificed to this god. Others suggest that the Lanzón was merely the dominant figure for worship.

Named after the Peruvian scientist, Julio C Tello, the **Tello obelisk** belongs to the earliest period of occupation of Chavín (c 100 BC). It represents a complex deity – perhaps a caiman-alligator – connected with the earth, water and all the living elements of nature. Carved on the body are the people, birds, serpents and felines that the divine beast has consumed.

The **Raimondi stela** was named after the Italian naturalist, who also gave his name to the famous plant (see box, page 108). It shows a feline anthropomorphic divinity standing with open arms and holding a staff in each hand.

Together, the stone figures at Chavín indicate that the resident cult was based principally on the feline, or jaguar, and secondarily on serpents and birds.

★**Chavín de Huantar** → *Colour map 3, B3.*
Tue-Sun 0900-1600, US$3.50, students half price, guided tours in Spanish for groups available for an extra charge. You will receive an information leaflet in Spanish at the entrance.

Chavín de Huantar, a fortress temple, was built about 800 BC. It is the only large structure remaining of the Chavín culture, which, in its heyday, is thought to have held influence from Cajamarca and Chiclayo in the north to Ayacucho and Ica in the south. In 1985, UNESCO designated Chavín a World Heritage Trust Site. The site is in good condition despite the effects of time and nature but becomes very crowded in high season. In order to protect the site some areas are closed to visitors. All the galleries open to the public have electric lights. The guard is also a guide and gives excellent explanations of the ruins.

The main attractions are the marvellous carved stone heads (*cabezas clavas*), the designs in relief of symbolic figures and the many tunnels and culverts, which form an extensive labyrinth throughout the interior of the pyramidal structure. The carvings are in excellent condition, and the best are now in the Museo Nacional Chavín. The famous Lanzón dagger-shaped stone monolith of 800 BC is found inside one of the temple tunnels.

Just north of the ruins, the town of Chavín, painted colonial yellow and white, has a pleasant plaza with palm and pine trees. There are a couple of good, simple hotels and restaurants here and a local *fiesta* in mid July. The **Museo Nacional Chavín** ① *1 km north of town and 1.6 km from the site, Tue-Sun, 0900-1700, US$3.50,* has a comprehensive collection of items gathered from several deposits and museums, including the Tello obelisk dating from the earliest period of occupation of Chavín (c 100 BC), and many impressive *cabezas clavas*.

Chavín to Huari

The road north from Chavín descends into the Mosna river canyon. The scenery is quite different from the other side of the Cordillera Blanca, very dry and hot. After 8 km it reaches **San Marcos**, the town that has been most heavily impacted by the huge **Antamina** gold mine. Hotels may be full with mine workers and public safety is a concern, so press on for 32 km to Huari.

Huari is perched on a hillside at 3150 m and has various simple hotels (\$ Huagancu 2, Jr Sucre 335, T043-630434, clean and good value) and restaurants. The **fiesta of Nuestra Señora del Rosario** takes place on 7th October, with festivities during the first two weeks of the month. There is a spectacular two- to three-day walk from Huari to Chacas via Laguna Purhuay inside Parque Nacional Huascarán. Alberto Cafferata of Caraz writes: "The Purhuay area is beautiful. It has splendid campsites, trout, exotic birds and, at its north end, a 'quenual' forest with orchids. This is a microclimate at 3500 m, where the animals, insects and flowers are more like a tropical jungle, fantastic for ecologists and photographers." A pleasant alternative for those who don't want to do the longer walk to Chacas is a day walk to Laguna Purhuay, starting at the village of Acopalca; a taxi from Huari to Acopalca costs US$3.50, to Puruhuay, US$14. The lake has a visitors' centre, food kiosk and boat rides.

★San Luis to Huaraz

From Huari the road climbs to the Huachacocha pass at 4350 m and descends to **San Luis** at 3130 m, 60 km from Huari. Here you'll find the **\$ Hostal Puñuri** (Ramón Castilla 151, T043-830408, with bath and hot water), a few basic restaurants, shops and a market.

Beyond San Luis there are a few options to take you back to Huaraz. The first is via **Chacas**, 10 km south of San Luis on a paved road. It has a fine church and celebrates the **Virgen de la Asunción** on 15 August, with bullfights, a famous *carrera de cintas* and fireworks. There are hostels (\$), shops, restaurants and a small market. A spectacular paved road and 4700-m-high tunnel through **Punta Olímpica** opened in 2013, connecting Chacas with Carhuaz in the Callejón de

Huaylas north of Huaraz. Alternatively, it is a three-day hike west from Chacas to Marcará via the Quebradas Juytush and Honda (lots of condors to be seen). Quebrada Honda is known as the *Paraíso de las Cascadas* because it contains at least seven waterfalls.

The second road route heads some 20 km north of San Luis, to where a road branches left to **Yanama**, 45 km from San Luis, at 3400 m. It has a good comfortable hotel, **Andes Lodge Peru**, T043-943 847423, www.andeslodgeperu.com ($$, full board available, excellent food and services, fabulous views). The village retains many traditional features and is beautifully surrounded by snow-capped peaks. There are superb views from the ruins above the town, reachable on a day hike. From Yanama the road continues west via the Portacheulo de Llanganuco pass to Yungay (see page 105).

North of San Luis

A longer circuit to Huaraz can be made by continuing from San Luis for 62 km to **Piscobamba**, which has a couple of basic hotels, a few shops and small restaurants. Beyond Piscobamba by 22 km is **Pomabamba**, worth a visit for some very hot natural springs (the furthest are the hottest). There are various hotels ($) near the plaza and restaurants. Pomabamba is also the terminus of one the variations of the **Alpamayo Trek**, see page 115.

From Pomabamba a dusty road runs up the wooded valley crossing the puna at Palo Seco, 23 km. The road then descends steeply into the desert-like Sihuas valley, passing through the village of Sicsibamba. The valley is crossed half an hour below the small town of **Sihuas**, a major connection point between the Callejón de Conchucos, Callejón de Huaylas, the upper Marañón and the coast. It has a few $ hotels and places to eat.

From Sihuas it is also possible to travel in the other direction, via Huancaspata, Tayabamba, Retamas and Chahual to Huamachuco along a road which is very poor in places and involves crossing the Río Marañón twice. Using this route, it is possible to travel from Cuzco to Quito through the Andes entirely by public transport. This journey is best undertaken in this direction, but it can take over two days (if it's not impassable) in the wet season.

Listings Huaraz–Chavín circuit

Where to stay

Chavín

$$-$ La Casona
Wiracocha 130, Plaza de Armas, T043-454116, www.lacasonachavin.com.pe.
In a renovated house with attractive courtyard, single, double and triple rooms, some with balcony overlooking Plaza or courtyard, nice breakfast, laundry, parking.

$$-$ R'ikay
On 17 de Enero 172N, T043-454068.
Set around 2 patios, modern, best in town, variety of room sizes, hot water, restaurant does Italian food in the evening. Recommended.

$ Hostal Chavín

Jr San Martín 141-151, half a block from the plaza, T043-454055.

Pleasant courtyard, hot water, will provide breakfast for groups, best of the more basic hotels but beds are poor.

$ Inca

Wiracocha 170, T043-754021, www.huaraz.com/hotelinca.

Rooms are cheaper without bath, good beds, hot water on request, nice garden.

Restaurants

Chavín

$$-$ Chavín Turístico

Middle of 17 de Enero.

The best in town, good *menú* and à la carte, delicious apple pie, nice courtyard, popular. Also run a hostal nearby.

$$-$ La Portada

Towards south end of 17 de Enero.

In an old house with tables set around a pleasant garden.

$ La Ramada

Towards north end of main street, 17 de Enero.

Regional dishes, also trout and set lunch.

Transport

Chavín

Bus

It is much easier to get to Chavín (even walking!) than to leave the place by bus. All buses to **Huaraz** (2 hrs from Chavín), originate in Huari or further afield. They pass through Chavín at irregular hours and may not have seats available. Buying a ticket at an agency in Chavín does not guarantee you will get a seat or even a bus. **Sandoval/Chavín Express** goes through around 1200, 1600 and 1700 daily, **Río Mosna** at 0430 and then

4 between 1600-2200. There are also services to **Lima**, 438 km, 12 hrs, US$14, with **Trans El Solitario** and **Perú Andino** daily, but locals prefer to travel to Huaraz and then take one of the better companies from there.

In the other direction, buses from Huaraz or Lima (such as **El Solitario**, which passes through Chavín at 1800) go on to **Huari**, with some going on to **San Luis**, a further 61 km, 3 hrs; **Piscobamba**, a further 62 km, 3 hrs; and **Pomabamba**, a further 22 km, 1 hr. The other way to reach places in the Callejón de Conchucos is to hop on and off the cars and combis that leave regularly from Chavín's main plaza, every 20 mins and 30 mins respectively, to **San Marcos**, 8 km, and **Huari**, 38 km.

Huari

Bus

Terminal Terrestre at Av Circunvalación Baja. To **Huaraz**, 4 hrs, US$5.50, **Sandoval/Chavín Express** 3 a day. Also runs to **San Luis** and **Lima**.

San Luís to Huaraz

There are daily buses between **Yanama** and **Yungay** over the 4767-m Portachuelo de Llanganuco (3 hrs, US$7.50), stopping at **Vaquería** (at the end of the Santa Cruz valley trek) 0800-1400, US$4, 2 hrs.

North of San Luís

Pomabamba

To **Piscobamba**, combis depart hourly, 1 hr, US$1.50; also combis to **Sihuas** (see below). **El Solitario** has a service to **Lima** on Sun, Mon and Thu at 0800, 18 hrs, US$15, via San Luis (4 hrs, US$5), Huari (6 hrs, US$7.50) and Chavín (9 hrs, US$9); **La Perla del Alto Mayo** goes from

Pomabamba to **Lima** via **Yungay** and **Huaraz** on Wed, Thu, Sat, Sun, 16 hrs.

Sihuas
To **Pomabamba**, combi from Av 28 de Julio near the market at 1100, 4 hrs, US$7 (returns 0200). To **Huaraz**, via Huallanca, with **Cielo Azul**, daily at 0830, 10 hrs, US$11. To **Tayabamba**, for the Marañón route north to Huamachuco and Cajamarca: **Andía** passes through from Lima on Sat and Sun at 0100,

La Perla del Alta Mayo passes through Tue, Thu 0000-0200; also **Garrincha** Wed, Sun around 0800; all 8 hrs, US$11, the beginning of a long wild ride. To **Huacrachuco**, **Andía** passes through Wed, Sat 0100. To **Chimbote**, **Corrival** on Wed, Thu and Sun morning, 9 hrs, US$9; **La Perla del Alta Mayo** Tue, Thu, Sun. To **Lima** (19 hrs, US$20) via Chimbote, **Andía** Tue, Sun 0200, Wed, Sat 1600; and 3 other companies once or twice a week each.

Callejón de Huaylas

hike to beautiful mountain lakes

Carhuaz and Mancos → *Colour map 3, B2.*
Carhuaz is a friendly, quiet mountain town with a pleasant plaza. There is very good walking to thermal baths, or up the Ulta valley. Market days are Wednesday and Sunday (the latter is much larger). The local fiesta of **Virgen de las Mercedes**, 14-24 September, is rated as among the best in the region. From Carhuaz it is 14 km to Mancos at the foot of Huascarán. The village has a dormitory at **La Casita de mi Abuela**, some basic shops and restaurants. After Mancos, the main road goes to **Yungay** (8 km north, 30 minutes).

★Yungay → *Colour map 3, A2.*
The town of Yungay was completely buried by a massive mudslide during the 1970 earthquake; a hideous tragedy in which 20,000 people lost their lives. The earthquake and its aftermath are remembered by many older residents of the Callejón de Huaylas. The original site of Yungay, known as Yungay Viejo, is desolate and haunting; it has been consecrated as a *camposanto* (cemetery). The new settlement is on a hillside just north of the old town. It has a pleasant plaza and a concrete market, good on Wednesday and Sunday. The **Virgen del Rosario** fiesta is celebrated on 17th October, and 28th October is the anniversary of the founding of the town. The tourist office is on the corner of the Plaza de Armas. The main road continues 12 km north of Yungay to Caraz.

Lagunas de Llanganuco
The Lagunas de Llanganuco are two lakes nestling 1000 m below the snowline beneath Huascarán and Huandoy. From Yungay, the first you come to is Laguna Chinancocha (3850 m), the second Laguna Orconcocha (3863 m). The national park office is situated before the lakes at 3200 m, 19 km from Yungay. Accommodation is provided for trekkers who want to start the Llanganuco–Santa Cruz trek from here (see page 113). From the park office to the lakes takes about five hours (a steep climb). The last section is a nature trail, Sendero María Josefa (sign on the

road); it takes 1½ hours to walk to the western end of Chinancocha where there is a control post, descriptive trail and boat trips on the lake. Walk along the road beside the lake to its far end for peace and quiet among the quenual trees, which provide shelter for 75% of the birdlife found in the park.

Caraz → *Colour map 3, A2.*

This pleasant town at 2290 m is a good centre for walking and parasailing and is the access point for many excellent treks and climbs. Tourist facilities are expanding as a more tranquil alternative to Huaraz, and there are great views of Huandoy, Huascarán and surrounding summits in July and August. In other months, the mountains are often shrouded in cloud. In addition to its many natural attractions, Caraz is also developing a lively cultural scene. Events are organized by **Caraz Cultura** ⓘ *contact Ricardo Espinosa, T991-996136, carazcultura@gmail. com*. On 20 January is the fiesta **Virgen de Chiquinquirá**. In the last week of July is **Semana Turística**.

The **Museo Arqueológico Municipal** is on San Martín, half a block up from the plaza. The ruins of **Tumshukaiko** are 1½ km from the Plaza de Armas in the suburb of Cruz Viva, to the north before the turn-off for Parón. There are seven platforms from the Huaraz culture, dating from around 2000-1800 BC, but the site is in poor shape.

Treks around Caraz

Caraz has a milder climate than Huaraz and is more suited to day trips. A good day walk goes from Caraz by the lakes of Miramar and Pampacocha to Huaripampa, where you can get a pickup back to Caraz. A longer full-day walk with excellent views of Huandoy and Huascarán follows the foothills of the Cordillera Blanca east along the main Río Santa valley, from Caraz south through the villages of Chosica and Ticrapa. It ends at Puente Ancash on the Caraz–Yungay road, from where frequent transport goes back to Caraz.

From Caraz a narrow, rough road goes east 32 km to beautiful ★**Laguna Parón** (US$3.50), in a cirque surrounded by several massive, snow-capped peaks, including Huandoy, Pirámide Garcilazo and Caraz. The gorge leading to it is spectacular. It is a long day trek for acclimatized hikers (25 km) up to the lake at 4150 m, or a four- to five-hour walk from the village of Parón, which can be reached by combi (US$2). Camping is possible. A taxi from Caraz to the lake costs US$40-45 for four passengers. **Pony's Expeditions** have a pool of well-trained drivers who make daily departures to Laguna Parón at 0800 (US$60 for four, including one-hour visit to the lake and one-hour walk). You could also hire a bike (US$18 per day), take a car up and then ride back down. There is no trail around the lake and you should not attempt to circumnavigate it, as the shore is slippery and dangerous, particularly on the southern side; tourists have been killed here.

Many other excellent trekking opportunities in both the Cordillera Blanca and Cordillera Negra can be accessed from Caraz. Those described in detail on pages 113-121 are but a few of the most popular routes. There are also ample opportunities to venture further afield.

★Puyas raymondii at Winchos

A large stand of *Puya raimondii* can be seen in the Cordillera Negra southwest of Caraz. Beyond Pueblo Libre is a paved road which heads west via Pamparomás and Moro to join the Panamerican highway south of Chimbote. The *Puya raymondii* plants are located at a place called **Winchos**, after 45 km (1½ hours). There are far-reaching views of the Cordillera Blanca and west to the Pacific. The plants are usually in flower May or October. Take warm clothing, food and water. You can also camp near the puyas and return the following day. The most popular way to visit is to rent a bike (US$18 per day), travel up by public transport (see below), and then ride back down in four or five hours. Or form a group (eg via the bulletin board at **Pony's Expeditions**, Caraz) and hire a car which will wait for you (US$60 for five). From Caraz, a minibus for Pamparomás leaves from

Treks from Caraz

ON THE ROAD
A blooming century

The giant *Puya raimondii*, named after Antonio Raimondi, the Italian scholar who discovered it, is a rare and strikingly beautiful plant.

Often mistakenly referred to as a cactus, it is actually the largest member of the bromeliad family (which includes the pineapple) and is found in only a few isolated areas of the Andes. One of these areas is Huascarán National Park, particularly the Ingenio and Queshque gorges, the high plateaus of Cajamarquilla, along the route leading to Pastoruri in the Pachacoto gorge and by the road from Caraz to Pamparomas.

At its base, the *Puya* forms a rosette of long, spiked, waxy leaves, 2 m in diameter. The distinctive phallic flower stalk of the plant can reach a height of 12 m. The plant takes an incredible 100 years to bloom, after which it withers and dies, but, during the flowering period, as many as 20,000 blooms can decorate a single plant. Groups of *Puya raimondii* blooming together create a spectacular picture against the dramatic backdrop of the Cordillera Blanca.

Ramón Castilla y Jorge Chávez around 0830, two hours, US$3 (get there at about 0800 as they often leave early). From the pass (El Paso) or El Cruce it is a short walk to the plants. Return transport leaves between 1230 and 1300. If you miss the bus, you can walk back to Pueblo Libre in four hours, to Caraz in six to eight hours, but it is easy to get lost and there are not many people to ask directions along the way.

Listings Callejón de Huaylas *map p109*

Tourist information

Note that the national park office (page 97) is principally administrative, with no information for visitors.

Caraz

The **tourist office** (Plaza de Armas, next to the municipality, T043-391029 ext 143), has limited information. There are 3 ATMs in the centre.

Where to stay

Carhuaz

$$ pp Casa de Pocha
1.5 km out of town towards Hualcán, at foot of Nevado Hualcán, ask directions in town, T943-613058 (mob 1800-2000), www.socialwellbeing.org/lacasadepocha.htm.
Including breakfast and dinner, country setting, entirely solar and wind energy powered, hot water, sauna and pool, home-produced food (vegetarian available), horses for hire, camping possible, many languages spoken. Book in advance.

$$ El Abuelo
Jr 9 de Diciembre 257, T043-394456,
www.elabuelohostal.com.
Modern, comfortable 3-star, laundry,
restaurant, large garden with organic
fruit and veg, parking, credit cards
accepted. Knowledgeable owner is
map-maker, Felipe Díaz.

$ Hostal Señor de Luren
Buin 549, 30 m from Plaza de Armas,
T043-668806.
Hot water, safe motorcycle parking,
very hospitable.

$ 4 family-run *hospedajes* operate as
part of a community development
project. All have private bath and hot
water. The better 2 are: **Hospedaje
Robri** (Jr Comercio 935, T043-394505)
and **Alojamiento Las Torresitas**
(Jr Amazonas 603, T043-394213).

Yungay

$ Complejo Turístico Yungay
(COMTURY)
Prolongación 2 de Mayo 1012,
2.5 km south of the new town, 700 m
east of main road in Aura, the only
neighbourhood of old Yungay that
survived, T043-788656.
Nice bungalows, pleasant country
setting, hot water, fireplace,
restaurant with regional
specialities, camping possible.

$ Hostal Gledel
Av Arias Graziani, north past plaza, T043-
793048, www.huaraz.com/gledel.
Owned by Sra Gamboa, who is
hospitable and a good cook, shared
bath, hottish water, no towels or soap,
cheap meals prepared on request,
nice courtyard.

Caraz

Where to stay
1 Backpacker Los Ponys
2 Caraz Dulzura
3 Chavín
4 Hostal La Casona
5 La Alameda
6 La Perla de los Andes
7 Los Pinos Lodge
8 O'Pal Inn

Restaurants
1 El Turista
2 Entre Panes
3 Heladería Caraz Dulzura
4 Jeny
5 La Punta Grande
6 La Terraza
7 Panificadora La Alameda
8 Venezia

$ Hostal Sol de Oro
Santo Domingo 7, T043-493116,
www.huaraz.com/soldeoro.
Most rooms with bath, hot water,
comfortable, breakfast and dinner on
request, good value, best in town.

Lagunas de Llanganuco

$$$$-$ Llanganuco Mountain Lodge
Lago Keushu, Llanganuco Valley, close to
Huascarán park entrance (booking office
in Huaraz: Gamarra 699), T943-669580,
www.llanganucomountainlodge.com.
2 luxury rooms, 2 standard rooms
and 10-bed dormitory. Room rate is
seasonal and full board with a packed
lunch, dorm beds can be with or
without meals, modern, camping area,
excellent food in restaurant, helpful
staff, fine views and limitless possibilities
for trekking (equipment rental and
logistics), British-owned.

Caraz

$$$-$$ Los Pinos Lodge
Parque San Martín 103 (also known as
Plazuela de la Merced), T043-391130,
www.lospinoslodge.pe.
Nice comfortable rooms, patio,
gardens, parking, cosy bar, tourist
information. Recommended.
Also have a nearby annex nearby
called **Caraz Backpacker** ($).

$$$-$$ O'Pal Inn
Km 265.5, 5 min south of Caraz, T043-
391015, www.opalsierraresort.com.
Scenic, family bungalows, suites and
rooms, swimming pool, includes
breakfast, restaurant, games room.

$$-$ La Alameda
Av Noé Bazán Peralta 262, T043-391177,
www.hotellaalameda.com.

Comfortable rooms, hot water, ample
parking, pleasant gardens.

$ Caraz Dulzura
Sáenz Peña 212, about 12 blocks
from the city centre, T043-392090,
www.hostalcarazdulzura.com.
Modern building in an old street,
hot water, comfortable, airy rooms,
restaurant and bar.

$ Chavín
San Martín 1135 just off the plaza,
T043-391171.
Get a room overlooking the street,
many others have no window. Warm
water, breakfast extra, guiding service,
tourist info.

$ Hostal La Casona
Raymondi 319, 1 block east from the
plaza, T043-391334.
With or without bath, hot water,
lovely little patio, noisy at night.

$ La Perla de los Andes
Daniel Villar 179, Plaza de Armas,
next to the cathedral, T043-392007,
http://huaraz.com/perladelosandes.
Comfortable rooms, hot water, helpful,
average restaurant.

$ San Marco
San Martín 1133, T043-391558.
Comfortable rooms with private
or shared bath, hot water, patio.

Restaurants

Carhuaz

$$ La Bicharra
Just north of Carhuaz on main road,
T943-780893.
Innovative North African/Peruvian
cooking, lunch only, busy at weekends,
call ahead to check if they are open
on weekdays.

Yungay

$$ Alpamayo
Av Arias Graziani s/n.
At north entrance to town, good
for local dishes, lunchtime only.

$ Café Pilar
On the main plaza.
Good for juices, cakes and snacks.

Caraz

$$ Venezia
Av Noé Bazán Peralta 231, T043-784813.
Good home-made pasta, Italian owner.

$$-$ Entre Panes
*Daniel Villar 211, half a block from
the plaza. Closed Tue.*
Variety of excellent sandwiches,
also meals. Good food, service
and atmosphere.

$$-$ La Punta Grande
*D Villar 595, 10 mins' walk from centre.
Closes 1700.*
Best place for local dishes.

$$-$ La Terraza
Jr Sucre 1107, T043-301226.
Good *menú* as well as pizza, pasta,
juices, home-made ice cream,
sandwiches, sweets, coffee and drinks.

$ Jeny
*Daniel Villar on the plaza next to
the Cathedral.*
Local fare at reasonable prices,
ample variety.

Cafés

Café de Rat
Sucre 1266, above Pony's Expeditions.
Breakfast, vegetarian dishes, good
pizzas, drinks and snacks, darts, travel
books, nice atmosphere.

El Turista
*San Martín 1117. Open in morning and
evening only.*
Small, popular for breakfast, ham
omelettes and ham sandwiches
are specialities.

Heladería Caraz Dulzura
D Villar on the plaza.
Home-made ice cream.

Panificadora La Alameda
D Villar y San Martín.
Good bread and pastries, ice cream,
popular with locals. The excellent
manjar blanco for which the town
earned its nickname 'Caraz dulzura' is
sold here and at several other shops on
the same street.

Bars and clubs

Caraz

Airu Resto Bar
*At Los Pinos Lodge, Parque San Martín.
Open 1800-2200.*
Serves wines and piscos.

Shopping

Caraz
There's fresh food in the market. Some
dried camping food is available from
Pony's Expeditions, who also sell
camping gaz canisters and white gas.

What to do

Caraz
Agencies in Caraz arrange treks in the
Cordillera Huayhuash, as well as more
local destinations.
Apu-Aventura, *Parque San Martín 103,
5 blocks west of plaza, T043-391130,
www.apuaventura.pe.* Range of
adventure sports and equipment rental.

Pony's Expeditions, *Sucre 1266, near the Plaza de Armas, T043-391642, www.ponyexpeditions.com. Mon-Sat 0800-2200*. Owners Alberto and Aidé Cafferata are knowledgeable about treks and climbs. They arrange local tours, offer accommodation at **Pony's Lodge ($$)** and **Backpacker Los Ponys ($)**, trekking, transport for day excursions, and rental of a 4WD vehicle with driver (US$125 per day plus fuel). Also maps and books for sale, equipment hire and mountain bike rental (US$18 for a full day). Highly recommended.

Transport

Carhuaz

All transport leaves from the main plaza. To **Huaraz**, colectivos and buses leave 0500-2000, US$1, 40 mins. To **Caraz**, 0500-2000, US$1, 1 hr. Buses from Huaraz to **Chacas** in the Cordillera Blanca, 87 km, 4 hrs, US$5.75, pass through Carhuaz about 40 mins after leaving Huaraz, then continues to Punta Olímpica from where there are excellent views. The dirt road is not in good condition due to landslides (can be closed in the wet season). **Renzo** daily buses pass through en route to **San Luis** (see page 102), a further 10 km, 1½ hrs.

Yungay

Buses and colectivos run all day to **Caraz**, 12 km, US$0.50, and **Huaraz**, 54 km, 1½ hrs, US$1. To the **Llanganuco lakes**, combis leave when full, especially 0700-0900, from Av 28 de Julio 1 block from the plaza, 1 hr, US$2.50. To **Yanama**, via the Portachuelo de Llanganuco Pass, 4767 m, 58 km, 3½ hrs, US$5; stopping at María Huayta (for the Llanganuco–Santa Cruz trek), after 2 hrs, US$3. To **Pomabamba**, via Piscobamba,

Trans Los Andes, daily at 0700-0730, the only company with a ticket office in Yungay; **Transvir** and **La Perla de Alta Mayo** buses coming from Huaraz, stop in Yungay at 0730 if they have room, 6-7 hrs, US$6. The buses descend to Puente Llacma, where it is possible to pick up buses and combis heading south to **San Luis**, **Chacas** and **Huari**.

Caraz

To **Lima**, 470 km, daily, US$11-30, 10-11 hrs via Huaraz and Pativilca, 9 companies: **El Huaralino** (T996-896607), **Huaraz Buss** (T943-469736), **Zbuss** (T043-391050), **Cooperativa Ancash** (T043-391126), all on Jr Cordova, also **Rochaz** (Pasaje Olaya, T043-794375), **Cavassa** (Ctra Central, T043-392042), **Yungay Express** (Av Luzuriaga, T043-391492), **Móviltours** (east end of town, www.moviltours.com.pe) and **Rodríguez** (Daniel Villar, T043-635631).

To **Chimbote**, Yungay Express, via Huallanca, Casma and Cañon del Pato, 3 daily, US$9, 7 hrs, sit on right for best views. To **Trujillo**, via Casma with Móviltours. To **Huaraz**, combis leave from a terminal on the way out of town, where the south end of C Sucre meets the highway, daily 0400-2000, 1¼ hrs, US$2, no luggage racks, you might have to pay an extra seat for your bag. To **Yungay**, 12 km, 15 mins, US$0.70. To **Huallanca** and **Yuramarca** (for the Cañon del Pato), combis and cars leave from Córdova y La Mar, 0700-1600, US$2.50. To **Cashapampa** (for the Santa Cruz valley) colectivo/minbus from Ramón Castilla y Jorge Chávez, Caraz, leave when full from 0600 to 1530, 1½ hrs, US$2. To **Parón** (for the walk to Laguna Parón), colectivos leave from Ramón Castilla y Jorge Chávez, close to the market, 1 hr, US$2.

Classic treks
in the cordilleras

popular treks with spectacular views

★The Llanganuco–Santa Cruz trek is one of the finest and most heavily used walks in the Cordillera Blanca, offered by all tour agencies in Huaraz and Caraz. It usually takes three to five days depending on your starting point and which alternative options you choose along the way. Starting in Cashapampa, you climb more gradually to the 4750 m Punta Unión Pass, then down to Vaquería or the Llanganuco lakes beyond. Along this 'clockwise' route (as described below) the climb is gentler, giving more time to acclimatize, and the pass is easier to find. On the other hand, if you start in Vaquería and finish in Cashapampa, you ascend for one day, rather than three in the other direction. The area receives heavy trekker traffic; please remove all your own rubbish.

Day 1 Caraz to Llamacorral (3850 m) Taking a combi to **Cashapampa** covers the first 600 m (1½ hours) of the trip (see Caraz Transport, page 112). Services in Cashapampa include shops, campsites and transport; arrieros and their mules can be hired (for prices, see page 97). The local community charges a fee for every trekker on the Santa Cruz hike. A recommended arriero is **Mellan Leiva Pariachi** (Caserío de Shuyo, Cashapampa). From here it's a 10-km, 900-m climb to the Llamacorral campsite (four hours).

Day 2 Llamacorral to Taullipampa (4250 m) This is an easy day, perfect for acclimatizing (a total of 12 km, climbing about 400 m). The trail leads to the Ichiccocha and Jatuncocha lakes, both providing shelter for many water birds and exotic plants. Beyond the lakes there is a quisuar forest, providing perfect shade for lunch. A side trip to the north (left) of the main valley takes a series of switchbacks to the **Alpamayo Base Camp**. After 45 minutes and climbing some 200 m, the circle of glaciers and snow peaks comes into full view. Go no further unless you plan to camp here. If returning to the main trail, look on the left of the trail (east) for a tiny path that will take you to **Taullipampa**, the next campsite. It's only 3 km to the camp, which is one of the most beautiful in the whole region, surrounded by snowy peaks, a silent river and incredible plants.

Day 3 Taullipampa to Huaripampa (3750 m) Make an early start for the **Punta Unión Pass**, the highest point on the trail, at 4750 m. The 4-km trail makes a series of switchbacks, but at a gentle pace you will reach this point in two to three hours. From the campsite the pass seems to be just a notch on the rock ridge right of Taulliraju (5850 m) but once there, the view is a 360° panorama of the snow peaks. The descent starts steeply, then traverses the granite slabs close to the ridge, before another series of switchbacks drive to the far left of the valley to descend on the lake below, another nice spot for lunch. Now the trail becomes slippery, crossing grass-like meadows towards **Quebrada Huaripampa**. After about two hours, a granite tower on your left is your sign to look for the bridge to cross the river. Now, with the river on your right, you will reach the **Quebrada Pariá**. This is a good campsite, with great views of Pariá mountain. It's usually crowded in July and August so, for more privacy, continue 2 km down the valley to camp at **Quenoapampa**. This is a spot at the end of the quenoal forest and a great campsite, despite the mosquitoes before sunset. For most travellers, the next campsite, some 3 km away, known as **Cachina Pampa** (3750 m), is a better option as it makes a shorter fourth day to catch the early buses back to Yungay. Total distance from the pass is 9 km, some three to four hours, descending 1000 m.

Day 4 For those who have only four days, the exit is at **Vaquería**, a group of houses at the side of the Yanama to Yungay road. Descend for 4 km in about one hour to the bridge on your right, climb to the left until you meet the fork to Colcabamba, take the right path steeply upwards and after 1½ hours you will meet the road. Yanama to Yungay combis can be caught at Vaquería (daily 0800-1400, US$4, two hours). In case of emergency, there is a solar-powered telephone at Colcabamba, available 0900-1800. Buy a phone card for the *teléfono rural*.

If you're on the five-day trek, at Vaquería, continue along the road for some 4 km to a green meadow, a toilet block (or what is left of it) and a huge rock forming a sort of cave (**Pampamachay**, 3870 m). This is a good campsite. If you have energy enough and want to gain on the next day, continue by taking the first short cut on the right. Walk uphill across the trail through bushes to the **Paccha Pampa** campsite (4120 m), named after the waterfalls by the campsite.

Day 5 Portachuelo to Llanganuco lakes (3850 m) A final climb reaches the Portachuelo Pass at 4767 m, in about two hours. You can see, on a clear day, more snow peaks than on any of the previous days, including the twin peaks of Huascarán, four summits of Huandoy, two of Pisco, two of Chacraraju, three of Yanapaccha and the giant Chopicalqui. The trail to the lakes starts on the south (left) of the pass, then after 5 km you reach the area of **Cebollapampa**, a popular campsite for climbers going to Cerro Pisco. At this point, cars are available to take you to Yungay. If you wish, pause on the way down at the Llanganuco lakes (see page 105).

a dramatic and demanding trek, not for the faint-hearted

★This difficult but spectacular trek can begin from either Cashapampa or from the more remote, smaller community of Hualcayan. Starting the trek from Hualcayan avoids 2½ to three hours' (7 km) fairly pleasant hike along the base of the mountains from Cashapampa, but supplies in this village are very limited (cookies, cola, candles; better to stock up in Caraz) and it may not be easy to organize arrieros at short notice. Once on the trek you can either hike directly across the range to Pomabamba (as described below – allow at least seven days), returning to Huaraz by bus, or extend the trek into a circuit of Alpamayo returning from Huilca via the Yanta Quenua and Santa Cruz valleys. For this second option allow at least 12 days.

Do not underestimate either route. They take in spectacular, constantly changing mountain vistas, including picture-postcard views of Alpamayo (5947 m), Quitaraju and the Pucajirca range. They cross three major, very steep mountain passes over 4700 m, plus an assortment of smaller challenges.

Day 1 Cashapampa to Hualcayan (four to 4½ hours) After 20 minutes' hiking north along the unpaved road from Cashapampa to Hualcayan, the badly dilapidated **Baños Termales Huancarhuas** come into view in the valley below. These are passed after one to 1½ hours of easy walking, first crossing a rushing stream in the valley floor. Beyond the baths the route climbs gently uphill, following the road beneath the mountains. There are a few shortcuts on trails along the way and you pass through traditional villages and fields. Cacti, spider plants, bromeliads and flowers are everywhere, not to mention the ubiquitous stands of eucalyptus. Views of the Cordillera Negra include a rich agricultural tapestry of small holdings and villages. After about three hours, a trail turns a little to the north, crossing a steep quebrada, just before a final one-hour steep climb to **Hualcayan** (3139 m). If you ask politely, you may be able to camp next to

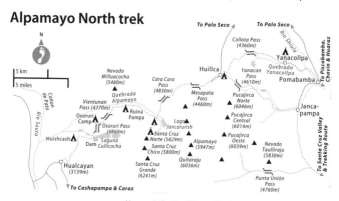

Alpamayo North trek

To Palo Seco
To Palo Seco
Collota Pass (4360m)
Rio Shiula
Yanacollpa
To Piscobamba, Chavin & Huaraz
Huillca
Yanacon Pass (4610m)
Quebrada Yanacollpa
Pomabamba
Nevado Milluacocha (5480m)
Cara Cara Pass (4830m)
Mesapata Pass (4460m)
Pucajirca Norte (6046m)
Janca-pampa
Quebrada Alpamayo
Vientunan Pass (4770m)
Ruina Pampa
Laguna Jancarurish
Pucajirca Central (6014m)
Osoruri Camp
Osoruri Pass (4860m)
Santa Cruz Norte (5829m)
Pucajirca Oeste (6039m)
Santa Cruz Valley & Trekking Route
Huishcash
Laguna Cullicocha
Santa Cruz Chico (5800m)
Alpamayo (5947m)
Nevado Taulliraju (5830m)
Dam
Hualcayan (3139m)
Santa Cruz Grande (6241m)
Quitaraju (6036m)
Punta Unión Pass (4760m)
To Cashapampa & Caraz
Cañon de Pato
Rio Santa
5 km
5 miles
N

the football pitch and beneath the ancient terraces that rise above the village; a community fee may be charged.

Day 2 Hualcayan to Huishcash (2½ hours) Heading east into the mountains you soon leave the road, following a zigzag trail as it climbs steeply, heading towards a large waterfall. Quickly gaining height, the trail keeps to the south of the waterfall for the first hour before crossing an adobe bridge to the north bank above the cascade. Views of the Cañón del Pato below, not to mention the Cordillera Negra across the valley, become increasingly more impressive as you climb above Hualcayan. After two hours, the path begins taking a more direct route, slowly climbing north towards a small patch of polylepis woodland. A sign marks the limit of Parque Nacional Huascarán at 3710 m. Thirty minutes later, heading north, you begin crossing a large landslide area and just beyond that you reach the beautiful remnant of polylepis woodland just mentioned. Beyond the forest there's an open pasture area, which makes a good stopping point for lunch and also a very good camping spot. (Note that the next potential campsite is by Laguna Cullicocha (see below), 3½ hours away: very high and cold.) If you decide to stay at **Huishcash** you could explore **Laguna Yanacocha**, only 1.65 km away but a steep 400 m below; a sign just beyond Huishcash points the way.

Day 3 Huishcash to Quebrada Vientunan (5½ to six hours) At the sign to Laguna Yanacocha, walk up the winding trail heading away from the direction in which the sign is pointing, straight up the hill in front of you. Fifteen minutes later you cross a small stream on an adobe bridge passing a small 'walking man' trail sign. This sign also names this pampa as Huishcash (4200 m), as well as listing various prohibitions: no fires, no fishing, no booze, no rubbish, etc. Some 1½ hours after the Huishcash lunch/camping spot, a sign indicates 2.7 km to Laguna Cullicocha and, in another direction, 7 km to Laguna Yanacocha. On the left is a black, canyon-like feature, full of dense native vegetation below, but barren on exposed ridges and faces. Not far beyond the last signpost the path runs just to the left, underneath a black hill on top of the pass and in between the two black mountains above the dark valley. Lots of polylepis woodland covers the inaccessible parts of this gorge.

Roughly 3½ hours after leaving Huishcash you come to the Duke Energy hydro station and the potential campsite in front of **Laguna Cullicocha**. This station is always staffed. Before arriving at the station, follow the steep right-hand side of the gorge, passing (but not following) a water drainage channel. The campsite itself is set in a landscape of smooth sculpted rocks backed by spectacular views of the Laguna Cullicocha and, behind the lake, the icy walls of the Santa Cruz massif: **Santa Cruz Norte** (5829 m), **Chico** (5800 m) and **Santa Cruz Grande** (6241 m, also referred to as **Nevado Pucaraju**). The rocks and high altitude make for a cold and uncomfortable campsite but, if you are very polite, the station attendant may let you stay in the station's spare accommodation. The next good campsite is a couple of hours' hike further, on the far side of one of the trek's major passes.

Head north, following trail markers just to the west of the Cullicocha hydro station, with great views again of the Santa Cruz mountains and the lakes below. After about

15 minutes the trail begins to swing more to the east towards Santa Cruz Norte and begins to zigzag higher above the lakes towards the pass. Thirty to 40 minutes after the station, the route starts to turn north through a jagged rocky area, heading up towards the pass. From here you have a good view down into the glacial moraine of Santa Cruz. Fifty minutes after Cullicocha, a knife-edge ridge on the top of the first pass, **Osoruri** (4860 m), is reached. A great vista of the mountains of the **Milluacocha** massif opens up, with the trail twisting into the valley below you on your right. Condors may be seen here. Between Osoruri and Nevado Milluacocha the valley of the **Quebrada Alpamayo** plunges beneath you, its floor around 1700 m below. Turning east-northeast you descend into the steep, bowl-like valley, underneath the next pass, Punta Vientunan. This, with shelter and water, is as good a campsite as any.

Day 4 Vientunan to Alpamayo (six to seven hours) Climb steeply in switchbacks on the far wall of the valley to reach the next pass, **Punta Vientunan** (4770 m). Before climbing, at the bottom of the valley, a sign points to Ruina Pampa, 5.2 km away. You reach the pass after a little more than an hour's climb. A very long descent follows Vientunan Pass, at least 1¼ hours of knee stress, before beginning to approach the bottom of the Quebrada Alpamayo. A few traditional houses mark a small settlement and, on the far side of the valley, an extensive area of terraces hints at a long history of habitation. A signpost gives the distance to the base camp at **Nevado Alpamayo** as 10.5 km to the east up the valley, and the distance to the Ruinas de Auquis Puquio as 13 km to the west. Take the east route up the valley deeper into the heart of the mountains. The valley floor soon begins to open up, passing the unrestored walls of **Ruina Pampa** (another potential camping spot) and continuing along the valley's right-hand side fairly constantly for around 10 km until reaching an official camping spot, marked by another signboard. Surrounded by magnificent mountains on all sides, the site is positioned just before the turn to the south where the valley swings towards Lago Jancarurish and the glacial moraines. In good weather the classic northwest face of **Alpamayo** is visible, but for the best views of the mountain, give yourself some time the following day to ascend the moraine to the south.

Day 5 Alpamayo viewpoint (optional) Heading south up the valley, a brief climb to the summit of the moraine affords fabulous views of the turquoise **Lago Jancarurish**, vast cliffs and a spectacular cascade pouring from Alpamayo and its glacier above. Avalanches sometimes rumble down to the far side of the lake, a spectacular and very humbling sight. Glance to the west and you'll find views of **Santa Cruz** and her sister peaks, perhaps from their most striking angle. Hiking further up the valley on the right-hand side will bring you to the climbers' base camp, and all the beauty and hazards that the world of ice and snow entails.

Day 6 Alpamayo to Huillca (6½ to seven hours) From the official campsite below Lago Jancarurish, cross to the north side of the Quebrada Alpamayo, then bear left, heading north towards the Cara Cara Pass, but zigzagging up on the left-hand (west) side of the valley. The initial climb is steep but offers increasingly panoramic views of the surrounding peaks, including **Quitaraju** to the south, an impressive mountain often hidden by rocky outcrops from the valley floor. After about an hour of climbing, the trail leads into a flatter valley, with a small lake on its right-hand side. Beyond this flatter section, the final push up to the pass is a steep scree slope, almost a scramble in the last moments. It should take a couple of hours to reach the chilly, windswept **Cara Cara Pass** (4830 m). There's not a lot of room to manoeuvre up there and the wind can be fierce, but with awe-inspiring peaks all around, Cara Cara offers perhaps the most jaw-dropping vista on the trek.

On the far side of the pass, descend roughly east-northeast, following the trail down through steep rocky ground. This valley appears to have a slightly wetter climate than Quebrada Alpamayo, with cushion mosses and many flowers. A couple of small ruins are passed in the higher sections of the valley. The descent from the pass is fairly steep for the first 45 minutes, then flattens out into a damp puna environment, with thick ichu grass everywhere and occasional boggy patches. Follow the left flank of the valley to the northeast. A couple of hours after the pass, the trail reasserts its easterly course, crossing to the right-hand side of the valley and climbing towards the small Mesapata Pass. At the same time the Quebrada Mayobamba swings sharply to the north, away from your route. After another hour (five hours after starting out) you reach the summit of **Mesapata** (4460 m), to be rewarded by yet another imposing range, the ice-bound peaks of the **Pucajirca** massif. Below you lies the **Quebrada Tayapampa** and, on the river's left-hand bank, a rough road heading northeast. Descend into the valley and follow the road until it crosses the river and opens up into the wide valley of **Huillca**. Here you'll find a traditional, almost totally self-sufficient settlement of three Quechua families, all carving a rugged existence from animal herding, with large groups of alpacas, sheep, horses and cattle grazing the valley. With permission from one of these families, it's possible to camp on the eastern side of the valley, beyond the Yanta Quenua stream. Note that not even the basic highland staples such as potatoes may be available here. Always treat the inhabitants of this valley and their extraordinary culture with respect. At the same time, make sure you store all valuables inside your tent.

Options from Huillca At Huillca, you have the choice of either continuing east to the far side of the mountains and reaching **Pomabamba** via the Collota Pass (as described in detail below), or turning southeast up the **Yanta Quenua valley**. The latter route will take you in a couple of days over the 4610-m Yanacon Pass, via Quebrada Yanajanca, the Jancapamapa Valley and Quebrada Tuctubamba, to join the classic Santa Cruz trekking route (see page 113) close to the small Laguna Huecrucocha. Heading west from Huecrucocha will lead you in two or three days over the Alto de Pucaraju (4640 m) and Punta Unión (4760 m, see page 114) passes and through the Santa Cruz valley, completing what's generally termed the **Alpamayo Circuit**.

You can also reach Pomabamba via the Yancon Pass, by following the broad boggy valley to **Jancapampa** village, from where there are combis to Pomabamba (Mon-Sat at 0730 and 1300, more frequent on Sun, US$2, 1 hr, often full). Whichever route you take to Pomabamba, you can rest and re-supply there, then take the combi to Jancapampa (from Pomabamba Mon-Sat at 0600 and 1200) to continue along the Alpamayo Circuit.

Finally, there is also a road running north and east from Huillca to Pomabamba via Palo Seco, but this is a very long way around and there is no regular transport.

Day 7 Huillca to Quebrada Yanajanca (five to six hours) The trail to Pomabamba via the Collota Pass starts in the Huillca valley's southeast corner, zigzagging up the hill to the northeast before swinging more to the north. The top of the first pass is reached after around 50 minutes, the route commanding spectacular views of the Pucajirca snow peaks and passing through a small patch of polylepis woodland. Reaching the top of the pass (there's no name on the Alpenverin Map, but let's call it **Punta Shuitucocha** for clarity) you are presented with a view of a second valley to the east. This valley has two lakes, the more southerly, larger of which is **Laguna Shuitucocha**. The trail now follows a route between the two lakes, then up the hill to the far side, taking a generally east-northeastly course along the left-hand edge of the hills. After around 2½ hours you'll reach the bleak 4360-m **Collota Pass**, crowned by a large cross.

A steep descent to the east leads towards a trail/rough road. A long descent down this valley on the left (north) bank leads into a lush, jungle-like landscape. The valley becomes increasingly heavily populated, the trail crossing over onto the right bank of the river, passing some small shops, before re-crossing the river and heading through the main part of the **Yanacollpa** village. Some families in the village and slightly beyond it will allow you to camp or rent a room for a small fee. Keep a close eye on your gear when staying close to the village. Alternatively, camp before crossing the bridge just before Yanacollpa to avoid fees and locals hanging around your tent asking for goods, medicine, money, matches, candies, etc.

Day 8 Yanacollpa to Pomabamba Just a few hours' trek this morning, first crossing the river, following its course down the right-hand bank of the Yanacollpa until it meets the Río Shiula, then following the water downstream to the southeast to your destination. Make certain that just before **Pomabamba** you cross the river to the north side; this route will take you right into the town centre. If you want to relax after the trek, there are some good thermal baths close to Pomabamba (see page 103).

Cordilleras Huayhuash and Raura

remote mountains just waiting to be explored

The Cordillera Huayhuash, lying south of the Cordillera Blanca, has azure trout-filled lakes interwoven with deep *quebradas* and high pastures around the hem of the range. It is perhaps the most spectacular cordillera for its massive ice faces that seem to rise sheer out of the puna's contrasting green. You may see tropical parakeets in the bottom of the gorges and condors circling the peaks. The area offers fantastic scenery and insights into rural life.

The cordillera is approached from four points: **Chiquián** in the north is a town of narrow streets and overhanging eaves; **Oyón**, with links to Cerro de Pasco, lies to the southeast; **Churín** is to the south, and **Cajatambo**, a small market town with a beautiful 18th-century church and a lovely plaza, lies to the southwest. Note that the road out of Cajatambo is not for the faint-hearted. For the first three to four hours it is no more than a bus-width, clinging to the cliff edge.

★Huayhuash trekking circuit

The complete circuit is very tough; allow ten to 12 days. There are up to eight passes over 4600 m, depending on the route. Fees are charged by every community along the way, adding up to about US$80 for the entire circuit; take soles in small denominations and insist on getting a receipt every time. A half-circuit is also possible, and there are many other options. (Figures in the text and on the map indicate the most usual camping sites.)

Buy all your food and supplies in Huaraz as there are only basic supplies in Chiquián and almost nothing in the hamlets along the route. Ask for mules (US$6 per day) or horses (US$7 per day) at the hotels or restaurants in Chiquián, but note that it may take a day to bring the mules to your starting point from Llamac or Pocpa where they are kept. A guide for the Huayhuash is Sr Delao Callupe; ask for him in Chiquián.

The trail head is at **Cuartel Huain** (1) between Matacancha and the **Punta Cacanan Pass** (the continental divide at 4700 m). This northernmost point on the trek gives access to the village of **Janca**, to **Laguna Mitucocha** (2) and to the eastern flank of the Cordillera. A very steep short cut on scree takes you through

Cordilleras Huayhuash & Raura

the gap in the northern spur of the range above Matacancha and Janca village on the other side. This could save two or three hours.

The eastern side of the Cordillera is a chain of passes, lakes and stunning views of **Jirishanca Chico**, **Yerupajá Chico**, **Yerupajá** (Peru's second highest peak at 6634 m) and **Siulá Grande**. From Janca, a small side valley leads off **Quebrada Mitucocha** to **Punta Carhuac** (4650 m) and beyond to **Laguna Carhuacocha**, with magnificent camping (3) and views. Following on from there are **Punta Carnicero** (4600 m) – a section of Inca road and petroglyphs are found nearby – the twin lakes of **Azulcocha** and **Atoqshaico** (just beyond the pass) and **Huayhuash village** (4 – one house).

This is the regular route, but an alternative route is also open, following round Laguna Carhuacocha, passing Laguna Siulá and emerging on the regular route just before Huayhuash village. This trail gained popularity thanks to Joe Simpson's classic book, Touching the Void; there are no maps and it is for experienced trekkers only. A guide is recommended as the weather can change very suddenly.

The next pass, **Portachuelo Huayhuash** (4750 m, the continental divide), overlooks the superb southward line of pyramidal peaks and rounded ice caps of the **Cordillera Raura**. A path leads from **Laguna Viconga** below (5 – near the dam), over a pass and hugs the western flank of the Raura all the way to **Oyón**. (Transportes Javier run a daily bus from **Raura** to Cerro de Pasco in the Central Highlands, seven hours, US$5.50; there are also daily buses from Oyón.) Thirty-two kilometres southwest of Oyón is **Churín**, which boasts the 'best thermal baths in Peru'. There is also a small thermal pool 1 km past the outflow of Viconga, along the trail to Cajatambo. Note that water is released from the Viconga dam daily 0500-1100, and you cannot ford the outflow during this time. If you are bailing out at **Cajatambo** (6), it is downhill all the way from Laguna Viconga, apart from a short sting in the tail at the end.

Those continuing the circuit must cross the **Punto Cuyoc** (5000 m), sometimes snowbound, with outstanding 360° views. This is the highpoint of the circuit in every sense of the word. There follows a long, gentle descent into the **Quebrada Huanacpatay** (6 on the full circuit) and an optional one-day side trip up the valley of the **Río Huayllapa** to **Laguna Jurau** and **Laguna Sarapococha**, both beautiful lakes.

The route continues downhill to the village of **Huayllapa** (with shop and basic lodging and meals); just before town it turns north to begin climbing to the **Tapush Pass** (4800 m) below the summit of **Diablo Mudo** (also known as **Suerococha**), via **Huatiac** (7).

After the pass you reach **Cashpapampa** (8), from where you head east to the **Yaucha Pass** (4800 m, outstanding views), then north, by way of the **Quebrada Huacrish**, to **Laguna Jahuacocha**, which lies beneath **Yerupajá** and nevados **Jirishanca** and **Rondoy**. The lake offers the most idyllic campsite (9) in the Cordillera. It can also be reached from **Llamac**, by crossing over the Punta Llamac Pass at 4300 m, southeast of that town: first head southwest along a path just beneath the cemetery and zigzag up above the town. Llamac is also used as a starting point for the trek. You can camp on the football pitch (US$1.50 per night) and drinking water is available from the water source that is 200 m on the trail north to Pocpa; ask locals.

The 4800-m **Sambunya Pass**, beneath Rondoy, leads to the descent to the town of **Rondoy** (10), Matacancha and the trail head.

Where to stay

There are various hotels ($) and some
good restaurants around the plaza
in Cajatambo. The following are all in
Chiquián:

$ Hostal San Miguel
Jr Comercio 233, T043-447001.
Nice courtyard and garden, clean, many
rooms, popular.

$ Hotel Huayhuash
28 de Julio 400, T043-447049.
Private bathroom, hot water, restaurant,
laundry, parking, modern, great views,
information and tours.

$ Los Nogales de Chiquián
*Jr Comercio 1301, T043-447121, http://
hotelnogaleschiquian.blogspot.com.*
Traditional design, with private or shared
bath, hot water, cafeteria, parking.
Recommended.

Restaurants

**$ El Refugio de Bolognesi and
Yerupajá**
Tarapacá, Chiquián.
Both offer basic set meals.

$ Panificadora Santa Rosa
Comercio 900, on the plaza, Chiquián.
For good bread and sweets, has coin-
operated phones and fax.

Transport

Coming from Huaraz, the road is now
paved beyond Chiquián to Huansala,
on the road to Huallanca (Huánuco).
Private vehicles can sometimes be
hired in Chiquián or Llamac (less likely)
to take you to the trailhead at Cuartel
Huain; otherwise you'll have to walk.

Chiquián
To **Huaraz**, buses leave the plaza at 0500
daily, US$1.75, except **Trans El Rápido**,
Jr Figueredo 216, T043-447049, at 0500
and 1330, US$3.65. Also colectivo to
Huaraz 1500, 3 hrs, US$2.45 pp. There
is also a connection from Chiquián to
Huallanca (Huánuco) with buses from
Lima in the early morning and combis
during the day, which leave when full,
3 hrs, US$2.50. From Huallanca there
are regular combis on to **La Unión**, 1
hr, US$0.75, and from there transport to
Huánuco.

Cajatambo
Buses to **Lima** daily at 0600, US$9, with
Empresa Andina (office on plaza next to
Hostal Cajatambo), **Tour Bello** (1 block
off the Plaza) and **Turismo Cajatambo**
(Jr Grau 120; or Av Carlos Zavala 124
corner of Miguel Aljovin 449, Lima, T01-
426 7238).

North Coast

Peru's north coast could well be described as the Egypt of South America. This is a region of numerous monumental ruins, built by the many highly skilled pre-Inca cultures that once thrived here.

The ground-breaking discovery at Caral is now open to visitors. Not far from Trujillo, Chan Chán was the capital of the Chimú Kingdom; its crumbling remains still represent the largest adobe city in the world. The Huaca de la Luna and the Huaca Cao Viejo of the Moche Empire are revealing fabulous, multicoloured friezes of gods from the first millennium AD. Further north, near Chiclayo, the adobe brick pyramids of Túcume, Sipán and Sicán rise massively from the coastal plains. The wealth from some of their tombs is now displayed in state-of-the-art museums.

But it's not all pyramids and royal tombs. The elegant city of Trujillo is one of the finest examples of colonial architecture in the country. There are charming towns, such as Huanchaco, with its bizarre-looking reed fishing rafts, and Chulucanas, with its famous pottery. Up and down the coast the seafood is wonderful and the hospitality unrivalled. In addition, the northern seaboard enjoys a rain-free climate all year and has Peru's finest beaches for bathing and surfing. Around Tumbes, the most northerly regional capital, four reserves protect mangroves, equatorial dry forest and tropical forest, each with its share of endangered species.

Best for
Archaeology ▪ Beaches ▪ Seafood

Footprint picks

★ **Caral**, page 129

This site may be the oldest city in South America.

★ **Sechín**, page 129

The 500 monoliths here depict a gruesome battle in graphic detail.

★ **Trujillo**, page 135

The city's mansions, with their elaborately carved wooden balconies, are among the finest in Peru.

★ **Huanchaco**, page 141

Hang out with other travellers at this appealing surfing village.

★ **El Brujo**, page 152

This ancient complex was a ceremonial centre for up to 10 cultures.

★ **Lambayeque and Ferreñafe**, pages 158 and 162

These colonial towns are a good base for exploring the surrounding sites.

★ **Northern beaches**, page 178

Enjoy some of the best surf and warmest water in Peru.

★ **Tumbes' natural parks and reserves**, page 180

Four protected natural areas are home to unique ecosystems.

ECUADOR

Santuario Nacional
los Manglares de Tumbes
Puerto Pizarro
Tumbes
Aguas Verdes
Zona Reservada
de Tumbes
Zorritos
Cancas
Punta Sal
Máncora
Los Organos
Cabo Blanco
Talara
Sullana
Colán
Paita
Catacaos
Sechura
Bayovar
Parque Nacional
Cerros de Amotape
Alamor
Tambo
Grande
Frias
Chulucanas
Canchaque
Piura
Vice
Sechura
Desert
Olmos
La Tina
Ayabaca
Espíndola
Namballe
Huancabamba
Reventazón
Motupe
Apurlec
Túcume
Mórrope
Ferreñafe
Lambayeque
Pimentel
Sta Rosa
Puerto Etén
Chiclayo
Sipón
Zaña
Monsefú
Chochope
Sto Tomás
San Miguel
de Pallaques
Chota
Santa María
de Nieve
Sameriza
Chiriaco
Aramango
Bagua Chica
Bagua Grande
Jaén
Chamaya
Pucará
Lonya Grande
Pedro Ruiz
Chachapoyas
Leymebamba
Celendín
Barranca
San Ramón
La Libertad
Jeberos
Nuevo Cajamarca
Moyobamba
Lamas
Tarapoto
Sacanche
Pacasmayo
Chepén
Contumazá
Cajamarca
San Juán
Cajabamba
Huamachuco
Pto Chicama
El Brujo
Ascope
Otusco
Huanchaco
Chan Chán
Trujillo
Salaverry
Virú
Simbal
Santiago
de Chuco
Huacas del Sol
& de la Luna
Tauca
Retamas
Mollepata
Tayabamba
Sihuas
Huancaspata
Tanguche
Chimbote
Nepeña
Chuquicara
Huallanca
Pamparomas
Caraz
Tres Cruces
Cashapampa
Chacas
Huari
Quivilla
Pacific Ocean
Playa Tortugas
Casma
Sechín
Pariacoto
La Merced
Huaraz
Recuay
Chavinillo
Culebras
Huarmey
Huayllapampa
Marca
Chiquián
Conococha (4100m)
Raura
Chasquitambo
Cajatambo
Cochas
Paramonga
Pativilca
Barranca
Caral
Huaura
Huacho
Supe
Sayán
Huancahuasi
Churín
Reserva Nacional
Loma de Lachay
Chancay
Aucallama
Chillón
Callao
LIMA

Footprint picks

N

50 km
50 miles

Essential North Coast

Finding your feet

The transport hubs of the region are Trujillo, Chiclayo and Piura. All have regular flights and bus services to and from Lima. It can be a long haul across the desert, so if you are short on time then flying to the north coast is convenient.

Best *ceviche*

This marinated raw fish dish is a quintessential element of Peruvian cuisine. Try it at one of the following:
La Choza Náutica, Lima, page 63
Lobo del Mar – Octavio Otani, Lima, page 67
Rosa Náutica, Lima, page 66
Cevichería Puerto Mori, Trujillo, page 146
El Sombrero, Huanchaco, page 147
San Felipe, Colán, page 171

Getting around

Once you are up north, bus travel is the best way to get around. Trujillo is best explored on foot, although taxis are readily available. The major sites outside the city, Chan Chán, the Moche pyramids and Huanchaco, are easily reached by public transport, but take care when walking around.

A number of recommended guides run tours to these and other places. From Chiclayo it is easy to visit Lambayeque's museums, Sipán and Túcume by public transport or on a local tour; Sicán is a full-day tour from Chiclayo including Ferreñafe and Pómac. Public transport is your best bet for travel from Piura north to the beaches and Ecuador.

When to go

The summer months are December to April and can be very hot, especially around Piura. Hotels around Máncora are heavily booked at this time and prices can increase by 100% or more, especially for Christmas, Easter and other holidays. Surfing is best from November to March. There may be sea mists from May to October, especially south of Trujillo, but Piura's climate is very pleasant at this time, although nights can be cold and the wind piercing. This is also a good time to visit the nature reserves around Tumbes. Keep an eye on weather reports; El Niño events tend to affect the north coast more adversely than elsewhere.

Time required

One to three weeks, depending on how many centres you choose to visit.

Weather Trujillo

January	February	March	April	May	June
26°C 19°C 2mm	25°C 18°C 10mm	27°C 19°C 15mm	25°C 17°C 0mm	23°C 16°C 1mm	22°C 16°C 0mm

July	August	September	October	November	December
22°C 15°C 1mm	21°C 15°C 6mm	21°C 15°C 0mm	22°C 15°C 0mm	23°C 15°C 2mm	23°C 17°C 8mm

North of
Lima

Between Lima and Pativilca there is a narrow belt of coastal land deposited at the mouths of the rivers. The Pan-American Highway parallels the coast all the way to the far north, with feeder roads branching off it along various valleys to the east.

Lima to Chimbote
awesome prehistoric ruins along the Panamericana

Chancay Valley
Just north of Ancón, the Pasamayo sand dune, stretching for 20 km, comes right down to the seashore. The old road that snakes above the sea is spectacular, but is closed except to commercial traffic and buses. The toll road (four lanes, toll about US$2.65), which goes right over the top, gives good views of the nearby coast and valleys.

After the dune is the Chancay Valley, the name of which is associated with an extensive culture whose artefacts can be seen in many museums in the capital. About 20 km beyond Chancay is a turning to Sayán, after which is a track signposted to the Lomas de Lachay in the Reserva Nacional de Lachay.

Reserva Nacional de Lachay
T01-339 8342, www.sernanp.gob.pe. Daily 0830-1730. US$3.35, children US$1. Ask to be let off the bus at Km 105, from where it is 3 km to the guard post.

This small reserve (5070 ha) is a typical example of loma ('fog vegetation') habitat and protects several important species. During the winter months, fog caused by the Humboldt Current drives inland, rises and condenses into a dew suffient to sustain seasonal plants and endemic birds, such as the Raimondi's yellow finch and thick-billed miner. Within just 5 km the landscape changes from barren desert to a green carpet, resonating with birdsong. The area is most beautiful in September and October when the plants are in bloom. There is a visitor centre, trails, camping and picnic areas.

Huara valley
The Pan-American Highway by-passes both **Huacho** and **Puerto Huacho**, 19 km to the east. The beaches south of the town are clean and deserted. Inland from Huacho is another route to Sayán, which continues to the spa town of Churín.

The town of Huaura, just beyond Huacho, was where General San Martín first proclaimed the country's independence from Spain, eight months prior to the official declaration of Independence in Lima. The house with the balcony from which he made the proclamation is a small museum.

★Caral

25 km east of the Panamericana (Km 184); after 18.5 km, a track leads across the valley to the ruins (30 mins), though the river may be impassable Dec-Mar. Information: Proyecto Especial Caral, T01-205 2500 (Lima), www.caralperu.gob.pe. Daily 0900-1600. US$4, US$7 per group; all visitors must be accompanied by an official guide and not stray from the marked paths.

A few kilometres before Barranca, a signed turning to the east at Km 184 leads up the Supe valley to the UNESCO World Heritage Site of **Caral**. This ancient city, 26 km from the coast, dates from about 2600 BC. Many of the accepted theories of Peruvian archaeology have been overturned by Caral's age and monumental construction. It appears to be the oldest city in South America (a claim disputed by the Miravalles site, in the department of Cajamarca). The dry desert site lies on the southern fringes of the Supe valley, along whose flanks are 32 more ruins, 19 of which have been explored. Caral covers 66 ha and contains eight significant pyramidal structures. To date seven have been excavated by archaeologists from the University of San Marcos, Lima, who are undertaking careful restoration on the existing foundations to re-establish the pyramidal tiers.

It is possible to walk around the pyramids on marked paths. A viewpoint provides a panorama of the whole site. Allow at least two hours for your visit. Handicrafts are sold in the car park. You can stay or camp at the **Casa del Arqueólogo**, a community museum in Supe (at the turn-off to Caral), which provides information on the Caral culture and the progress of the excavations.

Barranca to Huarmey

Barranca is by-passed by the Highway but is an important transport hub for the region so you may find yourself there to change buses. Some 4 km beyond the turn-off to Huaraz at Pativilca, beside the Panamericana, are the well-preserved ruins of the Chimú temple of **Paramonga** ① *US$1.80; caretaker may act as guide.* Set on high ground with a view of the ocean, the fortress-like mound is reinforced by eight quadrangular walls rising in tiers to the top of the hill.

Between Pativilca and Chimbote the mountains come down to the sea. The road passes by a few very small protected harbours in tiny rock-encircled bays, such as **Huarmey**, with a fine beach and active hostel.

★Sechín and around

5 km north of Casma, off the road to Huaraz. Daily 0800-1700 (photography best around midday). US$1.80 (childrenUS$0.35, students US$1.40); ticket also valid for the Max Uhle Museum by the ruins and other sites in the Casma Valley, including Chanquillo. Mototaxi from Casma, US$2.85 each way for 2 passengers, US$8.55 return including wait.

This archaeological site in the Nepeña Valley, north of Casma, is one of the most important ruins on the Peruvian coast. It consists of a large square temple completely faced with about 500 carved stone monoliths narrating, it is thought, a gruesome battle in graphic detail. The style is unique in Peru for its naturalistic vigour. The complex as a whole is associated with the pre-Chavín Sechín culture, dating from about 1600 BC. Three sides of the large stone temple have been excavated and restored, but you cannot see the earlier adobe buildings inside the stone walls because they were covered up and used as a base for a second storey, which has been completely destroyed.

Casma and around → *Colour map 3, B2.*

Sechín is accessed from the city of Casma (*population: 22,600*), which has a pleasant Plaza de Armas, several parks and two markets including a good food market. However, this is not a safe city, so stay instead in **Tortugas**, 10 minutes away. This is a pleasant place to spend a day at the beach and enjoy the seafood.

South of Casma on the south bank of the Río Casma, is **Chanquillo**, a 2300-year old structure on a hilltop. It consists of three concentric stone walls with rectangular and circular buildings inside the interior wall. Beyond the ruins, stretching for over 300 m along a ridge are 13 towers (2 to 6 m high). Studies suggest a close solar alignment between the main ruins and the towers, making this by far the oldest known solar observatory in the Americas. Access is along a secondary road off the Panamericana at Km 361. If driving there, 4WD is recommended.

Chimbote to Callejón de Huaylas → *Colour map 3, A2.*

The port of Chimbote (*population: 296,600*) serves the national fishing industry; the smell of its fishmeal plants is overpowering. If that's not enough to put you off staying here, the city is also unsafe. Take extensive precautions; always use taxis from the bus station, and avoid staying overnight if possible.

Just north of Chimbote, a road branches northeast off the Pan-American Highway and goes up the Santa valley following the route of the old Santa Corporation Railway which used to run as far as **Huallanca** (not to be confused with the town southeast of Huaraz), 140 km up the valley. At **Chuquicara**, three hours from Chimbote (paved – very rough thereafter), is Restaurante Rosales, a good place to stop for a meal (you can sleep here, too, but it's very basic). There are also places to stay and eat at Huallanca, and fuel is available. At the top of the valley by the hydroelectric centre, the road goes through the very narrow and spectacular **Cañón del Pato**. You pass under tremendous walls of bare rock and through almost 40 tunnels, but

> **Tip...**
> If arriving in Chimbote from Caraz via the Cañón del Pato there is usually time to make a connection to Casma or Trujillo/Huanchaco and avoid overnighting in Chimbote. If travelling to Caraz from Chimbote, take the **Línea** 0600 service or earlier from Trujillo to make the 0830 bus up the Cañón del Pato. If overnighting is unavoidable, head south to Casma for the night, but buy your ticket to Caraz the day before.

the flow of the river has been greatly reduced by the hydroelectric scheme. After this point the road is paved to the Callejón de Huaylas and south to Caraz and Huaraz. For bus services along this route, see Transport, page 133.

A faster route to Huaraz, paved and also very scenic, branches off the Pan-American Highway at **Casma**. It climbs to **Pariacoto**, with basic lodging, and crosses the Cordillera Negra at the **Callán Pass** (4224 m). The descent to Huaraz offers great views of the Cordillera Blanca. This beautiful trip is worth taking in daylight; sit on the right for the best views. The road has many dangerous curves requiring caution. For bus services along this route, see Transport, page 133.

An alternative road for cyclists (and vehicles with a permit) is the 50-km private road known as the 'Brasileños', used by the Brazilian company Odebrecht which has built a water channel from the Río Santa to the coast. The turn-off at Km 482 on the Pan-American Highway is 35 km north of the Santa turning and 15 km south of the bridge in Chao. It is a good all-weather road via Tanguche. Permits are obtainable from the Chavimochic HQ at San José de Virú, US$7.50, or from the guard at the gate on Sunday.

Listings North of Lima

Where to stay

Barranca to Huarmey

$ Jaime Crazy
Manuel Scorza 371 y 373, Sector B-8, Huarmey, T043-400104, JaimeCrazyPeru on Facebook.
A hostel offering trips to beaches, archaeological sites, farming communities, volunteering and all sorts of activities.

Casma and around
Hotel prices are higher in Jan and Feb.

$$ Hostal El Farol
Túpac Amaru 450, Casma, T043-411064, www.elfarolinn.com.
Very nice, rooms and suites, swimming pool, pleasant garden, very good restaurant, parking, information.

$$ Hostal Gabriela
Malecón Grau Mz 6, Lt 18, Tortugas, T043-631302, misateinversiones@gmail.com.

Pleasant 10-room hotel, lounge with ocean views, good restaurant with extensive menu, seafood, local and international dishes.

$$ Tarawasi
1a Línea Sur, Centro, Tortugas, T043-782637, tarawasitortugas@hotmail.com.
Small family run *hospedaje*, pleasant atmosphere, 2 terraces with ocean views, good restaurant serves Peruvian and Mediterranean food.

$ El Dorado
Av Garcilazo de la Vega Mz J, Lt 37, 1 block from the Panamericana, Casma, T043-411795, http://eldoradocasma. blogspot.com.
With fan, pool, restaurant and tourist information.

$ Las Dunas
Luis Ormeño 505, Casma, T043-711057.
An upgraded and enlarged family home, welcoming.

Chimbote to Callejón de Huaylas

There are plenty of hotels in Chimbote, so try to negotiate a lower rate.

$$ Cantón
Bolognesi 498, T043-344388.
Modern, higher quality than others, has a good but pricey chifa restaurant.

$$ Ivansino Inn
Av José Pardo 738, T043-321811, www.ivansinoinn.com.
Includes breakfast, comfortable, modern.

$ Hostal El Ensueño
Sáenz Peña 268, 2 blocks from Plaza Central, T043-328662.
Cheaper rooms without bath, very good, safe, welcoming.

$ Hostal Karol Inn
Manuel Ruiz 277, T043-321216.
Hot water, good, family run, laundry, cafetería.

$ Residencial El Parque
E Palacios 309, on plaza, T043-345572.
Converted old home, hot water, nice, secure.

Restaurants

Huara valley
Good restaurants in Huacho include **Cevichería El Clásico** (Calle Inca s/n, daily 1000-1800), and **La Estrella** (Av 28 de Julio 561).

Casma and around
The best restaurants are at **Hostal El Farol** and at the hotels in Tortugas. Cheap restaurants are on Huarmey. The local ice cream, *Caribe*, is available at Ormeño 545.

$$ Tío Sam
Huarmey 138.
Specializes in fresh fish, good ceviche.

What to do

Casma and around
Akela Tours, *Lima A3-3, T990-283145, www.akelatours.com.* Good tours of Sechín, trips to the desert and beaches, sandboarding; run by Monika, an archaeologist.
Sechín Tours, *Hostal Monte Carlo, Casma, T043-411421, renatotours@yahoo.com.* Organizes tours in the local area. The guide, Renato, only speaks Spanish but has knowledge of local ruins.

Transport

Huara valley
Bus
AméricaMóvil (Av Luna Pizarro 251, La Victoria, Lima, T01-423 6338; in Huacho T01-232 7631) and **Zeta** (Av Abancay 900, Lima, T01-426 8087; in Huacho T01-239 6176) run every 20-30 mins **Lima–Huacho**, daily 0600 to 2000, 2½ hrs, US$6 (more expensive at weekends).

Caral
Empresa Valle Sagrado Caral buses to the site leave the terminal in Barranca (Berenice Dávila, cuadra 2), US$2.75 shared, or US$35 private service with 1½ hrs at the site. A taxi from Barranca to the ruins costs US$10 one way. Tours from Lima usually allow 1½ hrs at Caral, with a 3-hr journey each way, stopping for morning coffee and for lunch in Huacho on the return. If you don't want to go back to Lima, you'll have to get to Barranca to continue your journey.

Barranca to Huarmey
Bus
Bus companies have their offices in Barranca, so buses tend to stop there (opposite El Grifo service station at the

end of town) rather than at Pativilca or Paramonga. To **Lima,** 3½ hrs, US$7.50. To **Casma,** 155 km, several daily, 2½ hrs, US$6. To **Huaraz**, take a minibus from C Lima in Barranca to the gas station in Pativilca where you can catch a bus, colectivo or truck along the good paved road to Huaraz. From Barranca buses run only to **Paramonga port** (3 km off the Highway, about 15 mins from Barranca); from there you can get a taxi to the Paramonga ruins, US$9 (including wait); otherwise it's a 3-km walk.

Casma and around
Bus
América Express and **Tres Estrellas** run frequent services from Lima to **Chimbote** (see Chimbote below) stopping in Casma, 370 km, 6 hrs, US$11-18; other companies going to Chimbote or Trujillo might drop you off by the highway. In the other direction, many of the buses to **Lima** stop briefly opposite the petrol station, block 1 of Ormeño or, if they have small offices, along blocks 1-5 of Av Ormeño.

To **Chimbote**, 55 km, it is easiest to take the **Los Casmeños** colectivos, which depart when full from between the Plaza de Armas and Banco de la Nación, 45 mins, US$2.15. To **Trujillo** and **Chiclayo**, it is best to go first to Chimbote bus station and then take an **América Express** bus.

To **Huaraz**, 150 km via **Pariacoto**, 4 hrs, US$9, with **Transportes Huandoy**

(Ormeño 166, T043-712336) daily 0700, 1100 and 1400, or **Yungay Express** (by the Ovalo near the Repsol petrol station) daily 0600, 0800 and 1400; also colectivos from the same Ovalo, US$11, 3 hrs.

Chimbote
Bus
The bus station is 4 km south of town on Av Meiggs. Under no circumstances should you walk to the centre: minibus, US$0.50, taxi US$1.50. There are no hotels near the terminal; some companies have ticket offices in the centre.

To/from **Lima**, 420 km, 5½ hrs, US$15-20, frequent service with many companies, eg hourly with **América Express**, several daily with **Tres Estrellas**. To **Trujillo**, 130 km, 2 hrs, US$6, **América Express** every 20 mins till 2100, these continue to **Chiclayo**.

To **Huaraz,** most companies, with the best buses, go the 'long way round': down the Panamericana to Pativilca, then up the main highway, 7 hrs, US$14; the main companies start in Trujillo and continue to **Caraz**. The fastest route, however, is via Pariacoto, 5 hrs, US$11, with **Trans Huandoy** (Etseturh, T043-354024) at 0600, 1000 and 1300, and **Yungay Express** at 0500, 0700 and 1300. Alternatively, you can travel to **Caraz** via the Cañón del Pato, 6 hrs, US$12, with **Yungay Express** at 0830; sit on the left-hand-side for the best views.

Trujillo
& around

The capital of La Libertad Department, 548 km from Lima, Trujillo disputes the title of second city of Peru with Arequipa. It has an urban population of over 1.5 million, but the compact colonial centre has a small-town feel. The greenness surrounding the city is a delight against the backcloth of brown Andean foothills and peaks. Founded by Diego de Almagro in 1534 as an express assignment ordered by Francisco Pizarro, it was named after the latter's native town in Spain. Nearby are some of Peru's most important Moche and Chimú archaeological sites and a stretch of the country's best surfing beaches. *Colour map 3, A1.*

a colonial city with ancient archaeology on its doorstep

★City centre

The focal point is the pleasant and spacious **Plaza de Armas**, whose buildings, and many others in the vicinity, are painted in bright pastel colours. The prominent sculpture represents agriculture, commerce, education, art, slavery, action and liberation, crowned by a young man holding a torch depicting liberty. Fronting it is the **Cathedral** ⓘ *daily 0700-1230, 1700-2000*, dating from 1666, with religious paintings and sculptures displayed next door in the **museum** ⓘ *Mon-Fri 0900-1300, 1600-1900, Sat 0900-1300, US$1.45*. Also on the Plaza are the **Hotel Libertador**, the colonial-style Sociedad de Beneficencia Pública de Trujillo and the Municipalidad. The **Universidad de La Libertad**, second only to that of San Marcos at Lima, was founded in 1824. The colonial-style **Casa Urquiaga (or Calonge)** on the plaza now houses the **Banco Central de Reserva** ⓘ *Pizarro 446, Mon-Fri 0930-1500, Sat-Sun 1000-1330, free 30-min guided tour; take passport*, which contains valuable pre-Columbian ceramics. Another beautiful colonial mansion is **Casa Bracamonte (or Lizarzaburu)** ⓘ *Independencia 441*, which houses the Seguro Social de Salud del Perú and has occasional exhibitions. Opposite the Cathedral on Independencia, is the **Casa Garci Olguín** (Caja Nuestra Gente), recently restored but boasting the oldest façade in the city and Moorish-style murals. Near the Plaza de Armas is the spacious 18th-century **Palacio Iturregui**, now occupied by the **Club Central** ⓘ *Jr Pizarro 688, restricted entry to patio, daily 0830-1000, US$1.85*, an exclusive social club with a private collection of ceramics. **Casa Ganoza Chopitea** ⓘ *Independencia 630*, which now houses a pizzeria (see Restaurants, below), is considered architecturally the most representative of the viceroyalty in the city. It combines baroque and rococo styles and is also known for the pair of lions that adorn its portico.

Other mansions still in private hands include **Casa del Mayorazgo de Facalá** ⓘ *Pizarro 314 (Scotiabank), another entrance on Bolognesi, Mon-Fri 0915-1230*. **Casa de la Emancipación** ⓘ *Jr Pizarro 610 (Banco Continental), Mon-Sat 0900-1300, 1600-2000*, is the building where independence from Spain was planned and was the first seat of government and congress in Peru. The **Casa del Mariscal de Orbegoso** now houses the **Museo de la República** ⓘ *Orbegoso 553, daily 0930-2000*. It is owned by the BCP bank and holds temporary exhibitions. **Museo Haya de la Torre (Casa del Pueblo)** ⓘ *Orbegoso 664, Mon-Sat 0900-1300, 1600-2000*, is a small, well-presented museum about the life of the founder of the APRA party who was one of the leading 20th-century socialists in the Americas. He was born in the house, which now holds a cinema club once a week.

One of the best of the many churches is the 17th-century **La Merced** ⓘ *Pizarro 550, daily 0800-1200, 1600-2000*, with picturesque moulded figures below the dome. The church and monastery of **El Carmen** ⓘ *Colón y Bolívar, Mass Sun 0700-0730*, has been described as the 'most valuable jewel

Tip...
The city is generally safe, but take care beyond the inner ring road, Av España, as well as at bus stops, terminals, ATMs and internet cafés.

of colonial art in Trujillo', but is rarely open except for Mass. **La Compañía** ⓘ *near Plaza de Armas*, is now an auditorium for cultural events.

Museo de Arqueología ⓘ *Junín 682 y Ayacucho, Casa Risco, T044-249322, Mon-Fri 0830-1430, US$1.85*, houses a large and interesting collection of thematic

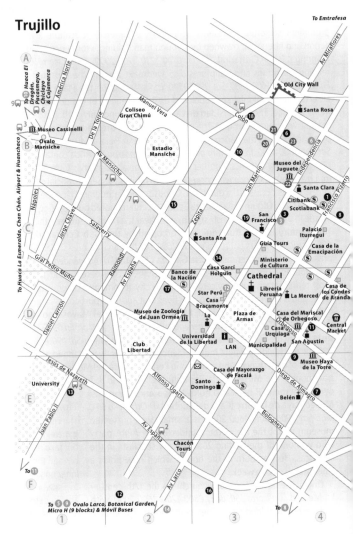

Trujillo

To Emtrafesa

Old City Wall

Santa Rosa

Huaca El Dragón, Pacasmayo, Chiclayo & Cajamarca

Museo Cassinelli

Ovalo Mansiche

Coliseo Gran Chimú

Manuel Vera

Colón

Estadio Mansiche

Museo del Juguete

Santa Clara

San Martín

Citibank
Scotiabank

San Francisco

Palacio Iturregui

Santa Ana

Guía Tours

Casa de la Emancipación

Ministerio de Cultura

Banco de la Nación

Cathedral

Casa Garci Holguín

Librería Peruana La Merced

Casa de los Condes de Aranda

Museo de Zoología de Juan Orméa

Star Perú
Casa Bracamonte

Plaza de Armas

Casa del Mariscal de Orbegoso

La

Casa Urquiaga

Central Market

Universidad de la Libertad

San Agustín

Club Libertad

LAN

Municipalidad

Casa del Mayorazgo de Facalá

Museo Haya de la Torre

Santo Domingo

Belén

University

Alfonso Ugarte

Jesús de Nazareth

To Huaca La Esmeralda, Chan Chán, Airport & Huanchaco

Av España

Chacón Tours

To Ovalo Larco, Botanical Garden, Micro H (9 blocks) & Móvil Buses

exhibits. The **Museo del Juguete** ① *Independencia 705 y Junín, Mon-Sat 1000-1800, Sun 1000-1300, US$1.85, children US$0.70*, is a toy museum containing examples from prehistoric times to 1950, collected by painter Gerardo Chávez. Downstairs is the **Espacio Cultural Angelmira** with a café bar ① *daily 0900-*

Where to stay 🛏
1 Casa de Clara *F6*
2 Chan Chán Inn *A5*
3 Colonial *C4*
4 Continental *D4*
5 El Gran Marqués *F2*
6 El Mochilero *B4*
7 Gran Bolívar *B5*
8 Hostal El Centurión *F4*
9 Hostal Malibú *F2*
10 Hostería El Sol *A1*
11 Kallpa *F1*
12 Libertador *D3*
13 Munay Wasi Hostel *B3*
14 Res Vanini *F2*
15 Turismo *D5*

Restaurants 🍴
1 Asturias, Café Oviedo, Demarco & Romano *C4*
2 Café Amaretto *C3*
3 Casona Deza *C4*
4 Cevichería Puerto Mori *B4*
5 Chelsea *B5*
6 Dulcería Doña Carmen *B4*
7 El Chileno *E4*
8 El Kluv *C4*
9 El Mochica *E4*
10 El Sol *B3*
11 Juguería San Agustín *D4*
12 Le Nature *F2*
13 Pizzería Pizzanino *E1*
14 Rincón de Vallejo *C3*
15 Rincón de Vallejo 2 *C2*
16 Romano-Rincón Criollo *F3*
17 Sabor Supremo *D2*
18 Sal y Pimienta *B3*
19 Trujillo Señorial *C3*

Bars & clubs 🎵
20 Canana *B3*
21 El Estribo *B4*
22 Juguete *C4*
23 Stradivarius *B4*

Transport 🚌
1 Buses to Huaca del Sol y de la Luna *D6*
2 Combi A to Chan Chán & Huanchaco *E2, E5*
3 Combis A & B; & Micros B, H & H-Corazón: to Chan Chán & Huanchaco *B1*
4 Combi B & Micro B: to Chan Chán & Huanchaco *A4, B3*
5 Micro H to Chan Chán & Huanchaco *E1*
6 El Dorado *B1*
7 Flores *A5*
8 Ormeño *A5*
9 Tarapoto Tours *B1*

BACKGROUND

Masters of sculpture

One of the most remarkable pre-Inca civilizations was that of the Moche people, who evolved during the first century AD and lasted until around AD 750. Though these early Peruvians had no written language, they left a vivid record of their life and culture in beautifully modelled and painted ceramics.

Compared with the empires of their successors, the Chimú and Inca, the realm of the Moche was very small, covering less than 250 miles of coast from the valleys of Lambayeque to Nepeña, south of present-day Chimbote. The Moche harnessed rivers spilling from the Andean cordillera, channelling them into a network of irrigation canals that watered the arid valleys along this seemingly inhospitable stretch of coast. The resultant lush fields produced plentiful crops, which, along with the sea's bountiful harvest of fish and seafood, gave the Moche a rich and varied diet. With the leisure allowed by such abundant food, Moche craftsmen invented new techniques to produce their artistic masterpieces. It is these ancient pottery vessels that have made the greatest contribution to our understanding of this civilization.

These masters of sculpture used clay to bring to life animals, plants and anthropomorphic deities and demons. They recreated hunting and fishing scenes, combat rituals, elaborate ceremonies and sexual intercourse (sometimes with contraception). They depicted the power of their rulers as well as the plight of the sick and invalid.

Ritual combat is a common theme in their work: prisoners of war are apparently brought before congregations where their throats are cut and

2300; in a restored *casona*; it's worth a visit. **Museo de Zoología de Juan Ormea** ⓘ *Jr San Martín 368, T044-205011, Mon-Fri 0900-1800, US$0.70*, has interesting displays of Peruvian animals.

Outskirts

Gerardo Chávez also opened the **Museo de Arte Moderno** ⓘ *Av Industrial, 3.5 km from centre, T044-215668, Mon-Sat 0930-1700, Sun 0930-1400, US$3.50, students half price*, which has some fine exhibits, a peaceful garden and friendly staff. The basement of the **Cassinelli garage** ⓘ *Av N de Piérola 607, T044-231801, behind a petrol station, daily 1000-1300, 1430-1800, US$2.45*, contains a private collection of Mochica and Chimú pottery which is recommended. There is also a **botanical garden** ⓘ *Mon-Sat 0800-1700, free,* about half a block beyond the Ovalo Larco, southwest of the city centre.

Huacas del Sol and de la Luna

Proyecto Huaca de la Luna, Jr San Martín 380, Trujillo, T044-221269, www.huacas. com. Daily 0900-sunset (last entry 1600); access by 1-hr guided tour only (English, French or Spanish); groups can be up to 25 people and quite rushed. US$4 (students

their blood offered to those present. Decapitation and dismemberment are also shown.

Moche potters were amazingly skilled at reproducing facial features, specializing in the subtle nuances of individual personality. In addition to these 3D sculptures, the Moche potter was skilled at decorating vessels with low-relief designs. Among the most popular scenes are skeletal death figures holding hands while dancing in long processions to the accompaniment of musicians. The potters also developed a technique of fine-line painting scenes on ceramic vessels. Over a period of several centuries the painters became increasingly skillful at depicting complex and lively scenes with multiple figures. Because of their complexity and detail, these scenes are of vital importance in reconstructing Moche life.

The early introduction of moulds and stamps brought efficiency to the production of Moche ceramics. By pressing moist clay into the halves of a mould, it was possible to produce an object much more rapidly than by hand. Similarly, the use of stamps facilitated the decoration of ceramic vessels with elaborate low-relief designs. Mould-making technology thus resulted in the repeated duplication of individual pieces. Since there were almost no unique ceramic objects, elaborate ceramics became more widely available and less effective as a sign of power, wealth and social status of the élite.

Although among the most sophisticated potters in Spanish America, the Moche did not use ceramics for ordinary tableware. Neither do their ceramics show many everyday activities, such as farming, cooking and pottery making. This is because Moche art expresses the religious and supernatural aspects of the culture.

US$2, children US$0.40), booklet in English or Spanish US$2.85; all tickets are sold at the Museo Huacas de Moche – see below.

A few kilometres south of Trujillo are the huge and fascinating Moche pyramids, the Huaca del Sol and the Huaca de la Luna. Until the Spaniards destroyed a third of it in a vain search for treasure, Huaca del Sol was the largest man-made structure in the western hemisphere, at 45 m high. It consisted of seven levels, with 11 or 12 phases of construction over the first six centuries AD. Today, about two thirds of the pyramid have been lost and it is closed to the public.

Huaca de la Luna, 500 m away, received scant attention until extensive polychrome moulded decorations were uncovered in the 1990s. The colours on these remarkable geometric patterns and deities have faded little and it is now possible to view impressive friezes of the upper four levels on the northern exterior wall of the *huaca*. The highest mural is a 'serpent' which runs the length of the wall; beneath it there are repeated motifs of 'felines' holding decapitated heads of warriors, then repeated motifs of 'fishermen' holding fish against a bright blue background and, next, huge 'spider/crab' motifs. The bottom two levels show dancers or officials grimly holding hands and, below them, victorious warriors following naked prisoners past scenes of combat, and two complex scenes, similar to those at Huaca Cao Viejo at El Brujo (see page 152). Combined with intricate, brightly painted two-dimensional motifs in the sacrificial area atop the huaca, and with new discoveries in almost every excavation, Huaca de la Luna is now a truly significant site well worth visiting.

The **Templo Nuevo**, or Plataforma III, represents the period 600 to 900 AD and has friezes in the upper level showing the so-called Rebellion of the Artefacts, in which weapons take on human characteristics and attack their owners. Also visit the **Museo Huacas de Moche** ⓘ *5 mins' walk from Huaca de la Luna, www.huacasdemoche.pe, daily 0900-1600, US$1, students US$0.75, children US$0.40,* the site museum. Three halls display objects found in the huacas, including beautiful ceramics, arranged thematically around the Moche culture, the cermonial complex, daily life, the deities of power and of the mountains and priests who worshipped them. Food is available on Sunday at the nearby town of Moche.

The visitors' centre (T044-834901) has a café showing videos and a souvenir shop and good toilets. In an outside patio, craftsmen reproduce ceramics in designs from northern Peru.

Chan Chán
5 km from Trujillo centre. Daily 0900-1600. Site may be covered up if rain is expected. Tickets cost US$3.80 (US$2 with ISIC card), children US$0.35, and are valid for Chan Chán, Huaca El Dragón and Huaca La Esmeralda for 2 days. Official guides, US$10, wait by the souvenir shops; toilets here too.

The imperial city of the Chimú domains was once the largest adobe city in the world. The vast, crumbling ruins consist of 10 great compounds built by Chimú kings, with perimeter walls up to 12 m high surrounding sacred enclosures with usually only one narrow entrance. Inside, rows of storerooms contained the agricultural wealth of the kingdom, which stretched 1000 km along the coast from near Guayaquil to the Carabayllo Valley, north of Lima. The Incas almost certainly copied this system and used it in Cuzco where the last Incas continued building huge enclosures. The Chimú surrendered to the Incas around 1471 after 11 years of siege.

Tip...
There are police at the entrance to the site, but it is a 25-minute walk from there to the ticket office. If you're not on a tour, you are advised to take one of the vehicles that wait at the entrance as it is not safe to walk to the ticket office. On no account should you walk beyond Chan Chán to Buenos Aires beach, nor walk on the beach itself, as there is serious risk of robbery and of being attacked by dogs.

Most of the compounds contain a huge walk-in well which tapped the ground water, raised to a high level by irrigation further up the valley. Each compound also included a platform mound which was the burial place of the king, his women and his treasure, presumably maintained as a memorial.

The dilapidated city walls enclose an area of 28 sq km containing the remains of palaces, temples, workshops, streets, houses, gardens and a canal. What is left of the adobe walls bears either well restored or modern fibreglass fabrications of moulded decorations showing small figures of fish, birds, fishing nets and various geometric motifs. Painted designs have been found on pottery unearthed from the debris of a city ravaged by floods, earthquakes and *huaqueros* (grave looters). The **Ciudadela de Nik-An** (formerly called Tschudi) is the part that visitors see.

The **site museum** ⓘ *on the main road, 100 m before the turn-off, daily 0830-1630, US$1*, has objects found in the area, with displays and signs in Spanish and English.

The partly restored temple, **Huaca El Dragón** ⓘ *daily 0930-1630 (in theory); combis from Huayna Cápac y Los Incas, or Av España y Manuel Vera marked 'Arco Iris/La Esperanza', taxi US$2*, is on the west side of the Pan-American Highway in the district of La Esperanza. It dates from Huari to Chimú times (AD 1000-1470) and is also known as **Huaca Arco Iris** (rainbow), after the shape of friezes which decorate it.

The poorly preserved **Huaca La Esmeralda** is at Mansiche, between Trujillo and Chan Chán, behind the church and near the Mall Aventura shopping centre. Buses to Chan Chán and Huanchaco pass the church at Mansiche.

★**Huanchaco** → *See map, page 142.*

An alternative to Trujillo is this fishing and surfing village, full of hotels, guesthouses and restaurants. It is famous for its narrow pointed fishing rafts, known as *caballitos* (little horses) *de totora*, made of totora reeds and depicted on the pottery of Mochica, Chimú and other cultures. Unlike those used on Lake Titicaca, they are flat, not hollow, and ride the breakers rather like surfboards. You can see fishermen returning in their reed rafts at about 0800 and 1400 when they stack the boats upright to dry in the fierce sun. Fishermen offer trips on their *caballitos* for US$1.75; be prepared to get wet. Groups should contact Luis Gordillo (El Mambo, T044-461092). Overlooking Huanchaco is a huge church (1535-1540), whose belfry affords extensive views. **El Quibishi**, at the south end of the beach, is the main *artesanía* market and also has a food section.

Listings Trujillo and around *maps p136 and p142*

Tourist information

Useful websites include http://
trujilloperu.xanga.com and www.
laindustria.com.

Gobierno Regional de la Libertad
*Dirección de Turismo, Av España 1800,
T044-296221.*
Information on regional tourism.

Municipalidad de Trujillo
*Sub-Gerencia de Turismo, Av España 742,
T044-244212, anexo 119, sgturismo@
munitrujillo.gob.pe.*

Indecopi
*Santo Toribio de Mogrovejo 518,
Urb San Andrés II etapa, T044-295733,
sobregon@indecopi.gob.pe.*
For tourist complaints.

iPerú
*Diego de Almagro 420, Plaza de Armas,
T044-294561, iperutrujillo@promperu.
gob.pe. Mon-Sat 0900-1800, Sun
0900-1300; also at Huaca de La Luna.
Daily 0900-1300.*

Tourist Police
*Independencia 572, in the Ministerio de
Cultura building, policia_turismo_tru@
hotmail.com. Mon-Sat 0800-2000.*

Provide useful information and can
help with reports of theft, some staff
speak English.

Huanchaco

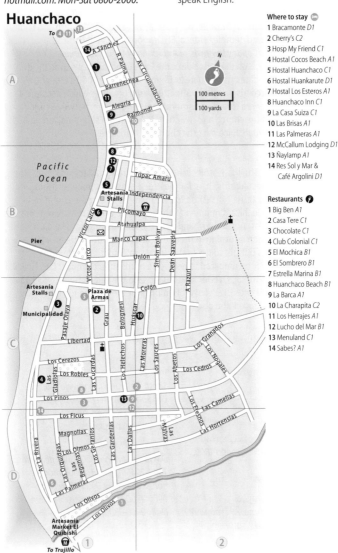

To ④ ⑪ ⑬
⑭ A. Sánchez
① H. Palma
Av. Circunvalación
Barrenechea
⑪
Alegría
⑨ Raimondi ⑩
⑦

*Pacific
Ocean*

⑧
⑫
⑦
⑤
Artesanía
Stalls
Víctor Larco
Independencia
⑥ Pilcomayo
Atahualpa
Manco Capac
Unión
Simón Bolívar
Dean Saavedra
Túpac Amaru

Pier

Artesanía
Stalls
⑤ Plaza de
Armas
③
Municipalidad
② Grau
Bolognesi
Huáscar
Colón
A. Razuri
⑩

Pasaje Olaya
Libertad
Los Cerezos
Los Robles
④ Las Gladiolas
Las Cucardas
Los Helechos
Los Moreras
Las Sauces
Los Abetos
Los Granados
Los Nopales
Los Cedros
Los Pinos
⑧
⑬ ⑨
③
⑫
⑭
Los Ficus
Magnolias
Los Olmos
Los Geranios
Las Gardenias
Las Dalias
Las Malvas
Las Fresnos
Las Camelias
Las Hortensias

Av. La Rivera
Las Orquídeas
Las Begonias
Las Palmeras
⑥
Los Olivos
Los Olivos ①

Artesanía
Market El
Quibishi
To Trujillo ① ②

Where to stay

1 Bracamonte *D1*
2 Cherry's *C2*
3 Hosp My Friend *C1*
4 Hostal Cocos Beach *A1*
5 Hostal Huanchaco *C1*
6 Hostal Huankarute *D1*
7 Hostal Los Esteros *A1*
8 Huanchaco Inn *C1*
9 La Casa Suiza *C1*
10 Las Brisas *A1*
11 Las Palmeras *A1*
12 McCallum Lodging *D1*
13 Ñaylamp *A1*
14 Res Sol y Mar &
   Café Argolini *D1*

Restaurants

1 Big Ben *A1*
2 Casa Tere *C1*
3 Chocolate *C1*
4 Club Colonial *C1*
5 El Mochica *B1*
6 El Sombrero *B1*
7 Estrella Marina *B1*
8 Huanchaco Beach *B1*
9 La Barca *A1*
10 La Charapita *C2*
11 Los Herrajes *A1*
12 Lucho del Mar *B1*
13 Menuland *C1*
14 Sabes? *A1*

N

100 metres
100 yards

Trujillo

$$$$ Casa Andina Private Collection
Av El Golf 591, Urb Las Flores del Golf III,
T01-213 9739, www.casa-andina.com.
Large multi-storey luxury hotel, part of
a nationwide chain, located outside the
centre. All facilities.

$$$$ El Gran Marqués
Díaz de Cienfuegos 145-147,
Urb La Merced, T044-481710,
www.elgranmarques.com.
Price includes breakfast, modern,
minibar, pool, sauna, jacuzzi, restaurant.

$$$$ Libertador
Independencia 485, Plaza de Armas,
T044-232741, www.libertador.com.pe.
Modern hotel in historic building, lovely
place to stay. Comfortable rooms,
excellent service, swimming pool in a
flower-filled patio, sauna, cafetería and
restaurant, breakfast extra, excellent
buffet lunch on Sun.

$$$ Gran Bolívar
Bolívar 957, T044-222090,
www.granbolivarhotel.net.
In converted 18th-century house,
restaurant and room service, café, bar,
laundry, gym, parking.

$$$-$$ Kallpa
Díaz de las Heras s/n, Urb Vista Hermosa,
T044-281266, www.kallpahotel.pe.
A smart boutique hotel, welcoming,
English spoken, well below usual
boutique hotel prices.

$$ Colonial
Independencia 618, T044-258261,
www.hostalcolonial.com.pe.
Attractive but small rooms, hot showers,
basic breakfast, good restaurant,
especially for set lunch. Recommended.

$$ Continental
Gamarra 663, T044-241607, www.
perunorte.com/hcontinental.
Modern but old-fashioned hotel
opposite the market, with hot water,
good breakfast, helpful, safe.

$$ Hostal El Centurión
Paraguay 304, Urb El Recreo, T044-
201526, www.hostalelcenturion.com.
About 20 mins' walk from the Plaza,
modern, good rooms, well kept, safe but
no a/c, simple restaurant, good service.

$$ Hostal Malibú
Av Larco 1471, Urb La Merced, T044-
284811, www.hostalmalibu.com.
Variety of rooms, restaurant,
room service, mini-bar, laundry,
massage, currency exchange.
Also sister hotel of same name
at Av Larco 1000, Huanchaco.

$ Casa de Clara
Cahuide 495, T044-243347,
http://trujilloperu.xanga.com.
Backpackers' hostal, hot water, good
food, helpful, information, lodging
packages with meals and tours, laundry
service, use of kitchen with permission
and charge for gas, meeting place and
lots going on, many languages spoken
(see Clara Bravo and Michael White,
What to do, below). Restaurants nearby.

$ Chan Chán Inn
Av Ejército 307, T044-298583,
chanchaninn@hotmail.com.
Close to several bus terminals so noisy,
with or without breakfast, popular
with backpackers, café, laundry, money
exchange, information.

$ El Mochilero
Independencia 887, T044-297842,
Elmochilerotrujilloperuoficial
on Facebook.

A variety of dorms and rooms, only one with bath, electric showers, breakfast US$1.75, fridge for guests' use. Tours arranged, information.

$ Hostería El Sol
Brillantes 224, Urb Santa Inés, T044-231933, hosteriaelsol@gmail.com, near bus terminals on Av Nicolás de Piérola.
With hot shower, restaurant, all meals available.

$ Munay Wasi Hostel
Jr Colón 250, T044-231462, www.munaywasihostel.com.
Family-run hostel within Av España, private and shared rooms (US$10 pp), book exchange, tourist information, fully-equipped kitchen.

$ Residencia Vanini
Av Larco 237, outside Av España, T044-200878, enriqueva@hotmail.com.
Youth hostel in a converted private house, a good option but not in the centre, some rooms with bath, others with shared shower.

$ Turismo
Gamarra 747, T044-244181.
Central, good services, restaurant, parking, travel agency.

Huanchaco

$$$-$$ Bracamonte
Los Olivos 160, T044-461162, www.hotelbracamonte.com.pe.
Comfortable, modern, contemporary decor, good, pool, secure, good restaurant offers lunch *menú* and some vegetarian dishes, English spoken, laundry service, games room. Highly recommended.

$$$-$$ Hostal Huankarute
La Rivera 312, T044-461705, www.hostalhuankarute.com.

On the seafront, with small pool, bar, sun terrace, bicycle rental; some rooms larger, more luxurious and more pricey, all with ocean view. Recommended.

$$$-$$ Las Palmeras
Av Larco 1150, sector Los Tumbos, T044-461199, www.laspalmeras dehuanchaco.com.
One of the best, rooms with terrace, hot water, dining room, pool and gardens. Rooms on top floor with sea view cost more than ground floor rooms with pool view.

$$ Hostal Huanchaco
Larco 185 on Plaza, T044-461272, www.huanchacohostal.com.
With hot water, pool, good but pricey cafetería, video, pool table.

$$ Hostal Los Esteros
Av Larco 618, T044-461300, www.losesteroshuanchaco.com.
Rooms with sea view for 1-4 people, hot water, laundry, restaurant, safe parking, bicycle hire, can arrange surfing and *caballitos de totora* trips.

$$ Residencial Sol y Mar
La Rivera 400, T044-461120, ctsolymar1@hotmail.com.
Breakfast extra, with pool, restaurant and garden.

$$-$ Hostal Cocos Beach
Av Larco 1500, Los Tumbos, T044-461023, www.hostelcocosbeach.com.
Opposite the beach, rooms with beds and bunks, hot water, restaurant, surfing lessons, car rental, tours arranged.

$$-$ Huanchaco Inn
Los Pinos 528, T044-461158.
Rooms with and without bath, hot water, use of kitchen, laundry service, small pool.

$ Cherry's
Los Pinos 448, T044-462066.
Owner Juan Carlos speaks English, rooms with private or shared bath, hot water, kitchen, shop, bar, roof terrace, laundry, even a small swimming pool.

$ Hospedaje My Friend
Los Pinos 533, T044-461080.
Dorm rooms with shared bath upstairs, with hot water, TV room, information. Tours arranged, but service is erratic. Popular place with surfers, good for meeting others and for a meal in the restaurant on ground floor (open 0800-1800).

$ La Casa Suiza
Los Pinos 308, T044-461285, www.lacasasuiza.com.
This Huanchaco institution has a variety of rooms with/without bath, breakfast US$3, BBQ on the roof, book exchange.

$ Las Brisas
Raymondi 146, T044-461186, www. facebook.com/lasbrisashuanchaco.
Hot water, café, comfortable.

$ McCallum Lodging
Los Ficus 460, T044-462350, http:// mccallumlodginghouse.wordpress.com.
Private rooms and dorms, hot water, hammocks, home-cooked meals available and recipes shared, laundry, baggage and surfboard storage, family atmosphere, highly considered by locals and tourists.

$ Ñaylamp
Av Víctor Larco 123, northern end of seafront in El Boquerón, T044-461022, www.hostalnaylamp.com.
Rooms set around a courtyard with patios and garden, others have sea view, dorms, hammocks, good beds, hot water, camping, tents available to hire, laundry, safe, Italian food, good breakfasts.

A speciality is *shambar*, a thick minestrone made with pork. On sale everywhere is *turrón*, a nougat-type sweet. All along Pizarro are restaurants to suit all tastes and budgets. On the west side of the central market at Grau y Ayacucho are several small, cheap restaurants.

Trujillo

$$$ Romano-Rincón Criollo
Estados Unidos 162, Urb El Recreo, 10-min walk from centre, T044-244207.
Northern Peruvian cuisine, *menú* for US$5.60, smart.

$$$-$$ El Mochica
Bolívar 462.
Good typical food with live music on special occasions.

$$ Casona Deza
Independencia 630, T044-434866, CasonaDezaCafe on Facebook. Mon-Sat 0800-2200, Sun from 0900.
An atmospheric pizzeria in a restored colonial house with period furniture and a patio surrounded by frescoes.

$$ Chelsea
Estete 675, T044-257032. Daily 1145-1645, 1700-0100.
Restaurant/bar. Buffet Criollo US$8.70, special shows on Fri (live music, fee US$3.50) and Sat (Marinera dance show, US$5.25). Recommended.

$$ Demarco
Pizarro 725.
Popular at midday for lunchtime menus and for its cakes and desserts, good service.

$$ Le Nature
Marcelo Corne 338, in a residential district off Av Larco, T044-209674. Mon-Thu

1000-2200, Fri, Sun 1000-1600,
Sat 1900-2200.
Probably the best vegetarian food
in town.

$$ Pizzería Pizzanino
Av Juan Pablo II 183, Urb San Andrés,
opposite University.
Good for pizzas, pastas, meats, desserts,
evening only.

$$ Romano
Pizarro 747.
International food, good *menú*,
breakfasts, coffee, excellent
milkshakes, cakes.

$$-$ Cevichería Puerto Mori
Estete 482, T044-346752.
Very popular, they serve only good
seafood. At the same location are
2 more fish restaurants, but not of
the same quality.

$ Asturias
Pizarro 741.
Nice café with a reasonable *menú*,
good pastas, cakes and sandwiches.

$ Café Oviedo
Pizarro 737.
With soups, vegetarian options, good
salads and cakes, helpful.

$ El Sol
Zepita 203, T044-345105. Mon-Sat 0800-
2200, Sun 0800-1600.
Vegetarian, lunch *menú* and à la carte.

$ Juguería San Agustín
Bolívar 526.
Good juices, good *menú*, sandwiches, ice
creams, popular, excellent value. Also at
Av Larco Herrera y Husares de Junín.

$ Rincón de Vallejo
Orbegoso 303.
Good *menú*, typical dishes, very crowded at
peak times. 2nd branch at Av España 736.

$ Sabor Supremo
Diego de Almagro 210, T044-220437.
Menú US$1.75, also à la carte, vegetarian
food, vegan on special request.

$ Sal y Pimienta
Colón 201.
Very popular for lunch, US$1 and
US$1.85, close to buses for Huanchaco
and Chan Chán.

$ Trujillo Señorial
Gamarra 353, T044-204873.
Mon-Sat 1300-1530.
Restaurant and hotel school,
good *menú* US$2.60-3, food
nicely presented, good value.

Cafés

Café Amaretto
Gamarra 368.
Smart, good selection of real
coffees, "brilliant" cakes, sweets,
snacks and drinks.

Casona Deza
Independencia 630.
Comfortable café/bar selling home-
made pasta and pizza and good coffee
in an old mansion.

Dulcería Doña Carmen
San Martín 814.
Serves local specialities such as *alfajores*,
budin, *king kong*, etc.

El Chileno
Ayacucho 408.
Café and ice cream parlour, popular.

El Kluv
Junín 527 (next to Metro Market).
Italian owned, fresh, tasty pizzas
at noon and in the late afternoon.

Fitopán
Bolívar 406.
Good selection of breads, also serves
lunches. Has 3 other branches, see
www.fitopan.com.

Huanchaco
There are about 30 restaurants on the
beachfront. Recommended on Av
Larco are **Estrella Marina** at No 740, **Los
Herrajes** at No 1020, and **Lucho del Mar**
at No 750; all **$$**. Many close in the low
season and at night.

$$$ Big Ben
*Av Larco 1884, El Boquerón, T044-
461378, www.bigbenhuanchaco.com.
Daily 1130-1730.*
Seafood and international cuisine,
very good.

$$$ Club Colonial
*La Rivera 514, on the beachfront,
T044-461015. Daily 1100-2300.*
A smart restaurant and bar, French-
speaking Belgian owner.

$$$ El Mochica
Av Larco 700, T044-461963.
Same owners and quality as the
restaurant in Trujillo, rebuilt in 2014.

$$$ Huanchaco Beach
Av Larco 800, T044-461484.
One of the best quality in town,
popular with tours.

$$$-$$ El Sombrero
*Av Larco 510, T044-462283,
www.restaurantelsombrero.com.*

Smart restaurant serving good ceviche
and seafood, most tables have great sea
view. Has another branch at Av Mansiche
267, Trujillo.

$$ Casa Tere
Plaza de Armas, T044-461197.
For best pizzas in town, also pastas,
burgers and breakfasts.

$$ La Barca
Raimondi 117, T044-461855.
Very good seafood, well-run, popular.

$$ Sabes?
*Av Larco 920, T044-461555, http://
sabesbar.com. Opens at 2000.*
Pub with food, internet café, popular,
British-owned.

$$-$ Menuland
Los Pinos 250, T044-461032.
Managed by a German/Peruvian couple
who speak English, German and Italian.
Peruvian and international dishes,
breakfast, lunch *menú* for US$1.75. Also
has 2 double rooms ($), book exchange.

$ La Charapita
Huáscar 162.
Modest but popular restaurant serving
large portions.

Cafés

Argolini
Av Rivera 400.
Convenient for people staying in the
Los Pinos/Los Ficus area for fresh bread,
cakes, ice cream, coffee and juices.

Chocolate
Av Rivera 772. Daily 0730-1900.
Dutch/Peruvian management, serves
breakfast, also some vegetarian food,
coffee and cakes. Also offers B&B.

Bars and clubs

Trujillo

Bar/Café Juguete
Junín y Independencia.
Open until midnight.
An old-style café serving good
coffee as well as alcohol. Has a
pasta restaurant attached.

Bar/Café Stradivarius
Colón 327. Open in the evenings only.
An attractive café with sofas,

Canana
San Martín 788, T044-232503.
Bars and restaurant, disco, live music at
weekends (US$1.50-3), video screens
(also has travel agency). Recommended,
but take care on leaving.

El Estribo
San Martín 809, T044-204053.
A club playing a wide variety of genres
and attracting a mixed crowd.

Festivals

Trujillo
The 2 most important festivals are the
National Marinera Contest (end of
Jan) and the **Festival Internacional de
La Primavera** (last week of Sep), with
cultural events, parades, beauty pageants
and Trujillo's famous **Caballos de Paso**.

Huanchaco
May **Festival del Mar**, a celebration of the
disembarkation of Taycanamo, the leader
of the Chimú period. A procession is made
in Totora boats during the 1st week.
29 Jun **San Pedro**, patron saint of
fishermen. His statue is taken out to sea
on a huge totora-reed boat. There are
also surf competitions.
Carnival and **New Year** are also
popular celebrations.

Shopping

Trujillo
Bookshops
Librería Peruana, *Pizarro 505, just off the
Plaza.* Has the best selection in town,
plus postcards; ask for Sra Inés Guerra
de Guijón.
There are also 3 branches of **SBS**:
on Jr Bolívar 714; in Mall Aventura,
Av Mansiche block 20, and in Plaza Real
Mall, Prol Av César Vallejo (behind UPAO
University), California (take taxi or green
California micro A).

Handicrafts
120 Artesanía por Descubrir, *Las
Magnolias 403, California, www.tienda120.
blogspot.com.* Art gallery designs and
handmade crafts, near Real Plaza.
APIAT, *Av España y Zela.* The largest craft
market in the city, good for ceramics,
totora boats, woodwork and leather,
competitive prices.
Artesanía del Norte, *at Dulcería
La Libertad, Jr Pizarro 758, and at the
Huacas del Sol y de la Luna, www.
artesaniadelnorte.com.* Sells items mostly
designed by the owner, Mary Cortijo,
using traditional techniques.
Trama Perú, *Pizarro 754, T044-243948,
www.tramaperu.com. Daily 1000-2200.*
High-quality, hand-made art objects,
authorized Moche art replicas.

Markets
Mercado Central, *Gamarra, Ayacucho
and Pasaje San Agustín.*
Mercado Unión, *between Av Santa and
Av Perú.* A little safer than others; also
repairs shoes, clothes and bags.

What to do

Trujillo

Tour operators

Prices vary and competition is fierce so shop around for the best deal. Few agencies run tours on Sun and often only at fixed times on other days. Groups are usually large. City tours, 2-2½ hrs for US$3.50 pp. To Chan Chán, El Dragón and Huanchaco, 4-4½ hrs for US$8-9 pp. To Huacas del Sol and de la Luna, 2½-3 hrs for US$8-9 pp. To El Brujo, 4-5 hrs for US$27-34 pp. Prices do not include entrance fees.

Chacón Tours, *Av España 106-112, T044-255212. Sat afternoon and Sun morning.* Recommended for flights etc, not local tours.

Tour guides

Many hotels work on a commission basis with taxi drivers and travel agencies. If you decide on a guide, make your own direct approach and always agree what is included in the price. The Tourist Police (see Tourist information, above) has a list of guides; average cost US$7 per hr. Beware of cowboy outfits herding up tourists around the plazas and bus terminals for rapid, poorly translated tours. Also beware scammers offering surfing or salsa lessons and party invitations.

Alfredo Ríos Mercedes, *riosmercedes@hotmail.com, T949-657978.* Speaks English.

Clara Bravo and Michael White, *Cahuide 495, T044-243347, http://trujilloperu.xanga.com, microbewhite@yahoo.com.* Clara is an experienced tourist guide who speaks Spanish, English, German and understands Italian and runs small group tours daily: archaeological tour US$20 for 6 hrs, city tour US$7 pp, US$53 per car to El Brujo,

with extension to Sipán, Brüning Museum and Túcume possible (tours in Lambayeque involve public transport, not included in cost). Clara works with **Michael White**, who provides transport and is very knowledgeable about tourist sites.

Gustavo Prada Marga, *at Chan Chán.* An experienced guide.

Jannet Rojas Sánchez, *Alto Mochica Mz Q 19, Trujillo, T949-344844.* Speaks English, enthusiastic. Also works for **Guía Tours** (Independencia 580, T044-234856).

José Soto Ríos, *Atahualpa 514, dpto 3, T949-251489.* Speaks English and French.

Luis Ocas Saldaña, *Jr José Martí 2019, T949-339593, guianorteperu@hotmail.com.* Very knowledgeable, helpful, covers all of northern Peru.

Huanchaco

Surfing

There are plenty of surf schools. Equipment rental is US$8.75/day; single lesson, US$14-15.50.

Casa Amelia, *Av Larco 1150, T044-461351, http://casaamelia.net.*

Indigan, *Deán Saavedra 582 (next to soccer field), T044-462591.* Jhon and Giancarlos Urcía for lessons, surf trips and rentals. Also offer lodging at their home.

Muchik, *Av Larco 650, T044-462535, www.escueladetablamuchik.com.* Instructors Chico and Omar Huamanchumo are former surf champions. They arrange trips to other surf sites and also offer repairs.

Olas Norte, *Los Ficus 450, see Facebook.* Individual and group lessons, prices include full equipment.

Onechako, *Av La Ribera Norte, escuelasurfonechako@hotmail.com.* Owner Tito Lescano. *Caballito de totora* riding lessons. Surf trips to other surf beaches in the North. Restaurant/bar.

Yenth Ccora, *Av Larco 500, T949-403871, http://yenthccora.blogspot.co.uk*. Surfing equipment manufacture, repair, rental and surfing school.

Air

The **airport** is west of the city; access to town is along Av Mansiche. Taxi to city hotels, US$6-8.

To **Lima**, 1 hr, daily flights with **LAN**, **Star Perú** and **Avianca/TACA**. The military **Grupo Aéreo 42** (J Alfonso Ugarte 642, Centro Cívico, T995-566264) has passenger flights on 2 routes in the north: Trujillo–Chiclayo–Chachapoyas–Tarapoto–Chiclayo–Trujillo (2 a week) and Trujillo–Chiclayo–Cajamarca–Mendoza–Juanjui–Tarapoto–Yurimaguas–Iquitos (out Wed, return Thu), plus Iquitos–Yurimaguas–Tarapoto–Chiclayo–Trujillo on Sun.

Bus

Local Micros (small buses with 25 or more seats) and combis (up to 15 passengers) on all routes within the city cost US$0.50-0.60; colectivos (6 passengers) charge US$0.50 and tend to run on main avenues starting from Av España. In theory, they are not allowed in the city centre. For transport to the archaeological sites, see below.

To **Huanchaco**, there are 2 combi routes (A and B; both take 25 mins), run by the **Caballitos de Totora** company (white and black), and 4 micros (A, B, H and H-Corazón; 45-60 mins), run by

Transportes Huanchaco (red, yellow and white). They run 0500-2030, every 5-10 mins, US$0.75. The easiest place to pick up any of these combis or micros is Ovalo Mansiche, 3 blocks northwest of Av España in front of the Cassinelli museum. Combi A takes the southerly route on Av España, before heading up Av Los Incas. Combi B takes the northerly route on Av España.

Long distance The **Terminal Terrestre de Trujillo** (TTT), or Terrapuerto, is to the southeast of the centre, at Km 558 on the Panamericana Norte, beyond Ovalo La Marina. It was completed in 2014 and bus companies are gradually relocating here, although at the time of writing, many were still using their private terminals. On arrival, take a taxi from the terminal and insist on being taken to your hotel of choice.

To **Lima**, 561 km, 9-10 hrs in the better class buses, average fare US$22-32; 10 hrs or more in the cheaper buses, US$11-16. There are many bus companies doing this route, among those recommended are: **Cruz del Sur** (Amazonas 437, between Av Ejército and Miraflores, T044-720444), the only one with a morning service from Lima to Trujillo at 0800; **Turismo Díaz** (TTT); **Línea** (Av América Sur 2857, T044-297000), 3 levels of service; **Flores** (Av Ejército 346, T044-208250); **Ittsa** (TTT), good service; **Móvil** (TTT, T044-245523 and at Av América Sur 3959, T044-286538), and **Oltursa** (TTT, T044-263055), 3 *bus cama* services to Lima.

To **Puerto Chicama**, combis from Santa Cruz terminal (Av Santa Cruz, 1 block from Av America Sur), US$2, 1½ hrs; also **Dorado** buses (Av N de Piérola 1062, T044-291778), US$2, via Chocope (US$0.75) and Paiján (US$0.60).

> **Tip...**
> On Friday-Sunday nights the better bus services must be pre-booked two to three days in advance.

Small **Pakatnamú** buses leave when full, 0400-2100 (from Av N de Piérola 1092, T044-206594), to **Pacasmayo**, 102 km, 1¼ hrs, US$5.50.

To **Chiclayo**, 4 hrs from Trujillo, from US$5.50, several companies, including **Emtrafesa** (Av Túpac Amaru 185, T044-471521) and **Línea** (from Carrión by Av Mansiche, T044-235847), both hourly. To **Jaén**, 9 hrs. To **Piura**, 6 hrs, US$15 (**Ittsa**'s 1330, or **Línea**'s 1415 buses are good choices). **Ittsa** also goes to **Talara**, 2200, 9 hrs, US$16.

Direct buses to **Huaraz**, 319 km, via Chimbote and Casma (169 km), with **Línea** and **Móvil**, 8 hrs, US$17-30. There are also several buses and colectivos to **Chimbote**, with **América Express** (from Av La Marina 315), 135 km, 2 hrs, US$6, departures every 30 mins from 0530 (ticket sales from 0500); leave Trujillo before 0600 to make a connection to Huaraz from 0800 in Chimbote (see page 133). Ask Clara Bravo and Michael White (see Guides, above) about transport to Caraz avoiding Chimbote: a worthwhile trip via the Brasileños road and Cañon del Pato.

To **Cajamarca**, 300 km, 7-8 hrs, US$10-27, with **Línea** and **Emtrafesa** at 2145. To **Huamachuco**, 170 km, 5-6 hrs, see page 193.

Taxi
Taxis in town charge US$1 within Av España and US$1.20 within Av América; always use official taxis, which are mainly yellow, or cooperative taxis, which have the company logo on the side. Beware of overcharging; check fares with locals. A taxi from in front of **Hotel Libertador** will charge US$12 per

hr to tour around the city, about the same as a tour with an independent guide or travel agent for 1-2 people.

Huacas del Sol and de la Luna
There are combis every 15 mins from Ovalo Grau in Trujillo and, less safe, from Galvez y Los Incas, but they drop you a long walk from the site. Taxis charge about US$5; there are few at the site so ask your driver to wait.

Chan Chán
Take any transport between Trujillo and Huanchaco (see above) and ask to get out at the turn-off, US$0.50; then get onward transport from the entrance to the ticket office, US$1. Do not walk from the turn-off to the ticket office. A taxi from Trujillo to the site is US$5; from Huanchaco, US$3.

Huanchaco
From Huanchaco, micro A goes to the 28 de Julio/Costa Rica junction in **Trujillo** where it turns west along Prolongación César Vallejo, passing the UPAO university and Plaza Real shopping centre, continuing to the Av El Golf (the terminus for the return to Huanchaco on almost the same route). On other routes from Huanchaco to Trujillo centre, ask the *cobrador* to let you off near C Pizarro on Av España. To reach the **Línea, Móvil Tours** and southern bus terminals in Trujillo, take micro H from Huanchaco; it also goes to Ovalo Grau where you can catch buses to the Huacas del Sol and de la Luna. For **Cruz del Sur, Ormeño and Flores** bus services, take combi or micro B from Huanchaco.

★El Brujo

3 km from Magdalena de Cao. Daily 0900-1600. US$4 (US$2 with ISIC card, children US$0.35). Shops and toilets at the entrance. See www.fundacionwiese.com.

A complex collectively known as El Brujo, 60 km north of Trujillo, is considered one of the most important archaeological sites on the north coast. Covering 2 sq km, it was a ceremonial centre for up to 10 cultures, including the Moche. Excavations here will, no doubt, continue for many years. Trujillo travel agencies run tours and there is a trail system for exploring the site.

Huaca Cortada (or El Brujo) has a wall decorated with stylized figures in high relief. Huaca Prieta is, in effect, a giant rubbish tip dating back 5000 years, which once housed the original inhabitants of the area. It was first investigated by the US archaeologist Junius Bird in the late 1940s, leading him to establish the chronology of prehistoric Peru that prevails today and cementing the place of this unremarkable *huaca* in Peruvian history.

Huaca Cao Viejo has extensive friezes, polychrome reliefs up to 90 m long, 4 m high and on five different levels. The mummy of a tattooed, pregnant woman, La Señora de Cao, dating from AD 450, was found here. Her mausoleum, with grave goods, can be visited in an excellent purpose-built museum. In front of Cao Viejo are the remains of one of the oldest Spanish churches in the region. It was common practice for the Spaniards to build their churches near these ancient sites in order to counteract their religious importance.

Puerto Chicama

Surfers claim that Puerto Chicama (Malabrigo), 70 km north of Trujillo (turn off the Panamericana at Paiján) is the best surf beach in Peru, with the longest left-hand point-break in the world. The best waves are from March to October (high point May/June). The town has a 1-km-long fishing pier, huge, abandoned warehouses and the remains of a railway to Casa Grande cooperative left over from the town's sugar-exporting days. There are a few *hospedajes* and simple places to eat in town itself (shop early by the market for fresh seafood), but the best places to stay and eat are in Distrito El Hombre, the clifftop south of town (eg **Chicama**, Arica 625); avoid the shacks that line the beach.

Pacasmayo and around → *Colour map 1, C2.*

Pacasmayo, 102 km north of Trujillo, is the port for the next oasis north. It has a nice beachfront with an old Customs House and a very long pier. Away from the front Pacasmayo is a busy commercial centre. Resort **El Faro** is 1 km away, with surfing at the point and kite- and windsurfing closer to town. There are maritime festivals at New Year and Semana Santa. Some 20 km further north on the Panamericana is the main road connection from the coast to Cajamarca (see page 193) at a junction called **Ciudad de Dios**.

About 30 to 40 minutes from the Panamericana towards the ocean, near the Río Jequetepeque, are the ruins of **Pacatnamú**, comparable in size to Chan Chán. It consists of pyramids, a cemetery and living quarters of nobles and fishermen, possibly initiated in the Chavín period. There is evidence also of Moche and Chimú occupation. No excavations are taking place and the site is more or less abandoned. Likewise, where the Highway crosses the Jequetepeque, the signed ruins of **Farfán** are closed to the public. The city was separate from Pacatnamú, but probably of the same period. It has yielded important Inca burials.

Chepén and around

The next town north is Chepén. The town itself is not particularly fascinating but **Cerro Chepén**, towering over it, is the site of an ancient fortress from the Middle Horizon (late Moche/Huari). The fortress contains the ruins of what may be a palace, surrounded by other buildings. The unexcavated site could have been the main station in a chain of lookout posts along the north coast.

A little further north is **San José de Moro** (70 km from Chiclayo), whose archaeological site is open to the public. It consists of a ceremonial centre and cemetery from the late Moche and transitional Moche/Lambayeque period (http://sanjosedemoro.pucp.edu.pe). About 1000 tombs have been found, including those of priestesses. The site is a couple of blocks from the town's main plaza where there is a museum. The guardian of the site can open the museum; entry is free, but please give a tip. He also has his own workshop reproducing the pottery, characterized by fineline painting, found at the site. Harvard University holds an annual field course here in the summer.

Listings Coast north of Trujillo

Where to stay

El Brujo

$ Hospedaje Jubalu
Libertad 105, Magdalena de Cao,
T995-670600.
With hot water. There's no internet in town and limited shopping.

Puerto Chicama

The following are in Distrito El Hombre (several close out of season):

$$$ Chicama Beach
T044-576130, www.chicamabeach.com.
3-star, hot water, swimming pool for kids and adults, restaurant, bar, laundry, parking, open all year.

$$$ Chicama Surf Resort
T044-576206, www.chicamasurf.com.
Exclusive, with surfing classes, boats to the waves, spa, restaurant, infinity pool, open all year.

$ Hostal Los Delfines
T943-296662.
Owner Tito Venegas. Guests can use well-equipped kitchen, rooms with balcony, hot water, spacious.

In town there are several cheaper places; **Hostal El Naipe** (Tacna 395), is arguably the best.

Pacasmayo

$$ La Estación
Malecón Grau 69, T044-521515,
www.hotellaestacion.com.pe.
Restaurant on ground floor, all meals extra, 4 rooms with terrace overlooking sea, internet, fan, good beds.

$$ Libertad
Leoncio Pardo 1-D, T044-521937,
www.hotellibertad.com.pe.
2 km from beach by petrol station, with breakfast, Wi-Fi and internet, safe, restaurant/bar, parking, efficient and nice.

$$ Pakatnamú
Malecón Grau 103, T044-522368,
hotelpakatnamu@hotmail.com.
Older building on seafront, 1 suite, newer rooms have seaview, with breakfast.

$ Duke Kahanamoku
Ayacucho 44, T044-521889,
www.eldukepacasmayo.com.
Surfing place, with classes and board rental, breakfast extra, hot water, Wi-Fi, free internet.

Restaurants

El Brujo

$ El Brujo
Plaza de Armas, Magdalena de Cao.
Best place to eat in town and accustomed to providing meals for tourists.

$ Café Antojitos
At entrance to Plaza de Armas,
Magdalena de Cao.
Run by a women's cooperative, specializing in sugar-based snacks.

Transport

El Brujo

The complex can be reached by taking one of the regular buses from Trujillo to **Chocope**, US$1.25, every 10 mins, 1 hr, and then a colectivo to **Magdalena de Cao**, US$0.75 (leave when full), 15 mins, then a mototaxi taking up to 3 people to the site, US$7.50 including 1½ hr wait. Unless you particularly like Peruvian public transport, it is more convenient to go on a tour.

Puerto Chicama
Buses stop just off Plaza Central, opposite the Comisaria.

Lambayeque
Region

Lambayeque Region, sandwiched between the Pacific and the Andes, is a major agricultural zone, especially for rice and sugar cane. It boasts a distinctive cuisine and musical tradition, and an unparalleled ethnographic and archaeological heritage. Excavations at the region's adobe pyramid cities, which include Sipán, Tucumé, Sicán and many less well-known sites, are uncovering fabulous treasures. Interspersed with the area's monumental archaeological sites are pleasant colonial towns like Lambayeque and Ferreñafe. This region is also gaining recognition as an important ornithological destination, with good birdwatching in the carob forests at Pómac and Chaparrí and in the transitional zones on the road that climbs to Porculla Pass and the mountains.

Since its foundation in the 16th century, Chiclayo has grown to become a major commercial hub with a population of 750,000. Its witchcraft market is famous, but it is best known for the spectacular cache of prehispanic archaeological treasures found on its doorstep.

Sights

On the Plaza de Armas is the 19th-century neoclassical **Cathedral**, designed by the English architect Andrew Townsend. The private **Club de la Unión** is on the Plaza at the corner of Calle San José. The Palacio Municipal contains a Centro Documental de la Memoria Histórica de Chiclayo. Continue five blocks north on Balta, the busiest commercial street, to the **Mercado Modelo**, one of northern Peru's liveliest and largest daily markets. Don't miss the market stalls off Calle Arica on the south side, where ritual paraphernalia used by traditional curers and diviners (*curanderos*) are sold: herbal medicines, folk charms, curing potions and exotic objects, including dried llama fetuses, to cure all manner of real and imagined illnesses. At **Paseo Artesanal Colón**, south of the Plaza, shops sell handicrafts in a quiet, custom-built open-air arcade. Another relaxing spot here is the **Paseo de las Musas**, with its gardens and imitation Greek statues.

Monsefú and the coast

The traditional town of **Monsefú**, southwest, is known for its music and handicrafts; there's a good market, four blocks from the plaza. The stalls open when potential customers arrive (see also Festivals, page 166).

Beyond Monsefú are three ports serving the Chiclayo area. **Pimentel**, 8 km from Chiclayo, is a beach resort which gets very crowded on Sundays and during the summer (US$4 to rent a chair and sunshade). Most of the seafront has been bought up by developers, but the main plaza is an oasis of green. There are several seafood restaurants (**El Muelle de Pimentel**, Rivera del Mar cuadra 1, T074-453142, is recommended). You can walk along the restored pier for US$0.25. Sea-going reed boats (*caballitos de totora*) are used by fishermen and may be seen from the pier returning late morning or afternoon on the beach.

The surfing between Pimentel and the **Bayovar Peninsula** is excellent, reached from Chiclayo (14.5 km) by a road branching off from the Pan-American Highway. Nearby **Santa Rosa** has little to recommend it, other than to see the realities of fishing life, and it is not safe to walk there from Pimentel. The most southerly port, 24 km by road from Chiclayo, is **Puerto Eten**, a quaint

Tip...

The ruined Spanish town of **Zaña**, 51 km south of Chiclayo, was destroyed by floods in 1720, and sacked by English pirates on more than one occasion. There are ruins of 5 colonial churches and the convents of San Agustín, La Merced and San Francisco.

place with some wooden buildings on the plaza. Its old railway station has been declared a national heritage monument. The adjacent roadstead, Villa de Eten, is a centre for panama hat-making, but is not as picturesque.

Chiclayo

100 metres
100 yards

N

Where to stay 🛏
1 Costa del Sol C3
2 Embajador A3
3 Gran Hotel Chiclayo B1
4 Hosp Concordia C3
5 Hosp San Eduardo C3
6 Inti B2
7 Muchik Hostel B3
8 Pirámide Real C3
9 Santa Rosa B2
10 Sicán C2
11 Sol Radiante C2
12 Sunec C2

Restaurants 🍴
1 Balta 512 C3
2 Boulevar B2
3 Café 900 C3
4 Café Astoria C2
5 D'Onofrio C3
6 El Huaralino C1
7 Fiesta B1
8 Hebrón C3
9 Kaprichos A3
10 La Panadería B2
11 La Parra C3
12 La Plazuela B1
13 Las Américas B3
14 Roma C3
15 Tradiciones C2

Transport 🚌
1 Brüning Express to Lambayeque B1
2 Cial C1
3 Civa C3
4 Colectivos to Lambayeque A2
5 Colectivos to Puerto Etén A3
6 Cruz del Sur C3
7 Emtrafesa C3
8 Línea C2
9 Móvil C1
10 Oltursa B1
11 Tepsa C2
12 Transportes Chiclayo B1

ON THE ROAD

King Kong in Lambayeque

Vintage movie fans will wonder what the icon of early cinema is doing in all the confectionary shops of northern Peru. King Kong, it seems, is alive and well here in the 21st century.

Back in the 1920s, the story goes, one Señora Victoria Mejía de García, who lived on Calle San Roque in Lambayeque, used to prepare and sell home-made sweets in order to finance her charity work. Among these delicacies were giant *alfajores* (biscuits filled with toffee and other sweets), which were soon dubbed 'King Kong' in the heyday of the popular film.

Señora Victoria's family eventually built her cottage industry into a major enterprise and their San Roque brand of King Kongs (www.sanroque.com.pe) is considered by many to be the best, among countless others. You will see them in the shops and hear them being touted by many loud vendors at the bus stations: "*Hay kinkones!*" – "gorilla biscuits for sale".

★Lambayeque

About 12 km northwest of Chiclayo is Lambayeque, a good base from which to explore the Chiclayo area. Its narrow streets are lined by colonial and Republican houses, many retaining their distinctive wooden balconies and wrought-iron grillwork over the windows, although many are in very bad shape. On Calle 2 de Mayo don't miss **Casa de la Logia o Montjoy**, whose 64-m-long balcony is said to be the longest in the colonial Americas. It has been restored and can be visited (free). At 8 de Octubre 345 is **Casona Descalzi** ⓘ *T074-283433, daily 1100-1700*, which is well preserved as a good restaurant. It has 120 carved iguana heads on the ceiling. **Casona Iturregui Aguilarte**, at No 410, is, by contrast, seriously neglected. Also of interest are the 16th-century **Complejo Religioso Monumental de San Francisco de Asís** and the baroque church of the same name, which stands on Plaza de Armas 27 de Diciembre.

The reason most people visit is to see the town's two museums. The older of the two is the **Brüning Archaeological Museum** ⓘ *daily 0900-1700, US$2.75, a guided tour costs an extra US$10*, in a modern building, which specializes in Mochica, Lambayeque/Sicán and Chimú cultures. Three blocks east is the more recent **Museo de las Tumbas Reales de Sipán** ⓘ *Av Juan Pablo Vizcardo y Guzmán 895, T074-283977, www.museotumbasrealessipan.pe, Tue-Sun 0900-1700, US$3.55, moto taxi from plaza US$0.60*. It's shaped like a pyramid. The magnificent treasure from the tomb of 'The Old Lord of Sipán' (see box, page 159), and a replica of the Lord of Sipán's tomb are displayed here. A ramp from the main entrance takes visitors to the third floor, from where you descend, mirroring the sequence of the archaeologists' discoveries. There are handicrafts for sale outside and in the museum shop, and there's also a tourist office ⓘ *Tue-Sun 1000-1400*.

At Lambayeque the new Pan-American Highway branches off the old road for 190 km, heading north across the **Sechura Desert**, a large area of shifting

ON THE ROAD
Old Lord of Sipán

The excavations at Sipán by the archaeologist Walter Alva revealed a huge number of riches in the shape of 'El Señor de Sipán'. This well-documented discovery was followed by an equally astounding find dating from AD 100. The tomb of the 'Old Lord of Sipán', as it has come to be known, predates the original Lord of Sipán by some 200 years, and could well be an ancestor of his.

Some of the finest examples of Moche craftsmanship have been found in the tomb of the Old Lord. One object in particular is remarkable; a crab deity with a human head and legs and the carapace, legs and claws of a crab. The gilded piece is over half a metre tall – unprecedented for a Moche figurine. This crab-like figure has been called Ulluchu Man, because the banner on which it was mounted yielded some of the first samples yet found of this ancient fruit.

The ulluchu fruit usually appears in scenes relating to war and the ritual offering of a prisoner's blood. One theory is that the ulluchu, part of the papaya family, has anticoagulant properties that are useful in preventing clotting before a man's blood is offered.

sands separating the oases of Chiclayo and Piura. If you're travelling this route, stop off in **Mórrope**, 20 km north of Lambayeque, to see one of the earliest churches in northern Peru. **San Pedro de Mórrope** (1545), an adobe and *algarrobo* structure on the plaza, contains the tomb of the cacique Santiago Cazusol.

> **Tip...**
> Solo cyclists should not cross the desert as muggings have occurred. Take the safer, inland route to Piura via Olmos. In the desert, there is no water, fuel or accommodation. Do not attempt this alone.

Sipán
Turn-off is well signposted in the centre of Pomalca. Daily 0900-1700. Tombs and museum, US$2.85; guide at site US$8 (may not speak English). To visit the site takes about 3-4 hrs. There are comedores outside the site.

At this imposing complex a short distance east of Chiclayo, excavations since 1987 in one of three crumbling pyramids have brought to light a cache of funerary objects considered to rank among the finest examples of pre-Columbian art. Peruvian archaeologist Walter Alva, former leader of the dig, continues to probe the immense mound that has revealed no less than 16 royal tombs filled with 1800-year-old offerings worked in precious metals, stone, pottery and textiles of the Moche culture (circa AD 1-750). In the most extravagant Moche tomb, El Señor de Sipán was discovered, a priest clad in gold (ear ornaments, breast plate, etc), with turquoise and other valuables.

In another tomb were found the remnants of what is thought to have been a priest, sacrificed llama and a dog, together with copper decorations. In 1989 another richly appointed, unlooted tomb contained even older metal and ceramic artefacts associated with what was probably a high-ranking shaman or spiritual leader, called 'The Old Lord of Sipán'. Three tombs are on display, with replicas of the original finds. **Museo de Sitio Huaca Rajada** ⓘ *daily 0900-1700, US$2.85*, concentrates on the finds at the site, especially Tomb 14 (the 'Sacerdote-Guerrero', or Priest-Warrior), the decorative techniques of the Moche and the roles that archaeologists and local communities play in protecting these precious discoveries. You can wander around the previously excavated areas of the Huaca Rajada to get an idea of the construction of the burial mound and adjacent pyramids. For a good view, climb the large pyramid across from the excavated Huaca Rajada.

Ventarrón

A 4000-year-old temple, Ventarrón, was uncovered about 20 km from Sipán in 2007 by Walter Alva; his son, Ignacio, is now in charge of the dig. It predates Sipán by some 2000 years and shows three phases of development. Its murals, which appear to depict a deer trapped in a net, are claimed to be the oldest in the Americas and there is evidence of cultural exchange with as far away as the Amazon. A project to build a site museum and improve access is underway; until then, entry with guide is US$2.

Chaparrí Reserve

75 km from Chiclayo, for day visits T978-896377, www.chaparri.org. US$10.50 entry to the reserve; groups of 10 accompanied by a local guide. Mototaxi from Chongoyape to Chaparrí, US$10.

East from Pomalca, just before Chongoyape, is the turning to the Chaparrí private ecological reserve, 34,000 ha, set up and run by the Comunidad Muchik Santa Catalina de Chongoyape. Visitors can go for the day or stay at the **EcoLodge Chaparrí** (see Where to stay, page 164). All staff and guides are locals, which provides work and helps to prevent littering. There are no dogs or goats in the area so the forest is recuperating; it contains many bird and mammal species of the dry forest, including white-winged guan and spectacled bear. There is a Spectacled Bear Rescue Centre where bears rescued from captivity live in semi-wild enclosures. The Tinajones reservoir is good for birdwatching.

Túcume

T074-835026, www.museodesitiotucume.com. Daily 0800-1700. US$4.50, students US$1, children US$0.30, plus guide US$7. Mototaxi from highway/new town to ruins, US$0.75.

About 35 km north of Chiclayo, not far from the Panamericana and Túcume Nuevo, lie the ruins of this vast city built over 1000 years ago. A short climb to the two *miradores* on **Cerro La Raya** (or **El Purgatorio**) offers the visitor an unparalleled panoramic vista of 26 major pyramids, platform mounds, walled citadels and residential compounds flanking a ceremonial centre and ancient cemeteries. One of the pyramids, Huaca Larga, where excavations are still being undertaken, is the longest adobe structure in the world, measuring 700 m long, 280 m wide and over 30 m high. There is no evidence of occupation at Túcume before the

BACKGROUND

A tale of fish and demons

Among the many legends that abound in this part of northern Peru are stories about the hill that dominates the site at Túcume and the origins of its two names: Cerro La Raya (Ray Hill) or El Purgatorio (Purgatory).

The first name, Cerro La Raya, refers to the indigenous legend of a manta ray that lived in a nearby lake. The local children constantly tormented the fish by throwing stones at it, so, to escape this torment, the poor creature decided to move to the hill and become part of it. The lake then disappeared and, ever since, the hill has been enchanted.

The second name derives from the conquering Spaniards' attempts to convert the indigenous people to the Christian faith. The Spanish invaders encountered fierce local resistance to their religion and came up with the idea of convincing the people of Túcume that the hill was, in fact, purgatory. They told the locals that there was a demon living on the hill, who would punish anyone not accepting the Roman Catholic faith.

In order to lend some credence to this tale, a group of Spaniards set out one dark, moonless night and built a huge bonfire at the foot of 'El Purgatorio', giving it the appearance of an erupting volcano and convincing the locals that any unbelievers or sinners would be thrown alive into the flames of this diabolical fire.

As if that wasn t enough to terrify the local populace, the Spanish also concocted the fiendish tale of 'El Carretón', an enormous wagon pulled by four great horses that would supposedly speed forth from the bowels of 'El Purgatorio' on the darkest of nights. Driven by a dandily dressed demon boss, and carrying his equally dandy demon buddies, this hellish vehicle careered round the town of Túcume making a fearsome racket. Any poor unbelievers or sinners found wandering the streets would immediately be carted off and thrown into the flames of purgatory.

Sicán or Lambayeque people who developed the site AD 1000-1375. Thereafter the Chimú conquered the region, establishing a short reign until the arrival of the Incas around 1470. The Incas built on top of the existing structure of **Huaca Larga** using stone from Cerro La Raya.

Among the other pyramids which make up this huge complex are: **Huaca El Mirador** (90 m by 65 m, 30 m high), **Huaca Las Estacas**, **Huaca Pintada** and **Huaca de las Balsas**, which is thought to have housed people of elevated status such as priests. A walkway leads around the covered pyramid and you can see many mud reliefs including fishermen on rafts.

Apart from the *miradores*, not much of the site is open to view, as lots of archaeological study is still going on. However, a site museum opened in 2014 with displays of many objects found at the site, including miniature offerings relating to the prehispanic gods and mythology of Lambayeque, items relating to the last

Inca governor of Túcume and a room detailing the history of the region from pre-Columbian times to the present. There is also a shop.

The town of **Túcume Viejo** is a 20-minute walk beyond the site. Look for the side road heading towards a park, opposite which is the ruin of a huge colonial church made of adobe and some brick. The surrounding countryside is pleasant for walks through mango trees and fields of maize. **Fiesta de la Purísima Concepción**, the festival of the town's patron saint, takes place eight days prior to Carnival in February, and also in September.

★Ferreñafe

The colonial town of Ferreñafe, 20 km northeast of Chiclayo, is worth a visit, especially for the **Museo Nacional Sicán** ① *T074-286469, Museo-Nacional-Sican on Facebook, Tue-Sun 0900-1700, US$4, students half price, good explanations in Spanish, café and gift shop.* This excellent museum on the outskirts of town houses objects of the Sicán (Lambayeque) culture from near Batán Grande. To get there, take a mototaxi from the centre, 5 mins, US$1.75, or, from Chiclayo, catch a combi from Avenida N de Piérola towards Batán Grande; these pass the museum every 15-20 minutes, taking 40 minutes, US$1.

Sicán (El Santuario Histórico Bosque de Pómac)

20 km beyond Ferreñafe along the road to Batán Grande (from the Panamericana another entrance is near Túcume), dalemandelama@gmail.com. Daily 0900-1700. Free; a guide (Spanish only) can be hired with transport, US$3.45, or horses for hire US$6. Food and drinks are available at the visitors' centre, and camping is permitted.

El Santuario Histórico Bosque de Pómac includes the ruins of **Sicán**. Visiting is not easy because of the arid conditions and distances involved: it is 10 km from the visitors' centre to the nearest *huaca* (pyramid). A two-hour guided tour of the area includes at least two *huacas*, some of the most ancient carob trees and a mirador that affords a beautiful view across the emerald-green tops of the forest with the enormous pyramids dramatically breaking through.

Sicán has revealed several sumptuous tombs dating to AD 900-1100. The ruins comprise some 12 large adobe pyramids, arranged around a huge plaza, measuring 500 m by 250 m, with 40 archaeological sites in total. The city of the Sicán (or Lambayeque culture) was probably moved to Túcume (see above), 6 km west, following 30 years of severe drought and then a devastating El Niño-related flood in AD 1050-1100. These events appear to have provoked a rebellion in which many of the remaining temples on top of the pyramids were burnt and destroyed. The forest itself has good birdwatching possibilities.

Tip...
There is a pleasant dry forest walk to Huaca I, with shade and the chance to do some bird- and lizard-watching.

Olmos and around

On the old Pan-American Highway 885 km from Lima, **Olmos** is a tranquil place surrounded by endless lemon orchards; there are several hotels and a **Festival de Limón** in the last week in June. A paved road runs east from Olmos over the Porculla Pass, branching north to Jaén and east to Bagua Grande (see page 226). Olmos is the best base for observing the critically endangered white-winged guan, a bird thought extinct for 100 years until its rediscovery in 1977. The old Pan-American Highway continues from Olmos to Cruz de Caña and Piura.

Listings Chiclayo and around *map p157*

Tourist information

Chiclayo

iPerú
Siete de Enero 579, T074-205703,
iperuchiclayo@promperu.gob.pe.
Mon-Sat 0900-1800, Sun 0900-1300; also
in Lambayeque at Museo de las Tumbas
Reales de Sipán, Tue-Sun 1000-1400.
There are tourist kiosks on the Plaza and on Balta.

Indecopi
Los Tumbos 245, Santa Victoria, T074-206223, aleyva@indecopi.gob.pe.
Mon-Fri 0800-1300, 1630-1930.
For complaints and tourist protection.

Tourist police
Av Sáenz Peña 830, T074-236700, ext 311. Daily 24 hrs.
Are very helpful and may store luggage and take you to the sites themselves.

Ferreñafe

Mincetur
On the Plaza de Armas, T074-282843, citesipan@mincetur.gob.pe.
Helpful.

Where to stay

Chiclayo

$$$ Costa del Sol
Balta 399, T074-227272,
www.costadelsolperu.com.
Non-smoking rooms, smart, small pool, sauna, jacuzzi, Wi-Fi, ATM. **Páprika** restaurant, good value Sun buffets, vegetarian options.

$$$ Gran Hotel Chiclayo
(Casa Andina Select)
Villareal 115, T511-2139739,
www.casa-andina.com.
Large, modern hotel for corporate and leisure guests, pool, safe car park, changes dollars, jacuzzi, entertainments, restaurant. Now operated by Casa Andina.

$$$ Inti
Luis Gonzales 622, T074-235931,
www.intihotel.com.pe.
More expensive rooms with jacuzzi, family rooms available, welcome cocktail, airport transfer included, parking, safe and fridge in room, restaurant, helpful staff.

$$$ Sunec
Izaga 472, T074-205110,
www.sunechotel.com.pe.
Modern hotel in a central location, parking and small pool, opened in 2013.

$$ Embajador
7 de Enero 1388, 1½ blocks from Mercado Modelo, T074-204729, http://hotelembajadorchiclayo.com.
Modern, bright, good facilities, 20 mins' walk from centre, small comfortable rooms, small restaurant, excellent service, free pick-up from bus office, tours arranged.

$ Hospedaje Concordia
7 de Enero Sur 235, Urb San Eduardo, T074-209423.
Rooms on 2nd floor bigger than 3rd, modern, pleasant, no meals, laundry service, view of Parque San Eduardo.

$ Hospedaje San Eduardo
7 de Enero Sur 267, Urb San Eduardo, T074-208668.
No meals, colourful decor, modern bathrooms, fan, Wi-Fi, public phone, quiet, hot water.

$ Muchik Hostel
Vicente de la Vega 1127.
Singles, doubles and dorm, with fan, pleasant common area, safe.

$ Pirámide Real
MM Izaga 726, T074-224036.
Compact and spotless, good value, no meals, safe in room, fan, very central.

$ Santa Rosa
L González 927, T074-224411.
Rooms with windows are bright and spacious, best at rear. Hot water, fan, laundry, good value.

$ Sicán
MM Izaga 356, T074-208741, hsican@hotmail.com.
With breakfast, hot water, fan, comfortable, restaurant and bar, laundry, parking, welcoming and trustworthy.

$ Sol Radiante
Izaga 392, T074-237858.
Hot water, comfortable, pleasant, family-run, laundry, tourist information. Pay in advance.

Lambayeque

$$$ Hostería San Roque
2 de Mayo 437, T074-282860, www.hosteriasanroque.com.
In a fine, extensive colonial house, beautifully refurbished, helpful staff, bar, swimming pool, lunch on request. Single, double, triple, quad rooms and dorm for groups of 6, $.

$ Hostal Libertad
Bolívar 570, T074-283561, www.hostallibertad.com.
1½ blocks from plaza, big rooms, fridge, secure.

$ Hostal Real Sipán
Huamachuco 664, opposite Brüning Museum.
Modern, an option if arriving late at night.

Mórrope

$$-$ La Casa del Papelillo
San Pedro 357, T955-624734, lacasadelpapelillo@gmail.com, www.airbnb.es/rooms/89079.
3 rooms in a remodelled 19th-century home, one with private bath, includes breakfast, communal areas, cultural events, discounts for community volunteer work. Owner Cecilia is knowledgeable and helpful.

Chaparrí Reserve

$$$$ EcoLodge Chaparrí
T984-676249 or in Chiclayo T074-452299, www.chaparrilodge.com.

A delightful oasis in the dry forest, 6 beautifully decorated cabins (more being built) and 5 double rooms with shared bath, built of stone and mud, nice and cool, solar power. Price is for 3 meals and a local guide for one day, first-class food. Sechuran foxes in the gardens; hummingbirds bathe at the pool about 0600 every day. Recommended.

Túcume

$$ pp Los Horcones
T951-831705, www.loshorcones detucume.com.
Rustic luxury in the shadow of the pyramids, with adobe and algarrobo rooms set in lovely garden with lots of birdlife. Good food, pizza oven, breakfast included. Note that if rice is being grown nearby in Jan-May there can be a serious mosquito problem.

Olmos

$$$ Los Faiques
Humedades Alto, Salas, T979-299932, www.losfaiques-salas.com.
Very pretty place in a quiet forest setting, buffet breakfast, excellent restaurant.

$ El Remanso
San Francisco 100, T074-427158, elremansolmos@yahoo.com.
Like a hacienda, with courtyards, small pool, whitewashed rooms, colourful bedding, flowers and bottled water in room, hot water (supposedly). Price is full board, good restaurant. Charming owner. There are several other places to stay in town.

Restaurants

Chiclayo
For delicious, cheap *ceviche*, go to the **Nativo** stall in the Mercado Central,

a local favourite. For ice cream, try **D'Onofrio** (Balta y Torres Paz). **La Panadería** (Lapoint 847), has a good choice of breads, including *integral*, snacks and soft drinks.

$$$ El Huaralino
La Libertad 155, Santa Victoria.
Wide variety, international and creole, but mixed reports of late.

$$$ Fiesta
Av Salaverry 1820 in 3 de Octubre suburb, T074-201970, www. restaurantfiestagourmet.com.
Gourmet local dishes, excellent food and service, beautifully presented, daily and seasonal specials, fabulous juices, popular business lunch place.

$$$ Sabores Peruanos
Los Incas 136. Tue-Sun 1200-1700.
Great Peruvian seafood and meat dishes.

$$ Balta 512
Balta 512, T074-223598.
First-class local food, usually good breakfast, popular with locals.

$$ Boulevar
Colón entre Izaga y Aguirre.
Good, friendly, *menú* and à la carte.

$$ Hebrón
Balta 605.
For more upmarket than average chicken, but also local food and *parrilla*, good salads. Also does an excellent breakfast and a good buffet at weekends.

$$ Kaprichos
Pedro Ruíz 1059, T074-232721.
Chinese, delicious, huge portions.

$$ Las Américas
Aguirre 824. Daily 0700-0200.
Good service.

$$ Roma
Izaga 706. Open all day.
Wide choice, breakfasts, snacks and meals.

$$ Tradiciones
7 de Enero Sur 105, T074-221192. Daily 0900-1700.
Good variety of local dishes, including ceviche, and drinks, pleasant atmosphere and garden, good service.

$ Café 900
MM Izaga 900, www.cafe900.com.
Appealing atmosphere in a remodelled old house, good food, popular with locals, sometimes has live music.

$ Café Astoria
Bolognesi 627. Daily 0800-1200, 1530-2100.
Breakfast, good-value *menú*.

$ La Parra
Izaga 746.
Chinese and creole *parrillada*, very good, large portions, cheerful.

$ La Plazuela
San José 299, Plaza Elías Aguirre.
Good food, seats outside.

Lambayeque
A Lambayeque speciality is the 'King Kong', a giant *alfajor* biscuit filled with manjar blanco and other sweets. San Roque brand (www.sanroque.com.pe), sold throught Peru, is especially good.

$$ Casona Descalzi
Address above.
Lunch only. Good menu, including traditional northern dishes.

$$ El Cántaro
2 de Mayo 180.
Lunch only. For traditional local dishes, à la carte and a good *menú*.

$$ El Pacífico
Huamachuco 970, T074-283135.
Lunch only. Renowned for its enormous plates of *arroz con pato* and *causa norteña*.

$$ El Rincón del Pato
A Leguía 270.
Lunch only. Offers 40 different duck dishes.

$$-$ Sabor Norteño
Bolívar 440.
One of the few restaurants open in the early evening.

$ Café Cultural La Cucarda
2 de Mayo 263, T074-284155.
Evening only. Small alternative café, decorated with rescued antiques, delicious pastries, pies and cakes. Recommended.

Festivals

6 Jan **Reyes Magos** in Mórrope, Illimo and other towns, a recreation of a medieval pageant in which pre-Columbian deities become the Wise Men.
4 Feb **Túcume** devil dances.
14 Mar **El Señor Nazareno Cautivo**, in Lambayeque and Monsefú, whose main celebration of this festival is **14 Sep**.
Mar/Apr **Holy Week**, traditional Easter celebrations and processions in many villages.
2-7 Jun **Divine Child of the Miracle**, Villa de Eten.
27-31 Jul **Fexticum** in Monsefú, traditional foods, drink, handicrafts, music and dance.
5 Aug Pilgrimage from the mountain shrine of **Chalpón** to **Motupe**, 90 km north of Chiclayo; the cross is brought down from a cave and carried in procession through the village.

24 Dec-1 Jan Christmas and New Year processions and children dancers (*pastorcitos* and *seranitas*) can be seen in many villages, including Ferreñafe, Mochumi, Mórrope.

What to do

Chiclayo
Tour operators
Lambayeque's museums, Sipán and Túcume can easily be visited by public transport (see below). Local operators run 3-hr tours to Sipán; Túcume and Lambayeque (5 hrs); Sicán is a full-day tour including Ferreñafe and Pómac. There are also tours to Zaña and coastal towns.
InkaNatura, *Manuel María Izaga 730, of 203, T979-995024, www.inkanatura.net. Mon-Fri 0915-1315, 1515-1915, Sat 0915-1315*. Historical and nature tours throughout northern Peru. Good service.

Sicán (El Santuario Histórico Bosque de Pómac)
Horse riding
Rancho Santana, *Pacora, T979-712145, www.cabalgatasperu.com*. Relaxing tours on horseback, half-day (US$15.50), 1-day (US$22.50) or 3-day tours to Santuario Bosque de Pómac, Sicán ruins and Túcume, Swiss-run (Andrea Martin), good horses. Also $ a bungalow, a double room and camping (tents for hire) at the ranch with safe parking for campervans. Frequently recommended.

Transport

Chiclayo
Air
José Abelardo Quiñones González airport is 1 km from town, T074-233192; taxi from centre US$4. Arrive 2 hrs before flight; be prepared for manual search of

hand luggage; no restaurant or bar in departure lounge.

Daily flights to/from **Lima** and **Piura** with **LAN** (MM Izaga 770) and **StarPerú** (MM Izaga 459, T074-225204), direct or via **Trujillo**. The military **Grupo Aéreo 42** (Av Balta 901, T979-975537) has passenger flights between Chiclayo, Trujillo and Iquitos; see page 150 for routes and schedules.

Bus
Local Combis to **Monsefú** cost US$0.75 from Balta y Pedro Ruiz, or Terminal Epsel (Av Castañeda Iparraguirre s/n). Combis to **Pimentel** leave from Av L Ortiz y San José, US$1.10. Colectivos to **Lambayeque**, US$0.75, 25 mins, leave from Pedro Ruíz at the junction with Av Ugarte; also **Brüning Express** combis from Vicente de la Vega entre Angamos y Av L Ortiz, every 15 mins, US$0.50, or **Trans Lambayeque** colectivo from Plaza Elias Aguirre, US$0.90. Combis to **Sipán** leave from Plaza Elías Aguirre and from terminal Epsel, US$1, 1 hr. To **Chongoyape** for Chaparrí Reserve, take a public bus from Leoncio Prado y Sáenz Peña (1¼ hrs, US$1.50), then a mototaxi to **Chaparrí**, US$10. Combis to **Tucumé** leave from Av Leguía, 15 m from Angamos, US$1, 45 mins. Colectivos to the centre of **Ferreñafe** leave from Terminal Epsel every few mins, or from 8 de Octubre y Sáenz Peña, 40 mins, U$1. Combis to **Batán Grande** depart from Av N de Piérola, and pass the museum in Ferreñafe every 15-20 mins, 40 mins, US$1.

Long distance There is no central terminal; most buses stop outside their offices on Bolognesi. To **Lima**, 770 km, US$25-36, with **Civa** (Av Bolognesi 714, T074-223434); **Cruz del Sur** (Bolognesi

888, T074-225508); **Ormeño** (Haya de la Torre 242, 2 blocks south of Bolognesi, T074-234206); **Ittsa** (Av Bolognesi 155, T074-233612); **Línea** (Bolognesi 638, T074-222221), *especial* and *bus cama* service; **Móvil** (Av Bolognesi 195, T074-271940), goes as far as Tarapoto; **Oltursa** (ticket office at Balta e Izaga, T074-237789, terminal at Vicente de la Vega 101, T074-225611); **Tepsa** (Bolognesi 504-36 y Colón, T074-236981) and **Transportes Chiclayo** (Av L Ortiz 010, T074-223632). Most companies leave from 1900 onwards.

To **Trujillo**, 209 km, with **Emtrafesa** (Av Balta 110, T074-600660), every 15 mins, 4 hrs, US$5.50, and **Línea**. To **Piura**, 4 hrs, US$5.50, **Transportes Chiclayo** leave 15 mins throughout the day; also **Línea** and **Emtrafesa** and buses from the **Cial/Flores** terminal (Bolognesi 751, T074-239579). To **Sullana**, US$8.50. To **Tumbes**, US$9, 9-10 hrs; with **Cial, Cruz del Sur** or **El Dorado**. Some companies on the route northwards arrive full from Lima. Many buses go on to the **Ecuadorean border** at **Aguas Verdes**. Go to the *Salida* on Elías Aguirre, mototaxi drivers know where it is; be there by 1900. All buses stop here after leaving their terminals to try and fill empty seats, so discounts may be possible. To **Cajamarca**, 260 km, US$9-20, eg **Línea**, 4 a day; others from Tepsa terminal (Bolognesi y Colón, eg **Días**, T074-224448). To **Chachapoyas**, US$13.50-25, with **Civa**, 1730 daily, 10-11 hrs; **Transervis Kuelap** (Tepsa station), 1830 daily; **Móvil**, at 2000. To **Jaén**, US$7.75-9.60, many companies; **Móvil charges** US$11.55-15.50. To **Tarapoto**, 18 hrs, US$25-29, with **Móvil**, also **Tarapoto Tours** (Bolognesi 751, T074-636231). To **Guayaquil**, with **Civarun** at 1825, *semi-cama* US$34.75, *cama* US$42.50, also **Super Semería**, US$25, 12 hrs, via Piura, Máncora, Tumbes; they also go to **Cuenca**.

Taxi
Mototaxis are a cheap way to get around: US$1 to anywhere in the city. Chiclayo to **Pimentel**, US$6, 20 mins. Taxi colectivos to **Eten** leave from 7 de Enero y Arica.

Lambayeque
Some major bus lines have offices in Lambayeque and can drop you off there. There are numerous combis between Lambayeque and Chiclayo (see above). Combi to **Túcume**, US$0.75, 25 mins.

Far northwest

From the historic city of Piura north to the border with Ecuador, the Peruvian coast is hardly green, but this is as green as it gets. It is also washed by the warmest water, and bathing is possible from December to April. Beaches in this area are popular with locals, *limeños* and foreign tourists alike, and the resort town of Máncora is a magnet for surfers and party animals from far and wide. Further north, accessed from the border town of Tumbes, are several natural reserves protecting mangroves and other habitats not found anywhere else in the country. Inland from Piura, and a world apart, is the Inca archaeological site of Aypate, as well as the high, cold, misty and mystical lakes of the Huaringas.

Piura and around → *Colour map 1, B1.*

a proud and historic city

Piura was founded in 1532, three years before Lima, by the conquistadors left behind by Pizarro. The city has public gardens and two well-kept parks, Cortés and Pizarro (also called Plaza de las Tres Culturas); the latter has a statue of the man himself. Old buildings are kept in repair and new buildings blend with the Spanish style of the old city. Three bridges cross the Río Piura to Castilla: the oldest is the pedestrian-only Puente San Miguel from Calle Huancavelica; another is from Calle Sánchez Cerro, and the newest is from Avenida Panamericana Norte at the west end of town.

Sights

On the **Plaza de Armas** is the **cathedral** ⓘ *daily 0800-1200,1700-2030*, with a gold-covered altar and paintings by Ignacio Merino. A few blocks away is **San Francisco** ⓘ *Mon-Sat 0900-1200, 1600-1800*, where the city's independence from Spain was declared on 4 January 1821, nearly eight months before Lima. **Casa Museo Grau** ⓘ *C Tacna 662, opposite the Centro Cívico, T073-326541, Mon-Fri 0800-1300, 1530-1800, Sat-Sun 0800-1200, US$0.70*, is the birthplace of Admiral Miguel Grau, hero of the War of the Pacific with Chile. The museum contains a model of the *Huáscar*, the largest Peruvian warship in the War of the Pacific, which was built in Britain. It also contains interesting old photographs. The small **Museo Municipal Vicús** ⓘ *Sullana, near Huánuco, Tue-Fri 0900-1700, Sat 0900-1300, Sun 0900-1200*, includes

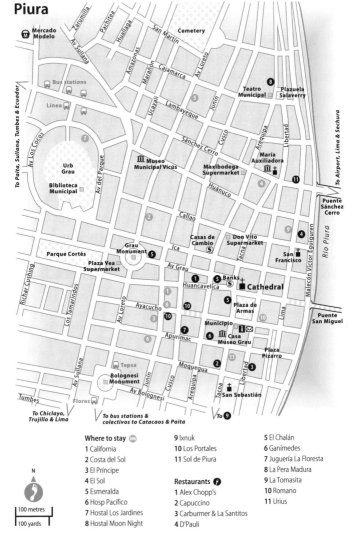

Piura

To Paita, Sullana, Tumbes & Ecuador
To Airport, Lima & Sechura
To Chiclayo, Trujillo & Lima
To bus stations & colectivos to Catacaos & Paita

Mercado Modelo
Cemetery
Bus stations
Línea
Teatro Municipal
Plazuela Salaverry
Urb Grau
Biblioteca Municipal
Museo Municipal Vicús
Maxibodega Supermarket
María Auxiliadora
Parque Cortés
Grau Monument
Casas de Cambio
Don Vito Supermarket
San Francisco
Plaza Vea Supermarket
Plaza de Armas
Banks
Cathedral
Municipio
Casa Museo Grau
Plaza Pizarro
Tepsa
Bolognesi Monument
San Sebastián
Flores
Puente Sánchez Cerro
Río Piura
Puente San Miguel

Streets: Zarumilla, Pachitea, Huallaga, San Martín, Av Sullana, Amazonas, Manantón, Cajamarca, Av Loreto, Ucayali, Lambayeque, Junín, Sánchez Cerro, Cusco, Arequipa, Libertad, Av Los Cocos, Av del Parque, Huánuco, Callao, Ica, Tacna, Malecón Victor Eguiguren, Av Grau, Huancavelica, Richar Cushing, Los Tamarindos, Av Loreto, Ayacucho, Apurímac, Lima, Moquegua, Av Bolognesi, Av Sullana, Junín, Cusco, Arequipa, Tacna

N
100 metres
100 yards

Where to stay 🛏
1 California
2 Costa del Sol
3 El Príncipe
4 El Sol
5 Esmeralda
6 Hosp Pacífico
7 Hostal Los Jardines
8 Hostal Moon Night
9 Ixnuk
10 Los Portales
11 Sol de Piura

Restaurants 🍴
1 Alex Chopp's
2 Capuccino
3 Carburmer & La Santitos
4 D'Pauli
5 El Chalán
6 Ganímedes
7 Juguería La Floresta
8 La Pera Madura
9 La Tomasita
10 Romano
11 Urius

a Sala de Oro (closed weekends, US$1.45) with 60 gold artefacts from the local Vicús culture and an art section.

Catacaos

Twelve kilometres southwest of Piura, Catacaos is famous for its *chicha*, *picanterías* (local restaurants, some with music) and for its crafts, including tooled leather, gold and silver filigree jewellery, wooden articles and straw hats (expensive). The town has splendid celebrations during Holy Week. About 2 km south of Catacaos is the **Narihuala** archaeological site ⓘ *Tue-Sun 0830-1630, US$0.70, children will guide you for a tip, mototaxi from Catacaos US$1.80*, which consists of deteriorated adobe pyramids of the Tallán culture (AD 900-1400) and a site museum.

Paita and around

Paita, 50 km from Piura, is the major fishing port for the area and is flanked on three sides by a towering, sandy bluff. Looming over Paita is a small colonial fortress built to repel pirates, who attacked it frequently. Several colonial buildings survive. Bolívar's mistress, Manuela Sáenz, lived the last 24 years of her life in Paita, after being exiled from Quito. She supported herself until her death in 1856 by weaving, embroidering and making candy, after refusing the fortune left her by her husband. A pleasant day trip can be made to the fishing village of **Yasila**, south of Paita, where *potos*, large octopus, are fished and prepared for export.

Alternatively, head up the coast for 25 km to the holiday resort of **Colán**, reached by driving down a large, sandy promontory (turn off at Km 989). Near the base is a striking and lonely colonial church, with breathtaking architecture and beautiful paintings in good condition. It is claimed by some to be the oldest church in Peru, if not in South America. The key-holder can be found by asking in the adjoining village of San Lucas de Colán. The seafront houses in Colán stand on wooden stilts and are surrounded by palms. At high tide the beach almost disappears. The seawater is clear and warm (but beware of stingrays; drag your feet when entering the water) and the sunsets are spectacular. Colán has a choice of hotels and excellent seafood restaurants, although many are closed midweek and in low season ($$ **San Felipe** is very good).

Chulucanas and around

Sixty kilometres northeast of Piura and 10 km off the Piura–Olmos highway is the small town of Chulucanas, centre of a lemon- and orange-growing area. An ancient pottery technique was discovered here in the 1960s when graverobbers brought to light examples of pottery from the Vicus and Tallane cultures dating from the second half of the first millennium BC. A group of pottery specialists researched and experimented with forms and techniques based on the pre-Columbian finds to produce a very subtle and unusual effect. At first local potters imitated the forms of the Vicus pieces, but gradually they began to develop their own stylized figures. The most popular form is the 'Chichera', a fat lady who makes and sells *chicha*. The most highly prized pieces are signed and sold in galleries and shops in Lima and abroad. Excellent ceramics can also be bought in shops in town.

ON THE ROAD
The witch doctors of Las Huaringas

To take part in the ceremony, arrive in town and prepare to be approached almost immediately by a shaman's 'agent'. As dodgy as this sounds, the agent can help you by doing all preparations. Go to the tourist centre in the plaza beforehand and double check if the agent's witch doctor is trustworthy. You'll then hop in a van, travel to the doctor's house, agree on a price and commence the ceremony immediately. It is an outdoor affair involving hallucinogenic San Pedro cactus juice that is quite vile. Note that there have been reports of people experiencing flashbacks long after taking San Pedro. The ceremony lasts all night and participants dance, reveal and predict the future. The entire ceremony is very mellow and most witch doctors have the disposition of concerned uncles. A spartan meal is provided but you're advised to bring your own snacks. The next day involves a three-hour horse ride to a high mountain lagoon where near-skinny dipping and more ceremonies take place. You're back in Huancabamba (tired and cold) by late afternoon.

Towards Huancabamba and Las Huaringas

From the road to Olmos (see page 163), beyond the Chulucanas turn-off, a paved road leads east to **Canchaque,** 146 km from Piura. This is a delightful small centre for coffee, sugar cane and fruit production, situated at 1198 m. A 30-minute walk leads to Los Peroles de Canchaque, a natural water slide carved by the Chorro Blanco stream.

The road continues over a pass above 3000 m for 63 km to **Huancabamba** ⓘ *http://munihuancabamba.gob.pe*. This very pretty town in a wonderful setting at 1933 m hosts a tourist week in early July and the Virgen del Carmen festival in mid-July. It has three claims to fame. First, the predominance of European architecture, due to the fact that it was an important Spanish settlement in colonial times. Second, it is called '*la ciudad que camina*' (the walking town), because it is built on irregularly slipping strata that cause much subsidence, resulting in the fall of the bridge over the Río Huancabamba.

Its third, and by far most remarkable, claim to fame, is that Huancabamba is the base for reaching **Las Huaringas** (Guaringas) lakes to the north of town, at about 3500 m. Around these 14 lakes live the most famous witch doctors in Peru, to whom sick people flock from all over the country and abroad. The shamanic ceremony performed by the witch doctors is definitely off the gringo trail and is an unforgettable trip (see box, above). Horses to the lakes can be hired for US$6.50. There are also trips to the village of **San Antonio,** below Lago Carmen, and the village of **Salalá,** below Lago Shumbe. **Sondor** is a village 15 km south of Huancabamba, near the 20-m-high Sitán waterfall. South of Sondor, a track, impassable in the wet season, goes east to **Tabaconas** and the Jaén–San Ignacio road, see page 226.

Tourist information

Piura

Information is available from the very helpful staff at **iPerú** (Ayacucho s/n y C Libertad, edif Serpost, in a lane off the Plaza de Armas, T073-320249, iperupiura@promperu.gob.pe, Mon-Sat 0900-1800, Sun 0900-1300); there's another office in Arrivals at the airport (Indecopi Av Los Cocos 268, Urb Club Grau, T073-308549, apena@indecopi.gob.pe).

Where to stay

Piura

$$$$-$$$ Costa del Sol
Av Loreto 649, T073-302864,
www.costadelsolperu.com.
Centrally located, part of the Peruvian 1st class hotel chain, pool, restaurant.

$$$$-$$$ Los Portales
Libertad 875, Plaza de Armas, T073-321161, www.losportaleshoteles.com.pe.
Elegantly refurbished *casona* in the heart of the city, luxurious suites and rooms, includes welcome cocktail, the city's social centre pleasant terrace, nice pool.

$$$ El Príncipe
Junín 930, T073-324868.
Comfortable suite and rooms with a/c, fridge, airport transfers.

$$$ Esmeralda
Loreto 235, T073-331205,
www.hotelesmeralda.com.pe.
Variety of room sizes, frigobar, comfortable, good, restaurant.

$$$ Ixnuk
Ica 553, T073-322205, www.ixnuk.com.
Modern hotel with bright ample rooms, a/c, fridge, airport transfers.

$$$-$$ Sol de Piura
Tacna 761, T073-332395,
www.soldepiura.com.
Centrally located modern hotel, comfortable rooms with a/c, fridge, airport transfers.

$$ El Sol
Sánchez Cerro 411, T073-324971,
www.hotel-elsol.com.
A/c rooms, frigobar, small pool, snack bar, parking, front rooms can be noisy.

$$-$ Hostal Los Jardines
Av Los Cocos 436, Urb Club Grau, T073-326590, www.hotellosjardines.com.
Not far from the centre, parking, good value. `

$ California
Jr Junín 835, upstairs, T073-328789.
Shared or private bath, own water-tank, mosquito netting on windows, roof terrace.

$ Hospedaje Pacífico
Apurimac 717, T073-303061.
Simple comfortable rooms with fan, the newer ones on the top floors are the nicest, no breakfast, good value.

$ Hostal Moon Night
Junín 899, T073-336174.
Spacious, with or without bath, cold water, fan, no breakfast.

Paita and around

The following are all in Colán. Expect higher prices (even double) in high season 15 Dec-Mar.

$$$ Bocatoma Resort
Av Costanera Norte Co99, Colán, T975-366833, http://bocatomahotelresort.com.
A variety of thatch-roofed cabins for 2 to 7 people on a spit of land between the ocean and lagoons, with restaurant, pool and sports facilities.

$$$-$$ Luna Nueva
Av Costanera, Playa Esmeralda, Colán, T968-009232, www.lunanuevadecolan.com.
17-room hotel with pool, restaurant, rooms with ocean view are more expensive than those facing the pool, kayak rentals.

$$ Bungalows Spilberg
Av Costanera, Playa Esmeralda, Colán, T073-778578, www.colanbungalows spilberg.com.
Cabins for up to 6 persons, with fan, fridge, small pools, restaurant, conference facilities, well suited to families.

$ Hospedaje Frente al Mar
Playa Esmeralda, Colán, T073-703117.
Family-run lodging in chalet by the sea, rooms with cold shower, no breakfast, good value.

Towards Huancabamba and Las Huaringas
Canchaque and Huancabamba both have basic lodgings and eateries.
$ El Dorado on Huancabamba's plaza is good.

Restaurants

Piura

$$$ Carburmer
Libertad 1001, T073-332380.
Very good dinnersand pizza in a renovated colonial house.

$$$ La Tomasita
Tacna 853, T073-321957. Daily 0730-2300.
Very good *picantería* serving regional dishes including ceviche, *arroz con cabrito* (goat) and *seco de chavelo* (sun-dried meat), a/c.

$$$ Picantería La Santitos
In the same precinct as Carburmer.
Serves a wide range of traditional dishes for lunch.

$$ Alex Chopp's
Huancavelica 538, T073-322568. Daily 1200-2400.
A la carte dishes, seafood, fish, chicken and meats, beer.

$$ Capuccino
Tacna 786. Mon-Sat 1100-2300.
A la carte meals, plus a choice of coffees and sweets, pleasant ambience.

$$ Urius
Sánchez Cerro 210, T073-332581, www.uriusrestaurante.com. Daily 0700-1600.
Upmarket dining, regional and international dishes à la carte and a more economical menú. Part of a cooking school.

$$-$ Romano and El Otro Romano
Ayacucho 580, Mon-Sat 0730-2300 and Ayacucho 673, Tue-Sun 0900-1600.
Popular with locals, extensive menu, excellent set meal. Recommended.

$ Ganímedes
Apurímac 468-B. Mon-Sat 0730-2230, Sun 0900-2200.
A good vegetarian restaurant, very popular set lunch, à la carte is slow but well worth it, also pizza from 1800 and bakery with a wide selection of bread and sweet and savoury pastries.

Cafés and snack bars

D'Pauli
Lima 541. Mon-Sat 0900-1400, 1600-2130.
Sweets, cakes and sandwiches.

El Chalán
Several branches including Tacna 520 on Plaza de Armas, Grau 173, Grau 452 and others.
Sandwiches, sweets, fruit salad and very good ice cream,

Juguería La Floresta
Cusco 965. Mon-Sat 0900-1400, 1700-2100.
A selection of fresh fruit juices and natural food products.

La Pera Madura
Arequipa 168, next to Teatro Municipal, no sign. Daily 1700-2300.
For turkey sandwiches, tamales and other local specialities.

Catacaos
Among the town's *chicha picanterías*, **Chayo**, Jr San Francisco 497, is very good.

What to do

City tours, visits to craft towns, beaches, adventure sports (including surfing and sandboarding) and nature tours in the Piura highlands and desert are all available.

Piura

Canechi Tours, *C Tacna 349, p2, T073-311327, www.canechitours.com.*
Dry Forest Expeditions, *Jr Huancavelica 878, p2, T073-618391, www.dryforest expeditions.com.*
Piura Tours, *C Arequipa 978, T073-326778, piuratours@speedy.com.pe.* The manager Mario speaks good English.

Piura
Air
Capitán Guillermo Concha airport is in Castilla, 10 mins from the centre by taxi (US$1.80-2.50). It has gift shops and car rental agencies (see below). 8 daily flights to **Lima** with **Avianca/TACA** (Centro Comercial Real Plaza), **LAN** (Centro Comercial Open Plaza) or **Peruvian Airlines** (Libertad 777).

Bus
Local Colectivos have their stops near the Piura stations; they leave as they fill up. To **Catacaos**, colectivos from Jr Loreto 1292, 1 block from Ovalo Bolognesi, US$0.90, 20 min. To **Paita**, Trans Dora (T968-158086) from Prolongación Sánchez Cerro, next to Club de Tiro, every 20 mins, 1 hr, US$1.50; also from **Terminal Gechisa** (Prolongación Sánchez Cerro, opposite Proyecto Chira, T073-399322) and colectivos from Av Loreto block 12, by Jr Tumbes. Transfer in Paita for **Colán** and **Yacila**. To **Chulucanas**, Trans Dora from Prolongación Sánchez Cerro, next to **Club de Tiro**, every 30 mins, US$1.15, 45 mins; also from **Terminal El Bosque** in Castilla. To **Huancabamba**, with **San Pedro y San Pablo** (T073-349271), from **Terminal El Bosque**, Castilla, at 0730, 1330, 1830, 6 hrs; also **Civa** (T073-397991) from same terminal at 1030, 1800; and Turismo Express Norte (073-344330) from **Terminal Castilla**, at 0730, 1400, 1830.

Long distance Most long-distance bus companies are clustered along Av Sánchez Cerro, blocks 11-13, and Av Loreto, blocks 11-14; the latter is in a more pleasant area and closer to the centre. Some regional services run from **Terminal Gechisa**, Prolongación Sánchez Cerro (the road to Sullana), west of the city.

To **Lima**, 973 km, 14-15½ hrs, US$30-48. Most buses stop at the major cities on route: **Cruz del Sur** (Av Circunvalación 160, T073-337094); **Oltursa** (Bolognesi 801, T073-326666); **ITTSA** (Sánchez Cerro 1142, T073-333982); **Tepsa** (Loreto 1195, T073-306345); **Flores** (Av Loreto cuadra 12), 8 daily; several others.

To **Chiclayo** and **Lambayeque**, 209 km, 4 hrs, from US$5.50, with **Trans Chiclayo** (Sánchez Cerro 1121, T073-308455), every 30 min; **Línea** (Sánchez Cerro 1215, T073-303894, www.linea.pe), hourly; several others. To **Trujillo**, 7 hrs, 420 km, US$12.50-15, **Línea** at 1330 and 2300; to travel by day **ITTSA** at 0900 or change in Chiclayo; several others in the afternoon and around 2300.

To **Sullana**, 38 km, 30 mins, US$0.50, frequent service from **Terminal Gechisa** 0500-2200. To **Ayabaca**, 6 hrs, with **Transporte Vegas** (Panamericana C1 Lt10, Urb San Ramón, T073-308729) at 0730, 0830 and 1400, or **El Poderoso Cautivo** (Sullana Norte 7, Urb San Ramón, T073-309888) at 0730, 0840 and 1500.

To **Tumbes**, 282 km, 4½ hrs, US$7-8.50, **El Dorado** (Sánchez Cerro 1119, T073-325875), every 1-2 hrs; several others originating in cities to the south eg **Cruz del Sur**, **Cial** (Bolognesi 817, T073-304250), **CIVA** (Av Loreto 1401, T073-345451) and **Emtrafesa** (Los Naranjos 255, T073-337093, also to Chiclayo

and Trujillo); also colectivos, US$12. To **Máncora**, 187 km, US$5.50, 3 hrs, with **Eppo** (Av Panamericana 243, behind CC Real Plaza, T073-304543, www.eppo.com.pe), every 30 mins; or buses to Tumbes or Ecuador; colectivos from Terminal Gechisa, US$11. To **Cajamarca**, 467 km, US$18, 10 hrs, at 1900 with **Dias** (Av Loreto 1485, T073-302834, www.turdias.com), also to **Lima** at 1500.

To Ecuador To **Guayaquil** via Tumbes, US$15-20, 9 hrs, with **CIFA**, from the same terminal as **Dias** (Av Loreto 1485, T073-324144), at 0720, 1950, 2100, 2330; also **Super Semeria** (from the same terminal), at 2200, and **CIVA,** from Av Loreto 140, at 2040. To **Loja** via Macará, with **Transportes Loja,** from the same terminal as Ronco (Av Loreto 1241, T073-33260), at 0900 and 2100, US$15, 8-9 hrs; or with **Unión Cariamanga**, from Dias terminal, at 2000. To **Cuenca**, US$16, 10 hrs, with **Azuay**, from Ronco terminal, T962-647002), at 2100; or **Super Semeria**, from Dias terminal, at 2030.

Car hire
Ramos, T073-348668, www.ramos rentacars.com and **Vicus**, T073-342051, both outside the airport, several others.

Huancabamba and Las Huaringas
Ignacio León, who owns a bodega opposite **Hotel El Dorado** in Huancabamba, runs an early pick-up service to the outlying villages and takes trips at negotiable prices.

beach resorts and nature reserves en route to the border

Sullana and beyond

The Pan-American Highway forks at Sullana, 38 km north of Piura. Built on a bluff over the fertile Chira valley, the city is neither clean nor safe, so there is no reason to stop here. To the east the Panamericana crosses the Peru–Ecuador border at La Tina (see box, page 178) and continues via Macará to Loja and Cuenca. The excellent paved road is very scenic and is the best option if you want to visit the southern or central highlands of Ecuador.

The second branch of the Pan-American Highway is the coastal road which goes from Sullana northwest towards the oilfields around Talara, and then follows the coastline to Máncora and Tumbes. This is the more frequently used route to Ecuador. There is good surfing in the area, especially near **Negritos** to the south, where a gentle beach break and rolling thunder are separated by **Punta Balcones**, the westernmost point of South America. The impressive sea lion colony and the occasional dolphin make this an interesting spot.

> **Tip...**
> If you are driving from Piura to the border at La Tina, you can take a shortcut from Piura to Tambo Grande, bypassing Sullana along a paved road opened in 2014.

Ayabaca and around

Heading northeast from Sullana on the road to La Tina, there is a turn off after 100 km towards the pleasant highland town of **Ayabaca** (www.muniayabaca. gob.pe). The town is some 182 km northeast of Sullana at 2710 m. The plaza is dominated by the large church of **El Señor Cautivo de Ayabaca** (the captured Christ on his way to crucifixion). Many devotees make pilgrimages to his shrine, which is the most famous in northern Peru, especially on 12 October.

Northeast of Ayabaca is the 1200-ha **Bosque de Cuyas Nature Reserve** ⓘ *Information from Naturaleza y Cultura Internacional, Sullana, T073-502431, www. naturalezaycultura.org; contact Angel Seminario in Ayabaca, T073-471108*, which protects a remnant of cloudforest. One hundred and twenty-one species of bird have been identified here. Access is along a road north starting at **Los Cocos**, 5 km from Ayabaca on the road to Espíndola.

A rough road goes via Yanchalá (34 km), Samanguilla (49 km), and El Toldo (57 km) to Espíndola by the border with Ecuador. (There are no border facilities at Espíndola at the time of writing.) From Yanchalá there is access along a poor road (impassable in the rainy season) to **Aypate**, an impressive archaeological site on a mountain top. The important Inca settlement covered over 100 hectares, only two of which have been cleared. The *usnu* (platform) and temple of the sun are especially beautiful, and a mirador gives wonderful views. Pickups from Ayabaca charge US$45 return with several hours' wait. (It's a 20-minute walk from the end of the vehicle road to the ruins.) Alternatively, you can walk from Yanchalá in three hours or from Hualcuy in five hours (enquire about safety before setting out).

BORDER CROSSING
Peru–Ecuador

La Tina–Macará
The border crossing is problem-free and both sides are open 24 hours. Immigration, customs and other services are on either side of the international bridge. There are no money changers or ATMs right at the bridge, only at the park on the Ecuadorean side where vehicles leave for the border. On the Peruvian side, there is one *hospedaje* and several eating places on the road down to the bridge. Pickups charge US$0.50 per person, or US$1.50 for the whole vehicle from the bridge to Macará on the Ecuadorean side (2.5 km), a small city with all services.

There is no lodging at Aypate but the caretakers may offer basic hospitality or you can camp. Take food, water and warm clothing. Further east, near Samanguilla and El Toldo are the **Samanga** petroglyphs.

★ Talara to Máncora

From Talara, the Panamericana goes a few kilometres inland and leads north to Máncora. Closer to the shore, the old Panamericana gives access to lovely beaches and fishing towns that are a peaceful alternative to Máncora. Some 15 km from Talara is **Lobitos**, where high winds are excellent for surfing and kite-surfing. A further 16 km north is the small port of **Cabo Blanco**, accessed from El Alto, at Km 1137 on the main road. Its famous for its excellent sea-fishing and surfing (tubular waves suited to experts). There are several basic hotels, but the scenery has unfortunately been spoilt by numerous oil installations. The film of Ernest Hemingway's *The Old Man and the Sea* was shot here. Nearby, **Caleta El Ñuro** (Km 1140, 23 km from Máncora) is a small fishing village with a nice beach where a group of resident sea turtles are attracted by the fish scraps. You can swim with them for US$1.80. **Los Organos** ⓘ *www.losorganos.com, 13 km from Máncora*, is a small town and fishing port with a fine long sandy beach (Punta Veleros) and easy surfing at its southern end. There are lodgings in town and at the beach, banks and ATMs. **Vichayito**, 7 km south of Máncora, is accessed from Km 1150 or from Las Pocitas and is a lovely beach well suited to swimming, kite-surfing (April to November) and diving. It has a spa and a number of hotels and restaurants and more are being built. Separated by a headland from Vichayito is **Las Pocitas**, a stretch of beautiful beach with rocks, behind which little pools (or *pocitas*) form at low tide. It is another alternative to Máncora, just 4 km away, for those looking for tranquillity.

Máncora

Máncora, a resort stretching along the Pan-American Highway, is popular with young Limeños, Chileans and Argentines and also as a stop-off for travellers, especially surfers, on the Peru–Ecuador route. Development here has been rapid and haphazard. The resort is crowded and noisy during the December-February high season; beaches can get dirty; drugs and scams (many involving mototaxis) abound, and safety is a concern. Enquire locally about which sections of Máncora are currently safe. There is one bank and various ATMs in Máncora.

Just north of Máncora, a road goes inland following Quebrada Fernández to Parque Nacional Cerros de Amotape (see page 180), 25 km to the east. Along this route, 15 minutes from Máncora, is **Fundo La Caprichosa** (www.ecofundola caprichosa.com), which has a lodge ($$), swimming pools and four zip lines.

Punta Sal to Tumbes

At Km 1187, 22 km north of Máncora, is the turn-off for **Punta Sal**, marked by a large white arch (El Arco) over the road (2 km). Punta Sal boasts a 3-km-long white sandy beach and a more upmarket clientèle than Máncora, with accommodation (and prices) to match. There is no town centre and no banks, ATMs or restaurants independent of hotels, so it is very quiet in the low season.

Zorritos, 62 km north of Punta Sal and 27 km south of Tumbes, is an important fishing centre with a good beach. At **Caleta La Cruz**, 16 km southwest of Tumbes, is the only part of the Peruvian coast where the sea is warm all year. It was here that Pizarro landed in 1532. There are regular colectivos, US$0.30 each way, from Tumbes.

Tumbes → *Colour map 1, A2.*

The most northerly Peruvian city is Tumbes, 265 km north of Piura. Few tourists stop here since international buses take you directly north to Ecuador or south to the beaches or Piura. It does, however, provide access to important natural areas, which, due to the latitude, are rich in fauna and flora found nowhere else in Peru. There are four national protected areas, administered by **Sernanp** ⓘ *Panamericana Norte 1739, Tumbes, T072-526489; Los Cocos H-23, Urb Club Grau, Piura, T072-321668*, one along the shore and three inland; the latter combine to form the Reserva de Biósfera del Noroeste. The best time to visit the parks is the dry season, April to December.

The most striking aspect of the town itself is its bright and cheery modern public buildings: the **Malecón Benavides**, a long promenade beside the Tumbes river, has rainbow-coloured archways and a monstrous statue called El Beso (the Kiss); the Plaza de Armas sports a large structure of many colours, and even the **cathedral**, built in 1903 and restored in 1985, has green and pink stripes. Calles Bolívar and San Martín (Paseo de la Concordia) make for a pleasant wander, and there is a small artisans' market at the top end of San Martín (approaching Plaza Bolognesi). On Calle Grau, there are the tumble-down colonial houses, many of which are no longer in use.

> **Tip...**
> There is an **Ecuadorean Consulate** in Tumbes at Bolívar 129, p 3, Plaza de Armas, T072-525949, consultum@ speedy.com.pe, Mon-Fri 0800-1300.

★Santuario Nacional Los Manglares de Tumbes

Access from the town of Zarumilla (22 km north of Tumbes and 4 km southwest of Aguas Verdes), snmanglaresdetumbes@sernanp.gob.pe, entry US$3.50.

This Ramsar site protects 3000 ha of Peru's remaining 4750 ha of mangrove forest between the border with Ecuador in the north and the Estero Zarumilla in the south. From Zarumilla it is about 7 km to either the El Algarrobal Interpretation Centre or to Puerto 25. Mangroves are very rich ecosystems, supporting fish, crustaceans and birdlife. There are five species of mangrove, the main one being the red mangrove on whose roots edible conchas negras shellfish live. Some 148 bird species have been recorded, eight of which are resident, including the mangrove eagle. The mangroves are threatened by flooding during extreme rainy periods upriver and also by the expanding shrimp-farming industry. In the buffer zone by Puerto 25, two local associations, **Nueva Esperanza** ⓘ *T972-621223*, and **San Pedro** ⓘ *T972-981497*, offer basic lodging, meals based on products extracted from the mangrove and boat tours. There is also a short self-guided trail in the buffer zone, El Oscuro.

South of the reserve is Puerto Pizarro (13 km from Tumbes), a small fishing village near the mouth of the Río Tumbes, where boat trips can be arranged. Worth visiting is the **FONDEPES crocodile-breeding centre** ⓘ *www.fondepes. gob.pe*, a programme to protect the cocodrilo de Tumbes or American crocodile (Crocodylus Acutus), the largest on the continent and a UN red-data species.

> Tip...
> The mangroves can be visited any time of the year, but the dry season is best. To have the complete experience, stay long enough to visit the mangrove at both high and low tide. Be sure to take repellent.

★Reserva de Biósfera del Noroeste

Parque Nacional Cerros de Amotape ⓘ *pncerrosdeamotape@sernanp.gob.pe*. The national park protects 151,500 ha of Pacific tropical forest and, principally, the best preserved area of dry equatorial forest (a habitat rich in endemic species), shared with neighbouring southern Ecuador. It is located inland near the Ecuador border south of Tumbes and north of Sullana between 120 m and 1538 m altitude. There are six access points, one from the south, one from Máncora via Fernández and the others from Tumbes. Rica Playa (45 km from Tumbes or 40 km from Zorritos) is the most frequently used access point leading to trails and the dock on the Río Tumbes. At El Caucho, 51 km from Tumbes is a research station with displays about the flora and fauna of the park.

Over 1000 vegetable species have been identified here, most representative are the large ceibo (kapok) at higher elevations and the algarrobo (carob) lower down. The dry forest is often barren, but as soon as it rains, it turns green and vines cover everything, making it almost impenetrable. Over 200 species of bird have been identified here, including 14 endangered species.

Reserva Nacional Tumbes ⓘ *rntumbes@sernanp.gob.pe.* This 19,300-ha reserve lies southeast of Tumbes between the Ecuadorean border and Parque Nacional Cerros de Amotape and is accessed through the national park. It protects a transition area between the dry equatorial Forest and the Pacific tropical forest between 145 and 1200 m. The endangered *cocodrilo de Tumbes* (see Puerto Pizarro, above) is found along the Río Tumbes and is emblematic of this reserve. There are also 137 species of bird, including 33 endemics, and 20 species of mammals, including the howler monkey.

Coto de Caza El Angolo ⓘ *Club de Caza, Pesca y Turismo Piura, T073-333190, ccelangolo@sernanp.gob.pe.* Abutting Parque Nacional Cerros de Amotape to the southwest is this 65,000-ha game preserve (the only one in Peru), which shares the habitats and richness of the other reserves in this region. At Sauce Grande to the south is the only lodge in this area, administered by the Club de Caza. White-tailed deer are hunted May to November.

Listings North to Ecuador

Tourist information

Máncora

iPerú
*Av Piura 250, Thu-Sun 1000-1700.
See also www.vivamancora.com.*

Tumbes

iPerú
*Malecón III Milenio, p3, T072-506721,
Mon-Sat 0900-1800, Sun 0900-1300,
iperutumbes@promperu.gob.pe.*

Where to stay

Ayabaca

There are several simple places to eat and sleep.

$ Hotel Samanga
*On the plaza, T073-471049,
ssbc2@hotmail.com.*
A good choice.

Talara to Máncora

There are over 40 hotels in the area around Las Pocitas and Vichayito, south of Máncora. Most are more upmarket than those in town.

$$$$ Arennas
*Antigua Panamericana Norte, Km 1213,
T073-258240, www.arennasmancora.com.*
Smart, luxury pool or beachfront suites, all modern facilities, with central bar and restaurant serving imaginative dishes, beautiful pool, palm-lined beach frontage, very romantic.

$$$ Las Pocitas
*Antigua Panamericana Norte,
Km 1215, T998-139711, www.
laspocitasmancora.com.*
Great location, rooms with ocean views, lovely palm-lined beach, terrace, pool, restaurant and bar.

$$$ Máncora Beach Bungalows
*Antigua Panamericana Norte,
Km 1215, Lima T01-201 2060,
www.mancora-beach.com.*

Comfortable rooms with ceiling fan, terrace and hammocks, good restaurant, good value for this price range.

$$$ Puerto Palos
Antigua Panamericana Norte, 2 km south of Máncora (10 mins by mototaxi, US$2), T073-258199, www.puertopalos.com.
Variety of rooms, fan, suites have a/c. Excellent, nice pool overlooking ocean, hammocks, sunbeds, umbrellas, good restaurant. Friendly and hospitable.

$$ Marcilia Beach Bungalows
Antigua Panamericana Norte, Km 1212, T994-685209, www.marciliadevichayito.com.
Nice rustic bamboo cabins with ocean views, includes breakfast, family run.

Máncora
There are at least 50 hotels in and around Máncora, heavily booked in high season (Dec-Mar) when prices can increase by 100% or more. Many hotels have even higher rates for Christmas, New Year, Easter and Independence Day holidays when the resort is full to bursting.

The main strip of the Panamericana is known as Av Piura from the bridge for the first couple of blocks, then Av Grau to the end of town. The better hotels are at the southern end of town, with a small concentration of mid-range hotels just over the bridge. Hotels to the left look onto the beach directly in front of the best surf and often have beach entrances as well as road entrances. They are the most popular with tourists and are all noisy at night from nearby discos, which last until around 0200 Mon-Thu and 0600 Fri-Sun.

When checking into any hotel, expect to pay up front and make sure you get a receipt or you are likely to be asked to pay again the next time the receptionist sees you. Take every precaution with your valuables, theft is common. Mosquitoes are bad at certain times of the year, so take plenty of bug spray.

Máncora town

$$$ Don Giovanni
Pje 8 de Noviembre s/n, T073-258525, www.dongiovannimancora.com.
3-storey Indonesian-style beachfront hotel, includes breakfast, restaurant and ice cream parlour, kitesurfing classes available.

$$ Del Wawa
Beachfront, T073-258427, www.delwawa.com.
This relaxed and spacious Spanish-owned hotel is popular with serious surfers and kitesurfers. Hotel service poor, rooms noisy, food average, but great location and nice restaurants round the corner.

$$ Kon Tiki
Los Incas 200, T073-258138, www.kontikimancora.net.
On hill with lighhouse, great views, cabins with thatched roofs, hammocks, kitchen facilities, bar. Transport to/from bus station provided. Advance booking required.

$$ Las Olas
Beachfront, T073-258099, www.lasolasmancora.com.
Smart, cabin-style rooms, top floor rooms have best view of ocean, hammocks and gardens, includes breakfast.

$$ Punta Ballenas Inn
Km 1164, south of Cabo Blanco bridge at the south entrance to town, T072-630844, www.puntaballenas.com.

Lovely setting on beach, garden with small pool, expensive restaurant.

$$-$ Kokopelli Beachpackers
Av Piura 209, T073-258091,
www.hostelkokopelli.com.
Popular hostel 3 mins' walk from beach, with pool, bar, good food, good meeting place, lots of facilities. Rooms for 2, 4 or 8, mixed or female only, all with bath, hot water.

$$-$ Laguna Surf Camp
T01-99 401 5628, www.vivamancora.
com/lagunacamp.
50 m from the sea, thatched roofs, cabins sleeping up to 6 people (US$11 pp), also cabins around small communal area with hammocks, pool and restaurant. Good surf lessons, helpful staff.

$$-$ Loki del Mar
Av Piura 262, T073-258484,
www.lokihostel.com.
In the Loki group of hostels, seafront, bright white and modern muti-storey building, doubles with private bath or dorms with 4-6 beds and lockable closets, bar, restaurant, pool, lots of activities. Be ready for loud music and parties. Advance booking required.

$ Casa del Turista
Av Piura 224, T073-258126.
Family-run, TV, roof terraces giving sea views, good value and location. Recommended.

Quebrada Cabo Blanco
Crossing the bridge into Máncora, a dirt track leads downhill to the right, to the Quebrada Cabo Blanco, signed to La Posada Youth Hostel. The many hotels at the end of the track are badly lit for guests returning at night (robberies have occurred) but are relatively quiet and relaxing.

$$ Kimbas Bungalows
T073-258373, www.kimbas
bungalowsmancora.com.
Relaxed spot with charming thatched bungalows, Balinese influences, nice garden with hammocks, pool, some rooms have hot water, good value. Recommended.

$$ La Posada
T073-258328, http://hostellaposada.com.
IYHF affiliated hostel, dorms (US$20 pp), camping (US$12 pp) and rooms with private bath, fan, garden with hammocks, pool, cooking facilities, parking,

Punta Sal to Tumbes
There is a huge resort of the Colombian Royal Decameron group in Punta Sal, www.decameron.com.

$$$$ Punta Sal
Panamericana Norte, Km 1192,
Punta Sal Chica, T072-596700/540088,
www.puntasal.com.pe.
A beautiful complex of bungalows along a fine sandy beach, with pool, bar decorated with photos of big game fishing, fine restaurant. Most deals are all-inclusive, but massages and whale-watching trips are extra. Good food and service.

$$$-$ Waltako Beach Town
Panamericana 1199, Canoas de Punta Sal,
T998-141976, www.waltakoperu.com.
Thatched cabins for 2, 4 or 6 people, with kitchenette, porch and hammock. Camping on the beach if you bring your own tent. Restaurant and bar, bicycles, quad bikes and horses for hire. Volunteers welcomed for conservation and reforestation work.

$$ Hospedaje El Bucanero
At the entrance to Playa Punta Sal,
set back from the beach, T072-540118,
www.elbucaneropuntasal.com.

The most happening place in Punta Sal, popular with travellers, rates rise in high season, a variety of rooms, pool, restaurant, bar and gardens.

$$ Huá
On the beach at the entrance to Playa Punta Sal, T072-540023, www.hua-puntasal.com.
A rustic old wooden building, pleasant terrace overlooking ocean, hammocks, quiet, restful, good food, friendly service.

$$-$ Las Terrazas
Opposite Sunset Punta Sal, T072-507701.
One of the more basic and cheaper hotels in Punta Sal in operation since 1989, restaurant has sea view, some rooms better than others, those with own bath and sea view twice the price. Helpful owners.

$ Hostal Grillo Tres Puntas
Panamericana Norte, Km 1235, Zorritos, T072-794830, www.casagrillo.net.
On the beach, rustic bamboo cabins, quiet and peaceful. Great food prepared by Spanish chef-owner, León, who breeds Peruvian hairless dogs. Lukewarm showers, Wi-Fi in dining area, camping possible on the beach.

$ Hospedaje Orillas del Mar
San Martín 496, Cancas.
A short walk from Punta Sal Chica beaches, this is the best of the basic *hostales* lining the beach and Panamericana.

Tumbes
Note that Av Tumbes is still sometimes referred to by its old name of Teniente Vásquez. At holiday times it can be very difficult to find a room.

$$$ Costa del Sol
San Martín 275, Plazuela Bolognesi, T072-523991, www.costadelsolperu.com.
The only high-class hotel in town, minibars, a/c, good restaurant, garden, pool, excellent service. Parking for an extra fee. Rooms which look onto the Plaza Bolognesi are noisy.

$$ Lourdes
Mayor Bodero 118, 3 blocks from main plaza, T072-522966.
Welcoming place. Narrow corridor leading to cell-like rooms which are plushly decorated with a mixture of antique and modern furniture. Good bathrooms, fans in each room.

$$-$ Asturias
Av Mcal Castilla 307, T072-522569.
Comfortable, hot water, a/c or fan, restaurant, bar and laundry. Accepts credit cards.

$ Hostal Tumbes
Filipinas s/n, off Grau, T072-522203, or T972-852954.
Small, dark, basic but cleanish rooms with fans and bath. Good cheap option.

Restaurants

Máncora
Máncora is packed with restaurants: plenty of sushi, pizza and grills. Most are pricey; the cheaper places are north along Av Piura.

$$$ Pizzería Mamíferos
Av Piura 346. Tue-Sun 1800-2300.
Wood-fired pizzas and lasagne.

$$$-$$ Josil
Av Piura, near The Birdhouse. Closed Sun.
Very good Sushi bar.

$$$-$$ Tao
Av Piura. Closed Wed.
Good Asian food and curries.

$$ Angela's Place/Cafetería de Angela
*Av Piura 396, www.vivamancora.com/
deangela. Daily 0800-2300.*
A great option for a healthy breakfast or
lunch and heaven for vegetarians and
whole-food lovers: home-made bread,
yoghurts, fresh fruit, etc.

$$ Don César
*Hard to find, ask around or take a
mototaxi. Closed Sun.*
Good fresh seafood, very popular
with locals.

$ The Birdhouse
Av Piura.
This small open-air commercial centre
incorporates **Green Eggs and Ham**,
open daily 0730-1300 for great breakfasts
(US$3.35), including waffles, pancakes
or eggs and bacon, plus juice or coffee.
Directly underneath is **Papa Mo's** milk
bar, with comfy seats next to the sand
and a selection of drinks.

$ Café La Bajadita
Av Piura.
Has an impressive selection of delicious
home-made desserts and cakes.

Tumbes
There are cheap restaurants on the Plaza
de Armas, Paseo de la Concordia and
near the markets.

$$-$ Budabar
*Grau 309, on Plaza de Armas,
T072-525493.*
One of a kind chill-out lounge offering
traditional food and comfy seating with
outdoor tables and cheap beer, popular
in the evenings.

$$-$ Chifa Wakay
Huáscar 413. Open evenings only.
A large, well-ventilated smart restaurant
offering the usual Chifa favourites.

$$-$ Classic
Tumbes 185.
Look for it almost under the bridge
over the river, heading south. Popular
for local food.

$$-$ Los Gustitos
Bolívar 148.
Excellent menús and à la carte. Popular,
good atmosphere at lunchtime.

$ Cherry
*San Martín 116. Open 0800-1400,
1700-2300.*
Tiny café offering an amazing selection
of cakes and desserts, also fresh juices,
shakes, sandwiches, hot and cold drinks
and traditional *cremoladas* (fruit juice
with crushed ice).

$ Sí Señor
Bolívar 119 on the plaza.
Good for snacks, cheap lunch menus.

What to do

Máncora
Surfing on this coast is best Nov-Mar;
boards and suits can be hired from
several places on Av Piura, US$10 per
day. Many agencies on Av Piura offer day
trips to Manglares de Tumbes, as well as
private transport in cars and vans.
Iguanas Trips, *Av Piura 306, T073-632762,
www.iguanastrips.com.* Run by Ursula
Behr, offers a variety of adventure tourism
trips, horseriding and camping in the
nearby national parks and reserve zones.
Samana Chakra, *in the eponymous hotel,
T073-258604, www.samanachakra.com.*
Yoga classes, US$5 per hr.

Surf Point Máncora, *on the beach next to Hostal del Wawa.* Surf lessons US$17.50 per hr, kitesurfing (season Mar-Sep) US$50 per hr. Surfboard, body-board and paddle-board rentals.

Transport

Sullana
Bus
Several bus companies including **Ormeño** share a Terminal Terrestre outside the centre. It's best to take a taxi or mototaxi to and from the terminal. To **Tumbes**, 244 km, 4-5 hrs, US$8, several buses daily. To **Chiclayo** and **Trujillo** (see under Piura). To **Lima**, 1076 km, 14-16 hrs, several buses daily, most coming from Tumbes, luxury overnight via Trujillo with **Ittsa** (T073-503705), also with **Ormeño** and **Tepsa** (José de Lama 236, T073-502120). To **Máncora**, **Eppo**, frequent, 2½ hrs, US$4.50.

To the international bridge at **La Tina** (see box, page 178), shared taxis leave when full from the Terminal Terrestre La Capullana, off Av Buenos Aires, several blocks beyond the canal, US$5.40 pp, 1¾ hrs. Once on the Ecuador side, buses leave frequently from Macará for Loja, so even if you are not taking the through bus (see Piura, page 169), you can still go from Sullana to Loja in a day.

Ayabaca
There is transport to/from **Piura**, 6 hrs, with **Transporte Vegas** (T073-308729) and **El Poderoso Cautivo** (T073-309888). To reach **Aypate**, take a shared taxi from Prado y Bolognesi near the Ayabaca market to Yanchalá or Hualcuy, from where it's a 3- or 5-hr walk respectively.

Máncora
Bus
To **Sullana** with **Eppo**, every 30 mins, 0400-1830, US$4.50, 2½ hrs; to **Piura**, US$5.50, 3 hrs; also colectivos to **Piura**, 2 hrs, US$11. To **Tumbes** (and points in between), minibuses leave when full, US$5.50, 1½ hrs. Several companies to **Lima**, US$28-70, 18 hrs. To **Chiclayo**, **Tran Chiclayo**, US$17.50, 6 hrs. To **Trujillo**, US$25, 9 hrs.

To Ecuador To **Machala** (US$14, 5 hrs) and **Guayaquil** (US$17.50, 8 hrs), with **CIFA** and **Super Semería** at 0800, 1100 and 1300; Guayaquil direct at 2300 and 2330; several others, see Piura Transport. To **Cuenca**, **Super Semería** at 2300, US$20; or **Azuay** at 2330.

Punta Sal
Taking a taxi from Máncora to Punta Sal is the safest option, 20 mins, US$14; mototaxi 40 mins, US$10.

Tumbes
Air
Daily flights to and from **Lima** with **LAN** (Bolognesi 250).

Bus
Daily to and from **Lima**, 1320 km, 18-20 hrs, depending on stopovers, US$34-45 regular fare, or US$60 with **Cruz del Sur VIP** (Tumbes Norte 319, T072-896163). **Civa** (Av Tumbes 518, T072-525120) has several buses daily. Cheaper buses usually leave 1600-2100, more expensive ones 1200-1400. Except for the luxury service, most buses to Lima stop at major cities en route. Tickets to anywhere between Tumbes and Lima sell quickly, so if arriving from Ecuador you may have to stay overnight.

BORDER CROSSING
Peru–Ecuador

Aguas Verdes–Huaquillas

The best way to cross this border is on one of the international buses that run between Piura, Máncora or Tumbes in Peru and Huaquillas, Machala, Guayaquil or Cuenca in Ecuador. If travelling from further south in Peru, do not take a bus all the way to the border; change to an Ecuador-bound bus in Piura, Máncora or Tumbes. Formalities are only carried out at the new bridge, far outside the border towns of Aguas Verdes (Peru) and Huaquillas (Ecuador). There are two border complexes called CEBAF (Centro Binacional de Atención Fronteriza), open 24 hours, on either side of the bridge. Both complexes have Peruvian and Ecuadorean immigration officers so you get your exit and entry stamps in the same place. If crossing with your own vehicle, however, you may have to stop at both border complexes for customs.

If you do not take one of the international buses then the crossing is hot and harrowing. Transport between the two sides via the new bridge and border complex is inconvenient and expensive: taxis charge US$2.50-5 from the bridge to Huaquillas across the border, and in the other direction, US$17 to Tumbes city or airport; US$50 to Punta Sal, and US$60 to Máncora. Travellers often fall victim to thefts, muggings, shakedowns by minor officials and countless scams on both sides. Never leave your baggage unattended and do your own arithmetic when changing money. Those seeking a more relaxed crossing to or from Ecuador should consider La Tina–Macará (page 178) or Namballe–Zumba (page 229).

Piura is a good place for connections in the daytime.

To **Sullana**, 244 km, 3-4 hrs, US$8, several buses daily. To **Piura**, 4-5 hrs, 282 km, US$7-8.50, with **El Dorado** (Piura 459, T072-523480) every 1-2 hrs; **Trans Chiclayo** (Tumbes 466, T072-525260) and **Cruz del Sur**. Colectivos **Tumbes/Piura** (Tumbes N 308, T072-525977) are a faster option, 3½ hrs, US$12 pp, leave when full. To **Chiclayo**, 552 km, 7-8 hrs, US$9, several each day with **Cruz del Sur**, **El Dorado** and others. To **Trujillo**, 769 km, 10-11 hrs, from US$15, with

Ormeño (Av Tumbes s/n, T072-522228), **Cruz del Sur**, **El Dorado**, **Emtrafesa** (Tumbes Norte 596, T072-522894).

To Ecuador CIFA (Av Tumbes 958) runs to **Machala**, US$4, and **Guayaquil**, 5 hrs, 4 a day, luxury bus at 1000, US$8.50. For other options, see Piura Transport. If you cannot cross on an international bus (the preferred option), then take a taxi from Tumbes to the international bridge beyond Aguas Verdes (see box, above), 17 km, US$12, and from there to **Huaquillas** across the border, US$2.50-5.

Northern Highlands

This vast area stretches from the western foothills of the Andes across the mountains and down to the fringes of the Amazon jungle. It contains spectacular pre-Columbian ruins, some of them built on a massive scale unequalled anywhere in the Americas.

A good road rises from the coast to the city of Cajamarca, where the Inca Atahualpa was captured by the Spanish. Despite the proximity of a huge gold mine, the city has a pleasant colonial centre, with comfortable hotels and good restaurants. Close by are the hot springs where Atahualpa used to bathe and a number of pre-Inca sites.

Beyond Cajamarca, an exceptionally tortuous road winds its way east to Chachapoyas. This is a pleasant, friendly little city at the centre of a region full of fantastic archaeological treasures whose mysteries are only just being uncovered. There are fortresses, enigmatic cities and strange burial sites; not to mention the spectacular 771-m Gocta waterfall and a muddy but beautiful trek to Laguna de los Cóndores.

From Chachapoyas there are three options: continue east on one of Peru's most beautiful roads to the tropical town of Tarapoto; return to the coast at Chiclayo, or head north to Ecuador via Jaén and San Ignacio.

Best for
Archaeology ▪ Birdwatching ▪ Trekking ▪ Waterfalls

Footprint
   picks

★ **Marca Huamachuco**, page 193

One of the top 10 archaeological sites in Peru, this is home to the oldest-known buildings to have more than two storeys.

★ **Los Baños del Inca**, page 197

Atahualpa tried the effect of these waters on a war wound and his bath is still there.

★ **Museo Leymebamba**, page 204

One of the finest archaeology museums in the country houses superb collections of mummies and *quipus*.

★ **Kuélap**, page 208

This spectacular pre-Inca walled city is said to contain three times more stone than the Great Pyramid at Giza in Egypt.

★ **Gocta**, page 212

This gorgeous 771-m waterfall surrounded by cloudforest may be the third highest in the world.

★ **Road to the jungle**, page 220

The ride from Chachapoyas to Yurimaguas via Moyobamba and Tarapoto is as spectacular as any in Peru.

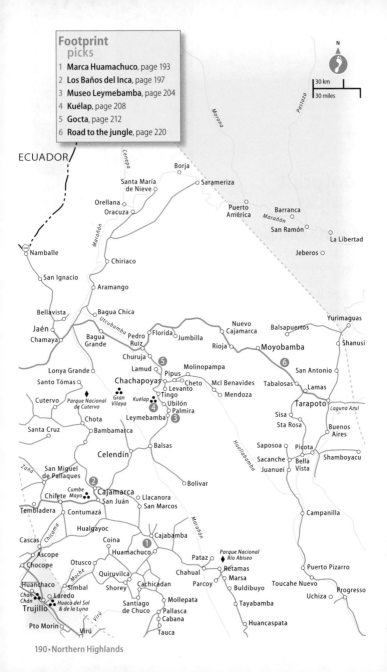

ECUADOR

30 km
30 miles

N

Borja
Santa María de Nieve
Sarameriza
Orellana
Oracuza
Puerto América
Barranca
Marañón
San Ramón
La Libertad
Jeberos

Namballe
Chiriaco
Cenepa
Morona
Pastaza

San Ignacio
Aramango
Marañón

Bellavista
Bagua Chica
Nuevo Cajamarca
Balsapuertos
Yurimaguas

Jaén
Bagua Grande
Pedro Ruíz
Florida
Jumbilla
Rioja
Moyobamba
Shanusi

Chamaya
Utcubamba
Churuja
Lamud
Molinopampa
San Antonio

Lonya Grande
Pipus
Chachapoyas
Cheto
Mcl Benavides
Tabalosas
Lamas

Santo Tomás
Gran Vilaya
Levanto
Tingo
Mendoza
Tarapoto
Laguna Azul

Cuervo
Parque Nacional de Cuervo
Kuélap
Ubilón
Palmira
Sisa

Chota
Leymebamba
Sta Rosa
Buenos Aires

Santa Cruz
Bambamarca
Huallabamba
Saposoa
Picota
Shamboyacu

Celendín
Balsas
Sacanche
Bella Vista

San Miguel de Pallaques
Juanueí

Cumbe Mayo
Cajamarca
San Juan
Bolívar

Chilete
Llacanora
San Marcos

Tembladera
Contumazá
Campanilla

Cascas
Chicama
Hualgayoc
Cajabamba
Marañón

Coina
Humachuco
Patáz
Parque Nacional Río Abiseo
Puerto Pizarro

Ascope
Otusco
Chahual
Retamas
Toucahe Nuevo

Chocope
Moche
Quiruvilca
Marsa
Progresso

Huanchaco
Simbal
Cachicadan
Parcoy
Buldibuyo
Uchiza

Chan Chan
Laredo
Shorey
Santiago de Chuco
Mollepata
Tayabamba

Huaca del Sol & de la Luna
Trujillo
Pallasca
Cabana
Huancaspata

Pto Morín
Virú
Virú
Tauca

Essential Northern Highlands

Getting around

Long-distance buses connect the major centres and crossroads, including Cajamarca, Celendín, Chachapoyas, Pedro Ruíz, Moyobamba, Tarapoto and Jaén. Cars and vans are also common (and useful) for reaching out-of-town destinations, especially in the Chachapoyas region and further east. The archaeological sites around Chachapoyas are spread over a large area, so the easiest way to visit them is on a tour. Some of the more remote sites can only be reached by trekking.

When to go

Cajamarca has a pleasant climate year round, with warm days and chilly nights. Carnival in Cajamarca can be particularly messy and violent, so it is not the best time for sightseeing around the city. Hotels are also likely to be fully booked at this time. More sedate festivals in the city include Easter and Corpus Christi in May. November to April is the wet season in the Northern Highlands when travel can be difficult, although the Chachapoyas area may be cloudy at any time of year. The climate becomes more tropical the further east you go.

Time required

One to three weeks, depending on how many areas you choose to visit.

Weather Cajamarca

January	February	March	April	May	June
21°C	21°C	21°C	20°C	21°C	21°C
7°C	7°C	7°C	7°C	5°C	3°C
140mm	60mm	140mm	130mm	40mm	10mm

July	August	September	October	November	December
21°C	22°C	22°C	22°C	22°C	22°C
3°C	3°C	5°C	7°C	6°C	6°C
9mm	9mm	10mm	40mm	60mm	40mm

Cajamarca
& around

To the northeast of Trujillo is Cajamarca, an attractive colonial town surrounded by lovely countryside. It was here in 1532 that Pizarro ambushed and captured Atahualpa, the Inca emperor. This was the first showdown between the Spanish and the Incas and, despite being greatly outnumbered, the Spanish emerged victorious. Only one Inca building remains in the city, the so-called Ransom Chamber, but the city has a pleasant colonial centre and some interesting archaeological sites nearby. Change has come fast to Cajamarca: the nearby Yanacocha gold mine (www.yanacocha.com.pe) has brought new wealth to the town but also major ecological disruption and social problems. The city is also the hub of tourism development for the whole *Circuito Turístico Nororiental*, which encompasses Chiclayo, Cajamarca and Chachapoyas.

don't miss the extensive ruins at Marca Huamachuco

The main route from the coast to Cajamarca is via Ciudad de Dios, a junction some 20 km north of Pacasmayo (see page 152) on the Panamericana. The 175-km paved road branches off the highway soon after it crosses the Río Jequetepeque. Terraced rice fields and mimosas may often be seen in bloom, brightening the otherwise dusty landscape.

A quicker route is on the old road (now paved) via Huamachuco and Cajabamba; it takes two hours from Huamachuco to Cajabamba and three hours from Cajabamba via San Marcos to Cajamarca (as opposed to nine hours via Ciudad de Dios). This road is also more interesting, passing over the bare *puna* before dropping to the Huamachuco valley.

Huamachuco → *Colour map 3, A2.*

This colonial town is located at 3180 m, 181 km from Trujillo. It was formerly on the royal Inca Road and has the largest main plaza in Peru, with fine topiary and a controversial modern **cathedral**. On Sundays there is a colourful **market**, with dancing in the plaza. **Museo Municipal Wamachuko** ⓘ *Sucre 195, Mon-Sat 0900-1300, 1500-1900, Sun 0900-1200, free,* displays artefacts found at nearby **Cerro Amaru** and **Marca Huamachuco** (see below). The extensive Huari ruins of **Wiracochapampa** are 3 km north of town (45 minutes' walk), but much of the site is overgrown.

★ Marca Huamachuco

Access along a poor road, off the road to Sanagorán, 5 km from Huamachuco (there is an archway at the turn-off). Daily 0900-1700; a minimum of 2 hrs is needed, or 4 hrs to really explore. US$1. Carry all food and drink with you. Mototaxi from Huamachuco to the turn-off, US$2, or combi to Sanagorán.

The Marca Huamachuco ruins surely rank among the top 10 archaeological sites in Peru. It is an extensive site, 3 km long, dating back to at least 300 BC though many structures were added later. Its most impressive features are: **El Castillo**, a remarkable circular structure with walls up to 8 m high located at the highest point of the site. This and other structures are the oldest-known buildings in Peru to extend to more than two storeys and may have reached five storeys. The outer defensive wall, which is accessible where it bisects the hill halfway along, also reaches up to 8 m in height. It consists of two parallel walls with gallery rooms in between. The **Convento** complex consists of five circular structures of varying sizes located towards the northern end of the hill. These are later constructions dating back to AD 600-800. The largest one has been partially reconstructed by the INC and provides an interesting insight into how they must once have appeared,

Tip...

In dry weather, 4WDs can make it to the top of the site, but it is generally much faster to walk on the mule trail that starts just after the archway.

with two or three parallel outer walls, gallery rooms between them and several other internal structures. It has been suggested that these buildings housed the privileged members of an elite class.

It seems likely that Marca Huamachuco existed for many centuries as the centre of an autonomous religious cult, separate from the activities of the Chachapoyans to the north and east. The site was certainly used as much as a ceremonial centre as it was for defensive purposes. Some theories suggest that the Huari-Tiahuanaco culture (AD 600-1100) may have developed from the north, out of places such as Marca Huamachuco and Yaino, and then spread south, rather than the other way round. Apparently, the chronology of the sites fits much better with this theory, but, if it's correct, it would require a complete reassessment of the Huari-Tiahuanuco culture.

Some 3 km before the ruins you will pass the remarkable **Cerro Amaru** on the left. It would seem that the whole of this relatively small hilltop was adapted to store water by placing an impermeable layer of clay around it. Wells on the summit (known as '**Los Chiles**') provided access to the water within; these can still be viewed. The hill almost certainly acquired major religious and cultural significance within the Huari-Tiahuanaco Empire and became a place of pilgrimage and sacrifice in times of drought.

Cajabamba

Cajabamba is a small market town and a useful stop-over point between Huamachuco and Cajamarca. A thermal bath complex, **La Grama**, is 30 minutes by combi (US$1) from Cajabamba, with a pool, very hot individual baths and an adjoining small *hostal*.

Listings Trujillo to Cajamarca

Where to stay

Huamachuco

$$ Real
Bolívar 250, T044-441402, www. hotelrealhuamachuco.com.
Modern, sauna, majority of fittings are wood, pleasant with good service.

$$ Santa María
Grau 224, T044-348334.
An enormous, sparsely furnished edifice offering the best-quality rooms in town, with restaurant.

$$-$ Hostal Santa Fe
San Martín 297, T044-441019, www.actiweb.es/luisnv83/.
Good value, hot water, parking, restaurant.

$ Hostal Huamachuco
Castilla 354, on the plaza, T044-440599.
With private or shared hot showers, small rooms but large common areas, good value, has parking.

Cajabamba

$ Hostal Flores
Leoncio Prado 137, Plaza de Armas, T076-551086.

With electric shower, cheaper without bath, clean but rooms are gloomy, nice patio; no breakfast.

Restaurants

Huamachuco

$$-$ Bull Grill
R Castilla 364.
Smart place specializing in meat dishes, with a cool bar at the back.

$ Café Somos
Bolognesi 665.
Good coffee, large turkey/ham sandwiches and excellent cakes.

$ Doña Emilia
Balta 384, on Plaza de Armas.
Good for breakfast and snacks.

$ El Viejo Molino
R Castilla 160.
Specializes in local cuisine, such as cuy.

Cajabamba

$ Cafetería La Otuscana
Grau 929. Daily 0730-2200.
Good bakery, sweets and sandwiches.

$ Don Lucho
Jr Leoncio Prado 227.
Good local trout and other à la carte dishes.

Festivals

Huamachuco

2nd wk Aug Founding of Huamachuco. Festival with spectacular fireworks and amazing, aggressive male dancers, called *turcos*.

Transport

Huamachuco
Bus
To/from **Trujillo**, 170 km, 5-6 hrs, US$9-15 (see page 135): the best service is **Fuentes** (J Balta 1090, Huamachuco, T044-441090 and Av R Palma 767, Trujillo, T044-204581); **Tunesa** (Suárez 721, T044-441157). To **Cajabamba**, with **Trans Los Andes** (Pje Hospital 109), 3 combis a day, 2 hrs, US$7.50.

Cajabamba
Bus
Several companies run buses and combis to **Cajamarca**, 127 km, US$7.50-8, 3 hrs.

Sights around Cajamarca → *Colour map 1, C3.*

follow in Atahualpa's fateful footsteps

Cajamarca is a beautiful colonial town and the most important in the northern highlands. It's also a great place to buy handicrafts, although nowadays you'll find soapstone carvings of miners with power drills alongside more traditional figures. Outside town are several good haciendas offering bed, board and rural pursuits, while at the Baños del Inca, just up the road, you can unwind as the steam from the thermal waters meets the cool mountain air.

City centre
The **Plaza de Armas**, where Atahualpa was executed, has a 350-year-old fountain, topiary and gardens. The **Cathedral** ⓘ *daily 0800-1000, 1600-1800*, opened in 1776 and is still missing its belfry, but the façade has beautiful baroque carving in stone.

On the opposite side of the plaza is the 17th-century church of **San Francisco** ⓘ *Mon-Fri 0900-1200, 1600-1800*, older than the Cathedral and with more interior stone carving and elaborate altars. The attached **Museo de Arte Colonial** ⓘ *Mon-Sat 1430-1800, US$1, entrance is behind the church on Amalia Puga y Belén*, is filled with colonial paintings and icons. The guided tour of the museum includes entry to the church's spooky catacombs.

The group of buildings known as **Complejo Belén** ⓘ *Tue-Sat 0900-1300, 1500-1800, Sun 0900-1300. US$5 (valid for more than 1 day and for the Cuarto de Rescate; see below), guided tour for all the sites, US$2.85-8.50,* comprises the tourist office and Institute of Culture, two museums and the beautifully ornate church of Belén, considered the city's finest. The arches, pillars and walls of the nave are covered in lozenges (rombos), a design picked out in the gold tracery of the altar. Look up to see the inside of the dome, where eight giant cherubs support an intricate flowering centrepiece. The carved pulpit has a spiral staircase and the doors are intricately worked in wood. In the same courtyard is the **Museo Médico Belén**, which has a collection of medical instruments. Across

Cajamarca

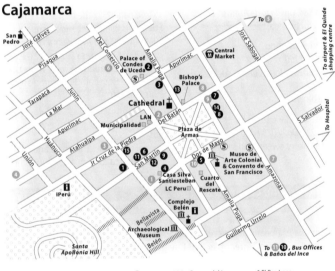

Where to stay	10 La Casona del Inca	6 El Pez Loco
1 Cajamarca	11 Los Balcones de	7 El Zarco
2 Costa del Sol	La Recoleta	8 Heladería Holanda
3 El Cabildo		9 Om-Gri
4 El Cumbe Inn	**Restaurants**	10 Pascana
5 El Ingenio	1 Bella's Café Lounge	11 Pizzería El Marengo
6 El Portal del Marqués	2 Casa Club	12 Pizzería Vaca Loca
7 Hosp Los Jazmines	3 Cascanuez	13 Querubino
8 Hostal Becerra	4 De Buena Laya	14 Salas
9 Hostal Perú	5 Don Paco	15 Sanguchón.com

the street on Junín and Belén is a maternity hospital from the colonial era, now the **Archaeological and Ethnological Museum**. It has a range of ceramics from all regions and civilizations of Peru.

To the east, the **Cuarto de Rescate (Ransom Chamber)** ⓘ *entrance at Amalia Puga 750, Tue-Sat 0900-1800, Sun 0900-1300*, is the room where Atahualpa was held prisoner. A red line on the wall is said to indicate where Atahualpa reached up and drew a mark, agreeing to have his subjects fill the room to that height, once with gold and twice with silver.

You can also visit the stone altar set high on **Santa Apolonia hill** ⓘ *US$0.60, take bus marked Santa Apolonia/Fonavi, or micro A*, from where Atahualpa is said to have surveyed his subjects. There is a road to the top, or you can walk up from Calle 2 de Mayo, using the steep stairway. The view is worth the effort, especially at sunrise (but go in a group).

Around the city centre are many fine old houses, with garden patios and elaborately carved doorways. Look out for the **Bishop's Palace**, across the street from the Cathedral; the **palace of the Condes de Uceda** ⓘ *Jr Apurímac 719 (now occupied by BCP bank, photography prohibited)*; and the **Casa Silva Santiesteban** ⓘ *Junín y 2 de Mayo*.

The Universidad Nacional de Cajamarca maintains an experimental arboretum and agricultural station, the **Museo Silvo-agropecuario** ⓘ *Km 2.5 on the road to Baños del Inca*, with a lovely mural at the entrance.

★Los Baños del Inca and around
6 km from Cajamarca, T076-348385, www.ctbinca.com.pe. Daily 0500-2000, entry US$0.70, baths US$1.75-2.10, sauna US$3.50, massage US$7. Combis marked Baños del Inca cost US$0.20, 15 mins; taxis US$2.30.

These sulphurous thermal springs are where Atahualpa bathed to try to cure a festering war wound; his bath is still there. The water temperature is at least 72° C, and the main baths are divided into five categories, all with private tubs and no pool (take your own towel; soaps are sold outside); many of the facilities are open to men- or women-only at certain times. Obey the instructions and only spend 20 minutes maximum in the water. The complex is renewed regularly, with gardens and various levels of accommodation (see Where to stay, below).

A nice 13-km walk downhill from the Baños del Inca will bring you **Llacanora** after two hours, a typical Andean village in beautiful scenery.

Alternatively, head north from the *baños* to the **Ventanillas de Otusco** ⓘ *8 km from Cajamarca, daily 0800-1800, US$1.10, combi US$0.20*, part of an old pre-Inca cemetery that has a deteriorating gallery of secondary burial niches. There are good day walks in this area and local sketch maps are available.

From Otusco, a road leads 20 km to **Ventanillas de Combayo** ⓘ *occasional combis on Mon-Sat; more transport on Sun when a market is held nearby, 1 hr*. These burial niches are more numerous and spectacular than those at Otusco, being located in an isolated, mountainous area and distributed over the face of a steep, 200-m-high hillside.

Cumbe Mayo

Cumbe Mayo, 20 km southwest of Cajamarca, is famous for its extraordinary, well-engineered pre-Inca channels, running for 9 km across the mountain tops at 3600 m. This hydraulic irrigation system is said to be the oldest man-made construction in South America. The sheer scale of the scene is impressive, backed by the huge rock formations known as Los Frailones ('big monks') and others. On the way to Cumbe Mayo is the Layzón ceremonial centre.

It is possible to walk from Cajamarca to Cumbe Mayo in three to four hours, although you're advised to take a guide or join a tour group. The trail starts from the hill of Santa Apolonia (see above) and goes straight through the village and up the hill. At the top of the mountain, leave the trail and take the road to the right to reach the canal. The walk is not difficult and you do not need hiking boots, but it is cold (best weather May to September). Take warm clothing and a good torch. The locals use the trail to bring their goods to market.

Tip...
There is no bus service to Cumbe Mayo; taxi US$15. Guided tours run from 0830 to 1400 and are recommended in order to see all the pre-Inca sites.

Porcón

The Porcón rural cooperative, with its evangelical faith expressed on billboards, is a popular excursion, 30 km northwest of Cajamarca. It is a tightly organized community, with carpentry, bakery, cheese and yoghurt-making, zoo and vicuñas. A good guide helps to explain everything. If you're not taking a tour, contact **Cooperativa Agraria Atahualpa Jerusalén** ⓘ *Chanchamayo 1355, Fonavi 1, T076-825631.* At Km 8 along the road to Porcón is **Huambocancha**, a town specializing in stone sculptures. Combis run from Cajamarca market, US$0.75, 30 minutes.

Kuntur Wasi

Site museum in San Pablo US$1.75, ruins US$2.50.

Some 93 km west of Cajamarca is the mining town of Chilete, 21 km north of which on the road to San Pablo is Kuntur Wasi. The site was devoted to a feline cult and consists of a pyramid and stone monoliths. There are two basic hostales in Chilete, with very limited facilities.

Parque Nacional de Cutervo

This remote national park, about 260 km north of Cajamarca via twisting mountain roads, was the first to be created in Peru in 1961. Despite its small size (only 8214 ha), divided into northern and southern sections, it protects a wide variety of rare or endemic plants and animals in the cloudforests of the Cordillera de los Tarros, including the mountain tapir, the spectacled bear and the Andean cock of the rock. The area is particularly well known for its caves, which harbour colonies of rare oil birds or *guácharos* (Steatornis caripensis). These large birds with a wingspan of nearly 1 m, use their screeching calls as a form of echo location to guide them through the pitch darkness. The caves also support a rare species of fish, the *bagre de las cavernas* (Astroblepus rosei).

Combis leave Cajamarca for **Cutervo**, from where it's possible to reach the village of San Andrés de Cutervo. Check at the local police station regarding park entry regulations. From San Andrés it is about one hour's hike to the oil birds' cave. It may be possible to hire local guides, and some Cajamarca agencies offer tours.

Listings Cajamarca *map p196*

Tourist information

Information is available from: **iPerú** (Jr Cruz de Piedra 601, T076-365166, iperucajamarca@promperu.gob.pe, Mon-Sat 0900-1800, Sun 0900-1300); **Dirección Regional de Turismo** and **Ministerio de Cultura**, in the Conjunto Monumental de Belén (Belén 631, T076-362601, Mon-Fri 0900-1300, 1500-1730), and the **Sub-Gerencia de Turismo** (Av Alameda de los Incas, Complejo Qhapac Ñan, opposite UNC university on the road to Baños del Inca, T076-363626, www.municaj.gob.pe). The **University tourist school** (Del Batán 289, T076-361546, Mon-Fri 0830-1300, 1500-2200) also offers free advice and leaflets.

Where to stay

$$$$ Costa del Sol
Cruz de Piedra 707, T076-362472,
www.costadelsolperu.com.
On the Plaza de Armas, part of a Peruvian chain, with airport transfer, welcome drink; restaurant, café and bars, pool, spa, casino, business centre.

$$$ El Ingenio
Av Vía de Evitamiento 1611-1709, T076-368733, www.elingenio.com.
Colonial style buildings 1½ blocks from El Quinde shopping mall. With restaurant, solar-powered hot water, spacious, quiet and relaxed, generous breakfast.

$$ Cajamarca
Dos de Mayo 311, T076-362532,
hotelcajamarca@gmail.com.
3-star in beautiful colonial mansion, sizeable rooms, hot water, food excellent in **Los Faroles** restaurant.

$$ El Cabildo
Junín 1062, T076-367025.
Includes breakfast, in historic monument with patio and modern fountain, full of character, elegant local decorations, comfortable, breakfast served.

$$ El Cumbe Inn
Pasaje Atahualpa 345, T076-366858,
www.elcumbeinn.com.
Includes breakfast and tax, comfortable, variety of rooms, hot water, evening meals on request, small gym, will arrange taxis, very helpful.

$$ El Portal del Marqués
Del Comercio 644, T076-368464,
www.portaldelmarques.com.
Attractive converted colonial house, laundry, safe, parking, leased restaurant **El Mesón del Marqués** has good lunch *menú*. Casino with slot machines.

$$ La Casona del Inca
2 de Mayo 458-460, Plaza de Armas, T076-367524, www.casonadelincaperu.com.
Upstairs, old building, traditional style, some rooms overlooking plaza, some with interior windows, good beds, breakfast in café on top floor, tours, laundry.

$$ Los Balcones de la Recoleta
Amalia Puga 1050, T076-363302,
hslosbalcones@speedy.com.pe.
Beautifully restored 19th-century house, central courtyard full of flowers, some rooms with period furniture, internet.

$ Hospedaje Los Jazmines
Amazonas 775, T076-361812.
In a converted colonial house with courtyard and café, 14 rooms with hot water, all profits go to disabled children, guests can visit the project's school and help.

$ Hostal Becerra
Del Batán 195, T076-367867.
With hot water, modern, pleasant, will store luggage until late buses depart.

$ Hostal Perú
Amalia Puga 605, on Plaza, T076-365568.
With hot water, functional rooms in old building around central patio used by **El Zarco** restaurant, wooden floors, credit cards taken.

Los Baños del Inca

$$$$-$$$ Laguna Seca
Av Manco Cápac 1098, T076-584300,
www.lagunaseca.com.pe.
In pleasant surroundings with thermal streams, private hot thermal baths in rooms, swimming pool with thermal water, restaurant, bar, health spa with a variety of treatments, disco, horses for hire.

$$$ Hostal Fundo Campero San Antonio
2 km off the Baños road (turn off at Km 5), T076-368237.
An old *hacienda*, wonderfully restored, with open fireplaces and gardens, 15 mins walk along the river to Baños del Inca, riding on *caballos de paso*,

own dairy produce, fruit and vegetables, catch your own trout for supper; try the *licor de sauco*.

$$-$ Los Baños del Inca
See above, T076-348385.
Various accommodation: bungalows for 2 to 4 with thermal water, fridge; **Albergue Juvenil**, not IYFH, hostel rooms with bunk beds or double rooms, private bath, caters to groups, basic. Camping possible. Restaurant offers full board.

Restaurants

$$$ Pascana
Av Atahualpa 947.
Well-known and recommended as the best in town, near the Qhapac Ñan Municipality. Their **Taberna del Diablo** is the top disco in town.

$$$ Querubino
Amalia Puga 589, T076-340900.
Mediterranean-style decoration, a bit of everything on the menu, including pastas, daily specials, breakfasts, cocktails, coffees, expensive wines otherwise reasonable, popular.

$$ Casa Club
Amalia Puga 458-A, T076-340198.
Daily 0800-2300.
Menú, including vegetarian, and extensive selection à la carte, family atmosphere, slow but attentive service.

$$ Don Paco
Amalia Puga 390, T076-362655.
Opposite San Francisco. Typical, including novo andino, and international dishes, tasty food, desserts, drinks.

$$ El Pez Loco
San Martín 333.
Recommended for fish dishes.

$$ Om-Gri
San Martín 360, near the Plaza de Armas.
Opens 1300 (1830 Sun).
Good Italian dishes, small, informal,
French spoken.

$$ Pizzería El Marengo
Junín 1201, T368045 for delivery.
Good pizzas and warm atmosphere.

$$ Salas
Amalia Puga 637, on the main plaza,
T076-362867. Open 0800-2200.
A Cajamarca tradition: fast, attentive
service, excellent local food (try their *cuy
frito*), best *tamales* in town, very popular.

$$-$ De Buena Laya
2 de Mayo 343.
With a rustic interior, popular with
hostales, offers Novo Cajamarquino
cuisine; lunchtime *menú* US$3.50.

$$-$ El Zarco
Jr Del Batán 170, T076-363421.
Sun-Fri 0700-2300.
Breakfast, good vegetarian dishes,
excellent fish, also has short *chifa*
menu, very popular.

$ Pizzería Vaca Loca
San Martín 330.
Popular, best pizzas in town.

Cafés

Bella's Café Lounge
Junín 1184, T076-345794.
For breakfasts, sandwiches, great
desserts and coffee from Chanchamayo,
Wi-Fi, a place to linger, check emails and
relax, owner Raul speaks English. Popular
with visitors to the city.

Cascanuez
Amalia Puga 554.
Great cakes, extensive menu including
humitas, breakfasts, ice creams and
coffees, highly regarded.

Heladería Holanda
Amalia Puga 657 on the Plaza de Armas,
T076-340113.
Dutch-owned, easily the best ice creams
in Cajamarca, 50 flavours (but not all on
at the same time); try *poro poro*, *lúcuma*
or *sauco*, also serves coffee. 4 branches,
including at Baños del Inca. Ask if it is
possible to visit their factory. They assist
deaf people and single mothers.

Sanguchón.com
Junín 1137.
Best burgers in town, sandwiches,
also popular bar.

Feb Carnaval. Cajamarca's pre-Lent
festivities are spectacular and regarded
as among the best in the country; they
are also perhaps the most raucous.
Mar Palm Sun. The processions in
Porcón, 16 km to the northwest, are
worth seeing.
24 Jun San Juan in Cajamarca, Chota,
Llacanora, San Juan and Cutervo.
Jul Agricultural fair is held at Baños
del Inca.
Oct Festival Folklórico in Cajamarca on
the 1st Sun.

Handicrafts
Specialities including gilded mirrors
and cotton and wool saddlebags
(*alforjas*). Items can be made to order.
The **Mercado Central** at Amazonas y
Apurímac is colourful and worth a visit
for *artesanía*. There are also stalls at the

Belén complex (Belén and/or 2 de Mayo) and along the steps up to Santa Apolonia hill. Other options for a good range of local crafts are the **Feria Artesenal** (Jr El Comercio 1045, next to the police office) and **El Molino** (2 de Mayo).

What to do

Agencies around the Plaza de Armas offer trips to local sites and further afield, trekking on Inca trails, riding *caballos de paso* and handicraft tours. Prices are roughly as follows: Cumbe Mayo, US$6.50-8.50, 4-5 hrs at 0930; Porcón, US$6.50-8.50, 4-5 hrs at 0930; Otusco, US$4.50-7, 3-3½ hrs at 1530; city tour, US$7, 3 hrs at 0930 or 1530. Kuntur Wasi is a full day trip. There are also 2 day/3 night tours to Kuélap and Cutervo National Park.

Cumbemayo Tours, *Amalia Puga 635 on the plaza, T076-362938*. Standards tours, guides speak English and French.
Mega Tours, *Amalia Puga 691 on the plaza, T076-341876, www.megatours.org*. Conventional tours, full day and further afield, ecotourism and adventures.

Transport

Air
The airport is 5 km from town; taxi US$8. There are flights to/from **Lima**, with **LC Peru** (Comercio 1024, T076-361098), Sun-Fri, and **LAN** (Cruz de Piedra 657). The military **Grupo Aéreo 42** (Amalia Pugla 605, T970-029134) has passenger flights to Cajamarca originating in Trujillo or Iquitos; see page 150 for routes and schedules.

Bus
Buses in town charge US$0.35. Bus companies have their own ticket offices and terminals; many are on Av Atahualpa blocks 2-6, a 20-min walk from the Plaza de Armas.

To **Lima**, 870 km, 12-14 hrs, US$27-53, many daily with **Civa** (Ayacucho 753, T076-361460), **Cruz del Sur** (Atahualpa 606, T076-361737) and **Línea** (Atahualpa 318, T076-363956), **Móvil** (Atahualpa 405, T076-340873), **Tepsa** (Sucre y Reina Forje, T076-363306) and **Turismo Días** (Av Evitamiento s/n, T076-344322), including several luxury services.

To **Trujillo**, 295 km, 7 hrs, US$10-27, regular buses daily 0900-2230, with **Emtrafesa** (Atahualpa 315, T076-369663), Línea and **Turismo Días**; most continue to Lima via Chimbote. To **Chiclayo**, 265 km, 6 hrs, US$9-20, several buses daily with **Línea** and **Turismo Días**; you have to change buses to go on to Piura and Tumbes. To **Celendín**, 107 km, 3½ hrs, US$6, usually 2 a day with **CABA** (Atahualpa 299, T076-366665), **Royal Palace's** (Reina Forje 130, T076-343063) and **Rojas** (Atahualpa 309, T076-340548). To **Chachapoyas**, 336 km, 11-12 hrs, US$18, with **Virgen del Carmen** (Atahualpa 333A, T983-915869), at 0500, via **Leymebamba**, US$11.55, 9-10 hrs; the route follows a paved road through beautiful countryside.

Taxi
US$2 within city limits. Mototaxis, US$0.75. Radio taxi: **El Sol**, T076-368897, 24 hrs; **Taxi Super Seguro**, T076-507090.

Chachapoyas
& around

The Region of Amazonas contains the archaeological riches of the Chachapoyans, also known as Sachupoyans. Here lie the great pre-Inca cities of Vilaya (not yet developed for tourism) and the immense fortress of Kuélap, among many others. It is also an area of great natural beauty with waterfalls, notably Gocta, cliffs and caves. This region is called 'La Ceja de la Selva' (eyebrow of the jungle). Its beautiful scenery includes a good deal of virgin cloudforest (although other sections are sadly deforested), as well as endless deep, dry canyons traversed by hair-raising roads. The temperature is always in the 20°Cs during the day, but the nights are cool at 3000 m. Many ruins are overgrown with ferns, bromeliads and orchids and are easily missed.

The central geographic feature of the region, and its boundary with neighbouring Cajamarca, is the great Río Marañón, one of the major tributaries of the Amazon. Running roughly parallel to the mighty Marañón, one range to the east, is the gentler valley of the Utcubamba, home to much of the area's ancient and present population. Over yet another cordillera to the east, lie the isolated subtropical valleys of the province of Rodríguez de Mendoza, the origin of whose inhabitants, has been the source of much debate (see box, page 210).

East from Cajamarca

Cajamarca is a convenient starting point for the trip east. The road is paved but prone to landslides in the rainy season. It follows a winding course through the mountains, crossing the wide and deep canyon of the Río Marañón at Balsas. The road climbs steeply with superb views of the mountains and the valleys below. The fauna and flora are spectacular as the journey alternates between high mountains and low forest.

Celendín → *Colour map 3, B2.*

East from Cajamarca, this is the first town of note, with a pleasant plaza and cathedral that is predominantly blue. The fascinating local market on Sunday is held in three distinct areas. From 0630 till 0730 there's a **hat market** by the Alameda, between Ayacucho and 2 de Mayo at Jorge Chávez, at which you can see hats at every stage of production. Then, at 0930 the **potato market** takes place at 2 de Mayo y Sucre, and, at the other end of town, there's a **livestock market** on Túpac Amaru. The **Virgen del Carmen** festival takes place from 16 July to 3 August. The most popular local excursion is to the hot springs and mud baths at **Llanguat**, 20 km away (US$2.75 by limited public transport).

> **Tip...**
> The **Multired** ATM beside the **Banco de la Nación** on 2 de Mayo in Celendín may not accept all foreign cards; take cash.

★Leymebamba and around → *Colour map 1, C4.*

There are plenty of ruins – many of them covered in vegetation – and good walking possibilities around this pleasant town at the source of the Utcubamba River. **La Congona**, a Chachapoyan site, is well worth the effort, with stupendous views (see below). Archaeological sites to the south of Leymebamba include **La Petaca**, **La Joya** and **Diablo Huasi**. There are also caves with petroglyphs at Chururco, 2½ hours walk from Pomacochas (not to be confused with Pomacochas on the road to Tarapoto), reached by taxi for US$5.40.

In 1996 six burial *chullpas* were discovered at **Laguna de los Cóndores**, a spectacular site in a lush cloudforest setting. The chullpas contained 219 mummies and vast quantities of ceramics, textiles, woodwork, *quipus* and everyday utensils from the late Inca period, now housed in the excellent **Museo Leymebamba** ⓘ *outside San Miguel, on the road to Celendín, T041-816803, www.museoleymebamba.org, Tue-Sun 0930-1630, entry US$5.75, (taxi from Leymebamba US$2.75, mototaxi US$2).* It is beautifully laid-out and very informative, and the collection of mummies and quipus is superb. To get there from Leymebamba, walk to the village of 2 de Mayo, ask for the trail to San Miguel, then take the footpath uphill; the road route is much longer.

It is also possible to visit Laguna de los Cóndores itself; the trip takes 10 to 12 hours on foot and horseback from Leymebamba. An all-inclusive tour for the three-day muddy trek can be arranged at Leymebamba hotels (ask for Sinecio or Javier Farge) or with Chachapoyas operators, US$70 per person.

Sites around Chachapoyas

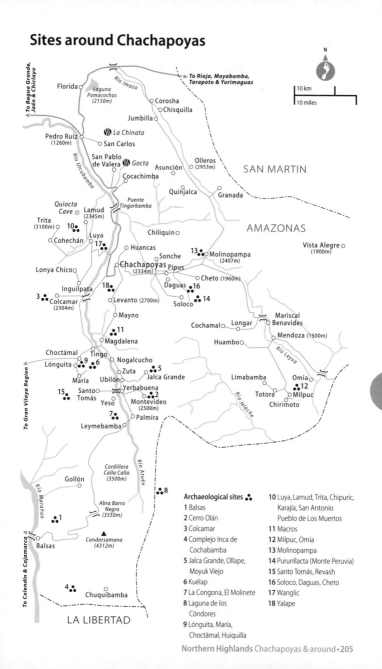

To Bagua Grande, Jaén & Chiclayo

To Rioja, Moyabamba, Tarapoto & Yurimaguas

N

10 km
10 miles

Florida
Laguna Pomacochas (2150m)
Río Imaza
Corosha
Chisquilla
Jumbilla
Pedro Ruiz (1260m)
La Chinata
San Carlos
San Pablo de Valera   Gocta
Río Utcubamba
Cocachimba
Asunción
Olleros (2953m)
SAN MARTIN

Quiocta Cave
Lamud (2345m)
Puente Tingorbamba
Quinjalca
Granada
AMAZONAS

Trita (3100m)
10
Luya
17
Cohechán
Chiliquin
Huancas
Sonche
13   Molinopampa (2407m)
Vista Alegre (1900m)
Chachapoyas (2334m)
Pipus
Cheto (1960m)
Lonya Chico
Inguilpata
18
Daguas   16
3   Colcamar (2304m)
Levanto (2700m)
Soloco   14
Mayno
11
Magdalena
Cochamal   Longar   Mariscal Benavides
Choctámal
Tingo
Nogalcucho
Mendoza (1500m)
Lónguita
9
Zuta
5   Jalca Grande
Río Leyva
María
Ubilón
2   Yerbabuena
Huambo
Limabamba
Omia
15   Santo Tomás
Yeso
Montevideo (2500m)
12   Milpuc
7   Palmira
Totora
Chirimoto
Leymebamba
Río Jelache

To Gran Vilaya Region

Cordillera Calla Calla (3500m)
Río Atuén
Gollón
8
Abra Barro Negro (3550m)
Condorsamana (4312m)
1
Balsas
4   Chuquibamba
LA LIBERTAD

To Celendín & Cajamarca
Río Marañón

Archaeological sites

1 Balsas
2 Cerro Olán
3 Colcamar
4 Complejo Inca de Cochabamba
5 Jalca Grande, Ollape, Moyuk Viejo
6 Kuélap
7 La Congona, El Molinete
8 Laguna de los Cóndores
9 Lónguita, María, Choctámal, Huiquilla
10 Luya, Lamud, Trita, Chipuric, Karajía, San Antonio Pueblo de Los Muertos
11 Macros
12 Milpuc, Omia
13 Molinopampa
14 Purunllacta (Monte Peruvia)
15 Santo Tomás, Revash
16 Soloco, Daguas, Cheto
17 Wanglic
18 Yalape

BACKGROUND
Chachapoyas

The Chachapoyan Empire began about AD 0 and covered an area bounded by the rivers Marañón and Huallaga, as far as Pataz in the south and Bagua in the north. Theories about the culture suggest that its cities, highways, terracing, irrigation, massive stonework and metal-craft were all fully developed. Socially the Chachapoya were organized into chiefdoms, which formed war alliances in the case of external aggression. Archaeologists claim that this region overwhelms even Machu Picchu and its neighbouring Inca sites in grandeur and mystery. By some counts, its 'lost' and uncharted cities, such as Pueblo Alto, near the village of Pueblo Nuevo (25 km from Kuélap) and Saposoa in the northeast of San Martín department, exceed three dozen. By far the majority of these cities, fortresses and villages were never discovered by the Spanish. In fact many had already returned to the jungle by the time the conquistadors arrived in 1532.

The German ethnologist and former mayor of Chachapoyas (2006-2010), Doctor Peter Lerche, has carried out extensive research on Chachapoyan cultures. In an article in *National Geographic*, September 2000, 'Quest for the Lost Tombs of the Peruvian Cloud People', Doctor Lerche writes about the discovery of a Chachapoya tomb named the 'White House' and gives a good general introduction to the history and archaeology of the region.

La Congona

One of the most impressive outings from Leymebamba is to the Chachapoyan site of La Congona, to the west of the town.

The site is a brisk three-hour walk starting at the lower end of 16 de Julio. A vehicle road and the remaining sections of an old path climb steeply from town to the village of Fila San Cristóbal. Continue straight on, on a trail past the football field (not the road to the right); it undulates before descending to the large, flat pasture of Tío Pampa, about 30 minutes past the village. Turn left at the end of the pasture and follow a streambed with white sand; then climb to a ridge and follow it left. There are many structures spread on the hills here; aim for the middle of three peaks, covered in vegetation and identified by a white limestone cliff. The most impressive structures are clustered in a small area, impossible to see until you are right there. Turn right off the main trail, and go through a gate to get there. If the landowner is there, he appreciates a contribution. The views are stupendous and the ruins worth the effort; allow one to two hours to explore them at leisure. There are some 30 decorated round stone houses (some with evidence of three storeys) and a watch tower. It is supposed to be the only site displaying all three Chacha friezes – zigzag, rhomboid and Greek stepped.

There are two other sites, **El Molinete** and **Pumahuanyuna**, nearby. All three can be visited in a day, but a guide is advisable to explain the area and show the way to the ruins as it is easy to get lost.

Around Yerbabuena

The road to Chachapoyas follows the Utcubamba River north. In the mountains rising from the river at Yerbabuena (important Sunday market, basic *hospedaje*) are a number of archaeological sites. Before **Yerbabuena**, a road heads east to **Montevideo** (basic *hospedaje*) and beyond to the small village of San Pedro de Utac, where you can hike up to the impressive but overgrown ruins of Cerro Olán.

On the other side of the river, west of Yerbabuena, are burial *chullpas* from the Revash culture (AD 1250). They are reached from either **San Bartolo** (30-45 minutes' walk) or along a trail starting past **Puente Santo Tomás** (1½ to two hours' walk).

The town of **Jalca Grande** (or La Jalca), at 2800 m, is reached along a road going east at **Ubilón**, north of Yerbabuena. Jalca Grande has the remains of a Chachapoyan roundhouse, a stone church tower, a small **museum** with ceramics and textiles, and one very basic *hospedaje*.

Tingo to Kuélap

Situated at the junction of the Tingo and Utcubamba rivers, 40 km north of Leymebamba and 37 km south of Chachapoyas, Tingo (altitude: 1800 m) is the access point for Kuélap. A road climbs steeply from Tingo to Choctámal, where it divides. The right branch provides access to the southern part of Gran Vilaya (see page 211); the left branch climbs east to Lónguita, María, Quizango and Kuélap. It is also possible to walk to Kuélap from María (two to 2½ hours), Choctámal (four to five hours) and Tingo, although this last is a strenuous, five-hour uphill slog and only fit hikers should try to ascend and descend in one day on foot. Take waterproofs, food and drink, and start early as it gets very hot. In the rainy season it is advisable to wear boots; at other times it is hot and dry. Take all your water with you as there is nothing on the way up. See also Transport, page 218.

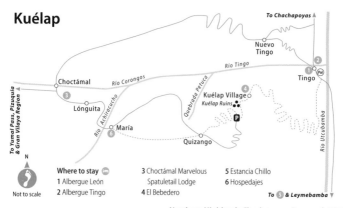

Kuélap

To Chachapoyas

Nuevo Tingo

Río Tingo

Choctámal

Río Corongos

Río Tingo

Tingo

Río Achirecucho

Lónguita

Quebrada Petaca

Kuélap Village

Kuélap Ruins

El Bebedero

P

María

Río Utcubamba

Quizango

To Yumal Pass, Pizquia & Gran Vilaya Region

N

Not to scale

Where to stay
3 Choctámal Marvelous Spatuletail Lodge
4 El Bebedero
5 Estancia Chillo
6 Hospedajes

1 Albergue León
2 Albergue Tingo

To ⑤ & Leymebamba

★Kuélap → See map, page 207.

Daily 0800-1700. US$4.30, guides available for US$7 per group (Rigoberto Vargas Silva has been recommended). The ticket office at the car park has a small but informative Sala de Interpretacion.

Kuélap is a spectacular pre-Inca walled city at 3000 m which was re-discovered in 1843. It was built continuously from AD 500 up to Inca times and is said to contain three times more stone than the Great Pyramid at Giza in Egypt. The site lies along the summit of a mountain crest, more than 1 km in length. The massive stone walls, 585 m long by 110 m wide at their widest, are as formidable as those of any pre-Columbian city. Some reconstruction has taken place, mostly of small houses and walls, but the majority of the main walls on all levels are original, as is the inverted, cone-shaped main temple. The structures have been left in their cloudforest setting, the trees covered in bromeliads and moss, the flowers visited by hummingbirds.

> **Tip...**
> There are plans to build a cablecar to Kuélap, which will make the site far more accessible to tourists; visit now to see it without the crowds.

Chachapoyas → Colour map 1, C4.

The capital of the Amazonas Region was founded in 1538 and retains its colonial character. The city's importance as a crossroads between the coast and jungle began to decline in the late 1940s, but archaeological and ecological tourism have grown gradually since the 1990s and have brought increasing economic benefits to the region.

The cathedral, with a lovely modern interior, stands on the spacious Plaza de Armas. **Ministerio de Cultura Museum** ① *Ayacucho 904, T041-477045, Mon-Fri 0800-1300, 1500-1700, free,* contains a small collection of artefacts and mummies, with explanations in Spanish. The **Museo Santa Ana** ① *Jr Santa Ana 1054, T041-790988, Sun-Fri 0900-1300, 1500-1800, US$2,* has colonial religious art and pre-Hispanic ceramics and textiles. Jr Amazonas, pedestrianized from the Plaza de Armas uphill to Plaza Burgos, makes a pleasant stroll.

Huancas

Autos leave from Jr Ortiz Arrieta 370 in Chachapoyas, daily 0600-1800, 20 min, US$1.15, or 2-hr walk.

Huancas is a small village to the north of Chacha where rustic pottery is produced. Walk uphill from the plaza to the **mirador** ① *1 km, US$0.70,* for magnificent views into the deep canyon of the Río Sonche, with tumbling waterfalls. There are crafts on sale here. At **Huanca Urco**, 5 km from Huancas, past the large prison complex, are ruins, remains of an Inca road and another *mirador* with fine views to Gocta waterfall in the distance.

Levanto

Due south of Chachapoyas, Levanto was built by the Spaniards in 1538, directly on top of the previous Chachapoyan structures, as their first capital of the area.

Nowadays Levanto is an unspoilt colonial village overlooking the massive canyon of the Utcubamba River. On a clear day, Kuélap can be seen on the other side of the rift. A 30-minute walk from Levanto towards Chachapoyas will bring you to the overgrown ruins of **Yalape**, which seems to have been a massive residential complex, extending over many hectares. Local people can guide you to the ruins.

Mendoza and around

A road heads east from Chachapoyas, reaching Mendoza after 2½ hours. The town is the centre of the coffee-producing region of Rodríguez de Mendoza. Close by are the caves at Omia, the Tocuya thermal baths, Mirador Wimba and the Santa Natalia waterfall. Also of interest is the Guayabamba Valley, where there is an unusually high incidence of fair-skinned people (see box, Vikings in the cloudforest?, page 210).

Chachapoyas

Where to stay
1 Aventura Backpackers Lodge *A1*
2 Belén *A1*
3 Casa Vieja *A1*
4 Casona Monsante *B2*
5 Chachapoyas Backpackers *B2*
6 El Dorado *A1*
7 Las Orquídeas *A1*
8 Posada del Arriero *B1*
9 Puma Urco *B2*
10 Quiocta *B2*
11 Revash *B2*
12 Rumi Huasi *A2*
13 Vilaya *B2*
14 Vista Hermosa *A1*
15 Xalca *B1*

Restaurants
1 Batán del Tayta *B2*
2 Dulcería Santa Elena *B2*
3 El Edén *A2*
4 El Tejado *A1*
5 Fusiones *A1*
6 Heladería San Antonio *B2*
7 Matalaché *B3*
8 Panadería Café San José *B2*
9 Paraíso de las Pizzas *A1*
10 Romana *B1*

Transport
1 Cars to Huancas & Mendoza *A2*
2 Cars to Lamud & Luya *A1*
3 Combis to Bagua Grande & Moyobamba *A1*
4 Combis to Pedro Ruiz *A1*
5 Trans Rollers to Kuelap & Pizuquia *A2*
6 Cars to Pedro Ruiz & Bagua Grande *A2*
7 Civa *A2*
8 Virgen del Carmen to Celendín & Cajamarca *A2*
9 Karlita to Leymebamba *A2*
10 Móvil Tours *B3*
11 El Expreso & Transervis Kuelap *B3*
12 GH Bus *A3*

ON THE ROAD
Vikings in the cloudforest?

The province of Rodríguez de Mendoza is home to fair-skinned, blond-haired, blue-eyed people who seem incongruous in this part of the world. Where did they come from?

For many decades, their origin was the subject of much speculation. One theory suggested they were the descendants of Vikings who arrived in South America via Easter Island around AD 1000. Another claimed they were the offspring of dissident conquistadors, who had strayed far from the mainstream of the conquest. Yet another hypothesis claimed that they might be descendants of Marrano Jews who fled the Inquisition in Lima during the 16th century.

DNA analysis eventually stripped away some of the romance. The inhabitants of Guayabamba were traced to one Spanish family who lived in the region for a long time. There is evidence that the people of Chirimoto were originally Italian and Spanish settlers from the 1820s. More wide-ranging but related research has compared the DNA of the mummies found at Laguna de Cóndores with Scandinavian bog people and other European mummies. This does not, however, explain everything. Why, for example, do married women here always cover their heads with a scarf, an uncommon custom in this part of the world?

Whatever their origin, you will find the people of the Guayabamba Valley to be very friendly and welcoming. Enjoy getting to know them.

It is a worthwhile four-hour hike from Mendoza to Huamanpata, a very pretty valley surrounded by forest; there's a lake here in the wet season, but this reduces down to a river in drier months. Robert Cabrerra (T949-305401) has cabins and camping, and he offers two-day tours from US$35 per person; contact him well in advance.

> **Tip...**
> South of the road from Chachapoyas to **Mendoza**, in the district of Soloco, is **Parjugsha**, Peru's largest cave complex, about 300 m deep and with some 20 km of galleries (10 km have been explored and connected). Spelunking experience is essential.

Luya and around

At Km 37 on the Chachapoyas–Pedro Ruiz road an unpaved road leads to the village of **Luya** where it divides. One branch goes north to **Lamud**, a convenient base for several interesting sites, such as San Antonio and Pueblo de los Muertos. Also worth visiting is the **Quiocta cave** ① *30 mins by car from Lamud, then a 10-min walk, US$2.* The cave is 560 m long, 23 m deep, and has four chambers with stalactites and stalagmites and a stream running through it. There are petroglyphs at the mouth, a man-made wall, human skulls set in depressions and other, partly buried, human remains. Tours to the cave can be arranged in Chachapoyas or through the Lamud tourist office.

The second road from Luya goes south and west to Cruzpata for access to **Karajía** ① *2½ hrs' walk from Luya or 30 mins from Cruzpata, US$2, take binoculars,* where remarkable, 2.5-m-high sarcophagi are set into an impressive cliff-face overlooking the valley. Other sites nearby include **Chipuric,** 1½ hours' walk from Luya, and **Wanglic,** a funeral site with large circular structures built under a ledge in a lush canyon with a beautiful waterfall nearby: a worthwhile excursion (1½ hours). Ask for directions in Luya, or take a local guide (US$7 a day). The road to Luya and Lamud is unpaved; see Chachapoyas Transport for how to get there.

Gran Vilaya

This area stretches west from the Río Utcubamba to the Río Marañón. Moist air pushing up from the Amazon Basin creates a unique biosphere of clouds and mist in which bromeliads and orchids thrive. It is near to the equator and over 3000 m above sea level, so the daytime temperature is an almost constant 22°C. While the Marañón valley is a desert, the peaks are always misted from June to September and often drenched in rain the rest of the year. This creates a huge variety of mini-ecological zones, each with its own flora and fauna, differentiated by altitude and by which flank of the mountain they are on.

The name Gran Vilaya was coined by US explorer, Gene Savoy, one of the candidates for the original 'Indiana Jones', who discovered an extensive set of ruined complexes in this region in 1985. There are about 30 sites spread over a vast area, 15 of which are considered significant. Among them are **Pueblo Alto, Pueblo Nuevo, Paxamarca** and **Machu Llacta.**

Gran Vilaya can be accessed from several points: via **Cohechán** (30 minutes' ride past Luya on the road to Cruzpata); via **Inguilpata** (on a road that branches south off the road to Luya); and via **Colcamar** (on a road that branches off the road between Tingo and Chachapoyas, just before it crosses to the east bank of the Utcubamba). The ancient roads in Gran Vilaya make for good trekking, and many Chachapoyas operators offer tours here. To trek across the area from north to south takes three to five days. Trails (and a road from Cohechán) run from the three northern access points to **Huaylla Belén,** a gigantic silted-in green valley at about 2800 m with a spectacular panorama of the river meandering below. It is the only large, flat area in the zone and can get frosts on clear nights. From here you cross the spine of the Andes on a 1.6-km Inca stairway, dropping into Gran Vilaya. You will pass many ruins near Vista Hermosa (3½ to four hours from Belén). From here, the 1600 to 1700 m climb to the **Yumal Pass** is "a killer", but from Yumal a road and the trail thankfully descend to Choctámal where there is lodging (see Where to stay below). The trek can be combined with a visit to Karajía (see above) and can also be done in reverse, starting in the south at the Yumal Pass, along the road that runs west from Choctámal to Pizuquia.

> **Tip...**
> To the south of Yumal, a trail goes from Llaucán (1.5 km west of Choctámal) to Yomblón. On the route is **Cerro Shubet** (3882 m), a striking flat-topped mountain with ruins and petroglyphs. The views from the top are excellent in good weather.

ON THE ROAD

Gocta Falls

Secrets of this size are hard to keep, yet the residents of the District of Valera, northwest of Chachapoyas, did not reveal the existence of Gocta, a 771-m waterfall, until the German Stefan Zimmendorff came across it in 2002. This spectacular waterfall, surrounded by cloudforest, is the source of the Río Cocahuayco, a tributary of the Utcubamba, and has two tiers: the upper waterfall is 231 m high, and the lower waterfall is 540 m high. The National Geographic Society's ranked Gocta third in the list, after Angel Falls in Venezuela and Tugela Falls in South Africa. Although there are other contenders for this distinction and no consensus on exactly where Gocta ranks in the world's waterfall hierarchy, the falls' great natural beauty make them unquestionably worth a visit.

Good trails on both sides of the river lead to the falls, with magnificent views along the way. Located on the eastern slopes of the Andes, the area is rich in fauna and flora: 20 species of mammals have been identified here, including two endemic primates; as well as 110 bird species and 355 plant species, including 41 species of orchid. In the words of Miles Buesst, "The World Waterfall Database gives Gocta itself a 'scenic rating' of 96%, which I think is ungenerous!"

Most operators in Chachapoyas offer tours of Gocta, and you can visit on your own from either Pedro Ruíz or Chachapoyas, see page 219).

★Gocta
Access from San Pablo de Valera or Cocachimba. Entry fee US$4, guides (compulsory), US$11.

South of Pedro Ruíz is the spectacular **Gocta waterfall**, one of the highest in the world at 771 m. (The upper waterfall is 231 m; the lower waterfall is 540 m.) From Chachapoyas, take the Pedro Ruiz road for 35 km to Cocahuayco (about 18 km before Pedro Ruiz) where there are two roads up to Gocta, along either bank of the Cocahuayco River. The first turn-off leads to the village of **San Pablo de Valera** at 1934 m (6 km from the main road, 20 minutes by car). From here, it is a one- to 1½-hour walk to a mirador, and then 30 to 60 minutes to the base of the upper falls, 6.3 km in total. The second turn-off, 100 m further along the main road, leads to the village of **Cocachimba** at 1796 m (5.3 km from the main road, 20 minutes). From here, it is a 1½- to 2½-hour walk (5.5 km) to the base of the lower waterfall, of which there is an impressive view. Both routes go through about 2 km of lovely forest; the San Pablo trail is somewhat flatter. A path connecting both banks starts on the San Pablo side at the mirador. This is a much smaller trail, quite steep and not signposted past the mirador. There is a suspension footbridge over the main river before the trail joins the Cocachimba trail about three quarters of the way to the base of the lower falls. To see both sides in one day you need to start very early, but this is a great way to get the full experience. Each community offers similar services: horses can be hired for US$11 (they can only go part of the way); rubber boots and rain ponchos are available for US$1.20 (it is always wet by the falls). The best time to visit is during the dry season from May to September; in the wet season the falls are more spectacular, but it is cold, rainy and the trails may be slippery.

Tip...
If you start the hike at San Pablo and finish at Cocachimba, arrange transport to return to San Pablo at the end of the day. Or, if you are staying in Cocachimba, arrange transport to San Pablo to begin the hike. The ride is about 30 minutes.

Several more waterfalls in this area are now becoming accessible, including **Yumbilla**, which is 895 m (124 m higher than Gocta) in eight tiers. For more information about expeditions to Yumbilla, other falls and related projects, see the Florida-based NGO, **Amazon Waterfalls Association** ⓘ *www.amazonwaterfalls.org*.

Listings Chachapoyas and around *maps p207 and p209*

Tourist information

Chachapoyas

iPerú
On the Plaza de Armas, T041-477292, iperuchachapoyas@promperu.gob.pe. Mon-Sat 0900-1800, Sun 0900-1300.

Mendoza
For information on the area, ask for Michel Ricardo Feijoó Aguilor in the Mendoza municipal office, mifeijoo@gmail.com; he can help arrange guides and accommodation. A recommended guide is Alfonso Saldana Pelaez, fotoguiaalsape@gmail.com.

Gocta
Community tourist information is available in both San Pablo, T041-631163, daily 0800-1730, and Cocachimba, T041-630569, daily 0800-1730.

Where to stay

Celendín

$$-$ Hostal Celendín
Unión 305, Plaza de Armas, T076-555041, hcgustavosd1@hotmail.com.
Some rooms with plaza view, central patio and wooden stairs, hot water, pleasant, has 2 restaurants: **Rinconcito Shilico** (2 de Mayo 816), and **Pollos a la brasa Gusys**.

$ Hostal Imperial
Jr Dos de Mayo 568, 2 blocks from the plaza, T076-555492.
Large rooms, good mattresses, hot water, Wi-Fi, parking, decent choice.

$ Loyer's
José Gálvez 410, T076-555210.
Patio with wooden balcony all round, nice, singles, doubles and family rooms.

$ Maxmar
Dos de Mayo 349, T076-555330.
Cheaper without bath, hot shower extra, basic, parking, good value, owners Francisco and Luis are very helpful.

$ Mi Posada
Pardo 388, next to Atahualpa bus,
T074-979-758674.
Includes breakfast, small cheerful
rooms, family atmosphere.

$ Raymi Wasi
Jr José Gálvez 420, T976-551133.
With electric shower, cheaper without,
large rooms, has patio, quiet, parking,
good value, restaurant and karaoke.

Leymebamba and around

$$$$-$$$ Kentitambo
Across the road from Museo
Leymebamba, T971-118273.
Accommodation in 2 comfortable
cabins, lovely grounds with
hummingbirds. **Kentikafe** offers
sandwiches, cake and coffee.

$$ La Casona
Jr Amazonas 223, T041-630301,
www.casonadeleymebamba.com.
Nicely refurbished old house with
balcony, attractive common area,
simple rooms with solar hot water,
arrange tours and horses.

$ Laguna de los Cóndores
Jr Amazonas 320, ½ a block from the
plaza, T041-797908.
Nice courtyard, breakfast available,
electric shower, also runs the shelter
at Laguna de los Cóndores and offers
tours of 1-8 days.

$ La Petaca
Jr Amazonas 426, on the plaza,
T999-020599.
Good rooms with hot water,
breakfast available, café, helpful.

Tingo to Kuélap

$$ Choctámal Marvelous Spatuletail Lodge
3 km from Choctámal towards
Kuélap at Km 20, T041-941-963327,
www.marvelousspatuletail.com.
Book in advance.
Heated rooms, hot showers, hot
tub, telescope for star-gazing. Meals
US$8-10. Offers horse riding and
a chance to see the endangered
marvellous spatuletail hummingbird.

$$ Estancia Chillo
5 km south of Tingo towards
Leymebamba, T041-630510/979-340444.
On a 9-ha farm, dinner and breakfast
included, with bath, hot water, transport,
horse riding. Friendly family, a lovely
country retreat. The walk from Chillo
to Kuélap is shorter than from Tingo.

$ Albergue León
Along the south bank of the Río Tingo,
just upriver from the highway, T941-
715685, hildegardlen@yahoo.es.
Basic, private or shared bath, electric
shower, guiding, arrange horses, run
by Lucho León who is knowledgeable.

$ Albergue Tingo
On the main highway, just north of the
Río Tingo, T941-732251.
Adequate rooms with electric
shower, restaurant.

Walking towards Kuélap from Tingo,
the last house to the right of the track
(**El Bebedero**) offers very basic rooms
with bed, breakfast and dinner, helpful.
It may be fully booked by archaeologists,
but **Gabriel Portocarrero**, the caretaker,
runs a hostel just below the ruins, basic,
friendly. **Sra Juanita** (T989-783432),
offers basic rooms in the home of
archaeologist Arturo Ruiz Estrada, with

shared bath, cold water, breakfast. The village of **María**, 2½ hrs from Kuélap on the vehicle road to Choctámal has 10 *hospedajes*, some with bath and hot water; meals available. All these places are in the $ range.

Chachapoyas

$$$ Casa Vieja
Chincha Alta 569, T041-477353, www.casaviejaperu.com.
Converted old house with lovely courtyard, very nicely decorated, all rooms different, comfy beds, family atmosphere, good service, living room and *comedor* with open fire, includes breakfast, good café, Wi-Fi and library. Repeatedly recommended.

$$$ Xalca
Jr Grau 940, T041-479106, www.laxalcahotel.com.
Built in colonial style with central patio, large comfortable rooms, parking, opened in 2014.

$$ Casona Monsante
Amazonas 746, T041-477702, www.lacasonamonsante.com.
Converted colonial house with patio, orchid garden, comfortable rooms decorated with antiques.

$$ Las Orquídeas
Ayacucho 1231, T041-478271, www.hostallasorquideas.com.
Converted home, pleasantly decorated rooms, hot water, large garden.

$$ Posada del Arriero
Grau 636, T041-478945, www.posadadelarriero.net.
Old house with courtyard nicely refurbished in modern style, although rooms are a bit plain, helpful staff.

$$ Puma Urco
Amazonas 833, T041-477871, www.hotelpumaurco.com.
Comfortable rooms, includes breakfast, TV, frigobar, Wi-Fi, **Café Café** next door, hotel and café receive good reports, run tours with **Turismo Explorer**.

$$ Vilaya
Ayacucho 734, T041-477664.
Ample carpeted rooms, parking.

$$-$ Quiocta
Amazonas 721, T041-477698.
Brightly painted rooms, hot water, family run.

$$-$ Revash
Grau 517, Plaza de Armas, T041-477391, revash9@hotmail.com.
Traditional house with patio, stylish decor, steaming hot showers, breakfast available, helpful owners, good local information, popular. Operate tours and sell local crafts.

$ Aventura Backpackers Lodge
Jr Amazonas 1416, www.chachapoyashostal.com.
Dorms with bunk beds, use of kitchen, good value.

$ Belén
Jr Ortiz Arrieta 540, Plaza de Armas, T041-477830, www.hostalbelen.com.
With hot water, nicely furnished, pleasant sitting room overlooking the Plaza, good value.

$ Chachapoyas Backpackers
Jr Dos de Mayo 639, T041-478879, www.chachapoyasbackpackers.com.
Simple 2- and 3-bed dorms with shared bath, electric shower, a good budget option, same owners as **Turismo Explorer** tour operator. Lovely family-run place. Recommended.

$ El Dorado
Ayacucho 1062, T041-477047,
ivvanovt@hotmail.com.
With bathroom, electric shower, helpful
staff, a good economical option.

$ Rumi Huasi
Ortiz Arrieta 365, T041-791100.
With and without bath, electric shower,
small rooms, simple and good.

$ Vista Hermosa
Puno 285, T041-477526.
Pleasant ample rooms, some have
balconies, electric shower, good value.

Levanto

$ Levanto Marvelous Spatuletail Lodge
Behind the church, T041-478838,
www.marvelousspatuletail.net.
2 circular buildings with tall thatched
roofs, 4 bedrooms with 2 external
bathrooms can accommodate up to
12 people, hot shower, lounge with
fireplace and kitchen, meals US$8-10,
must book ahead.

Luya and around

$ Hostal Kuélap
Garcilaso de la Vega 452, on the
plaza, Lamud.
With or without bath or hot water, basic.

Gocta
San Pablo
A new hotel Gocta was under
construction in 2015, just outside town
on the way to the falls, T984-007033,
with camping facilities already operating,
hot showers, lovely views.

$ Hospedaje Las Gardenias
T941-718660.
Basic rooms with shared bath, cold
water, economical meals available.

Cocachimba

$$$ Gocta Andes Lodge
Cocachimba, T041-630552 (Tarapoto
T042-522225), www.goctalodge.com.
Beautifully located lodge overlooking the
waterfall, ample rooms with balconies,
lovely terrace with pool, restaurant.
Packages available with other hotels
in the group.

$ Hospedaje Gallito de la Roca
T041-630048.
Small simple rooms with shared bath,
cold water, economical meals available.

$ Hospedaje Las Orquídeas
T041-631265.
Simple rooms in a family home, shared
bath, cold water, restaurant.

Restaurants

Celendín

$$-$ La Reserve
José Gálvez 313.
Good quality and value, extensive menu,
from Italian to *chifa*.

$ Carbón y Leña
2 de Mayo 410.
For chicken, *parrillas* and pizzas.

$ Juguería Carolin
Bolognesi 384. Daily 0700-2200.
One of the few places open early,
for juices, breakfasts and caldos.

Chachapoyas

$$$ Batán del Tayta
La Merced 604. Closed Sun.
Excellent innovative local cuisine,
generous portions. Recommended.

$$ El Tejado
Santo Domingo 424. Daily for lunch only,
but hours vary.

Excellent upscale *comida criolla*.
Large portions, attentive service, nice
atmosphere and setting. Good-value
menú ejecutivo on weekdays.

$$ Paraíso de las Pizzas
Chincha Alta 355. Open till 2200.
Good pizzas and pastas, family run.

$$-$ Romana
Amazonas 1091. Daily 0700-2300.
Choice of set meals and à la carte,
good service.

$ El Edén
*Grau by the market. Sun-Thu 0700-2100,
Fri 0700-1800.*
Simple vegetarian, a variety of dishes
à la carte and economical set meals.

$ Matalaché
*Ayacucho 616. Daily 0730-1530,
1800-2230.*
Famous for their huge *milanesa*
(breaded beef); also serves *menú*.

Cafés

Dulcería Santa Elena
Amazonas 800. Daily 0900-2230.
Old-fashioned home-made desserts.

Fusiones
*Chincha Alta 445. Mon-Sat
0730-1130, 1600-2100.*
Breakfast, fair-trade coffee, juices,
snacks, Wi-Fi, book exchange,
volunteer opportunities.

Heladería San Antonio
2 de Mayo 521 and Amazonas 856.
Good home-made ice cream; try the
lúcuma and *guanábana* flavours.

Panadería Café San José
Ayacucho 816. Mon-Sat 0630-2200.
Bakery and café, good breakfasts,
sweets and snacks.

What to do

Chachapoyas
The cost of full-day trips depends
on season (higher Jul-Sep), distance,
number of passengers and whether
meals are included. Several operators
have daily departures to Kuélap (US$15-
19, 3 hrs each way in vehicle, including
lunch stop on return, 3 hrs at the site);
Gocta, US$13.50-15; Quiocta and Karajía,
US$19-27, and Museo de Leymebamba
and Revash, US$31-39. All inclusive
trekking tours to Gran Vilaya cost about
US$46-50 pp per day.
Amazon Expedition, *Jr Ortiz Arrieta
508, Plaza de Armas, T041-798718, http://
amazonexpedition.com.pe.* Day tours and
multi-day treks.
Andes Tours, at **Hostal Revash**. Daily
trips to Kuélap and Gocta, other tours
to ruins, caves and trekking. Also less-
visited destinations, combining travel
by car, on horseback and walking.
Cloudforest Expeditions, *Jr Puno 368,
T041-477610, www.kuelapnordperu.com.*
English and German spoken.
Nuevos Caminos, *at Café Fusiones,
T041-479170, www.nuevoscaminos
travel.com.* Alternative community
tourism throughout northern Peru,
volunteer opportunities.
Turismo Explorer, *Jr Grau 509,
T041-478162.* Daily tours to Kuélap,
Gocta and other destinations,
trekking tours including Laguna de
los Cóndores and other archaeological
sites, transport service.
Vilaya Tours, *T041-477506, www.
vilayatours.com.* All-inclusive treks
to off-the-beaten-path destinations
throughout northern Peru. Run by
Robert Dover, a very experienced
and knowledgeable British guide,
book ahead.

Guides

Martín Chumbe, T941-994650, martin. chumbe@yahoo.es, or through **Restaurante Las Rocas**, Jr Ayacucho, at the Plaza. Specializes in longer trips.

Transport

Celendín
Bus

To **Cajamarca**, 107 km, 3½ hrs, with **Royal Palace's** (Jr Unión y José Gálvez, by Plaza de Armas), 1400 daily; also **CABA**, 2 a day, and **Rojas**, 3 a day. Cars to Cajamarca leave when full from Ovalo Agusto Gil, Cáceres y Amazonas, 2½ hrs, US$9 pp. They also go from the same place to **Chachapoyas**, 6 hrs, US$18 pp. **Virgen del Carmen** (Cáceres 112 by Ovalo A Gil, T076-792918) to Chachapoyas, daily at 0900, US$11.55, via **Leymebamba**, 6 hrs, US$7.75.

Leymebamba and around

To **Chachapoyas** (fills quickly, book ahead), 2½-3 hrs, cars US$7.75, *combis* US$4, with **Transportes Karlita** (Jr Amazonas corner 16 de Julio on the plaza), at 0400 and 0500; **Mi Cautivo** (Jr San Agustín ½ block from the plaza), Mon-Sat 0500 and 0700, Sun 1100 and 1700; **Hidalgo Tours** (Jr Bolívar 608), at 0500. **Virgen del Carmen** buses (Jr 16 de Julio at Plaza) from Cajamarca pass **Leymebamba** at about 1400 en route to Chachapoyas; from Chacha they pass at 0800 for **Celendín**, US$7.75, and **Cajamarca**, US$11.55, 8 hrs.

Tingo to Kuélap

The easiest way to visit Kuélap is on a tour from Chachapoyas (see above) or by hiring a vehicle with driver (US$45 per vehicle, or US$54 with wait). Alternatively, **Trans Roller's** combis

or cars depart from Grau y Salamanca in Chachapoyas at 0400 to **Tingo** (US$3.10, 1 hr), **Choctámal** (US$3.85, 1½ hrs), **Lónguita** (US$4.60, 2 hrs), **María** (US$6, 2½ hrs) and **Kuélap**, US$6, 3 hrs (only if they have enough passengers). Note that the car returns from Kuélap straight away (around 0700), so you will have to spend the night in the area (see Where to stay). There is also additional transport in combis or cars to María with **Sr José Cruz** (Grau 331) at 0530 (returns from María at 0800) and to Lónguita with **Trans Shubet** (Pasaje Reyes, off Grau) around 1400-1500. Cars bound for Magdalena with **Brisas del Utcubamba** (Grau 332, Chachapoyas) and transport going to/ from Yerbabuena or Leymebamba also pass through **Tingo**.

Chachapoyas
Air

There is an airport but flights are sporadic; enquire locally.

Bus

Regional For services to **Tingo**, **Choctámal** and **Kuélap**, see above. To **Leymebamba**, 83 km, 3 hrs, US$4 (reserve ahead) with **Transportes Karlita** (Salamanca cuadra 9) at 1300 and 1600; with **Mi Cautivo** (Pasaje David Reina y Grau), at 1200 and 1600; with **Hidalgo Tours** (Jr Grau corner Pasaje David Reina) at 1300. For **Revash**, to **Santo Tomás**, **Comité Santo Tomás** at 1000, 1300, 1500 (return at 0300, 0400, 0500), US$4.30, 3 hrs; get off at **Cruce de Revash** (near Puente Santo Tomás), US$4.30, 2½ hrs; or with the same company to **San Bartolo** at 1400 (return 0600), US$4.30, 3 hrs. To **Jalca Grande**, from Jr Hermosura y Salamanca, 2 combis depart Mon-Fri from 1330 onwards, US$4.30, 3 hrs (return 0300-0400). To **Levanto**, cars from Av Cuarto Centenario y Sociego southeast end of town, daily 1200-1300, US$2.90. To **Mendoza** (86 km), **Guayabamba**, Ortiz Arrieta 372, US$7.75, 2½ hrs, combis from same address US$6. To **Luya** and **Lamud**, from Libertad y Chincha Alta, cars 0400-1800, US$2.85; there are cars from Luya to Cruzpata, 0600-1700, US$3, 1 hr.

Long distance To **Lima** (20-22 hrs, US$44-52) the best service is **Móvil** (Libertad 464, T041-478545), daily at 1300. An alternative is **GH Bus** (tickets from Jr Grau entre Triunfo y Amazonas, T041-479200) from its station at C Evitamiento (take a taxi) at 1030. Móvil is also recommended to **Chiclayo** (9 hrs, US$15-25) and **Trujillo** (12 hrs, US$23-29), daily 1930. Other options to Chiclayo are **Civa** (Salamanca y Ortiz Arrieta, T041-478048) at 1815, **El Expreso** (Jr Unión 330), 1930 daily, and **Transervis Kuelap** (Jr Union 330, T041-478128), Tue and Sat at 1900, other days at 2000. **GH Bus** runs to Chiclayo at 2000 and to Trujillo at 1930. To **Celendín** (8-9 hrs, US$11.55) and **Cajamarca** (11-12 hrs, US$18) with **Virgen del Carmen** (Salamanca 956), 2000 daily.

Cars leave from Grau 310 y Salamanca, 0600-1800, and from Grau in front of the market, 1800-2200, to **Pedro Ruiz** (for connections to Chiclayo, Jaén, or Tarapoto), US$3.85, 1 hr, and to **Bagua Grande,** US$8.50, 2 hrs, for connections to Jaén. There are also combis to Pedro Ruiz, every 2 hrs 0600-1800, from Ortiz Arrieta 370, US$2, and **Diplomáticos** vans, as they fill 0500-1900, from Libertad cuadra 10. Combis/vans to Bagua Grande with **Evangelio Poder de Dios** (Jr Libertad 1048), US$6. This company also goes to **Moyobamba** (for connections to Tarapoto), 0700, US$9.75, 5 hrs.

Gocta
The easiest way to get to Gocta is with a tour from Chachapoyas; in high season there are also tours from Pedro Ruiz. A taxi from Chachapoyas costs US$30, or US$38 with 5-6 hrs wait. A taxi from Pedro Ruiz costs US$2 pp (there are seldom other passengers to share) or US$10 for the vehicle. **Sr Fabier**, T962-922798, offers transport service to **San Pablo**; call ahead to find out when he will be in Pedro Ruiz. A moto-taxi from Pedro Ruiz (5 Esq, along the road to Chachapoyas, 4 blocks from the highway) costs US$6, beware of overcharging and dress warmly; it is windy and cold. Arrange return transport ahead or at the tourist offices in San Pablo or Cocachimba, as it is difficult to get transport back from Cocahuayco to either Chachapoyas or Pedro Ruiz.

Chachapoyas to the Amazon
look out for birdlife on this dramatic journey to the jungle

From Chachapoyas the road heads north through the beautiful Utcubamba canyon for one hour to a crossroads at Pedro Ruíz, which has two hotels, other lodgings and some basic restaurants. From here, you can return to the coast, head to Jaén for Ecuador, or continue east to Tarapoto and Yurimaguas, making the spectacular descent on a paved road from high Andes to jungle.

★ **Pedro Ruiz to Moyobamba**

In the rainy season, the road east of Pedro Ruiz may be subject to landslides. This is a very beautiful journey, first passing **Laguna Pomacochas**, then leading to where the high Andes tumble into the Amazon Basin before your eyes. The descent from the heights of the Abra Patricia Pass to the Río Afluente at 1400 m is one of the best birdwatching areas in northern Peru. ECOAN ⓘ www.ecoanperu.org, has a private reserve at Km 364.5 aimed at conserving the critically endangered long-whiskered owlet (Xenoglaux loweryi) and other rare species. Further along, **Nueva Cajamarca** (reported unsafe), **Rioja** (198 km, with several hotels) and **Moyobamba** are growing centres of population, with much forest clearance beside the road.

Moyobamba → *Colour map 1, B5.*

Moyobamba, capital of the San Martín Region, is a pleasant town in the attractive Río Mayo valley. The area is renowned for its orchids: there is a Festival de la Orquídea over three days around 1 November. Among several places to see the plants is **Orquideario Waqanki** ⓘ www.waqanki.com, daily 0700-1800, US$0.55, where the orchids have been placed in trees. Just beyond are **Baños Termales San Mateo** ⓘ 5 km southeast, daily 0600-2200, US$0.55, which are worth a visit. Boat trips can be taken from **Puerto Tahuishco**, the town's harbour, a pleasant walk north of the centre.

Morro de Calzada ⓘ 13.5 km west of Moyobamba via Calzada, combi to the Calzada turnoff, US$0.55, mototaxi to the start of the trail US$2.50, is an isolated outcrop in white sand forest that is good for birdwatching. A path through forest leads to a lookout at the top (1½ hours), but enquire about safety beforehand.

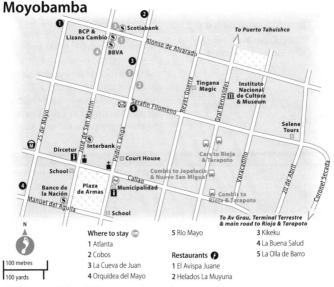

Moyobamba

Where to stay
1 Atlanta
2 Cobos
3 La Cueva de Juan
4 Orquídea del Mayo
5 Río Mayo

Restaurants
1 El Avispa Juane
2 Helados La Muyuna
3 Kikeku
4 La Buena Salud
5 La Olla de Barro

Lamas

Off the main road, 22 km northwest of Tarapoto, this small hill town has a Quechua-speaking native community, descendants of the Chancas people from the distant Central Highlands. Lamas is known as *'la ciudad de los tres pisos'* (the city of three storeys). On the top level, by the antennas, is a lookout with good views, a hotel-restaurant and a *recreo turístico*. The main town occupies the middle level, where there is a small **Museo Los Chankas** ⓘ *Jr San Martín 1157, daily 0830-1300, 1430-1800, US$1.15*, with ethnological and historical exhibits. Uphill from the museum is **El Castillo de Lamas** ⓘ *Mon-Sat 0900-1230, 1400-1800, Sun 0930-1830, US$2*, an art gallery and café set in a incongruous medieval castle. On the lower level is the neighbourhood of **Wayku**, where the native Chancas live. Some of the women wear traditional dress; you may see them at the market (largest on Sunday) in the main town early in the morning.

From Lamas you can visit several waterfalls including **Chapawanqui** ⓘ *US$1, taxi US$7, 15 mins, or take a car bound for Urcupata from Jr Lima corner 16 de Octubre, US$1 and get off at the turn-off*.

Tarapoto and around → *Colour map 1, C5.*

Tarapoto, the largest commercial centre in the region, with a population of 120,000, is a very friendly place. It stands at the foot of the forested hills of the **Area de Conservación Regional Cordillera Escalera** (149,870 ha), which is good for birdwatching and walking. Next to the conservation area and within easy reach of town is the 9-ha **El Amo del Bosque Sector** ⓘ *Urawasha, 5 km walk (9 km by car) from town, T042-524675 (after 1900)*, where the knowledgeable owner, Sr José Macedo, offers guided tours, and 20-hectare **Wayrasacha** ⓘ *6-km walk (10 km by car) from the city, T042-522261, www.wayrasacha.com.pe*, run by Peruvian-Swiss couple César Ramírez and Stephanie Gallusser, who offer day trips, overnight stays in a basic shelter and volunteer opportunities (English and French spoken).

Tarapoto to Yurimaguas

From Tarapoto it is 129 km to Yurimaguas on the Río Huallaga (see page 482), along a spectacular paved road. The road climbs through lush country reaching the 50-m **Ahuashiyacu Falls** ⓘ *US$1.15*, within the **Cordillera Escalera** conservation area after 15 km. This is a popular place with locals. Tours are available or there's transport from La Banda de Shilcayo. Past Ahuashiyacu, the road climbs to a tunnel – stop at the police control for good birdwatching (mototaxi US$6) – after which you descend through beautiful forest perched on rocky cliffs to Pongo de Caynarachi (several basic *comedores*), where the flats start. From Yurimaguas launches go to Iquitos (see page 486).

Tarapoto to Tingo María

The Carretera Marginal Sur heads south from Tarapoto, crossing the Río Mayo and then following the route of the Río Huallaga. East of the Huallaga, 52 km south of Tarapoto, **Laguna Azul** (also known as Laguna de Sauce) is a big lake with a choice of accommodation (eg $$$ **El Sauce Resort**, 3 blocks from the plaza, T042-522588, www.elsauceresort.com); there are motor boats for hire and a couple of waterfalls nearby. Further south, **Picota**, 59 km from Tarapoto on the Huallaga, is promoting itself as a tourist destination with access to several waterfalls, thermal baths and a cave with oilbirds. It has *alojamientos* and eateries. The road is paved from Tarapoto to **Juanjuí**, but the next section to **Tocache** is unpaved (about seven hours by bus) and is less safe than other parts of this road, although hold-ups may occur anywhere. Enquire about the current situation before travelling. From Tocache, the road continues paved to Tingo María (see page 477).

(see page 477)

Listings Chachapoyas to the Amazon *maps p220 and p223*

Tourist information

Moyobamba

Oficina Municipal de Información
Jr Pedro Canga 262, at Plaza, T042-562191 ext 541. Mon-Fri 0800-1300, 1430-1715. No English spoken.

Dircetur
Jr San Martín 301, T042-562043. Mon-Fri 0800-1300, 1430-1730.
Has leaflets and map, English spoken. Also see www.moyobamba.net.

Tarapoto

Oficina Municipal de Información
Jr Ramírez Hurtado, at plaza, T042-526188, Mon-Sat 0800-1300, 1500-2000, Sun 0900-1300.

Dircetur
Jr Angel Delgado Morey, cuadra 1, T042-522567.

Where to stay

Moyobamba

$$$ Puerto Mirador
Jr Sucre, 1 km from centre, T042-562050, www.hotelpuertomirador.com.
Buffet breakfast, lovely grounds, views overlooking river valley, pool, good restaurant, credit cards accepted.

$$ Orquídea del Mayo
Jr San Martín 432, T042-561049, orquideadelmayohostal@hotmail.com.
Modern comfortable rooms with bath.

$$ Río Mayo
Jr Pedro Canga 415, T042-564193.
Central, modern comfortable rooms, frigobar, small indoor pool, parking.

$$-$ El Portón
Jr San Martín 449, T042-866121, casahospedajeelporton@hotmail.com.
Pleasant modern rooms with fan, hot water, nice grounds with hammocks, kitchen facilities.

$ Atlanta
Alonso de Alvarado 865, T042-562063, atlantainn@hotmail.com.
Hot water, parking, fan, good value but front rooms noisy.

$ Cobos
Jr Pedro Canga 404, T042-562153.
Private bath, cold water, simple but good.

$ La Cueva de Juan
Jr Alonso de Alvarado 870, T042-562488, lacueva870@hotmail.com.
Small courtyard, private bath, hot water, central but reasonably quiet, good value.

Lamas

$ Hosp Girasoles
Opposite the mirador in the upper part of town, T042-543439, stegmaiert@yahoo.de.

Breakfast available, nice views, pizzeria and friendly, knowledgeable owners.

Tarapoto and around
There are several $ *alojamientos* on Alegría Arias de Morey, cuadra 2, and cheap basic hotels by the bus terminals.

$$$ Puerto Palmeras
Cra Belaúnde Terry, Km 614, T042-524100.
Private reserve outside town. Large, modern complex, popular with families, lots of activities and entertainment. Nice rooms, helpful staff, good restaurant, pleasant grounds with pool, mountain bikes, horses and small zoo, airport transfers.

$$$ Puma Rinri Lodge
Cra Shapaja–Chasuta, Km 16, T042-526694, www.pumarinri.com.
Lodge/resort hotel on the shores of the Río Huallaga, 30 km east of Tarapoto. Offers a variety of all-inclusive packages.

$$ Huingos Lodge
Prolongación Alerta cuadra 6, Sector Takiwasi, T042-524171, www.huingoslodge.com.
Nice cabins in lovely grounds by the Río Shilcayo. Fan, electric shower, frigobar, kitchen facilities, hammocks, HI-affiliated, mototaxi from bus stations US$1.55-2.

$$ La Patarashca
Jr San Pablo de la Cruz 362, T042-528810, www.lapatarashca.com.

Tarapoto

N

100 metres
100 yards

Where to stay	Restaurants	6 Real Grill
1 El Mirador	1 Café Plaza	
2 La Patarashca	2 Chifa Cantón	
3 La Posada Inn	3 El Manguaré	
4 Luna Azul	4 Helados La Muyuna	
5 San Antonio	5 La Patarashca Restaurant	

Very nice hotel with large rooms, cheaper without a/c, rustic, restaurant, electric shower, large garden with hammocks, tours arranged.

$$ Luna Azul
Jr Manco Capac 276, T042-525787, www.lunaazulhotel.com.
Modern, central, includes breakfast and airport transfers, with bath, hot water, a/c or fan, frigobar.

$$-$ El Mirador
Jr San Pablo de la Cruz 517, 5 blocks uphill from the plaza T042-522177, www.elmiradortarapoto.blogspot.com.
With bath, electric shower, fan, Wi-Fi, laundry facilities, breakfast available, hammocks on rooftop terrace with good views, tours arranged.
Family-run and very welcoming.

$$-$ La Posada Inn
San Martín 146, T042-522234, laposada_inn@yahoo.es.
Convenient but ageing hotel, a/c or fan, electric shower, fridge, nice atmosphere. **El Merendero** restaurant on ground floor.

$ San Antonio
Jr Jiménez Pimentel 126, T042-525563.
Rooms with private bath, hot water and fan, good value.

Restaurants

Moyobamba

$$-$ Kikeku
Jr Pedro Canga 450, next to casino. Open 24 hrs.
Good *chifa*, also *comida criolla*, large portions, noisy.

$$-$ La Olla de Barro
Pedro Canga 398. Daily 0800-2200.
Tourist place serving regional food and other Peruvian dishes.

$ El Avispa Juane
Jr Callao 583. Mon-Sat 0730-1600, Sun 0800-1500.
Regional specialities, menu Mon-Sat and snacks, popular.

$ La Buena Salud
25 de Mayo 227, by market. Sun-Fri 0800-1500.
Vegetarian set meals, breakfast and fruit juices.

Helados La Muyuna
Jr Pedro Canga 529.
Good natural jungle fruit ice cream.

Tarapoto
There are several restaurants and bars around Jr San Pablo de la Cruz on the corner of Lamas – a lively area at night.

$$$-$$ Chalet Venezia
Jr Alegría Arias de Morey 298, www.restaurantcafechaletvenezia.com. Tue-Sun 1200-2300.
Upmarket Italian-Amazonian fusion cuisine, wine list, elegant decor, interior or terrace seating.

$$$-$$ Real Grill
Jr Moyobamba on the plaza. Daily 0830-2400.
Regional and international food. One of the best in town.

$$-$ Chifa Cantón
Jr Ramón Castilla 140. Mon-Fri 1200-1600, Sat-Sun 1200-2400.
Chinese, very popular and clean.

$ El Manguaré
Jr Moyobamba corner Manco Cápac. Mon-Sat 1200-1530.
Choice of set meals and à la carte, good food and service.

Cafés

Café Plaza
Jr Maynas corner Martínez, at the plaza.
Daily 0730-2300.
Breakfast, coffee, snacks, juices,
Wi-Fi, popular.

Helados La Muyuna
Jr Ramón Castilla 271. Sun-Thu 0800-
2400, Fri 0800-1700, Sat 1830-2400.
Good natural ice cream, fruit salads
and drinks made with jungle fruits.

Festivals

Lamas
Lamas' **Easter** celebrations draw many
Peruvian visitors, as do the **Fiestas
Patronales** in honour of Santa Rosa de
Lima in the last week in Aug.

Transport

Chachapoyas to the Amazon
Pedro Ruíz
Bus
Many buses on the Chiclayo–Tarapoto
and Chiclayo–Chachapoyas routes
pass through town. Bus fare to
Chiclayo, US$11.50-19; to **Tarapoto**,
US$11.50-15.50. Cars or combis are
more convenient for Chacha or Bagua.
To **Jaén**, **Trans Fernández** bus from
Tarapoto passes Pedro Ruiz about 1400-
1500, or take a car to Bagua Grande and
transfer there.

Car, combi and van
To **Chachapoyas**, cars US$4, combis
US$2, 1 hr. To **Bagua Grande**,
cars US$4.75, combis US$4, 1hr. To
Moyobamba, cars US$10.70, 4 hrs.
To **Nueva Cajamarca**, cars US$9.75,
combis US$7.75, 3-3½ hrs. From Nueva

Cajamarca it's a further 20 mins to **Rioja**
by car, US$1.15, or combi, US$0.75. From
Rioja to **Moyobamba**, 21 km, 20 mins,
car US$1.15, combi US$0.75.

Moyobamba
Bus
The bus terminal is 12 blocks from the
centre on Av Grau (mototaxi US$0.55).
No services originate in Moyobamba;
all buses are en route to/from Tarapoto.
Several companies head west to **Pedro
Ruiz** (US$9, 4 hrs), **Jaén** (US$9, 7 hrs),
Chiclayo (US$15-US$23, 12 hrs). To
reserve a seat on a long-haul bus, you
may have to pay the fare to the final
destination even if you get off sooner.

Car, combi and van
Empresa San Martín (Benavides 276)
and **ETRISA** (Benavides 244) run cars
(US$1.15) and vans (US$0.75) to **Rioja,**
20 mins; to **Nueva Cajamarca**, 40 mins
(US$2, US$1.55) and **Tarapoto**, 2 hrs
(US$7.75, US$4); combis cost about 50%
less on all routes. To **Chachapoyas**,
Evangelio Poder de Dios (Grau 640),
at 1500, US$9.75, 5 hrs.

Tarapoto
Air
Taxi to town, US$3; mototaxi US$1.15. To
Lima, daily with **LAN** (Ramírez Hurtado
183, on the plaza, T042-529318), **Avianca/
TACA**, **Peruvian Airlines** and **Star Perú**
(San Pablo de la Cruz 100, T042-528765).
Star Perú to **Iquitos** daily (Mon, Wed, Fri
via Pucallpa), **LAN** to Iquitos Mon, Thu.
The military **Grupo Aéreo 42** (J Martínez
de Compagñon 688, T972-990630) has
passenger flights to Tarapoto originating
in **Trujillo** or **Iquitos**; see page 150 for
routes and schedules.

Bus

Buses depart from Av Salaverry, blocks 8-9, in Morales; mototaxi from centre, US$1.15, 20 mins.

To **Moyobamba**, 116 km, US$3.85, 2 hrs; to **Pedro Ruiz**, US$11.50-15.50 (companies going to Jaén or Chiclayo), 6 hrs; to **Chiclayo**, 690 km, 15-16 hrs, US$25-29; and **Lima**, US$46-52, *cama* US$64, 30 hrs. For **Chachapoyas**, go to Moyobamba and take a van from there (see above). To **Jaén**, US$13.50-15.50, 9-10 hrs, with **Fernández**, 4 a day. To **Piura** US$23, 16 hrs, with **Sol Peruano**, at 1200. To **Tingo María**, US$27, and **Pucallpa**, US$35, Mon, Wed, Fri 0500, Tue, Thu, Sat 0830, **Transamazónica**

and **Transmar** alternate days; there have been armed holdups on this route.

Car, combi and van

To **Lamas**, cars from Av Alfonso Ugarte, cuadra 11, US$1.45, 30 mins. To **Moyobamba**, cars with **Empresa San Martín** (Av Alfonso Ugarte 1456, T042-526327) and **ETRISA** (Av Alfonso Ugarte 1096, T042-521944); both will pick you up from your hotel, US$7.70, 2 hrs; combis with **Turismo Selva** (Av Alfonso Ugarte, cuadra 11), US$4, 2½ hrs. To **Yurimaguas**, **Gilmer Tours** (Av Alfonso Ugarte 1480), frequent minibuses, US$5.75, 2½ hrs; cars with **Empresa San Martín**, US$7.75, 2 hrs; **Turismo Selva** vans, US$4, 8 daily.

Chachapoyas to Ecuador

a scenic route and a straightforward border crossing

Bagua Grande and further west

This is the first town of note heading west from Pedro Ruiz. It has several hotels but is hot, dusty and unsafe; Pedro Ruiz or Jaén are more pleasant places to spend the night. From Bagua Grande the road follows the Río Chamaya, climbing to the Abra de Porculla (2150 m) before descending to join the old Pan-American Highway at **Olmos** (see page 163). From Olmos you can go southwest to Chiclayo, or northwest to Piura.

Jaén → *Colour map 1, B3.*

Some 50 km west of Bagua Grande, a road branches northwest at Chamaya to **Jaén**, a convenient stopover en route to the jungle or Ecuador. It is a modern city surrounded by rice fields, with a population of about 100,000. The **Museo Hermógenes Mejía Solf** ⓘ *2 km south of centre, T976-719590, Mon-Fri 0800-1400, mototaxi US$0.60,* displays pre-Columbian artefacts from a variety of cultures. Newly discovered temples at Monte Grande and San Isidro, close to Jaén, are revealing more finds, dating back possibly to 3500 BC.

San Ignacio to the border

A road runs north for 109 km to **San Ignacio** (only the first 55 km are paved), a pleasant town with steep streets in the centre of a coffee-growing area. The nearby hills offer excursions to waterfalls, lakes, petroglyphs and ancient ruins. West of San Ignacio is the **Santuario Tabaconas-Namballe** ⓘ *Sernanp, Huancabamba s/n, Sector Santiago, downhill from the centre in San Ignacio, T968-218439,* a 32,125-ha reserve at 1700-3800 m protecting the spectacled bear, mountain tapir and several ecosystems including the southernmost Andean *páramo*. From San Ignacio the unpaved road, being widened, runs 45 km through green hills to **Namballe** and the border with Ecuador (see box, page 229).

Where to stay

Bagua Grande

$$-$ Río Hotel
Jr Capac Malku 115, www.riohotel
baguagrande.blogspot.com.
A good choice if you can't avoid staying in Bagua Grande.

Jaén

$$ Casa del Sol
Mcal Castilla 140, near Plaza de Armas,
T076-434478, hotelcasadelsol
@hotmail.com.
Modern comfortable rooms with frigobar, parking, suites with jacuzzi.

$$ El Bosque
Mesones Muro 632, T076-431184,
hoteleraelbosque@speedy.com.pe.
On main road by bus terminals. Quiet rooms at the back, gardens, frigobar, solar hot water, pool, good restaurant.

$$ Hostal Valle Verde
Mcal Castilla 203, Plaza de Armas,
T076-432201.
Modern, large comfortable rooms, a/c or fan, hot water, frigobar, parking.

$$ Prim's
Diego Palomino 1341, T076-431039,
www.primshotel.com.
Includes breakfast, good service, comfortable, hot water, a/c or fan, frigobar, Wi-Fi, friendly, small pool.

$ Cancún
Diego Palomino 1413, T076-433511.
Good value rooms with hot water, fan.

$ Danubio
V Pinillos 429, T076-433110.
Older place, nicely refurbished, many different rooms and prices, some cheaper rooms have cold water only, fan, good.

San Ignacio to the border

$ Gran Hotel San Ignacio
Jr José Olaya 680 at the bottom of
the hill, San Ignacio, T076-356544,
granhotel-sanignacio@hotmail.com.
Restaurant for breakfast and good lunch *menú*, modern comfortable rooms, upmarket for San Ignacio.

$ Hostal Maldonado
Near the plaza, Namballe, T076-830011
(community phone).
Private bath (cheaper without), cold water, basic.

$ La Posada
Jr Porvenir 218, San Ignacio, T076-356180.
Simple rooms which are cheaper without bath or hot water, restaurant.

$ Sol de la Frontera
1 km north of Namballe, 4 km from
La Balsa, T976-116781, T01-247 8881 in
Lima, www.hotelsoldelafrontera.com.
British-run by Isabel Wood. Comfortable rooms in bungalows, bathtubs, gas water heaters, continental breakfast, set in 2.5 ha of countryside. A good option if you have your own vehicle or bring some food. Meals only available for groups with advance booking. Camping and campervans.

Restaurants

Jaén

$$-$ La Cabaña
Bolívar 1332 at Plaza de Armas.
Daily 0700-0000.
Daily specials at noon, à la carte
in the evening, popular.

$$-$ Lactobac
Bolívar 1378 at Plaza de Armas.
Daily 0730-0000.

Variety of à la carte dishes, snacks, desserts,
good *pollo a la brasa*. Very popular.

$ Cenfrocafé
San Martín 1528. Mon-Sat 0730-1330,
1600-2300.
Serve a variety of coffees, sandwiches,
humitas and desserts, Wi-Fi.

$ Ebenezer
Mcal Ureta 1360. Sun-Thu 0700-2130,
Fri 0700-1600.

Chachapoyas - Vilcabamba (Ecuador)

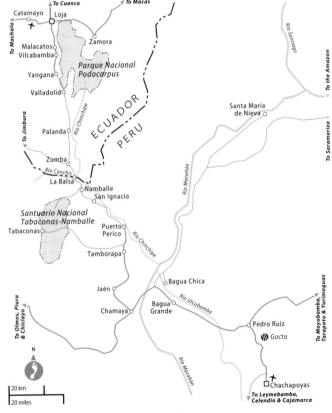

Namballe–Zumba

The border is 15 minutes from Namballe at **La Balsa** (taxi or moto-taxi, US$1.15), which has a simple lodging and *comedor*, a few small shops and money changers. To leave Perú, head directly to immigration (daily 0830-1300, 1500-2000); ask for the officer at his house if he is not at his desk). To enter Peru, visit immigration first, then get a stamp from the PNP (police), and return to immigration. *Rancheras* (open-sided buses) run from La Balsa to Zumba at 1200, 1700 and 1915 (US$1.75, 1¾ hrs) and from Zumba to La Balsa at 0800, 1430 and 1700. From Zumba there is onward transport to Vilcabamba and Loja; the road was being paved in 2015. There are Ecuadorean military controls before and after Zumba (keep your passport to hand), but in general this crossing is relaxed and straightforward.

Simple vegetarian restaurant serves economical midday *menú* and à la carte.

$ Gatizza
Diego Palomino 1503. Mon-Sat 0830-1800.
Tasty and varied *menú*.

Transport

Bagua Grande
Many buses en route to/from **Chiclayo**, **Tarapoto** or **Chachapoyas**. Cars to **Jaén** from Mcal Castilla y Angamos at the west end of town, US$4, combis US$2.50, 1 hr. From R Palma 308 at the east end of town, cars leave to **Pedro Ruiz**, US$4.60, combis US$4, 1 hr; to **Chachapoyas**, US$9.75, combis US$5.75, 2½ hrs.

Jaén
Bus, car and combi
Terminals are strung along Mesones Muro, blocks 4-7, south of centre. To **Chiclayo**, US$7.75-15.50, 6 hrs, many companies, **Móvil** more expensive than others. Cars to Chiclayo from Mesones Muro, cuadra 4, US$27, 5 hrs. To **Lima**, with **Móvil** at 1500, 16 hrs, *bus cama* US$46, *semi-cama* US$38.50; with **Civa** (tickets from Mcal Ureta 1300 y V Pinillos; terminal at Bolívar 935), 1700, US$35-42. Service to Lima also goes through **Trujillo**. To **Piura** via Olmos, with **Sol Peruano**, at 2200, US$15.50, 8 hrs. To **Tarapoto**, 490 km, US$13.50-15.50, 9-10 hrs, with **Fernández**, 4 a day. To **Moyobamba**, US$11.50-13.50, 7 hrs, same service as Tarapoto, likewise to **Pedro Ruiz**, US$6-7.75, 3½ hrs. To **Bagua Grande**, cars from Mesones Muro cuadra 6, 0400-2000, US$4, 1hr; combis from cuadra 9, US$2.50. To **Chamaya,** cars from Mesones Muro, cuadra 4, 0500-2000, US$1, 15 min. To **San Ignacio** (for Ecuador), cars from Av Pacamuros, cuadra 19, 0400-1800, US$7.75, 2 hrs; combis from cuadra 17, US$4.60, 3 hrs.

San Ignacio to the border
Bus
To **Chiclayo**, with **Civa** (Av San Ignacio 386), daily at 1830, US$11.55, 10-11 hrs; with **Trans Chiclayo** (Av San Ignacio 406), 1945 daily. To **Jaén**, from *óvalo* at south end of Av Mariano Melgar. To **Namballe** and **La Balsa**, cars leave from Sector Alto Loyola at north end of town, way above the centre, US$6 to Namballe, US$6.55 to La Balsa, 1½ hrs.

South Coast

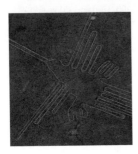

The desert coastline south of Lima has some distinctive attractions. The most famous, and perhaps the strangest, are the enigmatic Nazca Lines, whose origin and function continue to puzzle scientists.

Further north, the Ica Valley, with its wonderful climate, produces that equally wonderful grape brandy known as *pisco*. And, on the coast, the Paracas Peninsula, once home to one of Peru's most important ancient civilizations is now an internationally recognized marine reserve. As you bob in a boat to the Ballestas Islands to watch the seabirds, look for the giant Candelabra, drawn on the cliffs by unknown hands.

South of Nazca, on a small bay, is Puerto Inca, the seaport and fishing harbour for Cuzco in pre-colonial times. The major Inca road from here through the canyons to the sierra may have fallen into disuse, but several important paved roads now climb up from the coast to the highlands from Pisco, Nazca and Camaná. A rougher route from coast to sierra starts in the Cañete Valley, not far south of Lima, and climbs through the Yauyos to Huancayo. The road passes through stunning scenery and culturally fascinating villages where ancient languages are spoken.

Best for
Archaeological mysteries ▪ Birdwatching ▪ Pisco

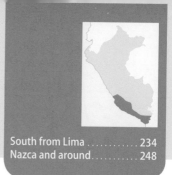

Footprint picks

★ **Cañete Valley**, page 235

Follow a rough road from the coast to the sierras, through miles of pre-Columbian terracing and spectacular natural scenery.

★ **Bodegas**, page 235 and 241

Watch *pisco* being made in the traditional way before sampling a glass.

★ **Ballestas Islands**, page 239

Spot sea birds, dolphins and evidence of an ancient culture.

★ **Nazca Lines**, page 249

Puzzle over these mysterious designs in the desert.

★ **Puerto Inca**, page 253

Visit the remains of the pre-Columbian port at the start of the Inca road to Cuzco.

Footprint picks

1 Cañete Valley, page 235
2 Bodegas, pages 235 and 241
3 Ballestas Islands, page 239
4 Nazca Lines, page 249
5 Puerto Inca, page 253

Essential South Coast

Finding your feet

The Pan-American Highway runs along the coast all the way south from Lima to the Chilean border and is the main transport artery for the South Coast. (The highway is soon to be a dual carriageway from Lima to Ica.) There are several important roads branching off it, east to the highlands: the highway from Nazca to Abancay is the main overland route from Lima to Cuzco; north of Nazca, another paved road runs from Pisco to Ayacucho in the Central Highlands, while to the south a highway leads from Camaná to Arequipa and Juliaca.

Getting around

There are frequent bus services south along the Pan-American Highway from Lima. Cars and vans provide local transport, although you will need a taxi to visit the bodegas around Ica. The Paracas Peninsula is best visited on a tour from either Pisco or Paracas. The Nazca Lines are best seen from the air. However, flights tend to be turbulent and can be dangerous, so you are advised to join a land-based tour or hire a taxi-guide.

When to go

The summer months are December to April. There may be sea mists May to October, although the Nazca Lines are far enough inland not to be affected. Here, the sun blazes year round by day and the nights are crisp. Ica has a very pleasant climate that allows grapes to thrive. Sandstorms can be a problem around the Paracas Peninsula, especially in August, when they can last for days.

Time required

You'll need one to two weeks thoroughly to explore, but a few days is enough time to see the Nazca Lines en route to elsewhere.

Weather Nazca

January	February	March	April	May	June
26°C 19°C 5mm	27°C 19°C 9mm	27°C 18°C 14mm	25°C 17°C 0mm	23°C 16°C 0mm	21°C 14°C 0mm

July	August	September	October	November	December
19°C 13°C 0mm	19°C 13°C 0mm	20°C 14°C 0mm	21°C 14°C 0mm	22°C 16°C 0mm	24°C 17°C 0mm

South from
Lima

There are a number of reasons to stop on the route south from Lima to Nazca. First are the beaches stretching south from the capital to San Vicente de Cañete, popular with surfers and sunbathers. From Cañete a road winds its way inland through extraordinary scenery towards Huancayo. Here, sandwiched between the main Pacific highway and one of the principal commercial centres of the Central Highlands, you will find a way of life quite different from mainstream Peru. Further south, Pisco is the access point for the Paracas marine reserve, while Ica is the centre of Peru's wine and pisco production.

Cañete Province

beaches, vineyards and a forgotten valley

Along the coast to Cañete

Beyond the beaches that are popular with Limeños the road passes near several towns. After El Silencio, the next notable beaches are **Punta Hermosa** at Km 39 and **Punta Negra**, Km 47, both popular with surfers. **San Bartolo** at Km 49 is very busy from New Year's Eve to March but is quiet at other times. All have plenty of places to eat. Most beaches have very strong currents and can be dangerous for swimming; if unsure, ask locals. Next is the fishing village of **Pucusana**, 57 km south of Lima. It is a working harbour with summer houses for Limeños. You can hire a boat for an hour's trip to see Humboldt penguins, sea cat otters, Inca terns, gulls, pelicans, cormorants, boobies and other seabirds; they are best seen close at hand near the rocks, not in the direction of the smelly factory.

Beyond **Chilca** (14 km south of Pucusana) famous for its figs, is **Asia**, an exclusive resort for wealthy Limeños, stretching from Km 92 to Km 104 and marked by a great wall. The 20 or so beaches are private, but the commercial centre adjoining the highway, with its smart restaurants and shopping, is open to all who can afford it.

Cañete and Quebrada de Lunahuana

About 150 km south of Lima, on the Río Cañete, is the prosperous market centre of **San Vicente de Cañete**. All the main services are within a few blocks of the plaza. A paved road runs inland, mostly beside the Río Cañete, through Imperial and Nuevo Imperial to **Lunahuaná** (40 km). This town is located 8 km beyond the Inca ruins of **Incawasi**, which used to dominate the valley. In the week Lunahuaná is very quiet, but on Sunday the town is full of life, with pisco tastings from the valley's bodegas, food and handicrafts for sale in the plaza and lots of outdoor activities.

⭐Several *bodegas* in the Cañete valley welcome visitors, including: Los Reyes ① *T01-435 5940, www. vinosypiscoslosreyes.com*, and Viña Santa María ① *T994-653790, www.bodegasantamaria.com*, in Condoray, and **Reyna de Lunahuaná** ① *T992-050846*, in Catapalla, which claims to be the oldest in the region.

> **Tip...**
> Throughout February and March you may still be able to see traditional methods of treading the grapes to the beat of a drum.

⭐Upper Cañete Valley

Beyond Lunahuaná the road ascending the Cañete Valley leaves the narrow flood-plain and runs 41 km, paved, through a series of gorges to the San Jerónimo bridge. A side road heads to Huangáscar and the village of Viñac, where **Mountain Lodges of Peru** has its **Viñak-Reichraming Lodge** (see Where to stay, page 237). The road beyond Huangáscar, from which you can see extensive areas of pre-Columbian agricultural terracing, is impassable from January to mid-March.

The main road carries on to the market towns of **Yauyos** (basic accommodation, 5 km off the road) and **Llapay**, a good base in the middle of the valley. Beyond Llapay, the Cañete valley narrows to an exceptionally tight canyon; the road squeezes between rock and rushing water. Near Alís, the road forks. The eastern branch climbs steeply to a 4600-m pass then drops down to Huancayo (see page 437), while the northern branch follows the Río Cañete deeper into the **Reserva Paisajística Nor Yauyos-Cochas** ① *contact Juan Carlos Pilco (pilco_traveler@hotmail.com) or the Sernanp regional office: RPNYC, Av Francisco Solano 107, San Carlos, Huancayo, T064-213064.* After the attractive village of **Huancaya,** the valley is transformed into one of the most beautiful upper valleys in all Peru, on a par with Colca. The river passes through high Andean terrain and descends through a series of absolutely clear, turquoise pools and lakes, interrupted by cascades and white water rapids. Culturally, the valley is fascinating for its dying indigenous languages and traditional ways of life, including perhaps the best pre-Columbian terracing anywhere in Peru.

Tourist information

Cañete and Quebrada de Lunahuana
For information on Cañete town, see
www.municanete.gob.pe, or the Oficina
de Turismo's Facebook page. There's
a **tourist office** in Lunahuaná in the
Municipalidad, opposite the church
(T01-284 1006, open daily).

Upper Cañete Valley
For details of accommodation in
Huancaya, call T01-810 6086/7,
or see www.huancaya.com.

Where to stay

Along the coast to Cañete

$$$ Casa Barco
Av Punta Hermosa 340, T01-230 7081,
www.casabarco.com.
A funky little hotel with pool, artworks,
private rooms with sea view, also has
shared rooms with shared bath ($)
and luxury suites. Meal plans available.

$$$ Peñascal Surf Hotel
Av Las Palmeras 258, Peñascal, San
Bartolo, T01-430 7436,
www.surfpenascal.com.
Price is for full board, including welcome
drink, Spanish lessons and transfer to
surfing area. Rooms overlook the sea,
cooking lessons available, seafood and
vegetarian meals, other sports and tours
offered, good, relaxing place.

$$$-$$ Hostal 110
Malecón San Martín Norte 110,
San Bartolo, T01-430 7559,
www.hostal110.com.
Apartments and rooms with great views,
very comfortable, 2 pools, also owns
Hostal 800 on the same beach.

$$ El Mirador
Distrito Turístico de Pucusana, T01-430
9228, www.elmiradordepucusana.com.
On a hill overlooking Pucusana town and
harbour, good value local food available.

$$ La Rotunda
Av Bolognesi 580, Punta Hermosa,
T01-230 7753, www.larotonda
puntahermosa.com.
Surf hostel above restaurant of same
name, on the boardwalk, large rooms,
good views, surfing lessons and
equipment available.

Cañete and Quebrada de Lunahuana
There are places to stay in San Vicente
de Cañete, and a range of options in
and around Lunahuaná, from large
family resorts and *casas de campo* to
campsites, plus many *restaurantes*
campestres. Note that prices may rise
at weekends and holidays.

$$$ El Molino Hotel y Restaurante
Malecón Araoz, Cra Cañete–
Lunahuaná, Km 39, T01-378 6062,
www.hotelelmolino.com.pe.
Modern hotel with well-appointed
rooms, local food in restaurant, gym,
gardens, riverside terrace, pool.

$$$ Rumiwasi
Cra Cañete–Yauyos, Km 38, Jita,
T01-284 1290, http://hotelrumiwasi
lunahuana.com.
Modern hotel with standard and
superior rooms, some with jacuzzi,
restaurant, swimming pool, riverside.

$$ Río Alto
Cra Cañete–Lunahuaná,
Km 38.5, Condoray, T01-284 1125,
www.rioaltohotel.com.

Just outside Lunahuaná, rooms for up to 4 people, restaurant, bar, swimming pool, rafting, biking and other sports, very pleasant.

$$-$ El Molle
Cra Cañete–Yauyos, Km 40, Condoray, T01-284 1096, www.hotelelmolle.net.
Double and family room, with restaurant and bar, swimming pool and gardens.

$ El Valle
Cra Cañete–Yauyos, Km 41.5, T01-378 6059.
Simple rooms with bath, hot water and TV at restaurant of the same name.

$ Hostal Casuarinas
Grau 295, near Lunahuaná's plaza, T01-284 1045.
Basic but clean hostal, rooms with bath and hot water, restaurant.

Upper Cañete Valley

$$$ Viñak-Reichraming Lodge
Mountain Lodges of Peru, T01-421 6952, www.refugiosdelperu.com.
A wonderful place to relax or go horse riding or walking, with superb views and excellent food. Prices are per person for full board.

$ Hostal Llapay
Llapay.
Basic but very friendly, will open at any hour, restaurant.

Festivals

Cañete and Quebrada de Lunahuana
Feb A **festival of adventure sports** is held in Lunahuaná.
1st weekend of Mar **Fiesta de la Vendimia** (grape harvest) in Lunahuaná.
Last week of Aug **Cañete festival**, with regional music and dancing.

What to do

Cañete and Quebrada de Lunahuana
Several agencies in Lunahuaná offer rafting and kayaking on the Río Cañete, especially at the *anexo* of San Jerónimo: Nov-Apr rafting is at levels IV-V; May-Oct is low water, levels I-II only.

Transport

Cañete Province
Soyuz bus runs between Lima and **Cañete** every 7 mins, US$5. There are combis between Cañete and **Lunahuaná**, US$2.75. Cars run from the Yauyos area to **Huancayo**, US$7.50. Ask locally where and when they leave. Public transport between villages is scarce and usually goes in the morning. When you get to a village you may have to wait till the early evening for places to open up.

Ica Region

go birdwatching around Paracas or visit the bodegas around Ica

In August 2007, an earthquake of 7.9 on the Richter scale struck the coast of Peru south of Lima, killing 519 people and injuring 1366; 58,500 homes were destroyed. Hardest hit was the region of Ica; in the port city of Pisco almost half of the buildings were destroyed. In October 2011, another earthquake, this time measuring 6.9 on the Richter scale, occurred just off the coast of Ica, leaving one dead, 1705 homeless and 515 damaged or destroyed houses.

Chincha Alto and El Carmen

Negro criollo culture thrives in the town of **Chincha Alta**, 35 km north of Pisco, where African slave labour once allowed the great haciendas to thrive (see box, page 542), and is celebrated at local festivals (see page 246). Chincha is also a good place to sample locally produced wine and pisco. One of the best *bodegas* is **Naldo Navarro** ⓘ *Pasaje Santa Rosa, Sunampe, 100 m west of the Panamericana, T056-271356, http://vinosnaldonavarro.com*, which offers guided tours and tastings. **Hacienda San José** is 9 km south of town in El Carmen (turn off the Panamericana at Km 203). It is a 17th-century sugar and cotton estate, with beautiful buildings, gardens and a small church. Tunnels run from the basement to link up with neighbouring *haciendas* and the old port of Tambo de Mora. These were used to facilitate the contraband trade in black slaves from Africa and to provide refuge from pirates. The extent of the tunnels was revealed after San José was severely damaged in the 2007 earthquake; since then it has been converted into a luxury hotel (see Where to stay, page 242), but the catacombs, where many of the slaves were interred, can be visited.

From Pisco to the sierras → *Colour map 5, B2.*

The largest port (*population: 82,250*) between Callao and Matarani, Pisco is located a short distance west of the Pan-American Highway and 237 km south of Lima. A 317-km paved road goes up the Pisco valley from the suburb of San Clemente to Ayacucho in the sierra, with a branch to Huancavelica. At Castrovirreyna it reaches 4600 m. The scenery on this journey is superb. The road passes one of the best-preserved Inca ruins in coastal Peru after 38 km: **Tambo Colorado** ⓘ *see www.facebook.com/TamboColorado for details of a French research project here*, includes buildings where the Inca and his retinue would have stayed. Many of the walls retain their original colours. On the other side of the road are the public plaza, the garrison and the messengers' quarters. The caretaker will act as a guide and has a small collection of items found on the site. You can visit Tambo Colorado on a guided tour from Pisco (US$15, minimum two people) or travel independently by taxi, bus or colectivo (see Transport, page 247).

Paracas National Reserve

Daily 1100-1500. US$1.75 pp. Tours (recommended) cost US$9 in a bus with 20 people.

Down the coast is the bay of **Paracas**, sheltered by the Paracas peninsula to the south and west. The peninsula, a large area of coast to the south and the Ballestas Islands are protected as a national reserve, with the highest concentration of marine birds in the world.

Paracas can be reached by the coast road from San Andrés, passing the fishing port and a large proportion of Peru's fishmeal industry. Alternatively, go down the Pan-American Highway for 14.5 km past the Pisco turning and

Tip...
Paracas means 'sandstorm' in Quechua; these can last for up to three days, especially in August. The wind gets up every afternoon, peaking at around 1500.

BACKGROUND

An economic mess

The islands lying off the coast of Peru are the breeding grounds for millions of sea birds, whose droppings have accumulated over the centuries. These piles of mineral-rich excrement were turned into piles of cash during the last century.

Though the ancient Peruvians knew of the benefits of guano – the name given to the natural fertilizer – and used it on their crops, it wasn't until 1840 that the vast deposits were exploited for commercial purposes. It was at this time that Peru began to trade abroad, particularly with France and England. Almost simultaneously, guano began to replace rare metals as the country's main export.

However, with the economy heavily based on the sales of bird droppings, Peru was caught in a vicious circle of borrowing money on future sales, then having to repay loans at vastly inflated rates. This unhealthy state of affairs was exacerbated in 1864 when Spain decided to occupy the guano islands of Chincha, thereby leaving the Peruvian government really up to its neck in it.

The main producers of guano are the guanay cormorant and the Peruvian booby. They gather in colonies on the islands, attracted by the huge shoals of anchovy that feed on the plankton in the cold water of the Humboldt current.

take the road to Paracas across the desert. In town is the **Museo Histórico de Paracas** ① *Av Los Libertadores Mz JI Lote 10, T955-929514*, with exhibits from the pre-Columbian culture of the region (see box, page 267).

The entrance to the reserve is at the south end of town on the main road. Just inside the reserve is the **Julio C Tello** site museum (named after the Peruvian archaeologist who first researched the Paracas culture). It was still being rebuilt in 2014, after the 2007 earthquake. Tours follow a route through the reserve, including to a *mirador* overlooking **La Catedral** rock formation, which collapsed in 2007. Longer tours venture into the deserts to the south. The tiny fishing village of **Lagunilla** is 5 km from the museum across the neck of the peninsula. Eating places there are poor value (watch out for prices in dollars), but almost all tours stop for lunch here. About 14 km from the museum is the pre-Columbian image known as **El Candelabro** (the candelabra), which has been traced into the hillside. It's at least 50 m long and is best seen from the sea; sit on the left side of the boat.

Trips to the ★**Islas Ballestas** leave from the jetties in Paracas town. The islands are spectacular, eroded into numerous arches and caves which give the islands their name (*ballesta* means archer's bow) and provide shelter for thousands of seabirds. You will see, close up, guano birds, pelicans, penguins, hundreds of inquisitive sea lions and, if you're lucky, dolphins swimming in the bay. Most boats are speedboats with life jackets, some are very crowded; wear warm clothing and

> **Tip...**
> It's advisable to see the peninsula as part of a tour from either Pisco or Paracas: it is not safe to walk alone and it is easy to get lost.

BACKGROUND

Textiles and trepanation

The Paracas Necropolis culture, which inhabited this region between 1300 BC and AD 200, is renowned for its finely woven textiles, in particular *mantos*, large decorated cloths, embroidered with anthropomorphic, zoomorphic and geometric designs. These *mantos* were used to wrap mummified bodies in their funerary bundles. Their discovery by anthropologists and archaeologists provided vital clues to this civilization. The bodies were often found to have trepanned skulls. Trepanation was a form of brain surgery performed by the Paracas people in which metal plates were inserted to replace broken sections of skull – a common injury among warring factions at that time. In addition, the Paracas culture practised the intentional deformation of infants' skulls for aesthetic reasons.

protect against the sun. The boats pass Puerto San Martín and the Candelabra en route to the islands.

Ica → Colour map 5, B2.

Ica, 70 km southeast of Pisco, is Peru's chief wine centre and is also famous for its *tejas*, a local sweet of *manjarblanco*.

Tip...
Birdlife on the Ballestas Islands includes some very rare species. The book *Las Aves del Departamento de Lima* by Maria Koepcke is useful. See also www.avesdelima.com/playas.htm.

It suffered less damage than Pisco in the 2007 earthquake, but one side of the Plaza de Armas did collapse. The **Museo Regional** ⓘ *Av Ayabaca, block 8 (take bus 17 from the Plaza de Armas, US$0.50), T056-234383 Mon-Wed 0800-1900, Thu-Sun 0900-1800, US$4, students US$2.15, tip guides US$4-5*, has mummies, ceramics, textiles and trepanned skulls from the Paracas, Nazca and Inca cultures. There's also a good, well-displayed collection of Inca *quipus* and clothes made of feathers. Behind the building is a scale model of the Nazca Lines with an observation tower, which is useful for orientation before visiting the lines themselves. The kiosk outside sells copies of motifs from ceramics and textiles.

Huacachina

From Ica, take a taxi for US$1.75 or colectivo from Bolívar block 2, return from behind Hotel Mossone, US$0.75.

About 5 km from Ica, round a palm-fringed lake amid amazing sand dunes, is the oasis and summer resort of Huacachina, a popular hang-out for people seeking a change from the archaeology and chill of the Andes. Plenty of cheap hostels and bars have opened, playing pop and grunge as opposed to pan-pipe music. Paddleboats can be rented, and sandboarding on the dunes has become a major pastime. For the inexperienced, note that sandboarding can be dangerous.

Pisco: a history in the making

A visit to Peru would not be complete without savouring a pisco sour, a cocktail made from *pisco* (a clear brandy, similar to *grappa*), mixed with lime or lemon juice, syrup, egg white and Angosturas bitters. Peruvians are mighty proud of their national tipple, which has turned out to be one of the few positive results of conquest (see also page 30).

Peru was the first conquered territory in Spanish America to produce wines and brandies. The cultivation of grapes began with the import of vine stalks from the Canary Islands, which were planted on the outskirts of Lima. The crop later reached Cuzco and Ayacucho in the Andes but it was in Ica that the enterprise really took off, owing to the region's exceptional climate.

A hundred years after the conquest, the wine and *pisco* trade had grown considerably. Ica sent its wine to Huamanga, Cuzco, Lima and Callao. And ships left from Pisco for ports in Central America, as well as Valparaíso and Buenos Aires.

Royal bans tried to halt the expansion of Peruvian vineyards because it endangered the Spanish wine industry. In 1629, the prohibition included the transport of Peruvian wines aboard Atlantic-bound ships. But despite the restrictions, the industry continued to expand during the 17th and 18th centuries.

Today several firms utilize modern procedures to manufacture and market larger quantities of *pisco*, but there are still many small, independent producers. Here the grapes are crushed by foot and the fermented grape juice is emptied into traditional Peruvian stills, called *falcas*, which are crucial to the process of true *pisco* production. More conventional wineries still rely on wood from the carob tree, a slow-burning fuel whose constant source of heat makes for a finer flavour, rather like food cooked over a charcoal fire.

Another important factor is the type of grape used. The Quebranta, brought to the Americas by the Spaniards, lends its unique characteristics to the making of renowned 'pure' *pisco*. There are also 'fragrant' *piscos* from Moscatel and Albilla varieties, 'Creole' *piscos* made with prime fragrant grapes and 'green' *piscos* made with partially fermented grape juice.

The Ica valley is still Peru's foremost producer of pisco and, together with Chincha, is the heart of a touristic Ruta del Pisco which comprises a number of bodegas (both industrial and artesanal), a museum and a school of technology and innovation. Nearby producer valleys are Pisco and Lunahuaná, while other centres include Moquegua, Vitor in Arequipa, Locumba in Tacna and Surco in Lima.

★ Bodegas around Ica

Local wine *bodegas* that you can visit include **La Caravedo** ⓘ *Panamericana Sur 298, T01-9833 4729*, with organic production and sophisticated presentation, and **El Carmen**, on the right-hand side when arriving from Lima, which has an ancient grape press made from a huge tree trunk. **El Catador** ⓘ *Fondo Tres Esquinas 102, Subtanjalla, 10 km outside Ica, T056-962629, elcatadorcristel@yahoo.es, daily 1000-*

1800, US$1.50, combi from the 2nd block of Moquegua, every 20 mins, US$0.75, taxi takes 10 mins, good tours in Spanish, has a shop selling wines, *pisco* and crafts associated with winemaking. In the evening there's a restaurant-bar with dancing and music. El Catador is best visited during harvest from late February to early April. Near El Catador is **Bodega Alvarez**, whose owner, Umberto Alvarez, is very hospitable. The town of Ocucaje is a popular excursion from Ica for tours of the **Ocucaje winery** ① *Ctra Panamericana Sur, Km 335.5, T01-251 4570, www.ocucaje. com,* which makes wines and *pisco.*

Listings Ica Region

Tourist information

Ica
Dirceture is at Av Grau 148 (T056-238710). Some tourist information is also available at travel agencies.

Where to stay

Chincha Alta
There are hotels and *hostales* along the Panamericana in Chincha, especially near the Soyuz bus terminal.

$$$ Casa Andina Classic Chincha Sausal
Panamericana Sur Km 197, T056-262451, www.casa-andina.com.
A modern hotel on the outskirts of Chincha Alta, with gardens, swimming pool and all facilities associated with this chain's style.

$$$ Hacienda San José
El Carmen, T056-313332, www. casahaciendasanjose.com.
See page 238.

Pisco

$$ Posada Hispana Hostal
Bolognesi 222, T056-536363, www.posadahispana.com.
Some rooms with loft and bath, also rooms with shared bath, hot water, can accommodate groups, comfortable, breakfast extra, **Café de la Posada** on site, information service, English, French, Italian and Catalan spoken.

$$-$ El Candelabro
Callao y Pedemonte, T056-532620, www.hoteleselcandelabro.com.
Modern and pleasant, with restaurant. All rooms have bath and fridge.

$$-$ Hostal San Isidro
San Clemente 103, T056-536471, http://sanisidrohostal.com.
With or without bath, hot water, safe, welcoming, nice pool and cafeteria, pizzeria, free laundry facilities, games room, English spoken, parking. Breakfast not included, free coffee in mornings, use of kitchen. Arranges dune buggy tours and other excursions.

$$-$ San Jorge Residencial
Jr Barrio Nuevo 133, T056-532885, www.hotelsanjorgeresidencial.com.
Smart and modern. Hot water, secure parking, breakfast is served in the restaurant, also lunch and dinner, swanky and spacious, café/bar in garden.

$ Hostal Los Inkas Inn
Prol Barrio Nuevo Mz M, Lte 14, Urb San Isidro, T056-536634.

Affordable rooms and dorms with private bath, fan, safes, rooftop games area, small pool.

$ Hostal Tambo Colorado
Av Bolognesi 159, T056-531379, www.hostaltambocolorado.com.
Welcoming, helpful owners are knowledgeable about the area, hot water, small café/bar, use of kitchen.

Paracas

$$$$ Hotel Paracas Luxury Collection Resort
Av Paracas 173, T056-581333, www.libertador.com.pe.
The famous Hotel Paracas has been reincarnated as a resort, with spa, pools, excellent rooms in cottages around the grounds, access to beach, choice of restaurants, bar.

$$$$ La Hacienda Bahía Paracas
Lote 25, Urb Santo Domingo, T01-213 1000, www.hoteleslahacienda.com.
Next to Doubletree but not connected, rooms and suites, some with access straight to pool, spa, choice of restaurants, bar.

$$$$-$$$ Doubletree Guest Suites Paracas
Lote 30-34, Urb Santo Domingo on the outskirts, T01-617 1000, www.doubletree.com.
Low rise, clean lines and a comfortable size, built around a lovely pool, on beach, water sports, spa, all mod cons and popular with families.

$$$ El Mirador
At the turn-off to El Chaco, T056-545086, www.elmiradorhotel.com.
Hot water, good service, boat trips arranged, meals available, large pool, tranquil gardens, relaxing.

$$$ Gran Palma
Av Principal Mz D lote 03, ½ block from plaza, T01-665 5932, www.hotelgranpalma.com.
Central, convenient for boats, best rooms have sea view, buffet breakfast on the terrace.

$$ Brisas de la Bahía
Av Principal, T056-531132, www.brisasdelabahia.com.
Good, family-run hostal, convenient position for waterfront and bus stops, ask for a back room, good breakfast.

$$ Los Frayles
Av Paracas Mz D lote 5, T056-545141, www.hostallosfrayles.com.
Variety of simple, well-kept rooms, ocean view, breakfast extra, roof terrace, tourist information, transfers to/from bus arranged.

$$ Mar Azul
Alan García Mz B lote 20, T056-534542, www.hostalmarazul.com.
Family-run hostal overlooking the sea, although most rooms face away from ocean, comfortable, hot water, breezy roof terrace with sea view for breakfast (included), helpful owner Yudy Patiño. Also **Ballestas Expeditions** for local tours.

$$ Santa María
Av Paracas s/n, T056-545045, www.hostalsantamariaparacas.com.
Smart rooms, hot water, no view. **El Chorito** restaurant, mainly fish and seafood. Also has **Santa María 2**, round the corner in lovely converted house (same contact numbers), not all rooms have view but has rooftop terrace. **Santa María 3**, under construction on the approach road, will have more facilities and pool.

$ Backpackers House
Av Los Libertadores, beside museum, T056-635623, www. paracasbackpackershouse.com.pe.
Rooms with and without bath, private and dorms, at high season prices rise to $$-$. Good value, comfortable, tourist information.

$ Hostal El Amigo
El Chaco, T056-545042, hostalelamigo@ hotmail.com.
Simple, hot water, no food, no internet but very helpful staff.

Ica
Hotels are fully booked during the harvest festival and prices rise. Many hotels are in residential neighbourhoods; insist taxis go to the hotel of your choice.

$$$$-$$$ Las Dunas
Av La Angostura 400, T056-256224, www.lasdunashotel.com. Lima office: Av Vasco Núñez de Balboa 259, Lima, T01-213 5000.
Variety of rooms and suites. Prices are reduced on weekdays. Packages available. Complete resort with restaurant, swimming pool, many sporting activities and full-day programmes.

$$$ Villa Jazmín
Los Girasoles Mz C-1, Lote 7, Res La Angostura, T056-258179, www.villajazmin.net.
Modern hotel in a residential area near the sand dunes, 8 mins from the city centre, solar heated water, restaurant, buffet breakfast, pool, tours arranged, airport and bus transfers, helpful staff, tranquil and very good.

$$ Princess
Santa Magdalena D-103, Urb Santa María, T056-215421, www.hotelprincess.com.pe.

Taxi ride from the main plaza, small rooms, hot water, frigobar, pool, tourist information, helpful, peaceful, very good.

$ Arameli
Tacna 239, T056-239107. 1 block from the Plaza de Armas.
A nice place to stay, good value, café on 3rd floor.

Huacachina

$$$ Mossone
East end of the lake, T056-213630, www.dmhoteles.pe.
Faded elegance, hacienda-style with a view of the lagoon, full board available, good buffet breakfast, large rooms, bilingual staff, lovely courtyard, bicycles and sandboards, large, clean swimming pool.

$$ Hostal Huacachinero
Av Perotti, opposite Hostal Salvatierra, T056-217435, http://elhuacachinero.com.
Spacious rooms, sparsely furnished but comfortable beds, nice atmosphere, pool, outside bar and restaurant, parking, offers tours and buggy rides.

$$ Hostería Suiza
Malecón 264, T056-238762, hostesuiza@terra.com.pe.
Overlooking lake, lovely grounds, quiet, safe parking.

$ Carola del Sur (also known as Casa de Arena II)
Av Perotti s/n, T056-237398.
Basic rooms, popular, small pool, restaurant/bar, hammocks, access to Casa de Arena's bigger pool, noisy at night, pressure to buy tours.

$ Casa de Arena
Av Perotti s/n, T056-215274.
Basic rooms and dorms, thin walls, bar, small pool, laundry facilities, board hire,

popular with backpackers but grubby,
check your bill and change carefully,
don't leave valuables unattended, disco
next door.

$ Desert Nights
Run by Desert Adventures (see What to do, below).
Good reputation, English spoken,
food available

$ Hostal Rocha
T056-222256, kikerocha@hotmail.com.
Hot water, with or without bath, family
run, kitchen and laundry facilities,
board hire, small pool, popular with
backpackers, but a bit run-down.

$ Hostal Salvatierra
T056-232352, http://salvaturgroup. galeon.com.
An old building, with or without bath,
not on waterfront, charming, pool,
relaxing courtyard, rents sandboards,
good value.

Restaurants

Pisco

$$-$ As de Oro
San Martín 472, T056-532010. Closed Mon.
Good food, not cheap but always full
at lunchtime, swimming pool.

$ Café Pirata
Callao 104, T056-534343. Mon-Sat 0630-1500, 1800-2200.
Desserts, pizzas, sandwiches, coffee and
lunch menu.

$ Chifa Lisen
Av San Martín 325, T056-535527. Daily 1230-1530, 1800-2200.
Chinese food and delivery.

Paracas
There are several eating places on
the Malecón by Playa El Chaco, all
with similar menus and prices (in our
$$ range), vegetarian options and open
for breakfast, including **Bahía**; **Brisa
Marina** (varied menu, mainly seafood),
and **Johnny y Jennifer**. Better value
menús are available at lunchtime on
the main road, eg at **Lobo Fino**. Higher
quality food within walking distance of
the centre can be found at the **Hotel
Paracas'** restaurant and trattoria, **$$$**,
both of which are open to the public.

Ica

$$-$ Anita
Libertad 133, Plaza de Armas.
Local dishes, breakfast, à la carte a bit
expensive for what's offered, but set
menus at US$4.50 are good value.

$ Carne y pescao
Av Juan José Elías 417, T056-228157.
Seafood and, at night, grilled chicken
and *parrilladas*.

$ D'lizia
Lima 155, Plaza de Armas, T056-237733, www.delizia.com.pe.
Also in the Patio de comidas at Plaza
Vea mall and in Urb Moderna. Modern
and bright, for breakfasts, lunches,
sandwiches, snacks, ice cream, cakes
and sweets, juices and drinks.

$ Plaza 125
C Lima 125, T056-211816.
On the plaza, regional and international
food as well as breakfast, good-value
set lunches.

$ Tejas Helena
Cajamarca 137.
The best *tejas* and locally made
chocolates are sold here.

Huacachina

$ La Casa de Bamboo
Av Perotti s/n, next to Hostería Suiza,
T056-776649.
Café-bar, English breakfast, marmite,
Thai curry, falafel, vegetarian and vegan
options, book exchange, games.

$ Moroni
T056-238471. Open 0800 till late.
Only restaurant right on the lake shore,
serving a variety of Peruvian and
international foods.

Festivals

Chincha Alta and around
End Feb **Verano Negro**. Famous festival
celebrating black and criollo culture.
Nov **Festival de las Danzas Negras** is
held in El Carmen, 10 km south.

Ica
Early Mar **Festival Internacional de la
Vendimia** (wine harvest).
Oct The image of **El Señor de Luren**
draws pilgrims from all Peru to a fine
church in Parque Luren on the 3rd Mon,
when there are all-night processions;
celebrations start the week before.

What to do

Paracas
There are agencies all over town offering
trips to the Islas Ballestas, the Paracas
reserve, Ica, Nazca and Tambo Colorado.
A 2-hr boat tour to the islands costs
US$13-15 pp, including park entrance
fee and tax, departure 0800. Usually,
agencies will pool 40 clients together
in 1 boat. An agency that does not pool
clients is **Huacachina**, based in Ica, with
an office in Paracas, T056-215582, www.
huacachinatours.com. Do not book tours
on the street.

Zarcillo Connections, *Independencia
A-20, Paracas, T056-536636, www.
zarcilloconnections.com*. With long
experience for trips to the Paracas
National Reserve, Tambo Colorado,
trekking and tours to Ica, Chincha and
the Nazca Lines and surrounding sites.
Agent for **Cruz del Sur** buses. Also has its
own hotel, **Zarcillo Paradise**, in Paracas.

Ica
Agencies offer city tours, trips to the
Nazca Lines, Paracas and Islas Ballestas,
plus dune buggies and sandboarding.
AV Dolphin Travel, *C Municipalidad
132, of 4, T056-256234, www.av-
dolphintravelperu.com.*
Desert Travel, *Lima 171, inside Tejas Don
Juan on Plaza, T056-227215,
desert_travel@hotmail.com.*
Ica Desert Trip, *Bolívar 178, T056-237373,
www.icadeserttrip.com*. Roberto Penny
Cabrera (speaks Spanish and English)
offers 1-, 2- and 3-day trips off-road into
the desert, archaeology, geology, etc.
4 people maximum, contact by email in
advance. Take toilet paper, something
warm for the evening, a long-sleeved
loose cotton shirt for daytime and long
trousers. Recommended, but "not for the
faint-hearted".

Huacachina
Dune buggies do white-knuckle,
rollercoaster tours for US$20 (plus a small
municipal fee); some start at 1000 but
most between 1600 and 1700 to catch
the sunset, 2½ hrs.
Desert Adventures, *Huacachina,
T056-228458, www.desertadventure.
net*. Frequently recommended for
sandboarding and camping trips into
the desert by 4WD and buggies, French,
English and Spanish spoken. Also to
beaches, Islas Ballestas and Nazca Lines

flights. Has an associated hostel (see Where to stay, above).

Pisco
Air
Capitán RE Olivera airport is being redeveloped from a military base into an alternative airport for Lima. Eventually, it is expected to become a major international hub.

Aerodiana (Av Casimiro Ulloa 227, San Antonio, Lima, T01-447 6824, www.aerodiana.com.pe) offers Nazca overflights from Pisco.

Bus
Buses drop passengers at San Clemente on Panamericana Sur (El Cruce); many bus companies and tour agencies have their offices here. It's a 10-km taxi ride from the centre, US$8, or US$10 to Paracas. Colectivos leave from outside Banco Continental (plaza) for El Cruce when full, US$2.

To Lima, 242 km, 4 hrs, US$7.50. The best company is Soyuz, every 7 mins from El Cruce. Ormeño has an office in Pisco plaza and will take you to El Cruce to meet their 1600 bus. Flores is the only company that goes into Pisco town, from Lima and Ica, but buses are poor and services erratic. To Ica, US$1.25, 45 mins, 70 km, with Ormeño; also colectivos. To Nazca, 210 km, take a bus to Ica and then change to a colectivo. To Ayacucho, 317 km, 8-10 hrs, US$12-20, several buses daily leave from El Cruce; book in advance and take warm clothing as it gets cold at night. To Huancavelica, 269 km, 12-14 hrs, US$12, with Oropesa,

coming from Ica. To Arequipa, US$17, 10-12 hrs, 2 daily.

To Tambo Colorado, buses depart from near the plaza in Pisco at 0800, US$2.50, 3 hrs; also colectivos, US$2 pp. Alight 20 mins after the stop at Humay; the road passes right through the site. For buses back to Pisco in the afternoon, wait at the caretaker's house.

Taxi
To Paracas about US$3; combis when full, US$1.75, 25 mins. To Tambo Colorado, US$30 (return).

Paracas
Cruz del Sur has 2 direct buses a day to its Paracas terminal, regular bus from US$9, luxury services US$30-35 from Lima, US$15 to Nazca. Agencies in Paracas sell direct transfers between Paracas and Huacachina, with Pelican Perú, at 1100 daily, US$7, comfortable and secure.

Ica
Bus
All bus offices are on Lambayeque blocks 1 and 2 and Salaverry block 3. To Pisco, US$1.25, 45 mins, 70 km, with Ormeño; also colectivos. To Paracas junction, US$1.15. To Lima, 302 km, 4 hrs, US$21-34, on upmarket buses, several daily including Soyuz (Av Manzanilla 130), every 7 mins, 0600-2200, and Ormeño (Lambayeque 180). To Nazca, 140 km, 2 hrs, several buses (US$3.50) and colectivos (US$5) daily, including Ormeño, Flores, 4 daily, and Cueva (José Elías y Huánuco), hourly 0600-2200; buses to Arequipa follow this route.

Nazca
& around

Set in a green valley amid a perimeter of mountains, Nazca's altitude puts it just above any fog which may drift in from the sea. Nearby are the mysterious, world-famous Nazca Lines and numerous other ancient sites.

Nazca town → *Colour map 5, B3.*

Nazca town lies 140 km south of Ica via the Pan-American Highway (444 km from Lima) and is the tourist centre for visiting the Nazca Lines. **Museo Antonini** ① *Av de la Cultura 600, eastern end of Jr Lima (10-min walk from the plaza or short taxi ride), T056-523444, cahuachi@terra.com.pe or CISRAP@numerica.it, daily 0900-1900 (ring the bell), US$6 including guide,* houses the discoveries of Professor Orefici and his team from the huge pre-Inca city at Cahuachi (see page 252), which, Orefici

Nazca

Where to stay 🛏
1 Alegría
2 Casa Andina Classic
3 Hosp Flores
4 Hostal Alegría
5 La Encantada
6 Maison Suisse
7 Majoro
8 Nasca
9 Nazca Lines
10 Oro Viejo
11 Paredones Inn
12 Posada de Don Hono
13 Posada Guadalupe
14 Sol de Nasca

Restaurants 🍴
1 Chifa Guang Zhou
2 Coffee Break
3 El Huarango &
   Travel Service
4 Kañada
5 La Choza
6 La Taberna
7 Los Angeles
8 Mamashana &
   Vía La Encantada
9 Panadería
10 Rico Pollo

believes, holds the key to understanding the Nazca Lines. Many tombs survived the *huaqueros* (tomb robbers), and there are displays of mummies, ceramics, textiles, amazing *antaras* (pan pipes) and photos of the excavations. In the garden is a prehispanic aqueduct. Recommended.

The **Maria Reiche Planetarium** ⓘ *Hotel Nazca Lines, T056-522293, shows daily usually at 1900 and 2115 in English, 2000 in Spanish, US$7 (students half price),* offers introductory lectures every night about the Nazca Lines, based on Reiche's theories (see below and box, page 250), which cover archaeology and astronomy. The show lasts about 45 minutes, after which visitors are able to look at the moon, planets and stars through telescopes.

Viktoria Nikitzhi, a colleague of Maria Reiche, gives one-hour lectures about the Nazca Lines at **Dr Maria Reiche Center** ⓘ*Av de los Espinales 300, 1 block from Ormeño bus stop, T965-888056, viktorianikitzki@hotmail.com, US$5.* She also organizes tours in June and December (phone in advance to confirm times or to ask about volunteer work).

Just south of town are the **Paredones ruins and aqueduct** ⓘ *US$3.55 (including El Telar Geoglyphs, Acueductos de Cantayoc, Las Agujas Geoglyphs and Acueductos de Ocongalla).* The ruins, also called Cacsamarca, are Inca on a pre-Inca base but are not well preserved. However, the underground aqueducts, built 300 BC-AD 700, are still in working order and worth seeing. A 30-minute to one-hour walk through Buena Fe (or organize a taxi from your hotel) will bring you to the Cantayoc, Las Agujas and El Telar sites, which consist of markings in the valley floor and ancient aqueducts descending in spirals into the ground. The markings consist of a triangle pointing to a hill and a telar (cloth) with a spiral depicting the threads. Climb the mountain to see better examples.

★Nazca Lines

Cut into the stony desert above the Ingenio valley north of Nazca are the famous Nazca Lines, thought to have been etched onto the Pampa Colorada sands by three different groups: the Paracas people (900-200 BC), the Nazcas (200 BC-AD 600) and the Huari settlers from Ayacucho (about AD 630). There are large numbers of lines, not only parallels and geometrical figures, but also recognizable designs, including a dog, an enormous monkey, birds (one with a wing span of over 100 m), a spider and a tree. They are best seen from the air (see What to do, page 256), but three of the huge designs – the Hands, the Lizard and the Tree – can also be viewed from the mirador, 17 km north of Nazca on the Pan-American Highway, paid for by Maria Reiche in 1976. (Travellers suggest the view from the hill 500 m back to Nazca is better.) The mirador is included on most tours; otherwise hire a taxi-guide to take you (US$5-8 per person), or you can hitch, but there is not always much traffic. Go early as the site gets very hot and busy by mid-morning. In January 1994 Maria

> **Tip...**
> Maria Reiche's book, *Mystery on the Desert*, is on sale in Nazca for US$10 (proceeds to conservation work). Another good book is *Pathways to the Gods: the mystery of the Nazca Lines*, by Tony Morrison (Michael Russell, 1978).

BACKGROUND

Guardian of the lines

The greatest contribution to our awareness of the Nazca Lines was made by Maria Reiche, who was born in Dresden in 1903 and died in Lima in 1998. The young German mathematician arrived in Peru in the early 1930s and lived and worked on the pampa for over 50 years, dedicating her life to removing centuries of windswept debris and carrying out painstaking survey work. She even used to sleep on the pampa.

Maria Reiche's years of meticulous measurement and study of the Lines led her to the conclusion that they represented a huge astronomical calendar. She also used her mathematical knowledge to determine how the many drawings and symbols could have been created with such precise symmetry. She suggested that those responsible for the Lines used long cords attached to stakes in the ground. The figures were drawn by means of a series of circular arcs of different radius. Reiche also contended that they used a standard unit of measurement of 1.30 m, or the distance between the fingertips of a person's extended arms.

As well as the anthropomorphic and zoomorphic drawings, there are a great many geometric figures. Reiche believed these to be a symbolic form of writing associated with the movements of the stars. In this way, the lines could have been used as a kind of calendar that not only recorded celestial events but also had a very important practical function, indicating the times for harvest, fishing and festivals.

Whatever the real purpose of the Nazca Lines, one fact remains indisputable: that their status as one of the country's major tourist attractions is largely due to the selfless work of Maria Reiche, the unofficial guardian of the Lines.

Reiche also opened a small site **museum** ⓘ *Km 421, 5 km from town, US$1; take micro from in front of Ormeño terminal (US$0.75, frequent).*

Origins of the Lines The Nazcas had a highly developed civilization which reached its peak about AD 600. Their polychrome ceramics, wood carvings and adornments of gold are on display in many of Lima's museums. The Paracas people represented an early phase of the Nazca culture, renowned for their superb technical quality and stylistic variety in weaving and pottery (see box, page 240). Geoglyphs made by the Paracas people in the desert near the Chincha valley (see above) have been studied by Charles Stanish and others. They appear to predate the Nazca Lines by some 300 years and indicate areas of ritual processions and activities, including ancient fairs. The Nazcas were succeeded by the Huari Empire, which in conjunction with the Tiahuanaco culture dominated much of Peru from AD 600-1000.

The German expert, Dr Maria Reiche, who studied the Lines for over 40 years, mostly from a step ladder, maintained that they represent some sort of vast astronomical pre-Inca calendar (see box, above). Other theories abound: that the Lines are the tracks of running contests (Georg A von Breunig, 1980, and

English astronomer Alan Sawyer); that they were used for ritualized walking (Anthony Aveni); that they represent weaving patterns and yarns (Henri Stierlin) and that the plain is a map of the Tiahuanaco Empire (Zsoltan Zelko). Johan Reinhard proposes that the Lines conform to fertility practices throughout the Andes, in common with the use of straight lines in Chile and Bolivia. William H Isbell proposed that the Lines are the

equivalent of pyramid building in other parts of Peru in the same period, with the added purpose of controlling population growth through mass labour.

Another theory, based on the idea that the Lines are best seen from the air, is that the ancient Nazcas flew in hot-air balloons (Jim Woodman, 1977, and, in part, the BBC series *Ancient Voices*). A related idea is that the Lines were not designed to be seen physically from above, but from the mind's eye of the flying shaman. Both theories are supported by pottery and textile evidence which shows balloonists and a flying creature emitting discharge from its nose and mouth. There are also local legends of flying men. The depiction in the desert of creatures such as a monkey or killer whale suggest the qualities needed by the shaman in his spirit journeys.

After six years' work at La Muña and Los Molinos near Palpa (see below) using photogrammetry, Peruvian archaeologist Johny Isla and Markus Reindel of the Swiss-Liechtenstein Foundation deduced that the lines on both the Palpa and Nazca plains were offerings dedicated to the worship of water and fertility, two elements which also dominate on ceramics and on the engraved stones of the Paracas culture. Isla and Reindel believe that the Palpa lines predate those at Nazca and that these lines and drawings are themselves scaled-up versions of the Paracas drawings. This research proposes that the Nazca culture succumbed not to drought, but to heavy rainfall, probably during an El Niño event.

In all probablility, there was no single, overriding significance to the Lines for the people who made them. Some of the theories attached to them may capture parts of their meaning, and, no doubt, more theories and new discoveries will be tested to cast fresh light on the puzzle.

Other excursions

More lines and designs of different periods are visible near **Palpa** (43 km north of Nazca), including La Muña and Los Molinos where extensive research has been carried out (see Origins of the Lines, above). The town itself is known as the Capital of Oranges. It has a municipal museum on the plaza with displays on the local area and its archaeology.

Overlooking Nazca town to the east is **Cerro Blanco**, the highest sand dune in the world at 2078 m. Tours to the dune start very early in the morning and involve a three-hour hike to the summit. Descents can be made on dune buggies, or by sandboarding or parapenting.

The Nazca area is dotted with over 100 ancient cemeteries, where the dry, humidity-free climate has perfectly preserved invaluable tapestries, cloth and mummies. At **Chauchilla** ① *30 km south of Nazca, last 12 km a sandy track, US$3*, *huaqueros* ransacked the tombs and left bones, skulls, mummies and pottery shards littering the desert. A tour takes about two hours and usually includes a visit to a small family gold-processing shop where very old-fashioned techniques are still used.

One hour west of the Nazca Lines along a rough dirt track, **Cahuachi** ① *US$3.50 entry, US$17 pp on a tour, US$12-15 in private taxi*, is a Nazca ceremonial site comprising some 30 pyramids. Only 5% of the site has been excavated so far, some of which has been reconstructed. Some believe it could be larger than Chan Chán, making it the largest adobe city in the world (see also Museo Antonini, above). Some 4 km beyond Cahuachi is a site called **El Estaquería**, thought to have been a series of astronomical sighting posts; more recent research suggests the wooden pillars were used to dry dead bodies and therefore it may have been a place of mummification.

On the coast west of Nazca, **Reserva Nacional de San Fernando** was established in 2011 to protect migratory and local land and oceanic wildlife, such as the Humboldt penguin, sea lions, the Andean fox, dolphins and whales. Condors and guanacos may also be seen, which is unusual for the coast. San Fernando is located in the highest part of the Peruvian coastal desert, where the Nazca Plate lifts the Continental Plate, generating moist accumulation in the ground with resulting seasonal winter flora and a continental wildlife corridor between the high coastal mountains and the sea. Full-day and two-day/one-night tours are offered by some agencies in town.

Towards Cuzco: Sondondo Valley

Two hours out of Nazca on the paved road to Abancay and Cuzco is the **Reserva Nacional Pampas Galeras** at 4100 m, which has a vicuña reserve and an interesting Museo del Sitio. There's also a military base and park guard here. Entry is free. At Km 155 is **Puquio**, which provides access to **Andamarca** and the surrounding villages of the **Sondondo Valley** in the south of the department of Ayacucho. This off-the-beaten-path area is gradually opening up to tourism. Local communities include: Andamarca, Cabana, Chipao, Aucara, Mayobamba and Sondondo.

Andamarca is said to be the place where Huascar was executed by his half-brother Atahualpa, following the bloody Inca civil war which preceded the arrival of the Spanish conquistadors. It is also home to the *danzantes de tijero*, who perform the unique 'scissor dance'. Sr Froila Ramos is a great source of information (ask around for him); entry to his private museum costs US$3.50. There is a **Mirador de Cóndores** at Km 13.5 on the road from Andamarca to **Chipao**, and *Puya raimondii* plants may be seen 1½ hours' walk uphill from Chipao. The Sondondo Valley contains 5600 ha of ancient agricultural terraces, both Huari and Inca, most still in use. There are many beautiful lakes around **Cabana**. The village of **Sondondo** was the birthplace of 16th-century chronicler Felipe Guamán Poma de Ayala.

Beyond Puquio along the road to Abancay and Cuzco, it's another 185 km to **Chalhuanca**. Fuel is available in both towns. There are wonderful views on this stretch, with lots of small villages, valleys and alpacas.

South of Nazca

Sacaco, 90 km from Nazca, has a museum built over the fossilized remains of a whale excavated in the desert. The fossil is 8 m long and thought to be over 4 million years old. If not visiting on a tour, take a bus towards Chala and ask to be let off at the right spot; the museum is a 2-km, shadeless walk from the Highway.

Lying on the coast, 98 km from Nazca and 7 km off the Panamericana, is **Puerto Lomas**, a fishing village with safe beaches that are popular in February and March. Before the Pan-American Highway was built, it used to be the harbour where steamers on the route from Lima to Arequipa would collect passengers from Nazca.

★Puerto Inca

10 km north of Chala. Taxi, US$8, or colectivo towards Nazca as far as the turn-off at Km 610, about US$6, beware overcharging.

Ten kilometres north of the fishing village of **Chala** on the coast are the large pre-Columbian ruins of **Puerto Inca**. This was the port for Cuzco. The site is in excellent condition: the drying and store houses can be seen as holes in the ground (be careful where you walk). On the right side of the bay is a cemetery; on the hill, a temple of reincarnation, and the Inca road from the coast to Cuzco is clearly visible. The road was 240 km long, with a staging post every 7 km so that, with a change of runner at every post, messages could be sent in 24 hours. The site is best appreciated when the sun is shining. Nearby Chala (173 km from Nazca) has many restaurants; **Antoquitos** is a good choice on the roadside, especially for *parihuela*.

Camaná and beyond

South of Chala, the Panamericana passes Atico and Ocoña before reaching **Camaná**, 222 km south of Chala and 5 km inland from the ocean. The main attraction here is the beaches, from 10 to 40 km away, which are very popular with *Arequipeños* from December to March. Camaná has a range of hotels and restaurants, and regular buses serve Arequipa and the coast north to Lima. Most bus agencies are on 300 block of Avenida Lima.

For the route south from Camaná to Moquegua, Tacna and the border with Chile, see page 298.

Listings Nazca and around *map p248*

Tourist information

Nazca

iPerú is located at the airport (iperunasca@promperu.gob.pe, daily 0700-1300, 1400-1600). The **tourist police** are at Av Los Incas cuadra 1, T056-522105. The ordinary **police** are at Av Los Incas, T056-522105 (T105 for emergencies).

Where to stay

Nazca

$$$ Casa Andina Classic
Jr Bolognesi 367, T01-213 9739,
www.casa-andina.com.
This recommended chain of hotels' Nazca property, offering standardized

Tip...
If arriving by bus, beware of touts who tell you that the hotel of your choice is closed, or full. If you phone or email, the hotel should pick you up at the bus station free of charge, day or night.

services in distinctive style. Bright, modern decor, central patio with palm trees, pool, restaurant.

$$$ Maison Suisse
opposite airport, T056-522434, www.nazcagroup.com.
Comfortable, safe car park, expensive restaurant, pool, suites with jacuzzi, good giftshop, shows video of Nazca Lines. Also has camping facilities. Its packages include flights over Nazca Lines.

$$$ Majoro
Panamericana Sur Km 452, T056-522490, www.hotelmajoro.com.
A charming old hacienda about 5 km from town past the airstrip so quite remote, beautiful gardens, pool, slow and expensive restaurant, quiet and welcoming, good arrangements for flights and tours.

$$$ Nazca Lines
Jr Bolognesi 147, T056-522293.
With a/c, rather dated rooms with private patio, hot water, peaceful, restaurant, safe car park, pool (US$9-10.50 pp includes sandwich and drink). Can also arrange package tours which include 2-3 nights at the hotel plus a flight over the lines and a desert trip.

$$$-$$ Oro Viejo
Callao 483, T056-521112, www.hoteloroviejo.net.
Has a suite with jacuzzi and comfortable standard rooms, nice garden, swimming pool, restaurant and bar. Recommended.

$$ Alegría
Jr Lima 166, T056-522497, www.hotelalegria.net.
Rooms with hot water, cafeteria serving breakfast, pool, garden, English, Hebrew, Italian and German spoken, laundry facilities, book exchange, restaurant, ATM, parking, bus terminal transfers. OK but can be noisy from disco and traffic. Also has a tour agency where guests are encouraged to buy tours (see What to do), flights and bus tickets.

$$ La Encantada
Callao 592, T056-522930, www. hotellaencantada.com.pe.
Pleasant modern hotel with restaurant, laundry and parking.

$$ Paredones Inn
Jr Lima 600, T056-522181.
1 block from the Plaza de Armas, modern, colourful rooms, great views from roof terrace, laundry service, bar, suites with minibar, microwave, jacuzzi, helpful staff.

$$ Posada de Don Hono
Av María Reiche 112, T056-506822, laposadadedonhono1@hotmail.com.
Small rooms and nice bungalows, good café, parking.

$ Hospedaje Flores
Grau 550, T056-521040.
Pleasant, family-run place, how water, Wi-Fi, parking.

$ Hostal Alegría
Av Los Incas 117, opposite **Ormeño** *bus terminal, T056-522497.*
Basic, hot water, hammocks, nice garden, camping, restaurant.

$ Nasca
C Lima 438, T056-522085, marionasca13@ hotmail.com.

Hot water, with or without bath, laundry facilities, newer annexe at the back, nice garden, safe motorcycle parking.

$ Posada Guadalupe
San Martín 225, T056-522249.
Family run, lovely courtyard and garden, hot water, with or without bath, good breakfast, relaxing. (Touts selling tours are nothing to do with hotel.)

$ Sol de Nasca
Callao 586, T056-522730.
Rooms with and without hot showers, restaurant, pleasant, but don't leave valuables in luggage store.

Towards Cuzco

$ Hostal Kondor Wasi
Mayobambo.
Next to the thermal baths.

$ Hotel Misky Puñuy
Puquio.
With private bath.

South of Nazca

$$$-$$ Puerto Inka
2 km along a side road from Km 610 Panamericana Sur (reservations T054-778458), www.puertoinka.com.pe.
Bungalows on the beautiful beach, hammocks outside, indoor games room, disco, breakfast extra, great place to relax, kayaks, boat hire, diving equipment rental, pleasant camping US$5, low season discounts, used by tour groups, busy in summer.

Restaurants

Nazca
There's a **panadería** at Bolognesi 387.

$$$-$$ Vía La Encantada
Bolognesi 282 (website as hotel above).

Modern, stylish with great food – fish, meat or vegetarian, good-value lunches.

$$-$ Mamashana
Bolognesi 270.
Rustic style with a lively atmosphere, for breakfast, grills, pastas and pizzas.

$$-$ La Choza
Bolognesi 290.
Nice decor with woven chairs and thatched roof, all types of food, live music at night. Single women may be put off by the crowds of young men hanging around the doors handing out flyers.

$$-$ La Taberna
Jr Lima 321, T056-521411.
Excellent food, live music, popular with gringos, it's worth a look just for the graffiti on the walls.

$ Chifa Guang Zhou
Bolognesi 297, T056-522036.
Very good.

$ Coffee Break
Bolognesi 219. Sun-Fri 0700-2300.
For real coffee and good pizzas.

$ El Huarango
Arica 602.
National and international cuisine. Relaxed family atmosphere and deliciously breezy terrace.

$ Kañada
Lima 160, nazcanada@yahoo.com.
Cheap, good *menú*, excellent pisco sours, nice wines, popular, display of local artists' work, email service, English spoken, helpful.

$ Los Angeles
Bolognesi 266.
Good, cheap, try the *sopa criolla*, and the chocolate cake.

$ Rico Pollo
Lima 190.
Good local restaurant with great chicken dishes.

Shopping

Nazca
There is a small market at Lima y Grau, the Mercado Central at Arica y Tacna and a Raulito supermarket at Grau 245.

Festivals

Nazca
29 Aug-10 Sep Virgen de la Guadalupe festival.

What to do

Nazca
Land-based tours
All guides must be approved by the Ministry of Tourism and should have an official identity card. Touts (*jaladores*) operate at popular hotels and the bus terminals using false ID cards and fake hotel and tour brochures. They are rip-off merchants who overcharge and mislead those who arrive by bus. Only conduct business with agencies at their office, or phone or email the company you want to deal with in advance. Some hotels are not above pressurising guests to purchase tours at inflated prices. Taxi drivers usually act as guides, but most speak only Spanish. Do not take just any taxi on the plaza for a tour; always ask your hotel for a reputable driver.
Air Nasca Travel, *Jr Lima 185, T056-521027.* Guide Susi recommended. Very helpful and competitive prices. Can do all types of tours around Nazca, Ica, Paracas and Pisco.
Algería Tours, *Lima 186, T056-523431, http://alegriatoursperu.com.* Offers inclusive tours. Guides with radio contact and maps can be provided for hikes to nearby sites. Guides speak English, German, French and Italian. They also offer adventure tours, such as mountain biking from 4000 m in the Andes down to the plain, sandboarding, and more.
Félix Quispe Sarmiento, *'El Nativo de Nazca'.* He has his own museum, Hantun Nazca, at Panamericana Sur 447 and works with the Ministerio de Cultura to offer tours off the beaten track. Can also arrange flights. Knowledgeable. Ask for him at Kañada restaurant.
Fernández family, *Hotel Nasca (see above).* Local tours; ask for the hotel owners and speak to them direct.
Huarango Travel Service, *Arica 602, T056-522141, huarangotravel@yahoo.es.* Tours around Ica, Paracas, Huacachina, Nazca and Palpa.
Mystery Peru, *Simón Bolívar 221, T01-435 0051, T956-691155, www.mysteryperu. com.* Owned by Enrique Levano Alarcón, based in Nazca with many local tours, also packages throughout Peru.
Nazca Perú 4x4, *Bolognesi 367 (in Casa Andina), T056-522928, or T975-017029.* Tubular 4WD tours to San Fernando National Reserve and other off-the-beaten-track locations.

Sightseeing flights
Small planes take 3-5 passengers to see the Nazca Lines. Flights last 30-35 mins and are controlled by air traffic personnel at the airport to avoid congestion. The price for a flight is around US$130 pp plus US$10 airport tax. Most tours include transport to the airport; otherwise it's US$5 by taxi or US$0.25 by bus. It is best to organize a flight with the airlines themselves at the airport. They will weigh you and select a group of passengers based on weight,

so you may have to wait a while for your turn. Make sure you clarify everything before getting on the plane and ask for a receipt. Also let them know in advance if you have any special requests.

Aero Diana, *Av Casimiro Ulloa 227, San Antonio, Lima, T01-447 6824, www.aero diana.com.pe.* Daily flights over the Lines.
Aero Paracas, *T01-641 7000, www.aero paracas.com.* Daily flights over the Lines.
Alas Peruanas, *T056-522444, http:// alasperuanas.com, or through Hotel Alegría.* Experienced pilots offer flights over the Nazca Lines as well as 1-hr flights over the Palpa and Llipata areas, where you can see more designs and other rare patterns (US$130 pp, minimum 3); Nazca and Palpa combined, US$250. See the website for promotional offers. All **Alas Peruanas** flights include the BBC film of Nazca.

Transport

Nazca
Air
The airport caters only for sightseeing flights.

> **Tip...**
> Be aware that fatal crashes by planes flying over the Lines do occur. Some foreign governments advise tourists not to take these flights and some companies will not provide insurance for passengers until safety and maintenance standards are improved.

Bus
It is worth paying extra for a good bus; there are reports of robbery on the cheaper services. Over-booking is common.

To **Lima**, 446 km, 7 hrs, several buses and colectivos daily, US$23-26. **Ormeño** (T056-522058) *Royal Class* at 0530 and 1330 from Hotel Nazca Lines, normal service from Av Los Incas, 6 a day; **Civa** (Av Guardia Civil, T056-523019), normal service at 2300; **Cruz del Sur** (Lima y San Martín, T056-720440), via Ica and Paracas, luxury service, US$39-55. To **Ica**, with **Ormeño**, 2 hrs, US$3.50, 4 a day. For **Pisco** (210 km), 3 hrs, buses stop 5 km outside town (see under Pisco, Transport), so change in Ica for direct transport into Pisco.

To **Arequipa**, 565 km, 9 hrs, US$19-22.50, or US$28-52 for *bus cama* services: **Ormeño**, from Av Los Incas, Royal Class at 2130, 8 hrs, also **Cruz del Sur** and **Oltursa** (Av los Incas 103, T056-522265), reliable, comfortable and secure on this route. Delays are possible out of Nazca because of drifting sand across the road or because of mudslides in the rainy season. Travel in daylight if possible. Book your ticket the previous day.

To **Cuzco**, 659 km, via **Chalhuanca** and **Abancay** (13 hrs), with **Ormeño**, US$50, and **Cruz del Sur**, 2015, 2100, US$50-70. The highway from Nazca to Cuzco is paved and is safe for bus travellers, drivers of private vehicles and motorcyclists.

Towards Cuzco: Sondano Valley
There are vans from **Puquio** to **Andamarca**, 65 km, 0600-0800, US$7, 2 hrs.

Arequipa & the Far South

canyons, condors and colonial architecture

The colonial city of Arequipa is the ideal place to start exploring southern Peru. The distinctive volcanic sillar stone used for building its churches, mansions and Plaza de Armas has given it the nickname 'White City'. In contrast, Arequipa's most famous colonial jewel, the Santa Catalina Convent, is painted in bright colours, a gorgeous little city within a city.

The city is, however, only one attraction in a region of towering volcanoes, deep canyons, terraced valleys and clear rivers well suited to rafting. Arequipa is the gateway to the Cotahuasi canyon, the world's deepest at 3354 m, and its more popular neighbour, Colca. There is excellent trekking and riding on the canyons' terraces and the calendar is full of festivals. Above all, Colca is a very good place to get a close-up view of the majestic condor rising on the morning thermals. On the altiplano there are lakes, herds of alpaca and vicuña and, at the World Heritage Site of Toro Muerto, the largest field of petroglyphs in the world.

From Arequipa routes lead west to Lake Titicaca and south to the Chilean border near Tacna via the pleasant city of Moquegua.

Best for
Architecture ▪ Food ▪ Scenery ▪ Trekking

Footprint
picks

★ **Santa Catalina Convent**, page 263

This beautifully restored convent and its treasure trove of art allows you to travel back in time and step into a Spanish colonial town.

★ **Museo Santuarios Andinos**, page 263

Meet 'Juanita', the Inca child mummy from the glaciers of Ampato, and learn about human sacrifice in pre-Columbian times.

★ **Casa Museo Vargas Llosa**, page 266

Let the Nobel laureate Mario Vargas Llosa tell you about his life, and meet some of the characters in his novels at this innovative modern museum.

★ **Colca Canyon**, page 282

Known as the best place in Peru to see the majestic condor, Colca also offers beautiful scenery, quaint indigenous villages set on pre-Columbian terraces and excellent trekking.

★ **Cotahuasi Canyon**, page 292

Still an off-the-beaten-path destination, the deepest canyon in the world is a land of green oases and hanging valleys amid arid slopes. It offers waterfalls, thermal baths and archaeological sites as well as great trekking and challenging kayaking.

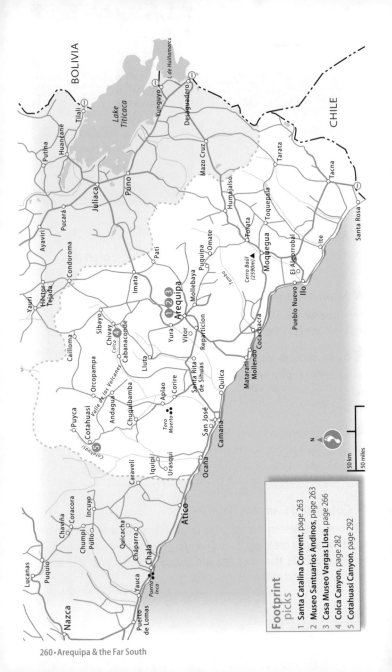

BOLIVIA

CHILE

Lake
Titicaca

Footprint
picks

1 Santa Catalina Convent, page 263
2 Museo Santuarios Andinos, page 263
3 Casa Museo Vargas Llosa, page 266
4 Colca Canyon, page 282
5 Cotahuasi Canyon, page 292

Essential Arequipa and the Far South

Finding your feet

Arequipa is the main commercial centre and transport hub for the south, with flights and long-distance buses to/from Lima and other major cities. 4M Express, www.4m-express.com, provides a useful service from Arequipa or Chivay east to Puno or north Cuzco. Head south from Arequipa to reach Moquegua and the coast, where both the Vía Costenera and the Pan-American Highway run down to the Chilean border.

Best Arequipeño restaurants

Crepísimo
Hatunpa
La Nueva Palomino
Tío Darío
Zig Zag

For details of these restaurants and information on Arequipeno cuisine, see pages 272-275.

Getting around

In Arequipa, the main places of interest and the hotels are within walking distance of the Plaza de Armas. If you are going to the suburbs, take a bus or taxi. Traffic can be chaotic, making the city noisy; perhaps a planned public transit system will help. Public buses run from Arequipa to both the Colca and Cotahuasi canyons, although tourist services may be more reliable. Buses and colectivos connect villages in the canyon areas; there are also numerous trekking opportunities.

When to go

The climate in Arequipa is delightful, with a mean daytime temperature in the low 20s. The sun shines on 360 days of the year and average annual rainfall is just 100 mm. In the Colca Canyon it rains January to April so this is not the best time to see condors or trek, although it makes the area green, with lots of flowers. May to December are drier but colder.

Time required

One to two weeks is enough time to explore the city and its surroundings. Allow at least two to three days to appreciate the Colca Canyon fully, more if you're planning on trekking.

Weather Arequipa

January	February	March	April	May	June
20°C 10°C 20mm	20°C 10°C 40mm	20°C 10°C 10mm	21°C 9°C 0mm	21°C 8°C 0mm	20°C 7°C 0mm

July	August	September	October	November	December
20°C 7°C 0mm	20°C 7°C 0mm	21°C 8°C 0mm	21°C 8°C 0mm	21°C 8°C 0mm	21°C 9°C 0mm

Arequipa

The city of Arequipa (population: one million) stands in a beautiful valley 1011 km from Lima, at the foot of the perfect cone of El Misti volcano (5822 m), guarded on either side by the mountains Chachani (6057 m), and Pichu-Pichu (5669 m). The city has fine Spanish buildings and many old and interesting churches built of sillar, a pearly white volcanic stone almost exclusively used in the construction of Arequipa. The city was re-founded on 15 August 1540 by an emissary of Pizarro, but it had previously been occupied by Aymara peoples and the Incas. It is the main commercial centre for the south and is a busy place.

There's an individual feeling to the Arequipa Region which, in part, stems from the stubborn pride of its people who have continuously attempted to gain more independence from Lima. Fellow Peruvians jokingly refer to it as the 'Independent Republic of Arequipa'.

beautiful buildings and fascinating museums in the 'White City'

The centre is known as Cercado; the Río Chili, spanned by four bridges, separates it from the suburbs to the west, among them the colonial district of Yanahuara.

Plaza de Armas

The elegant **Plaza de Armas** is faced on three sides by arcaded buildings with many restaurants, and on the fourth by the massive **Cathedral**, founded in 1612 and largely rebuilt in the 19th century. It is remarkable for having its façade along the whole length of the church (entrance on Santa Catalina and San Francisco). Inside is the fine Belgian organ and elaborately carved wooden pulpit. The Cathedral has a **museum** ① *www.museocatedralarequipa.org.pe, Mon-Sat 1000-1700, US$3.60*, which outlines the history of the building, its religious objects and art, and a bell tower. Behind the Cathedral is an alley with handicraft shops and places to eat.

★Santa Catalina Convent
Santa Catalina 301, T054-608282, www.santacatalina.org.pe. Mon, Wed, Fri-Sun 0800-1700 (last admission 1600), Tue and Thu 0800-2000, US$12.50, 1-hr tour US$7 for group up to 6, many guides speak English or German.

This is by far the most remarkable sight, opened in 1970 after four centuries of mystery. It is a complete miniature walled colonial town of over 2 ha in the middle of the city, where about 450 nuns lived in total seclusion, except for their women servants. The few remaining nuns have retreated to one section of the convent, allowing visitors to see a maze of cobbled streets and plazas bright with geraniums and other flowers, cloisters and buttressed houses. These have been painted in traditional white, orange, deep red and blue. The convent has been beautifully refurbished, with period furniture, paintings of the Arequipa and Cuzco schools and fully equipped kitchens. On Tuesday and Thursday evenings the convent is lit with torches, candles and blazing fireplaces: very beautiful. There is a good café, which sells cakes, sandwiches, baked potatoes and a special blend of tea.

★Museo Santuarios Andinos
La Merced 110, T054-215013, www.ucsm. edu.pe/santury. Mon-Sat 0900-1800, Sun 0900-1500, US$7.15 includes a 20-min video in English followed by a 1-hr guided tour (tip the guide), discount with student card.

This museum contains the frozen Inca mummies of child sacrifices found on Mount Ampato (see box, page 267). The mummy known as 'Juanita' is particularly

> **Tip...**
> There have been reports of taxi drivers colluding with criminals to rob both tourists and locals. Ask hotels, restaurants, etc, to book a safe taxi for you. Theft can be a problem in the market area and the park at Selva Alegre at quiet times. Be very cautious walking anywhere at night. The police are conspicuous, friendly, courteous and efficient, but their resources are limited.

Arequipa

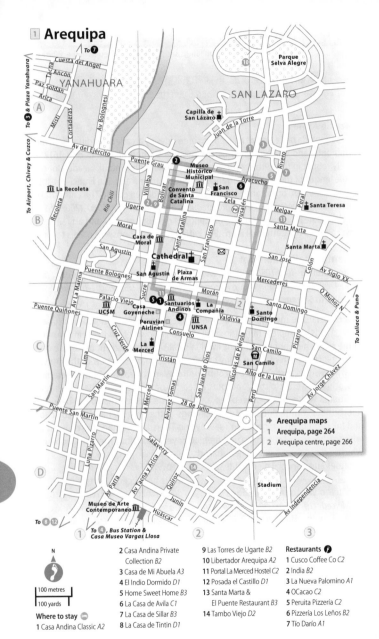

To ❼

Cuesta del Angel

YANAHUARA

Parque
Selva Alegre

SAN LÁZARO

Capilla de
San Lázaro

Museo
Histórico
Municipal

Convento
de Santa
Catalina

San
Francisco

Santa Teresa

La Recoleta

Casa de
Moral

Santa Marta

Cathedral

San Agustín

Plaza
de Armas

Puente Bolognesi

Santuarios
Andinos

La
Compañía

Casa
Goyeneche

Santo
Domingo

Peruvian
Airlines

UNSA

La
Merced

San Camilo

To ❽ ❿

Museo de Arte
Contemporáneo

Stadium

To ❹, Bus Station &
Casa Museo Vargas Llosa

➡ Arequipa maps
1 Arequipa, page 264
2 Arequipa centre, page 266

N

100 metres

100 yards

Where to stay
1 Casa Andina Classic A2

2 Casa Andina Private
  Collection B2
3 Casa de Mi Abuela A3
4 El Indio Dormido D1
5 Home Sweet Home B3
6 La Casa de Avila C1
7 La Casa de Sillar B3
8 La Casa de Tintin D1

9 Las Torres de Ugarte B2
10 Libertador Arequipa A2
11 Portal La Merced Hostel C2
12 Posada el Castillo D1
13 Santa Marta &
   El Puente Restaurant B3
14 Tambo Viejo D2

Restaurants ❼
1 Cusco Coffee Co C2
2 India B2
3 La Nueva Palomino A1
4 OCacao C2
5 Peruita Pizzería C2
6 Pizzería Los Leños B2
7 Tío Darío A1

fascinating as it is so well preserved and reveals a huge amount of information about Inca life and ritual practices. From January to April, Juanita is often jetting round the world and is replaced by other child sacrifices unearthed in the mountains. There has been talk of moving Juanita to a museum in the Colca Canyon.

Colonial houses

Arequipa is said to have the best preserved colonial architecture in Peru, apart from Cuzco. As well as the many fine churches, there are several seignorial houses with large carved tympanums over the entrances. Built as single-storey structures, they have mostly withstood earthquakes. They have small patios, no galleries, flat roofs and small windows, disguised by superimposed lintels or heavy grilles. Good examples are the 18th-century **Casa Tristán del Pozo**, or **Gibbs-Ricketts house** ⓘ *San Francisco 108, Mon-Sat 0900-1300, 1600-1800,* with its fine portal and puma-head waterspouts. It houses a bank and art gallery. **Casa de Moral** ⓘ *Moral 318 y Bolívar, Mon-Sat 0900-1700, Sun 0900-1300, US$1.80, US$1 for students,* also known as Williams House is now a bank and has a museum. **Casa Goyeneche** ⓘ *La Merced 201 y Palacio Viejo,* is also a bank office, but the guards will let you view the courtyard and fine period rooms.

Arequipa's churches

Among the many fine churches is **La Compañía** ⓘ *General Morán y Alvarez Thomas,* whose main façade (1698) and side portal (1654) are striking examples of the florid Andean *mestizo* style. To the left of the sanctuary is the **Capilla San Ignacio de Loyola** or **Capilla Real** (Royal Chapel) ⓘ *Mon-Fri 0900-1230, 1500-1930, Sat 1130-1230, 1500-1800, Sun 0900-1230, 1700-1800, mass daily 1200, US$1.80,* with a beautiful polychrome cupola. Also well worth seeing is the church of **San Francisco** ⓘ *Zela 103, Mon-Sat 0715-0900, 1600-200, Sun 0715-1245, 1800-2000.* There are religious art **museums** ⓘ *Mon-Sat 0900-1200, 1500-1800, US$1.80,* on either side of it, and also at the convent and at Templo de la Tercera Orden. Opposite San Francisco is the interesting **Museo Histórico Municipal** ⓘ *Plaza San Francisco 407, Mon-Fri 0800-1530, Sat-Sun 0900-1300, US$3.60,* with scale models of the façades of Arequipa's churches, much war memorabilia and some impressive photos of the city in the aftermath of several notable earthquakes.

The oldest district of Arequipa is **San Lázaro**, a collection of tiny climbing streets and houses quite close to the **Hotel Libertador**, where you can find the ancient **Capilla de San Lázaro** ⓘ *daily 0900-1700, US$1.80.*

La Recoleta
Jr Recoleta 117, T054-270966. Mon-Sat 0900-1200, 1500-1700. US$3.60.

This Franciscan monastery, built in 1647, stands on the other side of the river. A seldom-visited gem, it contains a variety of sights, including several cloisters, a religious art museum and a pre-Columbian art museum with ceramics and textiles produced by cultures of the Arequipa area. Most impressive however is the museum of Amazon exploration featuring artifacts and photos of early

Centro
Artesanal
Fundo
del Fierro

Museo
Histórico
Municipal

Puente Grau

Ayacucho

Convento
de Santa
Catalina

Instituto Cultural
Peruano-Norte
Americano

San
Francisco

Zela

Melgar

Instituto Cultural
Peruano Alemán

Tourist Police

Santa Marta

Ugarte

Ugarte

Moral

San José

La Casona
Chávez
de la Rosa

LAN

Cathedral

Casa
Tristán
del Pozo

Cambios

San Agustín

Patio del
Ekeko

Mercaderes

Cambios

Plaza
de Armas

Puente
Bolognesi

Morán

Municipal
& iPerú

➡ **Arequipa maps**
1 Arequipa, page 264
2 Arequipa centre, page 266

N

50 metres
50 yards

Where to stay
1 Casablanca Hostal B1
2 Casa de Melgar A2
3 Hostal Santa Catalina A1
4 Hostal Solar A2
5 La Casa de Margott A2
6 La Posada del Cacique A2
7 Le Foyer A1
8 Los Andes B&B B1
9 Sonesta Posadas
del Inca B1

9 Istanbul B1
10 La Alemana B1
11 La Canasta B2
12 La Trattoria del
Monasterio A1
13 Mandala A2
14 Pura Fruta A1
15 Ras El Hanout y
los 40 Sabores A1
16 Sandwichería Mamut B2
17 Zig Zag B2

Bars & clubs
18 Casona Forum &
Déjà Vu A1
19 Farren's B1
20 Museo del Pisco B1

Restaurants
1 Bóveda San Agustín B1
2 Café Capriccio B1, B2
3 Café Valenzuela B2
4 Chicha B1
5 Crepísimo, Chaqchao &
Alianza Francesa A1
6 El Asador A1
7 El Turko & Paladar 1900 B2
8 Hatunpa A1

Franciscan missionaries in the Amazon. The library, containing many antique books, is open for supervised visits during museum hours.

★Casa Museo Vargas Llosa
Av Parra 101, south of the centre, T054-283574. Tours Tue-Sun and hols at 1000, 1200, 1400 and 1600 (3-10 visitors). US$10.

The birthplace of Peru's Nobel laureate in literature, Mario Vargas Llosa (1936-), is now an innovative, modern museum. In holographic displays the writer himself tells you about the highlights of his life and career; during the 90-minute tour, you even get to meet some of the characters in his novels. Vargas Llosa's private library is now found at the **Biblioteca Regional** ⓘ *San Francisco 308, Mon-Sat 0830-2030.* For more information about the author, see page 558.

Other sights
Museo de Arte Contemporáneo ⓘ *Tacna y Arica 201, T054-221068, Tue-Fri 1000-1700, Sat-Sun 1000-1400, US$3.60,* in the old railway station, is dedicated to painting and photography from 1900 onwards. The building is surrounded by gardens and has a Sunday market. Universidad de San Agustín's **Museo Arqueológico UNSA** ⓘ *Alvarez Thomas y Palacio Viejo, T054-288881, Mon-Fri 0830-1600, US$0.70,* has an interesting collection of ceramics and mummies, tracing the region's history from pre-Columbian times to the Republican era. The Universidad Católica has a similar collection, which also includes textiles, at its **Museo de Arqueología UCSM** ⓘ *Cruz Verde 303, T054-221083, Mon-Fri 0830-1600, donations welcome.*

ON THE ROAD

Appeasing the gods

To the Incas, Nevado Ampato was a sacred god, described as one of the principal deities in the Colca Canyon region, who brought water and good harvests and, as such, claimed the highest tribute: human sacrifice.

In September 1995, Johan Reinhard of Chicago s Field Museum of Natural History, accompanied by Peruvian climber Miguel Zárate, whose brother Carlos is a well-known mountain guide, were climbing Ampato when they made a startling discovery. At about 6000 m they found the perfectly preserved mummified body of an Inca girl, wrapped tightly in textiles. They concluded that she had been ritually sacrificed and buried on the summit.

Mummies of Inca human sacrifices had been found before on Andean summits, but the girl from Ampato, nicknamed Juanita, was the first frozen Inca female to be unearthed and her body may be the best preserved of any found in the Americas from pre-Columbian times. The intact tissues and organs of naturally mummified, frozen bodies are a storehouse of biological information. Studies reveal how she died, where she came from, who her living relatives are and even yield insights about the Inca diet.

Juanita's clothes are no less remarkable. The richly patterned textiles serve as a model for depictions of the way noble Inca women dressed. Her *liclla* – a bright red and white shawl beneath the outer wrappings – has been declared "the finest Inca woman's textile in the world".

A subsequent ascent of Ampato revealed a further two mummies at the summit. One is a young girl and the other, though badly charred by lightning, is believed to be a boy.

The Incas not only appeased the mountain gods with the sacrifice of children, the Cabana and Collagua people even bound their children's heads to make them look like the mountains from which they believed they were descended. Nowadays, villages in the Colca continue to make offerings to the mountain gods for water and good harvests, but thankfully the gods have modified their tastes, now preferring *chicha* to children.

Yanahuara

In the district of **Yanahuara**, northwest of the centre across Puente Grau, is the mestizo-style church of **San Juan Bautista** ⓘ *Plaza de Yanahuara, daily 1700-1900, Mass Mon-Sat 0700, Sun 0700 and 1100,* completed in 1750, with a magnificent churrigueresque façade, all in sillar. On the same plaza is a *mirador* through whose arches there is a fine view of El Misti with the city at its feet, a popular spot in the late afternoon. Nearby, at the Yanahuara municipality is the **Museo Pre Inca de Chiribaya** ⓘ *Miguel Grau 402, Mon-Sat 0830-1900, Sun 0900-1500*, which has a good collection of vessels, gold objects and well-preserved textiles from the important pre-Inca Chiribaya culture (AD 800-1350), which extended from southern Peru to northern Chile and had its centre in Ilo, on the coast.

Around Arequipa

Some 3 km beyond the southwestern suburb of **Tingo**, beside the Río Sabandía on the Huasacanche road, is **La Mansión del Fundador** ① *daily 0900-1700, US$4.50*. Originally owned by the founder of Arequipa, Don Garcí Manuel de Carbajal, it has been restored as a museum with original furnishings and paintings; it also has a cafetería and bar.

About 8 km southeast of Arequipa is the **Molino de Sabandía** ① *US$3.60, ring bell for admission; round trip by taxi US$6*. This was the first stone mill in the area, built in 1621. It has been fully restored, and the guardian diverts water to run the grinding stones when visitors arrive. Adjoining Sabandía is the Inca site of **Yumina** ① *tourist fee of US$6 may be asked for on the bus to Chivay*, with many Inca terraces which are still in use.

Climbing El Misti and Chachani

At 5822 m, El Misti volcano offers a relatively straightforward opportunity to scale a high peak. There are three routes for climbing the volcano; all take two days. The northeast route starts from the Aguada Blanca reservoir, reached by 4WD, from where a four-hour hike takes you to the Monte Blanco camp at 4800 m. Then it's a five- to six-hour ascent to the top. Two hours takes you back down to the trail. The southwest route involves taking a 4WD vehicle to the trailhead at Pastores (3400 m), followed by a hike of five or six hours to a camp at 4700 m. A five-hour

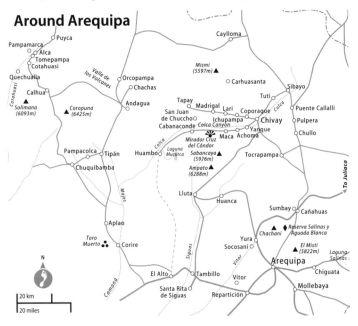

Around Arequipa

climb takes you to the summit, before a three-hour descent to the trail. A southern route (Grau) also starts at 3400 m, with a camp at 4610 m, followed by a five-hour hike to the summit and a two-hour descent.

Climbing Chachani (6057 m), northwest of El Misti, is also popular. This peak retains its icy covering longer than El Misti, though this is fast disappearing.

Remember that both summits are at a very high altitude and that this, combined with climbing on scree, makes it hard going for the untrained. Great care must be taken on the unstable rock left by deglaciation; serious accidents have occurred. Be prepared for early starts, and take plenty of water, food and protection against the weather. Favoured months are May to September. Always contact an experienced guiding agency or professional guide in Arequipa as you should never climb alone (see What to do, page 278).

Listings Arequipa *maps p264 and p266*

Tourist information

Indecopi (Hipólito Unanue 100-A, Urb Victoria, T054-212054, mlcornejo@indecopi.gob.pe).
iPerú (Portal de la Municipalidad 110, on the south side of Plaza de Armas, T054-223265, iperuarequipa@promperu.gob.pe, Mon-Sat 0900-1800, Sun 0900-1300, also in the airport Arrivals hall, T054-444564, daily 0630-2130).
Municipal tourist office (Portal de la Municipalidad 112 next to iPerú, Mon-Fri 0830-1530).
Tourist Police (Jerusalén 315, T054-201258, daily 24 hrs). Very helpful dealing with complaints or giving directions.

Where to stay

There are several economical *hostales* along Puente Grau and Ayacucho, near Jerusalén. Hostel chains include: **Che Lagarto** (www.chelagarto.com), **Flying Dog** (www.flyingdogperu.com), **The Point** (www.thepointhostels.com), and **Wild Rover** (www.wildroverhostels.com).

$$$$ Casa Andina Private Collection *Ugarte 403, T054-226907, www.casa-andina.com.*
Luxury hotel in a restored 18th-century mansion, former Casa de la Moneda. 5 large suites in colonial building, 36 rooms in modern extension off 2nd courtyard. Gourmet restaurant, room service, business centre, roof terrace with views.

$$$$ Libertador Arequipa *Plaza Simón Bolívar, Selva Alegre, T054-215110, www.libertador.com.pe.*
Large comfortable rooms, good service, swimming pool (cold), gardens, good meals, pub-style bar, cocktail lounge, squash court.

Tip...
On arrival, do not believe taxi drivers who say the hotel of your choice is closed or full in order to take you to another hotel which pays them a high commission. Instead, phone your preferred hotel in advance, or ring the doorbell and check for yourself.

$$$$ Sonesta Posadas del Inca
Portal de Flores 116, T054-215530,
www.sonesta.com/arequipa.
On Plaza de Armas, all the services
associated with this chain, comfortable
modern rooms, **Inkafé** restaurant and
bar overlooking plaza, good food, tiny
outdoor pool, business centre.

$$$ Casa Andina Classic
Jerusalén 603, T054-202070,
www.casa-andina.com.
Part of the attractive Casa Andina
chain, with breakfast, comfortable and
colourful, central, modern,
good restaurant, parking.

$$$-$$ La Casa de Margott
Jerusalén 304, T054-229517,
www.lacasademargott.com.
Family-run in a refurbished 19th-
century house, bright with a massive
palm tree in patio, spacious, convenient,
small bar/café, security box, heaters in
fancier rooms.

$$ Casablanca Hostal
Puente Bolognesi 104, a few metres
from the Plaza de Armas, T054-221327,
www.casablancahostal.com.
Super stylish *hostal*, lovely minimalist
rooms in a colonial building. Ambient
lighting, rooms with exposed stone
walls, most with balcony.

$$ Casa de Mi Abuela
Jerusalén 606, T054-241206,
www.lacasademiabuela.com.
An Arequipa tradition, in the same family
for several generations, suites with
bathtub and rooms, small swimming
pool, rooms at the back are quieter and
overlook the garden, English spoken,
parking, restaurant and piano bar, buffet
breakfast or evening snacks on patio
or in beautiful gardens, tour operator.
Warmly recommended.

$$ Hostal Solar
Ayacucho 108, T054-241793,
www.hostalsolar.com.
Colonial building, newer rooms in back
are bright, good breakfast served in nice
patio, sun lounge on roof, very secure,
multilingual staff.

$$ La Casa de Avila
San Martín 116, Vallecito, T054-213177,
www.casadeavila.com.
Rooms with hot water on 2 floors
around spacious, sunny garden,
computers for guests' use, can
arrange airport/bus station pick-up,
recommended Spanish courses held
in the garden and other activities.

$$ La Casa de Tintin
Urbanización San Isidro F1, Vallecito,
T054-284700, www.hoteltintin.com.
15 mins' walk, 5 mins by taxi from the
Plaza de Armas, Belgian/Peruvian-
owned, hot water, garden, terrace, sauna,
massage, laundry service, restaurant,
café and bar, mountain bike rental, v
ery pleasant and comfortable.

$$ Posada el Castillo
Pasaje Campos 105, Vallecito, T054-
201828, www.posadaelcastillo.com.
Dutch/Peruvian-owned, in an old house
decorated with utensils found in the
renovation, 20 mins by taxi from city
centre. Variety of rooms and suites,
some with balcony and view of El Misti,
wonderful breakfast in annexe, pool,
lovely gardens, a good choice.

$$ Santa Marta
Santa Marta 207, T054-243925,
www.hostalsantamarta.com.
Pleasant, comfortable hotel with nice
patio, modern rooms in back, arrange
airport and bus terminal transfers.

$$-$ Le Foyer
Ugarte 114, T054-286473,
www.hlefoyer.com.
Nicely refurbished old house, pleasant
common areas, colourfully decorated,
private rooms and US$9 pp in dorm,
book exchange, arrange tours, popular.

$$-$ Portal La Merced Hostel
La Merced 131, T054-330481,
PortalLaMercedHostel on Facebook.
Quiet, central, private rooms include
good breakfast, US$9 pp in dorms,
beds only so-so, good service, laundry,
travel agency.

$ Casa de Melgar
Melgar 108, T054-222459,
www.lacasademelgar.com.
18th-century building, excellent rooms
with bath, hot water (solar), courtyard,
good breakfast buffet.

$ El Indio Dormido
Av Andrés Avelino Cáceres B-9, T054-
*427401, http://members.tripod.com/h_*
indio_dormido/.
Close to bus terminals, free transport to
centre, kitchen, cafeteria, parking, laundry,
TV room, very helpful, family-run.

$ Home Sweet Home
Rivero 509A, T054-405982, www.
homesweethome-peru.com.
Family run, Cathy, who runs a travel
agency speaks Spanish, English,
French, very helpful, warm and inviting
atmosphere, substantial fresh breakfast
included. Private or shared bath, hot
water all day, simple rooms, no double
beds, kitchen and laundry facilities.

$ Hostal Santa Catalina
Santa Catalina 500, T054-243705,
www.hostalsantacatalinaperu.com.
On busy corner, rooms arranged around
a courtyard, roof terrace with great

views, helpful staff. Simple rooms
with fridge, private or shared bath,
security box. Can arrange trips and
accommodation in other cities.

$ La Casa de Sillar
Rivero 504, T054-284249,
www.lacasadesillar.com.
Nice refurbished 17th century stone
house, comfortable rooms, private or
shared bath, nice patio with plants,
ample kitchen facilities, terrace with
views, family run, tour operator.

$ La Posada del Cacique
Jerusalén 404, T054-202170,
posadadelcacique@ yahoo.es.
Well maintained, good value
and helpful, with roof terrace.

$ Las Torres de Ugarte
Ugarte 401, T054-283532.
Round the corner from Santa Catalina
convent, reflexology, roof terrace,
parking, safe, luggage store. Some rooms
are bungalow style in colonial part at
the back.

$ Los Andes Bed & Breakfast
La Merced 123, T054-330015,
www.losandesarequipa.com.
Good value, kitchen use, hot water,
large rooms with waxed wood floors
and minimalist decor, TV rooms,
pleasant roof terrace.

$ Lula's B&B
In Cayma, T054-272517, www.bbaqpe.com.
Same owners as Ari Quipay language
school, Lula (Peruvian) and her husband
(Swiss) speak Spanish, English, German
and French, with airport/bus terminal
pick-up, modern, charming, quiet,
meals available.

$ Tambo Viejo
Av Malecón Socabaya 107, IV Centenario,
T288195, www.tamboviejo.com.

5 blocks south of the plaza near the rail station. 15 rooms ranging from double with bath to dormitory, quiet, English and Dutch spoken, walled garden, choice of 8 fresh breakfasts (extra), vegetarian restaurant, safe deposit, coffee shop, bar, book exchange (2 for 1), money changed, tourist information for guests, bike rental, luggage store extra, tours and volcano climbs arranged. For a small fee, you can use the facilities if passing through. Free pick-up from bus terminal 0700-2300 (call when arriving), US$10 for airport pick-up.

Restaurants

Arequipa is proud of its cuisine; typical food is available in *picanterías* and at San Camilo market. There are also regional sweets and excellent chocolate, see Shopping, below. See also Arequipa's gastronomy, opposite.

$$$ Chicha
Santa Catalina 210, Patio del Ekeko int 105, T054-287360. Mon-Sat 1200-2300, Sun 1200-1800.
The menu of mostly local and fusion dishes is created by Gastón Acurio, fine dining in a historic building opposite Santa Catalina. In the same patio and also with an Acurio menu is **Tanta**, serving breakfast and snacks.

$$$ Paladar 1900
San Francisco 227. Mon-Sat 1200-2400, Sun 12-2300.
Stylish, contemporary design in a lovely refurbished old house. Peruvian-Asian fusion cuisine including sushi: interesting and tasty.

$$$ Zig Zag
Zela 210, T054-206020, www.zigzagrestaurant.com. Daily 1200-2400.

Lovely atmosphere and decor in a colonial house with arched ceilings, gourmet European/Peruvian fusion cuisine, specializes in meat (alpaca is recommended) and fish cooked on volcanic rock. Also offer a choice of set meals at midday. Delicious, very popular, book in advance.

$$$-$$ La Nueva Palomino
Pje Leoncio Prado 122, Yanahuara, T054-252393. Wed-Mon 1200-1700.
An Arequipa institution that has been in the same family for 3 generations, a very popular, large *picantería*, with a wide selection of local dishes, such as *rocoto relleno*, *cuy chactado* and *chupe de camarones*, accompanied by *chicha arequipeña*, made with purple corn, large portions. Expect queues at weekends.

$$$-$$ La Trattoria del Monasterio
Santa Catalina 309, T054-204062, www.latrattoriadelmonasterio.com. Mon-Sat 1200-1600, 1900-2300, Sun 1200-1600.
A fusion of Italian and Arequipeño styles and ingredients, in a cloister in the Convento.

$$$-$$ Ras El Hanout y los 40 Sabores
Santa Catalina 300 B-1, T054-212424, www.raselhanout40.com. Mon-Sat 1400-2300.
Nicely decorated Moroccan 'resto-lounge': tagines, keftas, salads, juices and world teas.

$$$-$$ Tío Darío
Pje del Cabildo 100, 2 blocks from the Yanahuara church, T054-270473, www.tiodario.com. Daily 1030-1630.
Very good ceviche and other seafood specialties with an Arequipeño touch, also meat dishes, outdoor seating in pleasant gardens with views.

Arequipa's gastronomy

One of the most important elements of the Arequipeño identity is its food. Very tasty and often spicy, Arequipa's dishes are a major component of internationally acclaimed Peruvian cuisine. Some of the better known dishes include:

adobo spicy pork stew served with *pan de tres puntas*, a local bread, and hot *rocoto* peppers.

chancho al palo pork roasted on a spit.

chupe de camarón freshwater shrimp chowder

cuy chactado crispy guinea pig with a corn breading, fried under stones and served with potatoes, *habas* (broad beans) and a hot *rocoto* sauce.

queso helado frozen milk with cinnamon.

rocoto relleno hot pepper stuffed with beef, vegetables, black olives and raisins, topped with cheese and served with *pastel de papa*, a potato pie, also topped with cheese and anis.

soltero a mixed vegetable and cheese salad.

These traditional dishes or *comida criolla* are served with *chicha*, a fermented corn drink, which in Arequipa, unlike other areas, is often made with purple corn. *Picanterías* are the restaurants specializing in traditional food and many good choices are found in and around the city. Local sweets include: marzipan, *alfajores arequipeños* (a crispy pastry filled with molasses) and fine chocolates.

The culinary delights of Arequipa go well beyond the *picantería*, with a fine selection of restaurants offering a fusion of Peruvian and international food. Since 2007, the Asociación Gastronómica de Arequipa, AGAR, has hosted FestiSabores, an annual gastronomic festival held for four days around the last weekend in October; the first of its kind in Peru. It is a great place to sample much of what Arequipa has to offer: traditional as well as fusion cuisine, regional sweets, wine and *pisco*, an organic food market, exhibits, music and folklore. Check www.festisabores.com for exact dates, location and additional information.

¡Buen provecho!

$$ Bóveda San Agustín
Portal San Agustín 127-129, T054-243596.
Daily 0700-2300.
Attractive bar downstairs, with an upstairs balcony overlooking the Plaza de Armas. Good breakfasts, lunches and evening specials.

$$ Crepísimo
Santa Catalina 208, at Alianza Francesa, T054-206620, www.crepisimo.com.
Daily 0800-2400.
Over 100 different sweet and savoury crepes with traditional and Peruvian flavours, plus salads, sandwiches, *menú* at lunch, great coffee and juices, drinks, magazines and board games, pleasant ambiance. Very tasty, recommended.

$$ Pizzería Los Leños
Jerusalén 407, T054-289179.
Daily 1700-2300.
The first wood-fired pizza in the city, plus pasta, original flavours with a touch of Peruvian home cooking, pleasant atmosphere and music.

$$-$ El Asador
Zela 201-B. Mon-Sat 1200-1500, 1730-2400.
Good value for alpaca steaks, *parrillada*, pleasant atmosphere, good music.

$$-$ Hatunpa
Ugarte 208. Mon-Sat 1230-2130.
Small place serving tasty dishes prepared with native potatoes with a choice of toppings, warm personalized service, very popular.

$$-$ Peruita Pizzería
Palacio Viejo 321, T054-212621.
Mon-Sat 1300-1500, 1730-2230.
Set lunch at midday and à la carte in the evening, very good wood-fired pizza and Italian dishes, Italian run.

$ El Puente
Santa Marta 207-A, Mon-Sat 0900-1700, and Bello Horizonte C-11B, across Puente Quiñones, behind Umacollo stadium, daily 0830-1800.
A choice of tasty vegetarian dishes, good value.

$ El Turko
San Francisco 223-25 and at the airport. Sun-Thu 0800-2400, Fri and Sat 0800-0300.
Bright café/bar selling kebabs, coffee, recommended breakfasts and good sandwiches.

$ India
Bolívar 502. Mon-Sat 1200-2100.
Very small restaurant serving tasty Indian cuisine, prepared by an Indian cook, many vegetarian dishes.

$ Istanbul
San Francisco 231-A. Daily 0800-2400.
Middle Eastern fast food, including a delicious falafel and other vegetarian dishes Also good coffee. In the same group as El Turko.

$ Mandala
Jerusalén 207. Mon-Sat 0900-2100.
Good-value vegetarian, breakfast, 3 set menus for lunch, dinner, friendly staff.

$ Sandwichería Mamut
Mercaderes 111. Daily 0900-2100.
Very tasty giant sandwiches with classic and typical Peruvian flavours and many different dressings.

Cafés

Café Capriccio
Mercaderes 121. Daily 0800-2200.
Not that cheap, but excellent coffee, cakes, etc. Very popular with local business people. **Capriccio Gourmet,** on Santa Catalina and at several shopping centres, is also good.

Café Valenzuela
Morán 114 and other locations. Mon-Sat 0800-2200, Sun 1630-2030.
Fantastic coffee (also sells beans and ground coffee), locals' favourite.

Chaqchao
Santa Catalina 204, p2, T054-234572.
Daily 1100-2100.
Coffee, desserts, organic chocolate. At 1500 and 1800 they offer fun chocolate-making classes (US$21), reserve ahead.

Cusco Coffee Co
La Merced 135 and Mall Aventura Plaza.
Good variety of coffees, cakes, average sandwiches, comfy sofas, Wi-Fi.

La Alemana
San Francisco 137 and at shopping centres. Mon-Thu 0800-2400, Fri-Sat 0800-0300.
Wide choice of sausages, plus very good *empanadas* and sandwiches. Good value and popular.

La Canasta
Jerusalén 115 in courtyard, no sign. Mon-Sat 0830-2000.
Excellent baguettes twice daily, also serves breakfast and delicious apple and brazil nut pastries, courtyard seating.

OCacao
Palacio Viejo 205 A. Mon-Fri 0900-2100, Sat 1000-2100.
Small café run by a Belgian *chocolatier*: coffee, sweets, excellent truffles and bonbons.

Pura Fruta
Mercaderes 121 and in Cayma. Mon-Sat 0800-2200, Sun 0900-1400.
A great variety of fruit juices and smoothies, coffee, fraps, yoghurt, salads, sandwiches, desserts.

Bars and clubs

Casona Forum
San Francisco 317, www.casonaforum.com.
Huge complex incorporating the **Retro Bar** (live music Tue-Sat from 1930), **Zero** pool bar for rock music, **Club Latino** for salsa dancing, **Club de los 80** (Thu-Sat from 2200) for 1980s music and lovely views, and **Forum**, an underground club with imitation waterfall and plants (Thu-Sat from 2200). Check the website for upcoming events.

Déjà Vu
San Francisco 319-B. Mon-Sat 1100-0200, Sun 1800-0100.
Popular café/restaurant and bar serving good food, including a set lunch. Hosts DJ evenings, movies and live music. Rooftop bar, weekend drinks specials.

Farren's
Pasaje Catedral.
Good meeting place, pool table, great music.

Museo del Pisco
Moral 229. Daily 1100-2400.
Bar where you can learn about the pisco culture and history, also tastings and mixology classes.

Festivals

A full list of the region's many festivals is available locally from **iPerú**.

10 Jan **Sor Ana de Los Angeles y Monteagudo**, festival for the patron saint of Santa Catalina monastery.
Mar-Apr **Semana Santa** celebrations involve huge processions every night, culminating in the burning of an effigy of Judas on Easter Sun in the main plazas of Cayma and Yanahuara, and the reading of his will, containing criticisms of the city authorities.
27 Apr The celebration of the apostle Santiago.
May is known as the **Mes de Las Cruces**, with ceremonies on hilltops throughout the city.
3 Aug A procession through the city bearing the images of Santo Domingo and San Francisco.
6-31 Aug **Fiesta Artesanal del Fundo El Fierro** is a sale and exhibition of *artesanía* from all parts of Peru, taking place near Plaza San Francisco.

ON THE ROAD

Ancient apparel

Four thousand years before the Spanish *conquistadores* set foot on Peruvian soil, the indigenous peoples excelled at the textile arts. Cotton was cultivated on the arid coast, but, up on the high Andean plain, there was a ready supply of fibre in the shape of the native camelids llamas, alpacas, vicuñas and guanacos. Alpacas and llamas were domesticated as early as 4000 BC and the wild camelids (guanacos and vicuñas) were used as clothing even further back by hunters who roamed the bleak, high Andean plateau. By 1500-1000 BC llamas were being used for ritual burial offerings, indicating their prestige.

Camelid fibre is easy to spin and dye and allowed the ancient weavers to develop extraordinarily fine spinning techniques. The pre-Columbian peoples prized the silky soft fibre of the alpaca, in particular. Living at altitudes of 4000 m, where temperatures can drop to -15°C, these animals have developed a coat that not only has thermal properties but is also soft and resistant. The majority of Peru's alpacas are in the hands of small breeders and indigenous communities who still herd and manage their animals in much the same way as their ancestors.

Alpaca-breeding and herding is the main economic activity of high-altitude regions, such as the Province of Carabaya in Puno. The textile arts tradition also continues. Fine woven and knitted garments can be found in specialized shops in main cities and tourist centres, see Shopping, below.

6-17 Aug Celebration of the city's anniversary on 15th, many events including a mass ascent of El Misti.
Oct-Nov FestiSabores, gastronomic festival around the last weekend in Oct, see Arequipa's gastronomy, page 273.
2 Nov Day of the Dead celebrations in cemeteries.

Shopping

The central **San Camilo market**, between Perú, San Camilo, Piérola and Alto de la Luna, is worth visiting.

Alpaca goods, textiles and crafts
Alpaca 21, *Jerusalén 115, of 125, T054-213425.* Recommended.
Ilaria, *Patio del Ekeko, Mercaderes 141.* Fine jewellery.

Fundo del Fierro, large handicraft market behind the old prison on Plaza San Francisco; it's worth a visit.
Kuna by Alpaca 111, *Patio del Ekeko, Mercaderes 141, www.kuna.com.pe or www.incalpaca.com.* High-quality alpaca and wool products. Also at Casona Santa Catalina, Santa Catalina 210, Local 1-2; in Hotel Libertador and at the airport. Shops in Lima, Cuzco and Puno.
La Comercial, *Mercaderes 236 (no sign), opposite Teatro Municipal.* Recommended for knitted goods, bags, etc.
Las Cláusulas de La Compañía, *Morán 140.* Handicrafts shopping centre in a colonial setting, containing many alpaca knitwear outlets including a factory outlet in the 2nd patio.
Michell y Cia, *Juan de la Torre 101, www.michell.com.pe.* Factory outlet, excellent

place for alpaca and other wool yarn in
huge variety of colours, also a clearance
room for baby and adult alpaca yarn.
Alpaca and pima cotton garments also
for sale at Sol Alpaca, Casona Santa
Catalina, Santa Catalina 210. 1920s
machinery on display. Branches in Lima
and Cuzco.
Millma's Baby Alpaca, *Pasaje Catedral
117, T054-205134, millmas@hotmail.
com*. 100% baby alpaca goods, run by
Peruvian family, high quality, beautiful
designs, good prices.

Bookshops
Librería El Lector, *San Francisco 213*.
Wide selection, including Peruvian
authors, book exchange in various
languages (2 for 1), stocks *Footprint*.
Librerías San Francisco *has branches at
Portal de Flores 138, San Francisco 102-106
and San Francisco 133-135*. Books on
Arequipa and Peru, some in English, also
expensive regional topographical maps.
SBS Book Service, *San Francisco 125,
T054-205317*. Has a good selection of
travel books, etc.

Shopping centres
There are several international style
malls in the suburbs of Cayma,
Paucarpata, Cerro Colorado and others.
Patio del Ekeko, *Mercaderes 141*.
A commercial centre with upmarket

restaurants and shops, cinema and
Museo de Arte Textil upstairs (Mon-Sat
1000-2030, Sun 1000-1530).

Sweets
Antojitos de Arequipa, *Morán 129.
An Arequipa institution.* Sells traditional
sweets. Also at Jerusalén 120, Portal
de Flores 144, the airport and all
shopping centres.
La Ibérica, *Jerusalén 136, www.laiberica.
com.pe*. Another Arequipa stalwart
since 1909. Top-quality chocolate, but
expensive. Outlets at Mercaderes 102,
Morán 112, Portal de Flores 130, the
airport and all shopping centres.
See also Cafés, above.

What to do

City tours
A cheap tour of the city can be made in
a *Vallecito* city bus, 1½ hrs for US$0.50.
It is a circular route which goes down
Jerusalén and San Juan de Dios. There
are 4 guides' associations, one of which
(**Adegopa**, Morán 118, Cláustros de la
Compañía, tienda 11, http://adegopa.
org) offers free promotional tours.
Panoramic bus tours are offered by
several companies (eg: www.bustour.
com.pe, www.tahuantinsuyotravel.com,
www.toursclassarequipa.com.pe),
US$12.50 for 2 hrs, US$16 for 4 hrs. Most
depart from Portal San Agustín, Plaza
de Armas, several times daily. **Free
walking tours** are offered daily at 1000
and 1500 by tourism students from the
**Universidad Nacional San Agustín
UNSA**; contact the Municipal Tourist
office, T9747-84999; also with **Free
Walking Tour Peru**, T9989-59566, www.
fwtperu.com, depart Plaza San Francisco
at 1030 and 1400, tips expected.

ON THE ROAD

Rafting around Arequipa

Río Chili (year-round, Grade II-IV): just outside Arequipa but highly water dependent and relying on dam releases to make it worthwhile. A fun half-day out if you need a break from the heat.

Río Colca (Jun, Grade IV-V): possibly even harder than the Cotahuasi, this rarely run expedition river has had its fair share of casualties in the past. Be prepared for rocks falling off the cliffs almost continuously, sandflies, storms and out-of-this-world whitewater. Recent seismic activity around Arequipa has caused major changes to several rapids; definitely book with the local experts.

Río Cotahuasi (May-Jun, Grade IV-V): this is a total expedition, including a long drive past Coropuna mountain, followed by 6 days of non-stop technical whitewater. The scenery is out of this world, including Wari terracing and ruins all in an incredibly deep desert canyon. Probably the best whitewater river on offer in Peru, only a handful of operators offer this trip and only one or two depart each year. Book early and only with companies who have plenty of experience.

Río Majes (all year, Grade II-III): where the Colca emerges from its gorge it joins the Río Majes and some day trips can be organized locally or from Arequipa. Good freshwater shrimp make up for the pretty average whitewater.

Climbing, cycling, rafting and trekking

Be sure to acclimatize before climbing and be wary of agencies wanting to sell you trips with very fast ascents.

Colca Trek, *Jerusalén 401 B, T054-206217, www.colcatrek.com.pe.* Knowledgeable and English-speaking Vlado Soto is one of the best guides for the Cotahuasi Canyon and is recommended for climbing, trekking and mountain biking in the Colca Canyon. He also rents equipment and has topographical maps.

Cusipata, *Jerusalén 402-A, T054-203966, www.cusipata.com.* Recommended as a very good local rafting operator, very popular half-day trips. Also 6-day trips on the Río Colca. May-Dec, Río Chili 1-day kayak courses, also trekking and mountain bike tours.

Expediciones y Aventuras, *Santa Catalina 219, T054-221653, www. expedicionesyaventuras.com.* Family-run adventure sports operator led by Gustavo Rondón. Experienced guides for rafting, kayaking, biking, climbing, trekking, sand-boarding, body-boarding and horse riding tours. Innovative 4x4 routes and camping tours to Colca, Valle de los Volcanes, Cotahuasi, protected areas and the coast; very helpful.

Mountrekk, *T054-601833, http:// mountrekk.com.* Run by Julver Castro, a climbing guide recommended as experienced and "full of energy".

Naturaleza Activa, *Santa Catalina 211, T054-695793, naturactiva@yahoo.com.* Experienced guides, knowledgeable, climbing and trekking.

Sacred Road Tours, *Jerusalén 400, T054-212332, www.sacredroad.com.* Arranges hiking and rock climbing in Colca Canyon and elsewhere, experienced guides led by Arcadio Mamani, equipment available.

Selern Services, *Urb Puerta Verde F13, José LB y Rivero, T054-348685, see*

Facebook. Trekking, adventure tourism, mountain climbing.

Volcanyon Travel, *C Villalba 414, T054-205078, volcanyon@terra.com.pe, see Facebook*. Trekking and some mountain bike tours in the Colca Canyon, also volcano climbing.

Zárate Aventuras, *Santa Catalina 204, of 3, T054-202461, www.zarateadventures.com/en*. Run by Carlos Zárate of the Mountaineering Club of Peru. Good family-run business that always works with qualified mountain guides. A specialist in mountaineering and exploring, with a great deal of information and advice and some equipment rental. Carlos also runs trips to one of the supposed sources of the Amazon, Nevado Mismi, as well as trekking in the Cotahuasi canyon, climbing tougher peaks such as Coropuna, rock climbing and rafting.

Tour operators

Many agencies on Jerusalén, Santa Catalina and around Plaza de Armas sell air and bus tickets and offer tours of Colca, Cotahuasi, Toro Muerto and the city. Prices vary greatly so shop around; check carefully what is included in the cheapest of tours and that there are enough people for the tour to run. Travel agents frequently work together to fill buses. Many tourists prefer to contract tours through their hotel. If a travel agency puts you in touch with a guide, make sure he/she is official. The following have been recommended as helpful and reliable:

Al Travel Tours, *Santa Catalina 203, of 7, T959-391436, www.aitraveltours.com*. Peruvian/Dutch tour operator offering cultural and adventure tours for groups or individuals, volunteer work and Spanish courses, large book exchange.

Andina Travel Service, *Jerusalén 309-A, T054-285477 and Santa Catalina 115-B, T054-234547*. Good 1- to 4-day tours of Colca Canyon, climbing and other adventure sports, guide Gelmond Ynca Aparicio is very enthusiastic. A good place to get information and a map of Cotahuasi.

Colca Explorer, *Mariscal Benavides 201, Selva Alegre (north of the centre), T054-202587, www.colca-explorer.com*. Agency associated with Amazonas Explorer in Cuzco, with many options in Colca and southern Peru: from classic local tours to horse riding, mountain biking, fishing in remote lakes, climbing, treks and visiting alpaca farms on the altiplano.

Colca Journeys, *C Rodríguez Ballón 533, Miraflores (northeast of the centre), T973-901010, www.colcajourneys.com*. Specializes in and operates tours to the Colca Valley and Cotahuasi Valley.

Giardino Tours, *at Casa de Mi Abuela (see above), T054-221345, www.giardino tours.com*. Professional company offering tours and transport, has own properties in Arequipa and Colca (eg delightful **La Casa de Mamayacchi** in Coporaque), community tourism options, good information.

Land Adventure, *Residencial La Peña A-20, Sachaca (southwest of the centre), T959-941570, www.landadventures.net*. 'Sustainable' tour operator with good guides for communities in Colca, trekking, climbing, downhill biking.

Pablo Tour, *Jerusalén 400-AB-1, T054-203737, www.pablotour.com*. Family-run agency, has connections with several hostals in Cabanaconde and knows the area well, 3-day mixed tours in the Colca Canyon with mountain biking, trekking and rafting, also climbing and sandboarding, free tourist information, topographical maps for sale, bus and hotel reservation service. Son Edwin Junco Cabrera can sometimes be found in the office; he speaks fluent French and English and is very helpful.

Vita Tours, *Jerusalén 302, T054-284211, www.vitatours.com.pe*. Tours in the Arequipa area, including to the coast, and in the Colca Canyon where they have a hotel, La Casa de Lucila in Chivay.

Transport

Taking a taxi from the airport or bus terminals to your hotel is recommended.

Air

Rodríguez Ballón airport is 7 km from the centre, T054-434834. 2 desks offer hotel reservations; also car rentals. Take a taxi to/from your hotel, 30 mins. Airport taxis charge US$9 to the centre; other taxis charge US$5.40 to/from the centre; best to use a radio taxi company listed below. The stop for local buses and combis (eg 'Río Seco', 'Cono-Norte' or 'Zamacola') is about 500 m from the airport, but this is not recommended with luggage.

To **Lima**, 1 hr 30 mins, several daily with **Avianca/TACA** (Centro Comercial Real Plaza, Av del Ejército, Cayma), **LAN** (Santa Catalina 118-C) and **Peruvian Airlines** (La Merced 202-B, also to **Tacna**). LAN also serves **Juliaca**, 30 mins. Avianca/TACA and LAN also serve **Cuzco**, 1 hr from Arequipa. **Peruvian Airlines** also serves **Tacna**. To **La Paz**, Mon, Wed and Fri with **Amazonas** (La Merced 121-B, www.amazonas.com).

Bus

There are 2 terminals at Av Arturo Ibáñez Hunter, south of the centre, 30 mins by city bus (not recommended with luggage, US$0.50), or 20 mins by taxi, US$2.50-3.60. The older **Terminal Terrestre**, T054-427792, has shops and places to eat. The newer **Terrapuerto**, across the car park, T054-348810, has a travel agency (T054-427852, daily 0600-1400, 2000-2300), which gives information and makes hotel reservations. Most luxury class services leave from the Terrapuerto. Terminal tax is US$0.55-.90. Some companies have offices in both terminals. **Flores**, with frequent service to Lima and throughout southern Peru, is in both terminals and also has a private terminal nearby at Av Forga y Av Los Incas. Note that buses may not depart from the terminal where you bought your ticket.

To **Lima**, 1011 km, 15-18 hrs, standard services US$18-29, luxury US$36-56. **Cruz del Sur** (T054-427375), **Enlaces** (T054-430333), **Tepsa** (T054-608079), **Ormeño** (T054-424187), **Oltursa** (T01-708-5000) are recommended. The road is paved but drifting sand and breakdowns may prolong the trip.

To **Nazca**, 566 km, 9-11 hrs, US$19-22.50 (US$30-52 on luxury services), several buses daily, mostly at night; most buses continue to **Ica** (US$30-42) and Lima. Also US$12 to **Chala**, 400 km, 6 hrs. Note that some companies charge a full fare to Lima for intermediate destinations. To **Moquegua**, 213 km, 4 hrs, US$6.50-12, several buses and

> **Tip...**
> Theft is a serious problem in the bus station area. Take a taxi to and from the bus station and do not wander around with your belongings. It is best not to arrive at night as you may find yourself stranded at the bus station.

colectivos daily. To **Tacna**, 320 km, 6-7 hrs, US$9-11, hourly with **Flores**, direct luxury service without stopping in Moquegua, US$16.

To **Cuzco**, all buses go via Juliaca, US$11-46, 10-11 hrs. Most companies go overnight (eg **Enlaces, Cial, Cruz del Sur, Oltursa** and **Ormeño**), but **Flores** and others travel in daytime, at 0715 and 1230.

To **Juliaca**, US$5.50 normal, US$7 semi-cama, US$9-27 cama, 5 hrs with **Julsa** (T054-430843), hourly 0300-2400, with **Flores**, 6-8 daily; some buses continue to Puno. To **Puno**, 297 km, 5-6 hrs, US$7-11, hourly with **Julsa**, 4 daily with **Flores**, at 0800 with **Cruz del Sur** (US$21-27), several others. **4M Express** (La Merced 125 Int 111, T054-452296, www.4m-express.com) offers a **tourist service** to Puno with stops at Pampa Cañahuas (vicuña observation), Vizcachani (rock formations) and Lagunillas (flamingo and other bird observation) daily at 1245, 6 hrs, US$27-35, includes bilingual guiding, snack and hotel pickup in Arequipa. They offer a similar service from Chivay to Puno and Cuzco (see Colca transport, page 291), so you don't necessarily have to travel via Arequipa. To **Puerto Maldonado** via Juliaca, US$21-36, 17-18 hrs, at 1530 with **Julsa**, **Wayra** (T959-390512) or **Mendivil** (T974-210329); more frequent departures from Juliaca.

To **Chivay**, with **Reyna** (T054-420770), **Trans Milagros** (T054-298090) and **Andalucía** (T054-486263), various departures daily, US$4.65, 3 hrs; most continue to **Cabanaconde**, US$6, a further 75 km, 2 hrs. **4M Express** provide private transport between Arequipa and Chivay on request.

Taxi
From US$1 for trips around town. Companies include: **Alo 45**, T054-454545; **Taxitel**, T054-266262; Real T054-426161; **Turismo Arequipa**, T054-458888.

Colca &
Cotahuasi canyons

watch condors cruising above this spectacular canyon

★The Colca Canyon is deep: twice as deep as the Grand Canyon. The Río Colca descends from 3650 m above sea level at Chivay to 3287 m at Cabanaconde. In the background looms the grey, smoking mass of Sabancaya (5976 m), one of the most active volcanoes in the Americas, and its more docile neighbours, Ampato (6265 m) and Hualca Hualca (6025 m). Unspoiled Andean villages lie on both sides of the canyon, inhabited by the Cabana and Collagua peoples, and some of the extensive pre-Columbian terraced fields are still in use. High on anyone's list when visiting the canyon is an early-morning trip to the Cruz del Cóndor to see these majestic birds at close quarters.

Arequipa to Chivay

From Arequipa there are two routes to **Chivay**, the first village on the eastern edge of the canyon. The old dirt route goes through Cayma and then runs north over the altiplano. About one hour from the city is a national vicuña reserve; if you're lucky, you can see herds of vicuñas near the road. This route affords fine views of the volcanoes Misti, Chachani, Ampato and Sabancaya.

The newer paved route is longer but quicker. It goes through Yura, following the railway. Cyclists should use the Yura road, as it's in better condition and has less of a climb at the start. The two routes join at **Cañahuas** where you can change buses to/from Juliaca or Chivay if you want to bypass Arequipa; the road from Cañahuas to Puno via Patahuasi, Imata and Juliaca is paved and has a daily tourist transport service (see Transport, below). It can be cold in the morning, reaching 4825 m in the Pata Pampa pass, but the views are worth it.

Reserva Salinas y Aguada Blanca
Headquarters: Los Jazmines 119, Urb Primavera, Arequipa, T054-257469, msalinasy aguadablanca@sernamp.gob.pe.

Between Arequipa and Chivay lies the almost 367,000-ha Reserva Salinas y Aguada Blanca, an important source of water for the dry Arequipa region. Misti, Chachani, Pichu Pichu and Ubinas volcanoes all lie within this scenic, high-altitude (3500-6075 m) reserve. Lakes in this Ramsar site include Laguna Salinas, the Aguada Blanca and El Frayle dams, and countless shallow ponds, home to flamingoes and other waterfowl. Among the fauna are important herds of vicuñas, a small group

Essential Colca Canyon

Finding your feet

To enter the canyon you must buy a tourist ticket for US$25 (valid for 10 days) at a checkpoint on the road to Chivay; you may be required to show this ticket at Mirador Cruz del Cóndor.

It is not always possible to join a tour in Chivay; it is best to organize it in Arequipa and travel with a group. Prices generally do not include the Colca entry ticket, meals other than breakfast nor entry to the baths.

From Arequipa a one-day tour to the mirador costs US$20-25. It departs Arequipa at 0300-0330, arrives at the Cruz del Cóndor at 0730-0830, followed by an expensive lunch stop at Chivay and back to Arequipa by 1800-1900. For many, especially for those with altitude problems, this is too much to fit into one day (the only advantage is that you don't have to sleep at high altitude). Two-day tours are about US$25-35 per person with an overnight stop in Chivay or Yanque; more expensive tours range from US$45 to US$90. Most agencies will have a base price for the tour and then different prices depending on which hotel you pick.

Trekking around the canyon

There are many hiking possibilities in the area, with *hostales* or camping for longer treks. Make sure to take enough water, or purification tablets, as it gets very hot and there is not a lot of fresh water available. Sun protection is also a must. Ask locals for directions as there are hundreds of confusing paths going into the canyon.

In Cabanaconde trekking and adventure sports can be organized quite easily at short notice. Buy food for longer hikes in Arequipa. Topographical maps are available at the **Instituto Geográfico Nacional** in Lima, and at **Colca Trek** or **Pablo Tour** in Arequipa. Economical trekking tours from Arequipa cost US$45-55 for two days, US$55-65 for three days; entry tickets and lunch on the last day are not included. Agencies pool their passengers and the tour quality is often poor. A private three-day trekking tour for two passengers costs about US$450 per person.

When to go

Conditions vary annually, but January to April is the rainy season, which makes the area green with lots of flowers. This is not the best time to see condors, however, or to go hiking as some treks are impossible if it rains heavily (this is very rare). May to December is the dry, cold season when there is more chance of seeing the birds.

Time required

Allow at least two to three days to appreciate the Colca Canyon fully, more if you plan on doing some trekking.

ON THE ROAD

How deep is your canyon?

The people of the Colca Canyon region were more than a little disgruntled when it was announced that the neighbouring Cotahuasi Canyon was deeper than Colca, taking its place as the deepest in the world, a distinction many Colca guides cling to tenaciously. But, how can you actually determine the depth of a canyon when there are different ways of measuring and no obvious international convention to follow?

Gonzalo de Reparaz Ruiz, a French-Basque geographer, was the first to study the hydrography of southern Peru in the 1960s. He was the one to crown Colca the deepest canyon, perhaps overlooking its neighbour. The depth of Cotahuasi was later determined by measuring the height of Nevado Solimana, the highest point on the eastern rim, then the highest point on the western rim opposite Solimana. The average of these two points is 3354 m above the Río Cotahuasi.

Cotahuasi's honour as the world's deepest canyon is disputed, with a long list of contenders in the Himalayas, Tibet and elsewhere. Generally, however, the depth of these canyons has been determined as the difference between the height of one high peak and the river, without taking into account the second rim; and some peaks are actually very far from the river.

Regardless of the exact depth of Cotahuasi and Colca, they are both spectacular canyons with much to offer the visitor.

of guanacos (an endangered species), Andean deer and several cats. Impressive rock formations, caves with rock art and thermal springs are also found. Within the reserve are several indigenous communities raising llamas and alpacas and mining salt deposits. Several roads provide access to the villages and park attractions, including the two roads to Chivay, the main road to Juliaca, which crosses the reserve, and an unimproved road to Puno. There is an interpretation centre in Tocra, between Cañahuas and Chivay, and rangers' stations at Cañahuas and Salinas Huito, by Laguna Salinas in the south of the reserve.

Chivay and around

Chivay (3650 m) is the gateway to the canyon, and its road bridge is the main link between the north and south sides (others are at Yanque and Lari). Crossing the river at Chivay going west to follow the canyon on the north side, you pass the villages of **Coporaque**, **Ichupampa** (a footbridge crosses the river between the two villages), **Lari**, **Madrigal** and **Tapay**.

In Chivay, the **Maria Reiche Planetarium and Observatory** ⓘ *in the grounds of the Casa Andina hotel, 6 blocks west of the Plaza between Huayna Capac and Garcilazo, www.casa-andina.com, US$6, discounts for students*, makes the most of the Colca's clear Southern Hemisphere skies with a powerful telescope and two 55-minute presentations per day at 1830 (Spanish) and 1930 (English). There is a Globalnet ATM close to the plaza. The hot springs of **La Calera** ⓘ *US$5.25 to bathe,* *half price to visit, regular colectivos (US$0.25), taxi (US$1.50) or a 1-hr walk from town,* are 4 km away and are highly recommended after a hard day's trekking.

Beyond the baths, the road continues northeast to **Tuti**, which has a small handicrafts shop and is the starting point for the trek to **Nevado Mismi (5598 m)**. This rugged mountain, about 15 km north of Ichupampa, is one of the sources of the Amazon (see box, page 286). It takes two days' hard trekking at high-altitude to reach the mountain through a very remote area rich in wildlife. Going with a tour or local *arriero* is recommended. Although it is very cold in the dry season, this is the preferred time of the year for the trek, as it can be very muddy in the rain. You can go around the mountain and make a loop ending at Lari.

Beyond Tuti is **Sibayo** (*pensión* and grocery store) from where a long circuit leads back to Arequipa, passing through **Puente Callalli**, **Chullo** and **Sumbay**. This is a little-travelled road, but the views, with vicuña, llamas, alpacas and Andean duck are superb.

Chivay to Cruz del Cóndor

From Chivay, the main road goes west along the south side of the Colca Canyon. The first village encountered is **Yanque** (8 km, excellent views), with an interesting church containing superbly renovated altar pieces and paintings; there's a museum on the opposite side of the plaza. A large thermal swimming pool is 20 minutes' walk from the plaza, beside the renovated colonial bridge that leads to the villages of Coporaque and Ichupampa on the other side of the canyon (US$0.75). The road west continues paved to **Achoma** and **Maca** (footbridge to Madrigal on the north side), which barely survived an earthquake in 1991. Then comes the tiny village of **Pinchollo**. From here it is a 30-minute walk on a dirt track to the **Hatun Infiernillo** geyser.

The Mirador at **Cruz del Cóndor**, where you may be asked to show your tourist ticket, overlooks the deepest point of the canyon. The view is wonderful and condors can be seen rising on the morning thermals (0900, arrive by 0800 to get a good spot) and sometimes in the late afternoon (1600-1800). Camping here is officially forbidden, but if you ask the tourist police in Chivay they may help. **Milagros'** 0630 bus from Chivay stops here very briefly at around 0800 (ask the driver), or try hitching with a tour bus at around 0600. Buses from Cabanaconde stop at about 0700 (**Andalucía**) or 0830 (**Reyna**); they leave Cabanaconde's plaza 30 minutes earlier.

Cabanaconde

From the Mirador it is a 20-minute ride in tourist transport or 40 minutes by local bus on a paved road to Cabanaconde at 3287 m. You can also walk: three hours by the road, or two hours via a short cut following the canyon. This is the last village in the Colca Canyon, friendly, typical but basic, although it does have 24-hour electricity. The views are superb and condors can be seen from the hill just west of the village, a 15-minute walk from the plaza. You'll also see agricultural terraces, arguably the most attractive in the valley, to the south of the village. Cabanaconde is an excellent base for visiting the region, with interesting trekking, climbing, biking and horse riding. Many are keen to encourage respectful tourism in the area and several locally owned tourism businesses have opened in the village.

ON THE ROAD

A source of controversy

For many centuries, the Marañón River in northern Peru was thought to be the source of the Amazon, since it is the tributary with the greatest volume of water. Later wisdom suggested that the serpentine Ucayali River was the source, as its many bends make it longer than the Marañón. In 1971 a *National Geographic*-sponsored expedition, led by acclaimed explorer Loren McIntyre, was the first to speculate that a branch of the Apurímac River, originating at Nevado Mismi in the Colca Canyon region, might be the longest of the Amazon's many tributaries. Several expeditions have since corroborated this claim, among them the Cousteau Amazon Expedition in 1982, the Amazon Source to Sea Expedition in 1986 (a highly entertaining account is found in *Running the Amazon*, by Joe Kane), a *National Geographic* expedition led by Andrew Pietowski in 2000, and a Brazilian expedition in 2007; the latter also measured the length of the Amazon to be 6800 km, the longest in the world.

Just as the scientific community was becoming confident that it had ascertained the source of the great river, in 2014 James Contos and Nicholas Tripcevich of the University of California (Berkley, USA) suggested that the true source is in the Cordillera Rumi Cruz, near Cerro Pasco in the Central Highlands of Peru, moving the honour of the most distant origin of the Amazon to the watershed of the Mantaro River.

Will we ever know the true source of the Amazon?

Treks around Cabanaconde

Two hours below Cabanaconde is **Sangalle**, an 'oasis' of palm trees and swimming areas where there are three campsites with basic bungalows and toilets. It's a beautiful spot, recommended. (It's three to 4½ hours back up; ask for the best route in both directions. Horses can be hired to carry your bag, US$5.85.)

A popular hike involves walking east on the Chivay road to the Mirador de Tapay (before Cruz del Cóndor), then descending to the river on a steep track (four hours, take care). Cross the bridge to the village of San Juan de Chuccho on the north bank, where you can stay and eat at a basic family hostel, of which there are several. From here, pass **Tapay** (also possible to camp here) and the small villages of Malata and Cosnirhua, all the time heading west along the north side of the Río Colca (take a guide or ask local directions). After about three hours' walking, cross another bridge to the south bank of the Río Colca, follow signs to Sangalle, spend the night and return to Cabanconde on the third day. This route is offered by many Arequipa and local agencies.

A longer hike from Cabanaconde goes to **Chachas** and takes four or five days. Follow a small path to the west, descending slowly into the canyon (three hours); ask locals for directions to **Choco**. Cross the Río Colca by the Puente Colgado (an Inca bridge) and ascend to Choco, 2473 m (five to six hours). From Choco climb high above the village to the pass at 5050 m and then down to Chachas at 3100 m (eight to 12 hours). There is a minibus daily at 1300 from Chachas to **Andagua** in the

Valley of the Volcanoes (see page 292). Otherwise it is a day's hike. This is a superb trek through untouched areas and villages, but you'll need camping equipment, food and lots of water, as there is hardly any on this trek.

Listings Colca Canyon

Tourist information

Tourist information and a map are available in Arequipa from the **Autoridad Autónoma del Colca** (Puente Grau 116, T054-203010, Mon-Fri 0830-1730). In Chivay, there is a very helpful **tourist office** in the Municipalidad on the west side of the plaza (closed at weekends). The tourist police, also on the plaza, can give advice about locally trained guides. There's a traveller's **Medical Center (TMC)** (Ramón Castilla 232, T054-531037). There's also a friendly **tourist information office** (Cabanaconde, T054-280212, that is willing to give plenty of advice, if not maps. It's a good place to find trekking guides and muleteers (US$30 a day mule and guide).

Where to stay

Note that only the fancier hotels and *hostales* have Wi-Fi and it is very slow.

Chivay and around

$$$ Casa Andina
Huayna Cápac s/n, Chivay, T054-531022, www.casa-andina.com.
Attractive cabins with hot showers and a cosy bar/dining area, a member of the recommended hotel chain, heating, parking.

$$$ Pozo del Cielo
C Huáscar B-3, Sacsayhuaman–Chivay, T054-531041 (Alvarez Thomas 309, Arequipa, T054-346547), www.pozodelcielo.com.pe.

Trekking around Cabanaconde

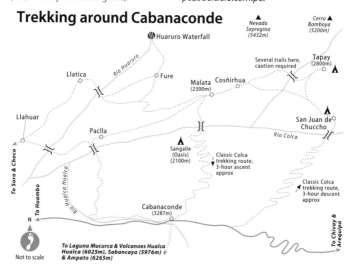

Very comfortable option, located over the Puente Inca from Chivay amid pre-Inca terraces. Warm rooms, good views, good service and restaurant.

$$ Colca Inn
Salaverry 307, Chivay, T054-531111, www.hotelcolcainn.com.
Good mid-range option, modern, decent restaurant, basic breakfast included or US$2.50 for buffet breakfast, some rooms with heaters, nice views from upper rooms. Also run the more upmarket **Hotel Colcallacta**.

$$ La Casa de Mamayacchi
In Coporaque, 6 km from Chivay on the opposite side of the river, T054-531004, www.lacasademamayacchi.com, reservations through Giardino Tours in Arequipa.
Part of the hotel is in an original Inca structure, nice rooms with heaters, lovely dining area, terraced garden, multi-day packages including transport.

$$ Posada del Colca
Salaverry 325, Chivay, T054-531040, laposadadelcolca@hotmail.com, also on Facebook.
Central, good rooms.

$ Hospedaje Restaurant Los Portales
Arequipa 603, Chivay, T054-531164.
Good value, though beds have rather 'floppy' mattresses. Restaurant downstairs.

$ La Casa de Lucila
M Grau 131, Chivay, T054-531109, http://vitatours.com.pe.
Small, refurbished, comfortable house, guides available, reserve ahead in high season.

$ La Pascana
Puente Inca y C Siglo XX 106, Chivay, T054-531001, hrlapascana@hotmail.com.

Excellent value on the northwest corner of the Plaza. Spacious en suite rooms overlook a pleasant garden, hot water, parking and a good restaurant.

$ Rumi Wasi
Sucre 714, 6 blocks from plaza (3 mins' walk), Chivay, T054-531146.
Good rooms, hot water, helpful.

Chivay to Cruz del Cóndor

$$$$ Colca Lodge
Across the river from Yanque, T054-531191 (office: Mariscal Benavides 201, Selva Alegre, Arequipa, T054-202587), www.colca-lodge.com.
Very relaxing, with beautiful hot springs beside the river, spend at least a day to make the most of the activities on offer. Day passes available. Rooms heated with geothermal energy, solar-heated water.

$$$$ Las Casitas del Colca
Av Fundo La Curiña s/n, Yanque, T959-672688, www.lascasitasdelcolca.com.
Luxury cottages made of local materials with underfloor heating and plunge pools. Has a gourmet restaurant, bar, vegetable garden and farm, offers cookery and painting courses, the spa offers a variety of treatments, swimming pool.

$$$ Collahua
Av Collahua cuadra 7, Yanque (office: Mercaderes 212, Galerías Gamesa, Arequipa, T054-226098), www.hotelcollahua.com.
Modern bungalows just outside Yanque, with heating, solar-powered 24-hr hot water and plush rooms, restaurant.

$$$ Eco Inn
Lima 513, Yanque, T054-837112, www.ecoinnhotels.com.
Perched high on a bluff with incredible views over the valley and restored

Ullo Ullo ruins. Large, comfortable rooms in cabins, restaurant open from 0530 for buffet breakfast, Wi-Fi in lobby and restaurant.

$$ Tradición Colca
Av Colca 119, Yanque, T054-781178 (office: C Argentina 108, Urb Fecia JL Bustamante y Rivero, T054-424926), www.tradicioncolca.com.
Adobe construction, gas stove, garden spa, massages, sauna, jacuzzi. Restaurant, bar, games room, observatory and planetarium (free for guests), horse riding from 2 hrs to 2 days, hiking tour to Ullu Ullu, bike rentals, travel agency in Arequipa.

$ Casa Bella Flor Sumaq Wayta Wasi
Cuzco 303, Yanque, T054-253586, www.casabellaflor.com.
Charming small lodge run by Sra Hilde Checca, flower-filled garden, tasteful rooms, good meals (also open to non-residents). Hilde's uncle, Gregorio, guides visitors to pre-Columbian sites.

$ Hospedaje Cruz del Cóndor
On the plaza in Achoma.
Also a campsite.

$ Hospedaje Refugio del Geyser
C Melgar s/n, behind municipality, Pinchollo, T959-007441.
Basic with good local information.

$ Rijchariy Colca Lodge
On the track leading down to the footbridge over the river, Yanque, T054-764610.
Great views, garden, comfortable rooms, restaurant.

Cabanaconde

$$ Kuntur Wassi
C Cruz Blanca s/n, on the hill above the plaza, T054-233120, www.arequipacolca.com.

Excellent 3-star, restaurant with fine traditional meals. Creative design, with rooms spaced between rock gardens and waterfalls. Viewing 'tower' and conference centre above. Owners Walter and María very welcoming and knowledgeable about treks.

$$ La Casa de Santiago
www.lacasadesantiago.com.
Upmarket small *hostal*, with views of the mountains and a large garden.

$$ Posada del Conde
C San Pedro, T054-440197, pdelconde@yahoo.com.
Smart hotel and lodge. Cheaper in low season, with hot shower, comfortable beds, good food. Local guides and horses for hire.

$ Hostal Valle del Fuego
1 and 2 blocks from the plaza on C Grau y Bolívar, T959-611241, www.valledelfuego.com.
Rooms with comfortable beds and dorms (US$7 pp, breakfast extra), laundry facilities, restaurant. Can arrange guides, pack animals, bike rentals. The Junco family have plenty of information and work with related establishments, including: **Pablo Tour in Arequipa,** where you can make reservations and get a Colca map; **Oasis Paradise** in Sangalle (discounts for clients of Valle del Fuego and related hotels); **Casa de Pablo Club** at the end of the street, and **La Casa de Santiago** (see above). They usually meet the incoming buses. Popular.

$ Pachamama Home
San Pedro 209, T054-767277, www.pachamamahome.com.
Backpacker hostel, rooms with and without bath, family atmosphere, hot water, lots of information, good bar/pizzería **Pachamama** next door, try the

Colca Sour, made from a local cactus. You can help with teaching and activities for village children.

$ Virgen del Carmen
Av Arequipa s/n, T054-830031, 5 blocks up from the plaza.
Hot showers, may even offer you a welcoming glass of *chicha*.

Trekking around Cabanaconde
Sangalle has 3 campsites with basic bungalows and toilets. In San Juan de Chuccho, **Hostal Roy** and **Casa de Rebelino** ($) are both good. US$2 will buy you a decent meal.

Restaurants

Chivay and around
Several restaurants serve buffet lunches for tour groups, US$5 pp, also open to the general public. Of the few that open in the evening, most have folklore shows and are packed with tour groups. When walking in the valley meals and drinks can be taken in any of the larger lodges. For local cheeses and dairy products, visit **Productos del Colca**, Av 22 de Agosto in the central market.

$$ El Balcón de Don Zacarías
Av 22 de Agosto 102 on plaza, T054-531108.
Breakfast, the best lunch buffet in town, à la carte menu, novo andean and international cuisine.

$$-$ McElroys's Irish Pub
On the plaza.
Bar run by a Peruvian and an Irishman, warm, good selection of drinks (sometimes including expensive Guinness), sandwiches, pizza, pasta and music. Mountain bikes for hire. Accepts Visa.

$$-$ Yaraví
Plaza de Armas 604.
Arequipeña food, vegetarian options and the most impressive coffee machine in town.

$ Innkas Café-Bar
Plaza de Armas 706.
Coffee, sandwiches, *menú*, pizzas, pool table, good atmosphere.

$ Ruadhri Irish Pub
Av Salaverry 202.
Nothing Irish about it, but still a popular hang-out offering pizzas, pastas and sandwiches, has happy hour and a pool table.

Cabanaconde

$$-$ Casa de Pablo Club
C Grau.
Excellent fresh juices and pisco sour, cable TV (football!), small book exchange and some equipment hire.

$ Las Brisas del Colca
Main plaza, T054-631593.
Pleasant, serves breakfast, tourist menu, à la carte dishes, juices and sandwiches.

$ Rancho del Colca
On plaza.
Mainly vegetarian.

Festivals

There are numerous festivals in the Colca region, many of which last several days and involve traditional dances and customs.

2-3 Feb **Virgen de la Candelaria**, celebrated in Chivay, Cabanaconde, Maca and Tapay.
Feb **Carnaval** in Chivay.
3 May **Cruz de la Piedra** in Tuti.

13 Jun San Antonio in Yanque and Maca.

14 Jun San Juan in Sibayo and Ichupampa.

21 Jun Anniversary of Chivay.

29 Jun San Pedro y San Pablo in Sibayo.

14-17 Jul La Virgen del Carmen in Cabanaconde.

25 Jul Santiago Apóstol in Coporaque.

26 Jul-2 Aug Virgen Santa Ana in Maca.

15 Aug Virgen de la Asunta in Chivay.

8 Dec Immaculada Concepción in Yanque and Chivay.

25 Dec Sagrada Familia in Yanque.

What to do

It is not always possible to join a tour in Chivay; it is best to organize it in Arequipa and travel with a group. In Cabanaconde trekking and adventure sports can be organized quite easily at short notice. See also Essential Colca Canyon, page 283.

Chivay

Ampato Adventure Sports, *Av Siglo XX 417, 2 blocks from the bus station*, T054-489156, www.ampatocolca.com. Offer information and rent good mountain bikes, but rarely open.

Colca-Turismo, *Av Salaverry 321*, T054-503368, guide Zacarías Ocsa Osca, zacariasocsa@hotmail.com. Seems to offer a professional service.

Cabanaconde

Agotour Colca, *T986-271212 (Pedro Samayani)*. An association of local guides.

Chiqui Travel & Expeditions, *Plaza de Armas s/n, next to the Municipalidad*, T958-063602. Private guide, professional and reliable, organizes trekking, biking

and horse riding, can also arrange for pack animals and make reservations.

Transport

Chivay and around
Bus

The bus station in Chivay is 3 blocks from the main plaza, next to the stadium. Combis and colectivos leave from the terminal behind the market to villages in the area except Pinchollo and Cabanaconde.

Reyna (Arequipa T054-420770), **Trans Milagros** (Chivay T054-531115) and **Andalucía** (Chivay T054-531106) have various departures daily to/from **Arequipa**, US$4.65, 3 hrs; most of these service start or end in **Cabanaconde**, a further 56 km, 2 hrs, US$1.80 to/from Chivay, US$6 to/from Arequipa. Buses leave Cabanaconde for Arequipa from 0730 to 1500 from the Plaza de Armas. None offers a secure service, so it may be better to join a tour bus. **4M Express** (see below) offers private transport to Arequipa on request. To **Cuzco**, take the 4M Express tourist service (see below) or a regular bus to Cañahuas and change there for a bus to Juliaca, then carry on to Cuzco.

Tourist service 4M Express, www.4m-express.com, has several routes departing from Hotel La Pascana on Chivay's plaza, all stop at places of interest along the way and include a snack. To **Puno** Terminal Terrestre, daily 1315, US$50, 6¼ hrs, stopping at Patapampa lookout, Chucura Volcano and Lagunillas (birdwatching). To **Cuzco**, direct route along a paved road via Tuti, Sibayo and Sicuani, Mon, Wed and Fri at 0700, US$65 (lunch extra), 10½ hrs, stopping at Castillos de Callalli rock formations, Yauri rock forest, Laguna de Langui (25 km long), Sicuani (lunch break) and dropping off at 4M's private station.

★At its deepest, at Ushua (just below the village of Quechualla), the Cotahuasi Canyon measures 3354 m from rim to river, making it 163 m deeper than the Colca Canyon and the deepest canyon in the world (see How deep is your canyon?, page 284). From this point, the only way along the canyon is by kayak, and it is through kayakers' reports that the area has come to the notice of tourists. The Reserva Paisajística Cañón de Cotahuasi protects the extensive Cotahuasi drainage, from the icy summits of Solimana and Huanzo (5445 m) to where it joins the Río Ocoña at 950 m. The canyon is very dry, especially from April to October when the contrast between the desert slopes and the green irrigated oases along the wider sections of the river valley and on the hanging valleys of its tributaries is particularly striking. Grapes, organic kiwicha (amaranth) and quinoa for export, avocados, citrus and other fruits are grown here. The side canyons are very impressive in their own right. Despite the arid climate and rugged geography, the canyon has been populated for centuries. There are a number of pre-Inca and Inca remains perched on terraces cut into the vertical canyon walls and segments of Inca trade routes from the coast to the highlands can still be seen. The area has several thermal baths, waterfalls, impressive rock formations, cacti and *Puya raimondii* bromeliad forests, and amazing views.

Towards Cotahuasi: Río Majes Valley

Southwest of Arequipa, a paved road branches off the Pan-American to the impressive Siguas Canyon and on to the agricultural valley and canyon of the Río Majes, a rafting destination. At the linear roadside town of **Corire** are several hotels and restaurants serving excellent freshwater shrimp.

Nearby is the world's largest field of petroglyphs at **Toro Muerto** ① *3 km from La Candelaria on a dirt road (6.5 km from Corire), US$2, van from the plaza in Corire Mon-Fri 0700, returning 1400, US$0.60, or taxi, US$10 incl 2-hr wait.* Access to the UNESCO World Heritage Site is signposted off the main road 1.5 km south of Corire, where a road turns east to the village of La Candelaria, 2 km from the main road. One block above the plaza is the archaeological site's office where the entry fee is collected. From here it is 3 km on a dirt road to the site entrance which provides the only shade in the area; the immense field of 5000 sculpted rocks in the desert lies beyond. The sheer scale of the 5-sq-km site is awe-inspiring and the view is wonderful. The higher you go, the more interesting the petroglyphs, though some have been ruined by graffiti. Don't believe the guides who, after the first few rocks, say the others are all the same. The designs range from simple llamas to elaborate human figures and animals. There are several styles which are thought to be Wari (AD 700-1100), Chuquibamba (AD 1000-1475) and Inca in origin. An extensive review of the designs is found in *Memorias del Arqueólogo Eloy Linares Málaga* (Universidad Alas Peruanas, 2011). Take plenty of water, sunglasses and sun cream. At least an hour is needed to visit the site.

Upriver from Corire, the paved road goes past a park with dinosaur prints to the regional centre of **Aplao**, which has a small museum containing Wari cultural objects from the surrounding area. A side road to the north leads to **Andagua** (see below), while the main road continues northwest to **Chuquibamba** (several places to stay and eat) in a scenic terraced valley, where the paving ends. Beyond Chuquibamba, the road climbs steeply to traverse the *puna* between Nevado Coropuna (6425 m) and Nevado Solimana (6093 m). The views are awe-inspiring, so it is well worth the effort to travel this route by day. At the Río Arma, a track leads to Andagua.

Andagua and around

Andagua at 3600 m is the access point for the **Valle de los Volcanes**, an extensive geological fault dotted with 85 volcanoes ranging in height from 30 cm to 350 m. They started to form some 250,000 years ago. The Andagua and Colca rivers cut through the prehistoric or lunar landscape. From Andagua a road goes north to **Orcopampa**, from where the thermal baths of Huancarama can be visited, and continues a long way around to Caylloma and Sibayo, to the north of the Colca Canyon (see page 285). Another road goes east of Andagua to **Chachas** (minivan daily), a picturesque little village on the edge of a lake. The area is heavily cultivated and there are perfect views of the valley from the top of the hill above town. It is possible to hike from Chachas to Choco and on to Cabanaconde via the Río Colca in four or five days, see page 286. A third road goes from Andaguas south to **Ayo**, Laguna Mamacocha and the Colca Canyon, near its deepest point.

Cotahuasi and the upper canyon

From Mirador Allhuay (3950 m) at the rim of the Cotahuasi Canyon, the road, now paved, winds down to the peaceful colonial town of Cotahuasi, nestled in a sheltered hanging valley at 2680 m, beneath Cerro Huinao. Its streets are narrow, with whitewashed houses. The Río Cotahuasi flows 1500 m below the town at the bottom of its great canyon.

Following the Río Cotahuasi to the northeast up the valley, you come to **Tomepampa** (10 km), a small town at 2700 m, with painted houses and a colonial church. The attractive hot springs of **Luicho** ⓘ *16.5 km from Cotahuasi, daily 0330-2130, US$1.80, 1 simple room for rent*, are a short walk from the road, across a bridge. There are three pools (33° to 38°C). The paved road ends at **Alca**, 20 km from Cotahuasi, at 2750 m, with several simple places to stay and eat. Above it are the small ruins of Kallak, Tiknay and a "stone library" of rock formations. All these places are connected by hourly combis from Cotahuasi (see Transport). **Puyca** ⓘ *23 km beyond Alca, combi from Alca at 0530, return at 1200, 1½ hrs, US$2.50, www. canyoncotahuasi.com*, is the last village of any significance in the valley, hanging on a hillside at 3560 m. Locals can guide you on treks in the area, and horses can be hired. Nearby, at 3700 m, are the extensive Wari ruins of **Maucallacta** (20-minute walk), the most important

Tip...

If you have a 4WD vehicle, this is a superb area for driving some rough roads, such as the circuit Arequipa–Aplao–Andagua–Orcopampa–Caylloma–Chivay–Arequipa.

in the Cotahuasi area. Beyond is **Churca** ⓘ *24 km from Puyca, van from Alca at 0530, return at 1200, 2-3 hrs, US$3.20,* from where you can walk to Lauripampa at about 4000 m in 20 minutes to see a vast prairie of *Puya raimondii* plants. On the opposite side of the river from Churca is Chincayllapa from where you can drive to the **Occoruro geysers** at 4466 m, also reached in a full-day walk from Puyca.

Along a tributary of the Cotahuasi, in a beautiful terraced side canyon north of Cotahuasi, is the village of **Pampamarca** ⓘ *at 3397 m, 28 km from Cotahuasi, daily bus from Cotahuasi at 0500 and 1630, returning 0600 and 1330, US$2, 2 hrs, accommodation in homestays.* There are excellent walking possibilities here. Attractions include the Wito rock formations, 90 m high Uskune waterfall, Josla thermal baths and, a bit further afield, the Fuysiri waterfalls.

Downstream from Cotahuasi

A rough, narrow road follows the Río Cotahuasi downriver for 28 km to Mayo. At Km 13 is the access to the powerful, 150-m **Cataratas de Sipia** ⓘ *2 km from the road, bus from Terminal Terrestre Tue-Thu and Sat 0630, Mon and Sun 0630 and 1330, Fri 0630 and 1400, US$1.45, 30 mins (return 2½-3 hrs later).* A good trail leads from the road to several lookouts over the three-tiered falls, which are the most visited attraction in the canyon; take care near the edge, especially if it is windy. The best light is at midday. You can also get an overview of the falls from the road, continuing past the turnoff to the top of the hill.

Beyond Sipia the road, carved into the canyon wall, leads to the hamlets of Chaupo and Rosariopampa, and, at Km 23, the cactus forest of **Judiopampa**, with trails. The road ends at **Mayo** ⓘ *return transport daily 0900, also 1600 Mon, Fri and Sun,* between two trails which climb to the village of **Velinga** (with homestays). A trail continues past the roadhead to the Niñochaca bridge over the Río Cotahuasi, beyond which is the dilapidated but extensive ruin of **Huaña** and, past another bridge, the charming village of **Quechualla** (9 km from Mayo, with homestays) at 1665 m. **Ushua**, the deepest part of the canyon, is below Quechualla, where you can also see two small waterfalls along a tributary stream. On the opposite side of the Cotahuasi from Quechuallaat 3417 m is the village of **Charcana** ⓘ *44 km from Cotahuasi, daily bus from Cotahuasi at 1500, returning 0600, US$3.20, 3 hrs,* on a terraced valley with views of Solimana and the canyon. It has a very basic *hospedaje* and homestays. Nearby are rock formations, including the Jaisampo stone arch, and rock art at Huancarama. The road continues to Sayla and Tauría. From Sayla, a road goes to the Region of Ayacucho. From Charcana, a trail leads to Picha and Quechualla; this is a very nice walk but you need a full day, so start very early.

Listings Cotahuasi Canyon

Tourist information

Cotahuasi
Grupo GEA (Bolognesi 104 by the plaza in Cotahuasi, T054-489409,

www.grupogea.org.pe), is an NGO that runs a sustainable development and tourism project in the area. It aims to improve access to and signs at tourist sites and to provide *turismo vivencial* homestays in the main towns throughout the area. They also publish a good map. Tourist information is available from **CONSETUR** (www. cotahuasituristico.com), represented in Cotahuasi by **Purek Tours** (C Arequipa 103, daily 0900-1300, 1400-2000), and in Arequipa by **Andina Travel** (see What to do, page 279). See also www. municipiolaunion.com. There are no ATMs in Cotahuasi but **Banco de la Nación on C Cabildo** changes US$ cash.

Where to stay

Río Majes Valley

$ Hostal Willy's
Av Progreso opposite the market, Corire, T054-472046 and Progreso y Morán, at the Plaza, Aplao, T959-476622.
Both modern buildings with comfortable rooms, no breakfast.

$ La Casa de Mauro
La Central, 12 km north of Aplao (combi service), T054-631076, www.star.com.pe/lacasademauro.
Simple cabins and camping (US$5.50 per tent) in a lovely rural setting, restaurant with 60 different shrimp dishes, run by the friendly Zúñiga family, rafting, trekking and conventional tours.

$ Montano
Ramón Castilla s/n, Corire, T054-472122.
Best rooms are at the back away from the road, some rooms are small, no breakfast, good value.

Andagua and around

There are several places to stay in Andagua; **Casa Grande** on the plaza is good, also **Restaurante Sarita**.

Cotahuasi and the upper canyon

For information about homestays in the towns outside Cotahuasi, contact Grupo GEA (see above).

$$ Valle Hermoso
Tacna 108-110, Cotahuasi, T054-581057, www.hotelvallehermoso.com.
Nice and cosy, includes breakfast, beautiful views of the canyon, comfortable rooms, large garden, meals with home-grown fruit and veg require advanced notice.

$ Casa Primavera
Tomepampa, T954-734056.
Family-run hostel with a flower-filled courtyard, some rooms with private bath, price includes breakfast, other meals on request, kitchen facilities, common areas, good value.

$ El Mirador
Centenario 100-A, Cotahuasi, T054-489417.
Pleasant rooms, great views, no breakfast, new section under construction in 2014.

$ Hatun Huasi
Centenario 309, Cotahuasi, T054-581054, www.hatunhuasi.com.
Popular *hostal* with a variety of rooms, nice small garden and common areas, breakfast extra, helpful owner Catalina Borda.

$ Don Justito
Arequipa110, ½ block below the plaza, Cotahuasi, T973-698053.
Ample functional rooms with and without bath, plenty of solar heated water, popular, good value economy option.

Restaurants

Cotahuasi and the upper canyon
There are many tiendas well-stocked with fruit, vegetables and local wine.

$$-$ Buen Sabor
C Arequipa, 1 block down from the plaza, Cotahuasi.
A la carte Peruvian dishes, caters to tourists.

$ Las Chombitas
C Zela, 1 block below C Arequipa, Cotahuasi, daily 0700-1700.
A choice of good *menús* at midday, popular.

What to do

Several tour operators in Arequipa, including **Cotahuasi Trek** (www. cotahuasitrek.com) run 4-day trips to Cotahuasi, taking in the main attractions. They can also organize adventure activities. **Amazonas Explorer** (www.amazonas-explorer. com) in Cuzco can organize 5-day kayaking expeditions on the Cotahuasi for experienced kayakers only.

Río Majes Valley
La Casa de Mauro Tours, *see Where to stay, T959-362340, www.star.com.pe/ lacasademauro.* Pancho Zúñiga offers rafting, trekking and 4x4 tours in the Majes, Cotahuasi and Colca areas.

Cotahuasi and the upper canyon
Purek Tours, *C Arequipa 103, Cotahuasi, T054-698081, cotahuasitours@gmail. com.* Biking, horse riding and 2- to 3-day trekking tours.

Transport

Río Majes Valley
Empresa Del Carpio buses to **Corire** and **Aplao** leave from the Terrapuerto in **Arequipa** about every 1½ hrs 0430-1900, 3-4 hrs, US$4.30; to **Chuquibamba** at 0515 and 1615, return 0500 and 1200, US$7.50, 6-7 hrs. For **Toro Muerto**, ask to be let out at the turnoff to La Candelaria. Cotahuasi-bound buses from Arequipa stop at the plaza in Corire (near the Del Carpio station), at the highway in Aplao and at the terminal in Chuquibamba. To **Camaná** on the coast (transfer here for Nazca and Lima), van from Aplao at 0800, passes Corire 0830, US$5.40, 2 hrs; returns from Camaná at 0400-0500. To **Andagua**, **Reyna** from Arequipa at 1600, via Corire and Aplao. There is a daily minivan from Andagua to **Chacas**.

Cotahuasi and the upper canyon
Destinations along the canyon are connected Mon-Sat 0600-1800 by hourly combis from Cotahuasi, fewer on Sun. Cotahuasi has a modern bus station (terminal fee US$0.35) 10 mins' walk from the plaza. Buses daily from **Arequipa** Terminal Terrestre, 10-11 hrs, US$11: **Cromotex** at 1700 and 1800; **Reyna** at 1630, also Fri at 0500 and Sun at1800; they stop for refreshments in Chuquibamba, about halfway. Both companies continue to **Tomepampa** and **Alca**; buses leave Alca for Arequipa around 1400 (you can get off at Cotahuasi). Return Cotahuasi to Arequipa, **Cromotex** at 1800 and 1900, **Reyna** at 1700, also Mon at 0600 and Fri at 1900. Doing the trip during the day is recommended. From **Lima**, Trans López (Sebatián Barranca 158, La Victoria, T01-332 1015), Sun at 0900, US$36, 20 hrs (passes Chuquibamba Mon 0500-0630); return Cotahuasi to Lima Tue 0700.

South of
Arequipa

From Arequipa, the main road to the coast goes southwest for 37 km to Repartición where it divides. One branch goes west from here for 54 km through a striking arid landscape before dividing again: northwest to the Majes and Cotahuasi areas (see above) or southwest to Camaná (170 km from Arequipa) on the coast (see page 253). The second branch from Repartición continues southwest for 15 km, where it also splits, one road leading southeast to Moquegua and the second south to Mollendo.

Mollendo and the Vía Costanera

Mollendo is a town with lots of character, brightly painted old wooden houses, a wrought-iron market and many well-maintained parks. From January to March, Mollendo comes to life with visitors who flock to its beaches. Playa Catarindo, in a small bay 2 km north of town, is reportedly good for bathing. There are many others but mind the powerful undertow. In the low season, however, the town is quiet and the beaches may be littered with rubbish.

The port of **Matarani** is 14.5 km northwest of Mollendo. From here south along the shore towards the Chilean border runs the very scenic Vía Costanera, an alternative to the Pan-American Highway. **Balneario Mejía**, 15 km south of Mollendo (70 km north of Ilo) along this route, has nice beaches and provides access to the **Santuario Nacional Lagunas de Mejía** ⓘ *5 km south of town, T988-648043, snlagunasdemejia@sernanp.gob.pe, visitor's site at the entrance, take repellent and sun protection*. This Ramsar site at the mouth of the Río Tambo has three lakes separated from the ocean by a narrow strip of land; a trail runs the length of it and there are several rustic observation towers. Some 195 species of bird have been identified here, including land, freshwater and seabirds; 85 of them are resident and the remainder migratory.

Moquegua and around → *Colour map 6, C2.*

This city lies 213 km from Arequipa in the narrow Moquegua river valley and enjoys a sub-tropical climate. The old centre, a few blocks above the Pan-American Highway, has winding, cobbled streets and 19th-century buildings. The Plaza de Armas, with its mix of ruined and well-maintained churches, colonial and republican façades and fine trees, is one of the most interesting small-city plazas in the country. Within the ruins of Iglesia Matriz is the **Museo Contisuyo** ① *Jr Tacna 294, on the Plaza de Armas, T053-461844, www.museocontisuyo.com, Wed-Mon 0800-1300, 1430-1730, Tue 0800-1200, 1600-2000, US$0.50,* which focuses on the cultures that thrived in the Moquegua and Ilo valleys, including the Huari, Tiahuanaco, Chiribaya and Estuquiña, who were conquered by the Incas. Artefacts are well displayed and explained in Spanish and English.

A highly recommended excursion is to **Cerro Baúl** (2590 m) ① *30 mins by colectivo, US$2,* a tabletop mountain with marvellous views and many legends, which can be combined with the pleasant town of Torata, 24 km northeast.

One of the most breathtaking stretches of the **Carretera Binacional** from Ilo to La Paz runs from Moquegua to Desaguadero at the southeastern end of Lake Titicaca. The road is fully paved and should be travelled in daylight. It skirts Cerro Baúl and climbs through zones of ancient terraces to its highest point at 4755 m. On the altiplano there are herds of llamas and alpacas, lakes with waterfowl, strange mountain formations and snow-covered peaks. At Mazo Cruz there is a PNP checkpoint where all documents and bags are checked. Approaching Desaguadero, the Cordillera Real of Bolivia comes into view.

Ilo and beyond

Ilo is located along the Vía Costanera, near the mouth of the Río Osmore, 90 km southwest of Moquegua (two hours by bus). It is Peru's southernmost port and is the Pacific terminus of both the **Carretera Interoceánica**, connecting Peru and Brazil via Juliaca, Macusani and Puerto Maldonado (see page 514), and the **Carretera Binacional** between Peru and Bolivia (see below). Ilo is a functional place with an oceanfront promenade. Air pollution from a copper smelter is a problem. At **Algarrobal** along the road to Moquegua is an archaeological site of the Chiribaya culture (AD 800-1350) with an on-site museum (www.centromallqui. pe/ilo/museochiribaya.html). Just south of town on a peninsula is the **Reserva Municipal Punta Coles** ① *entry only with a permit and accompanied by a park ranger, free,* which shelters sea lions and seabirds (including penguins).

Along the Vía Costanera to the south of Ilo are the **Humedales de Ite**, an area of wetlands where about 130 species of bird, both resident and visitor, have been recorded. In other parts, seabirds and sea lions can be seen on offshore islands. South of the fishing village of Puerto Grau, there are archaeological remains, including sections of Inca road and two adjoining stone circles known as the Reloj Solar. Before the road turns inland is the small resort of Playa Llostay. **Expediciones y Aventuras** in Arequipa offers private tours in this area.

BORDER CROSSING
Peru–Chile

Tacna–Arica

It is 56 km from Tacna to the Chilean city of Arica. The border post is 30 minutes from Tacna at Santa Rosa, open 0800-2300 Sunday to Thursday and 24 hours on Friday and Saturday. You need to obtain a Peruvian exit stamp at Santa Rosa before proceeding a short distance to the Chilean post at Chacalluta where you will get a Chilean entrance stamp. Formalities are straightforward and should take about 30 minutes in total. All luggage is X-rayed in both directions. No fruit or vegetables are allowed across the border. If you need a Chilean visa, get it from the Chilean consulate in Tacna (Presbítero Andía block 1, T052-423063, Monday-Friday 0800-1300). Money-changers can be found at counters in the international bus terminal; rates are much the same as in town. Remember that Peruvian time is one hour earlier than Chilean time from March to October; two hours earlier from September/October to February/March (varies annually).

Crossing by bus It takes one to two hours to travel from Tacna to Arica, depending on waiting time at the border. Buses charge US$2.50, and colectivo taxis, which carry five passengers, charge US$7.50 per person. All leave from the international terminal in Tacna throughout the day, although colectivos only leave when full. As you approach the terminal you will be grabbed by a driver or his agent and told that the car is "just about to leave". This is hard to verify as you may not see the colectivo until you have filled in the paperwork. Once you have chosen a driver/agent, you will be rushed to his company's office where your passport will be taken from you and the details filled out on a Chilean entry form. It is then 30 minutes to the Peruvian border post at Santa Rosa. The driver will hustle you through all the exit procedures. A short distance beyond is the Chilean post at Chacalluta, where again the driver will show you what to do. It's a further 15 minutes from Chacalluta to Arica's bus terminal. A Chilean driver is more likely to take you to any address in Arica.

Crossing by private vehicle Those leaving Peru by car must buy *relaciones de pasajeros* (official forms, US$0.45) from the kiosk at the border or from a bookshop; you will need four copies. At the border, return your tourist card to immigration (Migraciones), visit the PNP (police) office, return the vehicle permit to the SUNAT/Aduana office and finally depart through the checkpoints.

Tacna → *Colour map 6, C2.*

Thanks to its location, only 36 km from the Chilean border and 56 km from the international port of Arica, Tacna has free-trade status. (For details of the border crossing, see box, above.) It is an important commercial centre, and Chileans come here for cheap medical and dental treatment. Around the city the desert is gradually being irrigated to produce olives and vines; fishing is also important.

Tacna was in Chilean hands from 1880 to 1929, when its people voted by plebiscite to return to Peru. Above the city (8 km away, just off the Panamericana Norte) is the **Campo de la Alianza**, scene of a battle between Peru and Chile in 1880. The cathedral, designed by Eiffel, faces the Plaza de Armas, which contains huge bronze statues of Admiral Grau and Colonel Bolognesi. They stand at either end of the Arca de los Héroes, the triumphal arch which is the symbol of the city. The bronze fountain in the Plaza is said to be a duplicate of the one in the Place de la Concorde (Paris) and was also designed by Eiffel. The **Parque de la Locomotora** ① *knock at the gate under the clocktower on Jr 2 de Mayo for entry, daily 0700-1700, US$0.30,* near the city centre, has a British-built locomotive, which was used in the War of the Pacific. There is a very good railway museum at the station.

Around Tacna

Northeast of the city is the fruit-growing valley of the Río Caplina, known as Valle Viejo, where *tacneños* go for comida típica at weekends. It is 23 km to the thermal baths at **Calientes**, which have individual hot tubs and an outdoor pool, crowded at weekends. There is a restaurant on site. The archaeological site of **Miculla** beyond Calientes is set in the rocky valley of the Río Palca. Many excellent petroglyphs from various periods may be seen, as well as a fragment of ancient road. Also in the vicinity are two rope suspension bridges over the river (rebuilt with a steel cable core). Miculla covers about 20 sq km and is reputed to have mystical properties. It's a good place for star-gazing from June to September and, some say, for UFO sightings.

Listings South of Arequipa

Tourist information

Moquegua

Dircetur
Ayacucho 1060, T053-462236, www.dirceturmoquegua.gob.pe. Mon-Fri 0800-1630.
The regional tourist office. Its website has a calendar of upcoming events.

Ilo

Dircetur
Av Venecia 222, T053-481347. Mon-Fri 0800-1630.

Tacna

Dircetur
Blondell 50, p 2, T052-246944, www. turismotacna.com. Mon-Fri 0730-1530.
Provides a city map and regional information.

Immigration
Av Circunvalación s/n, Urb El Triángulo, T052-243231.

iPerú
San Martín 491, Plaza de Armas, T052-425514. Mon-Sat 0830-1800, Sun 0830-1300, iperutacna@promperu.gob.pe.
Also in the Arrivals hall at the airport (usually open when flights are scheduled to arrive), at the Terminal Terrestre

Internacional (Mon-Sat 0830-1500)
and at the border (Fri-Sat 0830-1600).

OGD Tur Tacna
Deústua 364, of 107, T052-242777.

Tourist police
*Pasaje Calderón de la Barca 353,
inside the main police station,
T052-414141 ext 245.*

Where to stay

Mollendo

$$ La Villa
*Mcal Castilla 366, T054-545051,
www.lavillahotelmollendo.com.*

Moquegua
Most hotels do not serve breakfast.

$ Alameda
Junín 322, T053-463971.
Includes breakfast, large comfortable
rooms, welcoming.

$ Hostal Adrianella
Miguel Grau 239, T053-463469.
Hot water, safe, helpful, tourist
information, close to market and
buses, bit faded.

$ Hostal Carrera
Jr Lima 320-A (no sign), T053-462113.
With or without bath, solar-powered
hot water (best in afternoon), laundry
facilities on roof, good value.

$ Hostal Plaza
Ayacucho 675, T053-461612.
Modern and comfortable, good value.

Tacna

$$$ Gran Hotel Tacna
*Av Bolognesi 300, T052-424193,
www.granhoteltacna.com.*

Disco, gardens, safe car park. The pool
is open to non-guests who make
purchases at the restaurant or bar.
English spoken.

$$ Copacabana
*Arias Aragüez 370, T052-421721,
www.copahotel.com.*
Good rooms, also has a restaurant
and pizzería.

$$ Dorado
*Arias Aragüez 145, T052-415741,
www.doradohoteltacna.com.*
Modern and comfortable, good
service, restaurant.

$$ El Mesón
*H Unanue 175, T052-425841,
www.mesonhotel.com.*
Central, modern, comfortable, safe.

$ Hostal Anturio
28 de Julio 194 y Zela, T052-244258.
Cafeteria downstairs, breakfast extra,
good value.

$ Hostal Bon Ami
2 de Mayo 445, T052-244847.
With or without bath, hot water
best in afternoon, simple, secure.

$ La Posada del Cacique
*Arias Aragüez 300-4, T052-247424,
laposada_hostal@hotmail.com.*
Antique style in an amazing
building constructed around
a huge spiral staircase.

$ Roble 18 Residencial
*H Unanue 245, T052-241414,
roble18@gmail.com.*
One block from Plaza de Armas. Hot
water, English, Italian, German spoken.

Restaurants

Mollendo
There are many restaurants along
Jr Comercio.

Moquegua

$ Moraly
*Lima y Libertad. Mon-Sat 1000-2200,
Sun 1000-1600.*
The best place for meals. Breakfast,
lunches, *menú* US$1.75.

Tacna

$$ DaVinci
*San Martín 596 y Arias Araguez,
T052-744648. Mon-Sat 1100-2300,
bar Tue-Sat 2000-0200.*
Pizza and other dishes, nice atmosphere.

$$ Il Pomodoro
*Bolívar 524 y Apurimac. Closed Sun
evening and Mon lunchtime.*
Upscale Italian serving set lunch on
weekdays, pricey à la carte in the
evening, attentive service.

$ Cusqueñita
Zela 747. Daily 1100-1600.
Excellent 4-course lunch, large
portions, good value, variety of choices.
Recommended.

$ Fu-Lin
*Arias Araguez 396 y 2 de Mayo.
Mon-Sat 0930-1600.*
Vegetarian Chinese.

$ Koyuki
Bolívar 718. Closed Sun evening.
Generous set lunch daily, seafood and
à la carte in the evening. Several other
popular lunch places on the same block.

$ Un Limón
Av San Martín 843, T052-425182.
Ceviches and variety of seafood dishes.

Cafés

Café Zeit
Deústua 150, CafeZeit on Facebook.
German-owned coffee shop, cultural
events and live music as well as quality
coffee and cakes.

Verdi
Pasaje Vigil 57.
Café serving excellent *empanadas* and
sweets, also set lunch.

Festivals

Moquegua
25 Nov **Día de Santa Catalina**.
The anniversary of the founding
of the colonial city.

Transport

Moquegua
Bus
All bus companies are on Av Ejército,
2 blocks north of the market at Jr Grau,
except **Ormeño** (Av La Paz casi Balta).
To **Lima**, US$30-42, 15 hrs, many
companies with executive and regular
services. To **Tacna**, 159 km, 2 hrs, US$6,
hourly buses with **Flores** (Av del Ejército
y Andrés Aurelio Cáceres). To **Arequipa**,
3½ hrs, US$7.50-12, several buses
daily. Colectivos for Tacna and
Arequipa leave when full from

> **Tip...**
> If you're travelling to La Paz, Bolivia,
> the quickest and cheapest route is
> via Moquegua and Desaguadero;
> it involves one less border crossing
> than via Arica and Tambo Colorado.
> There is a **Bolivian Consulate** in
> Tacna (Avenida Bolognesi 175, Urb
> Pescaserolli, T052-245121, Monday-
> Friday 0830-1630).

Av del Ejercito y Andrés Aurelio Cáceres; they charge almost double the bus fare – negotiate. To **Desaguadero** and **Puno**, **San Martín-Nobleza**, 4 a day, 6 hrs, US$12; colectivos to Desaguadero, 4 hrs, US$20, with **Mily Tours** (Av del Ejército 32-B, T053-464000).

Tacna

Air

The airport (T052-314503) is at Km 5 on the Panamericana Sur, on the way to the border. To go from the airport directly to Arica, call the bus terminal (T052-427007) and ask a colectivo to pick you up on its way to the border, US$7.50. Taxi from airport to Tacna centre US$5-6.

To **Lima**, 1½ hrs; daily flights with **LAN** (Apurímac 101, esq Av Bolognesi, T01-213 8200) and **Peruvian Airlines** (Av Bolognesi 670, p2, T052-412699), also to **Arequipa**.

Bus

There are 2 bus stations (T052-427007; local tax US$0.50) on Hipólito Unánue, 1 km from the plaza (colectivo US$0.35, taxi US$1 minimum). One terminal is for international services (ie Arica), the other for domestic; both are well organized, with baggage stores. It is easy to make connections to the border, Arequipa or Lima. To **Moquegua**, 2 hrs, US$6, and **Arequipa**, 6 hrs, frequent buses with **Flores** (Av Saucini behind the Terminal Nacional, T052-426691),

Tip...
Bus passengers' luggage is checked at **Tomasiri**, 35 km north of Tacna. Do not carry anything on the bus for anyone else. Passports may be checked at Camiara, a police checkpoint some 60 km from Tacna. **Sernanp** also has a post where any fruit will be confiscated in an attempt to keep fruit fly out of Peru.

Trans Moquegua Turismo and **Cruz del Sur**. Ask at the **Flores** office about buses along the Vía Costanera to Ilo. To **Nazca**, 793 km, 12 hrs, several buses daily, en route to Lima (fares US$3 less than to Lima). Several companies daily to **Lima**, 1239 km, 21-26 hrs, US$26-62 *bus-cama* with **Oltursa** or Civa; **Cruz del Sur** (T052-425729) charges US$43.

Buses to **Desaguadero**, **Puno** and **Cuzco** leave from Terminal Collasuyo (Av Internacional, Barrio Altos de la Alianz, T052-312538); taxi to centre US$1. **San Martín-Nobleza** in early morning and at night to **Desaguadero**, US$22, and **Puno**, US$18, 8-10 hrs.

Train

The station is at Av Albaracín y 2 de Mayo. In 2015 no trains were running on the cross-border line to Arica and it was estimated that over US$1 million worth of repairs would be needed before services could be restored.

Lake Titicaca

Straddling Peru's southern border with Bolivia are the deep, sapphire-blue waters of mystical Lake Titicaca, a favourite of school geography lessons. This gigantic inland sea covers up to 8500 sq km and is the highest navigable lake in the world, at an average 3810 m above sea level.

The Straits of Tiquina divide the lake in two: to the north, the larger Lago Mayor or Chucuito, and to the south, the smaller and shallower Lago Menor or Huiñamarca (Wiñaymarca). Titicaca's shores and islands are home to the Aymara, Quechua and Uros peoples. Here you can wander through old traditional villages where Spanish is a second language and where ancient myths and beliefs are still held dear.

The main city on the lake is Puno, where chilled travellers gather to stock up on warm woollies to keep the cold at bay. The high-altitude town is the departure point for the islands and is also well placed to visit the remarkable funeral towers of Sillustani and the peaceful Capachica Peninsula. When it is time to move on, make the beautiful journey from Puno to Cuzco by bus or train, or visit some parts of Peru that other travellers rarely reach: the remote northeastern shore of the lake and the magnificent cordilleras of Carabaya and Apolobamba.

Best for
Boat trips ▪ Festivals ▪ Handicrafts ▪ Local customs ▪ Scenery

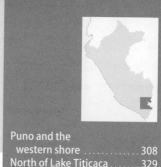

Footprint picks

★ **Fiesta de la Virgen de la Candelaria**, page 314
Early February is the time to experience Puno's folklore at its best.

★ **Sillustani**, page 318
Set on a beautiful peninsula on Lake Umayo, these impressive stone burial towers are up to 12 m high.

★ **Capachica Peninsula**, page 318
The community tourism programme gives visitors the opportunity to experience rural life around Lake Titicaca first hand.

★ **Juli and Pomata**, page 319
Anybody interested in religious architecture should visit these villages along the southwestern shore of Lake Titicaca.

★ **Amantaní**, page 326
Visit independently to spend time on the island after the tour groups have returned to Puno.

★ **Isla Suasi**, page 333
Leave the crowds and visit the northeast shore of Titicaca where you'll find Isla Suasi, a private island with a luxury hotel.

Shintuya
Pilcopata
Koshñipata   Quincemil
Marcapata
Tinqui
Ocongate
N Ausangate
(6384m)

Iñambiri
Mazuko
Loromayo
Lanlacuni Bajo
Ollachea
Ayapata
Macusani
Coasa
Combapata   Limbani
Racchi
Tinta   Sicuani
Maranganí   Nuñoa
La
Raya
El Descanso
Sta Rosa
Yauri   Héctor
Tejada   Ayavirí   Tirapata
Llalli   Azángaro
Condoroma   Pucará
Lampa
Juliaca
Deústua   Huata
Santa   Sillustani
Lucía
Imata   Puno
Chucuito
Cañahuas   Pichacani
Pati
Chiguata   L Salinas
Loripongo   Juli
Mollebaya   Puquina   Sorapa
Omate
MOQUEGUA   Mazo Cruz
Humajalso   L Loriscota
Torata   Pisacoma
Cerro Baúl
(2590m)
Moquegua   Toquepala   L Aricota
Tarata

Iñambari   Tambopata
National Reserve
Bahuaja-
Sonene
National Park
San Juán
del Oro
Sandia   Yanahuaya
Crucero
Potoni   Carabaya
Ananea
BOLIVIA
Muñani
Putina   Cójata
Arapa
L Arapa   Huancané
Taraco   Rosapata
Moho
Reserva   Tilali
Nacional   I Suasi
Titicaca   I Soto
I Amantaní   Llachón
I Taquile
Los Uros   Lake Titicaca
Acora
Ilave   Ilave
Pomata   Yunguyo
L de
Huiñamarca
Zepita
Desaguadero
Huenque

Footprint
picks

1 **Fiesta de la Virgen de la
   Candelaria**, page 314
2 **Sillustani**, page 318
3 **Capachica Peninsula**, page 318
4 **Juli and Pomata**, page 319
5 **Amantaní**, page 326
6 **Isla Suasi**, page 333

N

30 km
30 miles

Essential Lake Titicaca

Finding your feet

The regional airport is in Juliaca, 44 km north of Puno. Paved roads climb from the coastal deserts and oases to the high plateau around Lake Titicaca, either from Arequipa via Yura, Santa Lucía and Juliaca or from Moquegua via Desaguadero. The steep ascents lead to wide open views of pampas with agricultural communities, desolate mountains, small lakes and salt flats. It is a rapid change of altitude, so be prepared for some discomfort and breathlessness. The route to or from Cuzco, whether by rail or road, is also very beautiful and although the gradient is not as steep, it also reaches an altitude of 4321 m.

Getting around

In Puno, the main places of interest and many hotels are within walking distance of Jirón Lima and the plazas. Three-wheel *trici-taxis* are the best way to get to the train station, port or bus stations (about 10 to 15 minutes from the centre), especially if you have luggage or are not acclimatized to the altitude. Boats run regularly from the port to the most popular islands on the lake, and villages along the western shore are easily reached by public transport. Northwest of Puno, Juliaca is a major transport hub for paved roads to Cuzco and Arequipa and also has the only airport in the region. Transport along the under-visited north shore of the lake is less frequent, but that should not discourage you from travelling here.

When to go

Being so high up, Puno gets bitterly cold at night, and from June to August the temperature regularly drops below freezing. Days are bright and the midday sun is hot, but you can never be quite sure what weather is going to come off the lake. There is more rain from November to April. The first two weeks in February, when the Fiesta de la Candelaria takes place, and 4-5 November, when the emergence of the founding Incas from the lake is celebrated, are good times to visit, but crowded, too.

Time required

One to two weeks will give you the chance to explore the area around Puno including the most popular islands. Add more time to venture along the northeastern shore.

Weather Puno

Month	Temp high	Temp low	Rainfall
January	16°C	4°C	117mm
February	16°C	3°C	81mm
March	16°C	3°C	72mm
April	17°C	1°C	36mm
May	16°C	-2°C	3mm
June	16°C	-4°C	3mm
July	16°C	-6°C	0mm
August	16°C	-4°C	9mm
September	17°C	-1°C	12mm
October	18°C	1°C	24mm
November	17°C	2°C	45mm
December	17°C	3°C	51mm

Puno &
the western shore

Located on the northwest shore of Lake Titicaca at 3855 m, Puno is capital of its region and Peru's folklore centre, with a vast array of handicrafts, festivals and costumes and a rich tradition of music and dance. The city has a noticeable vitality, helped by the fact that students make up a large proportion of the 100,000-strong population. *Colour map 6, B2.*

Sights in Puno

Titicaca's tourist centre

Plaza de Armas and around

The **Cathedral** ⓘ *daily 0730-1200, 1500-1800, Sat until 1900*, completed in 1657, has an impressive baroque exterior, but an austere interior. Across the street from the Cathedral is the **Balcony of the Conde de Lemos** ⓘ *Deústua y Conde de Lemos, art gallery open Mon-Fri 0830-1230, 1330-1730* where Peru's Viceroy stayed when he first arrived in the city. The **Museo Carlos Dreyer** ⓘ *Conde de Lemos 289, Mon-Sat 0900-1900, US$5.40 includes 45-min guided tour,* has eight halls with archaeological and historical artefacts from pre-Inca to republican times.

The heart of the tourist scene is along Jirón Lima, between the Plaza de Armas and Plaza Pino, where it becomes a pedestrian mall. Many restaurants, cafés, bars, several hotels and other services are concentrated here and in the nearby streets.

North of the centre

A short walk up Independencia leads to the **Arco Deústua**, a monument honouring those killed in the battles of Junín and Ayacucho. Nearby, is a *mirador* giving fine views over the town, the port and the lake beyond. The walk from Jr Cornejo following the Stations of the Cross up a nearby hill, with fine views of Lake Titicaca, has been recommended, but be careful and don't go alone; the same applies to any of the hills around Puno, including Huajsapata and Kuntur Wasi; the latter is patrolled 0800-1200 and 1600-1800.

Lakeshore

From the Plaza de Armas Avenida Titicaca leads 12 blocks east to the lakeshore and port. From its intersection with Avenida Costanera towards the pier, one side of the road is lined with the kiosks of the **Artesanos Unificados de Puno**, selling crafts. Closer to the port are food kiosks. On the opposite side of the road is a shallow lake where you can hire **pedal boats** ⓘ *US$2.15 for up to 3 passengers for 20 mins*. At the pier are the ticket counters for transport to the islands. The **Malecón Bahía de los Incas**, a lovely promenade along the waterfront, extends to the north and south; it has a sundial and is a pleasant place for a stroll and for birdwatching.

The **Yavari** ⓘ *Av Sesquicentenario 610, Huaje, T051-369329, www.yavari.org, daily 0900-1700, free but donations welcome*, the oldest ship on Lake Titicaca, is berthed near the entrance to the **Sonesta Posada del Inca** hotel; you have to go through the hotel to get to it. Alternatively, a boat from the port costs US$2 return, with wait. The ship was built in England in 1862 and was shipped in kit form to Arica, then by rail to Tacna and by mule to Lake Titicaca, a journey that took six years. The *Yavari* was finally launched on Christmas Day 1870. Berthed near the *Yavari*, is the *MS Ollanta*, which was built in Hull (UK) and sailed the lake from 1926 to the 1970s. Another old ship moored near the port is the *MN Coya*, built in Scotland and launched on the lake in 1892.

Listings Puno *map p310*

Tourist information

Useful websites include www.munipuno.gob.pe (the municipal site) and www.titicaca-peru.com (in Spanish and French).

Dircetur
Ayacucho 684, T051-364976, dircetur@dirceturpuno.gob.pe.
Also has a desk at the Terminal Terrestre.

Indecopi
Jr Ancash 146, T051-363667, jpilco@indecopi.gob.pe.
Consumer protection bureau.

iPerú
Jr Lima y Deústua, near Plaza de Armas, T051-365088, iperupuno@promperu.gob.pe. Mon-Sat 0900-1800, Sun 0900-1300.
Helpful English- and French-speaking staff, good information and maps.

Tourist police
Jr Deústua 588, T051-352303, 24 hrs.
Report any scams, such as unscrupulous price changes, and beware touts (see page 579).

Where to stay

There are over 200 places to stay including a number of luxury hotels in and around the city. Prices vary according to season. Many touts try to persuade tourists to go to a hotel not of their own choosing. Be firm.

$$$$ Casa Andina Private Collection Puno
Av Sesquicentenario 1970, T051-363992, www.casa-andina.com.
This recommended chain's luxury lakeshore property.

$$$$ Libertador Lago Titicaca
On Isla Esteves linked by a causeway 5 km northeast of Puno (taxi US$3), T051-367780, www.libertador.com.pe.
Modern hotel with every facility, built on a Tiahuanaco-period site, spacious, good views, bar, restaurant, disco, good service, parking.

$$$$ Sonesta Posadas del Inca
Av Sesquicentenario 610, Huaje, 5 km from Puno on the lakeshore, T051-364111, www.sonesta.com/laketiticaca/.

62 rooms with heating, facilities for the disabled, local textile decorations, good views, **Inkafé** restaurant has an Andean menu, folklore shows.

$$$ Hacienda Plaza de Armas
Jr Puno 419, T051-367340, www.hhp.com.pe.
Tastefully decorated modern hotel overlooking the Plaza de Armas, small comfortable rooms, all with bathtub or jacuzzi, heater, safety box, restaurant.

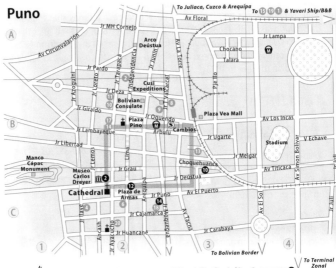

Puno

200 metres
200 yards

Where to stay
1 Casa Andina Private Collection Puno *A4*
2 Casa Andina Tikarani *B2*
3 Casona Colón Inn *Puno centre*
4 Conde de Lemos *C2*
5 El Buho *Puno centre*
6 Hacienda Plaza de Armas *C2*
7 Hacienda Puno *Puno centre*
8 Hostal Imperial & Los Uros *B3*
9 Hostal Italia *B2*
10 Hostal Los Pinos *B2*
11 Hostal Margarita *B2*
12 Hostal Pukara *Puno centre*
13 Inka's Rest *B3*
14 Intiqa *B2*
15 Libertador Lago Titicaca *A4*
16 Plaza Mayor *Puno centre*
17 Posada Don Giorgio *B2*
18 Posada Luna Azul *C2*
19 Sonesta Posadas del Inca *A4*
20 Tayka & Vylena Hostels *C1*
21 Tierra Viva Puno Plaza *Puno centre*

Restaurants
1 Cafetería Mercedes *Puno centre*
2 Casa del Corregidor *C2*
3 Chifa Nan Hua *B2*
4 Govinda *Puno centre*
5 IncAbar *Puno centre*
6 La Casona *Puno centre*
7 La Cayma *Puno centre*
8 La Estancia *Puno centre*
9 La Hostería *Puno Centre*
10 Loving Hut *C3*
11 Machupizza *Puno centre*

$$$ Hacienda Puno
Jr Deústua 297, T051-356109,
www.hhp.com.pe.
Refurbished colonial house, with
buffet breakfast, rooms and suites
with good bathrooms, restaurant
with local specialities, comfortable.

$$$ Intiqa
Jr Tarapacá 272, T051-366900,
www.intiqahotel.com.

Puno centre

Built around a sunny courtyard. Stylish,
rooms have heaters, dinner available,
professional staff.

$$$ Plaza Mayor
Deústua 342, T051-366089,
www.plazamayorhostal.com.
Comfortable, well-appointed, good big
beds, buffet breakfast, heating, restaurant.

$$$ Tierra Viva Puno Plaza
Jr Grau 270, 1 block from plaza, T051-
368005, www.tierravivahoteles.com.
Regional decor, heating, all rooms
non-smoking, central, business centre.

$$$-$$ Casona Colón Inn
Tacna 290, T051-351432,
www.coloninn.com.
Colonial style, good rooms, some
with bathtub, heating, good service.
Le Bistrot serves international and
Peruvian cuisine.

$$ Casa Andina Tikarani
Independencia 185, T051-367803,
www.casa-andina.com.
A central option. Heating, non-
smoking rooms, business centre.

$$ Conde de Lemos
Jr Puno 681, T051-369898,
www.condelemosinn.com.
Convenient, comfy suites and rooms
with bathtubs, heating, elevator, 1 room
has wheelchair access, restaurant.

$$ El Buho
Lambayeque 142, T051-366122,
www.hotelbuho.com.
Nice carpeted rooms, most with
bathtubs, heating, discount for
Footprint book owners, travel agency
for trips and flights, parking extra.

$$ Hostal Imperial
Teodoro Valcarcel 145, T051-352386,
www.hostalimperial.com.

Basic but big rooms, good hot showers, safety box, helpful, stores luggage, comfortable.

$$ Hostal Italia
Teodoro Valcarcel 122, T051-367706, www.hotelitaliaperu.com.
2 blocks from the train station. Cheaper in low season, good restaurant, small rooms, staff helpful.

$$ Hostal Pukara
Jr Libertad 328, T051-368448, www.pukaradeltitikaka.com.
Excellent, English spoken, helpful service, heating, central, quiet, free coca to drink in evening, American breakfast included, dining room on top floor, lots of stairs.

$$ Posada Don Giorgio
Tarapacá 238, T051-363648, www.posadadongiorgio.com.
Comfortable large rooms, nicely decorated, traditional architecture, heater extra.

$$ Posada Luna Azul
Cajamarca 242, T051-364851, www.posadalunaazul.com.
Comfortable carpeted rooms, heating, parking, luggage storage.

$$ pp MN Yavari
Muelle del Hotel Sonesta Posadas del Inca, T051-369329 (in Lima T01-255 7268), reservasyavari@gmail.com.
B&B is available on board this historic ship in 3 twin bunk rooms with shared bath. Dinner served on request downstairs in the Victorian saloon.

$ Hostal Los Pinos
Tarapacá 182, T051-367398, hostalpinos@hotmail.com.
Family run, helpful, breakfast available, cold rooms, heater on request, reliable hot water, laundry facilities, small book exchange, tours organized, good value.

$ Hostal Margarita
Jr Tarapacá 130, T051-352820.
Large building, family atmosphere, cold rooms, private or shared bath, heaters on request, helpful owner, tours can be arranged.

$ Hostal Vylena
Jr Ayacucho 503, T051-351292, hostalvylena20@hotmail.com.
Functional rooms, hot water during limited hours, breakfast available, luggage storage, economical.

$ Inka's Rest
Pasaje San Carlos 158, T051-368720, www.inkasrest.com.
Several sitting areas, heating, double or twin rooms with private or shared bath and US$9 pp in dorm, cooking and laundry facilities, a place to meet other travellers, reserve ahead.

$ Los Uros
Teodoro Valcarcel 135, T051-352141.
Private or shared bath, breakfast available, quiet at back, small charge to leave luggage, laundry, heating costs extra.

$ Tayka Hostel
Jr Ayacucho 515, T051-351427, www.taykahostel.com.
Simple lodging, private rooms include breakfast, shared rooms (US$9 pp) do not, electric showers, luggage storage.

Restaurants

Tourist restaurants, all offering alpaca, trout, *cuy* and international dishes, are clustered along Jr Lima.

$$$-$$ La Casona
Lima 423, p2, T051-351108, www.lacasona-restaurant.com.
Daily 1200-2130.
Upmarket tourist restaurant serving a wide choice of international dishes.

$$$-$$ Mojsa
Lima 635 p 2, Plaza de Armas,
mojsarestaurant.com.
Good international and *novo andino*
dishes, also has an arts and crafts shop.

$$$-$$ Tradiciones del Lago
Lima 418, T051-368140, www.tradiciones
delago.com. Daily 1000-2100.
Popular tourist restaurant serving
a great variety of à la carte dishes.

$$ IncAbar
Lima 348, T051-368031.
Open for breakfast, lunch and dinner,
interesting dishes in creative sauces,
fish, pastas, curries, café and couch bar,
nice decor.

$$ La Hostería
Lima 501, T051-365406.
Good set meal and à la carte dishes
including local fare like alpaca and *cuy*,
pizza, also breakfast.

$$ La Estancia
Libertad 137. Daily 1100-2200.
Grilled meat and à la carte Peruvian
dishes, large portions, very popular.

$$ Tulipan's
Lima 394. Mon-Sat 1100-2100,
Sun 1630-2030.
Sandwiches, juices and a lunchtime
menu are its staples. One of the few
places in Puno with outdoor seating in
a pleasant colonial courtyard, a good
option for lunch.

$$-$ Chifa Nan Hua
Arequipa 378. Daily 1200-2200.
Tasty Chinese, big portions.

$$-$ La Cayma
Libertad 216, T051-634226.
Open 1200-2200, closed Sat.

Good pizza, Peruvian and international
dishes, tasty set lunch, pleasant
atmosphere, good service.

$$-$ Loving Hut
Pje Choquehuanca 188.
Mon-Sat 1130-1530.
Daily choice of very tasty, creative
vegan dishes and salad bar.

$$-$ Machupizza
Tacna 279 and at Arequipa 409,
T951-390652. Mon-Sat 1800-2200.
Tasty pizza and other Italian dishes,
good value, popular with locals.

$$-$ Pizzería/Trattoria El Buho
Lima 349 and at Jr Libertad 386,
T051-356223. Open 1800 onwards.
Excellent pizza, lively atmosphere.

$ Govinda
Deústua 312. Closes at 2000.
Cheap vegetarian lunch *menú*.

$ Ukukus
Libertad 216 and Pje Grau 172,
T051-367373/369504.
Good combination of Andean and
novo andino cuisine as well as pizzas
and some Chinese *chifa* style.

Cafés

Cafetería Mercedes
Jr Arequipa 144.
Good menú, bread, cakes, snacks, juices.

Casa del Corregidor
Deústua 576, aptdo 2, T051-365603.
In restored 17th-century building,
sandwiches, good snacks, coffee,
good music, great atmosphere, nice
surroundings with patio. Also has a Fair
Trade store offering products directly
from the producers.

Ricos Café
Jr Arequipa 332 and Jr Moquegua 334.
Mon-Sat 0600-2130, Sun 1500-2130.
Café and bakery, great cakes, excellent coffees, juices and pastries, breakfasts and other dishes

Bars and clubs

Dómino
Libertad 443.
Happy hour Mon-Thu 2000-2130. "Megadisco", good.

Pachas
Lima 370.
Innovative bar.

Platinum
Libertad 521.
Club, popular with local youth.

Positive
Lima 382.
Drinks, large-screen TV, modern music, occasional heavy metal groups.

Festivals

★1st 2 weeks in Feb **Fiesta de la Virgen de la Candelaria.** On the 1st Sun, some 100 communities compete in an indigenous dance contest. The dances include *llameritos*, *wifala* and *ayarachis*. The following Sun and Mon colourfully attired dancers participate in a contest of *mestizo* folk dances such as *diablada*, *morenada*, *llamerada*, *caporales* and *saya*. A large procession takes place on 2 Feb, the main day. The nighttime festivities on the streets are better than the official functions in the stadium. The dates of the festival until 2020 are posted on www.titicaca-peru.com.
Mar/Apr **Good Fri**. A candlelit procession through darkened streets.

3 May **Festividad de las Cruces**. Celebrated with masses, a procession and the Alasitas festival of miniatures.
29 Jun Colourful festival of **San Pedro**, with a procession at Zepita (see page 321).
4-5 Nov Pageant dedicated to the founding of Puno and the emergence of Manco Cápac and Mama Ocllo from the waters of Lake Titicaca.

Shopping

Puno is the best place in Peru to buy alpaca wool articles; bargaining is appropriate. There are numerous outlets selling alpaca garments, paintings and other handicrafts in the centre. You will be hassled to buy along Jr Lima, so keep your wits about you.

Markets
Along the avenue leading to the port is the large **Mercado Artesanal Asociación de Artesanos Unificados** (daily 0900-1800). Closer to the centre are **Mercado Coriwasi** (Ugarte 150, daily 0800-2100) and **Central Integral de Artesanos del Perú (CIAP;** Jr Deústua 792, Mon-Sat 0900-1900). The **Mercado Central**, in the blocks bound by Arbulú, Arequipa, Oquendo and Tacna, has all kinds of food, including good cheeses as well as a few crafts. Beware pickpockets. **Súper Mico** (Jr Arbulú 119, opposite the market, daily 0800-2100) has a good selection of dried fruits, nuts and cereals.

What to do

To avoid paying above the odds for a tour by a *jalagringo*, ask to their ID card. Only use agencies with named premises, compare prices and only hand over money at the office, never on the street or in a hotel.

Pot luck

One of the most intriguing items for sale in Andean markets is Ekeko, the symbol of good fortune and plenty, and one of the most enduring and endearing of the Aymara folk legends.

He is a cheery, avuncular little chap, with a happy face to make children laugh, a pot belly because of his predilection for food, and short legs so he can't run away. His image, usually in plaster of Paris, is laden with sacks of grain, sweets, household tools, baskets, utensils, suitcases, confetti and streamers, rice, noodles and other essentials. Dangling from his lower lip is the ubiquitous lit cigarette. Believers say that these little statues only bring luck if received as gifts, not purchased. You can get one for your best friend at the Alacitas festival of miniatures, held in Puno around the first week of May.

Agencies organize trips to the Uros floating islands (see page 323, ½ day from US$5.50), the islands of Taquile (full day including Uros from US$11, US$21 on a fast boat) and Amantaní (2 days, see below), as well as to Sillustani (½ day from US$9) and other places. The standard tour is 2 days, 1 night, visiting the Uros, staying in either Taquile or Amantaní and then visiting the other island the next day (from US$27 pp). Choose an agency that allows you to pay direct for your lodging so you know that the family is benefiting. Make sure that you settle all details before embarking on the tour. Some agencies pool tourists. We have received good reports on the following:

All Ways Travel, *Casa del Corregidor, Deústua 576, p 2, T051-353979, and at Tacna 287, of 106, T051-355552, www. titicacaperu.com.* Good quality tours, very helpful, kind and reliable, speak German, French, English and Italian, towards the upper end of the price range. Among their tours is a unique cultural tour to the islands of Anapia and Yuspique in Lake Wiñaymarka, beyond the straits of Tiquina.

CEDESOS, *Centro para el Desarrollo Sostenible (Centre for Sustainable Development), Jr Moquegua 348 Int p 3, T051-367915, www.cedesos.org.* A non-profit NGO which offers interesting tours of Capachica peninsula (see page 318) with overnight stops in family homes, going to the less visited islands where there are few tourists.

Cusi Expeditions, *Jr T Varcarcel 155, T051-369072, reservascusi@terra.com.pe.* Experienced operator that owns most of the standard tour boats to the islands. You will very likely end up on a Cusi tour so it's best to buy from them directly to get the best price and the most accurate information.

Edgar Adventures, *Lima 328, T051-353444, www.edgaradventures.com.* English, German and French spoken, very helpful and knowledgeable, work with organized groups. Constantly exploring new areas, lots of off-the-beaten-track tours, eg kayaking tour of Llachón. Community-minded, promote responsible tourism. Consistently recommended.

Kontiki Tours, *Jr Melgar 188, T051-353473, www.kontikiperu.com.* Large receptive tour agency specializing in special interest excursions.

Nayra Travel, *Lima 419, of 105, T051-337934, www.nayratravel.com.* Small agency run by Lilian Cotrado and her helpful staff, traditional local tours and a variety of options in Llachón. Can organize off-the-beaten track excursions for a minimum of 2 people. Recommended.

Pirámide Tours, *Jr Rosendo Huirse 130, T051-366107, www.titikakalake.com.* Sells out of the ordinary and classic tours, flexible, personalized service, modern fast launches, very helpful, works only via internet, overseas clients.

Titikaka Explorers, *Jr Puno 633 of 207, T051-368903, www.titikaka-explorer. com.* Good service, helpful, works with organized groups.

Boats to the islands (see page 327) leave

Transport

Air
The regional airport is in Juliaca (see Transport, page 331). Airport transfers from/to **Puno** US$5.60 pp with **Camtur** (Jr Tacna 336, of 104, T951-967652) and **Rossy Tours** (Jr Tacna 308, T051-366709); many hotels also offer an airport transfer. Taxi from Puno to the airport, about US$25-28. Alternatively, take regular public transport to Juliaca (see below)

and then a taxi to the airport from there, but allow extra time for the minibuses to drive around Puno picking up passengers before leaving.

Boat
Boats to the islands (see page 327) leave from the terminal at the harbour; *trici-taxi* from centre, US$1. There are also boats to **Llachón**, Sat 1000, US$1.80, 3½ hrs.

To Bolivia Crillon Tours, Camacho 1223, La Paz, T+591 2-233 7533, www. titicaca.com, run luxury services by bus and hydrofoil between La Paz and Puno, with onward tours to Cuzco and Machu Picchu. They also have hotels on the Bolivian side of the lake and a luxury travel service on Uyuni salt lake (www. uyuni.travel). Office in the USA at 1450 Brickell Bay Dr, Suite 815, Miami, FL 33131.

Similar services, by catamaran, are run by **Transturin** (Jr Puno 633, of 3, Puno, www.transturin.com).

Bus
Local Small buses and vans for Juliaca, Ilave and towns on the lakeshore between Puno and Desaguadero, including Yunguyo, leave from the **Terminal Zonal** (Av Costanera 451; taxi to the centre, US$1.80). To **Juliaca**, 44 km, 1 hr, vans US$1.25, also from **Terminal Fátima** (Jr Ricardo Palma 225); they all go

to the *Salida a Cuzco*, outside the centre of Juliaca; for long-distance bus services to Juliaca, see below. To **Yunguyo**, hourly 0600-1900, 2½ hrs, US$2.90; if there are enough passengers, they may continue to the border at Kasani (see page 338), US$3.60.

Long-distance All long-distance buses leave from the **Terminal Terrestre** (1 de Mayo 703 y Victoria, by the lake, T051-364733). It has a tourist office. Platform tax, US$0.35. Taxi to the centre, US$1.80.

To **Juliaca**, 44 km, 1 hr, US$1 (see also Local transport, above); buses go to their own terminals in Juliaca. To **Puerto Maldonado**, several daily from Juliaca (see below). To **Arequipa**, 5-6 hrs via Juliaca, 297 km, US$7-11, hourly with **Julsa**, 4 daily with **Flores**, at 1500 with **Cruz del Sur** (city office at Jr Lima 394, T051-368524, US$21-27), several others. **Tourist service** with 3 stops (see Arequipa transport, page 281 for details), with **4M Express**, www.4m-express. com, from the Terminal Terrestre at 0600, 6 hrs, US$27-35 includes bilingual guiding, snack and hotel drop-off in Arequipa. The same company offers service with 3 stops direct to **Chivay** on the **Colca Canyon** (see Transport, page 291), without going to Arequipa, from the Terminal Terrestre at 0600, US$50, 6¼ hrs. To **Moquegua**, 5 hrs, US$9-18, and **Tacna**, 7 hrs, US$11-18. To **Lima**, 1011 km, 21-24 hrs, US$36-57, all buses go through Arequipa, sometimes with a change of bus (see Arequipa Transport, page 281).

To **Cuzco**, 388 km, 6-7 hrs, there are 3 levels of service, all via Juliaca: Regular, stopping in Juliaca, US$7-12; Direct, US$15-27, from Terminal Terrestre with **Tour Perú** (city office at Jr Tacna 285, www.tourperu.com.pe) at 0800 and

Tip...
It is advisable to travel between Puno and Cuzco by day, for safety as well as for the views.

2200, with **Cruz del Sur** at 2200 and with **Transzela** (www.transzela.com. pe) at 0815 and 2200; **Tourist service** with 5 stops (Pucará, La Raya, Sicuani for lunch, Raqchi and Andahuaylillas), US$45-50 (includes lunch, may or may not include entry tickets), 10 hrs. Several companies offer the tourist service; all depart from the Terminal Terrestre (except Turismo Mer): **Inka Express** (Terminal Terrestre and Jr Tacna 346, T051-365654), leaves 0700; **Turismo Mer** (Jr Tacna 336, T051-367223, www. turismomer.com) leaves from private terminal at Av Costanera 430, past the Terminal Zonal, at 0730; **Wonder Perú** (Terminal Terrestre and Jr Tacna 344, T051-353388) leaves 0715. In high season, reserve 2 days ahead.

To Bolivia (see box, page 338)
To **Copacabana** (via Kasani border), US$5.40-7, 3½ hrs, departures at 0700 or 0730 and 1430; continuing to **La Paz**, US$10-12.50 (from Puno), 10 hrs (including border and lunch stops); most services involve transferring to a Bolivian company in Copacabana. All companies have offices at the Terminal Terrestre from where they leave; some also have offices in the centre; some provide hotel pick-up. The better companies include: **Tour Peru** (Jr Tacna 285, of 103, T951-604189, www.tourperu.com.pe); **Panamericano** (Jr Tacna 245, T051-354001); **Huayruro Express** (Jr Arequipa 624, T051-366009), and **Titicaca** (Jr Tacna 285, of 104, T051-363830, www.titicacabolivia.com), which also has a 0600 departure. **Litoral**, at the

Terminal Terrestre, is cheaper, but thefts have been reported on its night buses.

To **La Paz**, direct via Desaguadero with **Tour Peru** at 0700, US$16, 5 hrs. To **Desaguadero**, from the Terminal Zonal in Puno, hourly vans 0600-1900, 2½ hrs, US$3.60. Taxi US$33.

Taxi
3-wheel trici-taxis cost about US$0.25 per km and are the best way to get around town.

Train
The train station is 3 blocks from Pl Pino. The railway runs from Puno to Juliaca (44 km), where it divides, to Cuzco (381 km) and Arequipa (279 km; no passenger service). **Andean Explorer** (La Torre 224, T051-369179, www.perurail.com, Mon-Fri 0700-1200, 1500-1800, Sat 0700-1500) runs services from Puno to **Cuzco**, US$161, or from Cuzco to Puno, US$268; both US$5 less in low season. Departures Mon, Wed, Fri (Apr-Oct) and Sat at 0800, arriving in Cuzco at about 1800; try to sit on the right-hand side for the views. The train stops at La Raya. In high season buy tickets several days in advance; passport required.

Around Puno

chullpas, churches and a peaceful peninsula

★Sillustani
32 km from Puno off the road to Juliaca. Daily 0830-1730. US$3.60. Tours from Puno, US$15-18, last about 3-4 hrs, and usually stop at a Colla house on the way, to see local products.

Near Puno are the *chullpas* (pre-Columbian funeral towers) of Sillustani in a beautiful setting on a peninsula in Lake Umayo. The scenery is barren, but impressive. John Hemming writes: "Most of the towers date from the period of Inca occupation in the 15th century, but they are burial towers of the Aymara-speaking Colla tribe. The engineering involved in their construction is more complex than anything the Incas built – it is defeating archaeologists' attempts to rebuild the tallest 'lizard' *chullpa*." Artefacts found in the tombs can be seen at the Museo Carlos Dreyer in Puno (see above). Handicraft sellers wait at the exit. There is a small community at the foot of the promontory.

There are more *chullpas* from the Lupaca and Colla kingdoms (AD 1100-1450) in **Cutimbo** ① *turnoff at Km 17 on the Puno–Moquegua road, daily 0830-1730, US$3*, where rock art and Inca ruins are also to be found.

> **Tip...**
> Photography at Sillustani is best in the afternoon light, though this is when the wind is strongest.

★Península de Capachica
The Península de Capachica encloses the northern side of the Bahía de Puno and is a great introduction to Lake Titicaca. The scenery is very pretty, with sandy beaches, pre-Inca terracing, trees and flowers. It is also good for hiking and mountain biking, and sailing boats can be hired. Some visitors consider the view

ON THE ROAD

Sacred lake

Lake Titicaca has played a dominant role in Andean beliefs for over two millennia. This, the highest navigable body of water in the world, is the most sacred lake in the Andes.

From the lakes profound, icy depths emerged the Inca creator deity, Viracocha. Legend has it that the sun god had his children, Manco Cápac and his sister, Mama Ocllo, spring from its waters to found Cuzco and the Inca dynasty.

The name Titicaca derives from the word *titi*, a mountain cat, and the Quechua word *caca*, meaning rock. The rock refers to the Sacred Rock on the Isla del Sol (on the Bolivian side), which was worshipped by the pre-Inca people on the island. The mountain cat inhabited the shores of the lake and is said to have visited the Isla del Sol occasionally. The ancient indigenous people saw the eyes of the mountain cat gleaming in the Sacred Rock and so named it Titicaca, or Rock of the Mountain Cat.

The *titi* has characteristics – such as its aquatic ability and the brilliance of its eyes – that conceptually link it with a mythological flying feline called *ccoa*. The role of the *ccoa* remains important in some part of the Andes. It was originally associated with the gods that controlled the weather and was is believed to throw lightning from its eyes, urinate rain, spit hail and roar thunder. Among indigenous people today, the *ccoa* is believed to live in the mountains as one of the mountain god's servants. It is closely involved in daily life and is considered the most feared of the spirits as it uses lightning and hail.

---

of the sunset from Capachica's Auki Carus hill to be even better than that from Taquile (see page 323). At the eastern end of the peninsula, the pretty farming villages of Llachón, Santa María and Ccotos have become a focus of community-based tourism. There are currently six organizations, each with a dozen or more families and links to different tour operators in Puno, Cuzco or abroad. Visitors share in local activities and 70% of all produce served is from the residents' farms. Throughout the peninsula the dress of the local women is very colourful, with four-cornered hats called *monteras*, matching vests and colourful *polleras*. Off the east coast of the peninsula is the island of **Ticonata**, whose community tourism association offers accommodation in round houses and various activities. It's a short boat ride from Ccotos, or from Amantaní (see page 326); motorboats from Puno take 3½ hours.

> **Tip...**
> Capachica is a great place to start your exploration of Lake Titicaca: it's relatively close to the airport and you can get to the islands or Puno by boat.

★ Western shore: Chucuito to Pomata

Anybody interested in religious architecture should visit the villages along the western shore of Lake Titicaca. An Inca sundial can be seen near the village of

Chucuito ⓘ *19 km from Puno, vans from Jr La Oroya 195 y Banchero Rossi, US$0.55, 25 mins*, which has houses with carved stone doorways and two interesting colonial churches: 16th-century Santo Domingo, the first in the region, and 17th-century La Asunción. Also here is the Inca Uyo, a fertility plaza filled with stone phalli. A lookout affords good views of the lake. Further south is the larger town of **Acora** (34 km), which provides access to a lovely peninsula with luxury hotels and the Charcas beaches. The important commercial centre of **Ilave** is 55 km from Puno.

Juli ⓘ *80 km, colectivo from Puno, US$1.60; returns from outside Juli market at Ilave 349*, has some fine examples of religious architecture. **San Pedro** on the plaza, is the only functioning **church** ⓘ *Mon, Wed-Sat 0800-1700, Tue for Mass only at 0700, Sun for Mass at 0730, 1100 and 1800, free, donations appreciated*. It contains a series of paintings of the saints, with the Via Crucis scenes in the same frame, and gilt side altars above which some of the arches have baroque designs. **San Juan Letrán** and **La Asunción** ⓘ *both daily 0830-1730, US$3*, are now museums containing paintings by artists from the Cuzco School of Art and from Italy. San Juan has two sets of 17th-century paintings of the lives of St John the Baptist and St Teresa, contained in sumptuous gilded frames, as well as intricate *mestizo* carving in pink stone. The nave at La Asunción is empty, but its walls are lined with

Cuzco - Puno - La Paz (Bolivia)

unlabelled paintings. The original murals on the walls of the transept can be seen. Its fine bell tower was damaged by earthquake or lightning. Outside is an archway and atrium which date from the early 17th century. Needlework, other weavings, handicrafts and antiques are offered for sale in town.

A further 20 km along the lake, atop a hill, is **Pomata** ① *bus from Juli US$0.90, US$3 from Puno*, whose red sandstone church of **Santiago Apóstol** ① *daily 0800-1200, 1300-1800, US$0.70 (if guardian is not there, leave money on table)*, has a striking exterior and beautiful interior, with superb carving and paintings.

To the Bolivian border
Past Pomata, the road south along the lake divides; one branch continues straight towards the Bolivian border at **Desaguadero**, via **Zepita**, where the 18th-century Dominican church is worth a visit. Desaguadero is a bleak place with simple restaurants and accommodation. Friday is the main market day, when the town is packed. There is a smaller market on Tuesday but at other times it is deserted.

The other branch of the road from Pomata follows the lakeshore to another border crossing on a peninsula near **Yunguyo** at Kasani. This crossing (via Copacabana and the Straits of Tiquina) is the most popular route from Puno to La Paz. Vans also depart from Yunguyo to Punta Hermosa, where you can catch a boat to Anapia in Lago Menor (see page 326). ►► *For details of both border crossings, see box, page 338.*

> **Tip...**
> There is a Bolivian consulate in **Yungayo** (Jr Grau 339, T051-856032, near the main plaza, Monday-Friday 0830-1500).

Listings Around Puno

Where to stay

Península Capachica
Families offer accommodation on a rotational basis and, as the community presidents change each year, the standard of facilities changes from year to year and from family to family. To be assigned to a family, go to the **Centro Artesanal** in Llachón. All hosts can arrange boat transport to Amantaní. Among those who offer lodging ($ per bed, meals extra) are: **Tomás Cahui Coila** (Centro Turístico Santa María Llachón, T951-691501, www.exploretiticaca.com); **Primo Flores** (Villa Santa María Tours, T951-821392, primopuno@hotmail.com);

Valentín Quispe (Asociación de Turismo Solidario Llachón, T951-821392, llachon@yahoo.com). But do recognize that there are other families who accept guests.

Western shore: Chucuito to Pomata

$$$$ Castillo del Titicaca
Playa de Charcas, 45 min from Puno, T950-308000, www.castillo.titicaca-peru.com.
Exclusive 5-room hotel on a rocky promontory overlooking the lake and surrounded by extensive terraced gardens. Luxurious apartments and rooms, one inside a castle, restaurant with lake views, full board. Belgian manager Christian Nonis is known for his work on behalf of the people of Taquile.

$$$$ Titilaka Lodge
Comunidad de Huencalla s/n, on a private peninsula near Chucuito, T01-700 5111 (Lima), www.titilaka.com.
Luxury boutique hotel in Relais et Châteaux group offering all-inclusive packages in an exclusive environment on the edge of the lake. Plenty of activities available; works with local Uros communities.

$$$ Taypikala
Sandia s/n, Chucuito and at Panamericana Sur Km 18, T051-792266, www.taypikala.com.
2 upmarket hotels near the lakeshore, suites with jacuzzi, fridge and fireplace, and heated rooms with bathtub and safety box; restaurant, pool, spa, water sports, gym, meditation and yoga areas.

$$ Las Cabañas
Jr Tarapacá 538, Chucuito, T951-751196, www.chucuito.com.
Rooms and ample cottages in nice grounds, breakfast included, other meals available. Owned by Sr Juan Palao, a knowledgeable local historian, busy at weekends, events held here; will collect you from Puno if you phone in advance.

$ Sra Nely Durán Saraza
Chucuito Occopampa, T951-586240.
2 nice rooms, 1 with lake view, shared bath, breakfast and dinner available, very welcoming and interesting.

To the Bolivian border

$ Hostal Isabel
San Francisco 110, near Plaza de Armas, Yunguyo, T951-794228.
With or without bath, nice rooms and courtyard, electric shower, parking, friendly. A few other cheap places to stay.

Transport

Península Capachica
Boat
There is only 1 weekly public boat between Puno and Llachón, departing **Puno** Fri 0900, returning from **Llachón** Sat 1000, US$1.80 each way, 3½ hrs. The daily 0800 boat from Puno to Amantaní may drop you off at Colata (at the tip of the peninsula), a 1-hr walk from Llachón; confirm details in advance. Returning to Puno, you can try to flag down the boat from Amantaní which passes Colata between 0830 and 0930. In Santa María (Llachón), boats can be hired for trips to **Amantaní** (US$29 return, 40 mins) and **Taquile** (US$32 return, 50 mins), minimum 10 passengers. If there is demand, passenger service costs US$1.80 pp, one way.

Road
Vans run daily 0700-1600 from Av Costanera y Jr Lampa in Puno to **Capachica**, 1½ hrs, US$1.45, where you get another van to **Llachón**; these leave when full, 30 mins, US$1; by mototaxi costs US$5.40, by taxi US$7.

To the Bolivian border
Hourly minibuses from Puno to **Yunguyo** may continue to the border at Kasani if there are enough passengers; there are also shared taxis (US$0.40 pp) and private taxis (US$2.50) from Yunguyo (Jr Titicaca y San Francisco, 1 block

> **Tip...**
> Don't take a taxi from Yunguyo to Puno without checking its reliability first; the driver may pick up an accomplice to rob passengers.

from Plaza de Armas) to **Kasani**, 5 mins (see also box, page 338). In the other directions, minibuses to **Puno** depart from Jr Cusco esq Arica, 1 block from Plaza 2 de Mayo, Yunguyo, hourly 0600-1900, 2½ hrs, US$2.90.

The islands

witness traditional life on the lake when the tour boats go home

The Uros

US$3 to land, 5 km northeast of Puno.

Of the estimated 80 Uros or 'floating islands' in Puno Bay, only about 15 are regularly visited by tourists. Today we can talk about two kinds of Uros people; those close to the city of Puno and easily accessible to tourism, and those on islands that remain relatively isolated. On the more far-flung islands, reached via narrow channels through the reed beds, the Uros do not like to be photographed and continue to lead relatively traditional lives outside the monetary economy. They hunt and fish and depend on trade with the mainland for other essentials. They also live off the lake's plants, the most important of which are the reeds they use for their boats, houses and the very foundations of their islands (see box, page 324). Their diet is very rich in fats. This, plus the high red corpuscle content, leads to the saying that they have black blood.

> **Tip...**
> The Uros people cannot live from tourism alone, so it is better to buy their handicrafts or pay for services rather than just to tip them.

Visitors to the floating islands will encounter more Uros women than men. These women wait every day for the tour boats to sell their handicrafts, while most of the men are out on the lake, hunting and fishing, although you may see some men building or repairing boats or nets. They glean extra income from tourists offering overnight accommodation in reed houses, selling meals and providing Uro guides for two-hour tours. Organized tour parties are usually given a boat-building demonstration and the chance to take a short trip in a reed boat. Some islanders will also greet boatloads of tourists with a song and will pose for photos. The islanders, who are very friendly, appreciate gifts of pens, paper, and other items for their two schools. This form of tourism on the Uros Islands is now well-established and, whether it has done irreparable harm or will ultimately prove beneficial, it takes place in superb surroundings. Take drinking water as there is none on the islands.

Taquile

US$3 to land, 37 km east of Puno. Contact Munay Taquile, the island's community-based travel agency, Titicaca 508, Puno, T051-351448, www.titicaca-taquile.com.

Isla Taquile is just 1 km wide but 6-7 km long. It has numerous pre-Inca and Inca ruins, and Inca terracing. The sunset from the highest point of the island (3950 m) is beautiful.

Full-day tours usually include a stop in Taquile along with Uros, and two-day tours to Amantaní also stop here either on the way there or back. This

ON THE ROAD
Like the fish and birds of the water

Titicaca's waters nourished great civilizations like the Tiahuanaco and Pukará and drew the Incas south in search of new lands and the origin of their own creation legend. But very little is known about a third people who made Titicaca their home. They were the Uros, the people of the floating islands. The ephemeral nature of their totora reed constructions and the watery world they inhabit make archaeological study impossible, and only their myths remain.

In their oral histories, the Uros say that their forefathers came from the south. We cannot know for certain when the Uros first arrived at Lake Titicaca, but it is thought that a great drought around AD 1200 provoked a series of massive migrations of entire peoples across the *altiplano*. In a scenario similar to the one predicted for parts of the world in the 21st century, conflicts arose as competition increased for water and fertile land.

The Uros found the fertile shores of the great lake occupied by other, much larger ethnic groups. According to Uro tradition, facing defeat by their established rivals, the Uros hid in the water among the reeds. Tired and cold, they cut the *totora* and, by binding the reeds together, made a number of rafts on which they slept.

Legend has it that when the Inca Pachacútec arrived to conquer the lake region he asked the Uros who they were. These people who had hunted and fished in the same way for generations replied as they always had, saying: We are the founders of the world, the first inhabitants of the planet. Our blood is black and we cannot drown. We are like the fish and birds of the water.

With the arrival of the Spanish in the 16th century, the Uros isolated themselves even more from the mainland. Persecuted by the invaders, they began to meld themselves more than ever to their lake environment and their only outside contact was with other ethnic groups onshore, with whom they exchanged fish and birds for agricultural products.

Recalling their childhood, some old Uros islanders still remember when the first tourists arrived. Fearing that the Spanish had returned, their grandparents told them to run and hide.

Times have changed on some of the floating islands where the Uros smile, pose for photographs, and then ask for a tip. After generations of intermarriage with their Aymara neighbours, one of South America's most ancient tribal groups is in fact now ethnically extinct. The last Uro died in 1959, and the Uros language died with her.

means there are lots people on the island around midday. For a more authentic experience, get a tour that stays overnight in Taquile, or go independently to have time to explore the island's six districts or *suyos* and to observe the daily flurry of activity around the boatloads of tourists: demonstrations of traditional dress and weaving techniques, the preparation of trout to feed the hordes. When the boats

A lasting tradition

One of the most enduring textile traditions in Peru is found among the people of Taquile. Each family possesses at least four different types of costume: for work, leisure, weddings and festivals.

For weddings, which all take place on 3 May, when the planet Venus – Hatun Chaska – is visible, the bridegroom wears a red poncho provided by the best man. As a single man he wore a half red, half white cap, but to signify his married status he wears a long red hat and a wide red wedding belt, or *chumpi*. His bag for coca leaves, *ch'uspa*, is also filled.

The bride wears a wide red hat (*montera*) and her hands are covered with a ritual cloth (*katana-oncoma*). A *quincha*, a small white cloth symbolizing purity, is hidden in her skirt. With her red wedding blouse (*gonna*), she wears a gathered skirt (*pollera*), made from 20 different layers of brightly coloured cloth. She also wears a belt (*faja*) and black cloak known as a *chukoo*.

The wool used for weaving is usually spun by the women, but on Taquile men spin wool, as well as knitting their conical hats (*chullos*). In fact, only the men on Taquile know how to knit. By the age of 10, a boy can knit his own Chullo Santa María, which is white-tipped to show single status. When he marries, or moves in with a woman, he adopts the red-tipped *chullo*, which is exclusive to the island. Today, much of the wool for knitting is bought ready-spun from factories in Arequipa.

leave, the island breathes a gentle sigh and people slowly return to their more traditional activities.

On Sunday, people from all the districts gather for a meeting in the main plaza after Quechua mass. There is an (unmarked) **museum of traditional costumes** on the plaza (see box, A lasting tradition, above) and a co-operative shop that sells exceptional woollen goods; they are not cheap, but of very fine quality. Each week different families sell their products. Other shops on the plaza sell postcards, water and dry goods. If you are staying over, you are advised to bring some food with you, particularly fruit, bread and vegetables, as well as water, plenty of small-value notes, candles, a torch, toilet paper and a sleeping bag. Take precautions against sunburn and take warm clothes for the cold nights.

Tip...
There are four docks on Taquile, so if you have trouble walking up many steps at high altitude, ask to be taken to a landing stage which requires less climbing.

★Amantaní
US$3 to land, 44 km northeast of Puno.

Another island worth visiting is Amantaní. It is very beautiful, peaceful and arguably less spoiled and friendlier than Taquile. There are three docks; the one on the northwest shore is closest to **Pueblo de Amantaní**, the main village. There are seven other villages on the island and ruins on both of its peaks, **Pacha Tata** (4115 m) and **Pacha Mama** (4130 m), from which there are excellent views. There are also temples. On the northwest shore, 30 minutes from the Pueblo, is the **Inkatiana,** a throne carved out of stone, eroded from flooding. The residents make beautiful textiles and sell them quite cheaply at the Cooperativa de Artesanos. They also make basketwork and stoneware. The people are Quechua speakers, but understand Spanish. Islanders arrange dances for tour groups for which visitors are invited to dress up in local clothes and join in. Small shops sell water and snacks.

Anapia and Yuspique
18 km from Punta Hermosa, contact Asociación de Turismo Anapia, Sra María Chávez Segales, T951-991164.

In the Peruvian part of the Lago Menor (see page 321) are the islands of **Anapia** (a friendly, Aymara-speaking community which maintains its traditions) and **Yuspique**, on which are ruins and vicuñas. The community has organized committees for tourism, motor boats, sailing boats and accommodation with families (from US$9 per person). You can visit Anapia independently (see Transport below) or take a tour with **All Ways Travel**, see page 315. On the island ask for José Flores, who is very knowledgeable about Anapia's history, flora and fauna. He sometimes acts as a guide.

Listings The islands

Where to stay

The **iPerú** office in Puno has a list of families offering accommodation in their homes.

The Uros
Accommodation costs from US$14 pp with simple meals extra or US$60 pp full board including tour. **René Coyla Coila**, T951-743533 is an official tour guide who can advise on lodgings. Some families you can contact are: **Elsa Coila Coila** (Isla Aruma Uros, T951-607147); **Cristina Suaña** (Kantati Uros, T951-695121); **Luis**

Carvajal (Qhanan Pacha, T951-835264); and **Silverio Lujano** (**Kamisaraki Inn Lodge**, Kamisaraki, T951-049493).

Taquile
The Community Tourism Agency **Munay Taquile** (T051-351448, www. titicaca-taquile.com) can arrange accommodation on the island. Someone will approach you when you get off the boat if you don't have anything booked in advance. Rates are from US$9 pp for bed only, from US$21 pp full board, or US$43 pp including transport and guiding. Some families have become

popular with tour groups and so have been able to build bigger and better facilities (with showers and loos), classified as *Albergue Rural* or *Hotel Rural*. As a result, families with more basic accommodation (*Casa Rural*) are often losing out on valuable tourist income. Instead of staying in the busy part of the island around the main square, consider staying with the Huayllano community on the south side of the island; contact **Alipio Huatta Cruz** (T951-668551 or T951-615239) or arrange a visit with **All Ways Travel** (see page 315).

Amantaní

The **Presidente del Comité Turístico de Amantaní** is Gerardo Yanarico, T951 848548. Rates are US$11-30 pp full board, or from US$29 pp including a tour. If you are willing to walk to more distant communities, you might get a better price and you are helping to share the income. Options include:
$$ Kantuta Lodge (T051-630238, 951-636172, www.kantutalodge.com), run by Richard Cari and family, full board; **Hospedaje Ccolono** (Occosuyo, T951-675918); **Eduardo Yucra Mamani** (Jatari, Comunidad Pueblo, T951-664577); or **Victoriano Calsin Quispe** (T051-360220/363320).

Restaurants

Taquile

There are many small restaurants around the plaza and on the track to the Puerto Principal, including Gerardo Huatta's **La Flor de Cantuta**, on the steps, and **El Inca** on the main plaza. Meals are generally fish, rice and chips, omelette and *fiambre*, a local stew. Meat is rarely available and drinks often run out. Breakfast consists of pancakes and bread.

Amantaní

The artificially low price of tours allows families little scope for providing anything other than basic meals, so take your own supplies.

Festivals

Taquile

The principal festivals are **2-7 Jun** and the **Fiesta de Santiago 25 Jul-2 Aug**, with many dances in between.

Amantaní

15-20 Jan **Pago a la Tierra** or **San Sebastián** is celebrated on the hills of the island. The festivities are very colourful, musical and hard-drinking. 9 Apr **Aniversario del Consejo** (the local council). 8-16 Aug **Feria de Artesanías**.

Transport

Purchasing one-way tickets gives you more flexibility if you wish to stay longer on the islands, but joining a tour is the most convenient way to visit, especially as it will include transport between your hotel and the port. 2-day tours to Uros, Amantaní and Taquile, including simple lodging and meals, start at US$27.

The Uros

Asociación de Transporte los Uros (T051-368024, aeuttal@hotmail.com, daily 0800-1600) runs motorboats from Puno to the islands, daily 0630-1630 or whenever there are 10 people, US$3.60. Agencies charge US$5.50-7 for a ½-day tour.

Taquile

Operaciones Comunales Taquile (T051-205477, daily 0600-1800) has boats at

0730 and 0800 in high season, stopping at the Uros on the way, returning at 1400 and 1430; in low season only 1 boat travels, US$7 return. Organized tours cost US$21-25.

Amantaní
Transportes Unificados Amantaní (T051-369714, daily 0500-1800) has 2 boats daily at 0815, 1 direct, the 2nd stopping at Uros; they return at 0800 the next day, one direct to **Puno**, the 2nd stopping at **Taquile** and continuing to Puno at 1200. Rates are US$7.50 Puno to Amantaní direct one way; US$11 return including stops at **Uros** and Taquile; US$3 Amantaní to Taquile one way. If you stop in Taquile on the way back, you can choose to continue to Puno at 1200 with the Amantaní boat or take a Taquile boat at 1400 (also 1430 in high season).

Anapia
Take a van from Parque Primero de Mayo in **Yunguyo** towards Tinicachi and alight at **Punta Hermosa**, just after Unacachi, US$0.55, 35 min. Boats leave Anapia for **Punta Hermosa** on Sun and Thu at 0600, returning from Punta Hermosa to Anapia on the same days between 1200 and 1300, US$1.25, 1½ hrs each way. To hire a boat from Punta Hermosa to Anapia costs US$29.

North of
Lake Titicaca

Heading north from Puno, the road crosses a range of hills to another coastal plain, which leads to Juliaca. This town is the main transport hub for journeys north to Cuzco or the jungle, west to Arequipa or east along the unspoiled northern shores of the lake.

Juliaca and around → *Colour map 6, B2.*

change buses here, then move on

Juliaca

Freezing cold at night, hygienically challenged and less than safe, Juliaca, 289 km northeast of Arequipa, is not particularly attractive. As the commercial focus of an area bounded by Puno, Arequipa and the jungle, it has grown very fast into a noisy chaotic place with a large, impermanent population of over 100,000, lots of contraband and more *trici-taxis* than cars. Monday, market day, is the most disorganized of all.

Lampa

The unspoiled friendly little colonial town of **Lampa**, 31 km northwest of Juliaca along an old road to Pucará, is known as the 'Pink City'. Being so close to Juliaca, it is a fine alternative place to stay for those seeking tranquility. It has a splendid church, **La Inmaculada** ① *daily 0900-1200, 1400-1600, US$3.60*, containing a copy of Michelangelo's 'Pietà' cast in aluminium, many Cuzqueña school paintings and a carved wooden pulpit. A plaster copy of the 'Pietà' and a mural depicting local history can be seen in the Municipalidad. **Kampac Museo** ① *Jr Alfonso Ugarte 462 y Ayacucho, T951-820085, daily 0700-1800, US$1.80*, a small private museum featuring an eclectic collection of sculptures and ceramics from a number of Peruvian cultures; the owner, Profesor Jesús Vargas, can be found at the shop opposite. Lampa has a small Sunday market and celebrates a fiesta of **Santiago Apóstol** on 6-15 December. There is a fine colonial bridge just south of the town and **La Cueva del Toro** cave with petroglyphs at Lensora, 4 km past the bridge. The Tinajani rock formations and stands of *Puya raimondii* plants south of Ayaviri (see below) can also be accessed from Lampa.

ON THE ROAD

Lampa: living in the past

Walking past Lampa's imposing pink-stone church and the colonial *casonas* with their terracotta finish which give the town its nickname, you can't help but wonder why this town is so different from others in the region. In the late 19th and early 20th centuries, the Lampa aristocracy did not allow the iron horse to trample upon its plains, so the Cuzco—Arequipa railway had to make a detour and go to Juliaca. With it went change and development. Lampa lost the importance it had held since colonial times becoming a tranquil town that time forgot, but always clinging tightly to its aristocratic air.

Listings Juliaca and around

Tourist information

Information is available from **Dircetur** (Jr Noriega 191, p 3, T051-321839, Mon-Fri 0730-1530) and **iPerú** (at the airport, iperupunoapto@promperu.gob.pe, open when flights arrive).

Where to stay

The town has water problems in dry season.

$$$-$$ Hotel Don Carlos
Jr 9 de Diciembre 114, Plaza Bolognesi, T051-323600, www.hotelesdoncarlos.com.
Comfortable, modern facilities, heater, good service, breakfast, restaurant and room service. Also has **Suites Don Carlos**, Jr M Prado 335, T051-321571.

$$ Royal Inn
San Román 158, T051-321561, www.royalinnhoteles.com.
Rooms and suites with heater and bathtub, good restaurant ($$-$).

$$ Sakura
San Román 133, T322072, hotelsakura@hotmail.com.

Quiet, basic rooms in older section with shared bath.

$$-$ Hostal Luquini
Jr Brasesco 409, Plaza Bolognesi, T051-321510.
Comfortable, patio, helpful staff, reliable hot water in morning only, motorcycle parking.

$ Yurac Wasi
Jr San Martín 1214.
Near Terminal Terrestre, good simple economical rooms, private or shared bath.

Lampa

$$ La Casona
Jr Tarapacá 271, Plaza de Armas, T999-607682, patronatolampa@yahoo.com.
Lovely refurbished 17th-century house, nice ample rooms with heaters and duvets, advanced booking required, tours arranged.

$ Hospedaje Estrella
Jr Municipalidad 540, T980-368700, juanfrien@hotmail.com.
Appealing rooms, with or without private bath, solar hot water, very friendly, breakfast available, parking.

Restaurants

$$ El Asador
Unión 113. Daily 1200-0100.
Regional dishes, chicken, grill
and pizza, good food and service,
pleasant atmosphere.

$ Delycia's
M Núñez 168. Closed Fri evening and Sat.
Good vegetarian set lunch with small
salad bar.

$ Nuevo Star
Bolívar 121. Daily 0600-2000.
Decent set meals.

$ Ricos Pan
Jr San Román y Jorge Chávez.
Good bakery with café, popular.

Shopping

La Dominical, a woollens market, is
held on Sun near the exit to Cuzco. The
handicrafts gallery, **Las Calceteras**, is
on Pl Bolognesi. Túpac Amaru market,
on Moquegua 7 blocks east of railway
line, is cheap.

Transport

Air
Manco Cápac airport, remodelled in
2014, is small but well organized. To/
from **Lima**, 1¾ hrs, 4-5 a day with **LAN**
(T051-322228 or airport T051-324448)
via **Arequipa** (30 mins), **Cuzco** and
direct; and 1-2 a day direct with **Avianca/
TACA**. Beware over-charging for ground
transportation. If you have little luggage,
regular taxis and vans stop just outside
the airport parking area. Taxi from Plaza
Bolognesi, US$2.75; taxi from airport
to centre US$3.60, or less from outside
airport gates. For transfers to/from Puno,
see page 316.

Bus
Local To **Puno**, minibuses leave when
full from Jr Brasesco near Plaza Bolognesi
throughout the day, US$1.25, 1 hr. To
Capachica, they leave when full from
Cerro Colorado market, 0500-1700, US$2,
1½ hrs. To **Lampa**, cars (US$1.25) and
vans (US$0.90) leave when full from the
Mercado Santa Bárbara area, eg. **El Veloz**
(Jr Huáscar 672 y Colón) or **Ramos** (2 de
Mayo y Colón), others nearby, 30 mins.
Vans to **Pucará** (US$1.25, 45 min), **Ayaviri**
(US$1.80, 1½ hrs) and **Azángaro** depart
from Terminal Virgen de Las Mercedes
(Jr Texas, corner San Juan de Dios); they
also stop at Paseo Los Kollas by the
exit to Cuzco to pick up passengers. To
Sicuani, take a bus bound for Cuzco (see
below) or **Chasquis** vans leave when full
from 8 de Noviembre 1368, by Paseo de
Los Kollas, US$5.40, 2½-3 hrs.

Long distance The Terminal Terrestre is
at the east end of San Martín (cuadra 9,
past the Circunvalación). To **Lima**, US$38
normal, US$43-70 cama, 20-22 hrs; with
Ormeño 1630, 2000, **Flores** or Civa at
1500, several others. To **Cuzco**, US$5.40
normal, US$9 semi-cama, US$12.50-17
cama, 5-6 hrs, with **Power** (T051-322531)
every 2 hrs, 0530-2330, **Flores** at 1200
and 1700, several others. To **Arequipa**,
US$5.50 normal, US$7 semi-cama,
US$9-27 cama, 4-5 hrs, with **Julsa** (T051-
331952) hourly 0300-2400, with Flores
6-8 daily, several others. To **Moquegua**
(7 hrs) and **Tacna** (8-9 hrs), US$9-11
semi-cama, US$12.50-15 cama, most
depart 1930-2030, with **San Martín** also
at 0745. To **Puerto Maldonado** along
the Interoceanic Highway, US$14-27,
12 hrs; several companies leave from
the Terminal Terrestre and then pick up
passengers at private terminals around
M Nuñez cuadra 11, 'El Triángulo', by the

exit to Cuzco: **Santa Cruz** (M Núñez y Cahuide, T051-332185) at 0900, 1400, 1800 and 1900; **Julsa** (Ferrocarril y Cahuide, T051-326602); **Wayra** at 2030; **ITSA** at 1730 and 1830; **Aguilas** at 1800.

To **Macusani, Alianza** (Av Ferrocarril y Cahuide) 1300, 1700, 1815, US$3.50, 3 hrs; **Jean** (M Núñez y Pje San José), 0845, 1330, 1800; also minibuses from Pje San José, leave when full, US$4.25.

Northeast shore of Lake Titicaca

discover beautiful, isolated communities off the beaten track

The northeast shore of Titicaca is beautiful, with terraced hills rising above coves on the lake. There are many Inca and pre-Inca ruins as well as pre-Inca roads to follow. In the warmer coves, where the climate is tempered by the lake, people lead traditional lives based on fishing and subsistence farming. Most of the people to the west of the Río Ramis are Quechua-speaking, while to the east are the Aymara speakers. Lodging and eateries in the towns along this route are generally basic; there are also water shortages.

Huancané and around

A paved road goes northeast from Juliaca across the *puna* for 56 km to **Huancané** (altitude 3825 m), which has a massive adobe church by its attractive plaza. There are good birdwatching possibilities 10 km southwest of town in the **Reserva Nacional del Titicaca,** where the road crosses the Río Ramis. The reserve protects extensive totora reed beds in which thousands of birds live. Nearby, a road goes north to Putina and the jungle, see page 337.

Ten kilometres east of Huancané, 1 km off the road to Moho, is the small town **Vilque Chico** ⓘ *combi from Huancané US$0.30, 15 mins*, from where a road goes northeast to Cojata on the Bolivian border (Ulla Ulla on the Bolivian side). Several undeveloped archaeological sites can be visited from here; **Cotañi** with one chullpa is one hour's walk away and the more extensive **Quiñalata**, two hours' walking; ask for directions or hire a taxi in town. There are no lodgings in Vilque Chico, only a couple of very basic eateries. Past Vilque Chico, the views are especially beautiful.

Moho and around

At Jipata, the road splits, providing two ways of getting to **Moho** (37 km from Huancané): the paved road inland goes over the hills and is the route the vans take, as it is shorter; the other route clings to the lakeshore, with lots of bends but beautiful views. Moho is known as the 'Garden of the Altiplano'. Maximizing the mild climatic benefits of the lake, the people here can grow roses and many other flowers. The plaza has rose bushes, topiary hedges and a colourful fountain. On a ridge top, two hours' climb from Moho is **Merka Marka** or 'old city', an impressive, undeveloped pre-Inca archaeological site, with gorgeous views of the lake and the altiplano, all the way to the glaciers on the Cordillera Apolobamba.

★Conima and Isla Suasi

Conima, 31 km from Moho, is a pleasant small town in a lovely setting overlooking the lake. It has a nice plaza with a fountain, colourful flowerbeds and an old stone tower by the church of San Miguel Arcángel. The main fiesta runs from 28-30 September. A 30-minute walk through worked fields leads down to a nice beach. Nearby is the Península de Huata with a stone monolith on the ridgetop.

Cambria, a village 3 km north of Conima, is the access point for **Isla Suasi** ① *www. islasuasi.pe, day visit US$25, includes transport from Cambria, arrange 24 hrs ahead*, a tiny, get-away-from-it-all, private island with a luxury hotel. The microclimate allows for beautiful terraced gardens, which are at their best from January to March. The non-native eucalyptus trees are being replaced by native varieties. You can take a community rowing boat around the island to see birds, or paddle yourself in one of the hotel's canoes. The island has some vicuñas, a small herd of alpacas and vizcachas. The sunsets from the highest point are out of this world.

Sucuni to Tilali

Along the shore 8 km to the southeast of Conima is the village of **Sucuni**. In the hills above are the hamlet of **Siani** and extensive pre-Inca ruins. The local community is developing a tourism project (**ATARSEM**, T950-079631/949-544466), including a hostel and guiding service. **Tilali** (7 km from Sucuni, 49 km from Moho), with a large plaza and basic accommodation, is the last town before the border. Near town is Península Huatasani, a good place for a walk offering spectacular views. A dirt road goes from Tilali to the border (see box, page 338) where a market is held on Wednesday and Saturday.

Listings Northeastern shore

Where to stay

$$$$ Hotel Isla Suasi
T051-351102 (office), T941-741347, www.islasuasi.pe.
The hotel is the only house on the island. Facilities are spacious, comfortable and solar-powered, price includes buffet breakfast, guided walk, birdwatching, canoe tour and sauna. Transport costs US$100 pp return, either by land from the airport or by private boat from Puno, including stops in Uros and Taquile, or a combination of the two.

$ Moho
On the plaza, Moho.
Municipal run hotel, basic rooms with solar heated shower (best in the afternoon), best choice among a poor lot.

Festivals

13-16 Sep The main fiesta in Moho is celebrated with dances, bands, bullfights, etc.

Transport

From Juliaca, minibuses for **Moho** via **Huancané** depart when full 0500-1800 from Jr Moquegua y Circunvalación, north of Mercado Tupac Amaru, US$2.15,

1½ hrs. Minibuses for **Conima** and **Tilali** depart when full from Jr Lambayeque y Av Circunvalación Este, also near the market, US$3.60, 3 hrs; these continue to the border on market days.

Puno to Cuzco

stop and savour the scenery on this well-trodden tourist route

The road Puno–Juliaca–Cuzco is fully paved. There is much to see on the way, but neither the regular daytime buses nor the trains make frequent stops. Tourist buses stop at the most important attractions, but to see these and other sights at a more relaxed pace, you will need to take local transport from town to town, or use your own car. There are plenty of places to stay and eat en route.

Pucará

The road and railway cross the altiplano, gradually climbing. At **Pucará**, 65 km northwest of Juliaca, are the colonial church of Santa Isabel and the **Complejo Arqueológico de Kalasaya** ① *1 km east of town, daily 0830-1730, US$3,* a ceremonial centre of the Pucará culture, which had its heyday from 250 BC to AD 380. The ruins consist of nine pyramids and an urban sector. There is also a **Museo Lítico**, with stelae, sculptures, ceramics and other artefacts. *Toritos de Pucará*, ceramic bulls that are placed on roofs throughout the region to bring good luck, are produced In Pucará. There is a basic *hospedaje* to stay in.

Ayaviri and around

The pleasant town of Ayaviri, 33 km from Pucará at 3930 m, is known for its mild creamy cheese and dish of *kankacho* (roast lamb served with potatoes). The church of San Francisco is in mestizo-baroque style. There are thermal baths near the centre.

Some 15 km south of town along a rough road towards Lampa are the interesting **Tinajani** rock formations; you can stay with Vicente Paloma and his family at **Fundo Checcachata** ① *information in Ayaviri at Jr Noguera 166, T976-955830, shelter US$5 pp, camping free, donations appreciated, meals on request,* a nice ranch amid the rock sculptures. A taxi from town costs US$12.50 or US$16 return with wait; on Saturday there are trucks. About 12 km beyond Tinajani, near the hamlet of **Huayatani**, there are slopes full of *Puya raimondii* bromeliads. Unfortunately some of the plants have been damaged, as the local people burn them so that their sheep don't get snagged in the lower leaves. Some 25 km beyond is **Vila Vila**, with an important Saturday market; the road continues to Lampa (see above).

Directly north of Ayaviri is the traditional town of **Orurillo** (3886 m), on the shores of the eponymous lake, where some 81 species of bird have been identified. Its adobe church, rich in art of the Cuzco School, dates to 1571, one of the earliest in the region. There is a colourful Tuesday market and the fiesta de la **Virgen del Rosario** is held on 7 October. Accommodation is in the simple **Hospedaje Municipal**.

Santa Rosa to Marangani

Along the main road to Cuzco, 42 km from Ayaviri is **Santa Rosa**, where knitted alpaca ponchos and pullovers and miniature llamas are made. A road branches off here to Nuñoa, where more *Puyas raimondii* can be seen.

At **La Raya** (4350 m), the highest pass between Juliaca and Cuzco, there is a crafts market by the railway. Trains stop here so passengers can admire the scenery. Up on the heights breathing may be a little difficult, but the descent along the Río Vilcanota is rapid. At **Aguas Calientes**, 10 km from La Raya along the railway, are steaming springs reaching 40°C, with thermal pools for bathing; the beautiful deposits of red ferro-oxide in the middle of the green grass is a startling sight. At **Marangani**, the river is wider and the fields greener, with groves of eucalyptus trees.

Sicuani

Located 38 km beyond La Raya pass at 3690 m is Sicuani, the main city in eastern Cuzco and a good base from which to visit the easternmost attractions of the region. It is an important commercial and agricultural centre and a transport hub. Excellent llama and alpaca wool products and skins are sold next to the pedestrian walkway and at the Saturday market. Around Plaza Libertad there are several hat shops. The tourist office (see below) has an excellent display of traditional outfits from all the districts of Canchis, which are among the most colourful in Cuzco.

▸▸ *For information about places between Sicuani and Cuzco, see page 381.*

Listings Puno to Cuzco

Tourist information

Sicuani

Tourist information office
At the Municipio, Plaza de Armas, T084-509257. Mon-Fri 0800-1300, 1430-1800.
Has pamphlets and very helpful staff.

Where to stay

Ayaviri

$ Gemely
Jr Tacna 510, Plaza de Armas, T051-503604.
Modern hotel in the centre of town, private or shared bath, rooms are cheaper if you don't want Wi-Fi, expensive for Ayaviri.

$ Hostal Imperio
Jr Grau 180, T051-563081.
Clean, simple, economical rooms with or without bath, solar hot water is best in the afternoon, patio, good value.

Sicuani

$ Jose's
Av Centenario 143, T084-351254.
Adequate *hostal* on the newer side of town, ample rooms, electric shower.

$ La Posada
Jr Tacna 219, T084-352191.
Modern *hostal* near the pedestrian walkway on the plaza side of the river, ample comfortable rooms, good value, new in 2014.

$ Samary

Av Centenario 138, T084-352201.
Family-run *hospedaje* on the newer side
of town, well maintained older place,
top floor rooms are the warmest, electric
shower, washing facilities, good value.

Restaurants

Ayaviri

There are a couple of places serving
kankacho, the local speciality, along the
highway west of the bus station; in town,
the most famous place is $ **Doña Julia**
at the plaza.

$ Tradiciones Las Américas

Jr Pacheco y Grau. Mon-Sat 0700-1800.
Large restaurant with indoor and
outdoor seating, good value set lunch
and *comida criolla* à la carte, large
portions, popular, go early.

Sicuani

$ La Miel

*Garcilazo de la Vega 231 y Comercio,
near the plaza. Mon-Sat 0930-2100.*
Good set meals, popular.

$ Wily's

*Av César Vallejo 102, p2, at the pedestrian
walkway. Daily 1200-2200.*
Popular grill and *pollería*, tasty, gets noisy.

Transport

Vans from Juliaca to **Pucará**, **Ayaviri**
and **Azángaro** depart from Terminal
Virgen de Las Mercedes (Jr Texas,
corner San Juan de Dios); they also stop
at Paseo Los Kollas by the exit to Cuzco
to pick up passengers.

Ayaviri

The Terminal Zonal in Ayaviri is by the
stadium near the highway, some distance
from the centre. Vans to Juliaca, US$1.80,
1½ hrs; to **Sicuani**, US$3.60, 2 hrs. A
couple of trucks leave from opposite
Colegio Mariano Melgar in Ayaviri (Sat
0630-0700), stopping in **Tinajani** (US$1,
30 mins), **Huayatani** (US$1.80, 1 hr) and
Vila Vila (2 hrs); return past Huayatani
around 1300; dress warmly. Vans to
Orurillo leave from Paradero Salcedo,
La Rinconada in Ayaviri (US$1.45, 1¼ hrs,
most frequent on Tue).

Sicuani

The bus terminal is in the newer part of
town, which is separated from the older
part and the Plaza by 3 bridges, the
middle one has a pedestrian walkway.
To **Juliaca**, Chasquis vans leave when
full, US$5.40, 2½-3 hrs. To **Cuzco**, 137 km,
US$3.60, 3 hrs. (The Sicuani terminals in
Cuzco are at Av Huayruropata, Wanchaq,
near Mercado Tupac Amaru.)

an exciting route for adventurous visitors

Macusani and the Cordillera Carabaya

A branch of the Interoceanic Highway, fully paved, runs together with the Juliaca–Cuzco road, before branching north across the vast alpaca-grazed altiplano. **Azángaro** (73 km from Juliaca) has the Templo de Tintiri, an adobe colonial church rich in art. Beyond is the cold regional centre of **Macusani**, 192 km from Juliaca, at 4400 m. The dramatic road then descends past the mining supply towns of **Ollachea** (with simple accommodation and eateries, a waterfall, thermal baths and pre-Inca ruins) and **San Gabán** (with petroglyphs and waterfalls) to **Puente Iñambari** (or Loromayo), where it converges with the other branches of the Interoceánica from Cuzco and Puerto Maldonado (see page 509). **Mazuko** (360 km from Juliaca), another mining town, is 5 km north of the junction. This off-the-beaten-path route through the **Cordillera Carabaya** connects Lake Titicaca and the southern jungle (see Transport, below).

This is an excellent area for those who want to explore. From Macusani you can see the glaciated summits of **Allincápac** (5780 m) and its neighbour **Chichicápac** (5614 m), which offer the climber a challenge. Between the two peaks lie a chain of beautiful lakes and valleys ideal for trekking. Northwest of Macusani is Quelcaya, a 13-km long glacier, the largest in the tropics. The peaks are surrounded by high *punas*, where thousands of alpacas are raised. There are many pre-Inca and Inca ruins and roads as well as colonial churches. The region is very rich in rock art, especially in the districts of Macusani and Corani. Here'll you also find the largest forest of rock formations in Peru, covering an area of 600 sq km. **Aymaña**, a village near **Corani**, provides access to part of this forest, the impressive **Bosque de Piedra de Llaylluwa**, and to rock art in the **Titulmachay Cave**. In addition to the vehicle road, these villages are connected by an Inca road which is in good shape and can be walked in a relaxed day. Richar Cáceres (T942-989821) in Macusani, is a recommended English-speaking mountaineer and guide, who is knowledgeable about the area.

> **Tip...**
> Detailed information about this area is found in *Carabaya: Paisajes y cultura milenaria* by Rainer Hostnig, 2010 (rainer.hostnig@gmail.com).

Sandia and the Cordillera Apolobamba

Further east, leading north from the northeastern shore of Titicaca near Huancané, another road goes towards the jungle. At **Putina**, 92 km from Juliaca, are **thermal baths** ⓘ *Tue-Sun 0400-2100, US$0.70*. Vicuñas can be seen at Picotani nearby, and *Puya raimondii* plants at Bellavista, 5 km from town. The road then crosses the beautiful Cordillera Apolobamba to **Sandia** (125 km from Putina), **San Juan del Oro** (80 km from Sandia) and **Putina Punco**, 40 km ahead. Beyond lies the remote **Parque Nacional Bahuaja-Sonene**, see page 513.

BORDER CROSSING
Peru–Bolivia

There are three different routes across the border from Puno. Remember that Peruvian time is one hour behind Bolivian time and that US citizens need a visa for Bolivia. These can be obtained at the Yunguyo border crossing or in advance from the Bolivian consulate in Puno (Jr Arequipa 136, T051-351251, Monday-Friday 0800-1400); consular visas take about 48 hours.

Puno–La Paz via Yunguyo and Copacabana The most frequently travelled route is along the southwest coast of Titicaca, from Puno to La Paz via Yunguyo (Peru) and Copacabana (Bolivia). The border villages on either side are called Kasani. This route is very scenic and involves crossing the Straits of Tiquina on a launch (there are barges for the vehicles) between Copacabana and La Paz. Almost all the tourist class bus services use this route.

Peruvian immigration (daily 0700-1830, Peruvian time) is five minutes' drive from Yunguyo and 500 m from the Bolivian immigration post (daily 0800-2000, Bolivian time). Minibuses from the Terminal Zonal in Puno to Yunguyo may continue to the border at Kasani if there are enough passengers. Otherwise there are shared and private taxis to Kasani from Yunguyo (see Transport, page 317). Minibuses (US$0.50) and taxis (US$3 or US$0.60 per person) run from Kasani to Copacabana (8 km, 15 minutes).

There is one ATM at Plaza 2 de Mayo in Yunguyo and a couple unreliable ones in Copacabana. The *casas de cambio* on the Peruvian side of the border offer slightly lower rates than those at the Plaza de Armas in Yunguyo, but better rates than the shops on the Bolivian side.

Listings Puno to the jungle

Where to stay

Macusani and Cordillera Carabaya
Given the altitude, Macusani is always cold. Choose a room with a window, since it will warm up a bit when it is sunny. The best place to stay in Aymaña is **Tambo Aymaña**, one of the inns set up by government for public servants working in the area; *hospedajes* in Corani are very basic.

$ Apu
Circunvalación Grau 113, 7 blocks from the plaza, opposite the coliseo, T951-241345.

Pleasant hotel with functional rooms, private or shared bath, good hot water supply, complementary hot drinks, parking.

$ El Arca de Noé
Jr Grau 224, T951-118021.
To match the name, a different pair of animals is painted on the ceiling of each room, simple rooms with private or shared bath, solar hot water in some rooms, but must request the valve be opened before each shower.

Puno–La Paz via Desaguadero A more direct route between Puno and La Paz is via the bleak town of **Desaguadero** (same name on both sides of the border), on the southwest coast of the lake. The Carretera Binacional, which joins La Paz with Moquegua and the Pacific port of Ilo, goes through Desaguadero, see page 298, but there is no need to stop here, as all roads to Desaguadero are paved and, if you leave La Paz, Moquegua or Puno early enough, you should be at your destination before nightfall. This particular border crossing allows you to stop at the ruins of Tiahuanaco in Bolivia along the way. The Peruvian border office is open daily 0700-1930; the Bolivian office, daily 0800-2030 (both local time). It is easy to change money on the Peruvian side where there are many changers by the bridge.

Puno–La Paz via Tilali and Puerto Acosta The most remote route is along the northeast shore of the lake, via Juliaca, Tilali (Peru) and **Puerto Acosta** (Bolivia). There are no immigration facilities at this border, only customs controls, so make sure you get an exit stamp at Migraciones in Puno (Ayacucho 280, T051-357103, Mon-Fri 0800-1300, 1500-1900), post-dated by a couple of days. From Juliaca there are minibuses to Tilali, the last village in Peru; these may continue to Puerto on market days (Wednesday and Saturday). At other times you may have to walk 3 km from Tilali to the frontier and then a further 10 km to Puerto Acosta in Bolivia. Try hitching to **Puerto Acosta** in order to catch the bus from there to La Paz daily at about 1400 (Bolivian time), more frequent service on Sunday, five hours, US$6. If you are in a hurry and miss the bus in Puerto Acosta, ask the truck to drop you off 25 km further into Bolivia at Escoma, from where there are frequent minivans to La Paz. You must get a preliminary entry stamp at the police station on the plaza in Puerto Acosta, then the definitive entry stamp at Migración in La Paz.

Restaurants

Macusani and Cordillera Carabaya

$ Don Freddy
Jr Alfonso Ugarte 407, p2.
Decent set meals, noisy TV.

$ Doña Lurdes
Jr Grau 208.
Good set meals. Bakery with sweets across the street.

Panadería El Carmen
Bolognesi 13 y Alfonso Ugarte, near the river.
A traditional bakery in the same family for four generations. Delicious *pan de piso*, pitta-like bread baked in the adobe oven. Worth a visit.

Transport

Macusani and Cordillera Carabaya
To **Juliaca**, US$3.50, 3 hrs; also minibuses US$4.25. Vans go as they fill from Macusani to **San Gabán**; some continue to **Puente Iñambari**. There is a daily bus from Macusani around 0400 to **Corani**, US$3, 2 hrs, and to **Aymaña**, US$3.60, 2½ hrs; return from Aymaña about 0900; more services on Fri.

Cuzco

Cuzco stands at the head of the Sacred Valley of the Incas and is the jumping-off point for the Inca Trail and famous Inca city of Machu Picchu. It's not surprising, therefore, that this is the prime destination for the vast majority of first-time visitors to Peru.

The ancient capital still has the remains of Inca stonework that now serves as the foundations for more modern dwellings. The Spanish transformed the city into a jewel of colonial achievement. Yet Cuzco today is not some dead monument; the local Quechua people bring Cuzco to life, with a combination of pre-Hispanic and Christian beliefs, and a long list of colourful festivals. Tourism is as much a part of Cuzco's personality as its Inca and colonial treasures. Colonial churches and extensive pre-Columbian ruins are interspersed with countless hotels, bars and restaurants that cater to the over one million international tourists who visit every year. Running southeast from the city, road and rail links to Lake Titicaca climb through the very scenic upper Vilcanota Valley. Although less famous than the lower Vilcanota (better known as the Sacred Valley of the Incas), this region offers fine archaeology, beautiful churches, congenial towns and excellent trekking. West of Cuzco, meanwhile, a few hours along the road to Abancay, is access to one of the area's greatest and, as yet, unexploited gems, the beautifully restored Inca city of Choquequirao.

Best for
Colonial architecture ▪ Inca archaeology ▪ Museums

Footprint
picks

★ **San Pedro Market**, page 352
Purchase local produce and crafts in an authentic market.

★ **Calle Hatun Rumiyoc**, page 352
This street of giant stones will transport you back to the Inca golden age.

★ **Church of San Blas**, page 353
Admire its beautifully carved cedar pulpit.

★ **Museo Inka**, page 353
Understand how the region has developed since pre-Inca times.

★ **Museo de Arte Precolombino**, page 353
See superb examples of art that define the world-view of their creators.

★ **Sacsayhuaman**, page 354
Don't miss this ceremonial centre on the northern outskirts.

★ **Ausangate trek**, page 384
Are you fit enough to tackle one of the most demanding treks in Peru?

★ **Choquequirao**, page 386
It's worth every drop of sweat required to trek there.

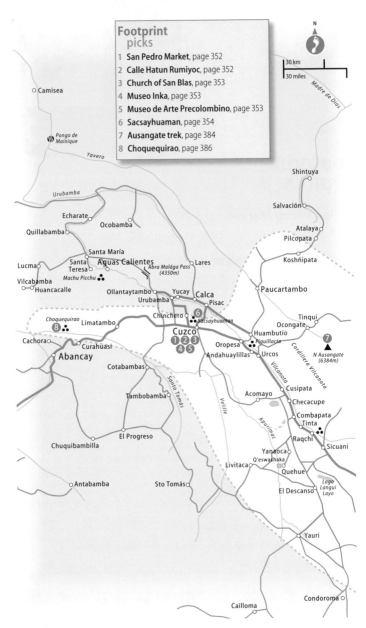

Footprint
picks

1 **San Pedro Market**, page 352
2 **Calle Hatun Rumiyoc**, page 352
3 **Church of San Blas**, page 353
4 **Museo Inka**, page 353
5 **Museo de Arte Precolombino**, page 353
6 **Sacsayhuaman**, page 354
7 **Ausangate trek**, page 384
8 **Choquequirao**, page 386

N

30 km
30 miles

Camisea

Pongo de Mainique

Yavero

Urubamba

Echarate

Ocobamba

Quillabamba

Santa María

Santa Teresa

Aguas Calientes

Lucma

Vilcabamba

Huancacalle

Machu Picchu

Lares

Abra Málaga Pass (4350m)

Ollantaytambo

Urubamba

Yucay

Calca

Pisac

Choquequirao

8

Limatambo

Chinchero

Cuzco

Sacsayhuaman

6

1 2 3
4 5

Cachora

Curahuasi

Abancay

Cotabambas

Oropesa

Piquillacta

Huambutío

Andahuaylillas

Urcos

Ocongate

Tinquí

N Ausangate (6384m)

7

Cordillera Vilcanota

Shintuya

Salvación

Atalaya

Pilcopata

Koshñipata

Paucartambo

Madre de Dios

Tambobamba

Santo Tomás

Vilcanota

Acomayo

Cusipata

Checacupe

Apurímac

Combapata

Tinta

Raqchi

Sicuani

Chuquibambilla

El Progreso

Velille

Yanaoca

Q'eswachaka

Livitaca

Quehue

Lago Langui Layo

El Descanso

Antabamba

Sto Tomás

Caylloma

Yauri

Condoroma

Cuzco city

The ancient Inca capital is said to have been founded around AD 1100. According to the central Inca creation myth, the Sun sent his son, Manco Cápac, and the Moon sent her daughter, Mama Ocllo, to spread culture and enlightenment throughout the dark, barbaric lands. They emerged from the icy depths of Lake Titicaca and began their journey in search of a place to found their kingdom. They were ordered to head north from the lake until a golden staff they carried could be plunged into the ground for its entire length. The soil of the altiplano was so thin that they had to travel as far as the valley of Cuzco where, on the mountain of Huanacauri, the staff fully disappeared and the soil was found to be suitably fertile. This was the sign they were looking for. They named this place Cuzco, meaning 'navel of the earth' according to popular legend, although there is no linguistic basis for this.

While the city is rapidly spreading over the hills that surround it, its heart, laid out much as it was in Inca times, is still discernible. The Incas conceived their capital in the shape of a puma and this can be seen from above: the Río Tullumayo forms the spine; Sacsayhuaman is the head, and the main city centre is the body. The best place for an overall view of the Cuzco Valley is from the puma's head – the top of the hill of Sacsayhuaman.

Essential Cuzco

Finding your feet

Respect the altitude: rest for several hours after arrival; eat lightly; don't smoke; drink plenty of water, and remember to walk slowly. There are too many sights in the city to see on a single visit; limit yourself to the highlights or to areas of particular interest. Note that many churches close to visitors on Sunday, and photography inside churches is generally not allowed.

Best luxury hotels

The Fallen Angel Guest House, Cuzco, page 356
Sonesta Posadas del Inca, Yucay, page 356
Casa Cartagena, Cuzco, page 357
El Monasterio, Cuzco, page 358
Palacio Nazarenas, Cuzco, page 358
El Albergue, Ollantaytambo, page 406

Getting around

The airport is to the southeast of the city; the road into the centre passes close to Wanchac station, at which trains from Puno arrive. The bus terminal is near the Pachacútec statue in Ttio district. If transport has not been arranged by your hotel on arrival, you are advised to travel by taxi from the airport, train or bus stations. You are also strongly advised to take a taxi when returning to your hotel at night. During the day, the centre of Cuzco is quite small and easy to explore on foot. Agencies offer guided tours of the city and surrounding archaeological sites, but visiting independently is not

difficult. There are regular buses from Cuzco to villages and towns throughout the region.

Visitors' tickets

A combined entry ticket, called **Boleto Turístico de Cusco (BTC)**, is available to most of the main sites of historical and cultural interest in and around the city, and costs as follows: 130 soles (US$46) for all the sites for 10 days; or 70 soles (US$25) for either the museums in the city (valid for two days); or Sacsayhuaman, Qenqo, Puka Pukara and Tambo Machay (one day); or Pisac, Ollantaytambo, Chinchero and Moray (two days). The BTC can be bought at **iCusco** (Portal Mantas 117-A, Monday-Saturday 0900-1700) and **Cosituc** (Avenida El Sol 103, of 102, Galerías Turísticas, T084-261465, daily 0800-1800, www.cosituc.gob.pe) or online at www.boletoturisticocusco.net, or at any of the sites included in the ticket. For students with an ISIC card the 10-day BTC costs 70 soles (US$25), only available at the Cosituc office upon presentation of the ISIC card. Take your ISIC card when visiting the sites, as some officials may ask to see it.

Two other combined entry tickets apply to churches and religious museums. The **Circuito Religioso Arzobispal (CRA)** costs 30 soles (US$11 for 10 days) and includes the Cathedral, Museo Arzobispal, San Blas and San Cristóbal. The **Circuito del Barroco Andino (CBA)** costs 25 soles (US$9 for seven days) and includes La Compañía in Cuzco and churches in Andahuaylillas, Huaro and Canincunca. Other churches and museums have individual entry fees.

Machu Picchu ruins and Inca trail entrance tickets are sold electronically at www.machupicchu.gob.pe, at the **Dirección Regional de Cultura Cusco** (Avenida de la Cultura 238, Condominio Huáscar, T084-236061, www.drc-cusco. gob.pe, Monday-Friday 0715-1600) and at other outlets listed on the machupicchu.gob.pe website.

Security

Police patrol the streets and stations, but still be vigilant. On no account walk back to your hotel after dark from a bar or club: strangle muggings and rapes do occur. Pay for the club's doorman to call you a taxi, and make sure that it is licensed. You should also take care at San Pedro market (otherwise recommended), in the San Cristóbal area and at out-of-the-way ruins. Also take precautions during Inti Raymi. Always go to the police when robbed, even though it will take you some time to go through the necessary procedures.

When to go

The wettest months are November to April. The months of June to September are clear and sunny by day, cold at night, but this is also high season when the city is very crowded. April and May are very pleasant. There are back-to-back festivals in June, including Inti Raymi, when Cuzco is very busy.

Time required

A minimum of two days is needed to acclimatize to the altitude and see the highlights, but you could easily spend two weeks or more exploring the city.

Weather Cuzco

Month	Max	Min	Rain
January	17°C	7°C	140mm
February	17°C	7°C	110mm
March	18°C	7°C	90mm
April	18°C	6°C	30mm
May	19°C	3°C	0mm
June	18°C	1°C	0mm
July	18°C	1°C	0mm
August	18°C	2°C	0mm
September	19°C	5°C	20mm
October	20°C	6°C	40mm
November	19°C	7°C	60mm
December	18°C	7°C	100mm

Since there are so many sights to see in Cuzco city, not even the most ardent tourist would be able to visit them all. Those with limited time, or who want a whistle-stop tour, should visit the cathedral, Qoricancha, La Compañía de Jesús, San Blas, La Merced, San Cristóbal (for the view) and Sacsayhuaman. If you visit one museum make it the Museo Inka, which has the most comprehensive collection.

Plaza de Armas

The heart of the city in Inca days was *Huacaypata* (the place of tears) and *Cusipata* (the place of happiness), divided by a channel of the Saphi River (no longer visible). Today, Cusipata is Plaza Regocijo and Huacaypata is the Plaza de Armas. This was the great civic square of the Incas, flanked by their palaces, and was a place of solemn parades and great assemblies. Each territory conquered by the Incas had some of its soil taken to Cuzco to be mingled symbolically with the soil of the Huacaypata, as a token of its incorporation into the empire. As well as the many ceremonies, the plaza has also seen its share of executions, among them the last Inca, Túpac Amaru, the rebel conquistador, Diego de Almagro the Younger, and the 18th-century indigenous leader Túpac Amaru II.

Around Plaza de Armas are colonial arcades and four great churches. To the northeast is the early 17th-century baroque **Cathedral** ⓘ *US$9 or CRA ticket, daily 1000-1800*. It was built on the site of the Palace of Inca Wiracocha (*Kiswarcancha*). The high altar is solid silver and the original altar *retablo* behind it is a masterpiece of Andean woodcarving. The Cathedral contains two interesting paintings: the first is the earliest surviving painting of the city, depicting Cuzco during the 1650 earthquake; the second, at the far right-hand end of the church, is a local painting of the Last Supper replete with Peruvian details, including *cuy* and *chicha*. In the sacristy are paintings of all the bishops of Cuzco. The choir stalls, by a 17th-century Spanish priest, are a magnificent example of colonial baroque art. The elaborate pulpit is also notable. Much venerated is the crucifix of El Señor de los Temblores, the object of many pilgrimages and viewed all over Peru as a guardian against earthquakes.

The tourist entrance to the Cathedral is through the church of **La Sagrada Familia** (also known as Jesús, María y José; 1733), which stands to the left of the Cathedral as you face it. Its gilt main altar has been renovated. The far simpler **El Triunfo**, on the right of the Cathedral, was the first Christian church in Cuzco, built on the site of the Inca Roundhouse (the *Suntur Huasi*) in 1536. It has a statue of the Virgin of the Descent that is reputed to have helped the Spaniards repel Manco Inca when he besieged the city in 1536.

On the southeast side of the plaza is the beautiful **La Compañía de Jesús** ⓘ *US$5, or CBA ticket, daily 0900-1750*, built in the 17th century on the site of the Palace of the Serpents (*Amarucancha*), residence of Inca Huayna Capac. Its twin-towered exterior is extremely graceful, and the baroque interior is rich in fine

ON THE ROAD

Inca stonework

Sacsayhuaman aside, there is much original Inca stonework in the streets of Cuzco, where it is incorporated into the foundations of more recent buildings; the most impressive examples are listed below. True Inca stonework is wider at the base than at the top and features ever-smaller stones as the walls rise, creating a 'batter' or tapering effect. Every wall has a perfect line of inclination towards the centre, from bottom to top. The curved stonework in the Temple of the Sun is probably unequalled anywhere in the world. Doorways and niches are trapezoidal. The Incas clearly learnt that the combination of these techniques helped their structures to withstand earthquakes, which explains why, in the two huge earthquakes of 1650 and 1950, Inca walls stayed standing while colonial buildings tumbled down.

Callejón Loreto, see below.
West wall of Santo Domingo, page 350.
Calle Ahuacpinta, page 351.
Calle Hatun Rumiyoc, page 352.
Calle San Agustín, to the east of the plaza.

murals and paintings, with a resplendent altar decorated in gold leaf. Outside the church, look for the **Inca stonework** in the Callejón Loreto, running southeast past La Compañía de Jesús from the main plaza, with the walls of the Acllahuasi (see below) on one side, and the **Amarucancha** on the other.

Santa Catalina and around

The church, convent and museum of **Santa Catalina** ① *Arequipa at Santa Catalina Angosta, Mon-Sat 0830-1730, Sun 1400-1700*, were built upon the foundations of the *Acllahuasi*, where Inca women chosen for their nobility, virtue and beauty were housed in preparation for ceremonial and domestic duties. The convent is a closed order, but the church and museum are worth visiting. Guided tours by English-speaking students (tip expected) will point out the church's ornate gilded altarpiece and beautifully carved pulpit and the museum's collection of Cuzqueño art.

Around the corner, **Museo Machupicchu (Casa Concha)** ① *Santa Catalina Ancha 320, T084-255535, Mon-Sat 0900-1700, US$7*, features objects found by Hiram Bingham during his initial excavations of Machu Picchu in 1912, which were returned by Yale University to the Peruvian government in 2010.

If you continue down Arequipa from Santa Catalina you come to Calle Maruri. Between this street and Santo Domingo is **Cusicancha** ① *US$1.75, Mon-Fri 0730-1600, sometimes open at weekends*, an open space showing the layout of the buildings as they would have been in Inca times.

Santo Domingo and Qoricancha

www.qorikancha.org. Mon-Sat 0830-1730, Sun 1400-1700 (closed holidays). Museo Qoricancha US$3.60; church free, multi-lingual guides charge US$11 for a 40-min tour.

This is one of the most fascinating sights in Cuzco. Behind the walls of a 17th-century Catholic church are the remains of Qoricancha, a complex that formed the centre of the vast Inca society. Its Golden Palace and Temple of the Sun were filled with such fabulous treasures of gold and silver that it took the Spanish three

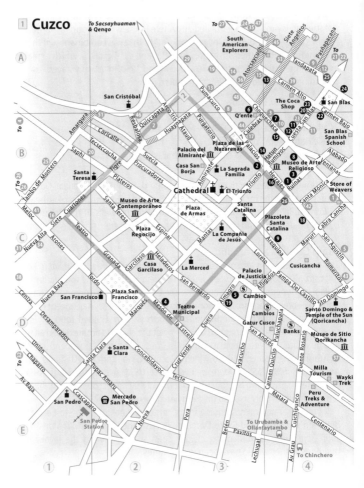

1 Cuzco

months to melt it all down. The Solar Garden contained life-sized gold sculptures of men, women, children, animals, insects and flowers, placed in homage to the Sun God. On the walls were more than 700 gold sheets weighing about 2 kg each. The conquistadors sent these back intact to prove to the King of Spain how rich their discovery was. There would also have been a large solar disc in the shape of a round face with rays and flames. This disc has never been found.

The first Inca, Manco Cápac, is said to have built the temple when he left Lake Titicaca and founded Cuzco with Mama Ocllo. However, it was the ninth

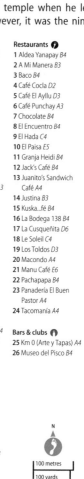

➡ **Cuzco maps**
1 Cuzco, page 348
2 Around Plaza de
   Armas, page 352

Where to stay 🛏
1 Albergue Casa Campesina C4
2 Albergue Municipal B2
3 Andenes al Cielo B4
4 Cahuide A1
5 Casa Andina Koricancha C4
6 Casa Andina Private
   Collection Cusco C5
7 Casa Andina San Blas B5
8 Casa Cartagena A3
9 Casa de la Gringa A4
10 Casa Elena B4
11 Casa San Blas &
   Tika Bistro B4
12 Casona Les Pleiades A4
13 El Arqueólogo & Divina
   Comedia Restaurant A3
14 El Balcón Colonial A3
15 El Grial A3
16 El Mercado C1
17 El Monasterio B3
18 Estrellita C5
19 Flying Dog Hostel A3
20 Hitchhikers B&B
   Backpackers Hostel B2
21 Hosp El Artesano
   de San Blas A4
22 Hosp Inka A4
23 Hostal Amaru B4
24 Hostal Casa de Campo A3
25 Hostal El Balcón B1
26 Hostal Killipata B1
27 Hostal Kuntur Wasi A3
28 Hostal Loki B1
29 Hostal María Esther A3
30 Hostal Pakcha Real A4
31 Hostal Qorichaska C1
32 Hostal Quipu D1
33 Hostal Tikawasi A3
34 Hostal Wayras C1
35 La Encantada A3
36 Los Apus Hotel
   & Mirador A3
37 Maison de la Jeunesse D4
38 Mamá Simona Hostel C1
39 Marani A4
40 Miracle Inn C6
41 Niños/Hotel Meloc C1
42 Novotel C4
43 Palacio del Inka
   Luxury Collection C4
44 Palacio Nazarenas B3
45 Pensión Alemana A3
46 Piccola Locanda &
   L'Osteria Restaurant B2
47 Quinua Villa Boutique A3
48 Rumi Punku A3
49 Sonesta Hotel Cusco E6
50 The Blue House A4
51 The Walk on Inn B2

Restaurants 🍴
1 Aldea Yanapay B4
2 A Mi Manera B3
3 Baco B4
4 Café Cocla D2
5 Café El Ayllu D3
6 Café Punchay A3
7 Chocolate B4
8 El Encuentro B4
9 El Hada C4
10 El Paisa E5
11 Granja Heidi B4
12 Jack's Café B4
13 Juanito's Sandwich
   Café A4
14 Justina B3
15 Kuska...fé B4
16 La Bodega 138 B4
17 La Cusqueñita D6
18 Le Soleil C4
19 Los Toldos D3
20 Macondo A4
21 Manu Café E6
22 Pachapapa B4
23 Panadería El Buen
   Pastor A4
24 Tacomanía A4

Bars & clubs 🍸
25 Km 0 (Arte y Tapas) A4
26 Museo del Pisco B4

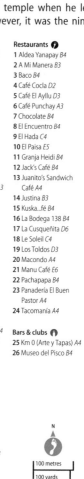

100 metres
100 yards

BACKGROUND

Inca society

Cuzco was the capital of the Inca empire – one of the greatest planned societies the world has known – from its rise during the 11th century to its death in the early 16th century. (See John Hemming's *Conquest of the Incas* and B C Brundage's *Lords of Cuzco* and *Empire of the Inca*.) It was solidly based on other Andean civilizations which had attained great skill in textiles, building, ceramics and working in metal. Immemorially, the political structure of the Andean *indígena* had been the *ayllu*, the village community; it had its divine ancestor, worshipped household gods, was closely knit by ties of blood to the family and by economic necessity to the land, which was held in common. Submission to the *ayllu* was absolute, because it was only by such discipline that food could be obtained in an unsympathetic environment.

All the domestic animals, the llama and alpaca and the dog, had long been tamed, and the great staple crops, maize and potatoes, established. What the Incas did – and it was a magnificent feat – was to conquer enormous territories and impose upon the variety of *ayllus*, through an unchallengeable central government, a willing spiritual and economic submission to the State. The common religion, already developed by the classical Tiwanaku culture, was worship of the Sun, whose vice-regent on earth was the absolute Sapa Inca. Around him, in the capital, was a religious and secular elite which never froze into a caste because it was open to talent. The elite was often recruited from chieftains defeated by the Incas; an effective way of reconciling local opposition. Even the

Inca, Pachacútec, who transformed it. When the Spaniards arrived, the complex was awarded to Juan Pizarro, the younger brother of Francisco, who willed it to the Dominicans when he was fatally wounded in the Sacsayhuaman siege. The Dominicans ripped much of the complex down to build their church. Walk first into the courtyard then turn around to face the door you just passed through. Behind and to the left of the paintings (representing the life of Santo Domingo Guzmán) is Santo Domingo. This was where the Temple of the Sun stood, a massive structure 80 m wide, 20 m deep and 7 m in height. The baroque cloister has since been excavated to reveal four of the original chambers of the great Inca temple – two on the west have been partly reconstructed in a good imitation of Inca masonry. The finest stonework is in the celebrated curved wall beneath the west end of Santo Domingo. This can be seen (complete with a large crack from the 1950 earthquake) when you look out over the Solar Garden. Excavations have revealed Inca baths below here and more Inca retaining walls. Still in the baroque cloister, close by and facing the way you came in, turn left and cross to the remains of the Temple of the Moon, identifiable by a series of niches. Beyond this is the so-called Temple of Venus and the Stars. Stars were special deities used to predict weather, wealth and crops. In the Temple of Lightning on the other

idol-gods of conquered peoples were brought to Cuzco, at once a form of homage and captivity.

The mass of the people were subjected to rigorous planning. They were allotted land to work, for their group and for the State; set various tasks (the making of textiles, pottery, weapons, ropes, etc) from primary materials supplied by the functionaries, or used in enlarging the area of cultivation by building terraces on the hill-sides. Their political organization was simple but effective. The family, and not the individual, was the unit. Families were grouped in units of 10, 100, 500, 1000, 10,000 and 40,000, each group with a leader responsible to the next largest group. The Sapa Inca crowned the political edifice; his four immediate counsellors were those to whom he allotted responsibility for the northern, southern, eastern and western regions (suyos) of the empire.

Equilibrium between production and consumption, in the absence of a free price mechanism and good transport facilities, must depend heavily upon statistical information. This the Incas raised to a high degree of efficiency by means of their quipus: a decimal system of recording numbers by knots in cords. Seasonal variations were guarded against by creating a system of state barns in which provender could be stored during years of plenty, to be used in years of scarcity. Statistical efficiency alone required that no one should be permitted to leave his home or his work. The loss of personal liberty was the price paid by the masses for economic security. In order to obtain information and to transmit orders quickly, the Incas built fine paved pathways along which couriers sped on foot. The whole system of rigorous control was completed by the greatest of all their monarchs, Pachacuti, who also imposed a common language, Quechua, as a further cementing force.

side of the courtyard is a stone; stand on it and you will appreciate how good the Incas were as stonemasons: all three windows are in perfect alignment. Another superb stretch of late Inca stonework is in Calle Ahuacpinta outside the temple, to the east, or left as you enter.

Around the corner from the site (but not part of it), **Museo de Sitio Qorikancha** (formerly Museo Arqueológico) ⓘ *Av El Sol, Mon-Sat 0900-1200, 1300-1700, Sun 0800-1400, entrance by BTC*, contains a limited collection of pre-Columbian items, Spanish paintings of imitation Inca royalty dating from the 18th century, and photos of the excavation of Qoricancha.

Southwest of the Plaza de Armas

The church of **La Merced** ⓘ *Plazoleta Espinar, C Mantas, church Mon-Sat 0700-0800, 1700-2000, Sun 0700-1300, 1800-2000; monastery and museum Mon-Sat 0800-1200, 1400-1700, US$2*, was first built in 1534 and rebuilt in the late 17th century. Attached is a very fine monastery with an exquisite cloister. Inside the church are buried Gonzalo Pizarro, half-brother of Francisco, and the two Almagros, father and son. The church is most famous for its jewelled monstrance, which is on view in the monastery's museum during visiting hours.

Museo de Historia Regional ① *in the Casa Garcilaso, C Garcilaso y Heladeros, daily 0730-1700, entrance by BTC,* tries to show the evolution of the Cuzqueño school of painting. It also contains Inca agricultural implements, colonial furniture and paintings.

San Francisco ① *on Plaza San Francisco, 3 blocks southwest of the Plaza de Armas, daily 0600-0800, 1800-2000,* is an austere church reflecting many indigenous influences.

★**San Pedro market**, two blocks south of here, is popular with tourists but has only been slightly sanitized for their benefit. It remains a working market and is a pleasant and reasonably safe place to purchase local produce and crafts. In front of the market, the church of **San Pedro** ① *Mon-Sat 1000-1200, 1400-1700,* was built in 1688. Its two towers were made from stones brought from an Inca ruin.

★**Calle Hatun Rumiyoc**
This street, running northeast from the Plaza de Armas, contains some of the most imposing Inca masonry in Cuzco, including the famous 'Stone of 12 angles'

② Around Plaza de Armas

⇒ **Cuzco maps**
1 Cuzco, page 348
2 Around Plaza de Armas, page 352

(halfway along its second block, on the right-hand side going away from the Plaza). The huge stone has been precisely cut into a 12-sided polygon in order for it to fit perfectly with the surrounding stones.

The **Museo de Arte Religioso** ⓘ *Hatun Rumiyoc y Herrajes, daily 0800-1800, US$3.60 or CRA ticket*, is housed in the **Palacio Arzobispal**, which was built on the site of the palace occupied in 1400 by the Inca Roca. The museum contains a collection of colonial paintings and furniture, including the paintings by the indigenous master, Diego Quispe Tito, of a 17th-century Corpus Christi procession that used to hang in the church of Santa Ana.

★San Blas

The San Blas district, uphill from the centre to the northeast, is now firmly on the tourist map, thanks to its shops, galleries and good-value hotels and restaurants. Its main sight is the small, simple church of **San Blas** ⓘ *Plazoleta San Blas, Carmen Bajo, daily 0800-1800, US$3.60 or CRA ticket,* which has a beautiful *mestizo* pulpit, carved from a single cedar trunk; well worth seeing. **Museo Máximo Laura** ⓘ *Carmen Alto 133, T084-227383, http://museomaximolaura.com, daily 1000-2000,* displays 24 prize-winning exhibits by this celebrated textile artist, with workshop, gallery and shop.

★Museo Inka
Cuesta del Almirante 103, T084-237380. Mon-Fri 0800-1900, Sat 0900-1600. US$4.

The impressive **Palacio del Almirante**, just north of the Plaza de Armas, houses the Museo Inka, run by the Universidad San Antonio de Abad. The museum exhibits the development of culture in the region from pre-Inca, through Inca times to the present day, with displays of textiles, ceramics, metalwork, jewellery, architecture and technology. Don't miss the collection of miniature turquoise figures and other offerings to the gods. Weaving demonstrations are given in the courtyard.

★Museo de Arte Precolombino
Pl de las Nazarenas 231. Daily 0900-2200. US$7, US$3.50 with student card; under same auspices as the Larco Museum in Lima, MAP Café (see Restaurants, below).

Where to stay ⬤
1 Andean Wings *A1*
2 Casa Andina Catedral *C3*
3 Casa Andina Classic –
  Cusco Plaza *C2*
4 EcoPackers *A1*
5 El Procurador del Cusco *A2*
6 Hostal Resbalosa *A3*
7 Hostal Royal
  Frankenstein *B1*
8 La Casona Inkaterra *B3*
9 Loreto Boutique Hotel *C2*
10 Marqueses *B1*
11 Pariwana *C1*
12 Pirwa *B3*
13 Sonesta Posadas
  del Inca *B2*
14 The Point *C1*
15 Tierra Viva
  Cusco Plaza *A3*

Restaurants 🍴
1 Café El Ayllu *C1*
2 Café Halliy *A2*
3 Café Perla *C3*
4 Chicha & El Truco *B1*
5 Cicciolina *C3*
6 Dolce Vita *C3*
7 Dos por Tres *C1*
8 El Encuentro *A2, C3*
9 El Fogón *A2*
10 Fallen Angel restaurant
  & Guesthouse *B3*
11 Fusiones *C2*
12 Greens Organic *C3*
13 Inka Grill *B2*
14 Kushka...fé &
  Museo del Café *B2*
15 La Bondiet *C1*
16 La China *A1*
17 La Retama & Destinos
  Turísticos Tour Agency *B2*
18 Limo *B3*
19 MAP Café *B3*
20 Papacho's *C3*
21 Pucará *B2*
22 Sara *C3*
23 The Muse *C3*
24 Tunupa *B2*
25 Tupanachis *C1*
26 Víctor Victoria *A2*
27 Yahuu! Juice Bar *B2*

Bars & clubs 🍸
28 Cross Keys Pub *C3*
29 El Garabato &
  Ukuku's *B2*
30 Indigo *A2*
31 Los Perros Bar *A2*
32 Mama Africa &
  Inca Rail Ticket Office *B2*
33 Mythology *B3*
34 Norton's Pub *C3*
35 Paddy's Pub *C3*
36 Temple *A2*

Housed in the **Casa Cabrera** on the northwest side of the Plaza de las Nazarenas, this beautiful museum is set around a spacious courtyard and contains many superb examples of pottery, metalwork (largely in gold and silver), woodcarvings and shells from the Moche, Chimú, Paracas, Nazca and Inca cultures. There are some vividly rendered animistic designs, giving an insight into the way Peru's ancient people's viewed their world and the creatures that inhabited it. Every exhibit carries explanations in English and Spanish. Highly recommended.

Elsewhere on the plaza, the **Convento de las Nazarenas** is now a hotel. You can see the Inca-colonial doorway with a mermaid motif, but ask permission to view the lovely 18th-century frescos inside.

★ Sacsayhuaman

30-min walk from Plaza de las Nazarenas. Daily 0700-1730. Entry with BTC ticket. Students offer free guided tours; give them a tip.

There are some magnificent Inca walls in this ruined ceremonial centre, on a hill in the northern outskirts. The massive rocks weighing up to 130 tons are fitted together with absolute perfection. Three walls run parallel for over 360 m and there are 21 bastions. Sacsayhuaman was thought for centuries to be a fortress, but the layout and architecture suggest a great sanctuary and temple to the Sun, which rises exactly opposite the place previously believed to be the Inca's throne; this was probably an altar, carved out of the solid rock, with broad steps leading to it from either side. The hieratic, rather than the military, hypothesis was supported by the discovery in 1982 of the graves of priests, who would have been unlikely to be buried in a fortress. The precise functions of the site, however, will probably continue to be a matter of dispute as very few clues remain, owing to its steady destruction.

The site survived the first years of the conquest. Pizarro's troops had entered Cuzco unopposed in 1533 and lived safely at Sacsayhuaman, until the rebellion of Manco Inca in 1536 caught them off guard. The bitter struggle that ensued became the decisive military action of the conquest: Manco's failure to hold Sacsayhuaman cost him the war and the empire. The destruction of the hilltop site began after the defeat of Manco's rebellion. The outer walls still stand, but the complex of towers and buildings was razed to the ground. From then until the 1930s, Sacsayhuaman served as a kind of unofficial quarry of pre-cut stone for the inhabitants of Cuzco.

The site can be reached in 30 minutes by walking up Pumacurco from Plaza de la Nazarenas, or from the church of **San Cristóbal**, just north of the centre. The church was built by Cristóbal Paullu Inca to honour his patron saint. North of San Cristóbal, you can see the 11 doorway-sized niches of the great Inca wall of the **Palacio de Colcampata**, which was the residence of Manco Inca before he rebelled against the Spanish and fled to Vilcabamba.

Beyond Sacsayhuaman

Take a guide to the sites and visit in the morning for the best photographs. Entry by BTC ticket; carry it with you as there are roving ticket inspectors. To get there take the Pisac bus or the Señor del Huerto city bus up to Tambo Machay (US$0.70).

Along the road from Sacsayhuaman to Pisac, past a radio station, is the temple and amphitheatre of **Qenqo**, which has some of the finest examples of Inca stone carving *in situ*, especially inside the large hollowed-out stone that houses an altar. On the same road is **Puka Pukara**, known as the Red Fort, but more likely to have been a *tambo*, or post-house; it's worth coming here for the wonderful views alone. Nearby is the spring shrine of **Tambo Machay**, which is in excellent condition. Water still flows by a hidden channel out of the masonry wall, straight into a little rock pool traditionally known as the Inca's bath. You can visit the sites on foot, a pleasant walk of at least half a day through the countryside; enquire about safety beforehand, take water and sun protection, and watch out for dogs. Alternatively, catch a bus up, and walk back.

Listings Cuzco *maps p348 and p352*

Tourist information

iPerú is the most reliable source of information. Their main office and information desk is at the airport (T084-237364, daily 0600-1700). There is also an iPerú desk on Plaza de Armas (Portal de Harinas 177 at BCP Traveller Point, T084-252974, Mon-Fri 0900-1900, Sat-Sun 0900-1300) and a kiosk next to La Compañía church (Mon-Sat 0900-1300, 1400-1800). Other information sources include **iCusco/Dircetur** (Portal Mantas 117-A, next to La Merced church, T084-222032, Mon-Sat 0800-2000, Sun 0800-1300) and **South American Explorers** (Av Pardo 847, next to the US consulate, T084-245484, www.saexplorers.org, Mon-Fri 0930-1700, Sat 0930-1300; see also page 56). See also www.about cusco.com and www.cuscoonline.com.

The **tourist Police** (Plaza Túpac Amaru, Wanchac, T084-512351/235123) will prepare a denuncia (report for insurance purposes) for you. (These are available from the Banco de la Nación.) **Indecopi** (Av Manco Inca 209, Wanchac, T084-252987, toll-free 24-hr hotline T0800-44040, mmarroquin@indecopi.gob.pe) is the consumer protection bureau.

Where to stay

Cuzco has hundreds of hotels in all categories but the more expensive ones should nonetheless be booked several months in advance, particularly for the week around **Inti Raymi**, when prices are greatly increased. Prices given are for the high season in Jun-Aug. When there are fewer tourists, hotels may drop their prices by as much as half. Always check for discounts. Be wary of unlicensed hotel agents for medium-priced hotels who are often misleading about details; their local nickname is *jalagringos* (gringo pullers), or *piratas*. Many places will store your luggage when you go trekking, but always check valuables and possessions before and after depositing them with hotel/hostel staff.

International chain hotels in Cuzco include Best Western (www.bestwestern.com), **JW Marriott** (www.marriott.com), **Novotel** (www.novotel.com) and **Sonesta** (www.sonesta.com).

Around the Plaza de Armas

$$$$ Andean Wings
Siete Cuartones 225, T084-243166, www.andeanwingshotel.com.
In a restored 17th-century house, in the same group as Casa de la Gringa and Another Planet, 5-star, intimate, suites, some with jacuzzi, are individually designed (one is accessible for the disabled), spa, restaurant and bar.

$$$$ The Fallen Angel Guest House
Pl Nazarenas 221, T084-258184, www.fallenangelincusco.com.
A 4-room luxury hotel above the restaurant of the same name. Each suite is decorated in its own lavish style (with living room, dining room, bathroom, feather duvets, heating), very comfortable and a far cry from the usual adaptation of colonial buildings elsewhere in the city. With all amenities, excellent service.

$$$$ La Casona Inkaterra
Pl Las Nazarenas 113, T084-223010, www.inkaterra.com.
A private, colonial-style boutique hotel in a converted 16th-century mansion, built on the site of Manco Cápac's palace. 11 exclusive suites, all facilities, concierge service with activities and excursions, highly-regarded and the height of luxury.

$$$ Casa Andina Classic – Cusco Plaza
Portal Espinar 142, T084-231733, www.casa-andina.com.
40-room hotel near plaza, ATM and safe deposit box. Equally recommendable

are **Casa Andina Koricancha** (San Agustín 371, T084-252633), **Casa Andina Catedral** (Santa Catalina Angosta 149, T084-233661), and the **Casa Andina San Blas** (Chihuampata 278, San Blas, T084-263964), all of which are in the same vein.

$$$ Loreto Boutique Hotel
Pasaje Loreto 115, T084-226352, www.loretoboutiquehotel.com.
Great location; 12 spacious rooms with original Inca walls, upgraded to boutique status. Laundry service, will help organize travel services including guides and taxis, free airport pick-up.

$$$ Marqueses
Garcilaso 256, T084-264249, www.hotelmarqueses.com.
Spanish colonial style, with 16/17th-century style religious paintings and 2 lovely courtyards. Rooms have heavy curtains and some are a little dark; luxury rooms have bath and shower. Buffet breakfast.

$$$ Sonesta Posadas del Inca
Portal Espinar 108, T084-227061, www.sonesta.com.
Includes buffet breakfast, warmly decorated rooms with heating, safe, some rooms on 3rd floor have view of Plaza, very helpful, English spoken, restaurant with Andean food, excellent service.

$$$ Tierra Viva Cusco Plaza
Suecia 345, T084-245858, www.tierravivahoteles.com.
Boutique hotel in the former residence of Gonzalo Pizarro. Rooms and suites have comfortable beds, heating, minibar, safe, with excellent breakfast. Exemplary service, airport transfers.

$$-$ EcoPackers Hostel
Santa Teresa 375, T084-231800, www.ecopackersperu.com.

Ecologically friendly, well-regarded hostal in a colonial *casona*, double rooms with en suite or dorms for 4-18 people, communal kitchen, games room, bar, large-screen TV room, Wi-Fi, garage for bicycles or motorcycles.

$$-$ Pirwa Hostels
T084-244315, www.pirwahostels cusco.com.
This chain of hostels offers a range of rooms from private doubles with bath to dorms, in colonial buildings, lockers, 24-hr reception: **Pirwa Suecia** (Suecia 300) is the B&B branch; **Pirwa Posada del Corregidor** (Portal de Panes 151, Pl de Armas); **Pirwa Backpackers San Blas** (Carmen Alto 283), and **Pirwa Backpackers Colonial** (Pl San Francisco 360).

$ El Procurador del Cusco
Coricalle 440, Prolongación Procuradores, T084-243559, http:// hostelprocuradordelcusco.blogspot.com.
Youth hostel. Price includes use of the basic kitchen (no fridge) and laundry area, with or without bath, basic rooms, but upstairs is better, helpful, good value.

$ Hostal Resbalosa
Resbalosa 494, T084-224839, www.hostalresbalosa.com.
Private or shared bath, hot water in the mornings and evenings, ask for a room with a view, dorm beds, laundry facilities, full breakfast extra.

$ Hostal Royal Frankenstein
San Juan de Dios 260, 2 blocks from the Plaza de Armas, T084-236999, www.hostal-frankenstein.net.
Eccentric place but a frequent favourite, with private or shared bath, hot water, safe, kitchen, small charge for computer, heater and laundry, German-owned, German and English spoken.

$ Pariwana
Mesón de la Estrella 136, T084-233751, www.pariwana-hostel.com.
Variety of rooms in a converted colonial mansion with courtyard, from doubles with bath to dorms sleeping 10, also girls only dorm, restaurant, bar/lounge, English spoken, lots of activities.

$ The Point
Mesón de la Estrella 172, T084-252266, www.thepointhostels.com.
Dormitory accommodation, also has doubles and singles, hot showers, good party atmosphere.

Beyond the Plaza, including San Blas

$$$$ Casa Andina Private Collection Cusco
Plazoleta de Limacpampa Chico 473, T084-232610, www.casa-andina.com.
The most upmarket and comfortable in this group, in a 16th-century mansion with 4 courtyards, enriched oxygen available in the rooms, plus a gourmet restaurant serving local cuisine and a bar with an extensive pisco collection.

$$$$ Casa Cartagena
Pumacurco 336, T084-261171, www.casacartagena.com.
In a converted monastery and national heritage building, super-deluxe facilities with Italian design and colonial features, 4 levels of suite, **La Chola** restaurant, extensive complimentary Qoya spa, enriched oxygen system, and all services to be expected in a Luxury Properties group hotel.

$$$$ El Mercado
C Siete Cuartones 306, T084-582640, www.elmercadotunqui.com.
On the site of a former market close to the Plaza de Armas, owned by **Mountain**

Lodges of Peru, superior rooms and suites, restaurant, bar, helpful staff.

$$$$ El Monasterio (Belmond)
C Palacios 136, Plazoleta Nazarenas, T084-604000, www.monasteriohotel.com.
5-star, beautifully restored Seminary of San Antonio Abad (a Peruvian National Historical Landmark), including the baroque chapel, spacious comfortable rooms with all facilities (some rooms offer an oxygen-enriched atmosphere), very helpful staff (buffet breakfast open to non-residents, will fill you up for the rest of the day), good restaurants, lunch and dinner à la carte, business centre.

$$$$ Palacio del Inka Luxury Collection
Plazoleta Santo Domingo 259, T084-231961, www.libertador.com.pe.
5-star, good, especially the service, warm and bright, **Inti Raymi** restaurant, excellent, live music in the evening.

$$$$ Palacio Nazarenas (Belmond)
Plazoleta Nazarenas 144, T084-582222, www.palacionazarenas.com.
Housed in a beautifully restored building, outdoor swimming pool, spa, history booklet and cooking classes.

$$$$-$$$ Casa San Blas
Tocuyeros 566, just off Cuesta San Blas, T084-237900, www.casasanblas.com.

An international-standard boutique hotel with bright, airy rooms decorated with traditional textiles. Breakfast, served in the **Tika Bistro** downstairs. Pleasant balcony with good views, attentive service.

$$$ El Arqueólogo
Pumacurco 408, T084-232522, www.hotelarqueologo.com.
Helpful, French and English spoken, heating extra, will store luggage, garden, cafeteria and kitchen. Same group as **Vida Tours** (Ladrillo 425, T084-227750, www.vidatours.com). Traditional and adventure tourism.

$$$ Los Apus Hotel & Mirador
Atocsaycuchi 515 y Choquechaca, San Blas, T084-264243, www.losapushotel.com.
Includes airport transfer and breakfast, full of character, very clean and smart, central heating, disabled facilities.

$$$ Rumi Punku
Choquechaca 339, T084-221102, www.rumipunku.com.
An Inca doorway leading to a sunny courtyard, comfortable rooms, helpful staff, safe, sauna, jacuzzi, gym.

$$$-$$ Andenes al Cielo
Choquechaca 176, T084-222237, www.andenesalcielo.com.

At the foot of the San Blas district, 15 rooms in renovated historic home, most expensive rooms have fireplaces, all with either balconies or patios, heating. Buffet breakfast, free airport pick up, gym.

$$$-$$ Cahuide
Saphi 845, T084-222771,
www.hotelcahuide-cusco.com.
Hot water, good rooms and suites, quiet, good laundry service, helpful, good value breakfasts.

$$$-$$ Hostal Casa de Campo
Tandapata 298 (at the end
of the street), T084-244404,
www.hotelcasadecampo.com.
Some of the top rooms have a *lot* of steps up to them, hot water, includes bus/airport/rail transfer with reservations, 10% discount for Footprint book owners, safe deposit box, sun terrace, quiet, relaxing, all rooms have great views, Dutch and English spoken, take a taxi after dark.

$$$-$$ Hostal El Balcón
Tambo de Montero 222, T084-236738,
www.balconcusco.com.
Warm atmosphere, very welcoming, quiet, laundry, sauna, bar, meals on request, English spoken, wonderful views, beautiful garden.

$$$-$$ Hostal Tikawasi
Tandapata 491, T084-231609,
www.tikawasi.com.
Includes heating, family-run, lovely garden overlooking the city. Stylish, modern rooms with good views, comfortable beds.

$$$-$$ La Encantada
Tandapata 354, T084-242206,
www.encantadaperu.com.
Good beds, rooftop spa, fabulous views of the city. Swiss-Peruvian owned.

$$$-$$ Piccola Locanda
Resbalosa 520, T084-252551,
www.piccolalocanda.com.
Steep walk up from the Plaza de Armas, colourful Peruvian/Italian-run B&B. Rooftop terrace with 360° views, excellent restaurant **L'Osteria**, a TV room, pleasant courtyard. Private or shared bath. Associated with **Perú Etico** tour company and 2 children's projects.

$$$-$$ Quinua Villa Boutique
Pasaje Santa Rosa A-8, T084-242646,
www.quinua.com.pe.
A beautifully built living museum, 5 different apartments, each with a different theme and kitchen.

$$$-$ Hostal Amaru
Cuesta San Blas 541, T084-225933,
www.amaruhostal.com.

Private or shared bath. Price includes airport/train/bus pick-up. Oxygen, kitchen for use in the evenings, book exchange. Rooms around a pretty colonial courtyard, some with no windows, good beds, pleasant, relaxing, some Inca walls. Also has **$$ Hostal Amaru II** (Chihuampata 642, San Blas, T084-223521, www.amaruhostal2.com), and **$$-$ Hostería de Anita** (Alabado 525-5, T084-225933, www.amaruhostal.com/hosteria_de_anita), with rooms or dorm beds, safe, quiet, good breakfast.

$$ Casa Elena
Choquechaca 162, T084-241202,
www.casaelenacusco.com.
French/Peruvian hostel, very comfortable, helpful staff, good choice.

$$ Casona Les Pleiades
Tandapata 116, T084-506430,
www.casona-pleiades.com.
Small guesthouse in renovated colonial house, cosy and warm, generous hosts, hot water, video lounge and book exchange, café, free airport pickup with reservation, lots of info.

$$ El Grial
Carmen Alto 112, T084-223012,
www.hotelelgrial.com.
Family-run, 2 star hostel, in a 17th-century building, coffee shop, laundry service.

$$ Hostal Kuntur Wasi
Tandapata 352-A, San Blas, T084-227570,
www.hospedajekunturwasi.com.
Great views, cheaper without bath, use of kitchen and laundry (both extra), owner speaks a bit of English and is very helpful and welcoming, a pleasant place to stay.

$$ Hostal María Esther
Pumacurco 516, T084-224382,
http://hostalmariaesther.free.fr.
Very comfortable, helpful, garden.

$$ Hostal Qorichaska
Nueva Alta 458, some distance from centre, T084-228974,
www.qorichaskaperu.com.
Rooms are clean and sunny, the older ones have traditional balconies. Also has dorms, mixed and men or women only. Laundry service. A good choice.

$$ Marani
Carmen Alto 194, San Blas, T084-249462.
Full of character, set around a courtyard, breakfast available, Dutch-owned hostel associated with Hope Foundation (www.stichtinghope.org), which builds schools, helps teachers and hospitals, good value.

$$ Niños/Hotel Meloc
Meloc 442, T084-231424,
www.ninoshotel.com.
Modern decor in colonial building. Hot water, excellent breakfast extra, restaurant, laundry service, luggage store, English spoken, run as part of the Dutch foundation **Niños Unidos Peruanos** and all profits are invested in projects to help street children. Also has **Niños 2/Hotel Fierro** (C Fierro 476, T084-254611), with all the same features.

$$ Pensión Alemana
Tandapata 260, San Blas, T084-226861,
www.cuzco.com.pe.
Colonial-style modern building. Swiss owned, welcoming, comfortable, discount in low season.

$$-$ Flying Dog Hostel
Choquechaca 469, T084-253997,
www.flyingdogperu.com.
Shared and private rooms and family suites, bar, living room with TV and DVD, buffet breakfast.

$$-$ Hitchhikers B&B Backpackers Hostel
Saphi 440, T084-260079,
www.hhikersperu.com.
Located close to the plaza, mixture of dorms and 1- to 3-bed private rooms with private or shared bath, laundry service.

$$-$ Hostal Loki
Cuesta Santa Ana 601, T084-243705,
www.lokihostel.com/en/cusco.
Huge hostel in a restored viceroy's residence on the steep Cuesta Santa Ana, dorms and rooms set around a beautiful courtyard, comfortable beds, hot water, free internet. A great meeting place.

$$-$ Mamá Simona Hostel
Ceniza 364, San Pedro, near the market,
T084-260408.
Traditional old house with rooms around a courtyard, doubles (with heating) and dorms, duvets, shared bathrooms, hot water, towel rental, breakfast available, laundry service, helpful.

$$-$ The Walk on Inn
Suecia 504, T084-235065,
www.walkoninn.com.pe.
2 blocks from the Plaza, dorms and rooms with private or shared bathrooms, breakfast extra, laundry service, free airport/bus station pick-up.

$ Albergue Casa Campesina
Av Tullumayo 274, T084-233466.
Shared bath, lovely place, funds support the Casa Campesina organization (www.cbc.org.pe), which is linked to local *campesina* communities (see also Store of the Weavers under Shopping, below).

$ Albergue Municipal
Quiscapata 240, San Cristóbal, T984-769954, alberguemunicipalcusco@ hotmail.com.

Youth hostel. Dormitories and double rooms with shared bath, great views, bar, cafeteria, small cooking facilities, laundry, luggage store, very clean, pleasant and good value.

$ The Blue House
Kiskapata 291 (parallel and above Tandapata), T084-242407, www. thebluehouse.info.
Cosy family hostal, good value. Reductions for longer stays, meals (except breakfast) US$3, hot shower, DVDs, great views.

$ Casa de La Gringa
Tandapata y Pasñapacana 148, T084-241168, www.casadelagringa.com.
Each room individually decorated, lots of art and colour, 24-hr hot water, DVD, CD player in the common areas, heaters in the main lounges. See also **Another Planet** (Tour operators), below.

$ El Balcón Colonial
Choquechaca 350, T084-238129.
Family house, fairly basic rooms, hot showers, good home cooking, use of family kitchen, laundry facilities extra, comfortable, safe, generous hosts.

$ Estrellita
Av Tullumayo 445, parte Alta,
T084-234134.
Most rooms with shared bath, 2 with private bath, basic but excellent value, safe parking available for bikes.

$ Hospedaje El Artesano de San Blas
Suytucato 790, San Blas, T084-263968, manosandinas@yahoo.com.
Many bright and airy rooms overlooking courtyard, quiet, taxis leave you at Plaza San Blas, then it's a steep walk uphill for 5-10 mins.

$ Hospedaje Inka

*Suytuccato 848, T084-231995, http://
hospedajeinka.weebly.com.*
Taxis leave you at Plaza San Blas, walk
steeply uphill for 5-10 mins, or phone the
hostal. Private or shared bath. Wonderful
views, spacious rooms, very helpful
owner, Américo.

$ Hostal Killipata

*Killichapata 238, just off Tambo de
Montero, T084-236668.*
Family-run lodging with variety of room
sizes, private or shared bath, good
showers, hot water and fully equipped
kitchen. Breakfast is extra.

$ Hostal Pakcha Real

*Tandapata 300, San Blas, T084-237484,
www.hostalpakchareal.com.*
Family run, hot water, relaxed, with or
without bath. Breakfast, cooking and
laundry facilities extra. Airport/train/bus
pick-up, but call ahead if arriving late.

$ Hostal Quipu

*Fierro 495, T084-236179,
www.hostalquipu.com.*
Small pleasant rooms with private bath
and reliable hot water, sunny patio,
modern kitchen facilities, helpful staff,
good value.

$ Hostal Wayras

*Nueva Alta 451, T084-237930,
wayrashouse@hotmail.com.*
Small quiet place, best rooms on top
floor, cheaper with shared bath, solar hot
water, small kitchen, attentive owner.

$ Maison de la Jeunesse

*Av El Sol, Cuadra 5, Pasaje Grace, Edif San
Jorge (down a small side street opposite
Museo Sitio de Qoricancha), T084-235617,
hostellingcusco@hotmail.com.*
Double rooms with bath or a bed
in a dorm with shared bath; TV and
video room, lockers, cooking facilities
and hot water. Affiliated to HI (www.
hihostels.com).

$ Miracle Inn

Av Huáscar 102, T084-237129.
Ample rooms, those in front get traffic
noise, private bath, near Wanchac
market and not far from colonial centre,
functional and good value.

Restaurants

Around the Plaza de Armas
There are many good cheap
restaurants on Procuradores,
Plateros and Tecseccocha.

$$$ Chicha

*Plaza Regocijo 261, p 2 (above El Truco),
T084-240520. Daily 1200-2400.*
Specializes in regional dishes created by
restaurateur Gastón Acurio (see under
Lima, Restaurants), Peruvian cuisine of
the highest standards in a renovated
colonial house, at one time the royal
mint, tastefully decorated, open-to-view
kitchen, bar with a variety of pisco sours,
good service.

$$$ Cicciolina

Triunfo 393, 2nd floor, T084-239510.
Sophisticated cooking focusing largely
on Italian/Mediterranean cuisine,
impressive wine list. Good atmosphere,
great for a special occasion.

$$$ El Truco

Plaza Regocijo 261. Open 0900-0100.
Excellent local and international dishes,
buffet lunch 1200-1500, nightly folk
music at 2045.

$$$ Fallen Angel

*Plazoleta Nazarenas 320, T084-258184.
Sun from 1500.*
International and *Novo Andino* gourmet
cuisine, great steaks, genuinely

innovative interior design, worth checking out their events.

$$$ Fusiones
Av El Sol 106, T084-233341.
Open 1100-2300.
In the La Merced commercial centre, 2nd floor. *Novo Andino* and international cuisine in a chic contemporary setting, fine wines.

$$$ Greens Organic
Santa Catalina Angosta 135, upstairs, T084-243379.
Exclusively organic, but not wholly vegetarian, ingredients in fusion cuisine and a fresh daily buffet, very good.

$$$ Incanto
Santa Catalina Angosta 135, T084-254753. Daily 1100-2400.
Under same ownership as **Inka Grill** and with the same standards, restaurant has Inca stonework and serves Italian dishes (pastas, grilled meats, pizzas), and desserts, accompanied by an extensive wine list. Also Peruvian delicatessen.

$$$ Inka Grill
Portal de Panes 115, Pl de Armas, T084-262992.
Specializing in *Novo Andino* cuisine, also home-made pastas, wide vegetarian selection, live music, excellent coffee and home-made pastries 'to go'.

$$$ La China
Santa Teresa 364, 2nd floor, T084-506462.
Reportedly one of the best *chifas* in Cuzco.

$$$ La Retama
Portal de Panes 123, 2nd floor, T084-226372. Daily 1030-2200.
Good food (also *Novo Andino*) and service, buffet dinner with live music and dance 1930-2030, art exhibitions.

$$$ Limo
Portal de Carnes 236, T084-240668.
On 2nd floor of a colonial mansion overlooking the Plaza de Armas, Peruvian cuisine of the highest standard, with strong emphasis on fish and seafood, fine pisco bar, good service and atmosphere.

$$$ MAP Café
In Museo de Arte Precolombino, Plaza de las Nazarenas 231.
Café by day (1000-1830), from 1830 to 2200 serves superb international and Peruvian-Andean cuisine, innovative children's menu, minimalist design and top-class service.

$$$ Tunupa
Portal Confiturias 233, p 2, Pl de Armas.
Large restaurant, small balcony overlooking Plaza, international, Peruvian and *Novo Andino* cuisine, good buffet US$15, nicely decorated, cocktail lounge, live music and dance at 2030.

$$$ Tupananchis
Portal Mantas 180, T084-245159.
Tasty *Novo Andino* and fusion cuisine in a sophisticated atmosphere.

$$ Pucará
Plateros 309. Mon-Sat 1230-2200.
Peruvian and international food (no language skills required as a sample plate of their daily menu is placed in the window at lunchtime), nice atmosphere.

$$ Sara
Santa Catalina Ancha 370, T084-261691.
Vegetarian-friendly organic café bistro, stylish and modern setting, menu includes both traditional Peruvian dishes as well as pasta and other international dishes.

$$ Víctor Victoria
Tecseccocha 466, T084-252854.
Mon-Sat 0800-2200.

Set lunch with salad bar, Peruvian dishes, vegetarian options.

$ El Encuentro
Santa Catalina Ancha 384, and Tigre 130. Daily 0800-2200.
Breakfast, economical *menú* and à la carte. Good vegetarian food, very busy at lunchtime.

$ El Fogón
Plateros 365.
Huge local *menú del día*, good solid food at reasonable prices. Very popular.

Cafés

Café El Ayllu
Almagro 133, and Marqués 263.
Classical/folk music, good atmosphere, superb range of milk products, wonderful apple pastries, good selection for breakfast, great juices, quick service. A Cuzco institution.

Café Cocla
Mesón De La Estrella 137.
Excellent coffee, also sells organic coffee beans, works with several cooperatives in the Cuzco region.

Café Halliy
Plateros 363.
Popular meeting place, especially for breakfast, good for comments on guides, has good snacks and 'copa Halliy' (fruit, muesli, yoghurt, honey and chocolate cake), also good vegetarian *menú* and set lunch.

Café Perla
Santa Catalina Ancha 304, on the plazoleta, T084-774130.
Extensive menu of light meals, sandwiches, desserts and coffee, including beans for sale roasted on the premises. Popular.

Dolce Vita
Santa Catalina Ancha 366. Open 1000-2100.
Delicious Italian ice cream.

Dos por Tres
Marquez 271.
Popular for over 20 years, great coffee and cakes.

La Bondiet
Heladeros 118. Open 0730-2300.
Upmarket French café with a good selection of sweet and savoury pastries, *empanadas*, good sandwiches, juices and coffee. A local favourite.

Museo del Café
Espaderos 136, around a beautifully restored colonial courtyard.
Coffee, sweets and a chance get to know the coffee making process. Coffee accessories for sale.

Yahuu! Juice Bar
Portal Confituría 249. Daily 0700-2300.
Fresh inexpensive juices and smoothies as well as sandwiches.

Beyond the Plaza, including San Blas

$$$ A Mi Manera
Triunfo 393, T084-222219.
Imaginative *Novo Andino* cuisine with open kitchen. Great hospitality and atmosphere.

$$$ Baco
Ruinas 465, T084-242808.
Wine bar and bistro-style restaurant, same owner as Cicciolina. Specializes in BBQ and grilled meats, also veggie dishes, pizzas and good wines. Unpretentious and comfy, groups welcome.

$$$ Pachapapa
Plazoleta San Blas 120, opposite church of San Blas, T084-241318.

A beautiful patio restaurant in a colonial house, good Cusqueña and other dishes, at night diners can sit in their own, private colonial dining room, attentive staff.

$$$ Papacho's
Portal de Belén 115, upstairs, off Plaza de Armas, T084-245359. Daily 1200-2400.
Gastón Acurio's upmarket US-style diner with a Peruvian twist in the heart of colonial Cuzco.

$$$-$$ Divina Comedia
Pumacurco 406, T084-437640. Daily 1230-1500, 1830-2300.
An elegant restaurant just 1 block from the Monasterio hotel, diners are enter tained by classical piano and singing. Friendly atmosphere with comfortable seating, perfect for a special night out, reasonable prices.

$$$-$$ Granja Heidi
Cuesta San Blas 525, T084-238383. Mon-Sat 1130-2130.
Delicious yoghurt, granola, ricotta cheese and honey and other great breakfast options. Also vegetarian dishes, a very good midday *menú* and steak at night. Highly recommended.

$$ El Paisa
Av El Sol 819, T084-501717. Open 0900-1700.
Typical northern Peruvian dishes including *ceviche* and goat.

$$ Inka Panaka
Tandapata 140, T084-235034.
Artistic flair, gallery of local artists' work. *Novo Andino* cuisine, and tasty innovative treats. Several vegetarian options, also breakfast.

$$ Jack's Café
Choquechaca y San Blas, T084-806960.
Excellent varied menu, generous portions, relaxed atmosphere, can get very busy at lunchtime, expect a queue in high season.

$$ Justina
Palacios 110. Mon-Sat from 1800.
Good value, good quality pizzería, with wine bar. It's at the back of a patio.

$$ Kushka...fé
Choquechaca 131-A and Espaderos 142. Daily 0700-2300.
Great food in a nice setting, English spoken.

$$ La Bodega 138
Herrajes 138, T084-260272.
Excellent pizza, good salads and pasta. Warm and welcoming.

$$ La Cusqueñita
Tullumayo y Av Garcilazo.
A traditional *picantería* serving Cuzco specialties, live music and dance show daily.

$$ Le Soleil
C San Agustin 275, in La Lune hotel, T084-240543, www.restaurante lesoleilcusco.com. Closed Wed.
Excellent restaurant using local products to make classic French cuisine.

$$ Los Toldos
Almagro 171 and San Andrés 219, T084-229829 (deliveries).
Grilled chicken, fries and salad bar, also *trattoria* with home-made pasta and pizza, delivery.

$$ Macondo
Cuesta San Blas 571, T084-229415.
Interesting restaurant with an imaginative menu, good food, well-furnished, gay friendly.

$$ Tacomanía
Tandapata 917.
Serving tacos cooked to order with freshly made Mexican fillings. Owned by Englishman Nick Garret.

$$ The Muse
C Triunfo 338, 2nd floor, T084-242030.
Restaurant lounge serving an international menu, lots of veggie options, live music every night, balcony seating, Wi-Fi. British owner Claire is a great source of information.

$$-$ Aldea Yanapay
Ruinas 415, p 2.
Good café serving breakfast, lunch and dinner. Run by a charity which supports children's homes (www.aldeayanapay.org).

$ Café Punchay
Choquechaca 229, T084-261504.
German-owned vegetarian restaurant, with a variety of pasta and potato dishes, good range of wines and spirits, large screen for international sports and you can bring a DVD for your own private movie showing.

Cafés

Chocolate
Choquechaca 162.
Good for coffee and cakes, but don't miss the gourmet chocolates.

El Hada
Arequipa 167.
Excellent home-made ice cream, unique flavors such as orange cardamom and cinnamon.

Juanito's Sandwich Café
Qanchipata 596.
Great grilled veggie and meaty burgers and sandwiches, coffee, tea and hot chocolate. Juanito himself is a great character and the café stays open late.

Manu Café
Av Pardo 1046.
Good coffee and good food too.

Panadería El Buen Pastor
Cuesta San Blas 579.
Very good bread, *empanadas* and pastries, proceeds go to a charity for orphans and street children.

Bars and clubs

Bars

Cross Keys Pub
Triunfo 350 (upstairs), T084-229227, www.cross-keys-pub-cusco-peru.com. Open 1100-0130.
Run by Barry Walker of Manu Expeditions, a Mancunian and ornithologist, cosy, darts, cable sports, pool, bar meals, plus daily half price specials Sun-Wed, great pisco sours, very popular, great atmosphere, free Wi-Fi.

Indigo
Tecseccocha 2, p 2, T084-260271.
Shows 3 films a day. Also has a lounge and cocktail bar and serves Asian and local food. A log fire keeps out the night-time cold.

Km 0 (Arte y Tapas)
Tandapata 100, San Blas.
Mediterranean themed bar tucked in behind San Blas, good snacks and tapas, with live music every night (around 2200).

Los Perros Bar
Tecseccocha 436. Open 1100-0100.
Great place to chill out on comfy couches, excellent music, welcoming, good coffee, tasty meals available (including vegetarian), book exchange, English and other magazines, board

games. Has a take-away only branch at Suecia 368, open 2400 to 0600 for good quality, post-club food.

Museo del Pisco
Santa Catalina Ancha 398, T084-262709, www.museodelpisco.org. Daily 1100-0100.
A bar where you can sample many kinds of pisco; tapas-style food served.

Norton's Pub
Santa Catalina Angosta 116.
Daily 0700-0300.
On the corner of the Plaza de Armas, fine balcony, microbrews, sandwiches and light meals, cable TV, English spoken, pool, darts, motorcycle theme. Very popular.

Paddy's Pub
Triunfo 124 on the corner of the plaza. Open 1300-0100.
Irish theme pub, deservedly popular, good grub.

Clubs

El Garabato Video Music Club
Plateros 316. Daily 1600-0300.
Dance area, lounge for chilling, bar, live shows 2300-0030 (all sorts of styles) and large screen showing music videos.

Mama Africa
Portal de Panes 109.
Cool music and clubber's spot, good food with varied menu, happy hour till 2300, good value.

Mythology
Portal de Carnes 298, p 2.
Mostly an early '80s and '90s combination of cheese, punk and classic, popular. Food in served in the jungle-themed **Lek Café**. They also show movies in the afternoons.

Temple
Tecseccocha y Tigre. Open 2100-0600.
A big nightclub set in a covered courtyard with large bar and pool table. Live bands some nights.

Ukuku's
Plateros 316.
US$1.35 entry, very popular, good atmosphere, good mix of music including live shows nightly. Also has a **restaurant** on the premises.

Entertainment

Folklore
Centro Qosqo de Arte Nativo, *Av El Sol 604, T084-227901*. Regular nightly folklore show from 1900 to 2030, entrance on BTC ticket.
Teatro Inti Raymi (Saphi 605, nightly at 1845, US$4.50), well worth it. **Teatro Municipal** (C Mesón de la Estrella 149, T084-227321 for information 0900-1300 and 1500-1900). Plays, dancing and shows, mostly Thu-Sun. They also run classes in music and dancing Jan-Mar which are great value.

Festivals

See also A month of festivals, page 385.
Feb Carnival in Cuzco is a messy affair with flour, water, cacti, bad fruit and animal manure being thrown about in the streets.
Easter Mon El Señor de los Temblores (Lord of the Earthquakes). Procession starting at 1600 outside the Cathedral. A large crucifix is paraded through the streets, returning to the Plaza de Armas around 2000 to bless the tens of thousands of people who have assembled there.

2-3 May **Vigil of the Cross** takes place at all mountaintops with crosses on them, a boisterous affair.

Jun **Corpus Christi** (Thu after Trinity Sun). All the statues of the Virgin and the saints from Cuzco's churches are paraded through the streets to the Cathedral. The Plaza de Armas is surrounded by tables with women selling *cuy* (guinea pig) and a mixed grill called *chiriuchu* (*cuy*, chicken, tortillas, fish eggs, water-weeds, maize, cheese and sausage) and lots of Cusqueña beer.

24 Jun The pageant of **Inti Raymi**. The Inca festival of the winter solstice, is enacted in Quechua at 1000 at the Qoricancha, moving on to Sacsayhuaman at 1300. Tickets for the stands can be bought a week in advance from the Emufec office (Santa Catalina Ancha 325), US$80, less if bought Mar-May. Travel agents can arrange the whole day for you, with meeting points, transport, reserved seats and packed lunch. Those who try to persuade you to buy a ticket for the right to film or take photos are being dishonest. On the night before Inti Raymi, the Plaza de Armas is crowded with processions and food stalls. Try to arrive in Cuzco 15 days before Inti Raymi.

28 Jul **Peruvian Independence Day**. Prices shoot up during these celebrations.

Aug On the last Sun is the **Huarachicoy** festival at Sacsayhuaman, a spectacular re-enactment of the Inca manhood rite, performed in dazzling costumes by boys from a local school.

8 Sep **Day of the Virgin** is a colourful procession of masked dancers from the church of Almudena, at the southwest edge of Cuzco, near Belén, to the Plaza de San Francisco. There is also a splendid fair at Almudena, and a free bull fight on the following day.

1 Nov **All Saints' Day**, celebrated everywhere with bread dolls and traditional cooking.

8 Dec **Cuzco Day**. Churches and museums close at 1200.

24 Dec **Santuranticuy**, 'the buying of saints', with a big crafts market in the plaza, very noisy until early hours of the 25th. This is one of the best festivals with people from the mountains coming to celebrate Christmas in Cuzco.

Shopping

Arts and crafts

In the Plaza San Blas and the surrounding area, authentic Cuzco crafts still survive. A market is held on Sat. Many leading artisans welcome visitors. Among fine objects made are Biblical figures from plaster, wheatflour and potatoes, reproductions of pre-Columbian ceramics and colonial sculptures, pious paintings, earthenware figurines, festive dolls and wood carvings.

Cuzco is one of the great weaving centres of Peru and excellent textiles can be found at good value. Be very careful of buying gold and silver objects and jewellery in and around Cuzco. Do not buy condor feathers, painted or unpainted, as it is illegal to sell or purchase them. Condors are being killed for this trade. The prison sentence is 4 years.

Agua y Tierra, *Plazoleta Nazarenas 167, and Cuesta San Blas 595, T084-226951.* Excellent quality crafts from rainforest communities.

Apacheta, *San Juan de Dios 250, T084-238210, www.apachetaperu.com.* Replicas of Pre-Inca and Inca textiles, ceramics, alpaca goods, contemporary art gallery, books on Andean culture.

Mercado Artesanal, *Av El Sol, block 4.* Good for cheap crafts.

Pedazo de Arte, *Plateros 334B.* A tasteful collection of Andean handicrafts, many designed by Japanese owner Miki Suzuki.

La Pérez, *Urb Mateo Pumacahua 598, Huanchac, T084-232186.* A big co-operative with a good selection; they will arrange a free pick-up from your hotel.

Seminario, *inside Museo de Arte Precolombino, Plaza Nazarenas.* Sells the ceramics of Seminario-Behar (see under Urubamba, page 399), plus cotton, basketry, jewellery, etc.

Books and maps
Centro de Estudios Regionales Andinos Bartolomé de las Casas, *Av Tullumayo 465, T084-233472, www. cbc.org.pe. Mon-Sat 1100-1400, 1600-1900.* Good books on Peruvian history, archaeology, etc.

Jerusalem, *Heladeros 143, T084-235408, Mon-Sat 1000-1400, 1600-2000.* English and Spanish books, maps, guidebooks, postcards, book exchange (2 for 1). Helpful owner.

Maratón, *Av de la Cultura 1020, across the street from the university, T084-225387.* Wide selection of IGN topographical maps, of interest to trekkers and cyclists.

SBS Librería Internacional, *Av El Sol 864, T084-248106, www.sbs.com.pe, Mon-Fri 0900-2030, Sat 0930-1330.* Good selection of books and maps.

Camping equipment
For renting equipment, check with tour agencies. Check the equipment carefully as it is common for parts to be missing or damaged. A deposit is asked, plus credit card, passport or plane ticket. White gas (*bencina*), US$3 per litre, can be bought at hardware stores. Stove spirit (*alcoól para quemar*) is available at some pharmacies; cooking gas canisters can be found at hardware stores and camping shops.

Edson Zuñiga Huillca, *Mercado Rosaspata, Jr Abel Landeo P-1, T084-802831, 3 mins from Plaza de Armas. Open 24 hrs a day, 7 days a week.* Repair camping equipment and footwear, also equipment rental, English and Italian spoken.

Tatoo, *Espinar 144, T084-236703, www. tatoo.ws.* High-quality hiking, climbing and camping gear, not cheap, but international brand names and their own lines.

Fabrics and alpaca clothing
Alpaca Golden, *Portal de Panes 151, T084-251724, alpaca.golden@terra.com. pe. Also at Plazoleta Nazarenas 175.* Designer, producer and retailer of fine alpaca clothing.

The Center for Traditional Textiles of Cuzco, *Av El Sol 603, T084-228117, www.textilescusco.org.* A non-profit organization that seeks to promote, refine and rediscover the weaving traditions of the Cuzco area. Tours of workshops, weaving classes, you can watch weavers at work. Also run 3-day weaving courses. Over 50% of the price goes direct to the weaver. Recommended.

Hilo, *Carmen Alto 260, T084-254536.* Fashionable items designed individually and handmade on-site. Run by Eibhlin Cassidy, she can adjust and tailor designs.

Josefina Olivera, *Portal Comercio 173, Plaza de Armas. Daily 1100-2100.* Sells old textiles and weavings, expensive but worth it to save pieces being cut up to make other item.

Kuna by Alpaca 111, *Plaza Regocijo 202, T084-243233, www.kuna.com.pe.* High-quality alpaca clothing with outlets also in hotels El Monasterio, Libertador and Machu Picchu Sanctuary Lodge.

Store of Weavers (Asociación Central de Artesanos y Artesanas del Sur Andino Inkakunaq Ruwaynin), *Av Tullumayo 274, T084-233466.* Store run by 6 local weaving communities, some of whose residents you can see working on site. All profits go to the weavers themselves.

Food and natural products

Choco Museo, *Garcilaso 210, 2nd floor, also in Ollantaytambo,T084-244765, www.chocomuseo.com.* Offers chocolate-making classes and runs trips to their cocoa plantation.

The Coca Shop, *Carmen Alto 115, San Blas, T084-260774.* Tiny shop selling an interesting selection of sweets and chocolates made using coca leaf flour. There is also plenty of information about the nutritional values of coca leaves.

Dried Fruit Shop, *Meloq 482.* Mon-Sat. Good quality and prices for a large variety of dried fruits and nuts.

La Cholita, *Los Portales Espinar 142B.* Special chocolates made with local ingredients.

San Isidro, *San Bernardo 134.* Mon-Fri 0900-1300, 1600-1900, Sat 0900-1200. Excellent local dairy products (great natural yoghurt and a variety of cheeses), honey and jams.

Jewellery

Calas, *Siete Angelitos 619-B, San Blas.* Handmade silver jewellery in interesting designs and alpaca goods from the community of Pitumarca.

Cusco Ink, *Choquechaca 131.* Tattoo and piercing studio. Also sells Peruvian clothing and jewellery including a wide variety of gauges.

Ilaria, *Portal Carrizos 258, T084-246253.* Branches in hotels Monasterio,

Libertador and at the airport. For recommended jewellery and silver.

Inka Treasure, *Triunfo 375, T084-227470.* With branches at Av Pardo 1080, Plazoleta Nazarenas 159 and Portal de Panes 163. Also at the airport and the airport in Juliaca. Fine jewellery including goldwork, mostly with pre-Columbian designs, and silver with the owner's designs. Tours of workshops at Av Circunvalación, near Cristo Blanco. The stores also incorporte the work of famed jeweller Carlos Chakiras.

Spondylus, *Plazoleta San Blas 617, T084-226929.* A good selection of interesting gold and silver jewellery and fashion tops with Inca and pre-Inca designs.

Markets

Wanchac (Av Garcilaso, southeast of centre) and **San Pedro Market** (see page 352) sell a variety of goods.

El Molino, beyond the Terminal Terrestre, sells everything under the sun at knock-down prices, but quality is not guaranteed and there are no tourist items; it's fascinating but crowded, so go there by colectivo or taxi and don't take valuables.

Music

Taki Museo de Música de los Andes, *Hatunrumiyoc 487-5.* Shop and workshop selling and displaying musical instruments, owner is an ethno-musicologist. Recommended for anyone interested in Andean music.

What to do

There are many travel agencies in Cuzco. The sheer number and variety of tours on offer is bewildering and prices for the same tour can vary dramatically. In general you should only deal directly with the agencies themselves. Do not deal with guides who claim to be employed by agencies listed below without verifying their credentials. Be sure to ask whatever questions you may have in advance. Doing so by email offers the advantage of getting answers in writing but it may also be worth visiting a prospective operator in person to get a feeling for their organization. Competition among agencies can be fierce, but remember that the cheapest option is often not the best. For the latest information, consult other travellers returning from trips; trip reports for members of South America Explorers are also useful. Student discounts are only obtainable with an ISIC card.

City tours cost about US$10-15 for 4 hrs; check what sites are included and that the guide is experienced. Open sightseeing bus tour, about 1 hr, US$7; tickets sold from the Western Union office on Plaza de Armas (C del Medio, T979-340615). Various 'free' walking tours of Cuzco meet at the Plaza de Armas around midday, the guides expect a minimum tip, ask how much in advance.

In general visitors to Cuzco are satisfied with their tours. Independent travellers should keep in mind, however, that you can do any trek and visit any archaeological site on your own, except for the Inca Trail to Machu Picchu. Visiting independently requires more time, effort and greater language skills than taking a package tour, but it opens the door to a wealth of authentic experiences beyond the grasp of mass tourism.

For a list of recommended Tour operators for Manu, including Manu Expeditions, see page 508.

Inca Trail and general tours
Only a restricted number of agencies are licensed to operate Inca Trail trips. **Sernanp** (Av José Gabriel Cosio 308, Urb Magisterial, 1 etapa, T084-229297, www.sernanp.gob.pe) verifies operating permits (see Visitors' tickets, page 344, for Dirección de Cultura office). Unlicensed agencies will sell Inca Trail trips, but pass clients on to the operating agency. This can cause confusion and booking problems at busy times, so book your preferred dates as early as possible in advance. Note also that many companies offer treks as alternatives to the trails to Machu Picchu. These treks are unregulated, so it is up to clients to

Professional Tour Operator Peru

ANDINA TRAVEL
Treks & Eco Adventure

Working for sustainable tourism & community development. | www.andinatravel.com

LARES	RIVER RAFTING
INCA TRAIL	CUSTOMIZED ITINERARIES
TRADITIONAL TOURS	FILM PRODUCTIONS
JUNGLE TRIPS	MOUNTAIN BIKING

The only operators of all the sections of the whole Inca Trail to Machu Picchu. | /andinatravelcusco

Plazoleta Santa Catalina 219, Cuzco - Peru | phone/fax. 00 51 84 251892 | sales@andinatravel.com

ensure that the trekking company does not employ the sort of practices (such as mistreating porters, not clearing up rubbish) which are now prohibited on the trails to Machu Picchu. See Essential Inca Trail, page 420.

Amazon Trails Peru, *Tandapata 660, T084-437374, or T984-714148, www.amazontrailsperu.com.* Trekking tours around the area, including the Inca Trail, Salkantay and Choquequirao. Also well-equipped and well-guided trips to Manu.

Amazonas Explorer, *see below.* Run a high-quality 5-day/4-night Inca Trail trek, every Tue, Mar-Nov.

Andean Treks, *Av Pardo 705, T084-225701, www.andeantreks.com.* Manager Tom Hendrickson uses high-quality equipment and satellite phones. This company organizes itineraries, from 2 to 15 days with a wide variety of activities in this area and further afield.

Andina Travel, Treks & Eco-Adventures, *Plazoleta Santa Catalina 219, T084-251892, www.andinatravel.com.* Eco-agency with more than 10 years operating all local treks. Has a reputation in Cuzco for local expertise and community projects.

Big Foot, *Triunfo 392 (oficina 213), T084-233836, www.bigfootcusco.com.* Tailor-made hiking trips, especially in the remote corners of the Vilcabamba and Vilcanota mountains; also the Inca Trail.

Chaska, *Garcilaso 265 p 2, of 6, T084-240424, www.chaskatours.com.* Dutch-Peruvian company offering cultural, adventure, nature and esoteric tours. They specialize in the Inca Trail, but also llama treks to Lares, treks to Choquequirao.

Culturas Peru, *Tandapata 354A, T084-243629, www.culturasperu.com.* Swiss/Peruvian company offering adventure, cultural, ecological and spiritual tours. Also specialize in alternative Inca trails.

Destinos Turísticos, *Portal de Panes 123, oficina 101-102, Plaza de Armas, T084-228168, www.destinosturisticosperu.com.* The owner speaks Spanish, English, Dutch and Portuguese and specializes in package tours from economic to 5-star budgets. Advice on booking jungle trips and renting mountain bikes. Very helpful.

EcoAmerica Peru, *C Marquez 259, of 8, T084-255136, www.ecoamericaperu.com.* Associated with **America Tours** (La Paz, Bolivia). Owned by 3 experienced consultants in responsible travel, conservation and cultural heritage. Specializes in culture, history, nature, trekking, biking and birding tours. Knowledgeable guides, excellent customer service for independent

travellers, groups or families. Also sell tours and flights to Bolivia.

Enigma Adventure, *C Fortunato L Herrera 214, Urb Magisterial, 1a Etapa, T084-222155, www.enigmaperu.com.* Well-organized, innovative trekking expeditions including a luxury service, Inca Trail and a variety of challenging alternatives. Also cultural tours to weaving communities, Ayahuasca therapy, climbing and biking.

Explorandes, *Av Garcilaso, T084-238380, www.explorandes.com.* Experienced high-end adventure company. Arranges a wide variety of mountain treks, also arranges tours across Peru for lovers of orchids, ceramics or textiles. Award-winning environmental practices.

Fertur, *C San Agustín 317, T084-221304, www.fertur-travel.com. Mon-Fri 0900-1900, Sat 0900-1200.* Cuzco branch of the Lima tour operator, see page 75.

Gatur Cusco, *Puluchapata 140 (a small street off Av El Sol 3rd block), T084-245121, www.gaturcusco.com.* Esoteric, ecotourism, and general tours. Owner Dr José (Pepe) Altamirano is knowledgeable in Andean folk traditions. Excellent conventional tours, bilingual guides and transportation. Guides speak English, French, Spanish and German. They can also book internal flights.

Habitats Peru, *Condominio La Alborada B-507, T084-246271, www.habitatsperu.com.* Birdwatching and mountain biking trips offered by Doris and Carlos. They also run a volunteer project near Quillabamba.

Hiking Peru, *Portal de Panes 109, of 6, T084-247942, T984-651414, www.hikingperu.com.* 8-day treks to Espíritu Pampa; 7 days/6 nights around Ausangate; 4-day/3-night Lares Valley Trek.

Inca Explorers, *C Peru W-18, Ttio, T084-241070, www.incaexplorers.com.*

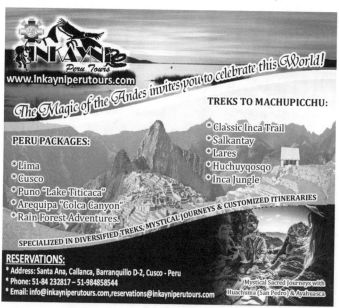

Specialist trekking agency for small group expeditions in socially and environmentally responsible manner. Also 2-week hike in the Cordillera Vilcanota (passing Nevado Ausangate), and Choquequirao to Espíritu Pampa.

InkaNatura Travel, *Ricardo Palma J1, T084-231138, www.inkanatura.com.* Offers tours with special emphasis on sustainable tourism and conservation. Knowledgeable guides.

Inkayni Tours, *Santa Ana Barranquillo, D2, T084-232817, www.inkayniperutours.com.* Offers trips and treks to Machu Picchu, city tours in Cuzco and alternative treks, such as Salkantay, Lares, Huchuy Qosqo.

Llama Path, *San Juan de Dios 250, T084-315925, www.llamapath.com.* A wide variety of local tours, specializing in Inca Trail and alternative treks, involved in environmental campaigns and porter welfare. Many good reports.

Mountain Lodges of Peru, *T084-243636 (Lima T01-421 6952), www.mountainlodgesofperu.com.* Offer a 7-day Machu Picchu Lodge-to-Lodge trek, going from purpose-built lodge to lodge. They also have a 5- or 7-day, Lodge-to-Lodge route from Lamay to Ollantaytambo via the Lares valley (http://laresadventure.com), with flexible options for each day's activities.

Peru Treks, *Av Pardo 540, T084-222722, www.perutreks.com.* Trekking agency initially set up by Englishman Mike Weston and his wife Koqui González. They pride themselves on good treatment of porters and support staff and have been consistently recommended for professionalism and customer care; a portion of profits go to community projects. The company specializes in trekking and cultural tours in the Cuzco region. Treks offered include Salkantay, the Lares Valley and Vilcabamba Vieja.

Q'ente, *Choquechaca 229, p 2, T084-222535, www.qente.com.* Their Inca Trail service is recommended. Also private treks to Salkantay, Ausangate, Choquequirao, Vilcabamba and Q'eros. Horse riding to local ruins costs US$35 for 4-5 hrs. Very good, especially with children.

Sky Travel, *Santa Catalina Ancha 366, interior 3-C, T084-240141, www.skyperu.com.* English spoken. General tours around city and Sacred Valley. Inca Trail with good-sized double tents and a dinner tent (the group is asked what it would like on the menu 2 days before departure). Other trips include Vilcabamba and Ausangate (trekking).

Southamerica Planet, *Garcilaso 210, of 201 T084-241424, www.southamerica planet.com.* Peruvian/Belgian-owned

agency offering the Inca Trail, other treks around Cuzco and packages within Peru, as well as Bolivia and Patagonia.

Tanager Tours, *T084-237254, Lima T01-669 0825, www.tanagertours.com.* Specializes in birdwatching tours throughout Peru but all will also arrange other tours. Owners live in Cuzco but currently no office. Most of their tours are arranged via the internet and they contact clients at their accommodation.

T'ika Trek, *no storefront, UK T07768-948366, www.tikatrek.com.* UK contact Fiona Cameron lived for many years in Peru and is a keen hiker and biker. With over 10 years in the Cuzco tourism business, Fiona provides high-quality personalized tours all over Peru as well as to the Galápagos Islands (Ecuador). Focus is on small groups and families.

Trekperu, *Av República de Chile B-15, Parque Industrial, Wanchac, T084-261501, www.trekperu.com.* Experienced trek operator as well as other adventure sports and mountain biking. Offers 'culturally sensitive' tours. Cusco Biking Adventure includes support vehicle and good camping gear (but providing your own sleeping bag).

United Mice, *Av Pachacútec 424 A-5, T084-221139, www.unitedmice.com.* Inca Trail and alternative trail via Salkantay and Santa Teresa, well-

established and reputable. Good guides who speak languages other than Spanish. Discount with student card, good food and equipment. City and Sacred Valley tours and treks to Choquequirao.

Wayki Trek, *Av Pardo 510, T084-224092, www.waykitrek.net.* Budget travel agency with a hostel attached, recommended for their Inca Trail service. Owner Americo Aquier knows the area very well. Treks to several almost unknown Inca sites and interesting variations on the 'classic' Inca Trail with visits to porters' communities. Also treks to Ausangate, Salkantay and Choquequirao.

Rafting, mountain biking and trekking

When looking for an adventure operator please consider more than just the price of your tour. Competition between companies in Cuzco is intense and price wars can lead to compromises in safety. Check the quality of safety equipment (lifejackets, etc) and ask about the number and experience of rescue kayakers and support staff. On large and potentially dangerous rivers like the Apurímac and Urubamba (where fatalities have occurred), this can make all the difference. Always use a licensed operator. See box, page 376.

ON THE ROAD
Staying safe when rafting

As the popularity of rafting has increased over the last few years, so too has the number of accidents, including fatalities, some due to negligence. The introduction of a new regulatory body in 2015 will, it is hoped, bring greater safety on what are some of the best whitewater runs anywhere in South America. Nevertheless rafting is an inherently dangerous sport so there are certain precautions you should observe.

As with many of Peru's adventure options, you get what you pay for. If price is all that matters to you, bear in mind the following: the cheaper the price, the less you get in terms of safety cover, experience of guides, quality of equipment, quantity and wholesomeness of food, emergency back up and environmental awareness (including proper disposal of waste). Choose only a rafting company legally registered in Peru, and check their safety record. Note that some companies with a poor safety record change their names.

You will often be required to show proof that your travel insurance will cover you for whitewater rafting. If you are unsure, check with your insurance company before you leave, as some policies have an additional charge. Very few policies cover Grade V rafting, so read the small print.

When signing up for a rafting trip, ask about the experience and qualifications of the guides or even, if possible, meet them. All guides should have some experience in rescue techniques, including whitewater rescue and wilderness first aid. Ask when they last took a course and what level they

Amazonas Explorer, *Av Collasuyo 910, T084-252846, http://amazonas-explorer. com*. Experts in rafting, inflatable canoeing, mountain biking, horse riding and hiking. English owner Paul Cripps has great experience. Most bookings from overseas, but they may be able to arrange a trip for travellers in Cuzco with advance notice. Rafting and inflatable canoeing includes the Urubamba, Apurímac and Tambopata rivers. Also offer the classic Inca Trail and various alternatives including Choquequirao to Machu Picchu. Multi-activity and family trips are a speciality. Mountain biking trips all use state-of-the-art equipment, expert guides and support vehicles where appropriate. All options are at the higher end of the market and are

highly recommended. Amazonas Explorer is a member of www.one percentfortheplanet.org, donating 1% of their turnover to a tree-planting project in the Lares watershed.
Apumayo, *Jr Ricardo Palma Ñ-11, Santa Mónica, Wanchac, T084-254816, www. apumayo.com. Mon-Sat 0900-1300, 1600-2000*. Urubamba rafting (from 0800-1530 every day); 3- to 4-day Apurímac trips. Also mountain biking to Maras and Moray in Sacred Valley, or from Cuzco to the jungle town of Quillabamba. This company also offers tours for disabled people, including rafting.
Apus Perú, *Cuichipunco 366, T084-232691, www.apus-peru.com*. Conducts most business by internet, specializes in alternatives to the Inca Trail, strong

achieved. Legislation demands that Grade IV+ guides hold the internationally recognized qualifications of Swift Water Rescue Technician and hold current first-aid certificates. At present there are a number of guides with the relevant qualifications, but you will only find them at companies who operate the longer, multi-day trips. Many Peruvian guides have worked overseas in the off-season, in Chile, Costa Rica, Europe and New Zealand. The more international experience your guide has, the more aware he will be of international safety practices. Unless you speak good Spanish, you should make sure the guides have a decent command of English; this is essential if you are going to understand their instructions. Also find out how many times they have rafted on this particular stretch of river.

Good equipment is essential. Under the new legislation, all rafting equipment will be checked regularly to ensure it meets basic safety standards. If possible, ask to see some of the gear provided. Basic essentials include self-bailing rafts for all but the calmest of rivers. Check how old your raft is and where it was made. Helmets should be provided and fit correctly. Life jackets must be of a lifeguard-recognized quality and be replaced regularly. Note that some new-looking life jackets are old ones, re-stuffed into new covers. Wetsuits or, at the very least, quality splash jackets should be provided as standard. Ask to see the first aid kit: what is in it and, most importantly, do they know how to use it? Satellite phones are essential on long trips in remote areas. You should also ask about tents and dry bags: how old are they? Do they leak? There is nothing worse than a soggy sleeping bag at the end of a hard day's rafting.

commitment to sustainability, well-organized. Associated with Threads of Peru NGO which helps weavers.
Pachatusan Trek, *Villa Union Huancaro G-4, B 502, T084-231817, www.pachatusan trek.com.* Offers a wide variety to treks, as alternatives to the Inca Trail, professional and caring staff, "simply fantastic".

River Explorers, *Pasaje Los Zafiros B-15, T084-260926 or T958-320673, www.riverexplorers.com.* An adventure company offering mountain biking, trekking and rafting trips (on the Apurímac, Urubamba and Tambopata). Experienced and qualified guides with environmental awareness.

Southern Crossings, *www.southern crossings.com*. Florida-based company offering mid- to high-end custom tours. Depart any day, cultural vacation packages, custom private and group tours.

Terra Explorer Peru, *T084-237352, www.terraexplorerperu.com*. Offers a wide range of trips from high-end rafting in the Sacred Valley and expeditions to the Colca and Cotahuasi canyons, trekking the Inca Trail and others, mountain biking, kayaking (including on Lake Titicaca) and jungle trips. All guides are bilingual.

Cultural tours

Milla Tourism, *Av Pardo 800, T084-231710, www.millaturismo.com. Mon-Fri 0800-1300, 1500-1900, Sat 0800-1300.* Mystical tours to Cuzco's Inca ceremonial sites such as Pumamarca and the Temple of the Moon. Guide speaks only basic English. They also arrange cultural and environmental lectures and courses.

Shamans and drug experiences

San Pedro and Ayahuasca have been used since before Inca times, mostly as a sacred healing experience. If you choose to experience these plants, only do so under the guidance of a reputable agency or shaman and always have a friend with you who is not partaking. If the medicine is not prepared correctly, it can be highly toxic and dangerous. Never buy from someone who is not recommended; never buy off the streets, and never try to prepare the plants yourself.

Another Planet, *Tandapata y Pasñapacana 148, San Blas, T084-241168, or T974-792316, www.anotherplanet peru.org*. Run by Lesley Myburgh, who operates mystical and adventure tours in and around Cuzco, and is an expert in San Pedro cactus preparation. She arranges San Pedro sessions for healing in the garden of her house outside Cuzco. Tours meet at La Casa de la Gringa, see Where to stay, above.

Etnikas Travel & Shamanic Healing, *Herrajes 148, T084-244516, www.etnikas. com*. A shamanic centre now offering travel for mind, body and spirit and the sale of natural products from the Andes and the jungle. Expensive but serious in their work.

Sumac Coca Travel, *San Agustín 245, T084-260311*. Mystical tourism, offering Ayahuasca and San Pedro ceremonies, and also more conventional cultural tourism. Professional and caring.

Private guides

As most of the sights do not have any information or signs in English, a good guide can really improve your visit. Either arrange this before you set out or contract one at the sight you are visiting. A tip is expected at the end of the tour. Tours of the city or Sacred Valley cost US$50 for half-day, US$65 full day; a guide to Machu Picchu charges US$80 per day. A list of official guides is held by **Agotur Cusco** (C Heladeros 157, Of 34-F, p 3, T084-233457). **South American Explorers** also has the contact details for recommended local guides. See also www.leaplocal.org.

Transport

Air

The airport is at Quispiquilla, near the bus terminal, 1.6 km from centre, airport information T084-222611/601. There are plans to build a new airport at Chinchero, 23 km northwest of the city (see page 399). The airport can get very busy; check in at least 2 hrs before your flight.

Flights may be delayed or cancelled during the wet season, or may leave early if the weather is bad. The Arrivals area has mobile phone rentals, ATMs, LAC Dollar money exchange, an Oxyshot oxygen sales stand, an **iPerú** office, phone booths, restaurant, cafeteria and a Tourist Protection Bureau desk. Hotel representatives and travel agents operate at the airport offering transport to particular hotels for arriving visitors without prior bookings; take your time to choose a hotel at a price you can afford. If you already have a booking, taxis and tourist minibuses meet new arrivals and (should) take you to the hotel of your choice: be insistent. A taxi to and from the airport costs US$5-7 (US$11 from the official taxi desk). Colectivos cost US$0.30 between Plaza San Francisco and the airport car park.

To **Lima**, 55 mins, over 30 daily flights with **Avianca/TACA**, **Star Perú**, **LAN** and **Peruvian Airlines**. To **Arequipa**, 30 mins daily with **LAN and Avianca**. To **Juliaca** (for Puno), 1 hr daily with **LAN**. To **Puerto Maldonado**, 30 mins, with **LAN** and **Star Perú**. To **La Paz**, **Peruvian Airlines** and **Amaszonas** (www.amaszonas.com), 1 hr, daily.

Bus
Long distance The busy, often crowded Terminal Terrestre is on Av Vallejo Santoni, block 2 (Prolongación Pachacútec). Colectivo from centre US$0.50 (not safe with luggage), taxi US$2-3. Platform tax US$0.50.

To **Lima,** US$35-65, a long ride (20-24 hrs) and worth paying for a comfortable bus. The route is via **Abancay** (US$7, 5 hrs) and **Nazca** (US$30, 13 hrs) on the Panamerican Highway. It is paved, but floods in the wet season often damage large sections. At night, take a

Tip...
If you're prone to travel sickness, take precautions on the way from Cuzco to Abancay; there are many curves but the scenery is magnificent.

blanket or sleeping bag to ward off the cold. Better companies to Lima include: **Molina**, daily at 2000; **Cruz del Sur** at 1400 and 1800; **Móvil Tours** at 1800 and **Oltursa** at 1600. **Bredde** has most frequent service (5 daily) to Abancay; others include **Turismo Ampay**, **Turismo Abancay** and **Expreso Huamanga**. **Los Chankas** to Abancay at 1930 continues to **Andahuaylas** (US$12.50, 9 hrs) and **Ayacucho** (US$22, 16 hrs).

To **Juliaca**, 344 km, US$5.40 normal, US$9 semi-cama, US$12.50-17 cama, 5-6 hrs, with **Power** every 2 hrs, 0530-2330; several others. The road is fully paved, but after heavy rain buses may not run. To **Puno**, 388 km, 6-7 hrs; there are 3 levels of service, all via Juliaca: regular, stopping in Juliaca, US$7-12; direct, US$15-27, with **Tour Perú** (www.tourperu.com.pe), Cruz del Sur or **Transzela** (www.transzela.com.pe); and tourist service with 5 stops (Andahuaylillas church, Raqchi, Sicuani for lunch, La Raya and Pucará), US$45-50 (includes lunch, may or may not include entry tickets; ask), 10 hrs. Several companies offer the tourist service; all leave from private terminals: **Inka Express** at 0700 from Av La Paz C-32, Urb El Ovalo, Wanchac, T084-247887; **Turismo Mer** at 0730 from Av La Paz A-3, Urb El Ovalo, Wanchac, T084-245171, www.turismomer.com.pe; and **Wonder Perú** at 0715 from Av 28 de Julio R2-1, Urb Ttio, Wanchac. In high season, reserve 2 days ahead. **Note** It is advisable to travel by day on the Juliaca-

Puno-Cuzco route, for safety as well as the views.

To **Arequipa** (via Juliaca), 521 km, 10-11 hrs, with **Cruz del Sur** at 2000 and 2030, US$37-47; **Cromotex** at 1900, 2000 and 2045, US$11-36; **Flores** at 0630 and 2030, US$11; **Power** at 0500 and 1700, US$11; many others, mostly at night. A tourist service direct to **Chivay** on the **Colca Canyon** is offered by **4M Express** (Av 28 de Julio, Urbanización Ttio, Wanchac, T054-452296, www.4m-express.com), Tue, Thu and Sat at 0700, US$65 (lunch extra); see Colca Canyon Transport, page 291, for details.

To **Puerto Maldonado**, **Móvil** at 1000 and 2100, US$18-30, 10-11 hrs; also **Transportes Iguazú**, **Machupicchu**, **Palomino** and **Mendivil**, several daily.

To the Sacred Valley There are 2 routes to Urubamba and Ollantaytambo: one via Pisac and Calca, the other via Chinchero. It is worth going on one and returning on the other. To **Pisac** (32 km, 1 hr, US$1.50), **Calca** (50 km, 1½ hr, US$1.50) and **Urubamba** (72 km via Pisac and Calca, 2 hrs, US$1.50), colectivos and minibuses from C Pututi near Av la Cultura (see map), leave when full 0600-1800. Buses returning from Pisac are often full; last one back leaves around 2000. Taxis charge about US$20 for the round trip to Pisac.

To **Chinchero** (23 km, 45 min US$2), **Urubamba** (50 km via Chinchero, 1½ hr, US$1.50), **Ollantaytambo** (70 km via Chinchero and Urubamba, 2 hrs, US$3.50-5), colectivos and minibuses from C Pavitos near Av Grau (see map). Taxi to Ollantaytambo US$22 one way.

Taxi

In Cuzco taxis are recommended when arriving by air, train or bus. They have fixed prices but you have to stay alert to overpricing (always agree on the price in advance): in the centre US$1.50 in town (50% more after 2100 or 2200). Safer and more expensive are radio-dispatched taxis with a sign on the roof, including **Aló Cusco**, T084-222222, **Ocarina**, T084-247080, and many others. Trips to **Sacsayhuaman**, US$10; ruins of **Tambo Machay** US$15-20 (3-4 people); day trip US$50-85.

Train

PerúRail uses Estación Wanchac (Av El Sol, T084-238722). The ticket office is open Mon-Fri 0700-1700, Sat, Sun and holidays 0700-1200, and offers direct information and sales for all PerúRail services. There is also a **Perú Rail** office at Portal de Carnes 214, open Mon-Fri 1000-2200, Sat, Sun and holidays 1400-2300 (take your passport or a copy when buying tickets). You can also buy tickets on www.perurail.com, at Lima airport (kiosk in domestic departures) or through a travel agent.

The *Andean Explorer* to **Puno** leaves Wanchac at 0800, Mon, Wed, Fri (Apr-Oct) and Sat, arriving at Puno around 1800; sit on the left for views. The train makes a stop to view the scenery at **La Raya**. Always check whether the train is running in the rainy season, when services may be cancelled. Cuzco to Puno costs US$268, Puno to Cuzco US$161; both US$5 less in low season. Meals are served on the train. When arriving in Cuzco, a tourist bus meets the train to take visitors to hotels whose touts offer rooms.

Trains to **Machu Picchu** and the **Sacred Valley** leave from Poroy, 7.5 km east of the centre, see page 418.

Around Cuzco

head upstream to avoid the crowds

The main road from Cuzco to Lake Titicaca and Arequipa follows the Río Vilcanota upstream to La Raya, the border with the neighbouring department of Puno. Along the route are archaeological sites, fascinating colonial churches, beautiful lakes and the majestic Ausangate massif, where you can do some serious high-altitude trekking.

Southeast of Cuzco

Between the villages of Saylla and Oropesa are the extensive **Tipón ruins** ① *5-km climb from village, US$3.60; take a combi to Oropesa, then a taxi*, which include baths, terraces, irrigation systems, possibly an agricultural laboratory and a temple complex, accessible from a path leading from just above the last terrace. **Oropesa**, whose church contains a fine ornately carved pulpit, is the national 'Capital of Bread'; try the delicious sweet circular loaves known as *chutas*.

Paucartambo and around

At **Huambutío**, north of the village of Huacarpay, the road divides, with one branch leading northwest to Pisac and the other heading north to Paucartambo, on the eastern slope of Andes. This remote town, 80 km east of Cuzco, has become a popular tourist destination with basic accommodation. In the Centro Cultural is the Museo de los Pueblos, with exhibits on the history, culture, textiles and society of the region, including the famous **Fiesta de la Virgen del Carmen** (Mamacha Carmen; see page 470). This is a major attraction, with masked dancers enacting rituals and folk tales. In the dry season, you can travel 44 km from Paucartambo, to **Tres Cruces**, along the Pilcopata road, turning left after 25 km. Come here for the sunrise in June and July, when peculiar climactic conditions make it appear that three suns are rising. Tour agencies in Cuzco can arrange transport and lodging.

Piquillacta

Daily 0700-1730, US$3.60. Buses to Urcos will drop you near the entrance.

Further on from Huacarpay are the extensive pre-Inca ruins of Piquillacta (which translates as the City of Fleas). This was an administrative centre at the southern end of the Huari Empire. The whole site is surrounded by a wall encompassing many enclosed compounds with buildings of over one storey; it appears that the walls were plastered and finished with a layer of lime. On the opposite side of the highway from Piquillacta is **Laguna de Huacarpay** (also known as Moina) and the ruins that surround it: Kañarakay, Urpicancha and the impressive Huari aqueduct of Rumicolca. A guide will help to find the more interesting structures. It's good to hike or cycle and birdwatch around the lake.

Andahuaylillas to Urcos

Buses from Cuzco to Urcos leave when full from Av de la Cultura y Pje Carrasco, opposite the Hospital Regional, US$1, 1 hr, passing Andahuaylillas en route.

Andahuaylillas, 32 km southeast of Cuzco, has a lovely shady plaza and beautifully restored early 17th-century **church** ⓘ *daily 0800-1800, on CBA ticket or US$5.50.* It's known as the 'Andean Sistine Chapel', due to its fabulous frescoes. There's also a splendid doorway and a gilded main altar. The next village, **Huaro**, also has a church whose interior is entirely covered with colourful frescoes. **Urcos**, meanwhile, is a chaotic commercial centre and transport hub; beware overcharging for everything here.

> **Tip...**
> South of Urcos, stop off at the villages of **Cusipata**, which has an Inca gate and wall, and **Checacupe**, which has a lovely church.

Cordillera Vilcanota

The Cordillera Vilcanota, east of Cuzco, is the greatest concentration of mountains and glaciers in southern Peru with at least four great peaks towering above 6000 m in densely packed icy masses. Viewed from the ruins of Sacsayhuaman, Ausangate, at 6384 m the range's loftiest member, is impressive even from a distance of nearly 100 km, but in the Vilcanota mountains Ausangate is just the beginning. The Vilcanota rise up from the northern altiplano, so treks into the region rarely, if ever, drop below 4000 m. Life is harsh for the communities who live in the shadow of these great peaks; knowledge of Spanish is often limited or non-existent, and the people's respect for ancient ways and the power of the apus (mountain spirits), runs strong.

A spectacular road from Urcos crosses the Eastern Cordillera to Puerto Maldonado in the jungle (428 km, see page 509). Some 82 km from Urcos, near the base of **Nevado Ausangate**, is the town of **Ocongate**, a friendly regional centre with most services and a good place to prepare for trekking. Beyond Ocongate, **Tinqui** is a smaller, colder town with basic places to stay and eat; it's the starting point for hikes around Ausangate (see below). From Mahauyani, 12 km beyond Tinqui, a wide trail runs 8.5 km up to the sanctuary of **Señor de Q'Olloriti** at 4700 m, where a massive festival is held each June (see A month of festivals, page 385); several Cuzco agencies offer tours. Above the Christian sanctuary are the glaciers of Nevado Cinajara, the original object of devotion and still considered a sacred site. There is good trekking in the area and few visitors outside the festival.

Continuing east, some 47 km after passing the snow line on the Hualla-Hualla pass, at 4820 m, the super-hot thermal baths of **Marcapata** ⓘ *173 km from Urcos, US$0.20,* provide a relaxing break. Beyond this point, what is arguably the most spectacular road in Peru descends the eastern flank of the Andes towards Puerto Maldonado (see page 509).

ON THE ROAD
The last bridge

The great Inca road which connected the vastness of the empire was built not only of monumental stones but also of humble straw. In a land incised by deep chasms and rushing rivers, roads are of little use without bridges, and the greatest Inca suspension bridges were made of straw rope.

The most famous of these, 45 m long and suspended 36 m above the water, crossed the canyon of the Río Apurímac not far from the current road between Cuzco and Abancay. It was first accurately measured and photographed in 1864 by the American explorer George Squire and immortalized 63 years later by Thornton Wilder in his novel, *The Bridge of San Luis Rey*. By then the great bridge was no more; sometime in the 1890s, after over 600 years of existence, it was abandoned and collapsed.

In an environment of intense solar radiation and heavy rainfall during part of the year, straw fibre degrades rapidly so Inca suspension bridges had to be rebuilt on a regular basis. Today that tradition continues in only one place, at Q'eswachaka, also on the Apurímac, about 200 km upstream from the bridge described by Squire and Wilder (see page 384). Every year in June, two weeks before *Inti-Raymi*, over 400 families from four communities join forces for four days to reconstruct their Inca bridge using ancestral tools and materials.

Each family is required to contribute 40 arms' length of cord made of twisted *q'oya*, a tough flexible highland straw. Exactly 30 strands of cord are carefully laid out alongside each another and twisted again into a thicker rope, which is, in turn, braided into the heavy cables which form the floor of the bridge. The cables are laboriously tensioned in an impressive effort requiring the brute force of 30 men. Then the taut cables are woven together into a single unit and covered with *chilca* sticks. Thin cords are strung from the handrails, also made of straw rope, to the floor to form the sides of the bridge.

Only the *chacacamayoc* (bridge-master) knows all the secrets of the process, handed down through countless generations of his family, and he constantly supervises the work of his companions. Throughout the construction period, a small but important group of Andean priests make offerings of coca leaves, alcohol and incense to *Pachamama* (Mother Earth) to propitiate a successful and accident-free effort. Even though women prepare most of the original cord, they are strictly forbidden to approach the bridge while it is under construction.

Once complete, the bridge is inaugurated with great ceremony and the event culminates with a day-long festival of food, drink, music and dance. In 2014 the bridge at Q'eswachaka was declared a UNESCO World Heritage Site.

★**Ausangate Trek** ① *Entry US$3.50 at Tinqui plus US$3.50 at each of 3 communities along the route.* The hike around the mountain of Ausangate is spectacular. There are two popular routes requiring three to six days. It is hard going, with a pass over 5000 m and camping above 4000 m, so you need to be fit and acclimatized. Temperatures in high season (April-October) can drop well below zero at night. It is recommended to take a guide and/or *arriero*. *Arrieros* and mules can be hired in Tinqui: US$12 per day for a guide, US$10 per mule, more for a saddle horse. *Arrieros* also expect food. Make sure you sign a contract with full details. Buy supplies in Cuzco or Ocongate. Maps are available at the IGN in Lima, **Maratón** in Cuzco (see Shopping above), or South American Explorers. Cuzco agencies and Hostal Tinqui (see Where to Stay, below) run tours from about US$120. Bring your own warm sleeping bag.

Q'eswachaka

At Combapata (50 km from Urcos) a paved road climbs west for 16 km, through a region of large highland lakes, to the cold regional centre of **Yanaoca** at 3950 m. Yanaoca has simple places to stay and eat, and provides access to the village of Quehue, 20 km further south. Near the village an Inca bridge spans the upper Río Apurímac at **Q'eswachaka**. The bridge, a UNESCO World Heritage Site, is 15 m long and is made entirely of straw, woven and spliced to form cables which are strung across the chasm. The bridge is rebuilt each year in June, during a unique and spectacular four-day event (see The last bridge, page 383). Cuzco operators offer tours during the festival or you can go on your own at any time of the year, although it's not safe to cross the bridge between December and June.

Raqchi and around

Continuing on the main road to Sicuani, **Tinta**'s church has a brilliant gilded interior and an interesting choir vault. **Raqchi** is the scene of the region's great folklore festival (see A month of festivals, opposite) and also the site of the **Viracocha Temple** ① *US$5.50, take a bus from Cuzco towards Sicuani, US$3.50.* John Hemming wrote: "What remains is the central wall, which is adobe above and Inca masonry below. This was probably the largest roofed building ever built by the Incas. On either side of the high wall, great sloping roofs were supported by rows of unusual round pillars, also of masonry topped by adobe. Nearby is a complex of barracks-like buildings and round storehouses. This was the most holy shrine to the creator god Viracocha, being the site of a miracle in which he set fire to the land – hence the lava flow nearby. The landscape is extraordinary, blighted by huge piles of black volcanic rocks."

You can do a homestay here with pottery classes and a walk to the extinct Quimsachata volcano. There is also simple accommodation in the nearby town of **San Pedro**, along the main road to Sicuani. Beyond San Pedro, the road continues southeast to Sicuani, La Raya and the department of Puno. For details see page 334.

ON THE ROAD

A month of festivals

By April most of the corn has been brought in and the large ears of *choclo cusqueño* set out to dry in the sun. May brings a change of climate and new potatoes are ready to be turned into *chuño* and *moraya* (two dehydrated forms of this staple food) as soon as overnight temperatures drop below freezing. If it has been a good harvest then sustenance is assured for the coming year, and the Quechua people are free to turn their attention to other pursuits. In the department of Cuzco June is the month of *fiestas*.

One of the first celebrations takes place at **Q'eswachaka** during the first weekend of the month, centred on the reconstruction of the Inca rope bridge (see box, page 383).

This is followed by the great pilgrimage of **Q'Olloriti**, the multitudinous Snow Star Festival held at a sanctuary at 4700 m in the Cordillera Vilcanota near Mahauyani. The festival pays simultaneous homage to a venerated image of Christ and the mountain deity *Apu Cinajara*. Q'Olloriti builds to a crescendo over two weeks, culminating on the Tuesday after Trinity Sunday (eight weeks after Easter Sunday). Many participants then make their way to the city of Cuzco (the more devout go on foot) for **Corpus Christi**, held two days later on Thursday. All the statues of the Virgin and saints from Cuzco's churches are paraded through the streets to the Cathedral and special foods are served.

The second or third weekend in June is the turn of Raqchi, where the **folklore dance festival** draws participants from all over Peru. Finally, on 24 June, is the greatest celebration of all: **Inti Raymi** (the solstice) in Cuzco, both an enduring link to ancient rites and beliefs as well as a major tourist event.

In addition to these best-known and heavily attended festivities, there are celebrations in towns and villages throughout the department of Cuzco. The dates vary from year to year and you should always confirm these locally in advance.

Listings Upper Vilcanota Valley

Where to stay

Andahuaylillas to Urcos
These are all in Andahuaylillas; the one decent hostal in Urcos (**$ El Amigo**, C Carpintero y Jr César Vallejo, T084-307064) is often full.

$ Hostal El Nogal
Plaza de Armas, T084-771164.
Small place with 3 warm bright rooms, shared bath, electric shower, restaurant.

$ Hostal Chiss
C Quispicanchis 216, T984-857294.
Economical accommodation in a family home with kitchen and washing facilities, shared bath, electric shower, some mattresses are poor. Effusively friendly owner, Sr Ladislao Belota.

Cordillera Vilcanota

$ Hostal Siesta
C Libertad, Ocongate, T996-603606.
Pleasant rooms with private or shared
bath, patio, very clean and good value.
Helpful owner Sr Raúl Rosas changes
US$ at fair rates.

$ Hostal Tinqui
*On the right-hand side as you enter
Tinqui from Ocongate, T974-327538,
Cuzco T084-227768, ausangate_tour@
outlook.com.*
Basic rooms with shared bath, cold water,
meals available. Sr Cayetano Crispín,
the owner, is knowledgeable
and can arrange guides, mules, etc.

A reliable source of trekking and
climbing information.

Transport

Paucartambo
Buses to Paucartambo leave from the
Paradero Control in the San Jerónimo
neighbourhood of Cuzco at 0800, 0900
and 1500, US$3.25, 3 hrs; also vans from
the same location, every half-hour 0600-
1800, US$4.25.

Cordillera Vilcanota
Buses to **Ocongate** (some continue
to **Tinqui**) leave from Av Tomasatito
Condemayta, corner of the Coliseo
Cerrado in Cuzco, every 30 mins, 0430-
1800, 3 companies, US$3.25, 2½ hrs.

Cuzco to Choquequirao

a site to rival Machu Picchu

West of Cuzco a road heads towards Abancay (see page 459) for access to
Ayacucho and the central highlands, or Nazca and the coast. There are enough
Inca sites on or near this road to remind us that the empire's influence spread to
all four cardinal points. Two kilometres before Limatambo a few hundred metres
from the road, are the ruins of Tarahuasi (76 km from Cuzco, US$6), comprising a
very well-preserved Inca temple platform, with 28 tall niches, and a long stretch
of fine polygonal masonry. The ruins are impressive, enhanced by the orange
lichen which gives the walls a honey colour.

Further along the Abancay road, 100 km from Cuzco, is the exciting descent
into the Apurímac canyon, near the former Inca suspension bridge that inspired
Thornton Wilder's *The Bridge of San Luis Rey*.

★ Choquequirao
Entry US$13.50, students US$6.75.

Choquequirao is another 'lost city of the Incas', built on a ridge spur almost 1600 m
above the Apurímac at 3100 m. It is reckoned to be a larger site than Machu Picchu,
but the buildings are more spread out. The main features of Choquequirao are
the **Lower Plaza**, considered by most experts to be the focal point of the city. The
Upper Plaza, reached by a huge set of steps or terraces, has what are possibly ritual
baths. A beautiful set of slightly curved agricultural terraces run for over 300 m
east-northeast of the Lower Plaza.

The **usnu** is on a levelled hilltop, ringed with stones and giving awesome 360° views. The **Ridge Group**, still shrouded in vegetation, is a large collection of unrestored buildings some 50-100 m below the usnu. The **Outlier Building**, thought to be the priests' residence, is isolated and surrounded on three sides by sheer drops of over 1.5 km into the Apurímac Canyon. It has some of the finest stonework in Choquequirao. The **Llama Terraces** are 200 m below and west of the Lower Plaza, a great set of agricultural platforms beautifully decorated with llamas in white stone. East of the Lower Plaza are two other very large and impressive groups of terraces built on nearly vertical slopes.

Tip...
Some tours allow insufficient time at Choquequirao (at least one full day is highly recommended), so enquire before you sign up.

Part of what makes Choquequirao so special is its isolation. At present, the site can only be reached on foot, a tough and exceptionally rewarding trek which attracts fewer than 50 hikers a day in high season and far fewer at other times. Sadly, there are plans to build a cablecar to Choquequirao which would convert it into a mass tourism alternative to Machu Picchu, although construction had not yet begun in early 2015.

The route to Choquequirao begins in (San Pedro de) **Cachora**, a village on the south side of the Apurímac, reached by a side road from the Cuzco–Abancay highway, shortly after Saywite. Take an Abancay-bound bus from Cuzco, four hours to the turn-off called Ramal de Cachora, where cars wait for passengers, then it's a 30-minute descent from the road to Cachora village. From the village you need at least a day to descend to the Río Apurímac then another day or two to climb up to Choquequirao, depending on your condition and how much weight you are carrying. Horses can be hired to carry your bags. Allow one or two days at the site. The route is well signed and in good condition, with several nice campsites (some with showers) en route.

You can either return to Cachora the way you came or continue two to four days from Choquequirao to Yanama, and then on to either Huancacalle (see page 424) or to Totora, Santa Teresa and Machu Picchu (see page 409). These treks are all long and demanding. Cuzco agencies offer all-inclusive trekking tours to Choquequirao; some continue to Yanama and Santa Teresa, fewer to Huancacalle.

Listings Cuzco to Choquequirao

Where to stay

$$ Casa de Salcantay
200 m below the Plaza, Cachora, T984-281171, www.salcantay.com.
Price includes breakfast, dinner available if booked in advance, very nice comfortable rooms, fantastic views. Dutch-Peruvian run, Dutch, English, German spoken. Very helpful owners Jan and Giovana can organize treks.

$$ Los Tres Balcones
Jr Abancay, Cachora, www.choquequirau.com.

Hostel designed as start and end-point for the trek to Choquequirao. Breakfast included, comfortable, hot showers, restaurant and pizza oven, camping. They run an all-inclusive 5-day trek to Choquequirao. May be closed when there is no group, book in advance.

$$-$ Casa Nostra
500 m below Cachora off the road to Capuliyoc, T958-349949, matteoagnusdei@libero.it.
Rooms with private bath and dorms, includes breakfast, other meals available, superb views, Italian-Peruvian run by Matteo and Judith, opened in 2014.

$ Hospedaje Salcantay
1 block above the Plaza, Cachora, T958-303055.
Simple rooms with clean shared bathrooms, warm water, large yard, good value.

Transport

Bus
From Cuzco take any bus towards Abancay; **Bredde** has 5 daily starting 0600, US$7, 4 hrs, to **Ramal de Cachora**. Colectivos from Ramal de Cachora to **Cachora** village, US$1.80, 30 min, beware overcharging. Colectivos also run all day from Prolongación Núñez in Abancay to Cachora, US$3.50, 1½ hrs. **Note** when travelling to Cachora, avoid changing vehicles in Curahuasi, where drivers have attempted to hold up tourists.

Sacred Valley
of the Incas

the Incas' country estates

As the Río Vilcanota flows north and west, it waters the agricultural heartland that provided the context for the great city of Cuzco. Here the Incas built country estates, temples, fortresses and other monumental works and, in the process, it became their 'Sacred Valley'.

The name conjures up images of ancient, god-like rulers who saw the landscape itself as a temple; their tributes to this dramatic land survive in places such as Machu Picchu, Ollantaytambo, Pisac and countless others. For the tourist, the most famous sights are now within easy reach of Cuzco and draw massive crowds, but there remains ample scope for genuine exploring, to see lost cities in a less 21st-century setting. If archaeology is not your thing, there are markets to enjoy, birds to watch, trails for mountain-biking and a whole range of hotels to relax in.

West of the towns of the Sacred Valley on a ridge above the Río Vilcanota lies the reason for most tourists' visit to Peru. The once 'lost city' of Machu Picchu has unquestionably been found, but it continues to inspire awe and admiration among the over one million visitors it receives each year. There are a wide variety of options for reaching the world-famous site, ranging from a luxurious train ride to the famous four- to five-day trek along the classic Inca Trail or one of its several alternatives.

Best for
Inca ruins ▪ Markets ▪ Rafting ▪ Relaxing ▪ Trekking

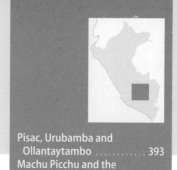

Footprint
picks

★ Pisac, page 395
The town's superb Inca fortress and very popular Sunday morning market make it a must for visitors.

★ Huchuy Cuzco, page 396
The impressive ruins of 'Little Cuzco' make for an interesting day visit, or they can be reached on a scenic one- or two-day trek from Tambo Machay.

★ Maras, page 400
From this village you can walk to both the Inca nursery at Moray and the ancient salt pans at Salineras.

★ Ollantaytambo, page 403
Spectacular ruins and a living Inca neighbourhood coexist with this town's international resort atmosphere.

★ Machu Picchu, page 411
No amount of tourism seems to tarnish the glow of the most famous archaeological site in South America.

★ Inca trails, page 419
As well as the classic trek to Machu Picchu, there are many other fascinating routes to explore.

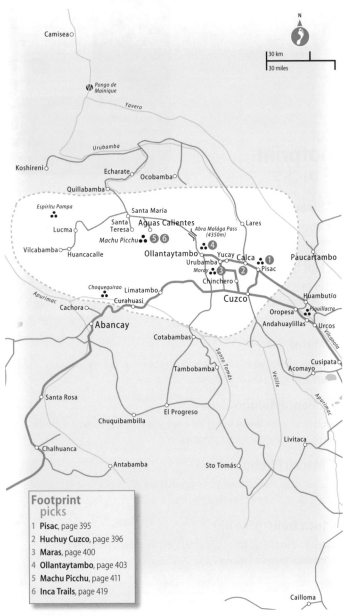

Camisea

Pongo de
Mainique

Yavero

Urubamba

Koshireni

Echarate   Ocobamba

Quillabamba

Espíritu Pampa   Santa María

Lucma   Santa   Aguas Calientes
         Teresa
         Machu Picchu   **5 6**

Vilcabamba   Huancacalle

Ollantaytambo   Abra Malága Pass
                 (4350m)   Lares

4

Yucay   Calca   **1**

Urubamba
Moray   **3**   **2**   Pisac
Chinchero

Choquequirao   Limatambo

Curahuasi   Cuzco

Cachora

Huambutío
Piquillacta
Oropesa
Andahuaylillas   Urcos

Abancay   Cotabambas

Vilcanota

Tambobamba   Santo Tomás

Veille

Cusipata

Acomayo

Santa Rosa

Chuquibambilla   El Progreso

Livitaca

Chalhuanca

Antabamba   Sto Tomás

Cailloma

30 km
30 miles

N

Pisac, Urubamba
& Ollantaytambo

The Río Vilcanota cuts its way through fields and rocky gorges beneath the high peaks of the cordillera. Brown hills, covered in wheat, separate Cuzco from this beautiful high valley, which stretches from Sicuani (on the road and railway to Puno) to the gorge of Torontoi, 600 m lower, northwest of Cuzco. That the river was of great significance to the Incas can be seen in the number of strategic sites they built above it: Pisac, Ollantaytambo and Machu Picchu among them. In addition to receiving large numbers of tourists throughout the year, Pisac, Urubamba and Ollantaytambo are also home to a thriving expat population from all over the world. Some have come to work in the tourist trade, some to retire, while others are attracted by the mystical energy of the region. Combined with the indigenous population of the Valley, their presence makes for an interesting and unusual mixture that gives each of the three main towns its own unique personality.

Essential Sacred Valley

Finding your feet

Many Machu Picchu trains terminate in Ollantaytambo, and the town is touristy and expensive as a result. Urubamba, 20 minutes away is a real Peruvian town and makes a more economical base for visiting the valley, with all services and transport throughout the region. Note that upstream from Pisac, the river is usually called the Vilcanota; downstream it may either be called the Vilcanota or the Urubamba – maps disagree.

Getting around

Many Cuzco agencies offer day tours to the Sacred Valley, US$25-30, but using public transport and staying overnight in Urubamba, Ollantaytambo or Pisac allows more time to see the ruins and markets. Paved roads, plentiful transport and a good selection of hotels and eating places make this a straightforward place to explore. You can choose either a quick visit from the city or, better still, linger for a few days to explore it on foot, by bike or on horseback.

When to go

The best time to visit is April to May or October to November. The high season is June to September when the days are clear and sunny but sites can be very crowded. The rainy season, from December to March, is cheaper and pleasant enough, although trekking routes may be wet and slippery.

Time required

Four days would allow a quick, whistle-stop tour of the main sights, but you'll need more time to do the area justice.

Weather Ollantaytambo

January	February	March	April	May	June
15°C 3°C 153mm	15°C 3°C 139mm	15°C 3°C 125mm	15°C 2°C 50mm	15°C 0°C 12mm	15°C -2°C 3mm

July	August	September	October	November	December
15°C -3°C 7mm	16°C -2°C 11mm	16°C 0°C 30mm	17°C 2°C 45mm	17°C 2°C 72mm	16°C 2°C 115mm

The road from Cuzco that runs past Sacsayhuaman and on to Tambo Machay (see page 355) climbs up to a pass, then continues over the pampa before descending into the densely populated Vilcanota valley. This road then crosses the river by a bridge at Pisac and follows the north bank to the end of the paved road at Ollantaytambo. It passes through Calca, Yucay and Urubamba, which can also be reached from Cuzco by the beautiful, direct road through Chinchero, see page 399.

★ **Pisac** → *Colour map 5, A5.*

Pisac, 30 km north of Cuzco, has a traditional Sunday morning **market**, at which local people sell their produce in exchange for essential goods. It is a major draw for tourists who arrive in their droves throughout the day. Pisac has

> **Tip...**
> At dusk you will hear, if not see, the *pisaca* (partridges), after which the place is named.

other, somewhat less crowded but more commercial markets every second day. Each Sunday at 1100 there is a Quechua Mass in the church on the plaza, where there is also a small, interesting **Museo Folklórico**. Elsewhere, the **Museo Comunitario Pisac** ⓘ *Av Amazonas y Retamayoc K'asa, museopisac@gmail.com, daily 1000-1700, free but donations welcome,* has a display of village life, created by the people of Pisac. There are many souvenir shops on Bolognesi. Local fiesta: 15 July.

High above the town on the mountainside is Pisac's superb **Inca fortress** ⓘ *1-hr walk from the plaza (30-min descent), daily 0700-1730, guides charge about US$5, you must show your BTC multi-site ticket to enter; combi US$0.75, taxi US$7 each way from near the bridge.* Walking up, although tiring, is recommended for the views and location. It's at least one hour uphill all the way, starting from the plaza and continuing past the Centro de Salud and a control post. The path goes through working terraces, giving the ruins a context. The first group of buildings is Pisaqa, with a fine curving wall. Climb then to the central part of the ruins, the Intihuatana group of temples and rock outcrops in the most magnificent Inca masonry. Here are the Reloj Solar ('Hitching Post of the Sun') – now closed because thieves stole a piece from it, palaces of the moon and stars, solstice markers, baths and water channels. From Intihuatana, a path leads around the hillside through a tunnel to Q'Allaqasa, the military area. At this point, a large area of Inca tombs in holes in the hillside can be seen across the valley. The end of the site is Kanchiracay, where the agricultural workers were housed. Road transport approaches from the Kanchiracay end; the drive up from town takes about 20 minutes. Even if you're going by car, do not rush as there is a lot to see and a lot of walking to do.

★Calca and Huchuy Cuzco

The second village on the road from Pisac towards Urubamba is **Lamay**, which has warm spring nearby that are highly regarded for their medicinal properties. Next is **Calca**, 18 km beyond Pisac at 3000 m, which has basic hotels and eating places around its large plaza and a bus terminal along the highway. The **Fiesta de la Vírgen Asunta** is held here on 15-16 August.

Dramatically located at 3700 m on a flat esplanade on the opposite side of the river are the impressive ruins of a small Inca town, **Huchuy Cuzco** ① *access from either Calca or Lamay (7 km southeast), then either by road or 3 hrs hiking on a good steep trail, entry US$8.* The views are magnificent. The ruins themselves consist of extensive agricultural terraces with high retaining walls and several buildings made from finely wrought stonework and adobe mud bricks. A lovely one- or two-day trek leads to Huchuy Cuzco from Tambo Machay (see page 355), the route once taken by the Inca from his capital to his country estate.

Valle de Lares

The Valle de Lares is renowned for its magnificent mountains, lakes and small villages, which make it perfect for trekking and mountain biking, although parts are undergoing rapid development. One route starts near an old hacienda in **Huarán** (6 km west of Calca at 2830 m), crosses two passes over 4000 m and ends at the hot springs near **Lares**. From this village, transport runs back to Calca.

The Sacred Valley

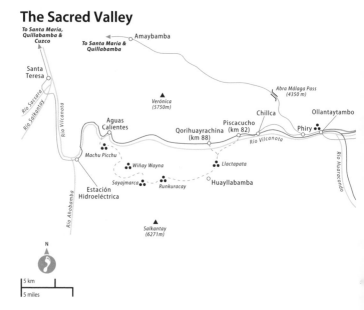

Alternatively, you can add an extra day and continue to Ollantaytambo, or start in Lares and finish in Yanhuara (between Urubamba and Ollantaytambo). Several agencies in Cuzco offer trekking and biking tours to the region (see page 375). Miguel Angel Delgado in Cuzco (T973-275881, mikyyuta@yahoo.com), has been recommended as a trekking guide for this area.

Yucay

About 3 km east of Urubamba, **Yucay** has two grassy plazas divided by the restored colonial church of Santiago Apóstol, with its oil paintings and fine altars. On the opposite side from Plaza Manco II is the adobe palace built for Sayri Túpac (Manco's son) when he emerged from Vilcabamba in 1558.

Listings Pisac to Yucay

Where to stay

Pisac

$$$ Royal Inka Pisac
Carretera Ruinas Km 1.5, T084-203064,
www.royalinkahotel.pe.

Converted hacienda with olympic-size swimming pool (US$3.50 per day), sauna and jacuzzi for guests only, very pleasant, provides guides. This chain also has **Royal Inkas I** and **II** in Cuzco.

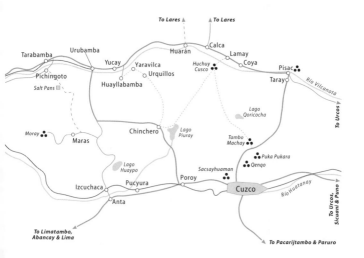

$$ Hostal Varayoc
Mcal Castilla 380, T084-223638,
luzpaz3@hotmail.com.
Renovated hotel around a colonial
courtyard with working bread
oven. Decor is smart and bathrooms
are modern.

$$ Melissa Wasi
15 mins walk from Pisac Plaza,
close to the river, T084-797589.
A family-run bed and breakfast
with rooms and small bungalows.
Very homely, English spoken.

$$ Paz y Luz
10-15 mins' walk from Pisac Plaza,
close to the river, T084-203204,
www.pazyluzperu.com.
American-owned, pleasant garden,
nicely designed rooms, breakfast
included. Diane Dunn offers healing
from many traditions (including Andean),
sacred tours, workshops and gatherings.

$$ Pisac Inn
At the corner of Pardo on the Plaza,
T084-203062, www.pisacinn.com.
Bright and charming local decor,
pleasant atmosphere, private and
shared bathrooms, hot water, sauna
and massage. Good breakfast, the
Cuchara de Palo restaurant serves
meals using local ingredients, plus
pizza and pasta, café.

$ Res Beho
Intihuatana 642, T084-203001.
Ask for room in main building,
good breakfast, owner's son will
act as guide to ruins at weekend.

Valle de Lares

$$$ The Green House
Km 60.2 Huarán, T984-770130,
www.thegreenhouseperu.com.

A charming, Wi-Fi-free retreat, only
4 rooms, breakfast included, comfortable
lounge, restaurant, small kitchen for guests,
beautiful garden, restricted internet.
No children under 10. Information on
walks and day trips in the area. Activities
include hiking, biking, horse riding and
rafting. Intimate, beautiful and relaxing.

Yucay

$$$$ Sonesta Posadas del Inca Sacred Valley
Plaza Manco II de Yucay 123, T084-201107,
www.sonesta.com.
Converted 300-year-old monastery is
like a little village with plazas, chapel,
69 comfortable, heated rooms, price
includes buffet breakfast. Lots of
activities can be arranged, canoeing,
horse riding, mountain biking, etc.
Inkafe restaurant is open to all, serving
Peruvian, fusion and traditional cuisine
with a US$15 buffet. Recommended.

$$$ La Casona de Yucay
Plaza Manco II 104, T084-201116,
www.hotelcasonayucay.com.
This colonial house was where
Simón Bolívar stayed during his
liberation campaign in 1824. With
heating, 2 patios and gardens,
Don Manuel restaurant and bar.

Restaurants

Pisac

$$-$ Miski Mijuna Wasi
On the Plaza de Armas, T084-203266.
Serves tasty local food, typical and
Novo Andino, also international dishes.
Has a *pastelería* also.

$$-$ Mullu
Plaza de Armas 352 and Mcal Castilla 375,
T084-208182. Tue-Sun 0900-1900.

Café/restaurant related to the Mullu store in Cuzco, also has a gallery promoting local artists.

$ Doña Clorinda
On the plaza opposite the church.
Tasty food, including vegetarian.

$ Valle Sagrado
Av Amazonas 116 (the main street where buses go towards Urubamba).
Good quality, generous portions and a lunchtime buffet that includes vegetarian options. Go early before the tour groups arrive.

Cafés

Panadería
Mcal Castilla 372.
Good wholemeal bread, excellent cheese *empanadas*.

Blue Llama Café
Corner of the plaza opposite Pisac Inn, T084-203135.
Cute, colourful café with a huge range of teas, good coffee, breakfasts and daily menus.

Ulrike's Café
C Pardo 613, T084-203195.
Has possibly the best apple crumble with ice cream, excellent coffee, smoothies and a wide range of international dishes. Good value 3-course daily *menú*. A good place to chill out.

Transport

Pisac
To **Urubamba**, US$1, 1 hr. To **Cuzco**, 32 km, 1 hr, US$1.50, last one back leaves around 2000; these buses are often full. There are also colectivos and minibuses.

Urubamba and around → *Colour map 5, A5.*

a good base for visiting the salt-pans

Like many places along the valley, Urubamba is in a fine setting at 2863 m with snow-capped peaks in view. The main road along the valley skirts the town, and the bridge for the road to Cuzco via Chinchero is just to the east.

Sights
The large market square is one block west of the main plaza. Calle Berriózabal, on the west edge of town, is lined with pisonay trees. There are many pottery studios in town, including **Seminario-Bejar Ceramic Studio** ⓘ *Berriózabal 111, T084-201002, www.ceramicaseminario.com.* Pablo Seminario and his workshop have researched pre-Columbian techniques and designs and now use them in their distinctive pottery. The tour of the of the workshops is highly recommended.

Chinchero
Church and archaeological site daily 0730-1800, BTC ticket (see page 344).

Chinchero (3762 m) is southeast of Urubamba along the more direct (western) road to Cuzco. It is a friendly town with an attractive church built on an Inca temple. The church has been restored to reveal the full glory of its interior paintings: ceiling, beams and walls are covered in beautiful floral and religious designs. Excavations have revealed many Inca walls and terraces around the town's plaza. Groups from Cuzco come to visit the church, ruins and several touristy textile centres in the town. Much of the area's character will change when the new airport for Cuzco is built nearby.

★Moray
9 km by road west of Maras. US$3.50 or by BTC ticket.

A paved road leads from the Chinchero–Urubamba road to the village of **Maras**, from where it's 9 km by unmade road or 5 km through the fields to the remote but beautiful site of Moray; ask in Maras for the best walking route. This site comprises three 'colosseums', used by the Incas, according to some theories, as a sort of open-air crop nursery; it is known locally as the 'laboratory of the Incas'. The great depressions contain no ruined buildings, but are lined with fine terracing. Each level is said to have its own microclimate. It is a very atmospheric place which, many claim, has mystical power, and the scenery is absolutely stunning. An alternative and more interesting way to get to Moray is from Urubamba via the Pichingoto bridge and the spectacular Inca salt pans (see above); the village of Maras is about 45 minutes further on. Tour companies in Cuzco offer cycle trips to Moray. There are no hotels at all in the area, so take care not to get stranded. See Transport, for further details on how to get there.

★Salineras
About 6 km west of Urubamba is **Tarabamba**, where a bridge crosses the Río Urubamba. Turn right after the bridge to reach **Pichingoto**, a tumbled-down village built under an overhanging cliff. Just over the bridge and before the town to the left of a small, walled cemetery is a salt stream. Follow the footpath beside the stream to Salineras, a small village below which are a mass of terraced **Inca salt pans** ⓘ *entry US$2.50, taxi from Urubamba, US$11.* There are over 5000 salineras and they are still in operation, producing highly regarded, light pink Maras salt. If you're walking to the salt pans, take water as this side of the valley can be very hot and dry.

Listings Urubamba and around

Tourist information

Tourist information is available at the bus terminal in Urubamba, Mon-Fri 0745-1630.

Where to stay

$$$$ Casa Andina Private Collection Sacred Valley
Paradero 5, Yanahuara, between Urubamba and Ollantaytambo, T984-765501, www.casa-andina.com.
In its own 3-ha estate, with all the facilities associated with this chain, plus **Valle Sagrado Andean Cottage** for family and long-stay accommodation, 'Sacred Spa', gym, planetarium, good restaurant, adventure options.

$$$$ Río Sagrado (Belmond)
Km 76 Ctra Cuzco–Ollantaytambo, T084-201631, www.riosagrado.com.
4 km from Urubamba, set in beautiful gardens overlooking the river with fine views. Rooms and villas, **Mayu**

Wilka spa, restaurant and bar, offers various packages.

$$$$ Sol y Luna
Fundo Huincho, west of town, T084-201620, www.hotelsolyluna.com.
Award-winning bungalows and suites set off the main road in lovely gardens, pool, excellent gourmet restaurant, wine tastings, spa, handicrafts shop. Also has **Wayra** lounge bar and dining room, open to non-guests, for freshly cooked, informal lunches. Entertainment includes paso fino horse shows, contemporary arts and circus shows (open to all). Arranges adventure and cultural activities and traditional tours. Profits go to **Sol y Luna** educational association.

$$$$ Tambo del Inka
Av Ferrocarril s/n, T084-581777, www. luxurycollection.com/vallesagrado.
A resort and spa on the edge of town, in gardens by the river. Completely remodelled with a variety of rooms and suites, fitness centre, swimming pools, **Hawa** restaurant, bar, business facilities and lots of activities arranged.

$$$ Casa Colibrí
2.5 km from town on road to Ollantaytambo, T084-205003, www.casacolibriecolodge.com.
Delightful, spacious rooms and casitas made of local stone, wood and adobe, set in beautiful gardens to attract bees, butterflies and hummingbirds. Very restful, hammocks, meditation room, excellent homegrown food, swings and table tennis, popular with couples, families and yoga groups.

$$ Las Chullpas
Querocancha s/n, 3 km from town, T084-201568, www.chullpas.pe.
Very peaceful, excellent breakfast, vegetarian meals, English and German spoken, Spanish classes, natural medicine, treks, riding, mountain biking, camping US$3 with hot shower. Mototaxi from town US$2.50, taxi (ask for Querocancha) US$4.

$$ Tambo de Oro
Av La Convención 113-B, T084-201450, www.hoteltambodelsol.com.
Ample modern rooms with bathtubs, beautiful garden, parking, good value.

$$ Urubamba Homestay
Jr Bolognesi 152, T084-509703, www.astongarciatours.com.
Three rooms with bath in a private home, includes breakfast, roof terrace, gardens, support community projects. British-run by Keith and Joan Parkin.

$ Hospedaje Buganvilla
Jr Convención 280, T084-205102, bukanvilla@hotmail.com.
Sizable rooms with hot water, breakfast on request, quiet, bright, lovely gardens, lively owners Raul and Mónica, good value, very pleasant.

$ Hospedaje Los Jardines
Jr Convención 459, T084-201331, www. hospedajelosjardines.blogspot.co.uk.
Attractive guesthouse with comfortable rooms, hot water, non-smoking, delicious breakfast US$3.25 extra (vegans catered for), safe, lovely garden, laundry. **Sacred Valley Mountain Bike Tours** also based here.

Chinchero

$$$-$$ La Casa de Barro
Miraflores 157, T084-306031, www.lacasadebarro.com.

Modern hotel, with heating, bar, restaurant serving 'fusion' food using organic local produce, tours arranged.

$ Mi Piuray
C Garcilaso 187, T084-306029, www. hospedajemipiuraycusco.com.
Simple rooms around a patio with flowers, private or shared bath, electric showers, kitchen facilities, meals on request, knowledgeable owner.

Restaurants

$$$ El Huacatay
Arica 620, T084-201790, www.el huacatay.com. Mon-Sat 1300-2130.
A small restaurant with a reputation for fine, creative fusion cuisine (local, Mediterranean, Asian). Lovely garden setting.

$$$ El Maizal
Av Conchatupa, the main road before the bridge, T084-201454. Daily 1200-1600.
Country-style restaurant, buffet service with a variety of Novo Andino and international choices, beautiful gardens, caters to tour groups.

$$$ Tunupa
On road from Urubamba to Ollantaytambo, on riverbank. Buffet lunch 1200-1500, US$15, dinner 1800-2030.
Same owners as Tunupa in Cuzco, colonial-style hacienda, excellent food and surroundings, pre-Columbian and colonial art exhibitions.

$$$ Tres Keros
Av Señor de Torrechayoc, T084-201701.
Novo Andino cuisine, try the lamb chops.

$$$-$$ Paca Paca
Av Mcal Castilla 640, T084-201181. Tue-Sun 1300-2100.

Varied selection of dishes including Peruvian fusion, also pizza, pleasant inviting atmosphere.

$$-$ Guyin
Comercio 453, T084-608838 for delivery. Daily 0500-2300.
Pizza, pastas and grill. Popular with local expats.

$$-$ Pizza Wasi
Av Mcal Castilla 857, Plaza de Armas, T084-434751 for delivery. Daily 1200-2300.
Good pizzas and pastas. Mulled wine served in a small restaurant with nice decor, good value.

$ Sweet Heart
Av Mcal Castilla 1028. Daily 0800-2300.
Good quality and value *menú* at midday, *à la carte* at night, couch seating.

Festivals

May and Jun are the harvest months, with many processions following ancient schedules.

1st week of Jun Urubamba's main festival, **El Señor de Torrechayoc**.
8 Sep Chinchero celebrates the **Day of the Virgin**.

What to do

Haku Trek, *contact Javier Saldívar, T984-613001, www.hakutrek.com*. Cooperative tourism project in the Chicón valley (the mountain valley above Urubamba), run by residents of the community, 1- and 2-day hiking trips based at a simple eco-lodge; profits fund reforestation of the area.
Perol Chico, *5 km from Urubamba at Km 77, T974-798 890/974-780020, www. perolchico.com*. Dutch/Peruvian-owned and operated stables offering 1- to 14-day horse riding trips. Good horses, riding is Peruvian paso style.

Bus

The Terminal is on the main road, 3 blocks west of the centre. To **Calca**, US$0.50, 30 min; and **Pisac**, US$1, 1 hr. To **Cuzco**, by bus, US$1.50, 1½ hrs via Chinchero or 2 hrs via Pisac; by van US$2; by car US$2.50. Frequent vans to **Ollantaytambo**, US$0.50, 30 min, all leave when full throughout the day.

Moray

Any bus between Urubamba and Cuzco via Chinchero passes the clearly marked turning to **Maras**; from the junction taxi colectivos charge US$2.50 pp to Maras, or you can walk all the way from here to Moray (see above). There is also public transport from Chinchero to Maras until 1700. A taxi to Moray and the salt pans (from where you can walk back to the Urubamba–Ollantaytambo road) costs US$25, including 1-hr wait.

Ollantaytambo → *Colour map 5, A5.*

the magnificent site of Manco Inca's last stand

The attractive but touristy town of Ollantaytambo is located at 2800 m at the foot of some spectacular Inca ruins and terraces and is built directly on top of an original Inca town. A great many visitors arrive by road from Cuzco to see the ruins and take the train from here to Machu Picchu.

Ollantaytambo town

Entering Ollantaytambo from the east, the road is built along the long Wall of 100 Niches. Note the inclination of the wall, which leans towards the road. Since it was the Incas' usual practice to build their walls leaning towards the interior of the building, it has been deduced that the road, much narrower then, was built inside a succession of buildings. The road leads into the Plaza de Armas. The Inca town, or *Llacta*, on which the present-day town is based can clearly be seen behind the north side of the plaza, where the original Inca *canchas* (blocks of houses) are almost entirely intact and still occupied. The road out of the plaza leads across a bridge to the colonial church with its enclosed *recinto*. Beyond are Plaza Araccama and the entrance to the archaeological site

> **Tip...**
> Traffic around the train station is chaotic every evening; take care not to be run-over on Avenida Ferrocarril.

★Ollantaytambo temple fortress

Daily 0700-1730; if possible arrive at 0700, before the other tourists. Admission by BTC visitor's ticket, which can be bought at the site. Guides are available at the entrance.

After crossing the great high-walled trapezoidal esplanade known as 'Mañariki', visitors to Ollantaytambo are confronted by a series of 16 massive, stepped terraces of the very finest stonework. These flights of terraces leading up above the town are superb, and so are the curving terraces following the contours of the rocks overlooking the river. These terraces were successfully defended by Manco Inca's warriors against Hernando Pizarro in 1536. Manco Inca built the wall above the site and another wall closing the Yucay valley against attack from Cuzco. Beyond these imposing terraces lies the so-called Temple of Ten Niches, a funeral chamber once dedicated to the worship of Pachacútec's royal household. Immediately above this are six monolithic upright blocks of rose-coloured rhyolite, the remains of what is popularly called the Temple of the Sun. The temple was started by Pachacútec, using Colla Indians from Lake Titicaca – hence the similarities of the monoliths facing the central platform with the Tiahuanaco remains. The massive, highly finished granite blocks at the top are worth the climb to see. The Colla are said to have deserted halfway through the work, which explains the many unfinished blocks lying about the site.

There are more Inca ruins in the small area behind the church, between the town and the temple fortress. Most impressive of these is the so-called Baño de la Ñusta (bath of the princess) made of grey granite. Some 200 m behind the bath, along the face of the mountain, are some small ruins known as Inca Misanca, believed to have been a small temple or observatory. A series of steps, seats and niches have

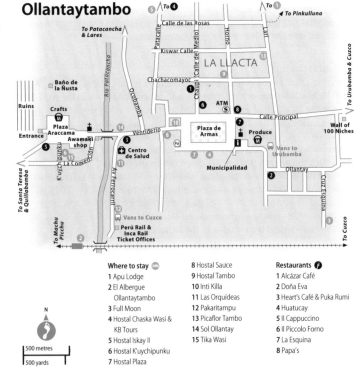

Ollantaytambo

Where to stay		
1 Apu Lodge	8 Hostal Sauce	**Restaurants**
2 El Albergue	9 Hostal Tambo	1 Alcázar Café
Ollantaytambo	10 Inti Killa	2 Doña Eva
3 Full Moon	11 Las Orquídeas	3 Heart's Café & Puka Rumi
4 Hostal Chaska Wasi &	12 Pakaritampu	4 Huatucay
KB Tours	13 Picaflor Tambo	5 Il Cappuccino
5 Hostal Iskay II	14 Sol Ollantay	6 Il Piccolo Forno
6 Hostal K'uychipunku	15 Tika Wasi	7 La Esquina
7 Hostal Plaza		8 Papa's

been carved out of the cliff. There is a complete irrigation system, including a canal at shoulder level, some 6 inches deep, cut out of the sheer rock face.

On the west side of the main ruins, a two-dimensional 'pyramid' has been identified in the layout of the fields and walls of the valley. A fine 750 m wall aligns with the rays of the winter solstice on 21 June. It can be appreciated from a high point about 3.5 km from Ollantaytambo.

Pinkulluna

At Pinkulluna, on the east side of Ollantaytambo and clearly visible from below, is an impressive collection of storehouses, or *colcas* perched on a steep slope. A marked path leads up from the end of Calle de las Rosas/T'ika K'ikllu, where it meets Calle Lari, in the Inca town. It's a relatively straightforward but steep climb on the stone steps. After 10 minutes the path divides, right to the buildings on a promontory and left to the *colcas*, a further 20-25 minutes (entry is free). The views are best seen in the morning, but are impressive at any time. You can continue climbing steeply from Pinkulluna on a rough trail which leads to a local summit. The views are wonderful but there are some difficult bits along the way and you should mind the weather on the exposed slopes.

Cachiccata

The stone quarries of Cachiccata are some 9 km from Ollantaytambo and can be seen by standing to the left of the six monolithic blocks of the Temple of the Sun, looking west-southwest across the valley. The stones that the Inca masons chose here had to be quarried, hewn into a rough shape and hauled across the valley floor and up to the temple by means of a ramp, which can still be seen. Between the ruins and the quarries more than 50 enormous stones that never reached their destination lie abandoned. They are known as the '*las piedras cansadas*', or 'the tired stones'. It takes about a day to walk to the Inca quarries on the opposite of the river and then return to Ollantaytambo, a very pleasant hike.

Tourist information

Tourist information is available at the **Municipio** on the plaza (T084-204030, ext 207, Mon-Fri 0800-1300, 1400-1700).

Where to stay

There are many hotels but they are often full, so it's best to book ahead in high season.

$$$$-$$$ El Albergue Ollantaytambo
Within the railway station gates, T084-204014, www.elalbergue.com.
Owned by North American artist Wendy Weeks. Also has **Café Mayu** in the station and a very good restaurant using ingredients from their own organic farm. Characterful rooms, rustic elegance, some larger than others, safety boxes, lovely gardens and a eucalyptus steam sauna. Books and crafts for sale. Private transport arranged to nearby attractions and Cuzco airport.

$$$ Hostal Sauce
C Ventiderio 248, T084-204044, www.hostalsauce.com.pe.
Smart, simple decor and views of the ruins from 3 of the 6 rooms as well as from the dining room, food from own farm.

$$$ Pakaritampu
C Ferrocarril s/n, T084-204020, www.pakaritampu.com.
Modern, well-appointed rooms, buffet breakfast, restaurant and bar, laundry, safe and room service. Adventure sports can be arranged. Lunch and dinner are extra. Excellent quality and service, but room 8 is next to the railway station car park.

$$$ Tika Wasi
C Convencion s/n, T084-204166.
Great location close to the archaeological site, garden, good service and comfortable rooms decorated in 'Inca style'.

$$$-$$ Picaflor Tambo
Larricalle s/n, T958-195240, www.picaflortambo.com.
6 comfortable rooms set around a small courtyard, charming and intimate, kitchen facilities, a good choice.

$$ Apu Lodge
Calle Lari, T084-797162, www.apulodge.com.
On the edge of town, great views of the ruins and surrounding mountains. Run by Scot Louise Norton and husband Arturo, good service, quiet, nice garden, good buffet breakfast, can help organize tours and treks. They work with Leap Local (www.leaplocal.org) guides project.

$$ Full Moon
Cruz Esquina s/n, T984-288877, reservas@fullmoonlodgeperu.com.
Quiet place away from the centre, rooms with private bath set around a large garden with hammocks, also camping US$5 pp. Caters to those seeking a San Pedro experience.

$$ Hostal Iskay II
Patacalle s/n, T084-204004, www.hostaliskay.com.
In the Inca town. Great location but car access is difficult. 6 rooms, hot water, free tea and coffee, kitchen. Good reports.

$$ Hostal K'uychipunku
K'uychipunku 6, T084-204175.
Close to Plaza Araccama, hot water, modern, some rooms with view, courtyard.

$$ Las Orquídeas
Av Ferrocarril s/n, T084-204032.
Hot water, fairly small but nice rooms,
flower-filled patio, discounts for 2 or
more nights.

$$-$ Sol Ollantay
*C Ventiderio s/n by the bridge between
the 2 plazas, T084-204130.*
Tastefullly renovated with good
views from most rooms, hot water.

$ Hostal Chaska Wasi
Plaza de Armas, T084-204045.
Private rooms and dorms, hammocks,
hot showers, free hot drinks, laundry,
popular. Owner Katy is very friendly.

$ Hostal Plaza Ollantaytambo
*beside the police station on
Plaza de Armas, T084-436741,
hostalplazaollantaytambo@gmail.com.*
Small modern rooms with private bath
and reliable hot water. Variable service,
all a bit improvised but great location
and value.

$ Hostal Tambo
*C Horno, north of the plaza, T984-
489094, www.hostaleltambo.com.*
Cheaper for groups, breakfast extra.
Once past the door you emerge into
a lovely garden full of fruit trees and
flowers. Small basic rooms for up to
3 people, shared bath downstairs in
the courtyard, hot water, good value.

$ Inti Killa
*just off Plaza de Armas, T948-356929,
intidante@gmail.com.*
Ample rooms with modern private
bath as well as dorms, pleasant and
good value.

There are restaurants all over town
offering *menú turístico*, pizzas, pastas,
juices and hot drinks.

$$$-$$ Puka Rumi
*Av Ventiderio s/n, above Heart's Café,
T084-204151. Daily 0700-2100.*
Serves a variety of international dishes,
pizza, salads, upmarket *menú*.

$$ Huatakay
*Patacalle s/n, a few blocks from centre,
T084-436723. Daily 0600-2100.*
Large restaurant serving *menú* and
regional specialties *à la carte*. Pleasant
setting, small camping area on the
grounds, US$7 per tent.

$$ Papa's
*C Horno at the plaza, T084-436700.
Daily 1100-2100.*
Restaurant and lounge serving
Tex-Mex, local dishes, pizzas, soups,
salads, and desserts.

$$ Heart's Café
*Av Ventiderio s/n, T084-204013, www.
heartscafe.org. Open 0700-2100.*
International and Peruvian dishes
including vegetarian, box lunch and
takeaway available, good coffee. All
profits to education and self-help
projects in the Sacred Valley. Popular,
tasty food but disappointing service.

$$ Il Cappuccino
Plaza Araccama.
Good coffee and continental and
American breakfasts. Also serves
menú turístico, lunch and dinner,
desserts, juices and light meals.

$$ Il Piccolo Forno
*C del Medio 120. Tue-Sun 1200-1500,
1800-2100.*

Very good Italian food and take-away pizza, as well as home baked bread, pies and cookies.

$$ La Esquina
C Principal at the corner of Plaza de Armas. Irregular hours.
Variety of international and Peruvian dishes, wide selection of sweets, popular.

$$-$ Alcázar Café
C del Medio, 50 m from Plaza, T084-204034.
Vegetarian, but also offers meat and fish, and pasta. Arranges excursions to Andean communities.

$ Doña Eva
C Ollantay facing the market. Sun-Fri 0700-2100, Sat 0700-1200.
Economical *menú* and *à la carte*, one of the few unpretentious places in town, popular with locals and travellers alike.

Festivals

6 Jan Bajada de Reyes Magos (Epiphany) is celebrated with dancing, a bull fight, local food and a fair.
End-May/early-Jun Fiesta del Señor de Choquekillca, patron saint of Ollantaytambo, has his festival 50 days after Easter, with several days of dancing, weddings, processions, masses, feasting and drinking.
Jun Ollanta-Raymi. A colourful festival on the Sun following Inti Raymi.
29 Oct The town's anniversary, with lots of dancing in traditional costume and many local delicacies for sale.

Transport

Bus
Vans leave all day for **Urubamba** from the produce market, 1 block east of the main plaza, US$0.50, 30 mins. Direct bus to **Cuzco** at 0715 and 1945, US$4; also **Cruz del Sur**, 3 a day, US$7. Vans to Cuzco leave from Av Ferrocaril above the railway station at 0715, 1100, 1630 and 2000, US$3.50, 1½ hrs. Taxi to Cuzco, US$22.

Train
Ollantaytambo is the point of departure for most trains to **Machu Picchu** (see Transport, page 418). The station is a 10-15 min walk from the Plaza, longer in the early evening when Av Ferrocaril is clogged with vehicles. There are **Perú Rail** and **Inca Rail** ticket offices outside the station and you must have a ticket to be allowed onto the platform.

Machu Picchu
& the Inca trails

There is a tremendous feeling of awe on first witnessing Machu Picchu. The ancient citadel (42 km from Ollantaytambo by rail) straddles the saddle of a high mountain (2380 m) with steep terraced slopes falling away to the fast-flowing Vilcanota river snaking its hairpin course far below in the valley floor. Towering overhead is Huayna Picchu, and green jungle peaks provide the backdrop for the whole majestic scene. Machu Picchu is a complete Inca city. For centuries it was buried in jungle, until Hiram Bingham stumbled upon it in 1911. It was then explored by an archaeological expedition sent by Yale University. The ruins – staircases, terraces, temples, palaces, towers, fountains and the famous Intihuatana (the so-called 'Hitching Post of the Sun') – require at least a day to explore. Take time to appreciate not only the masonry, but also the selection of large rocks used for foundations, the use of water in the channels below the Temple of the Sun and the beauty of the surrounding mountains. *Colour map 5, C5.*

Essential Machu Picchu

Getting there

The easiest way to get to Machu Picchu is by train from Poroy (near Cuzco) or Ollantaytambo to Aguas Calientes, from where you can walk or catch a bus to the ruins. Santa Teresa provides alternative access for those who have travelled by road from Ollantaytambo. The most strenuous but rewarding way to Machu Picchu is to hike one of the Inca trails (see page 419).

Tickets

The entrance fee for Machu Picchu only is 126 soles (US$45), or 63 soles (US$22.50) for Peruvians, citizens of other Andean Community nations, students with ISIC card, and visitors under age 18. Children under 8 enter for free. To climb Huayna Picchu you have to buy a ticket that includes site entry and the climb for 150 soles (US$54), specifying whether you are going to arrive 0700-0800 or 1000-1100 (only 400 people are allowed up at one time). There is also a Machu Picchu and Montaña ticket for 140 soles (US$50).

It is wise to reserve your ticket online in advance at **www.machupicchu. gob.pe**. You can also pay online (unless you need to show an ISIC card) with Visa or at branches of Banco de la Nación; the **Centro Cultural de Machu Picchu** (Av Pachacútec cuadra 1) in Aguas Calientes; **Dirección Regional de Cultura** in Cuzco (Av de la Cultura 238, Condominio Huáscar, T084-236061, www.drc-cusco.gob.pe, Mon-Fri 0715-1600); **AATC** (C Nueva Baja 424) in Cuzco; offices of **PerúRail** and **Inca Rail** in Cuzco, and **Hotel Monasterio** in Cuzco. Other websites offer tickets for sale at an inflated price. Do not buy (fake) tickets on the street in Cuzco.

On arrival

The site is open from 0600 to 1600. Officially, only 2500 visitors are allowed entry each day, but there may be more in high season, April through August. It is best to arrive early, although it is not possible to walk up to the ruins before the first buses arrive.

You can deposit your luggage at the entrance for a small fee. Guides are available at the site, US$80 for one to 10 people. Site wardens are also informative. The **Sanctuary Lodge** is located next to the entrance, with a self-service restaurant and the only toilets on the site.

Regulations

In an attempt to mitigate crowding, the authorities announced new regulations in 2014, but these had not been implemented by May 2015. They require that all visitors be accompanied by a guide, that they follow one of three established routes without turning back and that they limit stops at certain places to three to five minutes. There has also been talk of limiting entry to morning-, or afternoon-only tickets.

Advice and precautions

Take your own food, if you don't want to pay hotel prices, and take plenty of drinking water. Note that food is not officially allowed into the site and drink can only be carried in canteens/water bottles, not disposable containers. Toilets are only at the entrance. Take insect repellent and wear long clothes. Also take protection against the sun and rain.

★ Main site

Once you have passed through the ticket gate you follow a path to a small complex of buildings that now acts as the **main entrance** (1) to the ruins. It is set at the eastern end of the extensive **terracing** (2) that must have supplied the crops for the city. Above this point, turning back on yourself, is the final stretch of the Inca Trail leading down from **Intipunku** (Sun Gate), see page 422. From a promontory here, on which stands the building called the **Watchman's Hut** (3), you get the perfect view of the city (the one you've seen on all the postcards), laid out before you with Huayna Picchu rising above the furthest extremity. Go round the promontory and head south for the **Intipata** (Inca bridge), see page 422. The main path into the ruins comes to a **dry moat** (4) that cuts right across the site. At the moat you can either climb the long staircase that goes to the upper reaches of the city, or you can enter the city by the baths and Temple of the Sun.

The more strenuous way into the city is by the former route, which takes you past quarries on your left as you look down to the Urubamba on the west flank of the mountain. To your right are roofless buildings where you can see in close up the general construction methods used in the city. Proceeding along this level, above the main plazas, you reach the **Temple of the Three Windows** (5) and the **Principal Temple** (6), which has a smaller building called the **Sacristy** (7). The two main buildings are three-sided and were clearly of great importance, given the fine stonework involved. The wall with the three windows is built onto a single rock, one of the many instances in the city where the architects did not merely put their construction on a convenient piece of land. They used and fashioned its features to suit their concept of how the city should be tied to the mountain, its forces and the alignment of its stones to the surrounding peaks. In the Principal Temple, a diamond-shaped stone in the floor is said to depict the constellation of the Southern Cross.

Continue on the path behind the Sacristy to reach the **Intihuatana** (8), the 'hitching-post of the sun'. The name comes from the theory that such carved rocks (*gnomons*), found at all major Inca sites, were the point to which the sun was symbolically 'tied' at the winter solstice, before being freed to rise again on its annual ascent towards the summer solstice. The steps, angles and planes of this sculpted block appear to indicate a purpose beyond simple decoration, and researchers have sought the trajectory of each alignment. Whatever the motivation behind this magnificent carving, it is undoubtedly one of the highlights of Machu Picchu.

Climb down from the Intihuatana's mound to the **Main Plaza** (9). Beyond its northern end is a small plaza with open-sided buildings on two sides and on the third, the **Sacred Rock** (10). The outline of this gigantic, flat stone echoes that of the mountains behind it. From here you can proceed to the entrance to the trail to Huayna Picchu (see below). Returning to the Main Plaza and heading southeast you pass, on your left, several groups of closely packed buildings that have been taken to be **living quarters** and **Workshops** (11), **Mortar Buildings** (12; look for

1 Machu Picchu

To Huayna Picchu

Machu Picchu maps
1 Machu Picchu, page 412
2 Inca Trail, page 422

To Intipata (Inca Bridge)

Inca Trail

Ticket Gate

To Puente Ruinas &
Aguas Calientes

To Intipunku (Sun Gate)

N

50 metres
50 yards

1 Main entrance
2 Terracing 2
3 Watchman's Hut 3

4 Dry moat
5 Temple of the Three
   Windows
6 Principal Temple
7 Sacristry
8 Intihuatana
9 Main Plaza
10 Sacred Rock

11 Living quarters &
   workshops
12 Mortar buildings
13 Prison Group &
   Condor Temple
14 Intimachay
15 Ceremonial baths
   or Fountains

16 Principal Bath
17 Temple of the Sun
18 Royal Sector

Where to stay
1 Machu Picchu
   Sanctuary Lodge

the house with two discs let into the floor) and the **Prison Group** (13), one of whose constructions is known as the **Condor Temple**. Also in this area is a cave called **Intimachay** (14).

A short distance from the Condor Temple is the lower end of a series of **ceremonial baths** (15) or fountains. They were probably used for ritual bathing and the water still flows down them today. The uppermost, **Principal Bath** (16), is the most elaborate. Next to it is the **Temple of the Sun** (17), or Torreón. This singular building has one straight wall from which another wall curves around and back to meet the straight one, but for the doorway. From above it looks like an incomplete letter P. It is another example of the architecture being at one with its environment as the interior is taken up by the partly worked summit of the outcrop onto which the building is placed. All indications are that this temple was used for astronomical purposes. Underneath the Torreón a cave-like opening has been formed by an oblique gash in the rock. Fine masonry has been added to the opposing wall, making a second side of a triangle, which contrasts with the rough edge of the split rock. But the blocks of masonry appear to have been slotted behind another sculpted piece of natural stone, which has been cut into a four-stepped buttress. Immediately behind this is a two-stepped buttress. This strange combination of the natural and the man-made has been called the Tomb or Palace of the Princess. Across the stairway from the complex which includes the Torreón is the group of buildings known as the **Royal Sector** (18).

Huayna Picchu
There is access to the main path daily 0700-0800 and 1000-1100; latest return time 1500; max 200 people per departure. Check on www.machupicchu.gob.pe or with the Ministerio de Cultura in Aguas Calientes or Cuzco for current departure times and to sign up for a place.

Huayna Picchu, the mountain overlooking the site (on which there are also ruins), has steps to the top for a superlative view of the whole site, but it is not for those who are afraid of heights, and you shouldn't leave the path. The climb takes up to 90 minutes but the steps are dangerous after bad weather. Another trail to Huayna Picchu is via the Temple of the Moon, which consists of two caves, one above the other, with superb Inca niches inside. To reach the Temple of the Moon, take the marked trail to the left of the path to Huayna Picchu. It is in good shape, although it descends further than you think it should and there are very steep steps on the way. After the Temple it is safest to return to the main trail to Huayna Picchu, instead of taking a difficult shortcut. The round trip takes about four hours. Before doing any trekking around Machu Picchu, check with an official which paths may be used, or which are one-way.

Around Machu Picchu
The famous **Inca bridge** is about 45 minutes along a well-marked trail south of the Royal Sector. The bridge (on which you cannot walk) is spectacularly sited, carved into a vertiginous cliff-face. East of the Royal Sector is the path leading up

to **Intipunku** on the Inca Trail (60 minutes, fine views; see page 422). Climbing **Machu Picchu mountain** is another excellent and generally less crowded option which gives a completely different view of the site and surrounding valleys. The route is steep and takes up to three hours; a ticket for the site and the mountain costs 140 soles (US$50).

Aguas Calientes

The terminus of the tourist rail service to Machu Picchu, Aguas Calientes (official name Machu Picchu Pueblo) has grown from a handful of tin shacks along the railway in the 1980s, into an international resort village with countless multi-storey luxury hotels, restaurants advertising four-for-one happy hours, persistent massage touts and numerous services for the over one million tourists who visit every year. Although it is not to every traveller's taste, it may be worth spending the night here in order to visit the ruins early in the morning. Avenida Pachacútec leads from the plaza to the **thermal baths** ⓘ *at the upper end of town, daily 0500-2000, US$3.50,* which have a communal pool smelling of sulphur that's best early in the morning. There are showers for washing *before* entering the baths; take soap and shampoo, and keep an eye on valuables. The **Museo Manuel Chávez Ballón y Jardín Botánico** ⓘ *near the bridge to Machu Picchu, 25 min walk from town, daily 0900-1630, US$8,* displays objects found at Machu Picchu and local plants. There is also a **Butterfly House** ⓘ *access from Camping Municipal, see below, US$3.50.*

Tourist information

Aguas Calientes
iPerú (Av Pachacútec, by the plaza, T084-211104, iperumachupicchu@prompperu.gov.pe) provides tourist information Mon-Sat 0900-1300, 1400-1800, Sun 0900-1300.

Where to stay

$$$$ Machu Picchu Sanctuary Lodge
Reservations as for the Hotel Monasterio in Cuzco, which is under the same management (Belmond), T984-816956, www.sanctuarylodge.net.
Comfortable, good service, helpful staff, food well-cooked and presented. Electricity and water 24 hrs a day, prices are all-inclusive, restaurant

for residents only in the evening, but the buffet lunch is open to all. Usually fully booked well in advance, but try Sun night when other tourists find Pisac market a greater attraction.

Aguas Calientes

$$$$ Casa Andina Classic
Av Imperio de los Incas E-34, T084-211017, www.casa-andina.com.
Luxury chain hotel, rooms with heating and safety boxes, restaurant serving *novo-andino* cuisine, opened in 2014.

$$$$ Casa del Sol
Av Imperio de los Incas 608, on the railroad, T084-211118, www.hotelescasadelsol.com.
5-storey hotel with lift/elevator, different room categories with river or mountain

Aguas Calientes
(Machu Picchu Pueblo)

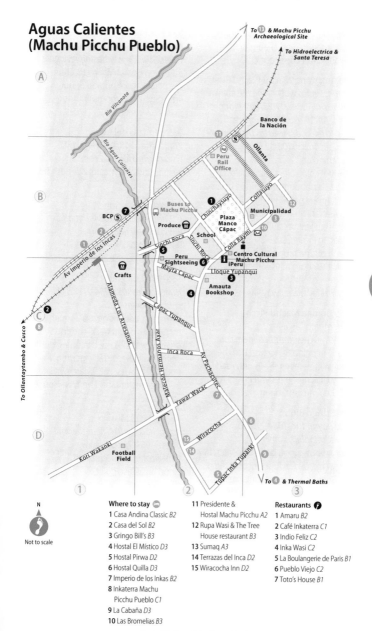

To ⑬ & Machu Picchu
Archaeological Site

To Hidroelectrica &
Santa Teresa

Río Vilcanota

Río Aguas Calientes

Banco de
la Nación

Ollanta

⑪

Peru
Rail
Office

Buses to
Machu Picchu

❶

Chinchaysuyo

Cotlasuyo

Municipalidad

❸

⑫

BCP Ⓢ

❼

Produce

Plaza
Manco
Cápac

Colla Raymi

⑩

Av Imperio de los Incas

Sinchi Roca

Sinchi Roca

School

❺

Peru
Sightseeing ❻

Centro Cultural
Machu Picchu
iPeru

Crafts

Mayta Cápac

Lloque Yupánqui

❸

❹

Amauta
Bookshop

Cápac Yupanqui

Inca Roca

Malecón Hermanos Ayar

Av Pachacutec

❼

Yawar Wacac

Wiracocha

❻

Túpac Inka Yupanki

⑮

❾

⑭

❺

To ❹ & Thermal Baths

❸

Kori Wakanki

Alameda Los Artesanos

Football
Field

❷

❶

❷

❽

To Ollantaytambo & Cusco

N

Not to scale

Where to stay
1 Casa Andina Classic B2
2 Casa del Sol B2
3 Gringo Bill's B3
4 Hostal El Místico D3
5 Hostal Pirwa D2
6 Hostal Quilla D3
7 Imperio de los Inkas B2
8 Inkaterra Machu
   Picchu Pueblo C1
9 La Cabaña D3
10 Las Bromelias B3

11 Presidente &
   Hostal Machu Picchu A2
12 Rupa Wasi & The Tree
   House restaurant B3
13 Sumaq A3
14 Terrazas del Inca D2
15 Wiracocha Inn D2

Restaurants
1 Amaru B2
2 Café Inkaterra C1
3 Indio Feliz C2
4 Inka Wasi C2
5 La Boulangerie de Paris B1
6 Pueblo Viejo C2
7 Toto's House B1

views, nice restaurant, beautiful spa. Shower service and changing room available after check out.

$$$$ Inkaterra Machu Picchu Pueblo
Km 104, 5 mins walk along the railway from town, T084-211122. Reservations from C Andalucía 174, Miraflores, Lima, T01-610 0400, or Plaza las Nazarenas 113 p2, in Cuzco, T084-234010, www. inkaterra.com.
Beautiful colonial-style bungalows in village compound surrounded by cloud forest, lovely gardens with a lot of steps between the public areas and rooms, pool, excellent restaurant, offer tours to Machu Picchu, several guided walks on and off the property. Good baggage service to coordinate with train arrivals and departures. Also has the Café Inkaterra by the railway line.

$$$$ Sumaq Machu Picchu
Av Hermanos Ayar Mz 1, Lote 3, T084-211059, www.sumaqhotelperu.com.
Award-winning 5-star hotel on the edge of town, between railway and road to Machu Picchu. Suites and luxury rooms with heating, restaurant and bar, spa.

$$$ Gringo Bill's
Colla Raymi 104, T084-211046, www.gringobills.com.
Pretty rooms, good beds, balconies, train-station pickup (on foot), lot of coming and going, good restaurant, breakfast from 0500, packed lunch available.

$$$ La Cabaña
Av Pachacútec 805, near thermal baths, T084-211048, www.lacabana machupicchu.com.
Variety of rooms, café, laundry service, helpful, popular with groups.

$$$ Presidente
Av Imperio de los Incas, at the old station, T084-211034, www.hostalpresidente.com.
Adjoining Hostal Machu Picchu, see below, more upmarket but little difference, rooms without river view cheaper.

$$$ Terrazas del Inca
Wiracocha M-18-4, T084-211117, www.terrazasdelinca.com.
Includes breakfast, safety deposit box, helpful staff.

$$$ Wiracocha Inn
C Wiracocha 206, T084-211088, www.wiracochainn.com.
Rooms and higher-priced suites, restaurant, helpful, popular with groups.

$$$-$$ Rupa Wasi
Huanacaure 105, T084-211101, www.rupawasi.net.
Charming 'eco-lodge' up a small alley off Collasuyo, laid back, comfortable, great views from the balconies, purified water available, organic garden, good breakfasts, half-board available, excellent restaurant, **The Tree House**, and cookery classes.

$$ Hostal El Místico
Av Pachacútec 814, near thermal baths, T084-211051, www. elmisticomachupicchu.com.
Good breakfast, quiet, new-wave-ish, comfortable.

$$ Imperio de los Inkas
Av Pachacútec 602, T084-211105, totemsito@gmail.com.
Functional, quiet, family-owned *hostal*, group rates, good value.

$$ Hostal Machu Picchu
Av Imperio de los Incas 135, T084-211065, sierrandina@gmail.com.

Functional, quiet, Wilber, the owner's son, has travel information, hot water, nice balcony over the Urubamba, grocery store.

$$ Hostal Quilla
Av Pachacútec 705, T084-211009, edwar_e.c.h@hotmail.com.
Adequate functional rooms, small terrace, pizzeria downstairs.

$ Las Bromelias
Colla Raymi 102, just off the plaza, T084-211145.
Rooms with private bath and hot water, some are small, family run, good value.

$ Hostal Pirwa
C Túpac Inka Yupanki 103, T084-214315, www.pirwahostelscusco.com.
In the same group as in Cuzco, Lima and elsewhere.

$ Jardines de Mandor
4 km from Aguas Calientes along the railway to Estacíon Hidroeléctrica, T940-188155, www.jardinesdemandor.com.
Relaxed rural lodging with simple rooms and a lovely garden, meals available, a delightful contrast to the buzz of Aguas Calientes.

Camping
The only official campsite (US$6 per tent) is in a field by the river, just below the former Puente Ruinas station. It has toilets and cold showers. There's an unpleasant smell from the nearby garbage-processing plant. Do not leave your tent and belongings unattended.

Restaurants

Aguas Calientes
The town is packed with eating places which double as bars, many of them are similar-looking *pizzerías*. Tax is often added as an extra to the bill. Simple economical set meals are served upstairs at the produce market, clean and adequate, daily 0600-1900. See also **The Tree House** restaurant at Rupa Wasi, above.

$$$ Café Inkaterra
On the railway, just below the Machu Picchu Pueblo Hotel.
US$15 for a great lunch buffet with scenic views of the river.

$$$-$$ Amaru
Chinchaysuyo on the Plaza.
Varied menu including pizza, nice location, Wi-Fi.

$$ Indio Feliz
C Lloque Yupanqui, T084-211090.
Great French cuisine, excellent value and service, set 3-course meal for US$20, good pisco sours, great atmosphere.

$$ Inka Wasi
Av Pachacútec.
Very good choice, has an open fire, full Peruvian and international menu available.

$$ Pueblo Viejo
Av Pachacútec (near plaza).
Good food in a spacious but warm environment. Price includes use of the salad bar.

$$ Toto's House
Av Imperio de los Incas, on the railway line.
Same owners as Pueblo Viejo. Good value and quality *menú*, buffet from 1130-1500.

Cafés

La Boulangerie de Paris
Jr Sinchi Roca by the footbridge. Open 0500-2100.

Coffee, sandwiches, quiche and great
French pastries.

Transport

Bus

Buses leave **Aguas Calientes** for Machu
Picchu as they fill daily 0530-1500,
25 mins, US$24 return, US$12 single,
children US$12, valid 48 hrs. The bus
stop and ticket office in Aguas Calientes
is on Malecón Hermanos Ayar y Av
Imperio de los Incas. Tickets can also
be bought in advance at **Consettur**
in Cuzco (Av Infancia 433, Wanchaq,
T084-222125, www.consettur.com),
which saves queuing when you arrive in
Aguas Calientes. Buses return from the
ruins to Aguas Calientes daily 0700-
1730. The walk up from Aguas Calientes
takes 1-2 hrs following a poor path and
crossing the motor road (take care).
The road is also in poor condition and
landslides can cause disruptions.

Train

Two companies operate services to
Machu Picchu, terminating at the
station in Aguas Calientes (Av Imperio
de los Incas: **PerúRail** (Av Pachacútec,
Wanchac Station, T084-581414, www.
perurail.com) runs trains from Poroy
(near Cuzco), from Urubamba and
from Ollantaytambo. **Inca Rail** (Portal
de Panes 105, Plaza de Armas, Cuzco,
T084-233030, or Lima T01-613 5288,
www.incarail.com) runs trains from
Ollantaytambo only. **Note** Services
may be disrupted in the rainy season,
especially Jan-Feb.

There are 4 classes of **PerúRail** tourist
train: **Vistadome** (recommended,

US$85 one-way from Poroy, US$75
from Urubamba or Ollantaytambo);
Expedition (US$73 one-way from
Poroy, US$63 from Ollantaytambo);
and the luxurious **Belmond Hiram
Bingham** service with meals, drinks and
entertainment (US$475 one way from
Poroy, US$795 round trip). Vistadome
and Expedition services are more
frequent from Ollantaytambo than
from Poroy or Urubamba. Seats can be
reserved even if you're not returning
the same day. These trains have toilets,
video, snacks and drinks for sale.

You must have your original passport
to travel on the trains to Machu Picchu.
Tickets for all trains may be bought at
Wanchac station and Portal de Carnes
214, Plaza de Armas, in Cuzco, at travel
agencies, or via PerúRail's website,
www.perurail.com.

Inca Rail has 4 trains a day from
Ollantayambo to Machu Picchu, 0640,
0720 (budget service), 1115 and 1636,
returning 0830, 1430, 1612 and 1900,
US$60 one way economy class, US$135
one way executive class. Carriages have
a/c and heating, snacks and drinks
served. In high season (1 Apr-31 Oct,
Christmas and New Year) a 1st class
service is added to the 0640, 1115
and 1636 trains and an exclusive Inca
Princess carriage can also be added
(US$300 return).The above are high-
season fares; they are slightly cheaper
in low season and at less convenient
hours and all are subject to change;
see company websites.

Tourists may not travel on the local
trains to Machu Picchu, except from
Santa Teresa, see page 427.

★The most impressive way to reach Machu Picchu is via the centuries-old Inca Trail that winds its way from the Sacred Valley near Ollantaytambo, taking three to five days. What makes this hike so special is the stunning combination of Inca ruins, unforgettable views, magnificent mountains, exotic vegetation and extraordinary ecological variety. This, the most famous trek in South America, is extremely popular and limited to 500 hikers a day, including guides and porters. It can only be done with a licensed tour operator or licensed private guide (the majority of trekkers sign up with an operator); independent trekking is not permitted. The Inca Trail is rugged and steep and you should be in reasonable physical shape. For most hikers, the magnificent views compensate for any weariness, but it is cold at night and weather conditions change rapidly.

The Classic Trail

The trek to Machu Picchu begins either at Km 82, **Piscacucho**, or at Km 88, **Qorihuayrachina**, at 2600 m. In order to reach Km 82 hikers are transported by their tour operator in a minibus on the road that goes from Ollantaytambo to Quillabamba. At Phiry the road divides; the left branch follows the north shore of the Río Vilcanota and ends at Km 82, where there is a bridge. Equipment, food, fuel and field personnel reach Km 82 (depending on the tour operator's logistics) for the Sernanp staff to weigh each bundle before the group arrives. Since many groups leave every day, it is convenient to arrive early. Km 88 can only be reached by train, which is slower than a bus, but you start your walk nearer to Llaqtapata and Huayllabamba.

The walk to **Huayllabamba**, following the Río Cusichaca, needs about three hours and isn't too arduous. Huayllabamba is a popular camping spot for tour groups, but there is another camping place about an hour ahead at **Llulluchayoc** (3200 m). A punishing 1½-hour climb further is **Llulluchapampa**, an ideal meadow for camping. If you have the energy to reach this point, it will make the second day easier because the next stage, the ascent to the first pass, **Warmiwañuska** (Dead Woman's Pass) at 4200 m, is tough; 2½ hours.

Afterwards take the steep path downhill to the **Pacaymayo** ravine. Beware of slipping on the Inca steps after rain. Tour groups usually camp by a stream at the bottom (1½ hours from the first pass). Camping is no longer permitted at **Runkuracay**, on the way up to the second pass. This is a much easier climb to 3900 m, with magnificent views near the summit in clear weather. **Chaquicocha** camp (3600 m) is about 30 minutes past the ruins at **Sayacmarca** (3500 m), about an hour beyond the top of the second pass.

A gentle two-hour climb on a fine stone highway leads through an Inca tunnel to the third pass. Near the top there's a spectacular view of the entire Vilcabamba range, and another campsite. You descend to Inca ruins at **Phuyupatamarca** (3650 m), well worth a long visit.

Essential Inca Trail

Equipment

Take strong footwear, rain gear and warm clothing, extra snacks, water and water-purification supplies, insect repellent, plastic bags, coverings, a good sleeping bag and a torch/flashlight. Equipment is provided by tour agencies, but always check what is included and what must be rented or brought from home; see also under Camping equipment, page 369. Maps of the Trail and area are available from Cuzco bookshops and **South American Explorers** in Lima or Cuzco. On most tours, porters will take the heavy gear; you should carry a day-pack for your water, snacks, etc.

Tours

Tour operators taking clients on any of the Inca Trails leading to the Machu Picchu must be licensed and have to pass an annual test. **Sernanp** (Av José Gabriel Cosio 308, Urb Magisterial, 1 etapa, T084-229297, www.sernanp.gob.pe) verifies operating permits. Unlicensed agencies will sell Inca Trail trips, but pass clients on to the operating agency. This can cause confusion and booking problems at busy times. There have been many instances of disappointed trekkers whose bookings did not materialize. Don't wait to the last minute, and check your operator's cancellation fees. Tour operators in Cuzco (see page 371) include transport to the start, equipment and food, as part of the total price for all treks that lead to Machu Picchu. Prices start at about US$680 per person for a four-day/three-night trek on the Classic Inca Trail and rise according to the level of service given. If the price is significantly lower, you should be concerned, as the company may be cutting corners. Operators pay US$15 per day for each porter and other trail staff; porters are not permitted to carry more than 20 kg.

Groups of up to seven independent travellers who do not wish to use a tour operator are allowed to hike the trails if they contract an independent, licensed guide to accompany them, as long as they do not contract any other persons such as porters or cooks.

Tickets

Current advice is to book your preferred dates as early as possible, between two months and a year in advance, depending on the season when you want to go, then confirm nearer the time. Don't wait to the last minute. Check your operator's cancellation fees before booking. Tickets cost US$80; students and children under 15, US$40. This is the price for all hiking trails (Km 82 or Km 88 to Machu Picchu, Salkantay to Machu Picchu, and Km 82 or Km 88 to Machu Picchu via Km 104) except for the Camino Real de los Inkas (from Km 104 to Wiñay-Wayna and Machu Picchu), for which the fee is US$47 (US$26 for students and children). Tour operators usually purchase tickets

Tip...

Make sure your train ticket for the return to Cuzco has your name on it (spelt absolutely correctly), otherwise you will have to pay for any changes.

for their clients or they can be bought at the **Dirección de Cultura** office in Cuzco (Avenida de la Cultura 238, Condominio Huáscar, T084-236061, www.drc-cusco. gob.pe, Monday-Friday 0715-1600) on presentation of a letter from the tour operator, including your full passport details. Tickets are non-refundable and cannot be changed, so make sure you provide accurate passport details to your tour operator. No tickets are sold at the entrance to any of the routes.

When to go

July and August is the height of the tourist season but the Trail is booked to capacity for most of the year. Check conditions in the rainy season from December to March (note that this can vary from year to year); the weather may be cloudy and the paths are very slippery and difficult in the wet. **The Trail is closed each February for cleaning and repair**.

Time required

Four days would make a comfortable trip (though much depends on the weather). Allow a further day to see Machu Picchu when you have recovered from the hike. Alternatively, you can take a five-day tour, which reaches Machu Picchu in the afternoon. The first two days of the Trail involve the stiffest climbing, so do not attempt it if you're feeling unwell.

Regulations and precautions

Littering is banned, as is carrying plastic water bottles (canteens only may be carried). Pets and pack animals are prohibited. Groups must use approved campsites only. You cannot take backpacks into Machu Picchu; leave them at the ticket office. Leave all your valuables in Cuzco and keep everything inside your tent, even your shoes. Security has, however, improved in recent years. Always take sufficient cash to tip porters and guides at the end (S/.50-100 each, but at your discretion).

From there steps go downhill to the magnificent ruins of **Wiñay-Wayna** (2700 m), with impressive views of the cleared terraces of Intipata. There is a campsite here that gets crowded and dirty. After Wiñay-Wayna there is no water and no camping till after Machu Picchu, near Aguas Calientes (see Where to stay, page 417). The path from this point goes more or less level through jungle for two hours before it reaches the steep staircase up to the **Intipunku**, where there's a fine view of Machu Picchu, especially at dawn, with the sun alternately in and out, clouds sometimes obscuring the ruins, sometimes leaving them clear. Groups try to reach Machu Picchu as early as possible to avoid the crowds, but this is usually a futile endeavour and requires a pre-dawn start as well as walking along the edge of the precipice in the dark.

Camino Real de los Inkas and other options

The Camino Real de los Inkas starts at Km 104, where a footbridge gives access to the ruins of Chachabamba and the trail, which ascends above the ruins of Choquesuysuy to connect with the main trail at Wiñay-Wayna. This first part is a steady, continuous ascent of three hours (take water). Many people recommend this short Inca Trail. It can be extended into a three-night trek by starting from Km 82, trekking to Km 88, then along the Río Urubamba to Pacaymayo Bajo and Km 104, from where you can join the Camino Real de los Inkas. Alternatively, good day hiking trails from Aguas Calientes run along the banks of the Urubamba.

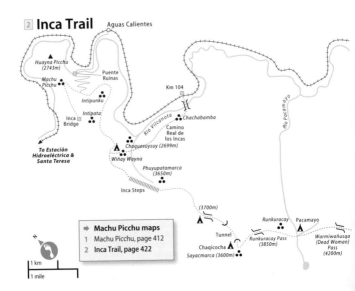

2 **Inca Trail**

Aguas Calientes

Huayna Picchu (2743m)

Machu Picchu

Puente Ruinas

Km 104

Intipunku

Intipata

Inca Bridge

Río Vilcanota

Chachabamba

Camino Real de los Incas

Río Pacamayo

To Estación Hidroeléctrica & Santa Teresa

Choquesuysuy (2699m)

Wiñay Wayna

Phuyupatamarca (3650m)

Inca Steps

(3700m)

Tunnel

Chaqicocha

Sayacmarca (3600m)

Runkuracay Pass (3850m)

Runkuracay

Pacamayo

Warmiwañusqa (Dead Woman) Pass (4200m)

➡ **Machu Picchu maps**
1 Machu Picchu, page 412
2 Inca Trail, page 422

N

1 km
1 mile

Salkantay treks

Two treks involve routes from Salkantay: one, known as the **High Inca Trail** joins the classic trail at Huayllabamba, then proceeds as before on the main Trail through Wiñay Wayna to Machu Picchu. To get to Salkantay, you have to start the trek in Mollepata, three hours northwest of Cuzco in the Apurímac valley. (**Ampay** buses run to Mollepata from Arcopata on the Chinchero road, or you can take private transport). Salkantay to Machu Picchu this way takes three nights.

The second Salkantay route, known as the **Santa Teresa Trek**, takes four days and crosses the 4500-m Huamantay Pass to reach the Santa Teresa valley, which you follow to its confluence with the Vilcanota. The goal is the town of Santa Teresa (see page 426).

Inca Jungle Trail

This route is offered by several tour operators in Cuzco and combines hiking with cycling and other activities. On the first day you cycle downhill from the Abra Málaga pass on the Ollantaytambo–Quillabamba highway to Santa María (see below) at 2000 m. This involves three to four hours of riding on the main road with speeding vehicles inattentive to cyclists; it's best to pay for good bikes and back-up on this section. Some agencies also offer white-water rafting in the afternoon. The second day is a hard 11-km trek from Santa María to Santa Teresa (see page 426). It involves crossing three adventurous bridges and bathing in the hot springs at Santa Teresa. The third day is a six-hour trek from Santa Teresa to Aguas Calientes. Some agencies offer ziplining near Santa Teresa as an alternative. The final day is a guided tour of Machu Picchu.

Qorihuayrachina
(Km 88, 2600m)

To Ollantaytambo

Wayna
Q'Ente

Llaqtapata
(2288m)

To Piscacucho (Km 82)
& Chilca

Río Cusichaca

Llulluchapampa

Llulluchayoc
(3 White Stones)

Huayllabamba
(2950m)

To Salkantay

Vilcabamba and around

discover the last refuge of the Incas

Santa María

A paved road runs from Ollantaytambo to Santa María, sometimes called Puente Chaullay, an important crossroads with basic places to stay and eat. This is a very beautiful journey, with snowy peaks on either side of the valley. The climb to the **Abra Málaga pass** (4350 m), west of Ollantaytambo, is steep with many tight curves – on the right is a huge glacier. Soon on the left, Nevado Verónica begins to appear in all its huge and snowy majesty. After endless zig-zags and breathtaking views, you reach the pass. The descent to the Vilcanota valley around Santa María shows hillsides covered in lichen and Spanish moss. From Santa María roads run to Quillabamba in the lowlands to the north; to Lucma, Pucyura, Huancacalle and Vilcabamba to the west, and to Santa Teresa to the south.

Huancacalle and around

West of Santa Maria, the tranquil little village of Huancacalle is the best base for exploring the last stronghold of the Incas (see box, opposite), including the nearby ruins of **Vitcos**, which were the palace of the last four Inca rulers from 1536 to 1572. **Yurac Rumi**, the sacred white rock of the Incas is also here. It is 8m high and 20 m wide and covered with intricate carvings. The 7-km loop from Huancacalle to Vitcos, the Inca terraces at Rosaspata, Yurac Rumi and back to Huancacalle makes a nice half-day hike. Several excellent longer treks begin or end in Huancacalle: from Choquequirao (see page 386) to Vilcabamba Vieja (Espíritu Pampa, see below), and to Machu Picchu via Santa Teresa (see page 426).

Towards Vilcabamba Vieja

The road continues west from Huancacalle, 5 km up to the chilly little village of **Vilcabamba**; there's no regular transport but you can hike through the pleasant countryside. There is a mission here run by Italians, with electricity and running water, where you may be able to spend the night; ask for 'La Parroquia'.

Beyond Vilcabamba the road runs a further 12 km to **Pampaconas**, start of the trail to the Vilcabamba Vieja ruins at **Espíritu Pampa**, a vast pre-Inca site with a neo-Inca overlay set in deep jungle at 1000 m. For background information about this unique site, see The last Incas of Vilcabamba, opposite. From Huancacalle a trip to Espíritu Pampa will take three or four days on foot. Give yourself at least

Vilcabamba

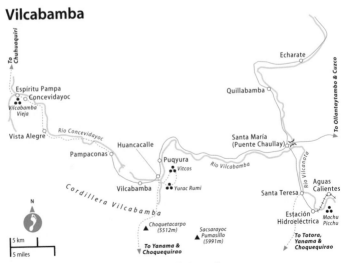

BACKGROUND
The last Incas of Vilcabamba

After Pizarro killed Atahualpa in 1532, the Inca empire disintegrated rapidly, and it is often thought that native resistance ended there. But, in fact, it continued for 40 more years, beginning with Manco, a teenage half-brother of Atahualpa.

In 1536, Manco escaped from the Spanish and returned to lead a massive army against them. He besieged Cuzco and Lima simultaneously, and came close to dislodging the Spaniards from Peru. Spanish reinforcements arrived, and Manco fled to Vilcabamba, a mountainous forest region west of Cuzco that was remote, but still fairly close to the Inca capital, which he always dreamed of recapturing.

The Spanish chased Manco deep into Vilcabamba, but he managed to elude them and continued his guerrilla war, raiding Spanish commerce on the Lima highway and keeping alive the Inca flame. Then, in 1544, Spanish outlaws to whom he had given refuge murdered him, ending the most active period of Inca resistance.

The Inca line passed to his sons. The first, a child too young to rule named Sayri Túpac, eventually yielded to Spanish enticements and emerged from Vilcabamba, taking up residence in Yucay near Urubamba in 1558. He died mysteriously – possibly poisoned – three years later.

His brother Titu Cusi, who was still in Vilcabamba, now took up the Inca mantle. Astute and determined, he resumed raiding and fomenting rebellion against the Spanish. But in 1570, Titu Cusi fell ill and died. A Spanish priest was accused of murdering him. Anti-Spanish resentment erupted, and the priest and a Spanish viceregal envoy were killed. Francisco de Toledo, the fifth Viceroy of Peru, reacted immediately, and his troops invaded Vilcabamba for the third and last time in 1572.

A third brother, Túpac Amaru, was now in charge. He lacked his brother's experience and acuity, and his destiny was to be the sacrificial last Inca. The Spanish overran the Inca's jungle capital and dragged him back to Cuzco in chains. There, Túpac Amaru, the last Inca, was publicly executed in Cuzco's main plaza.

The location of the neo-Inca capital of Vilcabamba was forgotten over the centuries, and the search for it provoked Hiram Bingham's expeditions and his discovery of Machu Picchu. Bingham discovered Vilcabama Vieja without realizing it, but the true location at Espíritu Pampa was only pinpointed by Gene Savoy in the 1960s and wasn't confirmed irrefutably until the work of Vincent Lee in the 1980s.

Sixpac Manco and *Forgotten Vilcabamba*, both by Vincent Lee (available in Cuzco), have accurate maps of all archaeological sites in the area and describe two expeditions into the region by the author and his party. Gene Savoy's book, *Antisuyo*, is also recommended reading.

a day at the site to soak up the atmosphere before continuing to **Chuhuanquiri** for transport back to Quillabamba and Cuzco. It is advisable to take local guides and mules, and to enquire in Cuzco and Huancacalle about public safety along the route. Distances are considerable and the going is difficult. The best time of year is May to November. Outside this period it is dangerous as the trails are very narrow and can be thick with mud and very slippery. There are no services along the route; bring all food and supplies including plenty of insect repellent, and take all rubbish with you back to Cuzco for disposal.

Santa Teresa

South of Santa María, this relaxed little town provides alternative access to Machu Picchu (via Estación Hidroeléctrica; see Transport, below) for those who do not wish to ride the train from Cuzco or Ollantaytambo, and makes a good base for activities in the area. Santa Teresa is located at the confluence of the Ríos Sacsara, Salkantay and Vilcanota, and its lower elevation at 1600 m creates a warm climate that is a pleasant change from the chill of Cuzco and trekking at high altitude. Many tour groups and independent travellers pass through or spend the night en route to or from Machu Picchu, and several popular treks go through here (see page 423). There are plenty of hotels, restaurants and most services. The **Colcamayo Thermal Baths** ① *2 km from town along the Río Vilcanota, Wed, Thu, Sat-Mon 0500-2300, Tue and Fri 1100-2300, US$1.75,* have crystal-clear warm pools in a pretty setting and an ice-cold waterfall; free camping nearby. There are several ziplines around town, including **Cola de Mono** (www.canopyperu.com), which is part of various tour itineraries.

> Tip...
> Many Cuzco agencies sell '**Machu Picchu By Car'** tours that go through Santa Teresa. You can also reach Santa Teresa by road on your own.

Listings Vilcabamba

Where to stay and eat

Huancacalle
Huancacalle has a few basic shops and eateries, although these are not always open; there's a better selection in Pucyura, 2 km north.

$ Sixpac Manco
Huancacalle, T971-823855, giorgio0909@hotmail.com.
A good simple hostal, with shared bath, electric shower, large garden, meals on request. It is managed by the Cobos family, who are very knowledgeable about the area and can arrange for guides and pack animals for trekking.

Santa Teresa
Mountain Lodges of Peru (www.mountainlodgesofperu.com) have a series of lodges on the Santa Teresa trek to Machu Picchu (see page 423).

$$-$ Hostal Yacumama
C Julio Tomás Rivas, T974-290605.
Rooms with private bath, hot water, breakfast available, restaurant next door.

$ Hospedaje El Sol
Av Av Calixto Sánchez, T084-637158.
Rooms of various sizes, all with private
bath and hot water.

$ Casa de Judas
*Av Calixto Sánchez by the Plaza,
T974-709058.*
Rooms with private bath and dorm, solar
hot water, opened in 2014, good value
economy option.

Transport

Santa María
To reach Santa María from Cuzco,
take a Quillabamba-bound bus
from the Terminal Terrestre, or a van
from C Almudena in the Santiago
neighbourhood, US$9, 4 hrs. From
Santa María there are vans to **Cuzco**
and **Quillabamba**, US$1.75, 1 hr, as well
as buses passing through between
Quillabamba and Cuzco (you can book
a seat in Santa María). Cars leave as they
fill throughout the day for **Santa Teresa**,
US$3.50, 45 min.

Huancacalle
Four companies leave Cuzco's bus
terminal for **Quillabamba**, US$7,
6 hrs, 233 km (**Ampay** is best). Then
take a colectivo from Quillabamba to
Huancacalle, 3 daily, US$5.50, 2½ hrs.
From Huancacalle to **Cuzco** you can
get off the colectivo at Santa María and
catch a Cuzco-bound bus from there, but
from Cuzco to Huancacalle you should
go all the way to Quillabamba because
the colectivos are usually full.

Santa Teresa
From Santa Teresa market, vans leave for
the **Estación Hidroeléctrica** at 0530-
0700 and 1200-1430, US$1.75, 30 min, to
meet the local train which runs to **Aguas
Calientes**, US$20 for tourists, 40 min.
There are **PerúRail** ticket offices at Santa
Teresa market (confirm current schedules
here) and at the Estación Hidroeléctrica,
which is not much more than a railway
siding. You can also walk 11 km along
the tracks from Estación Hidroeléctrica
to Aguas Calientes, a pleasant 3- to 4-hr
hike with great views and many birds,
but mind the passing trains.

Central Highlands

Stretching from the southern end of the Cordillera Blanca right up to Cuzco department, this area of stunning mountain scenery and timeless Andean towns and villages is a must for those who appreciate traditional, good-quality textiles and ceramics.

The main highlights include the cities of Huancayo and Ayacucho and the surrounding villages, which are the main production centres for handicrafts. Huancayo is still a little off the tourist compass but its festivals are very popular and not to be missed. Ayacucho hosts one of the largest and most impressive Holy Week celebrations in Latin America.

If you are seeking refuge from the Andean chill, the road through Tarma to the Selva Central is one of the most beautiful in Peru, leading to a relatively unexplored region of the country. More than just fabulous landscapes, this area also hides important pre-Inca sites, such as Kótosh (near Huánuco) and Huari (outside Ayacucho). Stretches of the Capaq Ñan – the Great Inca Road – run from the temple fortress of Huánuco Viejo and up the Yanahuanca Valley, serving as reminders of this imperial causeway. The Spaniards, too, have left their mark, with fine churches and mansions in Ayacucho.

Best for
Crafts ■ Festivals ■ Hair-raising journeys ■ Scenery

Footprint
picks

★ **Lima–Huancayo train journey**, page 433

Climb from the coast to the cordillera on a magnificent train ride through one of the highest railway tunnels in the world.

★ **Mantaro Valley**, page 438

This fertile valley is steeped in the ancient cultures of the Huanca and Inca civilizations.

★ **Ayacucho**, page 449

The city is famous for its Semana Santa celebrations, its splendid market and no less than 33 churches.

★ **Quinua**, page 456

The decisive Battle of Ayacucho was fought here on 9 December 1824, bringing Spanish rule in Peru to an end.

★ **Selva Central**, page 462

Between Tarma and La Merced the road drops 2450 m and the vegetation changes dramatically from temperate to tropical.

★ **Huánuco Viejo**, page 468

This was a major Inca city along the Capaq Ñan. It is nicely preserved and receives few visitors.

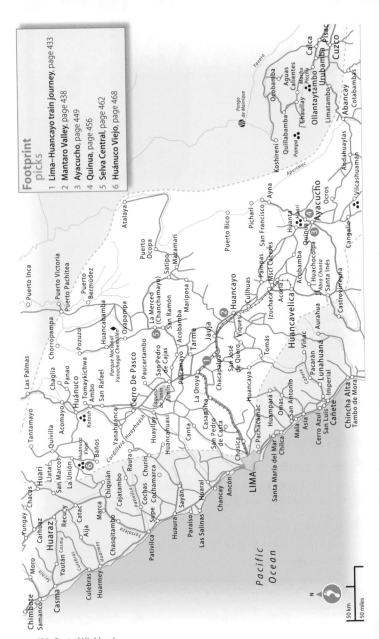

Footprint picks

1 Lima–Huancayo train journey, page 433
2 Mantaro Valley, page 438
3 Ayacucho, page 449
4 Quinua, page 456
5 Selva Central, page 462
6 Huánuco Viejo, page 468

Pacific Ocean

N

50 km
50 miles

Essential Central Highlands

Finding your feet

There are several options for getting to the Sierra and the views on whichever ascent you choose are beyond compare. The Central Highway and the railway run from Lima to Huancayo (335 km) but there are also paved roads from Pisco to Ayacucho and from Nazca to Abancay. You can also reach the Central Highlands from Cuzco (via Abancay and Andahuaylas) and from Huaraz (via La Unión and Huánuco), so Lima is not the sole point of access overland. If you prefer to fly, there are flights from Lima to Andahuaylas, Ayacucho, Jauja and Huánuco.

Getting around

If schedules allow, catch the train to Huancayo. You could continue by train to Huancavelica, although the paved road is a more comfortable option, if you can find a bus driver who doesn't scare the living daylights out of you. The rest of the region is best explored by bus or on a tour. Bear in mind that, apart from the major routes, roads in this region tend to be in poor condition, especially in the wet.

When to go

May to September is the dry season. November to April can be wet and travel can be difficult. Ayacucho's climate is lovely, with warm, sunny days and pleasant balmy evenings.

Time required

One or two weeks will allow you to see the best of this region, allowing for slow travel on some rough roads.

Weather Huancayo

Month	Temp (high)	Temp (low)	Rainfall
January	22°C	9°C	121mm
February	21°C	9°C	125mm
March	21°C	9°C	120mm
April	23°C	9°C	53mm
May	23°C	8°C	22mm
June	22°C	7°C	6mm
July	21°C	9°C	1mm
August	22°C	18°C	5mm
September	22°C	42°C	25mm
October	23°C	67°C	60mm
November	23°C	70°C	68mm
December	23°C	102°C	76mm

Lima to
Ayacucho

The Central Highway and the famous Central Railway
take you up from the coast to the thin air of the metal-
smelting zone of La Oroya. To get there you have to
follow some of the highest routes in the continent.
Beyond La Oroya are traditional towns and remains
of pre-Hispanic cultures on the altiplano. Huancayo
is the commercial centre of the region and the heart
of a valley whose villages concentrate on making
handicrafts and holding festivals. Head south towards
Ayacucho on difficult roads, either via the departmental
capital of Huancavelica, or through more remote but
magnificent scenery.

ON THE ROAD

★Central Railway

Constructed in the late 19th and early 20th centuries, this is the second-highest railway in the world and is a magnificent feat of engineering, with 58 bridges, 69 tunnels and six zigzags, passing beautiful landscapes. It's a great way to travel to the Central Highlands. The main line runs from Lima, via La Oroya, to Huancayo, and is run as an irregular tourist service, operated once or twice a month by Ferrocarril Centro Andino (Avenida José Gálvez Barrenechea 566, p 5, San Isidro, Lima, T01-226 6363, www.ferrocarrilcentral.com.pe). The train leaves Lima at 0700, reaching Huancayo 11 hours later; the return journey begins at 0700 or 1800, three or four days later; see the website for the next departure date. There are *turístico* (US$80 single, US$125 return) and *clásico* fares (US$40 single, US$70 return), sold online and by Lima and Huancayo agencies. Coaches have reclining seats and heating; there's also a restaurant, tourist information, toilets and a nurse with first aid and oxygen.

Beyond Huancayo trains run on a narrow gauge (3 ft) line 120 km to Huancavelica. They depart from a small station in the Huancayo suburb of Chilca (15 mins by taxi from the centre, US$2) three to four times a week, either as *Expreso* (*Tren Macho*; US$3), or *Autovagón*. Enquire locally about schedules, as they are constantly changing. This authentic Andean train journey on the *Tren Macho* takes seven long, uncomfortable hours and navigates 38 tunnels and 15 bridges. There are fine views as it passes through typical mountain villages where vendors sell food and crafts. In some places, the train has to reverse and change tracks.

Lima to Huancayo

ride the rails into the hills

The Central Highway more or less parallels the course of the railway between Lima and Huancayo (335 km). Chosica (www.chosica.com) is a chaotic town 45 km east of Lima at 860 m; it is increasingly becoming part of the big city.

Marcahuasi
3 hrs walk from San Pedro de Casta. Entry US$4, pack donkey US$8, horse US$10.

Up the Santa Eulalia valley, 40 km beyond **Chosica**, is Marcahuasi, a table mountain about 3 km by 1 km at 4000 m, near the village of **San Pedro de Casta**. There are three lakes, a 40-m-high 'monumento a la humanidad' and other mysterious lines, gigantic figures, sculptures, astrological signs and megaliths. Their origin is a mystery, although a widely accepted theory is that the formations are the result of wind erosion. The trail to Marcahuasi starts south of the village of San Pedro and climbs southeast. It's three hours' walk to the *meseta*; guides are advisable in misty weather. At shops in San Pedro you can buy everything for the trip, including bottled water. Take all necessary camping equipment for the trek. Tourist information is available at the municipality on the plaza and tours can be arranged with travel agencies in Lima.

Towards La Oroya

For a while, beyond Chosica, each successive valley looks greener and lusher, with a greater variety of trees and flowers. Between Río Blanco and **Chicla** (Km 127, 3733 m), Inca contour-terraces can be seen quite clearly. After climbing up from **Casapalca** (Km 139, 4154 m), there are glorious views of the highest peaks and of mines at the foot of a deep gorge. The road ascends to the Ticlio Pass, before the descent to **Morococha** and **La Oroya**. A large metal flag of Peru can be seen at the top of Mount Meiggs; this is not by any means the highest peak in the area, but through it runs the Galera Tunnel, 1175 m long, in which the Central Railway reaches its greatest altitude, 4782 m.

La Oroya (3755 m) is the main smelting centre for the region's mining industry. It stands at the fork of the Yauli and Mantaro rivers. Any traveller, but asthmatics in particular, should beware the pollution from the heavy industry, which can cause breathing difficulties. ▶ *For destinations to the northeast and north of La Oroya, see page 462.*

Jauja and around

The old town of **Jauja**, 80 km southeast of La Oroya at 3400 m, was Pizarro's provisional capital until the founding of Lima. It has a colourful Wednesday and Sunday market. The **Museo Arqueológico Julio Espejo Núñez** ⓘ *Jr Cusco 537, T064-361163, Mon and Wed 1500-1900, Sun 0900-1200, 1400-1700, donations welcome, knock on door of La Casa del Caminante opposite where the creator and curator lives,* is a quaint but endearing mix of relics from various Peruvian cultures, including two mummies, one still wrapped in the original shroud. The **Cristo Pobre** church is supposedly modelled on Notre Dame and is something of a curiosity. On a hill above Jauja there is a fine line of Inca storehouses, and, on hills nearby, the ruins of Huajlaasmarca, with hundreds of circular stone buildings from the Huanca culture. There are also ruins near the **Laguna de Paca** ⓘ *3.5 km from Jauja; combi from Av Pizarro, US$0.50.* The western shore is lined with restaurants, many of which offer weekend boat trips, US$1.

On the road south to Huancayo is **Concepción** at 3251 m, with a market on Sunday. From Concepción a branch road (6 km) leads to the **Convent of Santa Rosa de Ocopa** ⓘ *Wed-Mon 0900-1200 and 1500-1800, 45-min tours start on the hour, US$1.25; colectivos from the market in Concepción, 15 mins, US$0.50,* a Franciscan monastery set in beautiful surroundings. It was established in 1725 in order to train missionaries for the jungle. It contains a fine library with over 25,000 volumes, a biological museum and a large collection of paintings.

ON THE ROAD

Stairway to heaven

High in the central Andes of Peru, along the border between the departments of Lima and Junín, is Pariacaca, a particularly important mountain deity with two splendid summits rising to 5730 m and 5750 m. So great was the importance of this *Apu* (mountain god) that, according to the early 17th-century *Manuscrito de Huarochirí*, all wars were suspended in honour of its annual festival, when faithful from all over the Andean world would flock to visit it.

A great sanctuary on the slopes of Pariacaca was destroyed by the Spaniards in their frenzy to eradicate the old beliefs of the New World; its exact location is today a mystery. The sanctuary of Pariacaca was linked to another of equal importance at Pachacamac on the coast south of Lima by an ancient road – much older than the Inca Empire but greatly enhanced by it. The highest point of the road was crowned with a monumental stairway.

This superb architectural achievement survives to the present day and is located in the **Nor Yauyos Cochas Reserve**, accessed from Jauja, Cañete or Lima. (Some operators in Huancayo offer tours.) The stairway climbs over 300 m, from approximately 4400 to 4700 m above sea level, on 1800 stone steps, each three to four metres wide. Today, it is the focus of efforts to raise awareness of the many wonders still to be found along the *Capaq Ñan* (*Qhapaqñan*), the ancient road network that once linked the four corners of *Tawantinsuyo* – the Inca Empire. The *Capaq Ñan* was declared a UNESCO World Heritage site in 2014.

Listings Lima to Huancayo

Tourist information

Jauja

The Junín regional **tourist office** is located in the town (Jr Grau 528, T064-362897); for other information see www.jaujaperu.info.

Where to stay

Marcahuasi

Locals in San Pedro de Casta will put you up ($); ask at tourist information at the municipality. The best hotel in town is the $ **Marcahuasi**, just off the plaza. Rooms with private or shared bath; it also has a restaurant. There are 2 other restaurants in town.

Jauja

$ Hostal Manco Cápac
Jr Manco Cápac 575, T064-361620/ 99-974 9119.
Central, good rooms, private or shared rooms, garden, good breakfast and coffee.

$ Hostal María Nieves
Jr Gálvez 491, 1 block from the Plaza de Armas, T064-362543.
Safe, helpful, large breakfast, hot water all day, parking. Good.

Restaurants

Towards La Oroya

$$ El Tambo
2 km before town on the road from Lima.
Good trout and frogs legs, local cheese and *manjar*; recommended as the best in and around town; buses on the Lima route stop here.

Jauja

$ Centro Naturista
Huarancayo 138 (no sign).
Fruit salad, yoghurt, granola, etc, basic place.

$ D'Chechis
Jr Bolívar 1166, T064-368530.
Lunch only, excellent.

$ Ganso de Oro
R Palma 249, T064-362166.
Good restaurant in hotel of same name (which is not recommendable), varied prices, unpretentious.

$ La Rotonda
Tarapacá 415, T064-368412.
Good lunch menú and pizzas in the evening.

Transport

Most buses on the Lima–La Oroya route are full when they pass through Chosica.

Chosica
Colectivos for Chosica leave from Av Grau, **Lima**, when full, between 0600 and 2100, US$1. Colectivo taxi to La Oroya US$7.50, 3 hrs, very scenic, passing the 2nd highest railway in the world.

Marcahuasi
Bus
Minibuses to San Pedro de Casta leave **Chosica** from Parque Echenique, opposite market, 0900 and 1500, 4 hrs, US$3.50; return 0700 and 1400.

Towards La Oroya
Bus
To **Lima**, 4½ hrs, US$8. To **Jauja**, 80 km, 1½ hrs, US$2. To **Tarma**, 1½ hrs, US$2.50. To **Cerro de Pasco**, 131 km, 3 hrs, US$3. To **Huánuco**, 236 km, 6 hr, US$7.50. Buses leave from Zeballos, adjacent to the train station. Colectivos also run on all routes.

Jauja
Air
Francisco Carle airport is located just outside Jauja. **LC Peru** has 2 daily flights from **Lima**, 45 mins; price includes transfer to Huancayo.

Bus
Most companies have their offices on the Plaza de Armas, but their buses leave from Av Pizarro. To **Lima,** US$15, or with **Cruz del Sur** (Pizarro 220), direct, 6 hrs, US$22-29 *bus cama*.
To **Huancayo**, 44 km, 1 hr, US$2.25; combis to Huancayo from 25 de Abril y Ricardo Palma, 1¼ hrs, US$2.50.
To **Cerro de Pasco**, with **Turismo Central** from 25 de Abril 144, 5 hrs, US$6. **Turismo Central** also goes to **Huánuco**, 8 hrs, US$15. To **Tarma**, US$3, hourly with **Trans Los Canarios** and **Angelitos/San Juan** from Jr Tarma; the latter continues to **Chanchamayo**, US$8. Colectivos to Tarma leave from Junín y Tarma when full.

a nexus of traditional crafts and culture

Huancayo is the capital of the Junín Region and the main commercial centre for central inland Peru, with a population of over half a million. The city lies in the Mantaro Valley at 3271 m, surrounded by villages that produce their own original crafts and celebrate festivals all year round. People flock in from far and wide to the important festivals in Huancayo, with an incredible range of food, crafts, dancing and music.

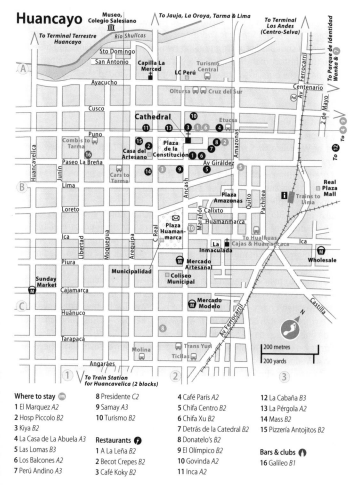

Huancayo

Where to stay
1 El Marquez *A2*
2 Hosp Piccolo *B2*
3 Kiya *B2*
4 La Casa de La Abuela *A3*
5 Las Lomas *B3*
6 Los Balcones *A2*
7 Perú Andino *A3*

8 Presidente *C2*
9 Samay *A3*
10 Turismo *B2*

Restaurants
1 A La Leña *B2*
2 Becot Crepes *B2*
3 Café Koky *B2*

4 Café París *A2*
5 Chifa Centro *B2*
6 Chifa Xu *B2*
7 Detrás de la Catedral *B2*
8 Donatelo's *B2*
9 El Olímpico *B2*
10 Govinda *A2*
11 Inca *A2*

12 La Cabaña *B3*
13 La Pérgola *A2*
14 Mass *B2*
15 Pizzería Antojitos *B2*

Bars & clubs
16 Galileo *B1*

Sights

The weekly Sunday market gives a little taste of Huancayo at festival time; it gets going after 0900. Jiron Huancavelica, 3 km long and four stalls wide, sells clothes, fruit, vegetables, hardware, handicrafts and traditional medicines and goods for witchcraft. There is also an impressive daily market behind the railway station and a large handicrafts market on Plaza Huanamarca, between Ancash and Real, offering a wide selection. However, in general, it is better to go to the villages themselves for local handicrafts. The **museum** ⓘ *at the Salesian school, Pje Santa Rosa 229, north of the river in El Tambo, Mon-Fri 0900-1300, 1500-1800, Sat 0900-1200, US$1.75,* has a good collection of ceramics from various cultures, as well as stuffed animals and miscellaneous curiosities. The **Parque de Identidad Wanka** ⓘ *on Jr San Jorge in the Barrio San Carlos northeast of the city, daily 0800-2000, entry free,* is a mixture of surrealistic construction interwoven with native plants and trees and the cultural history of the Mantaro Valley. It also has restaurants and craft stalls. On a hillside on the outskirts of town are the impressive, eroded sandstone towers of **Torre-Torre**; take a bus to Cerrito de la Libertad and walk up.

★ Mantaro Valley

The whole Mantaro valley is rich in culture. Near the small town of Huari are the ruins of **Warivilca** ⓘ *5 km from Huancayo, daily 1000-1200, 1500-1700 (museum mornings only), US$1.75, take a micro for Chilca from Av Ferrocaril,* with the remains of a pre-Inca temple of the Huanca tribe. The Museo de Sitio on the plaza houses deformed skulls and the modelled, painted pottery of successive Huanca and Inca occupations of the shrine.

East of the Río Mantaro, the villages of **Cochas Chico** and **Cochas Grande** ⓘ *11 km north of Huancayo, micros from the corner of Huancas and Giráldez, US$0.50,* are famous for *mate burilado*, or gourd carving. You can buy samples cheaply direct from manufacturers such as Pedro Veli or Eulogio Medina; ask around. There are beautiful views of the Valle de Mantaro and Huancayo from here.

Hualahoyo, near Cochas, has a little chapel with 21 colonial canvases. **San Agustín de Cajas** (8 km north of Huancayo) makes fine hats, and **San Pedro** (10 km) makes wooden chairs. **Hualhuas** (12 km) is known for its fine alpaca weavings which you can watch being made. The weavers take special orders, and small items can be finished in a day; negotiate a price.

The town of **San Jerónimo** is renowned for the making of silver filigree jewellery. It has a Wednesday market and a fiesta on the third Saturday in August. There are ruins two to three hours' walk above San Jerónimo, but seek advice before hiking to them.

Huancayo to Ayacucho

Between Huancayo and Huancavelica, **Izcuchaca** is the site of a bridge over the Río Mantaro. On the edge of town is a fascinating pottery workshop whose machinery is driven by a water turbine. There is also a small shop. It's a nice hike to the chapel on a hill overlooking the valley (one to 1½ hours each way).

Heading towards Ayacucho, there is a good road from Izcuchaca to the Quichuas hydroelectric scheme, but thereafter it is narrow with hair-raising bends and spectacular bridges. The scenery, however, is staggering. There is another fully paved route to Ayacucho which involves not so much climbing for cyclists. Cross the pass into the Mantaro valley on the road to **Quichuas**. Then continue to **Anco** and **Mayocc**, where there is accommodation. From here the road crosses a bridge after 10 km and in another 20 km reaches **Huanta** in the picturesque valley of the same name, see page 457.

Listings Huancayo and Mantaro Valley *map p437*

Tourist information

The regional office is in Jauja (see above). For city information contact **DIRCETUR** at the train station (T064-222575). **Indecopi** (Pje Comercial 474, El Tambo, T064-245180, abarrientos@indecopi.gob.pe) is the consumer protection office.

Where to stay

Huancayo
Prices may rise in Holy Week.
Note The Plaza de Armas is called Plaza Constitución.

$$$ Presidente
C Real 1138, T064-231275, http://huancayo.hotelpresidente.com.pe.
Helpful, classy, safe, serves breakfast, restaurant, convention centre.

$$$ Turismo
Ancash 729, T064-231072, http://turistases.hotelpresidente.com.pe/.
Restored colonial building, same owner as Presidente, with more atmosphere, elegant, rooms quite small, Wi-Fi extra, quiet. Restaurant ($$-$) serves good meals, fine service.

$$$-$$ El Marquez
Puno 294, T064-219202, www.elmarquezhuancayo.com.
Good value, efficient, popular with local business travellers, safe parking.

$$ Kiya
Giráldez 107, T214955, www.hotelkiya.com.
Comfortable although ageing, hot water, helpful staff. Spectacular view of Plaza.

$ Hospedaje Piccolo
Puno 239.
With hot water, good beds, well-kept.

$ La Casa de la Abuela
Prolongación Cusco 794 y Gálvez, T064-234383, www.incasdelperu.org/casa-de-la-abuela.
Doubles with or without private bath and dorms, 10 min walk from town. Hot shower, breakfast, laundry facilities, meals available, sociable staff, owner speaks English, good meeting place, games room, free pickup from bus station if requested in advance. Discount for Footprint Handbook readers.

$ Las Lomas
Giráldez 327, T064-237587.
Central location, basic rooms, hot water, good value, can arrange tours.

$ Los Balcones
Jr Puno 282, T064-214881.
Comfortable rooms, restaurant, hot water, helpful staff, elevator (practically disabled-accessible). View of the back of the Cathedral.

$ Peru Andino
Pasaje San Antonio 113-115, near Parque Túpac Amaru, in 1st block of Francisco Solano (left side of Defensoría del Pueblo), 10-15 mins' walk from the centre (if taking a taxi, stress that it's Pasaje San Antonio), T064-223956.
Hot showers, several rooms with bath, laundry and kitchen facilities, breakfast and other meals on request, safe area, cosy atmosphere, run by Sra Juana and Luis, who speak some English, organize trekking and mountain bike tours, bike hire, Spanish classes. Can pick up guests at Lima airport with transfer to bus station.

$ Samay
Jr Florida 285 (cdra 9 de Giráldez), T064-365259.
Hostel with shared bath, quiet (unless the little football field next door is being used), breakfast, laundry and kitchen facilities, garden, nice terraces on 3rd floor, helpful staff.

Huancayo to Ayacucho

$ Hostal Recreo Sol y Sombra
Quichuas.
Charming, small courtyard, helpful, basic.

Restaurants

Huancayo
Breakfast is served in Mercado Modelo from 0700. Better, more expensive restaurants serve typical dishes for about US$6, drinks can be expensive. Lots of cheap restaurants along Av Giráldez, and a large food court in Real Plaza mall.

$$ Detrás de la Catedral
Jr Ancash 335 (behind Cathedral as name suggests), T064-212969.
Pleasant atmosphere, excellent dishes. Charcoal grill in the corner keeps the place warm on cold nights. Considered by many to be the best in town.

$$ El Olímpico
Giráldez 199.
Long-established, one of the more upscale establishments offering Andean and *comida criolla*; the real reason to go is the owner's model car collection displayed in glass cabinets.

$$ La Cabaña
Av Giráldez 675, T064-223303. Daily 0900-2400.
Pizzeria, restaurant and bar, pastas, grill, juices and ice cream, wide variety of dishes, excellent atmosphere, Wi-Fi, home delivery US$2.

$$ Pizzería Antojitos
Puno 599.
Attractive, atmospheric pizzería with live music some nights.

$$-$ Chifa Xu
Giráldez 208.
Good food at reasonable prices, always a bustling atmosphere.

$ A La Leña
Ancash on Plaza Constitución.
Good rotisserie chicken and salads, popular.

$ Chifa Centro
*Giráldez 238, T064-217575. Another
branch at Av Leandra Torres 240.*
Chinese food, good service
and atmosphere.

$ Donatelo's
Puno 287.
Excellent pizza and chicken place,
with good atmosphere, popular.

$ Govinda
Jr Cusco 289.
Vegetarian restaurant and café, good
service, sells natural products. Nice
tranquil atmosphere with no blaring
TV, good concert videos instead.

$ La Pérgola
Puno 444, overlooking the plaza.
An oldie with a pleasant atmosphere,
4-course *menú*.

$ Mass
Real 549 and on block 10 of Real.
A clean place for *pollo a la brasa* with
good fast service.

Cafés

Becot Crepes
Av Real 471.
Savory and sweet crêpes to go, tasty
and cheap.

Café Koky
*Ancash y Puno, Ancash 235, and
Real Plaza Mall. Daily 0700-2300,
lunch 1230-1530.*
Good for breakfasts, lunches,
sandwiches, capuccino and pastries,
fancy atmosphere, free Wi-Fi.

Café París
Puno 254 and Arequipa 265.
Sofá-café and restaurant, good food
and atmosphere, many sweets, *menú*
at midday.

Inca
Puno 530.
Popular *fuente de soda*, with coffee,
Peruvian food, desserts, milkshakes.

Bars and clubs

Huancayo

Galileo Disco-Pub
Paseo La Breña 376.
Live music Wed through Sat,
good atmosphere.

Festivals

There are so many festivals in the
Mantaro Valley that it is impossible
to list them all. Nearly every day
of the year there is some sort of
celebration in one of the villages.

1-6 Jan **New Year** celebrations; also
La Huaconada dance festival in Mito.
20 Jan **San Sebastián y San Fabián**,
recommended in Jauja.
Feb There are carnival celebrations
for the whole month, with highlights
including **Virgen de la Candelaria**
and **Concurso Nacional de Huaylash**.
Mar-Apr **Semana Santa**, with
impressive Good Fri processions.
3-8 May **Fiesta de los Shapis**
in Chupaca.
May **Fiesta de las Cruces** throughout
the whole month.
15 Jun **Virgen de las Mercedes**.
24 Jun **San Juan Bautista**.
29 Jun **Fiesta Patronal**.
16 Jul **Virgen del Carmen**.
24-25 Jul **Santiago**.
4 Aug **San Juan de Dios**.
16 Aug **San Roque**.
30 Aug **Santa Rosa de Lima**.
8 Sep **Virgen de Cocharcas**.
15 Sep **Virgen de la Natividad**.
23-24 Sep **Virgen de las Mercedes**.

29 Sep **San Miguel Arcángel**.
4 Oct **San Lucas**.
28-30 Oct Culmination of month-long celebrations for **El Señor de los Milagros**.
1 Nov **Día de Todos los Santos**.
3-13 Dec **Virgen de Guadalupe**.
8 Dec **Inmaculada Concepción**.
25 Dec **Navidad** (Christmas).

Shopping

All crafts are made outside Huancayo in the many villages of the Mantaro Valley, or in Huancavelica. The villages are worth a visit to learn how the items are made.

Huancayo
See page 438 for details of Huancayo's markets; beware pickpockets. **Casa de Artesano** (on the corner of Real and Paseo La Breña, at Plaza Constitución), has a wide selection of good quality crafts in leather, ceramics, textiles and carved gourds.

What to do

Huancayo
Tour operators
American Travel & Service, *Plaza Constitución 122, of 2 (next to the Cathedral), T064-211181, T964-830220*. Wide range of classical and more adventurous tours in the Mantaro Valley and the central jungle. Transport and equipment rental possible. Most group-based day tours start at US$8-10 pp.
Hidden Peru, *no storefront, T064-101260 or 964-164979, andinismo_peru@yahoo.es*.
Incas del Perú, *Av Giráldez 675, T064-223303, www.incasdelperu.org*. Jungle, biking and hiking trips throughout the region as well as day trips to the Mantaro Valley. Also arranges flight/

train tickets and language and volunteer programmes (Spanish for beginners, US$50 for 5 days or US$185 per week, including accommodation at **Hostal La Casa de La Abuela** and all meals at **La Cabaña**); also home-stays and weaving, traditional music, Peruvian cooking and lots of other things. Very popular and recommended.
Marco Jurado Ames is a mountain guide who organizes adventure and cultural trips from Huancayo or Lima to the highlands and jungle, including trekking in the Mantaro valley, Huaytapallana and Pariacaca (Nor Yauyos Reserve); mountain biking and mountaineering all over Peru.
Peruvian Tours, *Plaza Constitución 122, p 2, of 1, T064-213069*. Next to the Cathedral and **American Travel & Service**. Classic tours of the Mantaro valley, plus day trips up to the Huaytapallana Nevados above Huancayo, plus long, 16-hr excursions to Cerro de Pasco and Tarma.

Transport

Huancayo
For train services, see Central Railway, page 433.

Bus
Terminal Terrestre Huancayo for buses to most destinations is 3 km north of the centre in the Parque Industrial. **Terminal Los Andes** (also known as **Terminal Centro-Selva**; Av Ferrocarril 151, T064-223367) serves mainly the Central Highlands and the jungle. Some companies have their own terminal in the centre, including **Turismo Central** (Jr Ayacucho 274, T064-223528). Most buses to the Mantaro Valley leave from several places around the market area, and from Av Ferrocarril. Buses to

Hualhuas and Cajas leave from block 3 of Pachiteca. Buses to Cochas leave from Amazonas y Giráldez.

There are regular buses to Lima, 6-7 hrs on a good paved road, US$13-25 with Oltursa. Other recommended companies with frequent service include Etucsa, Turismo Central, Mega Bus (Ancash 385, T064-225432) and Cruz del Sur (Terminal Los Andes). Travelling by day is recommended for the fantastic views and for safety, although most major companies go by night (take warm clothing).

To Ayacucho, 319 km, 9-10 hrs, US$13 with Molina (C Angaráes 334, T064-224501), 3 a day, recommended; 1 a day with Turismo Central (via Huanta) US$10-22; also Ticllas and Etucsa from Terminal Terrestre, US$5-10. There are 2 routes: 1 via Huanta, mostly paved; and the other via Huancavelica, partly paved with the remainder in poor condition, very difficult in the wet. Take warm clothing.

To Huancavelica, 147 km, 3 hrs, US$5. Many buses daily, including Transportes Yuri (Ancash 1220), 3 a day. The road is paved and offers a delightful ride, much more comfortable than the train (if you can find a driver who will not scare you to death). Shared taxis from Av Real cuadra 12, US$8 (US$10 on weekends), negotiable.

To Cerro de Pasco, 255 km, 5 hrs, US$7.50. Several departures. Alternatively, take a bus to La Oroya, about every 20 mins from Terminal Los Andes, or a shared taxi, US$5, 2 hrs. From La Oroya there are regular buses and colectivos to Cerro, US$8. The road to La Oroya and on to Cerro is paved and in good condition. To Huánuco, 7 hrs, Turismo Central, twice daily, US$20, good service.

To Tarma, Lobato and America from Terminal Los Andes, 5 hrs, US$10; some continue to La Merced. Also Turismo Central to La Merced, US$19. Minibuses and cars from outside the terminal, to Tarma US$6, to La Merced US$12, 3 hrs.

To Yauyos, cars at 0500 from Plaza de los Sombreros, El Tambo, US$7.50. It is a poor road with beautiful mountain landscapes before dropping to the valley of Cañete; cars go very fast.

To Jauja, 44 km, 1 hr. Colectivos and combis leave every few mins from Terminal Los Andes, US$2.50. Taxi to Jauja US$15, 45 mins.

To Tingo María and Pucallpa, daily with Turismo Central, US$27.

Huancavelica → Colour map 5, A3.

a colonial mountain town

Huancavelica is a friendly and attractive town at 3676 m, surrounded by huge, rocky mountains. It was founded in the 16th century by the Spanish to exploit rich deposits of mercury and silver, but it remains predominantly an indigenous town. There are beautiful mountain walks in the surrounding area.

Sights

The Cathedral, located on the Plaza de Armas, has an altar considered to be one of the finest examples of colonial art in Peru. Also very impressive are the five other churches in town, although most are closed to visitors. The church of San Francisco, for example, has no less than 11 altars. The **Ministerio de Cultura**

① *Plazoleta San Juan de Dios, Arica y Raimondi, T064-453420*, is a good source of information on festivals, archaeological sites, history, etc. It also runs courses and lectures on music and dancing, and has a small but interesting **Museo Regional** ① *T064-753420, Mon-Sat 0830-1300, 1430-1800*, with exhibits of archaeology, anthropology and popular art.

Bisecting the town is the Río Ichu. South of the river is the main commercial centre. On the hillside north of the river are the **San Cristóbal thermal baths** ① *Av Escalinata y 28 de Abril, daily 0600-1700, US$0.50 for private rooms, water not very hot (26° C), US$0.30 for the hot public pool, also hot showers, take a lock for the doors.* The pedestrian walkway up to the baths on Av Escalinata is full of figures illustrating the village festivals of the region and their typical characters. There are also thermal baths in Secsachaca, 1 km from town. The Potaqchiz hill, just outside the town, gives a fine view; it's about one hour walk up from San Cristóbal.

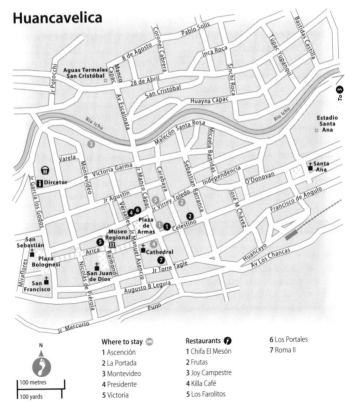

Huancavelica

Where to stay 🛌
1 Ascención
2 La Portada
3 Montevideo
4 Presidente
5 Victoria

Restaurants 🍴
1 Chifa El Mesón
2 Frutas
3 Joy Campestre
4 Killa Café
5 Los Farolitos
6 Los Portales
7 Roma II

100 metres
100 yards

Huancavelica to Ayacucho

The fully paved route from Huancavelica to Ayacucho (247 km) is one of the highest continuous roads in the world. The journey is a cold one but spectacular, as the road rarely drops below 4000 m for 150 km, with great views and many lakes en route. It goes via **Santa Inés** (4650 m), which is located 78 km south of Huancavelica on the main Pisco–Ayacucho road. Out of Huancavelica the road climbs steeply with switchbacks between herds of llamas and alpacas grazing on rocky perches. Around Pucapampa (Km 43) is one of the highest habitable *altiplanos* (4500 m), where the rare and highly prized ash-grey alpaca can be seen. Snow-covered mountains are passed as the road climbs to 4853 m at the Abra **Chonta** pass, 23 km before Santa Inés. By taking the turn-off to Huachocolpa at Abra Chonta and continuing for 3 km you'll reach one of the highest drivable passes in the world, at 5059 m. Nearby are two lakes (Laguna Choclacocha) which can be visited in 2½ hours.

The **Abra de Apacheta** at 4750 m is 52 km beyond Santa Inés, on the main road 98 km from Ayacucho. The rocks here are all the colours of the rainbow, and running through this fabulous scenery is a violet river. You can combine a tour to Santa Inés with the trip to Ayacucho (eg with Paccari Tours, see above).

A more adventurous route to Ayacucho is via Lircay and Julcamarca, along dirt roads with beautiful scenery all the way; see Transport, below, for bus services and accommodation options.

Listings Huancavelica *map p444*

Tourist information

Dircetur (Jr Victoria Garma 444, upstairs, T064-452938, Mon-Sat) is very helpful.

Where to stay

$$$ Presidente
Plaza de Armas, T064-452760, http://huancavelica.hotelpresidente.com.pe.
Lovely colonial building, higher-priced suites available, heating, parking, safe, laundry, buffet breakfast, very good restaurant (small and old-fashioned) and café.

$ Ascención
Jr Manco Capac 481 (Plaza de Armas), T064-453103.

Very comfortable, wooden floors, with or without bath, hot water, good value.

$ La Portada
Virrey Toledo 252, T064-453603.
Large rooms with private bath or small, basic rooms with shared bath with extra charge for TV. Lots of blankets, unlimited coca tea, helpful staff, good value, secure metal doors.

$ Montevideo
Av Malecón Santa Rosa 168, T967-980638.
Clean basic rooms. 4th-floor terrace has great views of the river and *malecón*.

$ Victoria
Virrey Toledo 133, next to the plaza.
Basic, functional, modern and clean, opened in 2014.

Huancavelica to Ayacucho
Santa Inés has **Alojamiento Andino**
($) and a very friendly restaurant, **El
Favorito**, where you can sleep. Several
others. For other accommodation on
this route, see Transport, below.

Restaurants

$$ Los Farolitos
*Jr Arica 202, Plazoleta San Juan de Dios.
Mon-Sat 0800-2200.*
Restaurant, café and bar serving good
food, juices & drinks. Small place with
tables on the pedestrian street, nice
atmosphere. Recommended.

$$-$ Roma II
*Manco Capac 580, T064-452608.
Open 1800-2300.*
Pizzas, smells delicious, friendly staff,
delivery available.

$ Chifa El Mesón
Manchego Muñoz 153, T064-453570.
Very popular, standard *chifa* fare.
Delivery available.

$ Frutas
Manchego 279.
Clean modern place serving fruit salads,
juices and sandwiches.

$ Joy Campestre
Av de los Incas 870.
Comida criolla and regional dishes served
in a leisurely country environment.

$ Killa Café
*Virrey Toledo, on Plaza de Armas opposite
the Cathedral. Evenings only.*
Good coffee, sandwiches and wine,
no noisy TV, free W-iFi, exhibition of
paintings for sale, nice and cosy.

$ Los Portales
Virrey Toledo 158, on Plaza de Armas.
Good breakfast, sandwiches and coffee,
giant fruit extracts (try the apple extract).

Festivals

**4-8 Jan Fiesta de los Reyes Magos y
los Pastores**.
2nd Sun in Jan Fiesta del Niño Perdido.
20 Jan-mid Mar Pukllaylay Carnavales,
celebration of the first fruits from the
ground (harvest).
Mar/Apr Semana Santa (Holy Week).
End May-Jun Toro Pukllay festival.
May and Aug Fiesta de Santiago in
all communities.
22-28 Dec Los Laijas or **Galas** (scissors
dance). This event is on UNESCO's World
Heritage list.

Shopping

Huancavelica is a major craft centre,
with a wide variety of goods produced
in surrounding villages. Handicraft
sellers congregate on the 4th block
of Victoria Garma and under Plaza
Santa Ana (*sótano*). Most handicrafts
are transported directly to Lima,
but you can still visit craftsmen in
neighbouring villages.

Qampaq Art, *Jr Arica 230, half block
from the Plaza*. Specializes in fine
alpaca textiles.

What to do

Cielo Azul, *Jr Manuel Ascencio Segura
140, on the plaza (former municipal
tourism office), T967-718802*. City tours
and many others, US$10-30 pp for a
group of 6.
Paccari Tours, *Av Ernesto Morales 637,
T978-978828, www.paccaritours.com.*
Offers city tours (also by bike), visits to

Uchkus Inkañan archaeological site, boating on one of the lakes, alpaca herding on the Puna, and historic mine tours. Owner Daniel Páucar is very helpful. **Willka Tours**, *Jr Carabaya 199, T967-758007, www.willkatours.com*. Variety of local tours.

Transport

Huancavelica
Bus
There is a **Terrapuerto** bus terminal in Ascensión, next to the EsSalud Hospital II in the west end of town. Many bus companies also have offices on, and leave from the east end of town, around Parque M Castilla (Santa Ana), between Manchego and O'Donovan.

To **Huancayo**, 147 km, 5 hrs, US$4, paved road, **Transportes Ticllas** (Manchego 686, T064-452787). Also shared taxis all day from Av Machego y González Prada and from the Terrapuerto, US$8 Mon-Thu, US$10 Fri-Sun, 3½ hrs. Most buses to Huancayo go on to **Lima**, 445 km, 13 hrs, minimum, US$14; there are several a day including **Molina** (Manchego 608, T064-454244). The other route is via **Pisco**, 269 km, 12 hrs, US$12, and **Ica**, US$13, 1730 daily, with **Oropesa** (Manchego 612, T064-369082), continuing to Lima. Buy your ticket 1 day in advance. The road is poor until it joins the Ayacucho–Pisco road, beyond which it is paved. Most of the journey is done at night; be prepared for sub-zero temperatures in the early morning as the bus passes snowfields,

then for temperatures of 25-30°C as the bus descends to the coast.

Train
Station at Av Ferrocarril s/n, T064-452898. To **Huancayo**, 3-4 times a week (see Huancayo Transport, page 442).

Huancavelica to Ayacucho
There is no direct transport from Huancavelica to Ayacucho, other than with **Molina** which passes through from Huancayo daily between 2230 and 2400, US$13. Otherwise you have to go to **Rumichaca** just beyond Santa Inés on the Pisco–Ayacucho road, with **San Juan Bautista**, 0430, 4 hrs, then take a minibus to Ayacucho, 3 hrs. Rumichaca has only a couple of foodstalls and some filthy toilets.

The alternative route to Ayacucho is to take a taxi or colectivo from Huancavelica with **Transportes 5 de Mayo** (Av Sebastián Barranca y Cercado) to the small village of **Lircay**, US$7.55, 2½ hrs. The village has an unnamed *hostal* ($) at Sucre y La Unión, with bath and hot water (much better than Hostal El Paraíso, opposite). **Transportes 5 de Mayo** continues from Lircay Terminal Terrestre hourly from 0430 to Julcamarca, 2½ hrs, US$6, where there is a colonial church and the very basic **Hostal Villa Julcamarca**, near the plaza (no tap water). From Julcamarca plaza, take a minibus to Ayacucho, US$4, 2 hrs.

The final, slow option to Ayacucho is to take the train to Izcuchaca, stay the night and continue by colectivo from there (see page 438).

Ayacucho
& around

The city of Ayacucho, the capital of its region, is famous for its hugely impressive Semana Santa celebrations, its splendid market and, not least, its plethora of churches – 33 of them no less – giving the city its alternative name La Ciudad de las Iglesias. A week can easily be spent enjoying Ayacucho and its hinterland. The climate is lovely, with warm, sunny days and pleasant balmy evenings. It is a hospitable, tranquil place, where the inhabitants are eager to promote tourism. It also boasts a large, active student population. *Colour map 5, A4.*

★Ayacucho is a large city but the interesting churches and colonial houses are all fairly close to the Plaza Mayor. Barrio Santa Ana is further away to the south; you can take a taxi or walk.

Plaza Mayor

The city is built round the Plaza Mayor, with the Cathedral, Municipalidad, Universidad Nacional de San Cristóbal de Huamanga (UNSCH) and various colonial mansions facing on to it. The **Cathedral** ① *daily 1000-1430, 1600-1900, Sunday Mass 1000,* built in 1612, has superb gold-leaf altars. It is beautifully lit at night. On the north side of the Plaza Mayor, at Portal de la Unión 37, is the **Casona de los Marqueses de Mozobamba del Pozo**, also called Velarde-Alvarez. Recently restored as the **Centro Cultural de la UNSCH**, it hosts frequent artistic and cultural exhibitions; see the monthly Agenda Cultural. The **Casona Chacón** ① *Portal de la Unión 28, in the BCP building,* displays temporary exhibitions. Jr Asamblea is pedestrianized for its first two blocks north of the plaza; on a parallel street is **Santo Domingo** (1548) ① *9 de Diciembre, block 2, Mass daily 0700-0800.* Its fine façade has triple Roman arches and Byzantine towers.

South of Plaza Mayor

Jr 28 de Julio is pedestrianized for two blocks south of the plaza. A stroll down 28 de Julio leads to the prominent **Arco del Triunfo** (1910), which commemorates victory over the Spaniards. Through the arch is the church of **San Francisco de Asís** (1552) ① *28 de Julio, block 3, daily for morning Mass and 1730-1830.* It has an elaborate gilt main altar and several others. Across 28 de Julio from San Francisco is the **Mercado de Abastos Carlos F Vivanco**, the packed central market. As well as household items and local produce, look out in particular for the stalls dedicated to cheese, breads and fruit juices. West of the market, **Santa Clara de Asís** ① *Jr Grau, block 3, open for Mass,* is renowned for its beautifully delicate coffered ceiling. It is open for the sale of sweets and cakes made by the nuns; go to the door at Nazareno 184, which is usually open.

One block east of Jr 28 de Julio, the 16th-century church of **La Merced** ① *2 de Mayo, open for Mass,* is the second oldest in the city. The high choir is a good example of the simplicity of churches in the early period of the Viceroyalty. **Casa Jáuregui**, opposite, is also called **Ruiz de Ochoa** after its original owner. Its outstanding feature is its doorway, which has a blue balcony supported by two fierce beasts with erect penises.

On the fifth block of 28 de Julio is the late 16th-century **Casona Vivanco**, which houses the **Museo Andrés A Cáceres** ① *Jr 28 de Julio 508, T066-812360, Mon-Fri 0900-1300, 1500-1700, US$0.70, US$1.25.* The museum has baroque painting, colonial furniture, republican and contemporary art, and exhibits on Mariscal Cáceres' battles in the War of the Pacific. Further south still, on a pretty plazuela,

Ayacucho

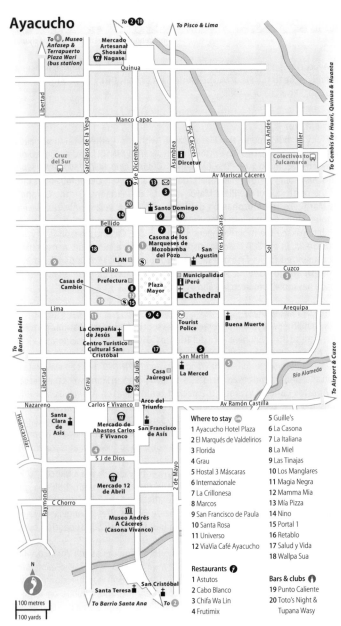

To **2 10**
To Pisco & Lima

To **5** , Museo
Anfasep &
Terrapuerto
Plaza Wari
(bus station)

Mercado
Artesanal
Shosaku
Nagase

Quinua

Libertad

Garcilaso de la Vega

Manco Capac

9 de Diciembre

Asamblea

Pje Cáceres

Los Andes

Miller

To Combis for Huari, Quinua & Huanta

Cruz
del Sur

Dircetur

Av Mariscal Cáceres

Colectivos to
Julcamarca

To Combis for Huari, Quinua & Huanta

11   **13**   ✉

20   ✝
14   Santo Domingo
Bellido   **6**   **16**

1   **7**   **19**
18   **8**   Casona de los
        LAN   Marqueses de
        Mozobamba   San
        del Pozo   Agustín

Tres Máscaras

Sol

Cuzco

9
Callao

Casas de   Prefectura
Cambio   **8**
        12
        15
Lima

Plaza
Mayor

Municipalidad
i iPerú
✝
Cathedral

Arequipa

11

La Compañía ✝
de Jesús
Centro Turístico
Cultural San
Cristóbal

9 **4**

Tourist
Police

✝
Buena Muerte

17

5
San Martín
✝
La Merced

Río Alameda

To Airport & Cuzco

To Barrio Belén

Libertad

Grau

28 de Julio

Casa
Jaúregui

12

Nazareno
Carlos F Vivanco

Arco del
Triunfo

Av Ramón Castilla

7

Santa
Clara
de
Asís

Mercado de
Abastos Carlos
F Vivanco

San Francisco
de Asís

S J de Dios

Raymondi

C Chorro

Mercado 12
de Abril

Museo Andrés
A Cáceres
(Casona Vivanco)

2 de Mayo

Santa Teresa ✝
To Barrio Santa Ana

San Cristóbal
✝

To **2**

N

100 metres
100 yards

Where to stay
1 Ayacucho Hotel Plaza
2 El Marqués de Valdelirios
3 Florida
4 Grau
5 Hostal 3 Máscaras
6 Internazionale
7 La Crillonesa
8 Marcos
9 San Francisco de Paula
10 Santa Rosa
11 Universo
12 ViaVia Café Ayacucho

Restaurants
1 Astutos
2 Cabo Blanco
3 Chifa Wa Lin
4 Frutimix

5 Guille's
6 La Casona
7 La Italiana
8 La Miel
9 Las Tinajas
10 Los Manglares
11 Magia Negra
12 Mamma Mia
13 Mía Pizza
14 Nino
15 Portal 1
16 Retablo
17 Salud y Vida
18 Wallpa Sua

Bars & clubs
19 Punto Caliente
20 Toto's Night &
Tupana Wasy

BACKGROUND
Ayacucho

The city was founded on 9 January 1539 by the invading Spaniards, who named it San Juan de la Frontera. This was changed to San Juan de la Victoria after the Battle of Chupas, when the king's forces finally defeated the rival Almagrist power. Despite these Spanish titles, the city always kept its original name of Huamanga. It became an important base for the army of the Liberator Simón Bolívar in his triumphant sweep south from the Battle of Junín. It was here, on the Pampa de Quinua, on 9 December 1824, that the decisive Battle of Ayacucho was fought, bringing Spanish rule in Peru to an end. Huamanga was, therefore, the first city on the continent to celebrate its liberty. In the midst of the massive festivities, the Liberator decreed that the city be named Ayacucho, meaning 'Place of the Dead'. For much of the 1980s and early 1990s, this title seemed appropriate as the Shining Path terrorized the local populace, severely punishing anyone they suspected of siding with the military. Those painful times are long past, and peace has returned to this beautiful colonial Andean city.

is **Santa Teresa** (1683) ⓘ *28 de Julio, block 6, daily Mass, usually 1600*, with its monastery. The nuns here sell sweets and crystallized fruits and a *mermelada de ají*, made to a recipe given to them by God; apparently it is not picante. **San Cristóbal** ⓘ *Jr 28 de Julio, block 6, rarely open*, was the first church to be founded in the city (1540), and is one of the oldest in South America. With its single tower, it is tiny compared with Santa Teresa, opposite.

Barrio Santa Ana

For a fascinating insight into Inca and pre-Inca art and culture, a visit to Barrio Santa Ana is a must. Here, about 200 families have workshops making *artesanías*: textiles, retablos, ceramics and work in stone. Their work is distributed through the galleries in the barrio. A good grasp of Spanish is essential to appreciate the galleries fully. Note that the galleries in the barrio are closed on Sunday.

Visit **Wari Art Gallery** ⓘ *Jr Mcal Cáceres 302, T066-312529*, run by Gregorio Sulca and his family, who will explain the Quechua legends, weaving and iconography. Next door is the Sulcas' **Instituto de Cultura Quechua**, which affords wonderful views of the city and surrounding hills from its roof. The Sulcas are renowned internationally. Also visit Edwin Pizarro ⓘ *T966-180666, artesretablos.ayacu7@ gmail.com*, for amazing altar-pieces

> **Tip...**
> For an insight into the recent history of this region and the violence surrounding the Sendero Luminoso campaign, visit **Museo de Anfasep** (Asociación Nacional de Familiares de Secuestrados Detenidos y Desaparecidos del Perú), which is located at Prol Libertad 1229, in the north of the city, 15 minutes' walk or a mototaxi ride from Mercado Artesanal Shosaku Nagase. Entry is free but a donation is appreciated.

(*retablos*) and **Julio Gálvez** ① *Plazoleta Santa Ana 12, T066-314278*, for remarkable sculptures in alabaster (*piedra de huamanga*).

Listings Ayacucho *map p450*

Tourist information

iPerú
Portal Municipal 45, on the Plaza, T066-318305, iperuayacucho@promperu.gob.pe. Mon-Sat 0900-1800, Sun 0900-1300.
Very helpful. Also has an office at the airport, open mornings only.

Dirección Regional de Industria y Turismo (Dircetur)
Asamblea 481, T066-312548. Mon-Fri 0800-1700.
Friendly and helpful.

Tourist Police
Arequipa cuadra 1, T066-312055.

Where to stay

$$$ Ayacucho Hotel Plaza
Jr 9 de Diciembre 184, T066-312202, www.dmhoteles.pe.
Spacious and elegant in a colonial *casona*, comfortable rooms, some suites have balconies overlooking the plaza. With restaurant, bar, cafetería, games room, conference rooms, parking. Helpful staff, organizes tours.

$$$-$$ Internazionale
Urb María Parado de Bellido Mz O, Lt 1, Emadi, T066-314701, www.internazionalehotel.pe.
Business-orientated, 5 mins drive from the centre, modern, junior suites with jacuzzi and roof terrace with great view of the city. Restaurant, free airport transfers, parking. Helpful staff.

$$$-$$ ViaVia Café Ayacucho
Portal Constitución 4, Plaza de Armas, T066-312834, www.viaviacafe.com.
Single, double and triple rooms with private bath, solar hot water 24 hrs, TV room, Spanish, Dutch and English spoken. The attached **ViaVia** restaurant and travellers' café overlooks the Plaza, offering international and Peruvian food, a lunch *menú*, lounge and live music on Sat, cultural events and tourist information.

$$ San Francisco de Paula
Jr Callao 290, T066-312353, www.hotelsanfranciscodepaula.com.
A bit like a museum with hallways filled with handicrafts and a nice patio, terrace with views, restaurant, parking, popular choice. Comfortable rooms and some suites with jacuzzi. Will book El Encanto de Oro in Andahuaylas.

$$ Santa Rosa
Jr Lima 166, T066-314614, www.hotelsantarosa.com.pe.
Lovely colonial courtyard in building with historical associations, roof terrace, warm rooms, attentive staff, car park, good restaurant with good value *menú*.

$$ Universo
Jr Grau 101, 1 block from the plaza, T066-313888.
Modern rooms, parking, laundry, meeting room, tour desk, helpful.

$ El Marqués de Valdelirios
Alameda Valdelirios 720, T066-317040.
Lovely colonial-style mansion facing a quiet park and the river, beautifully

furnished, hot water, meeting rooms, bar, airport pick-up, reserve at least 24 hrs in advance.

$ Florida
Jr Cuzco 310, T066-312565.
Small, central location, pleasant, quiet, patio with flowers, electric showers.

$ Hostal 3 Máscaras
Jr 3 Máscaras 194, T066-312921, www.hoteltresmascaras.galeon.com.
Newer rooms with bath better, but with less character, than the old ones without, nice colonial building with patio, hot water, breakfast extra, car park.

$ La Crillonesa
C Nazareno 165, T066-312350.
Good value, hot water, laundry facilities, great views from roof terrace, near produce market but quiet. Cooking lessons featuring typical Ayacucho gastronomy. Owner Carlos Manco is very friendly, helpful and has loads of information. He will act as a local tour guide and knows everyone. Recommended.

$ Marcos
9 de Diciembre 143, T066-316867.
Comfortable, modern, in a cul-de-sac half a block from the Plaza, quiet, hot water, laundry, includes breakfast in the cafetería.

Restaurants

Those wishing to try *cuy* should do so in Ayacucho as it's a lot cheaper than Cuzco. For a cheap, healthy breakfast, try *maca*, a drink of maca tuber, apple and quinoa, sold outside the market opposite Santa Clara, 0600-0800.

$$ Astutos
Jr Bellido 366, T066-326362 (reservations and delivery).
An upmarket traditional chicken restaurant and grill, also karaoke in a private room.

$$ Las Flores
Jr José Olaya 106, Plaza Conchopata, east of city in the 'gourmet neighbourhood'. Daily 0800-1800.
Specializes in *cuy*. Taxi US$1 from centre.

$$ Las Tinajas
Portal Independencia 65, T066-310128. Open 1200-2400.
Chicken grill and bar, large balcony overlooking the main square, very popular with locals, good service.

$$ Magia Negra
9 de Diciembre 293, T066-328289. Mon-Sat 1830-until last customer leaves.
Nice atmosphere, great music and pizzas, local paintings for sale.

$$ Mamma Mia
Jr 28 de Julio 262.
Excellent pizza, elegant and cosy, located on Plaza More, a nice spot where there are other restaurants and cafés, boutiques, jewellers and 4 karaoke pubs.

$$-$ La Casona
Jr Bellido 463. Open 0700-2230.
Dining under the arches and in dining room, regional specialities, try their *puca picante, mondongo* and *cuy*, and a wide menu.

$$-$ Los Manglares
Av 26 de Enero 415, T066-315900.
The best-established *cevichería* of several on this avenue, also does home delivery.

$$-$ Nino
Jr 9 de Diciembre 205, on small plaza opposite Santo Domingo church, T066-814537. Daily 0700-1900.

Quaint decor, terrace and garden (look for the owls in the trees); serves chicken, *parrillas*, pastas, very good pizzas, including take-away. Live music on weekends and holidays, large bar on the 1st floor.

$ Cabo Blanco
Av Maravillas 198, close to Shosaku Nagase market (see Shopping).
Open 0800-1800.
Ceviches, seafood and fish dishes, small place with personal service. Also serves, beers, wines and cocktails.

$ Chifa Wa Lin
Asamblea 257.
Very popular Chinese, said to be the best in town.

$ La Italiana
Jr Bellido 490, T066-317574.
Open 1700-2300.
Pizzería with a huge wood-burning oven for all to see.

$ Mía Pizza
Av Mcal Cáceres 1045, T066-313273.
Open 1030-1500,1800-0200.
Pizzas *a la leña*, pastas and karaoke (also has a bar to get you in the mood for singing). *Menú* at lunch time, good atmosphere, like an old tavern.

$ Retablo
Jr Asamblea 219, T066-528453.
Chicken, meat, burgers and more in a large modern locale. Always full with locals, good value.

$ Salud y Vida
San Martín 439. Mon-Sun 0830-1700.
Vegetarian *menú*, generous portions, good service.

$ Wallpa Sua
Jr Garcilazo de la Vega 240.
A good chicken place, also with *parrillas*.

Cafés
The **Centro Turístico Cultural San Cristóbal** (28 de Julio 178) has some expensive cafés, including **Lalo's** (café, pizza delivery service and bar) and **Café Express** (coffee specialists) as well as other restaurants and some interesting craft shops. There are tables in the pleasant courtyard.

Frutimix
Portal Independencia 56, and Jr 9 de Diciembre 427, www.frutimix.com.pe.
Shakes, frapps (Baileys, chocolate or frapuccino), modern and tasty.

Guille's
Jr San Martín 537. Daily 0800-1300, 1600-2200.
Coffee, sandwiches, smoothies, juices and desserts, pleasant and very good.

La Miel
Portal Constitución 11-12, on the Plaza.
Daily 1000-2300.
Good coffee, hot drinks, juices, shakes, cakes and snacks, also ice creams.

Portal 1
Portal Constitución 1.
A good café on the corner of the plaza serving snacks, light meals and ice cream.

Bars and clubs

Punto Caliente
Jr Asamblea 187. Daily from 1830 until the night is over.
Music, drinks, pizzas and karaoke, modern and upscale.

Tupana Wasy
Jr 9 de Diciembre 213, 3rd floor.
Live contemporary and traditional Andean music. On the 2nd floor is **Toto's Night**, another pub.

Festivals

The area is well-known for its festivals throughout the year. Almost every day there is a celebration in one of the surrounding villages; check with the tourist office.

Feb Carnaval. Reported to be a wild affair.

Mar/Apr Semana Santa begins on the Fri before Holy Week. There follows one of the world's finest Holy Week celebrations, with candle-lit nightly processions, floral 'paintings' on the streets, daily fairs (the biggest on Easter Sat), horse races and contests among peoples from all over central Peru. Prices double and all accommodation is fully booked for months in advance. Many people offer beds in their homes during the week. Look out for notices on the doors and in windows of transport companies.

25 Apr Anniversary of the founding of Huamanga province.

1-2 Nov Todos Los Santos and Día de los Muertos.

9 Dec Reenactment of the Battle of Ayacucho on the Pampa de Quinua.

Shopping

Handicrafts

Ayacucho is a good place to buy local crafts including filigree silver, which often uses *mudéjar* patterns. Also look out for little painted nativity scenes, carvings in local alabaster, harps, or the pre-Inca tradition of carving dried gourds. The most famous goods are carpets and *retablos*. In both weaving and *retablos*, scenes of recent political strife have been added to more traditional motifs. For carpets, go to Barrio Santa Ana (see page 451). Also recommended is **Familia Pizarro** (Jr UNSCH 278, Barrio Belén, T066-313294), who produce textiles, *piedra huamanga* (local alabaster) and carnival masks of good quality; all pieces are individually made. They also have rooms for visitors to stay and take classes.

Markets

Mercado 12 de Abril, Chorro y San Juan de Dios. For fruit and vegetables. **Shosaku Nagase**, Jr Quinua y Av Maravillas, opposite Plazoleta de María Parado de Bellido. A large handicraft market.

What to do

A&R Tours, *Jr 9 de Diciembre 130, T066-311300, www.viajesartours.com. Daily 0800-2000.* Offers tours in and around the city.

Fly Travel, *Jr 9 de Diciembre 118, T066-313282.* Offers tours along 2 main circuits. To the north: Wari-Quinua-Huanta; south: Vilcashuamán-Cangallo.

Morochucos Rep's, *Jr 9 de Diciembre 136, T066-317844, www.morochucos.com.* Dynamic company in business for over 30 years, with tours locally and to other parts of Peru, flight, train and bus tickets.

Urpillay Tours, *28 de Julio 262 (Plaza More), of 8, T066-315074, urpillaytours@ terra.com.* All local tours and flight tickets.

Wari Tours, *Lima 138, T066-311415.* Local tours.

Willy Tours, *Jr 9 de Diciembre 209, T066-314075.* Personal guides, also handles flight and bus tickets.

Transport

Air

The airport is to the east of the city along Av Castilla. Taxi from airport to city centre, US$3.

To/from **Lima**, 55 mins, with **LAN** (Jr 9 de Diciembre 115), 3 flights a week; **LC Peru** (Jr 9 de Diciembre 160, T066-316 012), daily; **StarPerú** (Portal Constitución 17, T066-316676).

Bus
Long distance Bus terminal **Terrapuerto Plaza Wari** (Av Javier Pérez de Cuéllar s/n, T066-311710) is 10 mins northwest of centre. All bus companies are here, but some may retain sales counters in the centre, including **Cruz del Sur** (Av Mcal Cáceres 1264, T066-312813).

To **Lima**, 8 hrs on a good paved road, via Ica, several companies US$14-22, including Expreso **Molina** (Jr 9 de Diciembre 459, T066-312984), 7 daily, 5 in the evening; **Cruz del Sur**, US$26 *regular*, US$37 *suite* and *VIP* services; **Tepsa**, US$37, presidential; **Internacional Palomino** (Jr Manco Cápac 216, T066-313899), morning service, US$13-26; **Los Chankas** (Jr Manco Cápac 450, T066-401943), at 2000 hrs, US$10-16. For **Pisco**, 332 km, take an Ica/Lima bus and get out at San Clemente (10 mins from Pisco), 5 hrs, same fare as Ica; then take a bus or combi.

To **Cuzco**, with **Los Chankas** (Jr Manco Cápac 450, T066-401943), at 0800 via Andahuaylas and Abancay, and at 2000 direct, US$20, some continue to **Puerto Maldonado**. Also **Celtur** (Pasaje Cáceres 174, T066-313194) at 1830, US$15.

To **Huancayo**, 319 km, 9-10 hrs, US$10-13, 3 daily with **Molina**, also **Turismo Central** (Jr Manco Cápac 413, T066-317873), US$13 at 2030. The road was being fully paved in 2014. The views are stunning.

For **Huancavelica**, Expreso **Molina** at 2100, US$13, 3hrs, continuing to Huancayo; you must pay the full fare to there.

Around Ayacucho

ancient cultures and independence battles

Huari
22 km north of Ayacucho on a good paved road. Daily 0800-1700, US$1. Combis leave from Paradero a Huari Quinua (corner of Jr Ciro Alegría y Jr Salvador Cavero), when full from 0700, 40 mins, US$1; or take a tour.

This site dates from the 'Middle Horizon' (AD 600-1000), when the Huari culture spread across most of Peru (see The Huari influence, opposite). This was the first urban walled centre in the Andes. The huge irregular stone walls are up to 3-4 m high, and rectangular houses and streets can be made out. The most important activity here was artistic: ceramics, gold, silver, metal and alloys such as bronze, which was used for weapons and for decorative objects. The ruins now lie in an extensive *tuna* cactus forest (don't pick the fruit). There is a museum at the site.

★Quinua
37 km northeast of Ayacucho. Combis to Huari (see above) continue to Quinua, a further 25 mins, US$0.75, or US$1.50 from Ayacucho; ask the driver to go all the way to the 'Obelisco' for an extra US$0.75.

BACKGROUND
The Huari influence

The city of Huari had a population of 50,000 and reached its apogee in AD 900. Its influence spread throughout much of Peru: north to Cajamarca; along the north coast to Lambayeque; south along the coast to Moquegua; and south across the sierra to Cuzco. Before the Inca invasion, the Huari formed a *chanca* – a confederation of ethnic groups – and populated the Pampas river and an area west of the Apurímac. This political agreement between the peoples of Ayacucho, Andahuaylas, Junín and Huancavelica was seen by the Incas in Cuzco as a threat. The Incas fought back around 1440 with a bloody attack on the Huari on the Pampa de Ayacucho, and so began a period of Inca domination. The scene of this massacre is still known as *Rincón de los Muertos*.

This village, 37 km northeast of Ayacucho, has a charming cobbled main plaza and many of the buildings have been restored. There is a small market on Sunday. The village's handicrafts are recommended, especially its ceramics; San Pedro Ceramics, at the foot of the hill, and Mamerto Sánchez (Jr Sucre) should be visited, but there are many others. Most of the houses have miniature ceramic churches on the roof. The Fiesta de la Virgen de Cocharcas is celebrated around 8th September. Nearby, on the Pampa de Quinua (part of a 300-ha *Santuario Histórico*), a 44-m-high obelisk commemorates the Battle of Ayacucho in 1824. A reenactment of the battle is held on 9 December, with college students playing the roles of Royalist and South American soldiers. Trips of about six hours can be arranged to Huari, La Quinua village and the Santuario Histórico for US$12 per person (minimum three people).

Huanta Valley

The town of Huanta, one hour from Ayacucho on the road to Huancayo, overlooks the valley and has a pleasant plaza with palms and other trees. It was in Huanta that the Pokras and Chancas warriors put up their last, brave fight against the Inca invasion. Huanta celebrates the Fiesta de la Cruz during the first week of May, with much music and dancing. Its Sunday market is large and interesting, and the permanent daily market is extensive. There are many places to eat around town, or you can take a combi from Parque Hospital in Huanta (US$0.15) to the Valley of Luricocha, 5 km away, which has a lovely, warm climate. The *recreos* (tourist restaurants) at Luricocha are famous for their platos típicos.

The area is notable as the site of perhaps the oldest known culture in South America, dating from 20,000 years ago. Evidence was found in the cave of Pikimachay, 24 km from Ayacucho, on the road to Huanta. It is a 30-minute walk from the road. The remains are now in Lima's museums.

Vilcashuamán and around

Full-day tours to these sites cost US$23 pp for 8 passengers, departing 0500. Alternatively, travel by bus or colectivo from Av Cuzco 350 (daily 0400-1500, 4 hrs, US$7.50) and stay overnight in one of the 3 basic but clean hotels ($).

The Inca ruins of **Vilcashuamán** are 120 km to the south, beyond Cangallo. Vilcashuamán was an important Inca provincial capital at the crossroads where the main road from Cuzco to the central coast met the empire's north–south highway. There are several monumental Inca buildings, including an intact *usnu*, a flat-topped pyramid which was used for religious ceremonies. The village of Vischongo is one hour from Vilcashuamán; it has a market on Wednesday. Other attractions in the area include **Intihuatana,** Inca baths of fine masonry, near a lake about one hour uphill from the village, and *Puya Raimondi* plants at Titankayuq, one hour's walk from Vischongo.

Southern Ayacucho

In the seldom-visited south of the department of Ayacucho, accessed from the town of Puquio along the paved highway between Cuzco and Nazca, is the **Sondondo Valley** a region of great natural beauty, archaeological and cultural interest, gradually opening up to tourism. For details see page 252. The south of Ayacucho department also provides alternate access to the Cotahuasi Canyon (page 292) in neighbouring Arequipa, an adventurous journey far off the beaten path.

Ayacucho to Cuzco

stop to stretch your legs on the journey to Cuzco

Beyond Ayacucho are two highland towns, Andahuaylas and Abancay, which are possible stopping or bus-changing places on the road to Cuzco. The road towards Cuzco climbs out of Ayacucho and crosses a wide stretch of high, treeless *páramo* before descending through Ocros to the Río Pampas (six hours from Ayacucho). It then climbs up to Chincheros, 158 km from Ayacucho, and Uripa, which has a good Sunday market. Ayacucho to Andahuaylas is 261 km on a paved road. It's in good condition when dry, but landslides may occur in the wet. The scenery is stunning. Daytime buses stop for lunch at Chumbes after 4½ hours, which has a few restaurants, a shop selling fruit, bread and refrescos, and some grim toilets.

Andahuaylas

Andahuaylas is about 80 km further on, in a fertile valley. It offers few exotic crafts, but beautiful scenery, great hospitality and a good market on Sunday. On the north side is the Municipalidad, with a small **Museo Arqueológico**, which has a collection of pre-Columbian objects, including mummies. A worthwhile excursion is to the **Laguna de Pacucha** ⓘ *colectivo from Av Los Chankas y Av Andahuaylas, at the back of the market, US$1, 40 mins.* On the shore is the town of Pacucha, which has a family-run hostal ($) on the road from the plaza to the lake and various places to eat. A road follows the north shore of the lake and climbs to **Sóndor** ⓘ *8-10 km from Pacucha, US$0.65; taxi from Andahuaylas, US$10, or colectivo towards Argama.* This Inca archaeological site at 3300 m has various buildings and small plazas leading up to a conical hill with concentric stone terracing and, at the summit, a large rock or *intihuatana*. **Sóndor Raymi** is celebrated here each year on 18-19 June. With any form of public transport, you will have to walk back to Pacucha, unless you are very lucky.

Abancay

Nestled between mountains in the upper reaches of a glacial valley, the town of Abancay is first glimpsed when you are many kilometres away. It is capital of the department of Apurimac, an important mining area. **Santuario Nacional de Ampay** ⓘ *5 km north of town on a paved road (take a colectivo to Tamburco and ask the driver where to get off), US$1.50,* has two lakes called Ankasccocha (3200 m) and Uspaccocha (3820 m), a glacier (receding rapidly) on Ampay mountain at 5235 m and a forest of endemic *Intimpa* trees (*Podocarpus glomeratus*). It's a two-day trek to the glacier, with overnight camping.

Saywite
3 km from the main road, Km 49 from Abancay. US$4, students US$2.

Beyond the town of Curahuasi, 126 km before Cuzco, is the large carved rock of Saywite. It is a UNESCO World Heritage Site. The principal monolith is said to represent the three regions of jungle, sierra and coast, with the associated animals and Inca sites of each. It is fenced in, but ask the guardian for a closer look. It was defaced, allegedly, when a cast was taken, breaking off many of the animals' heads. Six further archaeological areas stretch away from the stone and its neighbouring group of buildings.

Listings Ayacucho to Cuzco

Tourist information

Abancay
Information is available from the **tourist office** (Lima 206, daily 0800-1430) or **Dircetur** (Av Arenas 121, p1, T083-321664).

Where to stay

Andahuaylas

$ El Encanto de Apurímac
Jr Ramos 401 (near Los Chankas and other buses), T083-723527.
With hot water, very helpful.

$ El Encanto de Oro
Av Pedro Casafranca 424, T083-723066, www.encantodeoro.4t.com.
Modern, comfy, hot water, laundry service, restaurant, organizes trips on request. Reserve in advance.

$ Las Américas
Jr Ramos 410, T083-721646.
Near buses, bit gloomy in public areas, rooms are fine if basic, cheaper without bath, hot water, helpful.

$ Sol de Oro
Jr Juan A Trelles 164, T083-721152.
Good value, good

Abancay

$$-$ Turistas
Av Díaz Barcenas 500, T083-321017,
www.turismoapurimac.com.
The original building is in colonial
style, rooms a bit gloomy, breakfast
not included. Newer rooms on top
floor (best) and in new block are
more expensive, including breakfast.
Good restaurant ($$), wood panelled
bar, parking.

$ Apurímac Tours
Jr Cuzco 421, T083-321446.
Modern building, rooms with bath
have tiny bathrooms, hot water,
good value, helpful.

$ Hostal Arenas
Av Arenas 192, T083-322107.
Well-appointed rooms, good beds,
hot showers, helpful service, restaurant.

$ Imperial
Díaz Barcenas 517, T083-321538.
Great beds, hot water, spotless, very
helpful, parking, good value, cheaper
without bath or breakfast.

Restaurants

Andahuaylas

$ El Dragón
Jr Juan A Trellas 279.
A recommended chifa serving huge
portions, excellent value (same owner
as Hotel El Encanto de Apurímac).

$ Il Gatto
Jr G Cáceres 334.
A warm pizzería, with wooden furniture,
pizzas cooked in a wood-burning oven.

$ Nuevo Horizonte
Jr Constitución 426.
Vegetarian and health food restaurant,
open for breakfast.

Abancay

$ Focarela Pizzería
Díaz Bárcenas 521, T083-322036.
Simple but pleasant decor, pizza
from a wood-burning oven, fresh,
generous toppings, popular (ask
for *vino de la casa*!).

$ Pizzería Napolitana
Díaz Barcenas 208.
Wood-fired clay oven, wide choice
of toppings.

What to do

Abancay
Apurimak Tours, *at Hotel Turistas, see
Where to stay*. Run local tours and 1-
and 2-day trips to Santuario Nacional
de Ampay: 1-day, 7 hrs, US$40 pp for
1-2 people (cheaper for more people).
Also a 3-day trip to Choquequirao
including transport, guide, horses, tents
and food, just bring your sleeping-
bag, US$60 pp. The hotel can also put
you in touch with Carlos Valer, a very
knowledgeable and kind guide.

Transport

Andahuaylas
To **Ayacucho**, with **Los Chankas**
(Av José María Arguedas y Jr Trelles,
T083-722441) at 0600 and 1800 or
1840 (bus from Cuzco). To **Abancay**,
138 km, 5 hrs, with **Señor de Huanca**
(Av Martinelli 170, T083-721218), 3 a day,
US$6, or **Los Chankas** at 0630, US$7.50.
To **Cuzco**, with **San Jerónimo** (Av José
María Arguedas 425, T083-801767), via
Abancay, 1800 or 1830, also 1900 Sun,

US$22, or **Los Chankas**. To **Lima**, buses go via Ayacucho or Pampachiri and Puquio, US$20. On all night buses, take a blanket.

Abancay

The **Terminal Terrestre** is on Av Pachacútec, on the west side of town. Taxi to centre, US$1, or it's a steep walk. All buses leave from Terminal Terrestre but several companies have offices on or near the El Olivo roundabout at Av Díaz Bárcenas y Gamarra; others are on Av Arenas.

To **Cuzco**, 195 km, 4½ hrs, US$14-18, with **Bredde** (Gamarra 423, T083-321643), 5 a day; **Molina** (Gamarra 422, T083-322646), 3 a day; **San Jerónimo**, at 2130; **Los Chankas** (Díaz Bárcenas 1011, El Olivo, T083-321485) and several others. To **Lima**, **Oltursa**, US$66, or **Tepsa** US$71; several others. The scenery en route is dramatic, especially as it descends into the Apurímac valley and climbs out again. To **Andahuaylas**, Molina at 2330; **San Jerónimo** at 2130; **Señor de Huanca** (Av Arenas 198, T083-322377), 3 a day; also Los Chankas.

East & north of La Oroya

from highlands to jungle

★A paved road heads north from La Oroya towards Cerro de Pasco and Huánuco. Just 25 km north of La Oroya a branch turns east towards Tarma, then descends to the little-visited jungles of the Selva Central. This is a really beautiful run.

Tarma and around → *Colour map 3, C4.*

Founded in 1534, Tarma (60 km from La Oroya) is a growing city with a population of 55,000 but still has a lot of charm. The town is notable for its Semana Santa celebrations (see Festivals, below) and its locally made fine flower-carpets. There's a good, friendly market around calles Amazonas and Ucayali. The surrounding countryside is beautiful. Around 8 km from Tarma, the small town of **Acobamba** has *tapices* made in San Pedro de Cajas which depict the Crucifixion. There are

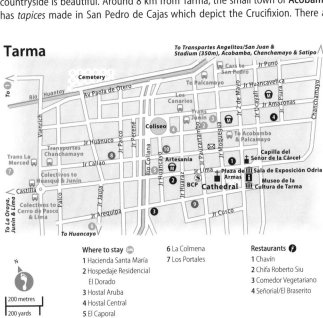

Tarma

Where to stay
1 Hacienda Santa María
2 Hospedaje Residencial
   El Dorado
3 Hostal Aruba
4 Hostal Central
5 El Caporal
6 La Colmena
7 Los Portales

Restaurants
1 Chavín
2 Chifa Roberto Siu
3 Comedor Vegetariano
4 Señorial/El Braserito

200 metres
200 yards

festivities during May. About 2 km beyond the town is the **Santuario de Muruhuay**, which has a venerated picture painted on the rock behind the altar.

Chanchamayo Province

Beyond Tarma the road is steep and crooked but there are few places where cars cannot pass one another. In the 80 km from Tarma to La Merced the road runs between great overhanging cliffs as it drops 2450 m and the vegetation changes dramatically from temperate to tropical. The first town in Chanchamayo Province is **San Ramón** (*population 25,000*), 11 km before La Merced. It has several hotels (\$\$\$-\$) and restaurants, and there are regular combis and colectivos between the two towns. **La Merced** (*population 20,000*) lies in the fertile Chanchamayo valley. Asháninka Indians can usually be found around the central plaza selling bows, arrows, necklaces and trinkets. There is a festival in the last week of September. There are several hotels (\$\$-\$) and restaurants.

Puerto Bermúdez and beyond → *Colour map 3, B5.*

About 25 km from La Merced along the road to **Oxapampa**, a road turns northeast to Villa Rica, centre of an important coffee-growing area. From here, a poor dirt road continues northeast to Puerto Bermúdez. This authentic jungle town, at the geographic centre of Peru, has grown up along the now seldom-used airstrip. It lies on the Río Pichis, an affluent of the Pachitea, and is a great base for exploring further into the Selva Central, with trips upriver to the Asháninka community. Tours are arranged by **Albergue Humboldt** (see Where to stay, below). The town is an access point to two extensive natural reserves: **Bosque de Protección San Matías-San Carlos** and **Reserva Nativa Sira**, both with primary forest. Note that the electricity supply is unreliable.

Fifty kilometres north of Puerto Bermúdez, **Ciudad Constitución**, also known as Palcazú, is a dusty town straddling the Río Palcazú. East of town are a few dilapidated old buildings being reclaimed by the jungle. They are the remains of President Belaúnde Terry's grandiose plans for the future national capital – a Peruvian Brasília that never happened. Beyond, the road continues north to join the Tingo María–Pucallpa road at Von Humboldt, 86 km before Pucallpa.

Listings Selva Central *map p462*

Tourist information

Tarma and around
The **tourist office** on the plaza (2 de Mayo 775, T064-321010, ext 107, turismo@munitarma.gob.pe, Mon-Fri 0800-1300, 1500-1800) is very helpful; see also www.tarma.info.

Chanchamayo Province
In La Merced, visit **Dircetur** (Pardo 110, San Ramón, T064-331265).

Where to stay

Tarma and around

\$\$\$ Hacienda Santa María
2 km out of town at Vista Alegre 1249, Sacsamarca, T064-321232.

A beautiful (non-working) 17th-century hacienda, beautiful gardens and antique furniture. Includes breakfast. Excellent guides for local day trips.

$$$ Los Portales
Av Castilla 512, T064-321411, www.losportaleshoteles.com.pe.
On the edge of town, hot water, heating, 1950s building with old furnishings, includes breakfast, good restaurant.

$$$-$$ Hacienda La Florida
6 km from Tarma, T064-341041, www.haciendalaflorida.com.
18th-century working hacienda owned by German-Peruvian couple Inge and Pepe, who also arrange excursions. Variety of rooms sleeping 1-4, adjoining family rooms, dorm for groups and an independent house; all with hot water, meals available, lots of home-grown organic produce. Also camping for US$5.

$$ Normandie
Beside the Santuario de Muruhuay, Acobamba, T064-341028, Lima T01-365 9795, www.hotelnormandie.com.pe.
Rooms with hot water, bar, restaurant, tours offered.

$ El Caporal
Lima 616, T064-323636, hostalelcaporal@yahoo.es.
Includes breakfast, good location, comfortable, hot water.

$ Hospedaje Residencial El Dorado
Huánuco 488, T064-321914, www.hospedajeeldoradotarma.com.
Hot water, rooms set round a patio, 1st floor better, safe, welcoming, secure parking.

$ Hostal Aruba
Jr Moquegua 452 near the market, T064-322057.

Hot water, nice rooms with tile floors, good value.

$ Hostal Central
Huánuco 614, T064-322625.
Cheaper without bath, hot water, laundry facilities, bit rundown but popular, has observatory (Fri 2000, US$1 for non-guests).

$ La Colmena
Jauja 618, T064-321157.
Well-maintained old building, convenient for Huancayo buses.

Puerto Bermúdez

$ Albergue Cultural Humboldt
By the river port (La Rampa), T063-963-722363, http://alberguehumboldt.free.fr.
The owner, Basque writer Jesús, has created a real haven for backpackers, with maps, library and book exchange. Rooms sleep 1-3, or there are hammocks and tents. Meals available, Spanish and Peruvian food. Jesús arranges tours, from day trips to camping and trekking in primary forest. Recommended.

Restaurants

Tarma and around

$ Chavín
Jr Lima 270 at Plaza de Armas. Daily 0730-2230.
Very good quality and variety in set meals (weekdays only), also à la carte.

$ Chifa Roberto Siu
Jr Lima 569 upstairs.
A good option for Chinese food, popular with locals.

$ Comedor Vegetariano
Arequipa 695. Open 0700-2100, but closed Fri after lunch and Sat.

Vegetarian, small and cheap, sells great bread.

$ Señorial/Pollería El Braserito
Huánuco 138.
Señorial is open daily 0800-1530, El Braserito, daily 1800-2300. Good *menú*, extensive choice of à la carte dishes.

Festivals

Tarma and around
The **Semana Santa** celebrations are spectacular, with a very colourful Easter Sun morning procession in the main plaza. Accommodation is hard to find at this time, but you can apply to the Municipalidad for rooms with local families.

What to do

Tarma and around
Katia Cerna, *Chanchamayo, T978-588827, katiacerna@hotmail.com.* Offers language classes, tours and accommodation. She is a recommended teacher.

Transport

Tarma and around
Bus
To **Lima**, 231 km (paved), 6 hrs, US$15, with the following companies: **Transportes Junín** (Amazonas 667; in Lima at Av Nicolás Arriola 198, T01-224 9220), 7 a day, with *bus cama* at night' **Trans La Merced** (Vienrich 420), 3 a day; **Trans Los Canarios** (Jr Amazonas 694), 2 daily starting in Tarma; **Transportes Chanchamayo** (Callao 1002, T064-321882), 2 a day, en route from Chanchamayo. To **Jauja**, US$2, and **Huancayo**, US$3, with **Transportes Angelitos/San Juan**, from the stadium, 0800-1800, every 1½ hrs; also **Trans Los Canarios** about 1 per hr, 0500-1800, and

Tip...
The local names for colectivos are 'carros' and 'stations'.

Trans Junín at 1200 and 2400; colectivos depart when full from Callao y Jauja, 2 hrs, US$4, and 3 hrs, US$6, respectively.
To **Cerro de Pasco**, **Empresa Junín** (Amazonas 450), 4 a day, 3 hrs, US$2.50; also colectivos when full, 2 hrs, US$4.
To **La Oroya**, buses leave from opposite the petrol station on Av Castilla block 5, 1 hr, US$1.50, while colectivos leave from the petrol station itself, 45 mins, US$2.
To **San Ramón**, US$1.75, 1½ hrs, with **Trans Junín**, 4 a day, continuing to La Merced, US$2.75, 2 hrs; also **Transportes Angelitos/San Juan**, 13 daily, 0600-2100, US$1.75; combis, US$1.75, and colectivos, US$4, depart from the stadium to La Merced. **Colectivos** and **Canary Tours combis** to **Acobamba** and up to **Muruhuay**, 15 mins, US$0.30 and US$0.45 respectively.

Chanchamayo Province
Air
Flights leave from San Ramón. There is a small airstrip where **Aero Montaña**, T064-331074 has air taxis that can be chartered (*viaje especial*) to the jungle towns, with a maximum of 3 people, but you have to pay for the pilot's return to base. Flights cost US$250 per hr. **Puerto Bermúdez** takes 33 mins. You can also just go to the air base, across the river, on the east side of town.

Bus
Many buses go to La Merced from **Lima**: **Expreso Satipo, Junín, La Merced** and **Chanchamayo** each have several buses during the day, US$8 *regular*, US$11 *cama* upper level, US$12.50 *cama* lower level,

7-8 hrs. To **Tarma**, with **Transportes Angelitos/San Juan**, hourly, 2½ hrs, US$1.75, or colectivos, just over 1 hr, US$4. To **Puerto Bermúdez**, **Empresa Transdife** and **Villa Rica** have 4WD pickups between 0400 and 0600 and may pick up passengers at their hotels. You must purchase tickets in advance, the vehicles get very full, US$14 in front, US$8 in the back (worth spending the extra money), 8-10 hrs or more.

some worthwhile sights en route to the Cordillera Blanca

A paved road runs 130 km north from La Oroya to Cerro de Pasco, crossing the great heights of the Junín pampa and the mining zone of Cerro de Pasco, before losing altitude on its way to the Huallaga Valley and Huánuco. On this route you can connect by road to the Cordillera Blanca via La Unión and Huallanca.

Pampas de Junín

The road runs up the Mantaro valley through canyons to the wet and mournful Junín pampa at over 4250 m, one of the world's largest high-altitude plains. An obelisk marks the battlefield where the Peruvians under Bolívar defeated the Spaniards in 1824. Blue peaks line the pampa in a distant wall. This windswept sheet of yellow grass is bitterly cold and the only signs of life are the youthful herders with their sheep and llamas. The road follows the east shores of Lago Junín. The town of **Junín** lies some distance south of the lake and has the desolate feel of a high *puna* town, bisected by the railway; it has several basic hotels. The **Junín National Reserve** ⓘ *US$5, ticket from Sernanp in Junín, Jr San Martín 138, T064-344146*, protects one of the best birdwatching sites in the central Andes where the giant coot and even flamingos may be spotted. It is easiest to visit from the village of Huayre, 5 km south of Carhuamayo, from where it is a 20-minute walk down to the lake. Fishermen are usually around to take visitors out on the lake.

Cerro de Pasco → *Colour map 3, B4.*

This long-established mining centre, 130 km from La Oroya, is not attractive, but is nevertheless very friendly. Copper, zinc, lead, gold and silver are mined here, and coal comes from the deep canyon of Goyllarisquisga, 42 km north of Cerro de Pasco. It is the highest coal mine in the world and its name translates as the 'place where a star fell'. The town is sited between Lago Patarcocha and the huge abyss of the mine above which its buildings and streets cling precariously. Nights are bitterly cold here at 4330 m.

Santuario Huayllay (Bosque de Piedras)

40 km southwest of Cerro de Pasco; information from Sernanp in Junín. US$1. Camping permitted. Minibuses to Huallay depart from Cerro de Pasco's terminal throughout the day, about 1 hr, US$1; last return 1800.

These unique weathered limestone formations at 4100-4600 m are in the shape of a tortoise, elephant, alpaca, and more. They can be explored on 11 tourist circuits through the rock formations. The village of **Huallay** is 6 km southwest of the sanctuary; it has a municipal hostel and other hotels. A festival of sports and music is held here on 6-8 September.

Towards Huánuco

The Central Highway from Cerro de Pasco continues northeast another 528 km to **Pucallpa** (see page 478), the limit of navigation for large Amazon river boats. The first part of this road has been rebuilt into an all-weather highway, and the sharp descent along the nascent **Río Huallaga** is a tonic to travellers suffering from *soroche*. The road drops 2436 m in the 100 km from Cerro de Pasco to Huánuco, most of it in the first 32 km. From the bleak high ranges the road plunges below the tree line offering great views. The only town of any size before Huánuco is **Ambo**. **Huánuco** itself is an attractive Andean town on the Upper Huallaga with an interesting market. Situated between the highlands and jungle at 1894 m, it has a particularly pleasant climate. ▶▶ *For the route from Huánuco to Tingo María, see page 477.*

Huánuco

Where to stay 🛏
1 El Roble
2 Grand Hotel Huánuco
3 Hostal Miraflores
4 Imperial
5 Las Vegas

Restaurants 🍴
1 Chifa Men Ji
2 Govinda
3 La Olla de Barro
4 Pizzería Don Sancho

Kótosh

5 km from Huánuco on the road west to La Unión. US$0.75, including a guide (in Spanish). Taxi from Huánuco, US$5 including a 30-min wait.

Investigations suggest that this archaeological site, at an altitude of 1912 m, was occupied for over 2000 years. Six distinct phases of occupation have been identified, the oldest of which dates back some 4000 years. The Temple of Crossed Hands dates from 2000 BC; it was at one time regarded as the 'oldest temple in the Americas'. There are three main temple buildings, some of which have been partly reconstructed, though the original 'crossed hands' sculpture is now in the Archaeology Museum in Lima. The site has an access bridge, is in good condition and has a small museum that gives clear explanations of Kótosh. A guide will take you around a marked circuit, which also passes through a small botanical garden of desert plants.

★Huánuco Viejo

2½ hrs' walk from La Unión. US$1.50. Taxi from La Unión, US$6.50-9.50 with wait.

From Huánuco, a spectacular but poor dirt road leads to **La Unión**, capital of Dos de Mayo district. It's a fast-developing town with a couple of simple hotels ($) and restaurants, but electricity can be a problem and it gets very cold at night.

On the pampa above La Unión are the Inca ruins of Huánuco Viejo (or Huánuco Pampa), a great temple-fortress with residential quarters. To get there, take the very steep path starting behind the market and climb towards the cross, which is at the edge of a plateau (this takes one hour). Continue straight through the village on the wide path. Note that, though the locals are friendly, some of their dogs are not always well disposed to strangers. The views of the pampa, surrounded on all sides by mountains, are beautiful. Seemingly at the foot of a mountain, in front and to your right, is the silvery metallic roof of a little chapel, behind which are the ruins, 4 km from the plateau's edge.

Huánuco Viejo was a major Inca settlement on the royal highway from Cuzco to Quito. The site has examples of very fine Inca stonework comparable with anything to be seen in Cuzco. This includes an *usnu* (ceremonial platform) measuring 30 m by 50 m and 4 m high, encased with superb stone blocks and with carved monkeys adorning the entrance and at one corner. The *usnu* is surrounded by a huge central plaza, 547 m by 370 m, which, possibly, had to accommodate large herds of animals. On the east side of the plaza are two *kallankas* (barracks), 84 m and 75 m long, nearly 10 m wide and two storeys high, with thatched roofs. Running from the *kallankas* down to the royal Inca quarters and Inca bath are a series of six fine stone gateways adorned with beautifully carved pumas. Illa Tupac used the site as his stronghold from which he mounted resistance against the Spanish from 1536 until at least 1542. The site was then largely forgotten by the outside world and left untouched until the mid-20th century. It is the only major Inca settlement on the royal highway not to have been built over by a colonial or modern town.

You can easily spend a whole day exploring the extensive site, which covers over 2 sq km and contains the remains of over 3500 structures, but allow a minimum of two hours. You should take warm clothing and be prepared for some violent thunderstorms.

One of the finest stretches of the Royal Inca Road, or Capaq Ñan, runs northwest from the site to the **Callejón de Conchucos**. Some tour operators in Huaraz (page 95) offer this trek.

Tourist information

Huánuco
The **tourist office** is on the plaza (Gen Prado 716, T062-512980). A website giving local information is www.webhuanuco.com.

Where to stay

Pampas de Junín
Carhuamayo is the best place to stay when visiting the reserve. **Gianmarco** (Maravillas 454) and **Patricia** (Tarapacá 862) are the best of several basic *hostales*. There are numerous restaurants along the main road.

Cerro de Pasco

$ Hostal Arenales
Jr Arenales 162, near the bus station, T063-723088.
Modern, TV, hot water in the morning.

$ Señorial
Jr San Martín 1, in the district of San Juan, 5 mins north of Cerro by taxi, T063-422802, hotelsenorial@hotmail.com.
The most comfortable in town, hot water, fine view across the mine pit.

$ Welcome
Av La Plata 125, opposite the entrance to the bus station, T063-721883.
Some rooms without window, hot water 24 hrs.

Huánuco

$$$ Grand Hotel Huánuco (Inka Comfort)
Jr D Beraún 775, T062-514222, www.grandhotelhuanuco.com.
With restaurant, pool, sauna, gym and parking.

$ El Roble
Constitución 629, T062-512515.
Without bath, cheap and good value.

$ Hostal Miraflores
Valdizán 560, T062-512848, www.granhostalmiraflores.com.
Hot water, private bathroom, quiet, safe, laundry service.

$ Imperial
Huánuco 581, T062-518737.
With hot showers, quiet and helpful. Recommended.

$ Las Vegas
28 de Julio 940, on Plaza de Armas, T062-512315.
Small rooms, hot water, restaurant next door. Good.

Restaurants

Cerro de Pasco

$ Los Angeles
Jr Libertad, near the market.
Excellent *menú* for US$1.50. Recommended.

$ San Fernando
Bakery in the plaza. Opens at 0700.
Great hot chocolate, bread and pastries.

Huánuco

$ Chifa Men Ji
28 de Julio, block 8.
Good prices, nice Chinese food.

$ Govinda
Prado 608.
Reckoned to be the best
vegetarian restaurant.

$ La Olla de Barro
Gral Prado 852, close to main plaza.
Serves typical food, good value.

$ Pizzería Don Sancho
Prado 645.
Best pizzas in town.

Festivals

Pampas de Junín
6 Aug Colourful ceremony to
commemorate the **Batalla de Junín**
(1824), which was fought on the nearby
Pampas de Junín, marking a decisive
victory in favour of the independence
of Peru and South America. The town
fills with visitors, prices rise and hotel
rooms are scarce.

Huánuco
20-25 Feb **Carnaval Huanuqueño.**
3 May **La Cruz de Mayo.**
16 Jul **Fiesta de la Virgen del Carmen.**
12-18 Aug **Tourist Week** in Huánuco.
28-29 Oct **Fiesta del Señor de Burgos,**
the patron of Huánuco.
25 Dec **Fiesta de los Negritos.**

Huánuco Viejo
27 Jul **Fiesta del Sol.** Major annual
festival at the site. Lodgings in La Unión
are almost impossible to find at this time.

Transport

Cerro de Pasco
Bus
There is a large bus station. To
Lima several companies including
Carhuamayo and **Transportes Apóstol
San Pedro,** hourly 0800-1200, plus
4 departures 2030-2130, 8 hrs, US$8. If
there are no convenient daytime buses,
you could change buses in La Oroya.
Buses leave when full, about every
20-30 mins, to **Carhuamayo** (1 hr, US$1),
Junín (1½ hrs, US$1) and **La Oroya**
(2½ hrs, US$2); colectivos also depart
with a similar frequency, 1½ hrs, US$2.50,
to La Oroya. To **Tarma, Empresa Junín,**
at 0600, 1500, 3 hrs, $2.50; colectivos
also depart hourly, 1½ hrs, US$4. To
Huancayo, various companies leave
throughout the day, 5 hrs, US$4. To
Huánuco, buses and cars leave when
full, about half hourly, 2½ hrs and 1½ hrs,
US$2 and US$4 respectively.

Huánuco
Air
The airport (T062-513066) is served by
flights from **Lima,** with **StarPerú** and
LCPeru (2 de Mayo 1355, T062-518113),
daily, 55 mins.

Bus
To **Lima,** US$18-25, 8 hrs, with **León
de Huánuco** (Malecón Alomía Robles
821), 3 a day; also **Bahía Continental**
(Valdizán 718), recommended, and
Transportes El Rey. The majority of
buses of all companies leave 2030-2200,
most also offer a bus at 0900-1000. A

colectivo to Lima, costing US$23, leaves
at 0400, arriving at 1400; book the night
before at Gen Prado 607, 1 block from
the plaza; recommended. To **Cerro de
Pasco**, 3 hrs, US$2, colectivos under
2 hrs, US$4; all leave when full from the
Ovalo Carhuayna on the north side of the
city, 3 km from the centre. To **Huancayo**,
7 hrs, US$6, with **Turismo Central**
(Tarapacá 530), at 2100. Colectivos run to
Tingo María, from block 1 of Prado close
to Puente Calicanto, 2½ hrs, US$5; also
Etnasa, 3-4 hrs, US2. For **Pucallpa**, take
a colectivo to Tingo María, then a bus
from there.

To **La Unión**, **Turismo Unión**, daily
0730, 7 hrs, US$5; also **Turismo Marañón**,
daily 0700; this is a rough road operated
also by **El Niño** colectivos (Aguilar 530),
which leave when full, US$7.15.

La Unión
Bus
To **Huánuco** with **Turismo Unión**
(Jr Comercio 1224), daily at 0600,
US$8, 7 hrs; also **Turismo Marañón**
(Jr Comercio 1309), daily at 0700 (no
afternoon/evening departures), and
El Niño colectivos (Jr Comercio 12,
T062-515952), 5 hrs. To **Huallanca** (for
access to Huaraz and the Cordillera
Blanca), combis leave from the market,
about hourly, when full and follow the
attractive Vizcarra valley, 1 hr, US$2.
El Rápido runs to **Huaraz** 0400, 4½ hrs,
US$8, or change in Huallanca.

Amazon Basin

The Amazon Basin covers a staggering 4,000,000 sq km. But despite the fact that 60% of Peru is covered by this green carpet of jungle, less than 6% of its population lives here, meaning that much of Peru's rainforest is still intact.

The area is home to countless plants and animals, including 2000 species of fish and 300 mammals. It also has over 10% of the world's 8600 bird species and, together with the adjacent Andean foothills, 4000 butterfly species. This incredible biological diversity is coupled with acute ecological fragility; any fundamental change to it habitats could have disastrous implications for the planet. Petroleum exploitation, gold mining and colonization from the highlands are perennial threats.

The two major tourist areas in the Peruvian Amazon are the northern and southern jungles. Northeastern Peru is dominated by flood plains and vast rivers, with much of the land regularly submerged. There are chances of seeing manatees, giant otters and pink and grey Amazonian dolphins. The Southern Amazon has faster-running rivers and rapids unsuited to dolphins and manatees, but the diverse forest habitats mean there are more bird species here. Moreover, in protected areas, tapir, giant anteaters, otters and primates are fairly easy to spot due to the lack of hunting pressure.

Best for
Ecotourism ▪ River trips ▪ Wildlife watching

Footprint
picks

★ **Pacaya-Samiria Reserve**, page 483

Travel by boat into this vast reserve to see numerous endangered species of mammal, bird and fish.

★ **Iquitos**, page 486

The isolated jungle city is a world-apart from the rest of the country and an excellent base for exploring the northern jungle; don't miss the market in Belén.

★ **Manu Biosphere Reserve**, page 501

Stay at a jungle lodge to experience the reserve's extraordinary natural diversity.

★ **Tambopata National Reserve**, page 512

Go birdwatching at the *collpas* and oxbow lakes.

ECUADOR

COLOMBIA

Pantoja

Marsella

Copal Urco

San Jacinto
Andoas

Intuto

Trompeteros

Mazán   *Amazonas*   Pebas

② Indiana

Iquitos   Caballococha   Leticia

San Pablo   Santa Rosa

Nauta

Borja

San Ramón

Lagunas   ◆ ① *Reserva Nacional Pacaya-Samiria*

BRAZIL

Balsapuertos

Yurimaguas

Moyobamba

Lamas   Tarapoto

Tocache Nuevo

L. Yarinacocha

Pucallpa

Aucayacu

La Morada   Aguaytía   Tournavista

Tingo María

Huaraz

Acomayo

Huánuco

Huancabamba   Atalaya

Cerro
De Pasco

San
Ramón

Junín   Mazamari

La Oroya   Tarma

Jauja

Huancayo

Iñapari

Iberia

Manu   ③ *Madre Dios*
Biosphere
Reserve   Boca Manu   Boca   Puerto
Itahuania   Colorado   Maldonado
Shintuya   Laberinto
LIMA   Atalaya   ④

Huancavelica   Ayna   *Bahuaja-Sonene*   *Tambopata*
Calca   *National Park* ◆   *National Reserve*

Ayacucho   Cuzco
Orcos

Ica

Nazca

Footprint
picks

1 **Pacaya-Samiria Reserve**, page 483
2 **Iquitos**, page 486
3 **Manu Biosphere Reserve**, page 501
4 **Tambopata National Reserve**, page 512

N

100 km

100 miles

Essential Amazon Basin

Getting around

Iquitos is the main transport and tourism hub in the northern Amazon. It has an airport with flights to/from Lima and several river ports; the main ports for long-distance services are Puerto Henry and Puerto Masusa, north of the centre. When travelling from the highlands, the roads end at Yurimaguas on the Río Huallaga and at Pucallpa on the Río Ucayali. From these towns onward transport is by boat.

In the southern Amazon the main hub is Puerto Maldonado, which has an airport with flights to/from Lima and Cuzco. Buses and tours from Cuzco travel either via Atalaya and Itahuania to reach Manu National Park, or via Quincemil on the Interoceanic Highway to reach Puerto Maldonado. Beyond Itahuania, transport is by river only, although this is due to change as road-building progresses. Beyond Puerto Maldonado, the Interoceanic Highway continues into Brazil.

When to go

April to October is the dry season; September is the best month to see flowers and butterflies in the northern jungle. November to March or April is the rainy season and can be oppressively hot; there are also more mosquitoes in the wet season. Expect some rain at any time of year.

Tip...

If you're venturing into the Peruvian Amazon, make sure you are properly equipped. Take a long-sleeved shirt, waterproof coat and shoes or light boots on jungle trips, plus binoculars and a good torch, as well as *espirales* to ward off the mosquitoes at night. 'Premier' is the most effective local insect repellent.

Time required

Allow one week to explore the northern jungle and one week in the southern jungle.

Weather Iquitos

Month	High	Low	Rainfall
January	31°C	22°C	260mm
February	30°C	22°C	250mm
March	30°C	22°C	290mm
April	30°C	22°C	300mm
May	30°C	22°C	260mm
June	29°C	22°C	300mm
July	29°C	21°C	160mm
August	30°C	22°C	160mm
September	31°C	22°C	190mm
October	31°C	22°C	230mm
November	31°C	22°C	240mm
December	31°C	22°C	250mm

Northern
Amazon

Cooled by winds sweeping down from the Andes but warmed by its jungle blanket, this region contains important tropical flora and fauna. It is a very varied landscape, with grasslands and tablelands of scrub-like vegetation, inaccessible swamps and forests up to 2000 m above sea level. The principal means of communication is by the many rivers, the most important being the Amazon, which rises high up in the Andes as the Marañón, then joins the Ucayali to become the longest river in the world. The northern tourist area is based on the River Amazon itself around the sizeable city of Iquitos. Although it has lost its rubber-boom dynamism, Iquitos is still at the heart of life on the river. There are jungle lodges upstream and down, each with its own speciality and level of comfort, but none is more than half a day away by fast boat. To get right into the wilds, head for Peru's largest national reserve, Pacaya-Samiria, accessed by boat from Iquitos or from the little town of Lagunas.

Huánuco to Tingo María

The journey to Tingo María from Huánuco, 135 km, is very dusty but gives a good view of the jungle. Some 25 km beyond Huánuco the paved road begins a sharp climb to the heights of Carpish (3023 m). A descent of 58 km brings it to the Río Huallaga again; it then continues along the river to Tingo María. Landslides along this section are frequent and construction work causes delays. Although this route is reported to be relatively free from terrorism, robberies do occur and it is advisable to travel only by day.

Tingo María → *Colour map 3, A4.*

Tingo María is situated on the Río Huallaga, in the Ceja de Montaña (literally 'eyebrow of the mountain'). The Cordillera Azul, the front range of the Andes, covered with jungle-like vegetation to its top, separates this transition zone from the jungle lowlands to the east. The meeting here of highlands and jungle makes the landscape extremely striking. Tingo María is isolated for days in the rainy season. Annual rainfall here is 2642 mm, but the altitude prevents the climate from being oppressive. Bananas, sugar cane, cocoa, rubber, tea and coffee are grown, but the main crop of the area is coca, grown on the *chacras* (small-holdings) in the countryside, and sold legitimately and otherwise in Tingo María.

The mountain that can be seen from all over the town is called La Bella Durmiente (the Sleeping Beauty). A small university outside the town, beyond the **Hotel Madera Verde**, has a little **museum-cum-zoo** ⓘ *free but a small tip is appreciated*; it also maintains botanical gardens in the town. About 6.5 km from Tingo, on a rough road, is a fascinating cave, the **Cueva de las Lechuzas** ⓘ *US$1 for the cave, take a torch, and do not wear open shoes; to get there, take a motorcycle-taxi from town, US$1.75, crossing the Río Monzón by new bridge*. There are many oilbirds in the cave and many small parakeets near the entrance.

Tingo María to Pucallpa

From Tingo María to the end of the road at Pucallpa is 255 km, with a climb over the watershed – the Cordillera Azul – between the Huallaga and Ucayali rivers. The road is in poor shape for most of the journey, but some paving has been completed and the entire route is scheduled to be improved by late 2015. Travel by day: it is safer and the views are tremendous as you go from the high jungle to the Amazon Basin; sit on the right-hand side of the bus. When the road was being surveyed it was thought that the lowest pass over the Cordillera Azul was over 3650 m high, but then an old document was discovered, stating that a Father Abad had found a pass through these mountains in 1757. As a consequence, the road goes through the **Boquerón del Padre Abad**, a gigantic gap 4 km long and 2000 m deep. At the top of the pass is a Peruvian customs house – the

Tip...
Tingo María is a main narco-trafficking centre and although the town is generally secure, it is not safe to leave it at night. Always keep to the main routes.

jungle land to the east is a free zone – beyond which the road bed is along the floor of a magnificent canyon. It is a beautiful trip through luxuriant jungle, ferns and sheer walls of bare rock, punctuated by occasional waterfalls plunging into the roaring torrent below. East of the foot of the pass the paved road goes over the flat pampa, with few bends, to the village of **Aguaytía**, where there is a narcotics police outpost, fuel station, accommodation and restaurants. From Aguaytía the road, paved in parts, continues for 160 km to Pucallpa – five hours by bus. There is a service station three hours before Pucallpa.

Pucallpa → *Colour map 3, A5.*

Pucallpa is a rapidly expanding jungle town on the Río Ucayali, navigable by vessels of 3000 tons from Iquitos, 533 nautical miles away. Different 'ports' are used depending on the level of the river; they are all just mud banks without any facilities (see Transport, below). The economy of the area includes sawmills, plywood factories, oil refinery, fishing and boat building. Large discoveries of oil and gas are being explored. The town is hot and dusty between June and November and muddy from December to May. **Museo Regional** ⓘ *Carretera Federico Basadre Km 4.2, Mon-Fri 0800-1630, Sat and Sun 0900-1730, park entry US$1.10,* in the **Parque Natural de Pucallpa** has examples of Shipibo ceramics, as well as some delightful pickled snakes and other reptiles.

> **Tip...**
> There is narcotics activity in the area; the city itself is safe enough to visit, but don't travel at night.

Lago Yarinacocha
Northeast of Pucallpa, 20 mins by colectivo or bus along Jr Ucayali, US$0.50, or 15 mins by taxi.

The main attraction in this area is **Lago Yarinacocha,** an oxbow lake linked to the Río Ucayali by a canal at the northern tip of its west arm. River dolphins can be seen here. **Puerto Callao**, also known as **Yarinacocha** or **Yarina**, is the main town at the southern tip, reached by road from Pucallpa. There are a number of restaurants and bars here and it is popular at weekends. From the town, a road continues along the western arm to **San José**, **San Francisco** and **Santa Clara** (bus US$0.75). The area is populated by the Shipibo people, who make ceramic and textile crafts. The area between the eastern arm of the lake and the Río Ucayali has been designated a reserve and incorporates the beautifully located **Jardín Botánico Chullachaqui** ⓘ *free, reached by boat from Puerto Callao to Pueblo Nueva Luz de Fátima, 45 mins, then 1-hr's walk.* For more information ask at Moroti-Shobo on the Plaza de Armas in Puerto Callao.

Tourist information

Tingo María

The **tourist office** is at Av Ericson 158, T062-562310, perucatapress@gmail.com. The **municipality** (Alameda Perú 525, T062-562058) also provides information, and the tourist police has an office in the municipal offices.

Pucallpa

Tourist information is available from **Dircetur** (Jr 2 de Mayo 111, T061-575110, Mon-Fri 0730-1300, 1330-1515) and from **Gobierno Regional de Ucayali** (GOREU; Raimondi block 220, T061-575018).

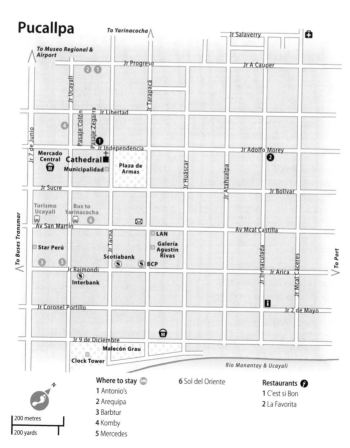

Pucallpa

Where to stay
1 Antonio's
2 Arequipa
3 Barbtur
4 Komby
5 Mercedes
6 Sol del Oriente

Restaurants
1 C'est si Bon
2 La Favorita

200 metres
200 yards

Where to stay

Tingo María

$$$-$$ Madera Verde
Av Universitaria s/n, out of town on the road to Huánuco, near the University, T062-562047.
Wooden chalets, cabins and rooms in beautiful surroundings, breakfast included, restaurant, 2 swimming pools, butterfly farm, free entry to wildlife rescue centre.

$$ Albergue Ecológico Villa Jennifer
Km 3.4 Carretera a Castillo Grande, 10 mins from Tingo María, T962-603509, www.villajennifer.net.
Danish/Peruvian-owned, includes breakfast, 2- to 4-night packages, US$50-90, and tours to local sites, pool, mini-zoo, birdwatching, restaurant, laundry service, phone ahead to arrange bus station pick-up. Rooms are surrounded by local flora, with lots of birdlife.

$$ Nueva York
Av Alameda Perú 553, T062-562406, joferjus@hotmail.com.
Central and noisy, cheaper without bath and TV, laundry, good value, restaurant.

Pucallpa

$$$ Sol del Oriente
Av San Martín 552, T061-575154.
Price includes breakfast and airport transfer, a/c, pool, mini-zoo, good restaurant, bilingual guides.

$$$-$$ Grand Hotel Mercedes
Raimondi 610, T061-575120, www.granhotelmercedes.com.
Pucallpa's 1st hotel, still family-run, with some refurbished rooms, modern facilities with old-fashioned ambiance, includes breakfast, hot water, a/c, fridge, pool, restaurant.

$$ Antonio's
Jr Progreso 545, T061-573721, www.antonioshotel.com.pe.
A variety of rooms and prices, garden, pool, jacuzzi, parking, airport pick-up.

$$ Komby
Ucayali 360, T061-571562, http://kombypucallpa.com.
Cold water, fan or a/c, ample rooms, pool, very noisy street but back rooms are quiet, good value, free airport pick-up.

$$-$ Arequipa
Jr Progreso 573, T061-571348, www.hostal-arequipa.com.
Good, a/c or fan, breakfast, comfortable, safe, restaurant, pool.

$ Barbtur
Raimondi 670, T061-572532.
Cheaper without bath, central, good beds, cold water, friendly but noisy.

Lago Yarinacocha

$$$ Yarina Ecolodge (Pandisho Amazon Ecolodge)
North of the village of 11 de Agosto, towards the northern tip of the eastern shore of the west arm, T061-799214, www. amazon-ecolodge.com (in Pucallpa, Pasaje Bolívar 261, T961-994227).
Prices are per person for full board, good resort with cabins by the lakeshore, includes packages of varying length and rainforest expeditions. Also has a lodge in Pacaya-Samiria, Amazon Green.

Restaurants

Pucallpa

$$-$ C'est si bon
Jr Independencia 560 y Pasaje Zegarra, Plaza de Armas. Daily 0800-2400.
Chicken, snacks, drinks, sweets, ice cream.

$$-$ La Favorita
Jr Adolfo Morey e Inmaculada,
T061-563712. Daily 0800-1600.
Regional and home cooking, good
set meals Mon-Sat and *parrilladas*
on Sun, popular.

Shopping

Pucallpa
Many Shibipo women carry and sell
their products around Pucallpa and
Yarinacocha. For local wood carvings
visit the workshop of **Agustín Rivas**
(Jr Tarapacá 861/863, above a small
restaurant; ask for it), whose work is
made from huge tree roots. **Artesanías
La Anaconda** (Pasaje Cohen by Plaza
de Armas) has a good selection of
indigenous crafts.

Festivals

Pucallpa
Local festivals are **Carnival** in Feb,
San Juan on 24 Jun, and the **Ucayali
regional fair** in Oct.

What to do

Pucallpa
**Usko Ayar Amazonian School of
Painting**, *Jr LM Sánchez Cerro 465-467,
T958-623871, see Facebook page.* Located
in the house of artist and healer Pablo
Amaringo, who died in 2009, the
renowned school provides art classes
for local people and is dependent upon
selling their art. It welcomes overseas
visitors for short or long stays to study
painting and learn Spanish and/or to
teach English to Peruvian students.

Transport

Tingo María
Air
To/from **Lima** Mon-Fri, 1 hr 10 mins,
with **LCPerú** (Av Raymiondi 571, Rupa
Rupa, T062-561672).

Bus
To **Huánuco**, 119 km, 3-4 hrs, US$2 with
Etnasa (not recommended due to theft
and drug-trafficking); instead take a
micro, US$2, or colectivo, US$5, 2 hrs,
several daily. Direct buses continue to
Lima, 10 hrs, with **Turismo Central**
(Raimondi cuadra 9, T062-562668; in
Lima at Av N Arriola 515, La Victoria,
T01-472 7565, www.turismocentral.com.
pe); **Transmar** (Av E Pimentel 147, T062-
564733; in Lima at Av 28 de Julio 1511
and Av N Arriola 197, T01-265 0190, www.
transmar.com.pe); **GM Internacional**
(Av Raimondi 740, T062-561895; in Lima
at Av 28 de Julio 1275, T01-715 3122,
www.gminternacional.com.pe), and
Bahía Continental (recommended,
T01-424 1539), US$18-30.
  To **Pucallpa**, 5 hrs, US$15 with **Ucayali
Express** colectivos (Raimondi y Callao)
and **Selva Express** (Av Tito Jaime 218,
T062-562380). Buses take 7-8 hrs, US$9.

Pucallpa
Air
To **Lima** and **Iquitos**, daily 1 hr, with **LAN**
(Jr Tarapacá 805, T061-579840), **Peruvian**
(Independencia 324, T061-505655) and
Star Perú (7 de Junio 865, T061-590585).
Airport taxis charge US$6 to town; other
taxis charge US$3.

Bus
There are regular bus services to **Lima**,
several companies, 18-20 hrs (longer in
the rainy season, Nov-Mar), including

Transmar (Av Raimondi 793, T061-579778); fares range from US$17.50 *regular* to US$43 for top level *bus cama*. To **Tingo María**, bus US$9, 7-8 hrs, bound for Lima, also **Etposa** (7 de Junio 843) at 1700; or by combi, 5 hrs, US$15, with **Turismo Ucayali** (7 de Junio 799, T061-593002) and **Selva Express** (Jr 7 de Junio 841, T061-579098). Take blankets as the crossing of the Cordillera at night is bitterly cold.

Ferry

Boats to all destinations dock around Puerto Inmaculada, 2 blocks downriver from the Malecón Grau, at the bottom of Jr Inmaculada, unless the water level is very high, in which case they dock at Puerto Manantay, 4 km south of town. A mototaxi to any of the ports costs US$0.75 from the Plaza de Armas; taxis charge US$3.

To **Iquitos** down the Ucayali and Amazon rivers, 3-4 days, longer if the water level is low when larger boats must travel only by day, hammock US$40, berth US$140 double. **Henry** is a large company with departures Mon, Wed, Fri and Sat from Puerto Henry at the bottom of Jr Manco Capac, by Jr Arica; their newer boats, *Henry 6* and *7*, have some cabins with private bath. Another good boat is *Pedro Martín 2* sailing from Puerto Inmaculada. You must ask around for the large boats to Iquitos. Departure times are marked on chalk boards on the deck. Schedules seem to change almost hourly. Do not pay for your trip before you board the vessel, and only pay the captain. Some boat captains may allow you to live on board for a couple of days before sailing. Bottled drinking water can be bought in Pucallpa, but not cheaply. See also, general hints for river travel, page 578.

Yurimaguas and Pacaya-Samiria

explore the waterways and wetlands

The Río Huallaga winds northwards for 930 km from its source to the confluence with the Marañón. The Upper Huallaga is a torrent, dropping 15.8 m per km between its source and Tingo María. In contrast, the Lower Huallaga moves through an enervation of flatness. Its main port, Yurimaguas, lies below the last rapids and only 150 m above the Atlantic Ocean yet is distant from that ocean by over a month's voyage. Between the Upper and Lower rivers lies the Middle Huallaga, the third of the river that is downstream from Tingo María and upstream from Yurimaguas.

Yurimaguas → *Colour map 1, B5.*

Yurimaguas is connected by road with the Pacific coast, via Tarapoto (120 km) and Moyobamba (see page 220). It's a very relaxed jungle town and, as the roadhead on the lower Río Huallaga, is an ideal starting point for river travel in the Peruvian Amazon. A colourful Mercado Central is open every morning, full of fruit and jungle animals, many, sadly, for the pot. The town's patron saint, La Santísima Virgen

> **Tip...**
> There are several banks with ATMs in town and **Casa de cambio Progreso** (Progreso 117) changes US$ cash.

de las Nieves, is celebrated from 5 to 15 August each year, which coincides with tourism week. Excursions in the area include the gorge of Shanusi and the lakes of Mushuyacu and Sanango.

★ Reserva Nacional Pacaya-Samiria

SERNANP, Jorge Chávez 930/942, Iquitos, T065-223555, www.pacayasamiria.org, Mon-Fri 0700-1300, 1500-1700. Entry US$2 for 1 day, US$23 for 3 days, US$46 for 7 days, payable at the ranger stations.

Northeast of Yurimaguas, this vast reserve is bounded by the rivers Marañón and Ucuyali, narrowing to their confluence near the town of Nauta. At 2,080,000 ha, it is the country's second-largest protected area. The reserve's waterways and wetlands provide habitat for several cats (including puma and jaguar), manatee, tapir, river dolphins, giant otters, black cayman, boas, 269 species of fish and 449 bird species. Many of the animals found here are in danger of extinction. There are 208 population centres in the area of the reserve, 92 within the park, the others in the buffer zone. Five native groups plus *colonos* live in the region.

The reserve can only be visited with an authorized guide arranged through a tour operator or a local community tourism association. Native guides generally speak only Spanish and native tongues. Most of the reserve is off-limits to tourists, but eight areas have been set up for visitors. These have shelters or camping areas; conditions are generally simple and may require sleeping in hammocks. Trips are mostly on the river and often include fishing. Four circuits are most commonly offered. All are rich in wildlife.

The basin of the Yanayacu and Pucate rivers is the most frequently visited area and includes Laguna El Dorado, an important attraction. This area is accessed from **Nauta** on the Marañón, two hours by paved road from Iquitos. It's three hours by *peque peque* or 1½ hours by *deslizador* from Nauta to the reserve. Note that Nauta has pirate guides, so it's best to arrange a tour with an operator.

The middle and lower Samiria is accessed from **Leoncio Prado** (which has a couple of *hospedajes*), 24 hours by *lancha* from Iquitos along the Marañón. Several lakes are found in this area.

The lower Pacaya, mostly flooded forest, is accessed from **Bretaña** on the Canal de Puinahua, a shortcut on the Ucuyali, 24 hours by *lancha* from Iquitos. This area is less frequently visited than others.

The Tibilo-Pastococha area in the western side of the park, also in the Samiria basin, is accessed from **Lagunas**, on the Río Huallaga. It's 10-12 hours by *lancha* or three hours by *deslizador* from Yurimaguas and 48 hours by *lancha* from Iquitos. All river traffic from Yurimaguas to Iquitos stops here.

Another way of visiting the reserve is on a cruise, sailing along the main rivers on the periphery of the park. These tours are offered by some Iquitos operators.

Tourist information

Yurimaguas

Ask for information at the **Municipalidad Provincial de Alto Amazonas** (Plaza de Armas 112-114, T065-351213), or see www.yurimaguas.net.

Pacaya-Samiria Reserve

General information and a list of authorized community associations and operators is found on the reserve's web page, at the reserve office in Iquitos and at iPerú in Iquitos.

Where to stay

Yurimaguas

$$$-$$ Río Huallaga
Arica 111, T065-353951,
www.riohuallagahotel.com.
Pleasant modern hotel overlooking the river, safety box, pool, bar, cinema, rooftop restaurant with lovely views.

$$-$ Hostal Luis Antonio
Av Jaúregui 407, T352062,
hostal_luis_antonio@hotmail.com
(also on Facebook).
Cold water, small pool, a/c at extra cost, breakfast, very helpful.

$$-$ Posada Cumpanama
Progreso 403, T065-352905, http://
posadacumpanama.blogspot.com.
Rooms cheaper with shared bath, breakfast extra, tastefully decorated, pool, very pleasant.

$ Hostal Akemi
Jr Angamos 414, T065-352237,
www.hostalakemi.com.
Decent rooms with hot water, cheaper without a/c, some with frigobar, restaurant, pool, helpful owner, good value.

$ Hostal El Caballito
Av Jaúregui 403, T065-352427.
Cold water, small bathroom, fan, pleasant, good value.

$ Hostal El Naranjo
Arica 318, T065-352650,
www.hostalelnaranjo.com.pe.
A/c or fan, hot water, frigobar, small pool, with restaurant.

Pacaya-Samiria Reserve

$$$$ Pacaya Samiria Amazon Lodge
Office at Urb Las Palmeras 09, Iquitos,
T065-225769, www.pacayasamiria.com.
pe.
Hatuchay hotel group. Beautifully designed lodge on a hill overlooking the Marañón, just inside the reserve but close to road and town. All buildings in indigenous style, with balconies and en-suite bathrooms, restaurant, bar. Community visits and specialist birdwatching trips included in the price, but boat trips (also included) can be long. Camping trips can be arranged deeper inside the reserve. Packages start at US$520 pp for 3-day/2-night programme.

$$$ Ecological Jungle Trips & Expeditions Tours
Office at Putumayo 163 p 2,
Iquitos, T965-783409/942-643020,
www.ecologicaljungletrips.com.
Delfín Lodge, 2½ hrs from Nauta on the Río Yarapa, is the base for tours to Pacaya-Samiria, 10 rooms. Programmes from 3 days to 7 days, tailored according to the interests of the guests.

$ Basic places in Nauta include **La Granja Azul** (near entrance to town) and **Nauta Inn** (Manuel Pacaya by Laguna Sapi Sapi, T065-411025).
$ Basic places in Lagunas include **Eco** (Jr Padre Lucero, near cemetery, T065-503703); **Hostal Miraflores** (Miraflores 1 block from plaza); **Samiria** (Jr José Cárdenas, near the market).

What to do

Yurimaguas
Huayruro Tours, *Río Huallaga Hotel, Yurimaguas; also at Alfonso Aiscorbe 2 in Lagunas, T065-401186, www.peruselva. com.* Tours to lakes, day and multi-day trips to Pacaya-Samiria.

Pacaya-Samiria
Community associations in many of the villages around the reserve run tours. Community tours cost about US$70 pp per day, compared to US$80 minimum for agency tours arranged in Iquitos. Make sure you know exactly what is included (park fees, lodging, food, transport, guide), what the trip involves (canoeing, walking, hunting, fishing) and the type of accommodation.
Consorcio Rumbo al Dorado, www. yacutayta.org, groups 3 communities in the Yanayacu-Pucate region. In the community of San Martín de Tipishca in the Samiria Basin are **Asiendes** (Asociación Indígena en Defensa de la Ecología Samiria), T965-861748, asiendesperu@hotmail.com (asiendes.

peru on Facebook) and **Casa Lupuna**. 5 associations operate in Lagunas; a tour operator is **Huayruro Tours** (see above). In Bretaña, the **Gallán family** offer tours.

Transport

Yurimaguas
Air
The military **Grupo Aéreo 42** (Bolívar 128, T981-664986) has passenger flights to Yurimaguas originating in Trujillo or Iquitos; see page 150 for routes and schedules.

Bus
The road to Tarapoto is paved. To **Lima**, with **Paredes Estrella** (Mariscal Cáceres 220), 0830 daily, 32-34 hrs, US$38.50, via **Tarapoto** (US$4), **Moyobamba** (US$7.75, 5-6 hrs), **Pedro Ruiz** (US$17.50), **Chiclayo** (US$27) and **Trujillo** (US$33). Also **Ejetur**, 0500 to Lima. Faster than the bus to **Tarapoto** are: **Gilmer Tours** (C Victor Sifuentes 580), frequent mini-buses, US$5.75, 2½ hrs; cars (eg **San Martín**) US$7.75; and combis (**Turismo Selva**, Mcal Cáceres 3rd block) US$4.

Ferry
There are 6 docks in all. To **Iquitos** from Embarcadero La Boca, 3 days/2 nights, best is **Eduardo/Gilmer** (Elena Pardo 114, T065-352552; see under Iquitos, Transport). To **Lagunas** for Pacaya Samiria Reserve, from Embarcadero Abel Guerra at 0900, US$11.55, 10 hrs.

★Iquitos stands on the west bank of the Amazon and is the chief town of Peru's jungle region. Some 800 km downstream from Pucallpa and 3646 km from the mouth of the Amazon, the city is completely isolated except by air and river. Its first wealth came from the rubber boom in the late 19th century and early 20th century, but now the main economic activities are logging, commerce and petroleum. The atmosphere of the city is completely different from the rest of Peru: hot, dirty, colourful, noisy and congested with the tens-of-thousands of mototaxis and motorcycles that fill the streets. Iquitos is the main starting point for tourists wishing to explore Peru's northern jungle. Here you can experience the authentic Amazon, from the lively streets of the city to the pink dolphins and Victoria regia water lilies of the river and its waterways.

Sights

The incongruous **Iron House/Casa de Fierro** stands on the Plaza de Armas, designed by Eiffel for the Paris exhibition of 1889. It is constructed entirely of iron trusses and sheets, bolted together and painted silver and was supposedly transported from Paris by a local rubber baron. It now houses a pharmacy. Of special interest in the city are the older buildings, faced with *azulejos* (glazed tiles). They date from the rubber boom of 1890 to 1912, when the rich merchants imported tiles from Portugal and Italy and ironwork from England to embellish their homes. The **Casa de Barro** on the Plaza (house of the controversial rubber baron Fitzcarrald; see box, page 488), is now a bank. **Museo Amazónico** ⓘ *Malecón Tarapacá 386, T065-234221, Mon-Sat 0800-1300, 1430-1730, Sun 0800-1230, free, some guides speak English, tip expected*, in the Prefectura, has displays of native art and sculptures by Lima artist Letterstein. The **Jardín Botánico del Instituto de Medicina Tradicional (IMET)** ⓘ *Pasaje San Lorenzo 205, Guayabamba, at Km 2 of Av Quiñónez, T065-265629, Mon-Sat till 1500*, has over 600 species of medicinal plants and a laboratory. Also worth visiting is the **Museo de Culturas Indígenas Amazónicas** ⓘ *Malecón Tarapacá 332, T065-235809, www.amazoneco.com, daily 0800-1930, US$5.25*, the private museum of Dr Richard Bodmer, who owns the **Casa Morey** hotel (see below). It celebrates cultures from the entire Amazon region; ask here about historic Amazonian boats, such as **Barco Ayapua** ⓘ *Plaza Ramón Castilla, T065-236072, US$5*, an early 20th-century vessel from the rubber boom era, fully restored for visits, expeditions and short trips. The waterfront by Malecón Maldonado, known as 'Boulevard', is a pleasant place for a stroll and gets busy on Friday and Saturday evenings.

Belén, the picturesque, lively waterfront district, is an authentic part of Amazon river life, but is not safe at night. Most of its huts were originally built on rafts to cope with the

> **Tip...**
> Iquitos has a **golf course** at Km 6 on the Zungaracocha road (T065-223599, daily 0600-1800). The green fee, US$25 per day, includes a set of clubs and a machete.

river's 10 m change of level during floods from January to July; now they're more commonly built on stilts. Arrive by 0700 to see people arriving with their forest fruits and fish to sell in the **Belén** market. On Pasaje Paquito are bars serving local

Iquitos

To ⑧ , Explorama Tours & ports (Embarcadero Turístico, Masusa & Bellavista)

To ① & offices of rápidos to Brazil

Craft Kiosks

Pevas
Carllao
Nanay
Samanez Ocampo
La Condamine
Nauta ⑯
Fitzcarraldo ㉓
Pevas
⑭
Napo
⑥
⑨ ⑪
Putumayo
② ⑪ Star Perú
⑮
③ ▪ Indecopi
④ Casa de Barro
⑳
Plaza de Armas ② ① ㉒ ⑧ Boulevard
㉑
Iron House/ Casa de Hierro ⑨ ① ⑩
Calvo de Araujo
Cathedral ✝ ⑱
Mercado Artesanal Anaconda
Mercado Central Ⓜ
Colombian Consulate ⑦
BCP Ⓢ LAN Muyuna
Peruvian Airlines
Sgto Lores
Brazilian Consulate
⑫
⑲
Morona
Interbank & Cambios Ⓢ
Museo Amazónico (Pol)
Ⓢ BBVA
Museo de Culturas Indígenas Amazónicas
Tacna
✉ ⑤
Supermarket
Brasil
Av Grau
Arica
Prospero
Ⓡ Huallaga
Malecón Tarapacá
Rio Itaya
Ricardo Palma
⑥ ⑩
④ Moore
⑮
⑰
⑩ ⑬
R Hurtado
Av M Cáceres
San Martín
To ⑬
Plaza de 28 de Julio
⑫
Ucayali
Bermúdez
To ⑭ , Airport & Nauta
To Belén & Market
To Immigration
Bolognesi

N

200 metres
200 yards

Where to stay 🛏
1 Casa Morey
2 El Dorado Isabel
3 El Dorado Plaza
4 El Sitio
5 Flying Dog Hostel

6 Green Track Hostel
7 Hostal El Colibrí
8 La Casa Fitzcarraldo
9 La Casona
10 Las Amazonas Inn
11 Marañón
12 Royal Inn
13 Samiria Jungle
14 Sol del Oriente
15 Victoria Regia

Restaurants 🍴
1 Antica Pizzería
2 Ari's Burger
3 Chef Paz
4 Chez Maggy Pizzería
5 Comedor Vegetariano
6 El Carbón
7 El Sitio
8 Fitzcarraldo
9 Helados Giornatta
10 Helados La Muyuna
11 Huasaí
12 La Gran Maloca

13 La Quinta de Abtao
14 María's Café
15 Mitos y Cubiertos
16 Norma Mía
17 Panadería Tívoli
18 Yellow Rose of Texas

Bars & clubs 🍸
19 Amazon Bistro
20 Arandú
21 Ikaro
22 Karma
23 Noa Noa

Rubber barons

The conquest and colonization of the vast Amazon Basin was consolidated by the end of the 19th century with the invention of the process of vulcanizing rubber. Many and varied uses were found for this new product and demand was such that the jungle began to be populated by numerous European and North American immigrants who came to exploit this resource boom.

The rubber tree grew wild in the Amazon but the indigenous peoples were the only ones who knew the forests and could find this coveted tree. The exporting companies set up business in rapidly expanding cities along the Amazon, such as Iquitos. They sent their slave hunters out into the surrounding jungle to find the native labour needed to collect the valuable rubber resin. These people were completely enslaved; their living conditions were intolerable, and they perished in their thousands, leading to the extinction of many indigenous groups.

One notable figure from the rubber boom was Fitzcarrald, son of an immigrant Englishman who lived on the Peruvian coast. He was accused of spying during the 1879 war between Peru and Chile and fled to the Amazon where he lived for many years among the indigenous people.

Thanks to Fitzcarrald, the isthmus between the basin of the Ucayali river and that of the Madre de Dios was discovered. Before this, no natural form of communication was known between the two rivers. The first steamships to go up the Madre de Dios were carried by thousands of indigenous workers across the 8-km stretch of land that separated the two basins. Fitzcarrald, one of the region's richest men, died at the age of 36 when the ship on which he was travelling sank.

The rubber barons lived in the new Amazonian cities. Every imaginable luxury was imported for their use: latest Parisian fashions for the women; finest foreign liqueurs for the men; even the best musical shows were brought over from the Old World. But after the boom came the bust: the heyday of Amazon rubber came crashing to an end in 1912 when rubber grown in the French and British colonies in Asia and Africa began to compete on the world market.

Perhaps Peru's 21st-century mining barons should take note…

sugar cane rum and places where shamans buy medicinal plants and other items for their ceremonies. The main plaza has a bandstand made by Eiffel. In the high season canoes can be hired on the waterfront for a tour of Belén, US$3 per hour. To get there take a mototaxi to Los Chinos and walk down to the port.

Around Iquitos

There is a pleasant beach, with white sand and palms, at **Tipishca** on the Río Nanay, reached in 20 minutes by boat from Puerto de Santa Clara near the airport; it gets quite busy at weekends. **Santa Rita**, reached from Puerto de Pampa Chica, on a turnoff from the airport road, is quieter. Also near the airport is the village of **Santo Tomás** ⓘ *turn left just before the airport, then take another left 300 m further on, then it's about 4 km to the village; mototaxi from Iquitos US$5.* It has a nice lake for swimming and renting canoes; beaches appear when the river is low, from July to September. The restaurants at the lake are very basic, so it's best to take your own food.

Pilpintuhuasi Butterfly Farm ⓘ *near the village of Padre Cocha, T065-232665, www.amazonanimalorphanage.org, Tue-Sun 1000-1600, guided tours at 0930, 1100, 1330 and 1500, US$7.75, students US$4, includes guided tour,* has butterflies, a small, well-kept zoo and a rescue centre, run by Austrian biologist Goody. (Next door is another butterfly farm run by Goody's ex-husband.) To get there catch a colectivo from Bellavista to Padre Cocha (20 minutes), then walk 15 minutes from there. If the river is high, speedboats can reach Pilpintuhuasi directly from Iquitos, US$25 return including waiting time; pay at the end.

The **Centro de Rescate Amazónico Acobia** ⓘ *Km 4.5 on the road to Nauta, http:// gonzalomatosuria.blogspot.com/p/fundacion-iquitos-centro-de-rescate_20.html, daily 0900-1500, US$6.75, must show ID,* is where orphaned and injured manatees are nursed until they can be released. It's a good place to see this endangered species. Further along the road to Nauta are several *balnearios*.

Allpahuayo-Mishana Reserve
SERNANP, Jorge Chávez 930/942, Iquitos, T065-223555, Mon-Fri 0700-1300, 1500-1700, reserve fees US$8.50, students US$6.25.

On the Río Nanay, some 25 km south of Iquitos by the Nauta road or two hours by boat from Bellavista, this reserve protects the largest concentration of white sand jungle (*varillales*) in Peru. Part of the Napo ecoregion, it has one of the highest levels of biodiversity in the Amazon basin. Among several endangered species are two primates and several endemic species. The area is rich in birds: 475 species have been recorded. Within the reserve at Km 25 is Zoocriadero BIOAM, a good birdwatching circuit in land belonging to the Instituto Nacional de Innovación Agraria (INIA). Just beyond is the **Jardín de Plantas Medicinales y Frutales** ⓘ *Km 26.8, daily 0800-1600, guiding 0800-1000;* with over 2400 species of medicinal plants. At Km 28, **El Irapay interpretation centre** ⓘ *Mon-Sat 0830-1430,* has a trail to Mishana village by the river.

Iquitos to the Brazilian/Colombia border
There are two ways to get to the 'tri-border' (see box, page 490): by fast launch (*rápido*), or by slow boat (*lancha*). Among the places passed on the way are Pebas, on the north bank, three hours from Iquitos. Pijuayal, a part of **Pebas**, is a military area. A further three hours downstream is San Pablo, a refuelling stop. After another hour you reach **Chimbote**, where there is a police and customs point. **Caballococha**, 45 minutes from Chimbote, is an atmospheric jungle town built on a small arm of the river, surrounded by tropical vegetation. Unfortunately it is not a place to stop since the surrounding area has become a centre for coca production and trafficking. The two-hour journey from Caballococha to Santa

BORDER CROSSING
Peru–Brazil–Colombia

Santa Rosa–Tabatinga–Leticia

Details on exit and entry formalities seem to change frequently, so when leaving Peru, check in Iquitos at Immigration (Mcal Cáceres 18th block, T065-235371, Monday-Friday 0800-1615) first or with the Capitanía at the port. It is vital that you check with the Brazilian or Colombian consulate before arriving at the tri-border whether you need a visa to enter the country. It is also advisable to get your visa before arriving at the frontier. Both countries have consulates in Iquitos: Brazil (Sargento Lores 363, T065-235151, cg.iquitos@itamaraty.gov.br. Monday-Friday 0800-1400); Colombia (Calvo de Araújo 431, T065-231461, http://iquitos.consulado.gov.co, Monday-Friday 0800-1400). Yellow fever vaccination certificates may be requested to enter any of the three countries.

Boats from Iquitos stop in Santa Rosa for Peruvian exit formalities. Migración is open daily 0730-1700. After clearing customs and getting your exit stamp, you can cross the rver by motorized canoe to **Tabatinga** (Brazil), US$1.75 per person, and **Leticia** (Colombia), US$1.65 per person, five minutes. Bear in mind that once you have an exit stamp from one country, you must get the entry stamp at your next destination within 24 hours; there are fines if you are late.

The immigration office in Tabatinga (Policia Federal, Avenida da Amizade 65, daily 0800-1200, 1400-1800) is about 1 km from the border; a taxi from the port costs US$9. In Leticia, Migración Colombia is located at the airport and is open Monday to Friday 0800-1700, Saturday and Sunday 0800-1500. A taxi from the centre of Leticia costs US$4, mototaxi US$2.50.

Onward travel If travelling into Brazil, there are about five boats a week downriver from Tabatinga to Manaus (three to four days, US$100 for a hammock, US$400 for a berth). There is also a jet boat once a week, which takes 38 hours. To travel to other parts of Colombia from Leticia, you have to fly.

Rosa is beautiful, with the rolling green hills of Colombia's **Amacayacu National Park** to your left. However, *rápidos* usually take the narrow, southern arm of the river, which does not give a view of Colombia, so check your route in advance.

Santa Rosa is a small Peruvian military base across the river from Leticia (Colombia) and Tabatinga (Brazil). It is the only place with a good beach, so it gets busy at weekends. It is prone to severe flooding in the rainy season. There are five basic hotels; Diana and Las Hamacas are reported better than the others.

The busy Brazilian port of **Tabatinga** is on the land border with **Leticia** (Colombia), a pleasant city with the best infrastructure in the area. There is no separation between the two and Avenida

Tip...
Reais and pesos colombianos are accepted in all three towns; soles are seldom used. There are ATMs in Tabatinga and Leticia, and the latter is the best place to change cash; TCs are not accepted anywhere.

da Amizade in Tabatinga becomes Avenida Internacional in Leticia. There are tourist offices at the land border. All three towns have accommodation and restaurants and people move freely between them with no border formalities. There is drug smuggling throughout the area and Tabatinga is particularly unsafe; do not go out here at night.

> **Tip...**
> If you are only visiting any of the towns for one day, there is no need to get stamped-in, but always keep your passport with you. Remember that Leticia and Santa Rosa are one hour behind Tabatinga.

Listings Iquitos and around *map p487*

Tourist information

iPerú (Jr Napo 161, of 4, T065-236144, iperuiquitos@promperu.gob.pe, Mon-Sat 0900-1800, Sun 0900-1300) also has a desk at the airport, open at flight times. If arriving by air, go to this desk first to get a list of hotels, a map and advice about the touts outside the airport. Both www.iquitosnews.com and www.iquitostimes.com have articles, maps and information; see also www.jungle-love.org. If you have a complaint about service, contact **Indecopi** (Putumayo 464, T065-243490, jreategui@indecopi.gob.pe, Mon-Fri 0830-1630); to report a crime, contact the **tourist police** (Sargento Lores 834, T065-242081).

Where to stay

Information on jungle lodges is given under What to do, as many work closely or exclusively with particular tour operators, see page 495.

Around Peruvian Independence Day (27 and 28 Jul) and Easter, Iquitos can get crowded and flight prices rise at this time.

$$$$ El Dorado Plaza
Napo 258 on main plaza, T065-222555, www.grupo-dorado.com.
Good accommodation and restaurant, bar, business-type hotel, pool, prices include service, small breakfast, welcome drink and transfer to/from airport. Also owns **$$$ El Dorado Isabel** (Napo 362, T065-232574).

$$$$ Samiria Jungle
Ricardo Palma 159, T065-223232, www.samiriajunglehotel.com.
Modern upmarket hotel, includes airport transfers, large suites and rooms, frigobar, bathtub, restaurant, bar, pool, meeting rooms.

$$$ Casa Morey
Raymondi y Loreto, Plaza Ramón Castilla, T065-231913, www.casamorey.com.
Boutique hotel in a beautifully restored historic rubber-boom period mansion. Great attention to detail, includes airport transfers, ample comfortable rooms, pool, good library.

$$$ Sol del Oriente
Av Quiñónez Km 2.5 on the way to the airport, T065-260317.
Airport transfers, pool, internet in hall, nice gardens, deco a bit kitsch.

$$$ Victoria Regia
Ricardo Palma 252, T065-231983,
www.victoriaregiahotel.com.
Free map of city, safe deposit boxes in
rooms, good restaurant, indoor pool.

$$$-$$ La Casa Fitzcarraldo
Av La Marina 2153, T065-601138,
http://casafitzcarraldo.com/.
Prices vary according to room. Includes
breakfast and airport transfer, with Wi-Fi,
satellite TV, minibar, 1st-class restaurant,
treehouse, pool in lovely gardens,
captive animals. The house is the home
of Walter Saxer, the executive-producer
of Werner Herzog's famous film, lots of
movie and celebrity memorabilia.

$$$-$$ Marañón
Fitzcarrald y Nauta 289, T065-242673,
http://hotelmaranon.com.
Multi-storey hotel, spotless
comfortable rooms, a/c, convenient
location, small pool.

$$ Royal Inn & Casino
Aguirre 793, T065-224244,
www.royalinncasinohotel.com.
Modern, comfortable, frigobar
and, bidet, airport transfer, good.

$$-$ Flying Dog Hostel
Malecón Tarapacá 592, T065-223755,
www.flyingdogperu.com.
Nice old house, pleasant 4 bed dorms
and private rooms with bath and a/c
or fan, clean kitchen, lockers.

$$-$ Hostal El Colibrí
Raymondi 200, T065-241737,
hostalelcolibri@hotmail.com.
1 block from Plaza and 50 m from the
river so can be noisy, nicely refurbished
house, a/c or fan, hot water, secure, good
value, breakfast extra, helpful staff.

$$-$ La Casona
Fitzcarald 147, T065-234 394,
www.hotellacasonaiquitos.com.pe.
In building dating from 1901, now
modernized, hot water, fan or a/c,
kitchen facilities, small patio, pool,
popular with travellers. Opposite, at
Fitzcarald 152, is **Hostal La Casona
Río Grande**, with smaller rooms, fan.
Transport to either from the airport
with advance reservation.

$ Green Track Hostel
Ricardo Palma 516, T950-664049,
www.greentrack-hostel.com.
Pleasant hostel, dorms with a/c or fan,
private rooms with and without bath,
free pick up with advanced booking,
terrace, Brazilian breakfast, English
spoken, helpful owners, tours arranged
to Tapiche Reserve (see below).

$ El Sitio
Ricardo Palma 541, T065-234932.
Fan, private bath, cold water, good value.

$ Las Amazonas Inn
*Ricardo Palma 460, T065-225367, las_
amazonas_inn_iquitos@yahoo.es.*
Simple rooms with electric shower, a/c,
kitchen facilities, breakfast available,
friendly owner.

Restaurants

Local specialities include palm heart
salad (*chonta*), or *a la Loretana* dish on
menus; also try *inchicapi* (chicken, corn
and peanut soup), *cecina* (fried dried
pork), *tacacho* (fried green banana and
pork, mashed into balls and eaten for
breakfast or tea), *juanes* (chicken, rice,
olive and egg, seasoned and wrapped
in bijao leaves and sold in restaurants)
and the *camu-camu*, an acquired taste,
said to have one of the highest vitamin
C concentrations in the world. Avoid

eating endangered species, such as paiche, caiman or turtle, which are sometimes on menus.

For a good local breakfast, go to the **Mercado Central**, C Sargento Lores, where there are several kioskos outside, popular and cheap. Try the local drink *chuchuhuasi*, made from the bark of a tree, which is supposed to have aphrodisiac properties (for sale at Arica 1046), and *jugo de cocona*, and the alcoholic *cola de mono* and *siete raíces* (aguardiente mixed with the bark of 7 trees and wild honey), sold at **Musmuqui** (Raymondi 382), Mon-Sat from 1900.

$$$ Al Frío y al Fuego
On the water, go to Embarcadero Turístico (El Huequito) and a boat will pick you up, T065-224862. Mon 1830-2300, Tue-Sat 1130-1600 and 1830-2300, Sun 1130-1600.
Good upscale floating restaurant with regional specialities.

$$$ Fitzcarraldo
Malecón Maldonado 103 y Napo.
Smart, typical food, also pizza, good pastas and salads.

$$$ La Gran Maloca
Sargento Lores 170, opposite Banco Continental. Closes 2000 on Sun, other days 2300.
A/c, high class regional food.

$$$-$$ Chef Paz
Putumayo 468, T065-241277. Mon-Sat 0800-midnight.
Excellent food including fish, shellfish, meat dishes, local specialities and their own jungle sushi.

$$ Ari's Burger
Plaza de Armas, Próspero 127.
Medium-priced fast food, breakfasts, popular with tourists but hygiene questionable.

$$ Yellow Rose of Texas
Putumayo 180. Open 24 hrs so you can wait here if arriving late at night.
Varied food including local dishes, Texan atmosphere, good breakfasts, lots of information, also has a bar, Sky TV and Texan saddle seats.

$$-$ Antica Pizzería
Napo 159. Sun-Thu 0700-2400, Fri-Sat 0700-0100.
"The best pizza in town" and Italian dishes, pleasant ambiance especially on the upper level.

$$-$ Arapaíma Gigas
Carretera a Zungarococha Km 4.5, opposite the golf course. Open for lunch at weekends.
Just outside the city, a restaurant with its own fish farm in a lake. They catch whatever you request and cook it immediately; ceviche de paiche on Sun. Mototaxi US$5.

$$-$ Chez Maggy Pizzería
Raymondi 177. Daily 1800-0100.
Wood-fired pizza and home-made pasta.

$$-$ La Quinta (5ta) de Abtao
Abtao 527. Closed Mon.
Small place serving ceviche of river fish and other dishes using local ingredients. Very good. Also does a good value lunch menu.

$ Comedor Vegetariano
Morona y Arica.
Small restaurant with a lot of vegetarian choices, US$3.35.

$ El Carbón
La Condamine 115. Open 1900-2300 only.
Grilled meats, salads, regional side-dishes such as tacacho and patacones.

$ El Sitio
Sargento Lores 404. Mon-Sat 1930-2230.
A simple place for *anticuchos* for all tastes including vegetarian, popular.

$ Huasaí
Fitzcarrald 131. Open 0715-1615, closed Mon.
Varied and innovative menu, popular, good food and value, go early.

$ Mitos y Cubiertos
Napo 337, by the Plaza. Mon-Sat midday only.
Generous lunches, good value.

Cafés

Helados Giornatta
Próspero, on Plaza de Armas.
Specializes in ice creams flavoured with fruits from the rainforest.

Helados La Muyuna
Jr Próspero 621.
Good natural jungle fruit ice cream. Second location on Napo near Malecón.

María's Café
Nauta 292. Tue-Sun 0800-1230.
Breakfasts, sandwiches, burgers, coffee and cakes, with desserts of the day.

Norma Mía
La Condamine 153.
Doña Norma has been making delicious cakes for over 30 years, also sells ice cream.

Panadería Tívoli
Ricardo Palma, block 3.
A variety of good bread and sweets.

Bars and clubs

Amazon Bistro
Malecón Tarapacá 268.
Upscale French bistro/bar on the waterfront, drinks, snacks, breakfasts and meal of the day. Trendy and popular. Live music at weekends.

Arandú
Malecón Maldonado.
Good views of the river.

El Pardo
Cáceres y Alzamora.
Huge place with live music; you dance along with 5,000 others. Bands play salsa, cumbia and música tropical. Only beer for sale; dirty toilets.

Ikaro
Putumayo 341.
Good Spanish rock music, internet.

Karma
Napo 138.
Cocktails, rock music and a happy hour.

Noa Noa
Pevas y Fitzcarrald.
Popular disco with cumbia and Latin music.

Festivals

5 Jan Founding of Iquitos.
Feb-Mar Carnival.
Jun Tourist week is the 3rd week.
24 Jun San Juan, the most important festival.
28-30 Aug Santa Rosa de Lima.
8 Dec Immaculate Conception (La Purísima), celebrated in Punchana, near the docks, Bellavista and Nanay.

Shopping

Hammocks in Iquitos cost about US$12. **Mercado Artesanal Anaconda**, by the waterfront at Napo is good for Amazon handicrafts, but be sure not to buy items that contain animal products. Also try the **Asociación de Artesanos El Manguaré**, which has kiosks on

Jr Nauta, block 1. **Mercado Artesanal de Productores** (4 km from the centre in the San Juan district, on the road to the airport; take a colectivo) is the cheapest in town with more choice than elsewhere.

For jungle clothing and equipment, visit **Comisesa** (Arica 348), and **Mad Mick's Trading Post** (Putumayo 163, top floor, next to the Iron House).

La Restinga, Raymondi 254, T065-221371, larestinga@gmail.com. This association sells t-shirts, books and soaps made by children. It also runs literacy workshops in Belén on Tue and Thu from 1430-1800, at which you can volunteer.

What to do

Jungle tours

Agencies arrange 1-day or longer trips to places of interest with guides speaking some English. Take your time before making a decision and don't be bullied by the hustlers at the airport (they get paid a hefty commission). You must make sure your tour operator or guide has a proper licence (check with iPerú). Do not go with a company which does not have legal authorization; there are many unscrupulous people about. Find out all the details of the trip and food arrangements before paying (a minimum of US$50 per day). Several companies have their own lodges, providing various levels of accommodation in the heart of the jungle (see below). All prices are negotiable, except tours run by **Muyuna**, **Heliconia Lodge** and **Explorama** (see below), who do not give commissions.

River cruises

There are several agencies that arrange river cruises in well-appointed boats.

> **Tip...**
> Some tours include visits to a Monkey Island (Isla de Monos), which claims to be a rescue centre for animals but often has animals that have been captured in the wild. Similarly, trips to Yagua or Bora indigenous communities merely provide a show of costume and dancing. Think twice about visiting such 'attractions'.

Most go to the Pacaya-Samiria region, very few towards Brazil. In addition to the vessels of Aqua and Delfín (see below), other options include La Amatista of the Dorado hotel group, the Aquamarina, Arapaima and Queen Violeta group and Estrella Amazónica. Contact a company like **Rainforest Cruises** (www.rainforestcruises.com), for options. Alternatively, speed boats for river trips can be hired by the hour or day at the **Embarcadero Turístico**, at the intersection of Av de la Marina and Samánez Ocampo in Punchana. Prices vary greatly, usually US$15-20 per hr, US$80 for speedboat, and are negotiable.

Shaman experiences

Iquitos is an important place for ayahuasca tourism. There are legitimate shamans as well as charlatans. **Karma Café** (Napo 138; see above) is the centre of the scene in town. See also the work of Alan Shoemaker (**Soga del Alma**, Rómulo Espinar 170, Iquitos 65, alanshoemaker@hotmail.com), who holds an International Amazonian Shamanism Conference every year. Before taking ayahuasca in a ceremony with a shaman, read the note in Practicalities, page 587.

Tour operators and jungle lodges

Amazon Yarapa River Lodge, *Av La Marina 124, www.yarapa.com*. On the Río Yarapa, award-winning in its use of ecofriendly resources and its work with local villages. Flexible and responsible. Its field laboratory is associated with Cornell University. Arranges trips to Pacaya-Samiria.

Aqua Expeditions, *Iquitos 1167, T065-601053, www.aquaexpeditions.com*. Luxury river cruises of 3, 4, or 7 nights on the *M/V Aria* (from US$2835 pp) and the *M/V Aqua* (from US$2685 pp), both designed by famous Peruvian architect Jordi Puig to look like floating town houses rather than boats, with massive picture windows in each a/c suite. Amazing food with local delicacies on the gourmet tasting menu, good shore excursions with knowledgeable local guides.

Chullachaqui Eco Lodge, *Raymondi 138, Iquitos, T965-705919, http:// amazoniantrips.com/chullachaqui-eco-lodge/.* 1 hr by speed boat up the Amazon on the Río Tapira. Thatched timber cabins, basic accommodation, private bath, communal dining room, hammock room, insect screens, tours with naturalist guides to see river dolphins and other wildlife.

Cumaceba Amazonia Tours, *Putumayo 184 in the Iron House, T065-232229, www.cumaceba.com*. Overnight visits to Cumaceba Lodge, 35 km from Iquitos, and tours of 1-4 nights to the Botanical Lodge on the Amazon, 80 km from Iquitos, birdwatching tours, ayahuasca ceremonies.

Curuhuinsi Eco Adventure Tours & Expeditions, *T965-013225, www. facebook.com/CuruhuinsiEcoAdventure ToursExpeditions*. Gerson Pizango is a local, English-speaking and award-winning guide who will take you to his village 2½ hrs by boat, from where you can trek and camp or stay and experience village life. Expert at spotting wildlife and knowledgeable about medicinal plants, he offers interesting and varied expeditions benefitting the community. In the village, accommodation is in a hut by the riverside where there are pink and grey dolphins. A private room with mosquito net costs US$50-70 pp per day depending on length of trip and size of party, includes food, water, camping gear, boots, raincoats, torches, binoculars, fishing rods, machetes.

Dawn on the Amazon, *Malecón Maldonado 185 y Nauta, T065-223730, www.dawnontheamazon.com*. Offers a variety of day tours around Iquitos on the luxurious 20 passenger *Dawn on the Amazon III* (US$199 pp). Also offer custom-made cruises for several days. Their wooden vessels are decorated with carvings of jungle themes. Also has a good bar/restaurant in town.

Delfín, *Av Abelardo Quiñones Km 5, San Juan Bautista, T065-262721, www. delfinamazoncruises.com*. Luxury cruises in the *Delfín I* and *Delfín II* (the cheaper of the 2), 3- and 4-night expeditions to Pacaya-Samiria, with daily activities including kayaking, bird- and wildlife-watching, fresh organic food, from US$2400 pp. Under same ownership as *Al Frío y al Fuego* restaurant in town.

Explorama Tours, *by the riverside docks on Av La Marina 340, T065-252530, www. explorama.com*. The biggest and most established operator, with over 40 years' experience. Frequently recommended. Their lodges are: **Ceiba Tops**, 40 km (1½ hrs) from Iquitos, a comfortable resort with 75 a/c rooms with electricity, hot showers, pool with hydromassage and beautiful gardens. The food is good and, as in all Explorama's properties, is served communally. There are attractive walks and other excursions, a recommended jungle experience for those who want their creature comforts, US$340 pp for 1 night/2 days.

Explorama Lodge at Yanamono, 80 km from Iquitos, 2½ hrs from Iquitos, has palm-thatched accommodation with separate bathroom and shower facilities connected by covered walkways, cold water, no electricity, good food and service. US$455 for 3 days/2 nights.

Explornapo Lodge at Llachapa on the Sucusai creek (a tributary of the Napo), is in the same style as Explorama Lodge, but is further away from Iquitos, 160 km (4 hrs), and is set in 105,000 ha of primary rainforest, so is better for seeing wildlife, US$1,120 for 5 days/4 nights (all 2014 basic prices). Nearby is the impressive canopy walkway 35 m above the forest floor and 500 m long, 'a magnificent experience and not to be missed'. It is associated with the Amazon Center for Tropical Studies (ACTS), a scientific station, only 10 mins from the canopy walkway. Close to Explornapo is the ReNuPeRu medicinal plant garden, run by a curandero.

Explor Tambos, 2 hrs from Explornapo, offer more primitive accommodation, 8 shelters for 16 campers, bathing in the river.

Heliconia Lodge, *Ricardo Palma 242; contact T01-421 9195, www.heliconialodge. com.pe.* On the Río Amazonas, 80 km downriver from Iquitos, surrounded by rainforest, islands and lagoons, this is a beautiful place for resting, birdwatching, looking for pink dolphins, jungle hikes. Organized packages 3 days/ 2 nights, US$282. Good guides, food and flexible excursions according to guest's requirements. The lodge has hot water, electricity for 5 hrs each day and a traditionally rustic yet comfortable design. Same management has bungalows 15 km from Iquitos on a lake.

Muyuna Amazon Lodge, *Putumayo 163, ground floor, T065-242858/T065-993 4424, www.muyuna.com.* 140 km upstream from Iquitos on the Río Yanayacu, before San Juan village. 1- to 5-night packages available. 2 nights/3 days is US$340 pp all-inclusive for 2-10 people. Trusted guides, high-quality accommodation, good food and service; very well organized, flexible and professional. Amenities are constantly updated with new ecological considerations. Birdwatching and camping trips into the forest. This area is less spoilt than some other parts of the forest downstream. **Centro de Rescate Amazónico** (see above) has released manatees here. Highly recommended.

Paseos Amazónicos Ambassador, *Pevas 246, T065-231618, www. paseosamazonicos.com*. Operates the **Amazonas Sinchicuy Lodge**, 1½ hrs from Iquitos on the Sinchicuy river, 25 mins by boat from the Amazon. The lodge consists of several wooden buildings with thatched roofs on stilts, cabins with bathroom, no electricity but paraffin lamps are provided, good food, and plenty activities, including visits to local villages. Recommended. They also have Tambo Yanayacu and Tambo Amazónico lodges, organize visits to Pacaya Samiria and run local tours. **Tapiche Reserve**, *Ricardo Palma 516, T065-600805/950-664049, office at Green Track Hostel (see above), www. tapichejungle.com*. On the Río Tapiche, a tributary of the Ucayali, 11 hrs upriver from Iquitos. Fully screened wood cabins with thatched roofs, custom designed trips according to the visitor's interests, 4-day/3-night and 5-day/4-night tours offered.

Transport

Air
Francisco Secada Vigneta airport, T065-260147 is southwest of the city; a taxi to the airport costs US$10; *mototaxi*, US$3.25. Most buses from the main road outside the airport go through the centre of town, US$0.75. To **Lima**, daily, with **LAN** (direct or via Tarapoto), **Peruvian Airlines** and **Star Perú** (direct or via Tarapoto, also daily to Pucallpa) and **TACA**. The military **Grupo Aéreo 42** has passenger flights to Iquitos originating in Trujillo; see page 150 for routes and schedules. They also fly occasionally to **Santa Rosa**.

Bus
To **Nauta**, **Trans del Sur** from Libertad y Próspero, daily 0530-1900, US$3.10, 2 hrs; also vans from Av Aguirre cuadra 14 by Centro Comercial Sachachorro, which leave when full, US$4, 1½ hrs.

Ferry
For general hints on river travel, see page 578. For information about boats, go to the corresponding ports of departure for each destination, except for speed boats to the Brazil/Colombian border which have their offices clustered on Raymondi block 3. When river levels are very high departures may be from alternative places.

Lanchas leave from Puerto Henry and Puerto Masusa, 2 km north of the centre, a dangerous area at night. Always deal directly with boat owners or managers; avoid touts and middle-men. All fares are negotiable; the first night's meal is not included. You can buy either a ticket to sling your hammock on deck, or for a berth in a cabin sleeping 2 to 4 people. It can be worth clubbing together and paying for a cabin in which to lock your belongings, even if you sleep outside in a hammock. A fabric hammock is essential. Board the boat many hours in advance to guarantee hammock space, and, if going on the top deck, try to get a space at the front. There are adequate washing and toilet facilities, but the food is basic and cooked in river water. Take your own supplies and plenty of prophylactic enteritis tablets. Also take insect repellent and a mosquito net, and a good book or two. If arriving in Iquitos on a regular, slow boat, take extreme care when disembarking. Things get very chaotic at this time and theft and pickpocketing is rife. Some of the newer boats have CCTV to deter theft.

To **Pucallpa**, 4-5 days upriver along the Amazon and Ucayali (can be longer if the water level is low), larger boats must travel only by day, hammock US$40, berth US$140 double. **Henry** (T065-263948) is a large company with 4 departures per week from Puerto Henry; *Henry 5, 6* and *7* have some cabins with bath. Another good boat is *Pedro Martín 2* from Puerto Masusa.

To **Yurimaguas**, 3-4 days upriver along the Amazon, Marañón and Huallaga, hammock space US$40, berth US$119-134 double. The **Eduardo/Gilmer** company, T065-960404, with 8 boats is recommended, sailing from Puerto Masusa several times a week, except Sun; *Eduardo I* and *Gilmer IV* have berths with bath for US$192.

To **Santa Rosa** (on the border with Brazil and Colombia; see page 490), the most convenient way to travel is by *rápido*, 8-10 hrs downriver, US$75, from the **Embarcadero Turístico** at 0600 Tue-Sun; be at the port 0445 for customs check, board 0500-0530. (In the opposite direction, boats leave Santa Rosa Tue-Sun at 0400 and take 10-12 hrs upstream; if you're coming from Brazil or Colombia get your immigration entry stamp the day before.) *Rápidos* carry life jackets and have bathrooms; a simple breakfast and lunch are included in the price. Luggage limit is 15 kg. Purchase tickets in advance from company offices in Iquitos: **Golfinho** (Raymondi 378, T065-225118, www.transportegolfinho.com) and **Transtur** (Raymondi 384, T065-

221356). *Lanchas* to Santa Rosa, which may continue to Islandia, leave from the Puerto Pesquero or Puerto Masusa (enquire at T065-250440), Mon-Sat at 1800, 2-3 days downriver, US$31 in hammock, US$50 in cabin; in the other direction they depart Santa Rosa Mon-Sat at 1200.

To reach the border with Ecuador you go to **Pantoja**, 5-7 days upriver on the Napo, a route requiring plenty of time, stamina and patience. There are irregular departures once or twice a month, US$38, plus US$3 per day for a berth if you can get one; for details call **Radio Moderna** in Iquitos (T065-250440), or T065-830055 (a private phone in Pantoja village). The vessels are usually cargo boats that carry live animals, some of which are slaughtered en route. Crowding and poor sanitation are common. Once in Pantoja, there is no public transport to **Nuevo Rocafuerte** (Ecuador), so you must hire a private boat, US$60. To shorten the voyage, or to visit the jungle towns along the way, go to **Indiana**, daily departures from **Muelle de Productores** in Iquitos, US$5, 45 mins, then take a mototaxi to **Mazán** on the Río Napo. From Mazán, there are *rápidos* to **Santa Clotilde**, US$31 includes a snack, 4-5 hrs, information from **Familia Ruiz** in Iquitos (T065-251410).

Tip...
There is no Ecuadorean consulate in Iquitos; get your visa in advance in your home country.

Southern
Amazon

The southern selva is mostly in Madre de Dios Region, which contains the Manu National Park (2.04 million ha), the Tambopata National Reserve (254,358 ha) and the Bahauja-Sonene National Park (1.1 million ha). The forest of this lowland region (Altitude: 260 m) is technically called Sub-tropical Moist Forest, which means that it receives less rainfall than tropical forest and is dominated by the floodplains of its meandering rivers. The most striking features are the former river channels that have become isolated as oxbow lakes. These are home to black caiman and giant otter and a host of other species. Other rare species living in the forest are jaguar, puma, ocelot and tapir. There are also howler monkeys, capybara, macaws, guans, currasows and the giant harpy eagle.

The relative proximity to Cuzco of Manu, in particular, has made it one of the prime nature-watching destinations in South America. Despite its reputation, Manu is heavily protected, with visitor numbers limited and a large percentage of the park inaccessible to tourists. Nevertheless, there is no need to worry that this level of management is going to diminish the quality of your jungle experience. There is more than enough in the way of birds, animals and plants to satisfy the most ardent wildlife enthusiast. Tambopata does have a town in the vicinity, Puerto Maldonado, but the suspension of oil exploration in 2000 led to a change of status for a large tract of this area, giving immediate protection to another of Peru's zones of record-breaking diversity.

As well as containing some of the most important flora and fauna on Earth, the region also harbours gold-diggers, loggers, hunters, drug smugglers and oil-men, whose activities have endangered the unique rainforest. Moreover, the construction of the *Interoceánica*, a road linking the Atlantic and Pacific oceans via Puerto Maldonado and Brazil, will certainly bring more uncontrolled colonization in the area, as seen so many times before in the Brazilian Amazon.

Manu Biosphere Reserve
Peru's premier wildlife-watching destination

★Few other reserves on the planet can compare with Manu for the diversity of life forms; it holds over 1000 species of birds and covers an altitudinal range from 200 m to 4100 m above sea-level. Giant otters, jaguars, ocelots and 13 species of primates abound in this pristine tropical wilderness; uncontacted indigenous tribes are present in the more remote areas, as are indigenous groups with limited access.

The reserve is one of the largest conservation units on Earth, encompassing the complete drainage of the Manu River. It is divided into the **Manu National Park** (1,692,137 ha), which only government-sponsored biologists and anthropologists may visit with permits from the Ministry of Agriculture in Lima; the **Reserved Zone** (257,000 ha) within the national park, which is set aside for applied scientific research and ecotourism; and the **Cultural Zone** (92,000 ha), which contains acculturated native groups and colonists along the Alto Madre de Dios and its tributaries, where the locals still employ their traditional way of life. Among the ethnic groups in the Cultural Zone are the Harakmbut, Machiguenga and Yine in the Amarakaeri Reserved Zone, on the east bank of the Alto Madre de Dios, who have set up their own ecotourism activities. Associated with Manu are other areas protected by conservation groups, or local people (for example the Blanquillo Reserved Zone) and some cloudforest parcels along the road. The **Nahua-Kugapakori Reserved Zone**, set aside for these two nomadic native groups, is the area between the headwaters of the Río Manu and headwaters of the Río Urubamba, to the north of the Alto Madre de Dios.

Essential Manu

Access to Manu

The Multi-Use Zone of Manu Biosphere Reserve is accessible to anyone and several lodges exist in the area (see page 504). The Reserved Zone is accessible by permit only, available from the Manu National Park office in Cuzco (see page 504); entry is strictly controlled and visitors must visit the area under the auspices of an authorized operator with an authorized guide. Permits are limited and reservations should be made well in advance. In the Reserved Zone the only permanent accommodation is in the comfortable **Manu Lodge** or the comfortable but rustic **Casa Machiguenga** in the Cocha Salvador area. In addition, several companies have tented safari camp infrastructures, some with shower and dining facilities, but all visitors sleep in tents. The entrance fee to the Reserved Zone is 150 soles per person (about US$55) and is included in package tour prices.

Tours to Manu usually enter by road, overnighting in a lodge in the cloudforest, and continue by boat (the route is described below). It is this journey from the highlands down through the various strata of habitat that sets it apart from many other visits to the jungle. At the end of the tour, passengers either return overland or fly back to Cuzco from Puerto Maldonado. There is an airstrip at Diamante, near Boca Manu, but there are no regular flights from Cuzco. Ask the tour operators in Cuzco if your tour will go overland or by air.

Beware of pirate operators on the streets of Cuzco who offer trips to the Reserved Zone of Manu and end up halfway through the trip changing the route "due to emergencies", which, in reality means they have no permits to operate in the area. Some unscrupulous tour guides will offer trips to see the uncontacted tribes of Manu; on no account make any attempt to view these very vulnerable people.

Tip...

It is not possible to arrange trips to the Reserved Zone of the National Park from Itahuania, owing to park regulations. All arrangements, including permits, must be made in Cuzco.

When to go

The climate is warm and humid, with a rainy season from November to March and a dry season from April to October. Cold fronts from the South Atlantic, called *friajes*, are characteristic of the dry season, causing temperatures to drop to 15-16°C during the day and to 13°C at night. Always bring a sweater at this time. The best time to visit is during the dry season when there are fewer mosquitoes and the rivers are low, exposing the beaches. This is also a good time to see birds nesting and to view animals at close range, as they stay close to the rivers and are easily seen. A pair of binoculars is essential and insect repellent is a must.

Cuzco to Manu and Puerto Maldonado via Pilcopata and Itahuania

Cuzco to Pilcopata The arduous 255 km trip over the Andes from Cuzco to Pilcopata takes about eight to 12 hours by bus or truck, or 10 hours to two days in the wet season. The scenery is magnificent. From Cuzco you climb up to the Huancarani pass (very cold at night) then drop to Paucartambo in the eponymous river valley. The road then ascends to a second pass (also cold at night), after which it goes down to the cloudforest and then the rainforest, reaching **Pilcopata** at 650 m on the border between the Regions of Cuzco and Madre de Dios.

Pilcopata to Itahuania After Pilcopata, the route is hair-raising and breathtaking, passing through **Atalaya**, the first village on the Alto Madre de Dios River and tourist port for hiring boats to Boca Manu; there are basic lodgings and restaurants here. The route continues to Salvación, where the park office and entrance are situated, plus some basic hostals and restaurants.

The road, which bypasses the previous port of **Shintuya**, continues as far as **Itahuania**, currently the starting point for river transport. The road is scheduled to continue to Nuevo Edén, 11 km away downriver, and to Diamante, so the location of the river port will be determined by road-building progress. Eventually, the road will go all the way to Boca Colorado. As it is, rain often disrupts wheeled transport.

Itahuania to Puerto Maldonado via Boca Colorado Cargo boats leave Itahuania for the gold-mining centre of Boca Colorado on the Río Madre de Dios, via Boca Manu (see below), but only when the boat is fully laden (see Transport, below). Very basic accommodation can be found in Boca Colorado, but it is not recommended for lone women travellers. From Colorado you can take a colectivo to Puerto Carlos, cross the river, then take another colectivo to Puerto Maldonado: 4½ hours in all.

Boca Manu and around → *Colour map 5, A6.*

Boca Manu is the connecting point between the rivers Alto Madre de Dios, Manu and Madre de Dios. It has a few houses and some food supplies. It is also the entrance to the Manu Reserved Zone and to go further you must be part of an organized group. The park ranger station is located in Limonal. You need to show your permit here. Camping is allowed if you have a permit.

Upstream on the Río Manu you pass the **Manu Lodge** on the Cocha Juárez after three or four hours (see Where to stay, below). You can continue to Cocha Otorongo in 2½ hours and Cocha Salvador, a further 30 minutes. The latter is the biggest lake with plenty of wildlife. From here it is two to three hours to Pakitza, the entrance to the National Park Zone, only accessible to biologists with a special permit.

Between Boca Manu and Boca Colorado is **Blanquillo**, a private reserve of 10,000 ha. Bring a good tent with you and all food if you want to camp and do it yourself, or alternatively accommodation is available at the **Tambo Blanquillo** (full board or accommodation only). Wildlife is abundant, especially macaws and parrots at the macaw lick near **Manu Wildlife Centre**. There are occasional boats to Blanquillo from Shintuya; six to eight hours.

Tourist information

Amazon Conservation Association (ACCA)
C Cesar Vallejo K-6, Urb Santa Mónica, Wanchaq, Cuzco, T084-222329, www. amazonconservation.org; also at Jr Cusco 499, T082-573237, Puerto Maldonado.
An NGO whose mission is to protect biodiversity by studying ecosystems and developing conservation tools while suporting local communities.

Asociación Peruana para la Conservación de la Naturaleza (APECO)
Parque José Acosta 187, p 2, Magdalena del Mar, Lima, T01-264 5804, apeco@apeco.org.pe.

Manu National Park Office
Av Cinco los Chachacomos F2-4, Larapa Grande, San Jerónimo, Cuzco, T084-274509, www.visitmanu.com. Mon-Fri.
Issues permits for the Reserved Zone.

Perú Verde
Ricardo Palma J-1, Santa Mónica, Cuzco, T084-226392, www.peruverde.org
This is a local NGO that can help with information and has free video shows about Manu National Park and Tambopata National Reserve. Friendly and helpful, with information on research in the jungle area of Madre de Dios.

Pronaturaleza
Doña Juana 137, Urb Los Rosales, Santiago de Surco, Lima, T01-271 2662; also in Puerto Maldonado at Jr Cajamarca cuadra 1 s/n, T082-571585, www.pronaturaleza.org.

Where to stay

Lodges in Manu
Most jungle lodges are booked as package deals for 3 days, 2 nights, or longer, with meals, transport and guides; see websites for offers.

Amazon Yanayacu Lodge
Cahuide 824, Punchana, T062-250822.
About 1 hr by boat above Diamante village on the southern bank of the Madre de Dios, close to a small parrot *collpa* (mineral lick). Using local river transport to arrive at the lodge rates are very reasonable, prices depend on length of stay. The lodge also offers several different itineraries in Manu.

Amazonia Lodge
On the Río Alto Madre de Dios just across the river from Atalaya, T084-816131, www.amazonialodge.com; in Cuzco at Matará 334, p 3, T084-231370.
An old tea hacienda run by the Yabar Calderón family, famous for its bird diversity and fine hospitality, a great place to relax, meals included, birding or natural history tours available, contact Santiago in advance and he'll arrange a pick-up.

Casa Machiguenga
Near Cocha Salvador, upriver from Manu Lodge.
Contact **Manu Expeditions** or **Apeco NGO**, T084-225595. Machiguenga-style cabins run by local communities with NGO help.

Erika Lodge
On the Alto Madre de Dios, 25 mins from Atalaya.
Offers basic accommodation and is cheaper than the other, more luxurious

lodges. Contact **Manu Ecological Adventures** (see below).

Manu Cloud Forest Lodge
At Unión, at 1800 m on the road from Paucartambo to Atalaya.

Owned by **Manu Nature Tours**, 6 rooms with 16-20 beds.

Manu Learning Centre
Fundo Mascoitania, a 600-ha reserve within the cultural zone, see Crees Tours, under What to do, below.

Manu Biosphere Reserve

Where to stay 🛏
1 Amazonia Lodge
2 Hosp Manu &
  Yine Lodge
3 Casa Machiguenga
4 Cock of the Rock
  Lodge
5 Erika Lodge
6 Manu Cloud
  Forest Lodge
7 Manu Lodge
8 Manu Wildlife Center
9 Pantiacolla Lodge
12 Amazon Yanayacu
  Lodge
20 Manu Learning Centre

Cultural Zone

Manu Lodge

On the Manu river, 3 hrs upriver from Boca Manu towards Cocha Salvador.
Run by **Manu Nature Tours** and only bookable as part of a full package deal with transport.

Manu Wildlife Center

2 hrs down the Río Madre de Dios from Boca Manu, near the Blanquillo macaw lick.
Book through **Manu Expeditions**, which runs it in conjunction with the conservation group **Peru Verde** (www.manuwildlifecenter.com). 22 double cabins, with private bathroom and hot water. Also canopy towers for birdwatching and a tapir lick.

Pantiacolla Lodge

30 mins downriver from Shintuya.
Owned by the Moscoso family.
Book through **Pantiacolla Tours** (see page 508).

Cuzco to Manu and Puerto Maldonado via Pilcopata and Itahuania

Turismo Indigena Wanamei

Av El Sol 814 p 2, of 212, Cuzco, T082-234608, T984-754708, or Av 26 de Diciembre 276, Puerto Maldonado, T082-572 539, www.ecoturismowanamei.com.
An initiative by the people of the Amarakaeri Communal Reserve, located between Manu and Tambopata. They offer 4- to 9-day trips starting and ending in Cuzco. Accommodation includes lodges, communities and camping. The trips aim not only to offer excellent wildlife viewing opportunities but also an insight in to the daily life of indigenous peoples. Knowledge of Spanish is an advantage.

$ Hospedaje Manu

Boca Colorado, on street beside football field.
Cell-like rooms, open windows and ceilings but comfy mattresses and mosquito netting.

$ Sra Rubella in Pilcopata

Very basic but friendly.

$ Yine Lodge

Next to Boca Manu airport.
A cooperative project run between Pantiacolla Tours and the Yine community of Diamante, who operate their own tours into their community and surroundings. Also **$ Hostal** in Boca Manu run by the community. Basic accommodation.

What to do

The following companies in Cuzco organize trips into the Multiple Use and Reserved Zones. Contact them for more details.

Amazon Trails Peru, *Tandapata 660, San Blas, Cuzco, T084-437374, or T984-714148, www.amazontrailsperu.com.* Operated by ornithologist Abraham Huamán, who has many years' experience guiding in Manu, and his German wife, Ulla Maennig. Well-organized tours to the National Park and Blanquillo clay lick, with knowledgeable guides, good boatmen and cooks, small groups, guaranteed departure dates. Runs 2 lodges in Manu. Also offers trekking in the Cuzco area.
Bonanza Tours, *Suecia 343, Cuzco, T084-507871, www.bonanzatoursperu.com.* 3- to 8-day tours to Manu with local guides, plenty of jungle walks, rafting, kayaking and camp-based excursions with good food. Tours are high quality and good value.

Crees Tours, *Urb Mcal Gamarra B-5, Zona 1, Cuzco, T084-262433, and 7/8 Kendrick Mews, London SW7 3HG, T+44 (0)20-7581 2932, www.crees-manu.org.* Tours from 4 days/3 nights to 9 days/8 nights to the **Manu Learning Centre**, a lodge accommodating 24 guests, 45 mins from Atalaya by boat. The lodge has all en suite rooms with hot showers; food is produced locally in a bio-garden. All tours spend the 1st night at the **Cock of the Rock Lodge**, on the road from Paucartambo to Atalaya. Tours are associated with the **Crees Foundation**, www.crees-foundation.org, a fully-sustainable organization which works with immigrant and indigenous communities to reduce poverty and protect biodiversity in the rainforest.

Expediciones Vilca, *Plateros 359, Cuzco, T084-244751.* Tours at economical prices. **Greenland Peru**, *Celasco Astete C-12, Cuzco, T084-246572, www.greenlandperu. com.* Fredy Domínguez is an Amazonian and offers good-value trips to Manu with comfortable accommodation and transport and excellent food cooked by his mother. Experienced, knowledgeable and enthusiastic, and he speaks English. **InkaNatura**, *Ricardo Palma J1, Cuzco; also in Lima at Manuel Bañón 461, San Isidro, T01-203 5000, www.inkanatura.com.* Tours to **Manu Wildlife Centre** (see above) and to **Sandoval Lake Lodge** in Tambopata (see below) with emphasis on sustainable tourism and conservation. Knowledgeable guides. They also run treks in Cuzco area.

Manu Adventures, *Plateros 356, Cuzco, T084-261640, www.manuadventures.com.* This company operates one of the most physically active Manu programmes, with options for a mountain biking descent through the cloudforest and 3 hrs of whitewater rafting on the way to **Erika Lodge** on the upper Río Madre de Dios. Jungle specialists.

Manu Expeditions and Birding Tours, *Jr Los Geranios 2-G, Urb Mariscal Gamarra, 1a Etapa, Cuzco, T084-225990, www.manuexpeditions.com.* Owned by ornithologist Barry Walker, 3 trips available to the reserve and **Manu Wildlife Center**.

Manu Nature Tours, *Av Pardo 1046, Cuzco, T084-252721, www.manuperu.com.* Boris Gómez Luna runs lodge-based trips. He is the owner of **Manu Lodge**, the only lodge in the Reserved Zone, open all year, situated on an oxbow lake, providing access to the forest, guides available; activities include river-rafting and canopy-climbing. Highly recommended for experiencing the jungle in comfort. Also part owns **Manu Cloudforest Lodge**.

Oropéndola, *Av Circunvalación s/n, Urb Guadalupe Mz A Lte 3, Cuzco, T084-241428,* www.oropendolaperu.org. Guide Walter Mancilla Huamán is an expert on flora and fauna. 5-, 7- and 9-day tours from US$800 pp plus park entrance. Good reports of attention to detail and to the needs of clients.

Pantiacolla Tours SRL, *Garcilaso 265, interior, p 2, of 12, Cuzco, T084-238323, www.pantiacolla.com.* Run by Marianne van Vlaardingen and Gustavo Moscoso. They have tours to the **Pantiacolla Lodge** (see Where to stay, page 506) and also 8-day camping trips. Pantiacolla has started a community-based ecotourism project, called the **Yine Project**, with the people of Diamante in the Multiple Use Zone.

Transport

Tour companies usually use their own vehicles for the overland trip from Cuzco to Manu, but it is possible to do it independently.

Cuzco to Manu and Puerto Maldonado via Pilcopata and Itahuania
Road and river
From the Coliseo Cerrado in Cuzco 3 buses run to **Pilcopata** Mon, Wed, Fri, returning same night, US$10. They

are fully booked even in low season. The best are **Gallito de las Rocas**; also **Unancha** from C Huáscar near the main plaza. Trucks to Pilcopata run on same days, returning Tue, Thu, Sat, 10 hrs in wet season, less in the dry. Only basic supplies are available after leaving Cuzco, so take all camping and food essentials, including insect repellent. Transport can be disrupted in the wet season because the road is in poor condition, although improvements are being made. A *camioneta* service between Pilcopata and **Salvación** connects with the buses, Mon, Wed, Fri. The same *camionetas* run **Itahuania−Shintuya−Salvacion** regularly, when there are sufficient passengers, usually once a day, also 2 trucks a day. On Sun, there is no traffic.

To reach **Boca Manu** you can hire a boat in Atalaya, several hundred dollars for a *peke peke*, more for a motor boat. It's cheaper to wait or hope for a boat going empty up to Boca Manu to pick up passengers, when the fare will be US$15 per passenger. Itahuania−Boca Manu in a shared boat is US$7.50; a private, chartered boat would be over US$100. From Itahuania, cargo boats leave for **Boca Colorado** on the Río Madre de Dios, via Boca Manu, but only when the boat is fully laden; about 6-8 a week, 9 hrs, US$20.

To reach **Puerto Maldonado** from Boca Colorado, catch a colectivo from near the football field for Puerto Carlos, 1 hr, US$5, for the ferry across the river, 10 mins, US$1.65; colectivos then run to Puerto Maldonado, 3 hrs, US$10, on a rough road with lots of stops; in Puerto Maldonado, contact **Turismo Boca Colorado** (Tacna 342, T082-573435).

Puerto Maldonado and the southeastern jungle

a worthy alternative to Manu

Puerto Maldonado is an important base for visiting the southeastern jungles of the Tambopata Reserve or departing for Bolivia or Brazil. It overlooks the confluence of the rivers Tambopata and Madre de Dios and, because of the gold mining and timber industries, the immediate surrounding jungle is now cultivated. A bridge, as part of the Interoceánica highway, has been built across the Río Madre de Dios; even before its completion, business activity in the town was growing fast.

Cuzco to Puerto Maldonado via Mazuko

This route is Cuzco−Urcos−Quincemil−Mazuko−Puerto Maldonado; it has been upgraded as part of the Interoceánica highway and its susceptibility to bad weather has declined. The changing scenery en route is magnificent.

Quincemil, 240 km from Urcos on the road to Mazuko, is a centre for alluvial gold-mining with many banks. **Hunt Oil** is building a huge oil and gas facility here; its exploration controversially overlaps the Amarakaeri Communal Reserve.

Puente Iñambari is the junction of three sections of the Interoceanic Highway, from Cuzco, Puerto Maldonado and Juliaca (see Puno to the jungle, page 337). However, this is only a small settlement and transport stops 5 km further north at **Mazuko**. In the evenings, Mazuko is a hive of activity as temperatures drop and the buses arrive.

The Highway beyond Mazuko cuts across lowland rainforest, large areas of which have been cleared by migrants engaged in small-scale gold mining. Their encampments of plastic shelters, shops and prostibars now line the Highway for several kilometres. A worthwhile stop on the route is the **Parador Turístico Familia Méndez** ⓘ *Km 419, 45 mins from Puerto Maldonado, www.paradormendez.com*, which prepares local dishes from home-grown ingredients and has a trail network in the surrounding forest.

Sights in Puerto Maldonado → *Colour map 6, A3.*

From the park at the end of Jirón Arequipa, across from the Capitanía, you get a good view of the two rivers and the stacks of lumber at the dockside. **El Mirador**

Puerto Maldonado

Where to stay 🛏	7 Hosp La Bahía	Restaurants 🍴	7 La Casa Nostra
1 Amarumayo	8 Paititi Hostal	1 Burgos's	8 Namaste
2 Anaconda Lodge	9 Perú Amazónico	2 Carne Brava	
3 Cabañaquinta &	10 Tambopata Hostel	3 D'Kaoba	Bars & clubs 🍸
Restaurant	11 Wasai & Restaurant	4 El Hornito/Chez Maggy &	9 El Asadero
4 Don Carlos		Le Boulevard	10 El Witite
5 Hosp El Bambú		5 Gustitos del Cura	11 T-Saica
6 Hosp Español		6 Kuskalla	12 Vikingo

ⓘ *at the junction of Av Fitzcarrald and Av Madre de Dios, Mon-Fri 0700-1200, 1500-2100, US$0.60*, is a 47-m-high tower with 250 steps and three platforms giving fine views over the city and surrounding rainforest. There is also a toilet at the top – no curtains – from which there is an equally fine view over the city! **Museo Huamaambi** ⓘ *26 de Diciembre 360, US$1*, contains photos and artefacts pertaining to the Harakmbut culture of central Madre de Dios. It is also home to **Fenamad**, a local organization for the protection of lands and cultures of people from jungle communities. **Mariposario (Butterfly House)** ⓘ *adjoining the airport entrance (a 5-min walk from the terminal building), daily 0800-1330, US$5*, breeds butterflies as part of a sustainable development project. Tours are self-guided. It's worth a visit if you arrive early for your flight, or if it is delayed, especially as the entrance fee gets you a seat in the cool reception area. Further along the airport road towards Puerto Maldonado is the **Serpentarium (Snake Farm)** ⓘ *daily 0800-1300, 1500-1800, US$2.50*, where you can see boas, bushmasters and fer-de-lances.

Tip...
Some 70% of the inhabitants of the Madre de Dios Region are involved in the collection of the prized Brazil nut. The harvest is from December to February, and the crop tends to be good on alternate years. Nuts are sold on the street in Puerto Maldonado, plain or coated in sugar or chocolate.

Around Puerto Maldonado

At Km 11 on the road to the Tambopata river is the **Amazon Shelter** ⓘ *T997-223958, www.amazonshelter.org*, a centre for the rehabilitation and conservation of wild animals.

For those interested in seeing a gold-rush town, a trip to **Laberinto** on the Madre de Dios is suggested; it has one hotel and several poor restaurants. At Km 13 on the Cuzco road (US$2 each way by mototaxi from town) is a pleasant recreational centre with a restaurant and natural pools where it's possible to swim. It gets busy at weekends.

The beautiful and tranquil **Lago Sandoval** ⓘ *entry US$9.50; boat hire from the Madre de Dios port, US$25 (minimum 2 people), plus petrol costs*, is a one-hour boat ride along the Río Madre de Dios, and then a 5-km walk into the jungle; parts of the first 3 km are on a raised wooden walkway, but boots are advisable. You must go with a guide, which can be arranged by the boat driver. Don't pay the boat hire fee until you are safely back at port.

Upstream from Lago Sandoval, towards Puerto Maldonado, is the wreck of a steamer that resembles the *Fitzcarrald*. It lies a few metres from the Madre de Dios in the bed of a small stream. The German director, Werner Herzog, was inspired to make his famous film *Fitzcarraldo* (1982) by the true story of rubber baron Carlos Fitzcarrald (1862-1897), who attempted to haul a boat from the Ucuyali to the Madre de Dios drainage basins (in what is now the Manu National Park) in order to find a way to transport rubber from the Madre de Dios region (see also page 488).

Trips can also be made to **Lago Valencia**, 60 km from Puerto Maldonado near the Bolivian border (four hours there, eight hours back). It is an oxbow lake with lots of wildlife and many excellent beaches and islands within an hour's boat ride. Mosquitoes are voracious, though. If you're camping, take food and water.

★Tambopata National Reserve
Sernanp, Av 28 de Julio 482, Puerto Maldonado, T082-573278.

The Tambopata National Reserve (TNR) lies between the rivers Madre de Dios, Tambopata and Heath. The area was first declared a reserve in 1990 and is a very reasonable alternative for those who do not have the time or money to visit Manu. It is a close rival in terms of seeing wildlife and boasts some superb oxbow lakes. Another highlight are the famous clay licks or *collpas*, where macaws and parrots gather to eat minerals which allow them to digest otherwise toxic seeds and fruits. There are a number of lodges here which are excellent for lowland rainforest birding. In an effort to ensure that more tourism income stays in the area, a few local families have established their own small-scale *casas de hospedaje*, which offer more basic facilities and make use of the nearby forest. If you're not visiting the reserve as part of a lodge package, it is quite easy to arrange a boat and guide

Tambopata National Reserve & Bahuaja-Sonene National Park

Where to stay 🛏
1 Casa de Hospedaje Mejía
2 Eco Amazonia Lodge
3 El Corto Maltés
4 Estancia Bello Horizonte
5 Explorers Inn

6 Inkaterra Reserva Amazónica Lodge
7 Posada Amazonas Lodge
8 Refugio Amazonas
9 Sandoval Lake Lodge
10 Tambopata Eco Lodge

11 Tambopata Research Centre
12 Wasaí Lodge

from Puerto Maldonado (see Tour operators, below), travelling up the Tambopata river or down the Madre de Dios.

Bahuaja-Sonene National Park
Sernanp, Libertad 1189, Puno, T051-363960, daranibar@sernanp.gob.pe, fee US$54 for 7-day visit.

Established in 1996, this national park stretches from the Río Heath (along the Bolivian border) across the Tambopata, incorporating the **Santuario Nacional Pampas del Heath**. There are no facilities in the park and visits are only possible with tour operators who offer seven-day rafting trips along the Río Tambopata. These start at Curva Alegre, downriver from Putina Punco, in the Puno Region (see page 337), camp on the shore of the river and finish at the **Tambopata Research Centre (TRC)**. It is an adventurous trip involving paddling through grade III and IV rapids. Sernanp has a list of authorized operators, including **Amazonas Explorer** and **River Explorers** (see Cuzco operators, pages 376 and 377). A more difficult access to the park is from the southeast near the Bolivian border, see page 337. There are lodges in the park's buffer zone, plus the **Heath River Wildlife Center**, run by **InkaNatura** ⓘ *www.inkantura.com*.

Río Las Piedras
Lying to the northeast of, and running roughly parallel to the Río Manu, this drainage runs some 700 km from rainforest headwaters in the Alto Purús region. The lower, more easily accessible section of the river, closer to Puerto Maldonado and outside state protection, runs through rich tropical forests, very similar to those in the Manu and Tambopata areas. Close to 600 species of birds, at least eight primate species and some of the Amazon's larger mammals – giant otter, jaguar, puma, tapir and giant anteater – are all present. Hunting pressure has resulted in wildlife being shyer than in Manu or Tambopata, but this remains an excellent wildlife destination. See www.arbioperu.org and www.relevantfilms.co.uk/propied/las-piedras/.

To Iberia and Iñapari
Daily public transport runs to **Iberia** and **Iñapari** on the border with Brazil. This section of the Interoceánica road takes a lot of traffic and can be dangerous for motorcyclists as a result. No primary forest remains along the road, only secondary growth and small *chacras* (farms). There are picturesque *caseríos* (settlements) that serve as processing centres for the brazil nut.

Iberia, Km 168, has three hotels, the best is $ **Hostal Aquino**, basic, cold shower; the others are **Hospedajes Casa Blanca** and **Delta** (Loreto 664). It's a small frontier town, much quieter and more laid back than Iñapari on the border. The old **Fundo María Cristina rubber plantation** ⓘ *5 mins south of town, US$0.50 by mototaxi*, is now a research centre and can be visited to see the whole rubber production process. Allow one hour.

Iñapari, at the end of the road, Km 235, has a growing problem with Haitian refugees trying to enter Brazil by the back door. Hundreds are stuck in transit. The

BORDER CROSSING
Peru–Brazil

Iñapari–Assis Brasil
Public transport stops near immigration in Iñapari where you get your Peruvian exit stamps, daily 0930-1300, 1500-1930 (Peruvian time). Note that there is also an immigration office in Puerto Maldonado (28 de Julio 465), which issues exit stamps. There is no Policía Federal office in Assis Brasil, so you have to travel on to Brasiléia to obtain your Brazil entry stamp from Policía Federal at the *rodoviária* (bus station). You must have a yellow fever certificate to enter Brazil.

From Brasiléia there are connections to Cobija in Bolivia, but there are no exchange facilities en route and poor exchange rates for Brazilian currency at Iñapari. Crossing between Peru and Bolivia on this route is not easy.

town has a basic hotel and a restaurant, but **Assis Brasil** across the border is much more attractive and has three hotels, two restaurants and shops. A suspension bridge now links the two countries.

Listings Southeastern jungle *maps p510 and p512*

Tourist information

Puerto Maldonado
There are **tourist offices** at the airport and at **Dircetur** (Urb Fonavi; take a moto-taxi to the 'Posta Médica', which is next door).

Where to stay

Cuzco to Puerto Maldonado
Accommodation is available in **Quincemil** at $ **Hotel Toni**, friendly, clean, cold shower, good meals. There are more options in Mazuko; $ **Hostal Valle Sagrado** is the best.

Puerto Maldonado
New hotels catering for business travellers are springing up.

$$$ Don Carlos
Av León Velarde 1271, T082-571029, www.hotelesdoncarlos.com.

Nice view over the Río Tambopata, a/c, restaurant, airport transfers, good.

$$$ Wasaí Lodge & Expeditions
Plaza Grau 1, T082-572290, www.wasai.com.
In a beautiful location overlooking the Madre de Dios, with forest surrounding cabin-style rooms, shower, small pool with waterfall, good restaurant (local fish a speciality). They can organize local tours and also have a lodge on the Río Tambopata (see page 517).

$$$-$$ Cabañaquinta
Cuzco 535, T082-571045, www. hotelcabanaquinta.com.
A/c or fan, frigobar, laundry, free drinking water, good restaurant, lovely garden, very comfortable, airport transfer. Request a room away from the Interoceanic Highway.

$$ Anaconda Lodge
600 m from airport, T982 611039 (mob), www.anacondajunglelodge.com.
With private or shared bath, Swiss/Thai-owned bungalows, hot showers, swimming pool, Thai restaurant or Peruvian food and pizza if you prefer, tours arranged, has space for camping, very pleasant, family atmosphere.

$$ Paititi Hostal
G Prada 290 y Av León Velarde, T082-574667, see Facebook page.
All mod-cons, executive and standard rooms. Reserve in advance.

$$ Perú Amazónico
Jr Ica 269, T082-571799, peruamazonico@hotmail.com.
Modern, comfortable and good.

$ Amarumayo
Libertad 433, 10 mins from the centre, T082-573860.
Comfortable, with pool and garden, good restaurant.

$ Hospedaje El Bambú
Jr Puno 837, T082-793880.
Basic and small but well-kept rooms with fan, family atmosphere, breakfast and juices not included in price but served in dining room. A good budget option.

$ Hospedaje Español
González Prada 670, T082-572381.
Comfortable, set back from the road, in a quiet part of town.

$ Hospedaje La Bahía
2 de Mayo 710, T082-572127.
Cheaper without bath or TV, large rooms, a good choice.

$ Tambopata Hostel
Av 26 de Diciembre 234, www.tambopatahostel.com.
The only real backpacker hostel in town, dorm beds, hammocks or camping. Nice atmosphere, they also organize local tours.

Around Puerto Maldonado
Most jungle lodges are booked as package deals for 3 days, 2 nights, or longer, with meals, transport and guides; see websites below for offers.

Lodges on the Río Madre de Dios

Casa de Hospedaje Mejía
T082-571428; contact Ceiba Tours, L Velarde 420, Puerto Maldonado, T082-573567, turismomejia@hotmail.com.
Attractive but basic rustic lodge close to Lago Sandoval, full board can be arranged, canoes are available.

Eco Amazonia Lodge
On the Madre de Dios, 1 hr down-river from Puerto Maldonado. Office at Jr Lambayeque 774, T082-573491; also Enrique Palacios 292, Miraflores, Lima, T01-242 2708, and Garcilazo 210, of 206, Cuzco, T084-236159, www.ecoamazonia.com.pe.
Basic bungalows and dormitories, good for birdwatching, has its own Monkey Island with animals taken from the forest.

El Corto Maltés
Billinghurst 229, Puerto Maldonado, T082-573831, www.cortomaltes-amazonia.com.
On the Madre de Dios, halfway to Sandoval which is the focus of most visits. Hot water, huge dining room, well run.

Estancia Bello Horizonte
20 km northeast of Puerto Maldonado, Loreto 252, T082-572748, www.estancia bellohorizonte.com.
In a nice stretch of forest overlooking the old course of the Madre de Dios,

now a huge aguajal populated with macaws. A small lodge with bungalows for 30 people, with private bath, hot water, pool, butterfly house. Transport, all meals and guide (several languages offered) included, US$220 for 3 days/2 nights. The lodge belongs to APRONIA, an organization that trains and provides employment for orphaned children. Suitable for those wanting to avoid a river trip.

Inkaterra Reserva Amazónica Lodge
45 mins by boat down the Madre de Dios. Contact: **Inkaterra,** *Andalucía 174, Miraflores L18, Lima, T01-610 0400; Plaza Nazarenas 167 p 2, Cuzco T084-245314, or Cuzco 436, Puerto Maldonado, www.inkaterra.com.*
Tastefully redecorated hotel in the jungle with suites and bungalows, solar power, good food in huge dining room supported by a big tree. Jungle tours in its own 10,000 ha plus a new canopy walk; also tours to Lago Sandoval.

Sandoval Lake Lodge
1 km beyond Mejía on Lago Sandoval, book through InkaNatura (see page 507).
Usual access is by canoe after a 3-km walk or rickshaw ride, huge bar and dining area, electricity, hot water. InkaNatura also has a lodge on the Río Heath, the **Heath River Wildlife Center**, about 4½ hrs from Puerto Maldonado by boat, but journey times depend on river levels. Just 10 mins from the lodge is a macaw and parrot clay lick. In the vicinity you can visit both jungle and savannah and in the latter are many endemic bird species. **InkaNatura** runs tours which combine both lodges.

> **Tip...**
> Some of the lodges along the Tambopata river offer guiding and research placements to biology and environmental science graduates. For more details send an SAE to **TReeS**: UK – J Forrest (PO Box 33153, London, NW3 4DR, www.tambopata.org.uk).

Lodges on the Tambopata
Lodges on the Tambopata are reached by vehicle to Bahuaja port, 15 km upriver from Puerto Maldonado by the community of Infierno, then by boat. Over 15 small lodges and *casas de hospedaje* along the Tambopata river are grouped together under the names: **Tambopata Ecotourism Corridor** and **Tambopata Homestays.** See lodge websites for prices of packages offered.

Explorers Inn
58 km from Puerto Maldonado (2½ hrs up the Río Tambopata; 1½ hrs return); book through **Peruvian Safaris,** *Alcanfores 459, Miraflores, Lima, T01-447 8888, www.peruviansafaris.com.*
Just before the La Torre control post, adjoining the TNR, in the part where most research work has been done, this is one of the best places in Peru for seeing jungle birds (580 plus species have been recorded) and butterflies (1230 plus species). There are also giant river otters, but you probably need more than a 2-day tour to benefit fully from the location. Tours through the adjoining community of La Torre. The guides are biologists and naturalists undertaking research in the reserve. They provide interesting wildlife-treks, including to the macaw lick (*collpa*).

Posada Amazonas Lodge
*1½ hrs by vehicle and boat upriver
from Puerto Maldonado; book through*
Rainforest Expeditions, *San Francisco de
Paula Ugariza 813, Of 201, San Antonio-
Miraflores, Lima, T01-241 4880/T01-997
903650, www.perunature.com.*
A collaboration between the tour
agency and the local native community
of Infierno. Attractive rooms with cold
showers, visits to Lake Tres Chimbadas,
with good birdwatching including
the Tambopata collpa. Offers trips to a
nearby indigenous primary healthcare
project where a native healer gives
guided tours of the medicinal plant
garden. Service and guiding is very
good. The **Tambopata Research
Centre**, the company's more intimate,
but comfortable lodge, is about 6 hrs
further upriver. Rooms are smaller than
Posada Amazonas, with shared showers,
cold water. The lodge is next to the
famous Tambopata macaw clay lick.
2 hrs from Posada Amazonas, Rainforest
Expeditions also has the **Refugio
Amazonas**, close to Lago Condenados.
It is the usual stopover for those visiting
the collpa. 3 bungalows accommodate
70 people in large, kerosene-lit, en suite
rooms with mosquito nets, well-
designed and run, atmospheric. There
are many packages at the different
lodges and lots of add-ons.

Tambopata Eco Lodge
*On the Río Tambopata; reservations office
at Nueva Baja 432, Cuzco, T084-245695;
operations office Jr Gonzales Prada 269,
Puerto Maldonado, T082-571726, www.
tambopatalodge.com.*
Rooms with solar-heated water, good
guides, excellent food. Trips go to Lake
Condenado, some to Lake Sachavacayoc,
and to the Collpa de Chuncho, guiding

mainly in English and Spanish, naturalists
programme provided.

Wasaí Lodge and Expeditions
*Río Tambopata, 120 km (3 hrs by
speedboat) upriver from Puerto
Maldonado; contact Las Higueras 257,
Residencial Monterrico, La Molina,
Lima 12, T01-436 8792, or Plaza Grau 1,
Puerto Maldonado, T082-572290,
www.wasai.com.*
Kayaking, zip line, fishing, photography
tours, mystic tours, wildlife observation,
volunteering, etc. Also tours to the
Colllpa de Chuncho and Lago Sandoval.
Guides in English and Spanish.

Lodges on the Río Las Piedras

Amazon Rainforest Conservation
Centre
*Contact Pepe Moscoso, Jr Los Cedros B-17,
Los Castaños, Puerto Maldonado, T082-
573655, www.laspiedrasamazontour.com.*
Roughly 8 hrs upriver, overlooking a
beautiful oxbow lake, Lago Soledad,
which has a family of giant otters.
Comfortable bungalows, with bath and
hot water. Activities include a viewing
platform 35 m up an ironwood tree, a
hide overlooking a macaw lick, and walks
on the extensive trail network. Most
trips break the river journey half way at
Tipishca Lodge (same website as above).

Las Piedras Biodiversity Station
T082-573922.
A small lodge in a 4000-ha concession
of 'primary' rainforest 90 km up the Río
Las Piedras. Visitors camp en route to
the lodge. 20 beds in 10 rooms, central
dining-room, shared bath, no electricity,
library, guiding in English/Spanish.
Minimum package is for 4 days/3 nights.
Birdwatching trips cost more.

Restaurants

Puerto Maldonado

$$-$ Burgos's
León Velarde 129.
Serves traditional dishes and has a good set lunch menu.

$$-$ Carne Brava
On the Plaza de Armas.
One of the smart new joints for a steak and chips.

$$-$ El Hornito/Chez Maggy
On the plaza.
Cosy, good pizzas, busy at weekends.

$$-$ Kuskalla
Av 26 de Diciembre 195.
Peruvian/Brazilian-fusion food with views of the Madre de Dios and Tambopata rivers.

$ D'Kaoba
Madre de Dios 439.
Serves the most delicious *pollos a la brasa* in town.

$ La Casa Nostra
Velarde 515.
Sells huge fruit juices for US$0.50, as well as *tamales, papas rellenas* and enormous fancy cakes, great coffee.

$ Namaste
Av León Velarde 469.
Moroccan and Indian food, sandwiches, breakfasts and set lunches, in chilled out surroundings.

Gustitos del Cura
Loreto 258, Plaza de Armas.
Thu-Tue 0800-2300.
Ice cream and juice parlour run by the APRONIA project for homeless teenagers, offering unusual flavours.

Bars and clubs

Puerto Maldonado

El Asadero
Arequipa 246, east side of Plaza.
Popular *menú* at lunchtime, great sandwiches later in the day, cool bar in the evening.

El Witite
Av León Velarde 153. Fri and Sat.
A popular disco playing latin music.

Le Boulevard
Behind El Hornito.
Live music, popular.

T-Saica
Loreto 335.
An atmospheric bar with live music at weekends.

Vikingo
León Velarde 158.
A popular bar and open-air disco.

What to do

Puerto Maldonado
Boat hire
Boat hire can be arranged through the **Capitanía del Puerto** (Río Madre de Dios, T082-573003).

Guides
All guides should have a carnet issued by the **Ministry of Tourism (DIRCETUR)**, which also verifies them as suitable for trips to other places and confirms their identity. Check that the carnet has not expired. Reputable guides are **Hernán Llave Cortez**, **Romel Nacimiento** and the **Mejía** brothers, all of whom can be contacted on arrival at the airport, if available. Also recommended are: **Carlos Borja Gama** (www.carlosexpeditions.com), a local guide offering specialist

birdwatching and photography trips as well as traditional jungle tours; he speaks several languages; **Víctor Yohamona** (T982-686279, victorguideperu@hotmail.com) who speaks English, French and German.

Local tour operators
Perú Tours (Loreto 176, T082-573 244). Organize local trips. See also **Ceiba Tours** (under Casa de Hospedaje Mejía, above).

Cuzco to Puerto Maldonado: via Urcos and Mazuko
Bus
The *Interoceánica* is paved all the way. There are many daily buses, US$18-30 (*económico* or *semi-cama*), 10-11 hrs, from the Terminal Terrestre in **Cuzco** with **Transportes Iguazú** (one of the cheapest, less reliable, no toilet), **Mendivil**, **Machupicchu**, **Palomino** and **Móvil Tours** (one of the better companies, T082-795785). All are on Av Tambopata, blocks 3 and 5 in Puerto Maldonado. There are also daily buses from **Mazuko** to Puerto Maldonado with **Transportes Bolpebra** and **Transportes Señor de la Cumbre**, 4 hrs, US$6. Several buses also run daily along the Interoceanic Highway from Arequipa and Juliaca, crossing the altiplano and joining the Cuzco–Puerto Maldonado section at Puente Iñambari, 5 km from Mazuko (see page 337 and page 280). There is regular traffic from Mazuko to Puerto Maldonado, including colectivos, 3 hrs, US$11.

Puerto Maldonado
Air
To **Lima**, daily with **LAN (León Velarde 503)** and **Star Perú** (León Velarde 151) via Cuzco. Moto-taxi from town to airport, US$2.25, taxi US$3.50, 8 km.

Bus and boat
For **Boca Manu** and **Itahuania** take a colectivo to **Boca Colorado** (see above) and then take a cargo boat (no fixed schedule). From Itahuania there is transport to Pilcopata and Cuzco. To **Iberia,** 2½ hrs, US$6.50, and **Iñapari,** 3½ hrs, US$8.50, daily combis from Jr Ica y Jr Piura; recommended companies are **Turismo Imperial** and **Turismo Real Dorado**; **Móvil** (see above) also has a daily service to **Rio Branco** (Brazil), 1200, US$35. To **Juliaca**, via Mazuko, San Gabán and Macusani, US$14-27, 12 hrs, with **Santa Cruz** (T951-298980) at 0600, 1330, 1630 and 1830; **Julsa** at 1530; **Mendivil** at 1600; **Wayra** at 1700; the last 3 continue to **Arequipa**, US$21-36, 17-18 hrs. Other companies on this route are **Aguilas** and **ITSA**. For all routes, ask around the bus offices for colectivo minibuses.

Motorcycle hire
Scooters and mopeds can de hired from **San Francisco** and others, on the corner of Puno and G Prado for US$1.75 per hr, off-road motorbikes cost US$3.50 per hr. Passport and driver's licence must be shown.

Background
Peru

History

Despite Peru's formidable geographical difficulties and frequent natural disasters, archaeologists have uncovered a pre-Columbian history of highly advanced societies that prevailed against these awesome odds. The coastal desert from Lambayeque department south to Paracas has revealed an 'American Egypt', although this has meant a bias towards the coastal region and a reliance on the contents of tombs for information. Knowledge of these tombs often only comes to light following their looting by gangs of *huaqueros* (grave robbers), incited by demand from the international antiquities market.

The Incas told the Spaniards that before they established their Tawantinsuyo Empire, the land was overrun by primitives constantly at war with one another. There were, in fact, many other civilized cultures dating back to before 2000 BC. The most accomplished of these were the Chavín and Sechín (circa 900-200 BC), the Paracas-Nazca (circa 200 BC-AD 500), the Huari-Tiahuanaco (circa 750 BC-AD 1000), and the Moche-Chimú (200 BC-AD 1400).

Early settlement

It is generally accepted that the earliest settlers in Peru were related to people who had crossed the Bering Straits from Asia and drifted through the Americas from about 20,000 BC. However, theories of early migrations from across the Pacific and Atlantic have been rife since Thor Heyerdahl's raft expeditions in 1947 and 1969-1970.

The earliest evidence of human presence has been found at three sites: Pikimachay near Ayacucho, Pachamachay in Junín and the Guitarrero Cave in the Callejón de Huaylas. All have a radiocarbon date prior to 9000 BC. It had been thought that village settlement in Peru, on the central coast at Pampa, dated from 2500 BC. The theory was that, between these two dates, people lived nomadically in small groups, mainly hunting and gathering but also cultivating some plants seasonally. Domestication of llamas, alpacas and guinea pigs also began at this time, particularly important for the highland people around the Titicaca basin. Caral, however, has overturned many of the accepted tenets of Peruvian archaeology for this period. Caral is a city, 20 km from the coast in the Supe Valley whose date is about 2600 BC. It is a monumental construction and appeared to be easily the oldest city in South America until this claim was disputed by the Miravalles site in the department of Cajamarca. Caral flourished for some 500 years. The evidence points to complex urban society beginning much earlier than previously thought and the city seems to have had a primarily religious, rather than warlike purpose. If these deductions are correct, they also upset some long-held beliefs about city-building worldwide being principally bellicose rather than peaceful.

The abundant wealth of marine life produced by the Humboldt Current, especially along the north coast, boosted population growth and settlement in this area. Around 2000 BC climatic change dried up the lomas ('fog meadows'), and drove sea shoals to deeper water. People turned to farming and began to spread inland along river valleys.

Origins of Andean civilization

From the second millennium BC to around the first century BC is known as the Formative Period (also called Preceramic Period VI and Initial Period) when the first signs of the high culture of Andean society appeared. During this period sophisticated irrigation and canal systems were developed, farming productivity increased and communities had more time to devote to building and producing ceramics and textiles. The development of pottery also led to trade and cultural links with other communities. Distribution of land and water to the farmers was probably organized by a corporate authority, and this may have led to the later 'Mit'a' labour system developed by the Incas.

Above all, this period is characterized by the construction of centres of urban concentration (Caral notwithstanding) that promoted labour specialization and the development of cultural expression. The earliest buildings built were huacas, adobe platform mounds, centres of cult or sacred power. Huaca Florida was the largest example of this period, near the Río Rimac, later replaced by Huaca Garagay as a major centre for the area. Similar centres spread along the north coast, such as El Aspero and Piedra Parada.

During this period, however, much more advanced architecture was being built at Kótosh, in the central Andes near Huánuco. Japanese archaeological excavations there in the 1960s revealed a temple with ornamental niches and friezes. Some of the earliest pottery was also found here, showing signs of influence from southern Ecuador and the tropical lowlands, adding weight to theories of Andean culture originating in the Amazon. Radiocarbon dates of some Kótosh remains are as early as 1850 BC.

Chavín and Sechín

For the next 1000 years or so up to circa 900 BC, communities grew and spread inland from the north coast and south along the northern highlands. Farmers still lived in simple adobe or rough stone houses but built increasingly large and complex ceremonial centres, such as at Las Haldas in the Casma Valley (dated at 1700 BC). As farming became more productive and pottery more advanced, commerce grew and states began to develop throughout central and north-central Peru, with the associated signs of social structure and hierarchies.

Around 900 BC a new era was marked by the rise of two important centres; **Chavín de Huantar** in the central Andes and **Sechín Alto**, inland from Casma on the north coast (some date the latter from 1600 BC).

Chavín takes its name from the site of Chavín de Huantar in the northern highlands. This was the first of several 'horizon styles' that were of the greatest importance in Peru and had very widespread influence. The other later ones, the Huari-Tiahuanaco and the Inca, were pan-Peruvian, affecting all parts of the country. The chief importance of Chavín de Huantar was not so much in its highly advanced architecture as in the influence of its cult coupled with the artistic style of its ceramics and other artefacts. The founders of Chavín may have originated in the tropical lowlands as some of its carved monoliths show representations of monkeys and felines.

Objects with Chavín traits have been found all along the coast from Piura to the Lurin valley south of Lima, and its cult ideology spread to temples around the same area. Richard L Burger of Yale University has argued that the extent of Chavín influence has been exaggerated. Many sites on the coast already had their own cult practices and the Chavín idols may have been simply added alongside. There is evidence of an El Niño flood that devastated the north coast around 500 BC. Local cults fell from grace as social order was disrupted and the Chavín cult was snatched up as a timely new alternative.

Chavín cult

The Chavín cult was paralleled by the great advances made at this time in textile production and in some of the earliest examples of metallurgy (whose origins have been attributed to some gold, silver and copper ornaments found in graves in Chongoyape, near Chiclayo, which show Chavín-style features). But earlier evidence has been discovered in the Andahuaylas region, dating from 1800 to 900 BC. The religious symbolism of gold and other precious metals and stones is thought to have been an inspiration behind some of the beautiful artefacts found in the central Andean area. The emergence of social hierarchies also created a demand for luxury goods as status symbols.

The cultural brilliance of Chavín de Huántar was complemented by its contemporary, **Sechín**. This huge granite-faced complex near Casma, 370 km north of Lima, was described by JC Tello as the biggest structure of its kind in the Andes. According to Michael Moseley of Harvard University, Chavín and Sechín may have combined forces, with Sechín as the military power that spread the cultural word of Chavín, but their influence did not reach far to the south where the Paracas and Tiahuanaco cultures held sway.

Upper Formative Period

The Chavín hegemony, which is also known as the Middle Formative Period (or Early Horizon), broke up around 300 BC. The 'unity' of this period was broken and the initial phase of the regional diversification of Andean cultures began. The process of domestication of plants and animals culminated in the Upper Formative Period. Agricultural technology progressed leading to an economic security that permitted a considerable growth in the centres of population. Among the many diverse stylistic/cultural groups of this period are: the Vicus on the north coast; Salinar in the Chicama valley; Paracas Necrópolis on the south coast; and Huarás in the Ancash highlands.

Paracas Necrópolis was the early phase of the Nazca culture and is renowned for the superb technical quality and stylistic variety in its weaving and pottery. The mantos (large, decorated cloth) rank amongst the world's best, and many of the finest examples can be seen in the museums of Lima. The extreme dryness of the desert here has preserved the textiles and ceramics in the mummies' tombs which have been excavated.

Paracas Necrópolis is, in fact, a cemetery located on the slopes of Cerro Colorado, in the Department of Ica, from which 429 funerary bundles were excavated. Each bundle is a mummy wrapped in many fine and rough textiles. Paracas Necrópolis corresponds to the last of the 10 phases into which Paracas ceramics have been divided. The previous ones, known as Paracas Cavernas, relate to the Middle Formative Period and were influenced by the Chavín cult.

Nazca culture

The Regional Development Period up to about AD 500, was a time of great social and cultural development. Sizable towns of 5000-10,000 inhabitants grew on the south coast, populated by artisans, merchants, government administrators and religious officials.

One of the most famous cultures of this period, or indeed of pre-Columbian history was the Nazca. The Nazca Lines are a feature of the region. Straight lines, abstract designs and outlines of animals are scratched in the desert surface forming a lighter contrast that can be seen clearly from the air. There are many theories as to how and why the lines were made but no explanation has yet been able definitively to establish their place in Peruvian history; for further details, see page 249). There are similarities between the style of some of the line patterns and that of the pottery and textiles of the same period. It is clear from the scale of the lines and the quality of the work that they were important to the Nazca culture.

In contrast to the quantity and quality of the Nazca artefacts found, relatively few major buildings belonging to this period have been uncovered in the southern desert. Dos Palmas is a complex of rooms and courtyards in the Pisco Valley, while Cahuachi in the Nazca Valley is a large area including adobe platforms, pyramids and a 'wooden Stonehenge' cluster of preserved tree trunks. Among the recently excavated sites are the architectural complex of Los Molinos, with large buildings, patios and passages, and the necropolis of La Muña, both near Palpa. As most of the archaeological evidence of the Nazca culture came from their desert cemeteries, little is known about the lives and social organization of the people. Alpaca hair found in Nazca textiles, however, indicates that there must have been strong trade links with highland people.

Moche culture

Nazca's contemporaries on the north coast were the militaristic Moche who, from about AD 100-800 built up an empire whose traces stretch from Piura in the north to Casma, beyond Chimbote, in the south. The Moche built their capital in the middle of the desert, outside present day Trujillo. It features the pyramid temples of the Huaca del Sol and Huaca de la Luna (see page 138). The Moche roads and system of way stations are thought to have been an early inspiration for the Inca network. The Moche increased the coastal population with intensive irrigation projects. Skillful engineering works were carried out, such as the La Cumbre canal, still in use today, and the Ascope aqueduct.

The Moche's greatest achievement, however, was its artistic genius. Exquisite ornaments in gold, silver and precious stones were made by its craftsmen. Moche pottery progressed through five stylistic periods, most notable for the stunningly lifelike portrait vases. A wide variety of ceremonial and everyday scenes were created in naturalistic ceramics, telling us more about Moche life than is known about other earlier cultures, and perhaps used by them as 'visual aids' to compensate for the lack of a written language.

A spectacular discovery of a Moche royal tomb at **Sipán** was made in February 1987 by Walter Alva, director of the Brüning Archaeological Museum, Lambayeque. Reports of the excavation in the National Geographic magazine (October 1988 and June 1990), talked of the richest unlooted tomb in the New World (see page 159). The find included semi-precious stones brought from Chile and Argentina, and seashells from Ecuador (the Moche were also great navigators).

The cause of the collapse of the Moche Empire around AD 600-700 is unknown, but it may have been started by a 30-year drought at the end of the sixth century, followed by one of the periodic El Niño flash floods (identified by meteorologists from ice thickness in the Andes) and finished by the encroaching forces of the Huari Empire. The decline of the Moche signalled a general tipping of the balance of power in Peru from the north coast to the southern sierra.

Huari-Tiahuanaco

The ascendant Huari-Tiahuanaco movement, from circa AD 600-1000, combined the religious cult of the Tiahuanaco site in the Titicaca basin, with the military dynamism of the Huari, based in the central highlands. The two cultures developed independently but, as had occurred with the Chavín-Sechín association, they are generally thought to have merged compatibly.

Up until their own demise around AD 1440, the Huari-Tiahuanaco had spread their empire and influence from Cajamarca and Lambayeque in the north and across much of southern Peru, northern Bolivia and Argentina. The Huari introduced a new concept in urban life, the great walled urban centre, the best example of which is their capital city, 22 km north of Ayacucho (see page 456). They also made considerable gains in art and technology, building roads, terraces and irrigation canals across the country.

The Huari-Tiahuanaco ran their empire with efficient labour and administrative systems that were later adopted and refined by the Incas. Labour tribute for state projects had been practised by the Moche and was further developed now. But the empire could not contain regional kingdoms who began to fight for land and power. As control broke down, rivalry and coalitions emerged, and the system collapsed.

Chimú culture

After the decline of the Huari Empire, the unity that had been imposed on the Andes was broken. A new stage of autonomous regional or local political organizations began. Among the cultures corresponding to this period were the Kuélap, centred in the Chachapoyas region (see page 208), and the Chimú.

The Chimú culture had two centres. To the north was Lambayeque, near Chiclayo, while to the south, in the Moche valley near present-day Trujillo, was the adobe walled city of Chan Chán. At 20 sq km, this was the largest pre-Hispanic Peruvian city (see page 140).

Chimú has been classified as a despotic state that based its power on wars of conquest. Rigid social stratification existed and power rested in the hands of the great Lord Siquic and the Lord Alaec. These lords were followed in social scale by a group of urban couriers who enjoyed a certain degree of economic power. At the bottom were the peasants and slaves. In AD 1450, the Chimú kingdom was conquered by the Inca Túpac Yupanqui, the son and heir of the Inca ruler Pachacuti Inca Yupanqui.

Inca Dynasty

The origins of the Inca Dynasty are shrouded in mythology. The best known story reported by the Spanish chroniclers talks about Manco Cápac and his sister rising out of Lake Titicaca, created by the Sun as divine founders of a chosen race. This was in approximately AD 1200. Over the next 300 years the small tribe grew to supremacy as leaders of the largest empire ever known in the Americas. The four territories of Tawantinsuyo, united by Cuzco as the umbilicus of the universe, were: Chinchaysuyo, north and northwest; Cuntisuyo, south and west; Collasuyo, south and east; Antisuyo, east.

At its peak, just before the Spanish Conquest, the Inca Empire stretched from the Río Maule in central Chile, north to the present Ecuador-Colombia border, containing most of Ecuador, Peru, western Bolivia, northern Chile and northwest Argentina. The area was roughly equivalent to France, Belgium, Holland, Luxembourg, Italy and Switzerland combined (980,000 sq km).

The first Inca ruler, Manco Cápac, moved to the fertile Cuzco region and established Cuzco as his capital. Successive generations of rulers were fully occupied with local conquests of rivals, such as the Colla and Lupaca to the south, and the Chanca to the northwest. At the end of Inca Viracocha's reign the hated Chanca were finally defeated, largely thanks to the heroism of one of his sons, Pachacútec Inca Yupanqui, who was subsequently crowned as the new ruler.

From the start of Pachacútec's own reign in AD 1438, imperial expansion grew in earnest. With the help of his son and heir, Topa Inca, territory was conquered from the Titicaca basin south into Chile, and all the north and central coast down to the Lurin Valley. The Incas also subjugated the Chimú, their highly sophisticated rivals on the coast (see above). Typical of the Inca method of government, some of the Chimú skills were assimilated into their own political and administrative system, and some Chimú nobles were even given positions in Cuzco.

Perhaps the pivotal event in Inca history came in AD 1527 with the death of the ruler, Huayna Capac. Civil war broke out in the confusion over his rightful successor. One of his legitimate sons, Huáscar, ruled the southern part of the empire from Cuzco. Atahualpa, Huáscar's half-brother, governed Quito, the capital of Chinchaysuyo. In 1532, soon after Atahualpa had won the civil war, Francisco Pizarro arrived in Tumbes with 167 conquistadors, a third of them on horseback. Atahualpa's army was marching south, probably for the first time, when he clashed with Pizarro at Cajamarca.

Francisco Pizarro's only chance against the formidable imperial army he encountered at Cajamarca was a bold stroke. He drew Atahualpa into an ambush, slaughtered his guards, promised him liberty if a certain room were filled with treasure, and finally killed him on the pretext that another Inca army was on its way to free him. Pushing on to Cuzco, Pizarro was at first hailed as the executioner of the traitorous Atahualpa, who had ordered the death of Huáscar in AD 1533. Panic followed, however, when the conquistadors set about sacking the city. The Spanish fought off with difficulty an attempt by Manco Inca to recapture Cuzco in 1536.

Inca society

The Incas were a small aristocracy numbering only a few thousand, centred in the highland city of Cuzco, at 3400 m. They rose gradually as a small regional dynasty, similar to others in the Andes of that period, starting around AD 1200. Then in the mid-1400s, they began to expand explosively under Pachacútec, a sort of Andean Alexander the Great, and later his son, Topa. Under 100 years later, they fell before the rapacious warriors of Spain. The Incas were not the first dynasty in Andean history to dominate their neighbours, but they did it more thoroughly and went further than anyone before them.

Empire building

Enough remains today of their astounding highways, cities and agricultural terracing for people to marvel and wonder how they accomplished so much in so short a time. They seem to have been amazingly energetic, industrious and efficient – and the reports of their Spanish conquerors confirm this hypothesis.

They must also have had the willing cooperation of most of their subject peoples, most of the time. In fact, the Incas were master diplomats and alliance-builders first, and military conquerors only second, if the first method of expansion failed. The Inca skill at generating wealth by means of highly efficient agriculture and distribution brought them enormous prestige and enabled them to 'out-gift' neighbouring chiefs in huge royal feasts involving ritual outpourings of generosity, often in the form of vast gifts of textiles, exotic products from distant regions, and perhaps wives to add blood ties to the alliance. The 'out-gifted' chief was required by the Andean laws of reciprocity to provide something in return, and this would usually be his loyalty, as well as a levy of manpower from his own chiefdom.

Thus, with each new alliance the Incas wielded greater labour forces and their mighty public works programmes surged ahead. These were administered through an institution known as mit'a, a form of taxation through labour. The state provided the materials, such as wool and cotton for making textiles, and the communities provided skills and labour.

Mit'a contingents worked royal mines, royal plantations for producing coca leaves, royal quarries and so on. The system strove to be equitable, and workers in such hardship posts as high altitude mines and lowland coca plantations were given correspondingly shorter terms of service.

Organization

Huge administrative centres were built in different parts of the empire, where people and supplies were gathered. Articles such as textiles and pottery were produced there in large workshops. Work in these places was carried out in a festive manner, with plentiful food, drink and music. Here was Andean reciprocity at work: the subject supplied his labour, and the ruler was expected to provide generously while he did so.

Aside from *mit'a* contributions there were also royal lands claimed by the Inca as his portion in every conquered province, and worked for his benefit by the local population. Thus, the contribution of each citizen to the state was quite large, but apparently, the imperial economy was productive enough to sustain this.

Another institution was the practice of moving populations around: inserting loyal groups into restive areas, and removing recalcitrant populations to loyal areas. These movements of *mitmakuna*, as they were called, were also used to introduce skilled farmers and engineers into areas where productivity needed to be raised.

Communications

The huge empire was held together by an extensive and highly efficient highway system. There were an estimated 30,000 km of major highway, most of it neatly paved and drained, stringing together the major Inca sites. Two parallel highways ran north to south, along the coastal desert strip and the mountains, and dozens of east-west roads crossing from the coast to the Amazon fringes. These roadways took the most direct routes, with wide stone stairways zig-zagging up the steepest mountain slopes and rope suspension bridges crossing the many narrow gorges of the Andes. The north-south roads formed a great axis that eventually came to be known as **Capaq Ñan** – 'Royal', or 'Principal Road', in Quechua – which exceeded in grandeur not only the other roads, but also their utilitarian concept. They became the Incas' symbol of power over men and over the sacred forces of nature. So marvellous were these roads that the Spaniards who saw them at the height of their glory said that there was nothing comparable in all Christendom.

Every 12 km or so there was a *tambo*, or way station, where goods could be stored and travellers lodged. The *tambos* were also control points, where the Inca state's accountants tallied movements of goods and people. Even more numerous than *tambos*, were the huts of the *chasquis*, or relay runners, who continually sped royal and military messages along these highways.

The Inca state kept records and transmitted information in various ways. Accounting and statistical records were kept on skeins of knotted strings known as *quipus*. Numbers employed the decimal system (although Italian engineer Nicolino De Pasquale claimed in 2006 the number system was based on 40), and colours indicated the categories being recorded. An entire class of people, known as *quipucamayocs*, existed whose job was to create and interpret these. Neither the Incas nor their Andean predecessors had a system of writing as we understand it, but there may have been a system of encoding language into *quipus*. Archaeologists are studying this problem today. History and other forms of knowledge were transmitted via songs and poetry. Music and dancing, full of encoded information that could be read by the educated elite, were part of every major ceremony and public event information was also carried in textiles, which had for millennia been the most vital expression of Andean culture.

Textiles

Clothing carried insignia of status, ethnic origin, age and so on. Special garments were made and worn for various rites of passage. It has been calculated that, after agriculture, no activity was more important to Inca civilization than weaving. Vast stores of textiles were maintained to sustain the Inca system of ritual giving. Armies and *mit'a* workers were partly paid in textiles. The finest materials were reserved for the nobility, and the Inca emperor himself displayed his status by changing into new clothes every day and having the previous day's burned.

Most weaving was done by women, and the Incas kept large numbers of 'chosen women' in female-only houses all over the empire, partly for the purpose of supplying textiles to the elite and for the many deities, to whom they were frequently given as burned offerings. These women had other duties, such as making *chicha* – the Inca corn beer that was consumed and sacrificed in vast quantities on ceremonial occasions. They also became wives and concubines to the Inca elite and loyal nobilities. And some may have served as priestesses of the moon, in parallel to the male priesthood of the sun.

Religious worship

The Incas have long been portrayed as sun-worshippers, but it seems that they were mountain-worshippers too. Research has shown that Machu Picchu was at least partly dedicated to the worship of the surrounding mountains, and Inca sacrificial victims have been excavated on frozen Andean peaks at 6700 m. In fact, until technical climbing was invented, the Incas held the world altitude record for humans.

Human sacrifice was not common, but every other kind was, and ritual attended every event in the Inca calendar. The main temple of Cuzco was dedicated to the numerous deities: the Sun, the Moon, Venus, the Pleiades, the Rainbow, Thunder and Lightning, and the countless religious icons of subject peoples which had been brought to Cuzco, partly in homage, partly as hostage. Here, worship was continuous and the fabulous opulence included gold cladding on the walls, and a famous garden filled with life-size objects of gold and silver. Despite this pantheism, the Incas acknowledged an overall Creator God, whom they called Viracocha. A special temple was dedicated to him, at Raqchi, about 100 km southeast of Cuzco. Part of it still stands today.

Military forces

The conquering Spaniards noted with admiration the Inca storehouse system, still well-stocked when they found it, despite several years of civil war among the Incas. Besides textiles, military equipment, and ritual objects, they found huge quantities of food. Like most Inca endeavours, the food stores served a multiple purpose: to supply feasts, to provide during lean times, to feed travelling work parties, and to supply armies on the march.

Inca armies were able to travel light and move fast because of this system. Every major Inca settlement also incorporated great halls where large numbers of people could be accommodated, or feasts and gatherings held, and large squares or esplanades for public assemblies.

Inca technology is usually deemed inferior to that of contemporary Europe. Their military technology certainly was. They had not invented iron-smelting, and basically fought with clubs, palmwood spears, slings, wooden shields, cotton armour and straw-stuffed helmets. They did not even make much use of the bow and arrow, a weapon they were well aware of. Military tactics, too, were primitive. The disciplined formations of the Inca armies quickly dissolved into melees of unbridled individualism once battle was joined. This, presumably, was because warfare constituted a theatre of manly prowess, but was not the main priority of Inca life. Its form was ritualistic. Battles were suspended by both sides for religious observance. Negotiation, combined with displays of superior Inca strength, usually achieved victory, and total annihilation of the enemy was not on the agenda.

Architecture

Other technologies, however, were superior in every way to their 16th century counterparts: textiles; settlement planning; and agriculture in particular with its sophisticated irrigation and soil conservation systems, ecological sensitivity, specialized crop strains and high productivity under the harshest conditions. The Incas fell short of their Andean predecessors in the better-known arts of ancient America – ceramics, textiles and metalwork – but it could be argued that their supreme efforts were made in architecture, stoneworking, landscaping, roadbuilding, and the harmonious combination of these elements.

These are the outstanding survivals of Inca civilization, which still remain to fascinate the visitor: the huge, exotically close-fit blocks of stone, cut in graceful, almost sensual curves; the astoundingly craggy and inaccessible sites encircled by great sweeps of Andean scenery; the rhythmic layers of farm terracing that provided land and food to this still-enigmatic people. The finest examples of Inca architecture can be seen in the city of Cuzco and throughout the Sacred Valley. As more evidence of Inca society is uncovered each year, our knowledge of these remarkable people can only improve.

Ruling elite

The ruling elite lived privileged lives in their capital at Cuzco. They reserved for themselves and privileged insiders certain luxuries, such as the chewing of coca, the wearing of fine vicuña wool, and the practice of polygamy. But they were an austere people, too. Everyone had work to do, and the nobility were constantly posted to state business throughout the empire. Young nobles were expected to learn martial skills, as well as read the quipus, speak both Quechua and the southern language of Aymara, and know the epic poems.

The Inca elite belonged to royal clans known as panacas, which each had the unusual feature of being united around veneration of the mummy of their founding ancestor – a previous Inca emperor, unless they happened to belong to the panaca founded by the Inca emperor who was alive at the time. Each new emperor built his own palace in Cuzco and amassed his own wealth rather than inheriting it from his forebears, which perhaps helps to account for the urge to unlimited expansion.

This urge ultimately led the Incas to overreach themselves. Techniques of diplomacy and incorporation no longer worked as they journeyed farther from the homeland and met ever-increasing resistance from people less familiar with their ways. During the reign of Wayna Cápac, the last emperor before the Spanish invasion, the Incas had to establish a northern capital at Quito in order to cope with permanent war on their northern frontier. Following Wayna Cápac's death came a devastating civil war between Cuzco and Quito, and immediately thereafter came the Spanish invasion. Tawantisuyo, the empire of the four quarters, collapsed with dizzying suddenness.

Conquest and after

Peruvian history after the arrival of the Spaniards was not just a matter of conquistadores versus Incas. The vast majority of the huge empire remained unaware of the conquest for many years. The Chimú and the Chachapoyas cultures were powerful enemies of the Incas. The Chimú developed a highly sophisticated culture and a powerful empire stretching for 560 km along the coast from Tumbes south to present-day Lima. Their history was well-recorded by the Spanish chroniclers and continued through the conquest possibly up to about 1600. The Kuélap/ Chachapoyas people were not so much an empire as a loose-knit "confederation of ethnic groups with no recognized capital" (Morgan Davis *Chachapoyas: The Cloud People*, Ontario, 1988). But the culture did develop into an advanced society with great skill in roads and monument building. Their fortress at Kuélap was known as the most impregnable in Tawantinsuyo. It remained intact against Inca attack and Manco Inca even tried, unsuccessfully, to gain refuge here against the Spaniards.

In 1535, wishing to secure his communications with Spain, Pizarro founded Lima, near the ocean, as his capital. The same year Diego de Almagro set out to conquer Chile. Unsuccessful, he returned to Peru, quarrelled with Pizarro, and in 1538 fought a pitched battle with Pizarro's men at the Salt Pits, near Cuzco. He was defeated and put to death. Pizarro, who had not been at the battle, was assassinated in his palace in Lima by Almagro's son three years later.

For the next 27 years each succeeding representative of the Kingdom of Spain sought to subdue the Inca successor state of Vilcabamba, north of Cuzco, and to unify the fierce Spanish factions. Francisco de Toledo (appointed 1568) solved both problems during his 14 years in office: Vilcabamba was crushed in 1572 and the last reigning Inca, Túpac Amaru, put to death.

For the next 200 years the Viceroys closely followed Toledo's system, if not his methods. The Major Government – the Viceroy, the Audiencia (High Court), and *corregidores* (administrators) – ruled through the Minor Government (indigenous chiefs put in charge of large groups of natives), a rough approximation to the original Inca system.

Towards independence

There was an indigenous rising in 1780, under the leadership of an Inca noble who called himself Túpac Amaru II. He and many of his lieutenants were captured and put to death under torture at Cuzco. Another indigenous leader in revolt suffered the same fate in 1814, but this last flare-up had the sympathy of many of the locally born Spanish, who resented their status, inferior to the Spaniards born in Spain, the refusal to give them any but the lowest offices, the high taxation imposed by the home government, and the severe restrictions upon trade with any country but Spain.

Help came to them from the outside world. José de San Martín's Argentine troops, convoyed from Chile under the protection of Lord Cochrane's squadron, landed in southern Peru on 7 September 1820. San Martín proclaimed Peruvian independence at Lima on 28 July 1821, though most of the country was still in the hands of the Viceroy, José de La Serna. Bolívar, who had already freed Venezuela and Colombia, sent Antonio José de Sucre to Ecuador where, on 24 May 1822, he gained a victory over La Serna at Pichincha.

San Martín, after a meeting with Bolívar at Guayaquil, left for Argentina and a self-imposed exile in France, while Bolívar and Sucre completed the conquest of Peru by defeating La Serna at the battle of Junín (6 August 1824) and the decisive battle of Ayacucho (9 December 1824). For over a year there was a last stand in the Real Felipe fortress at Callao by the Spanish troops under General Rodil before they capitulated on 22 January 1826. Bolívar was invited to stay in Peru, but left for Colombia in 1826.

Post-independence Peru

Following independence Peru attempted a confederation with Bolivia in the 1830s but this proved temporary. Then, in 1879 came the disastrous War of the Pacific, in which Peru and Bolivia were defeated by Chile and Peru lost its southern territory.

Economic change

Peru's economic development since independence has been based upon the export of minerals and foodstuffs to Europe and the United States. Guano, a traditional fertilizer in Peru and derived from the manure of seabirds, was first shipped to Europe in 1841. In the three decades that followed it became an important fertilizer in Europe and by the early 1860s over 80% of the Peruvian government's revenues were derived from its export. Much of this income, though, went to pay off interest on the spiralling national debt. By the 1870s the richer deposits were exhausted and cheaper alternatives to guano were being discovered. One of these was nitrates, discovered in the Atacama desert, but Peru's defeat by Chile in the War of the Pacific ensured that she would lose her share of this wealth.

After the decline of guano, Peru developed several new exports. In the 1890s the demand in Europe and USA for Amazonian rubber for tyres and for use in electrical components led to a brief boom in both the Brazilian and Peruvian Amazon. The Peruvian industry was based around the port of Iquitos. This boom was short-lived as cheaper rubber was soon being produced from plantations in the East Indies. Peru's colonial mineral exports, gold and silver, were replaced by copper, although ownership was mainly under control of foreign companies, particularly the US-based Cerro de Pasco Copper Corporation and Northern Peru Mining. Oil became another important product, amounting to 30% of Peruvian exports by 1930. Further exports came from sugar and cotton, which were produced on coastal plantations.

Social change

Independence from Spanish rule meant that power passed into the hands of the Creole elite with no immediate alternation of the colonial social system. The *contribución de indíginas* (the colonial tribute collected from the native peoples) was not abolished until 1854, the same year as the ending of slavery.

Until the 1970s land relations in the sierra changed very little, as the older landholding families continued to exert their traditional influence over 'their' peones. The traditional elite, the so-called '44 families', were still very powerful, though increasingly divided between the coastal aristocracy with their interests in plantation agriculture and trade, and the serrano elite, more conservative and inward looking.

The pattern of export growth did, however, have major social effects on the coast. The expansion of plantation agriculture and mining led to the growth of a new labour force; this was supplied partially by Chinese indentured labourers, about 100,000 of whom arrived between 1855 and 1875, partly by the migration of indigenous people from the sierra and partly by the descendants of black slaves.

Political developments

19th century

For much of the period since independence Peruvian political life has been dominated by the traditional elites. Political parties have been slow to develop and the roots of much of the political conflict and instability which have marked the country's history lie in personal ambitions and in regional and other rivalries within the elite.

The early years after independence were particularly chaotic as rival caudillos (political bosses) who had fought in the independence wars vied with each other for power. The increased wealth brought about by the guano boom led to greater stability, though political corruption became a serious problem under the presidency of José Rufino Echenique (1851-1854) who paid out large sums of the guano revenues as compensation to upper class families for their (alleged) losses in the Wars of Independence. Defeat by Chile in the War of the Pacific discredited civilian politicians even further and led to a period of military rule in the 1880s.

Early 20th century

Even though the voting system was changed in 1898, this did little to change the dominance of the elite. Voting was not secret so landowners herded their workers to the polls and watched to make sure they voted correctly. Yet voters were also lured by promises as well as threats. One of the more unusual presidents was Guillermo Billinghurst (1912-1914) who campaigned on the promise of a larger loaf of bread for five cents, thus gaining the nickname of 'Big Bread Billinghurst'. As president he proposed a publicly funded housing programme, supported the introduction of an eight hour day and was eventually overthrown by the military who, along with the elite, were alarmed at his growing popularity among the urban population.

The 1920s This decade was dominated by Augusto Leguía. After winning the 1919 elections Leguía claimed that Congress was plotting to prevent him from becoming president and induced the military to help him close Congress. Backed by the armed forces, Leguía introduced a new constitution which gave him greater powers and enabled him to be re-elected in 1924 and 1929. Claiming his goal was to prevent the rise of communism, he proposed to build a partnership between business and labour. A large programme of public works, particularly involving building roads, bridges and railways, was begun, the work being carried out by poor rural men who were forced into unpaid building work. The Leguía regime dealt harshly with critics: opposition newspapers were closed and opposition leaders arrested and deported. His overthrow in 1930 ended what Peruvians call the *Oncenio* or 11-year period.

The 1920s also saw the emergence of a political thinker who would have great influence in the future, not only in Peru but elsewhere in Latin America. José Carlos Mariátegui, a socialist writer and journalist, argued that the solution to Peru's problems lay in the reintegration of the indigenous people through land reform and the breaking up of the great landed estates.

The formation of APRA Another influential thinker of this period was Víctor Raúl Haya de la Torre, a student exiled by Leguía in 1924. He returned after the latter's fall to create the Alianza Popular Revolucionaria Americana (APRA), a political party which called for state control of the economy, nationalization of key industries and protection of the middle classes, which, Haya de la Torre argued, were threatened by foreign economic interests.

In 1932 APRA seized control of Trujillo; when the army arrived to deal with the rising, the rebels murdered about 50 hostages, including 10 army officers. In reprisal the army murdered about 1000 local residents suspected of sympathizing with APRA. APRA eventually became the largest and easily the best-organized political party in Peru, but the distrust of the military and the upper class for Haya de la Torre ensured that he never became president.

A turning point in Peruvian history occurred in 1948 with the seizure of power by General Manuel Odría, backed by the coastal elite. Odría outlawed APRA and went on to win the 1950 election in which he was the only candidate. He pursued policies of encouraging export earnings and also tried to build up working class support by public works projects in Lima. Faced with a decline in export earnings and the fall in world market prices after 1953, plus increasing unemployment, Odría was forced to stand down in 1956.

In 1962 Haya de la Torre was at last permitted to run for the presidency. But although he won the largest percentage of votes he was prevented from taking office by the armed forces who seized power and organized fresh elections for 1963. In these the military obtained the desired result: Haya de la Torre came second to Fernando Belaúnde Terry. Belaúnde attempted to introduce reforms, particularly in the landholding structure of the sierra; when these reforms were weakened by landowner opposition in Congress, peasant groups began invading landholdings in protest.

At the same time, under the influence of the Cuban revolution, terrorist groups began operating in the sierra. Military action to deal with this led to the deaths of an estimated 8000 people. Meanwhile Belaúnde's attempts to solve a long-running dispute with the International Petroleum Company (a subsidiary of Standard Oil) resulted in him being attacked for selling out to the unpopular oil company and contributed to the armed forces' decision to seize power in 1968.

The 1968 coup

This was a major landmark in Peruvian history. Led by General Juan Velasco Alvarado, the Junta had no intention of handing power back to the civilians. A manifesto issued on the day of the coup attacked the 'unjust social and economic order' and argued for its replacement by a new economic system 'neither capitalist nor communist'. Partly as a result of their experiences in dealing with the insurgency, the coup leaders concluded that agrarian reform was a priority.

Wide-ranging land reform was launched in 1969, during which large estates were taken over and reorganized into cooperatives. By the mid-1970s, 75% of productive land was under cooperative management. The government also tried to improve the lives of shanty-town dwellers around Lima, as well as attempting to increase the influence of workers in industrial companies. At the same time efforts were made to reduce the influence of foreign companies. Soon after the coup, IPC was nationalized, to be followed by other transnationals including ITT, Chase Manhattan Bank and the two mining giants Cerro de Pasco and Marcona Mining. After a dispute with the US government, compensation was agreed.

Understandably, opposition to the Velasco government came from the business and landholding elite. The government's crack-down on expressions of dissent, the seizure of newspapers and taking over of TV and radio stations all offended sections of the urban middle class. Trade unions and peasant movements found that, although they agreed with many of the regime's policies, it refused to listen and expected their passive and unqualified support. As world sugar and copper prices dropped, inflation rose and strikes increased. Velasco's problems were further increased by opposition within the armed forces and by his own ill-health. In August 1975 he was replaced by General Francisco Morales Bermúdez, a more conservative officer, who dismantled some of Velasco's policies and led the way to a restoration of civilian rule. Velasco Alvarado's land reforms marked a watershed in 20th-century Peruvian history, and he remains a hero to many *campesinos*.

Belaúnde returned to power in 1980 by winning the first elections after military rule. His government was badly affected by the 1982 debt crisis and the 1981-1983 world recession, and inflation reached over 100% a year in 1983-1984. His term was also marked by the growth of the Maoist movement **Sendero Luminoso** (Shining Path) and the smaller, Marxist **Movimiento Revolucionario Túpac Amaru** (MRTA).

Initially conceived in the University of Ayacucho, Shining Path gained most support for its goal of overthrowing the whole system of Lima-based government from indigenous highlanders and migrants to urban shanty towns. The activities of Sendero Luminoso and the MRTA were effectively curtailed after the arrest of both their leaders in 1992: Víctor Polay of MRTA and Abimael Guzmán of Sendero Luminoso. Although Sendero did not capitulate, many of its members in 1994-1995 took advantage of the Law of Repentance, which guaranteed lighter sentences in return for surrender, and freedom in exchange for valuable information. Meanwhile, MRTA was thought to have ceased operations.

In 1985 APRA, in opposition for over 50 years, finally came to power. With Haya de la Torre dead, the APRA candidate Alan García Pérez won the elections and was allowed to take office by the armed forces. García attempted to implement an ambitious economic programme intended to solve many of Peru's deep-seated economic and social problems. He cut taxes, reduced interest rates, froze prices and devalued the currency. However, the economic boom that this produced in 1986-1987 stored up problems as increased incomes were spent on imports. Moreover, the government's refusal to pay more than 10% of its foreign debt meant that it was unable to borrow. In 1988 inflation hit 3000% and unemployment soared. By the time his term of office ended in 1990 Peru was bankrupt and García and APRA were discredited.

Modern Peru

The Fujimori years

In presidential elections held over two rounds in 1990, **Alberto Fujimori** defeated the novelist **Mario Vargas Llosa** (see box, page 558). Fujimori, the son of Japanese immigrants and former dean of an agricultural college without an established political network behind him, failed to win a majority in either the senate or the lower house. Lack of congressional support was one of the reasons behind his dissolution of congress and the suspension of the constitution in 1992.

A new constitution was drawn up in 1993. Among its articles were the establishment of a single-chamber congress, the designation of Peru as a market economy and the favouring of foreign investment. As expected, Fujimori stood for re-election in 1995 and won by a resounding margin, about 65% of the votes cast. But the government's success in most economic areas did not appear to accelerate the distribution of funds for social projects. Rising unemployment and the austerity imposed by economic policy continued to cause hardship for many, despite the government's stated aim of alleviating poverty.

Dramatic events in 1996 thrust several of these issues into sharper focus: 14 Túpac Amaru terrorists infiltrated a reception at the Japanese Embassy in Lima, taking 490 hostages. Most were eventually released and negotiations pursued during a stalemate that lasted six months. The president took sole responsibility for the successful, but risky assault that freed all the hostages (one died of heart failure) and killed all the terrorists. By not yielding to Túpac Amaru, Fujimori regained much popularity.

But this masked the fact that no steps had been taken to ease social problems. It also deflected attention from Fujimori's plans to stand for a third term. Local and international observers voiced concern over his increasingly autocratic tendencies and state domination of the media. The opposition candidate boycotted the election and Fujimori won unopposed, but with scant approval.

The next bombshell was the airing of a secretly shot video showing Fujimori's close aide and head of the National Intelligence Service, Vladimiro Montesinos, handing US$15,000 to a congressman to persuade him to switch allegiances to Fujimori's coalition. Although Montesinos initially evaded capture, investigators began to uncover the extent of his empire, which held hundreds of senior figures in its web. His activities encompassed extortion, money-laundering, bribery, intimidation, alleged arms and drugs dealing and possible links with the CIA and death squads. Swiss bank accounts in his name were found to contain about US$70 million. In early 2001 he was eventually captured in Venezuela and returned to Peru where he was tried on, and convicted of, a multitude of charges.

Fujimori fled to Japan from where, on 20 November 2000, he sent Congress an email announcing his resignation. An interim president, **Valentín Paniagua**, was sworn in, and the government set about uncovering the depth of corruption

BACKGROUND
The high price of minerals

Since 2006 Peru has enjoyed unaccustomed social and political tranquility, due in large measure to an impressive economic boom. Various sectors of the Peruvian economy are thriving, among them tourism, but the current blush of prosperity is large due to the high world price of minerals which has encouraged widespread exploitation of the country's extensive ore deposits.

Peru's rapidly growing economy has drawn much praise from the international economic community and allowed the Humala government to increase funding for social programmes. But are these fat years really the best of times? The view from the ground, voiced by intellectuals, villagers and parish priests, among others, is "maybe not". Alongside the environmental upheaval caused by some of the world's largest open-pit mines, the social consequences of all the mining revenue have been less than positive.

Communities near the mines receive a canon *minero*, their own direct share of mining royalties, and the influx of this easy money has fostered unprecedented corruption in local governments. Cronies of those in office are appointed to sinecures and many people have abandoned their traditional activities, such as agriculture, to take on do-nothing municipal positions.

The seemingly endless flow of funds is squandered on showy but senseless projects, such as an oversize sports stadium for a tiny village, while more basic needs like sanitation are ignored. At the national level, one sees a great burst of vacuous consumer spending without any indication that the mining revenues are being re-invested in sustainable development.

Can you guess what will happen after the boom goes bust?

associated with Montesinos and Fujimori. In 2004, prosecutors sought to charge exiled Fujimori with authorizing death squads at Barrios Altos (1991) and La Cantuta (1992) in which 25 people died. This followed the Truth and Reconciliation Committee's report (2003) into the civil war of the 1980s and 1990s, which stated that over 69,000 Peruvians had been killed and multiple atrocities had been committed by insurgent groups and government forces alike.

With attempts to extradite Fujimori from Japan coming to nothing, prosecution could not proceed. Meanwhile Fujimori declared that he would be exonerated and stand again for the presidency in 2006. To this end he flew to Chile in November 2005 with a view to entering Peru, but the Chilean authorities jailed him for seven months and then held him on parole until an extradition request was finally approved in 2007. In December of that year the first of several trials began, Fujimori being charged with, but strenuously denying, the Barrios Altos and La Cantuta murders, kidnapping and corruption. He was found guilty of human rights abuses in 2009 and sentenced to 25 years in prison. Further convictons followed, but, despite his controversial time in power, advancing age and ill health, he still retains some popularity. His daughter, Keiko, has become

BACKGROUND

Constitution and government

Peru has a single chamber 120-seat congress. Men and women over 18 are eligible to vote, and registration and voting is compulsory until the age of 70. Those who do not vote are fined. The president, to whom is entrusted the executive power, is elected for five years. Since the Regionalization Law of 2002, Peru's territory has been divided into 26 units: 25 *regiones*, formerly called *departamentos* (a term that remains in common use) plus the Province of Lima. The regiones are subdivided into *provincias*, which are in turn made up of *distritos*. There are 195 *provincias* and 1840 *distritos* in Peru.

a major political player and came second to Ollanta Humala in 2011 presidential elections (see below).

From Fujimori to Humala

In the 2001 presidential elections, **Alejandro Toledo**, a former World Bank official of humble origins defeated ex-president Alan García. He pledged to heal the wounds that had opened in Peru during Fujimori's tenure, but his presidency was marked by slow progress on both the political and economic fronts. Nor could Toledo escape charges of corruption; accusations that he and his sister orchestrated voter fraud were upheld by a congressional commission. He completed his term of office but has been answering to additional corruption charges ever since.

The 2006 elections were again contested by Alan García and **Ollanta Humala**, a former military officer and unsuccessful coup leader who claimed support from Venezuela's Hugo Chávez and Evo Morales of Bolivia. García won in the second round, in part because many were suspicious of the 'Chávez factor' and the latter's interference in Peruvian affairs. Many were equally suspicious of García's ability to overcome his past record as president, but it turned out that the former populist had changed his stripes. In 2006 he signed a free trade agreement with the USA, which came into effect in 2009. The Peruvian economy showed exceptionally strong growth throughout most of his time in office, based almost exclusively on high international mineral prices, and mining interests became a dominant force in Peru (see box, The high price of minerals, opposite). Some of the mining revenues eventually trickled down to the poorer segments of society. After completing his term of office, García, like many of his predecessors, faced investigation on corruption charges.

In 2011, Ollanta Humala again ran for the presidency, this time with a more polished image and more moderate rhetoric than in the past. He defeated Keiko Fujimori in the second round with 51.5% of the vote. Humala had obtained the support of intellectuals and urban middle-class Peruvians, in addition to his traditional power base among poorer rural dwellers. Once in office, he quickly disappointed his former supporters with policies catering precisely to the international corporate interests (especially in the mining sector) whose influence he had previously decried. But with the economy still booming and his strengthening of various social programmes, he did not face much effective opposition.

Humala has faced criticism for weak leadershp, with his wife, Nadine Heredia, allegedly being the power behind the throne. She is a potential candidate, alongside Keiko Fujimori, Alan García and Alejandro Toledo for the 2016 presidential elections. Another prospective candidate is celebrity chef Gastón Acurio (see box, page 64), surely an indication of how much things have changed in Peruvian politics.

People

Peruvian society today is a melting pot of Native Andeans, Afro-Peruvians, Spanish, immigrant Chinese, Japanese, Italians, Germans and, to a lesser extent, indigenous Amazon tribes. The total population in 2007 was 28.2 million (INEI census statistics), with an annual average growth rate of 1.6%. The INEI estimates the total at 31.1 million in 2015. The urban population represents 73% of the total.

Criollos and mestizos

The first immigrants were the Spaniards who followed Pizarro's expeditionary force. Their effect, demographically, politically and culturally, has been enormous. They intermarried with the indigenous population and the children of mixed parentage were called *mestizos*. The Peruvian-born children of Spanish parents were known as *criollos*, though this word is now used to describe people who live on the coast, regardless of their ancestry, and coastal culture in general.

Afro-Peruvians

Peru's black community is based on the coast, mainly in Chincha, south of Lima, and also in some working-class districts of the capital. Their forefathers were originally imported into Peru in the 16th century as slaves to work on the sugar and cotton plantations on the coast. The black community represents between 2-5% of the total population. See also page 542.

Asian immigrants

There are two main Asian communities in Peru, the Japanese and Chinese. Large numbers of poor Chinese labourers were brought to Peru in the mid-19th century to work in virtual slavery on the guano reserves on the Pacific coast and to build the railroads in the central Andes. The culinary influence of the Chinese can be seen in the many *chifas* found throughout the country.

The Japanese community, now numbering some 100,000, established itself in the first half of the 20th century. The normally reclusive community gained prominence when Alberto Fujimori, one of its members, became the first president of Japanese descent outside Japan anywhere in the world. During Fujimori's presidency, many other Japanese Peruvians took prominent positions in business, central and local government. The nickname 'chino' is applied to anyone of Oriental origin.

Europeans

Like most of Latin America, Peru received many emigrés from Europe seeking land and opportunities in the late 19th century. The country's wealth and political power remains concentrated in the hands of this small and exclusive class of whites, which also consists of the descendants of the first Spanish families. There still exists a deep divide between people of European descent and the old colonial snobbery persists.

BACKGROUND
The Afro-Peruvian experience since 1532

The first person of African descent to arrive in the Americas came in 1492 with Christopher Columbus. He was a mulatto from Spain and a free man. During the next three centuries an estimated 15 million Africans arrived in the Americas as slaves. Francisco Pizarro brought the first black slaves to Peru. They were present at the capture of Atahualpa in Cajamarca in 1532 and saved the Spanish during Manco Inca's siege of Cuzco in 1536, when they put out the fire engulfing the great hall of Sunturwasi, where the *conquistadors* had taken refuge.

When Hernando de Soto returned to Spain in 1534 bearing Atahualpa's gold and silver ransom, he asked the crown for permission to take 100 slaves back to Peru. By 1550, their number had risen to 3000 – half of whom lived in Lima – and by 1640 to 30,000. In total, between 1532 and 1816, an estimated 100,000 African slaves were transported to Peru.

They were sent to replace an indigenous labour force ravaged by the destruction of its sociopolitical infrastructure and by European diseases. Some worked in the cities as servants, artisans or porters, others in the mines of Huancavelica or Potosí and the majority toiled on the coast in sugar cane plantations, cotton fields and vineyards.

Indigenous and African workers transformed Peru into the richest of all the Spanish colonies in the 16th and 17th centuries. Many fortunes, including that amassed by the Jesuits, were made using slave labour. The ownership of black slaves was a status symbol and even some Afro-Peruvians who had achieved their own freedom subsequently acquired slaves.

The location of Afro-Peruvian communities today reflects the colonial distribution of black labour. They are concentrated in the coastal areas once dominated by the great haciendas: Chincha, Cañete and Ica; the northern departments of Lambayeque and Piura, and the cities, especially Lima. Here, the vibrant culture created by slaves from diverse African heritages lives on in local art, music, dance, religion, food and folklore.

The wars of independence spread the libertarian ideal of emancipation. Promised their freedom, hundreds of Afro-Peruvians joined the republican armies, only to find their situation little changed in 1821 under the fledgling government. In 1854, Generals Ramón Castilla and José Rufino Echenique engaged in civil war and were in need of troops. To attract black recruits Echenique offered freedom to those who would join him and, in reply, Castilla announced the abolition of slavery, paying off landowners with awards raised from guano exports.

The 25,000 black slaves freed in 1854 were received by society with contempt and remained oppressed by labour laws. Racism continues to live on today. Colour is still identified with inferiority in everyday attitudes and in the poverty and marginalization of black communities and their lack of representation in government. Over 150 years after abolition, those who shared the hardships of the *conquistadors* have still not shared in either their glory or their wealth.

Peru has a substantial indigenous population, only smaller as a percentage of the total than Bolivia and Guatemala of the Latin American republics. The literacy rate of the indigenous population is the lowest of any comparable group in South America and their diet is 50% below acceptable levels. The highland communities bore the brunt of the conflict between Sendero Luminoso and the security forces, which caused thousands of deaths and mass migration from the countryside to provincial cities or to Lima. Many indigenous groups are also under threat from colonization, development and lost road-building projects. Long after the end of Spanish rule, discrimination, dispossession and exploitation are still a fact of life for many native Peruvians.

Quechua

Predominantly an agricultural society, growing potatoes and corn as their basic diet, they are largely outside the money economy. Today, there remain two enduring legacies of Inca rule; their magnificent architecture and their language, Quechua, which, although predating the Incas themselves, has become synonymous with the descendants of their subjects. Quechua is one of the key channels of continuity with the captivating pre-European past and indigenous identity of the Andes. Sadly, that continuity still takes the form of a distinctly underprivileged status in relation to the dominant Spanish and it is only the remoteness of many Quechua speakers which has preserved the language in rural areas. This isolation has also helped preserve many of their ancient traditions and beliefs. Most speakers today are bilingual in Spanish and Quechua is still losing ground fast. It remains primarily a spoken, in-group language, strongly bound up with the distinct indigenous identity, but unlike the Aymara (see below), the seven million or so Quechua-speakers have generally been much less successful in asserting themselves. There is no real sense of unity between the disparate groups of speakers scattered through Ecuador, Peru and Bolivia. Some recent developments in these three countries have at last been more positive. The language is now increasingly written and is being fitfully introduced in primary education, though the impact of Spanish, and polemics about standardization, continue to have a very disruptive effect. At least some Quechua-speaking communities, in Peru and elsewhere, are gradually recovering a long-deserved semblance of pride in their native tongue and culture.

Aymara

High up in the Andes, in the southern part of Peru, lies a wide, barren and hostile plateau, the *altiplano*. Prior to Inca rule Tiahuanaco on Lake Titicaca was a highly organized centre for one the greatest cultures South America has ever witnessed: the Aymara people. Today, the shores of this lake and the plains that surround it remain the homeland of the Aymara. The majority live in Bolivia, the rest are scattered on the southwestern side of Peru and northern Chile. The climate is so harsh on the *altiplano* that, though they are extremely hard working, their lives are very poor. They speak their own unwritten language, Aymara. More so than the scattered group of different peoples that speak Quechua, the Altiplano Aymara people form a compact group with a clear sense of their own distinct identity and in many respects have been able to preserve more of their indigenous traditions and belief system.

The Aymaras are a deeply religious people whose culture is permeated with the idea of the sacred. They believe that God, the Supreme Being, gives them security in their daily lives and this God of Life manifests him/herself through the deities, such as those of the mountains, the water, wind, sun, moon and wa'qas (sacred places). As a sign of gratitude, the Aymara give *wax'ta* (offerings), *wilancha* (llama sacrifices) and *ch'alla* (sprinkling alcohol on the ground) to the achachilas (the protecting spirits of the family and community), the Pachamama (Mother Earth), Kuntur Mamani and Uywiri (protecting spirits of the home).

The remote mountains of the bleak *altiplano* are of particular importance for the Aymara. The most sacred places are these high mountains, far from human problems. It is here that the people have built their altars to offer worship, to communicate with their God and ask forgiveness. The community is also held important in the lives of the Aymara. The achachila is the great-great grandfather of the family as well as the protector of the community, and as such is God's representative on earth.

The offerings to the sacred mountains take place for the most part in August and are community celebrations. Many different rituals are celebrated: there are those within the family; in the mountains; for the planting and the harvest; rites to ask for rain or to ask for protection against hailstorms and frosts; and ceremonies for Mother Earth.

All such rituals are led by Aymara Yatiris, who are male or female priests. The Yatiri is a wise person – someone who knows – and the community's spiritual and moral guide. Through a method of divination that involves the reading of coca leaves, they guide individuals in their personal decision-making.

Amazonian peoples

Before the arrival of the Europeans, an estimated six million people inhabited the Amazon Basin, comprising more than 2000 tribes or ethnic-linguistic groups who managed to adapt to their surroundings through the domestication of a great variety of animals and plants, and to benefit from the numerous nutritional, curative, narcotic and hallucinogenic properties of thousands of wild plants.

It's not easy to determine the precise origin of these aboriginal people. What is known, however, is that since the beginning of colonial times this population slowly but constantly decreased, mainly because of the effect of western diseases such as influenza and measles. This demographic decline reached dramatic levels during the rubber boom of the late 19th and early 20th centuries, due to forced labour and slavery.

Today, at the basin level, the population is calculated at no more than two million inhabitants making up 400 ethnic groups, of which approximately 200,000-250,000 live in the Peruvian jungle. Within the basin it is possible to distinguish at least three large conglomerates of aboriginal societies: the inhabitants of the varzea, or seasonally flooded lands alongside the large rivers (such as the Omagua, Cocama and Shipibo people); the people in the interfluvial zones or firm lands (such as the Amahuaca, Cashibo and Yaminahua) and those living in the Andean foothills (such as the Amuesha, Asháninka and Machiguenga).

The Amazonian natives began to be decimated in the 16th century, and so were the first endangered species of the jungle. These communities still face threats to their traditional lifestyles, notably from timber companies, gold miners and multinational oil and gas companies. There appears to be little effective control of deforestation and the intrusion of colonists who have taken over native lands to establish small farms. And though oil companies have reached compensation agreements with local communities, previous oil exploration has contaminated many jungle rivers, as well as exposing natives to risk from diseases against which they have no immunity.

Culture

Religion

Inca spirituality was displaced by Roman Catholicism from the 16th century onwards, the conversion of the inhabitants of the 'New World' to Christianity being one of the stated aims of the Spanish *conquistadores*. Today, statistics vary between 81% and 89% of the population declaring itself Catholic.

One of the first exponents of Liberation Theology, under which the Conference of Latin American Bishops in 1968 committed themselves to the 'option for the poor', was Gustavo Gutiérrez, from Huánuco. This doctrine caused much consternation to orthodox Catholics, particularly those members of the Latin American church who had traditionally aligned themselves with the oligarchy. Gutiérrez, however, traced the church's duty to the voiceless and the marginalized back to Fray Bartolomé de las Casas.

The Catholic Church faced a further challenge to its authority when President Fujimori won the battle over family planning and the need to slow down the rate of population growth. Its greatest threat, however, comes from the proliferation of evangelical Protestant groups throughout the country. Some 6% of the population now declare themselves Protestant and one million or more people belong to some 27 different non-Catholic denominations.

Although the vast majority of the population ostensibly belongs to the Roman Catholic religion, in reality religious life for many Peruvians is a mix of Catholic beliefs imported from Europe and indigenous traditions based on animism, the worship of deities from the natural world such as mountains, animals and plants.

Arts and crafts

Peru has a rich variety of handicrafts. Its geographic division into four distinct regions – coast, mountains, valleys and Amazon Basin – coupled with cultural differences, has resulted in numerous variations in technique and design. Each province, even each community, has developed its own style of weaving or carving.

The Incas inherited 3000 years of skills and traditions: gold, metal and precious stonework from the Chimú; feather textiles from the Nazca; and the elaborate textiles of the Paracas. All of these played important roles in political, social and religious ceremonies. Though much of this artistic heritage was destroyed by the Spanish conquest, the traditions adapted and evolved in numerous ways, absorbing new methods, concepts and materials from Europe while maintaining ancient techniques and symbols.

Textiles and costumes

Woven cloth was the most highly prized possession and sought after trading commodity in the Andes in pre-Columbian times. It is, therefore, not surprising that ancient weaving traditions have survived. In the ninth century BC camelid fibre was introduced into weaving on the south coast. This allowed the development of the textiles of the Paracas culture that consist of intricate patterns of animalistic, supernatural and human forms embroidered onto dark backgrounds. The culture of the Chancay valleys cultivated cotton for white and beige dyed patterned cloth in preference to the camelid fibres used by the Paracas and Nazca cultures. The Incas inherited this rich weaving tradition. They forced the Aymaras to work in *mit'as* or textile workshops. The ruins of some enormous *mit'as* can be seen at the temple of Raqchi, south of Cuzco (see page 384). Inca textiles are of high quality and very different from coastal textiles, being warp-faced, closely woven and without embroidery. The largest quantities of the finest textiles were made specifically to be burned as ritual offerings – a tradition which still survives. The Spanish, too, exploited this wealth and skill by using the mitas and exporting the cloth to Europe.

Prior to Inca rule Aymara men wore a tunic (*llahua*) and a mantle (*llacata*) and carried a bag for coca leaves (*huallquepo*). The women wore a wrapped dress (*urku*) and mantle (*iscayo*) and a belt (*huaka*); their coca bag was called an *istalla*. The *urku* was fastened at shoulder level with a pair of metal *tupu*, the traditional Andean dress-pins. Inca men had tunics (*unkus*) and a bag for coca leaves called a *ch'uspa*. The women wore a blouse (*huguna*), skirts (*aksu*) and belts (*chumpis*), and carried foodstuffs in large, rectangular cloths called *llicllas*, which were fastened at the chest with a single pin or a smaller clasp called a *ttipqui*. Women of the Sacred Valley now wear a layered, gathered skirt called a *pollera* and a *montera*, a large, round, red Spanish type of hat. Textiles continue to play an important part in society. They are still used specifically for ritual ceremonies and some even held to possess magical powers. One of the most enduring of these traditions is found among the Aymara people of Taquile island on Lake Titicaca.

Textile materials and techniques

The Andean people used mainly alpaca or llama wool. The former can be spun into fine, shining yarn when woven and has a lustre similar to that of silk, though sheep's wool came to be widely used following the Spanish conquest. A commonly used technique is the drop spindle. A stick is weighted with a wooden wheel and the raw material is fed through one hand. A sudden twist and drop in the spindle spins the yarn. This very sensitive art can be seen practised by women while herding animals in the fields.

Spinning wheels were introduced by Europeans and are now prevalent owing to increased demand. In Ayacucho and San Pedro de Cajas, centres of the cottage textile industry, the wheel is the most common form of spinning. Pre-Columbian looms were often portable and those in use today are generally similar. A woman will herd her animals while making a piece of costume, perhaps on a backstrap loom, or waist loom, so-called because the weaver controls the tension on one side with her waist with the other side tied to an upright or tree. The pre-Columbian looms are usually used for personal costume while the treadle loom is used by men for more commercial pieces.

The skills of dyeing were still practised virtually unchanged even after the arrival of the Spanish. Nowadays, the word *makhnu* refers to any natural dye, but originally was the name for cochineal, an insect that lives on the leaves of the nopal cactus. These dyes were used widely by pre-Columbian weavers. Today, the biggest centre of production in South America is the valleys around Ayacucho. Vegetable dyes are also used, made from the leaves, fruit and seeds of shrubs and flowers and from lichen, tree bark and roots.

Symbolism

Symbolism plays an important role in weaving. Traditionally every piece of textile from a particular community had identical symbols and colours that were a source of identity as well as carrying specific symbols and telling a story. One example is on the island of Taquile where the Inti (sun) and Chaska (Venus) symbols are employed as well as motifs such as fish and birds, unique to the island.

Animal figures dominated the motifs of the Chavín culture and were commonly used in Paracas textiles. Specimens of cotton and wool embroidery found in Paracas graves often show a puma as a central motif. Today, this and other pre-Columbian motifs are found on many rugs and wall-hangings from the Ayacucho region. Other symbols include Spanish figures such as horses and scenes depicting the execution of Túpac Amaru.

Pottery

The most spectacular archaeological finds in South America have been made in Peru. The Nazca culture (100 BC-AD 900) excelled in polychrome painting of vessels with motifs of supernatural beings, often with strong feline characteristics, as well as birds, fish and animals. Many of the Nazca ceramic motifs are similar to those found in Paracas textiles.

Moche or Mochica vessels combined modelling and painting to depict details of Moche daily life. Human forms are modelled on stirrup spout vessels with such precision that they suggest personal portraits. The Moche also excelled in intricate linear painting often using brown on a cream base.

Inca ceramic decoration consists mainly of small-scale geometric and usually symmetrical designs. One distinctive form of vessel that continues to be made and used is the arybola. This pot is designed to carry liquid, especially *chicha*, and is secured with a rope on the bearer's back. It is believed that arybolas were used mainly by the governing Inca elite and became important status symbols. Today, Inca-style is very popular in Cuzco and Pisac.

With the Spanish invasion many indigenous communities lost their artistic traditions, others remained relatively untouched, while others still combined Hispanic and indigenous traditions and techniques. The Spanish brought three innovations: the potter's wheel, which gave greater speed and uniformity; knowledge of the enclosed kiln; and the technique of lead glazes. The enclosed kiln made temperature regulation easier and allowed higher temperatures to be maintained, producing stronger pieces. Today, many communities continue to apply pre-Hispanic techniques, while others use more modern processes.

Jewellery and metalwork

Some of the earliest goldwork originates from the Chavín culture – eg the Tumi knife found in Lambayeque. These first appeared in the Moche culture, when they were associated with human sacrifice. Five centuries later, the Incas used Tumis for surgical operations such as trepanning skulls. Today, they are a common motif.

The Incas associated gold with the Sun. However, very few examples remain as the Spanish melted down their amassed gold and silver objects. They then went on to send millions of indigenous people to their deaths in gold and silver mines.

During the colonial period gold and silver pieces were made to decorate the altars of churches and houses of the elite. Metalworkers came from Spain and Italy to develop the industry. The Spanish preferred silver and strongly influenced the evolution of silverwork during the colonial period. A style known as Andean baroque developed around Cuzco embracing both indigenous and European elements. Silver bowls in this style – *cochas* – are still used in Andean ceremonies.

False filigree This was practised by some pre-Hispanic cultures. The effect of filigree was obtained with the use of droplets or beads of gold. True filigree work developed in the colonial period. Today, there are a number of centres. Originally popular in Ayacucho, the tradition continues in the small community of San Jerónimo de Tunan, near Huancayo. Here, silversmiths produce intricate filigree earrings, spoons and jewellery boxes. Catacaos near Piura also has a long tradition of filigree work in silver and gold.

Seeds, flowers and feathers These continue to be used as jewellery by many Amazonian peoples. Pre-Hispanic cultures also favoured particular natural materials; eg the sea shell spondylus was highly revered by the Chavín and Moche. It was found only along part of the Ecuadorean coast and must have been acquired through trade. The western fashion for natural or ethnic jewellery has encouraged production, using brightly coloured feathers, fish bones, seeds or animal teeth.

Woodcarving

Wood is one of the most commonly used materials. Carved ceremonial objects include drums, carved sticks with healing properties, masks and the Incas' *keros* – wooden vessels for drinking *chicha*. Keros come in all shapes and sizes and were traditionally decorated with scenes of war, local dances, or harvesting coca leaves. The Chancay, who lived along the coast between 100 BC and AD 1200, used *keros* carved with sea birds and fish. Today, they are used in some Andean ceremonies, especially during Fiesta de la Cruz, the Andean May festival.

Glass mirrors were introduced by the Spanish, although the Chimú and Lambayeque cultures used obsidian and silver plates, and Inca *chasquis* (messengers) used reflective stones to communicate between hilltop forts.

Transporting mirrors was costly so they were produced in Lima and Quito. Cuzco and Cajamarca then became centres of production. In Cuzco the frames were carved, covered in gold leaf and decorated with tiny pieces of cut mirror. Cajamarca artisans, meanwhile, incorporated painted glass into the frames.

Gourd-carving

Gourd-carving, or *mate burilado*, as it is known, is one of Peru's most popular and traditional handicrafts. It is thought even to predate pottery – engraved gourds found on the coast have been dated to some 4500 years ago. During the Inca empire gourd-carving became a valued art form and workshops were set up and supported by the state. Gourds were used in rituals and ceremonies and to make poporos – containers for the lime used while chewing coca leaves. Today, gourd-carving is centred around the small communities of Cochas Grande and Chico, near Huancayo.

The information on arts and crafts in this guidebook has been adapted from *Arts and Crafts of South America*, by Lucy Davies and Mo Fini, published by Tumi, 1994. Tumi ⓘ *Unit 2, Ashmead Business Centre, Ashmead Road, Keynsham, Bristol BS31 1SX, T0117-986 9216*, the Latin American Craft Centre, specializes in Andean and Mexican products and produces cultural and educational videos for schools. Tumi Music ⓘ *www.tumi.com*, specializes in different rhythms of Latin America.

Music and dance

The music of Peru can be described as the very heartbeat of the country. Peruvians see music as something in which to participate, and not as a spectacle. Just about everyone, it seems, can play a musical instrument or sing. Just as music is the heartbeat of the country, so dance conveys the rich and ancient heritage that typifies much of the national spirit. Peruvians are tireless dancers and dancing is the most popular form of entertainment. Unsuspecting travellers should note that once they make that first wavering step there will be no respite until they collapse from exhaustion.

Each region has its own distinctive music and dance that reflects its particular lifestyle, its mood and its physical surroundings. The music of the sierra, for example, is played in a minor key and tends to be sad and mournful, while the music of the lowlands is more up-tempo and generally happier. Peruvian music divides at a very basic level into that of the highlands (Andina) and that of the coast (Criolla). For a celebration of many Peruvian dance styles, see the film *Soy Andina* and its accompanying website www.soyandina.com. Made by Mitch Teplitsky in 2007 it documents two women, both living in the USA, rediscovering their roots in Peru through its music and traditions.

Highlands

When people talk of Peruvian music they are almost certainly referring to the music of the Quechua- and Aymara-speaking people of the highlands that provides the most distinctive Peruvian sound. The highlands themselves can be very roughly subdivided into some half dozen major musical regions, of which perhaps the most characteristic are Ancash and the north, the Mantaro Valley, Cuzco, Puno and the Altiplano, Ayacucho and Parinacochas.

Musical instruments Before the arrival of the Spanish in Latin America, the only instruments were wind and percussion. Although it is a popular misconception that Andean music is based on the panpipes, guitar and charango, anyone who travels through the Andes will realize that these instruments only represent a small aspect of Andean music. The highland instrumentation varies from region to region, although the harp and violin are ubiquitous. In the Mantaro area the harp is backed by brass and wind instruments, notably the clarinet. In Cuzco it is the charango and quena and on the *altiplano* the sicu panpipes.

The *quena* is a flute, usually made of reed, characterized by not having a mouthpiece to blow through. As with all Andean instruments, there is a family of quenas varying in length from around 15-50 cm. The sicu is the Aymara name for the *zampoña*, or panpipes. It is the most important pre-Hispanic Andean instrument, formed by several reed tubes of different sizes held together by knotted string. Virtually the only instrument of European origin is the Charango. When stringed instruments were first introduced by the Spanish, the indigenous people liked them but wanted something that was their own and so the charango was born. Originally, they were made of clay, condor skeletons and armadillo or tortoise shells.

Highland dances The highlands are immensely rich in terms of music and dance, with over 200 dances recorded. Every village has its fiestas and every fiesta has its communal and religious dances.

Comparsas are organized groups of dancers who perform for spectators dances following a set pattern of movements to a particular musical accompaniment, wearing a specific costume. They have a long tradition, having mostly originated from certain contexts and circumstances and some of them still parody the ex-Spanish colonial masters.

One of the most notable is the comical Auqui Auqui (*auqui* is Aymara for old man). The dance satirizes the solemnity and pomposity of Spanish gentlemen from the colonial period. Because of their dignified dress and manners they could appear old, and a humped back is added to the dancers to emphasize age. These little old men have long pointed noses, flowing beards and carry crooked walking sticks. They dance stooped, regularly pausing to complain and rub aching backs, at times even stumbling and falling. Another dance parody is the Contradanza, performed in the highlands of La Libertad.

Many dances for couples and/or groups are danced spontaneously at fiestas throughout Peru. These include indigenous dances which have originated in a specific region and ballroom dances that reflect the Spanish influence. One of the most popular of the indigenous dances is the **Huayno**, which originated on the *altiplano* but is now danced throughout the country. It involves numerous couples, who whirl around or advance down the street arm-in-arm, in a Pandilla. During fiestas, and especially after a few drinks, this can develop into a kind of uncontrolled frenzy.

Two of the most spectacular dances to be seen are the **Baile de las Tijeras** (scissor dance) from the Ayacucho/Huancavelica area, for men only, and the pounding, stamping **Huaylas** for both sexes. Huaylas competitions are held annually in Lima and should not be missed. Also very popular among indigenous and/or mestizo people are the Marinera, Carnaval, Pasacalle, Chuscada (from Ancash), Huaylas, Santiago and Chonguinada (all from the Mantaro) and Huayllacha (from Parinacochas).

Urban and other styles Owing to the overwhelming migration of peasants into the barrios of Lima, most types of Andean music and dance can be seen in the capital, notably on Sundays at the so-called 'Coliseos', which exist for that purpose. This flood of migration to the cities has also meant that the distinct styles of regional and ethnic groups have become blurred. One example is **Chicha music**, which comes from the *pueblos jóvenes*, and was once the favourite dance music of Peru's urban working class. Chicha is a hybrid of Huayno music and the Colombian Cumbia rhythm – a meeting of the highlands and the tropical coast.

Tecno-cumbia originated in the jungle region with groups such as Rossy War, from Puerto Maldonado, and Euforia, from Iquitos. It is a vibrant dance music which has gained much greater popularity across Peruvian society than *chicha* music ever managed. There are now also many exponents on the coast such as Agua Marina and Armonía 10. Many of the songs comment on political issues and Fujimori used to join Rossy War on stage. Tecno-cumbia has evolved into a more sophisticated form with wider appeal across Peruvian society. Listen to Grupo 5, from Chiclayo, for instance.

Coast

Música Criolla The music from the coast, could not be more different from that of the sierra. Here the roots are Spanish and African. The immensely popular **Valsesito** is a syncopated waltz that would certainly be looked at askance in Vienna and the **Polca** has also undergone an attractive sea change. Reigning over all is the **Marinera**, Peru's national dance, a splendidly rhythmic and graceful courting encounter and a close cousin of Chile's and Bolivia's Cueca and the Argentine Zamba, all of them descended from the Zamacueca. The Marinera has its 'Limeña' and 'Norteña' versions and a more syncopated relative, the Tondero, found in the northern coastal regions, is said to have been influenced by slaves brought from Madagascar. All these dances are accompanied by guitars and frequently the cajón, a resonant wooden box on which the player sits, pounding it with his hands. Some of the great names of 'Música Criolla' are the singer/composers Chabuca Granda and Alicia Maguiña, the female singer Jesús Vásquez and the groups Los Morochucos and Hermanos Zañartu.

Afro-Peruvian Also on the coast is the music of the small but influential black community, the 'Música Negroide' or 'Afro-Peruano', which had virtually died out when it was resuscitated in the 1950s, but has since gone from strength to strength, thanks to Nicomedes and Victoria Santa Cruz who have been largely responsible for popularizing this black music and making it an essential ingredient in contemporary Peruvian popular music. It has all the qualities to be found in black music from the Caribbean – a powerful, charismatic beat, rhythmic and lively dancing, and strong percussion provided by the cajón and the quijada de burro, a donkey's jaw with the teeth loosened. Its greatest star is the Afro-Peruvian diva Susana Baca. Her incredible, passionate voice inspired Talking Head's David Byrne to explore this genre further and release a compilation album in 1995, thus bringing Afro-Peruvian music to the attention of the world. Other notable exponents are the excellent Perú Negro, one of the best music and dance groups in Latin America, and the singer Eva Ayllón. In the footsteps of the dynamic Gotan Project (Argentine musicians who have taken a radical approach to the interpretation of the tango), Novalima, a group of internationally based Peruvian musicians, have produced new arrangements of many classic Afro-Peruvian tracks (see www.novalima.net). Some of the classic dances in the black repertoire are the Festejo, Son del Diablo, Toro Mata, Landó and Alcatraz. In the last named one of the partners dances behind the other with a candle, trying to set light to a piece of paper tucked into the rear of the other partner's waist.

Festivals

Fiestas (festivals) are a fundamental part of life for most Peruvians, taking place the length and breadth of the country and with such frequency that it would be hard to miss one, even during the briefest of stays. This is fortunate, because arriving in any town or village during these frenetic celebrations is a great Peruvian experience.

While Peru's festivals can't rival those of Brazil for fame or colour, the quantity of alcohol consumed and the partying run them pretty close. What this means is that, at some point, you will fall over, through inebriation or exhaustion, or both. After several days of this, you will awake with a hangover the size of the Amazon rainforest and probably have no recollection of what you did with your backpack.

Peruvian festivals also involve widespread balloons-filled-with-water fights, bags of flour and any other missile guaranteed to cause a mess. In the Amazon region various petroleum by-products are favoured ingredients, which can be bad news for smokers. Some travellers complain that they are being picked on, but to someone from the *altiplano*, a 6-ft tall, blond-haired gringo makes an easier target. So, don't wear your best clothes, arm yourself with plenty of water bombs, get into the spirit and have some fun!

With over 3000 fiestas, there are too many to mention them all. The main national ones are described on page 18, and details of local fiestas are given under the listings for each town.

Meaning of fiestas

It is only when they don their extravagant costumes and masks and drink, eat and dance to excess that the indigenous Peruvians show their true character. The rest of the time they hide behind a metaphorical mask of stony indifference as a form of protection against the alien reality in which they are forced to live. When they consume alcohol and coca and start dancing, the pride in their origins resurfaces. This allows them to forget the reality of poverty, unemployment and oppression and reaffirms their will to live as well as their unity with the world around them.

The object of the fiesta is a practical one, such as the success of the coming harvest or the fertility of animals. Thus the constant eating, drinking and dancing serves the purpose of giving thanks for the sun and rain that makes things grow and for the fertility of the soil and livestock, gifts from Pachamama, or Mother Earth, the most sacred of all gods. So, when you see the Aymara spill a little *chicha* (maize beer) every time they refill, it's not because they're sloppy but because they're offering a *ch'alla* (sacrifice) to Pachamama.

The participants in the dances that are the central part of the fiesta are dressed in garish, outlandish costumes and elaborate masks, each one depicting a character from popular myth. Some of these originate in the colonial period, others survive from the Inca Empire or even further back. Often the costumes caricature the Spanish. In this way, the indigenous people mock those who erased their heritage.

Literature

Quechua

The fact that the Incas had no written texts in the conventional European sense and that the Spaniards were keen to suppress their conquest's culture means that there is little evidence today of what poetry and theatre was performed in pre-conquest times. It is known that the Incas had two types of poet, the *amautas*, historians, poets and teachers who composed works that celebrated the ruling class' gods, heroes and events, and *haravecs*, who expressed popular sentiments. There is strong evidence also that drama was important in Inca society.

Written Quechua even today is far less common than works in the oral tradition. Although Spanish culture has had some influence on Quechua, the native stories, lyrics and fables retain their own identity. Not until the 19th century did Peruvian writers begin seriously to incorporate indigenous ideas into their art, but their audience was limited. Nevertheless, the influence of Quechua on Peruvian literature in Spanish continues to grow.

Colonial period

In 16th-century Lima, headquarters of the Viceroyalty of Peru, the Spanish officials concentrated their efforts on the religious education of the new territories and literary output was limited to mainly histories and letters.

Chroniclers such as Pedro Cieza de León (*Crónica del Perú*, published from 1553) and Agustín de Zárate (*Historia del descubrimiento y conquista del Perú*, 1555) were written from the point of view that Spanish domination was right. Their most renowned successors, though, took a different stance. Inca Garcilaso de la Vega was a mestizo, whose *Comentarios reales que tratan del origen de los Incas* (1609) were at pains to justify the achievements, religion and culture of the Inca Empire. He also commented on Spanish society in the colony. A later work, *Historia General del Perú* (1617) went further in condemning Viceroy Toledo's suppression of Inca culture. Through his work, written in Spain, many aspects of Inca society, plus poems and prayers have survived.

Writing at about the same time as Inca Garcilaso was Felipe Guaman Poma de Ayala, whose *El primer nueva corónica y buen gobierno* (1613-1615) is possibly one of the most reproduced of Latin American texts (eg on T-shirts, CDs, posters and carrier bags). Guaman Poma was a minor provincial Inca chief from Ayacucho province whose writings and illustrations, addressed to King Felipe III of Spain, offer a view of a stable pre-conquest Andean society (not uniquely Inca), in contrast with the unsympathetic colonial society that usurped it.

In the years up to Independence, the growth of an intellectual elite in Lima spawned more poetry than anything else. As criollo discontent grew, satire increased both in poetry and in the sketches that accompanied dramas imported from Spain. The poet Mariano Melgar (1791-1815) wrote in a variety of styles, including the yaraví, the love-song derived from the pre-Columbian *harawi* (from *haravek*). Melgar died in an uprising against the Spanish but played an important part in the Peruvian struggle from freedom from the colonial imagination.

After Independence

After Independence, Peruvian writers imitated Spanish *costumbrismo*, sketches of characters and lifestyles from the new Republic. The first author to transcend this fashion was Ricardo Palma (1833-1919), whose inspiration, the *tradición*, fused *costumbrismo* and Peru's rich oral traditions. Palma's hugely popular *Tradiciones peruanas* is a collection of pieces which celebrate the people, history and customs of Peru through sayings, small incidents in mainly colonial history and gentle irony.

Much soul searching was to follow Peru's defeat in the War of the Pacific. Manuel González Prada (1844-1918), for instance, wrote essays fiercely critical of the state of the nation: *Páginas libres* (1894), *Horas de lucha* (1908). José Carlos Mariátegui, the foremost Peruvian political thinker of the early 20th century, said that González Prada represented the first lucid instant of Peruvian consciousness. He also wrote poetry, some Romantic, some, like his *Baladas peruanas*, an evocation of indigenous and colonial history, very pro-Indian, very anti-White.

20th-century prose

Mariátegui himself (1895-1930), after a visit to Europe, considered the question of Peruvian identity. His opinion was that it could only be seen in a global context and that the answer lay in Marxism. With this perspective he wrote about politics, economics, literature and the indigenous question (see *Siete ensayos de interpretación de la realidad peruana*, 1928).

Other writers had continued this theme. For instance Clorinda Matto de Turner (1854-1909) intended to express in *Aves sin nido* (1889) her "tender love for the indigenous people" and hoped to improve their lot. Regardless of the debate over whether the novel achieves these aims, she was the forerunner by several years of the 'indigenist' genre in Peru and the most popular of those who took up González Prada's cause.

Other prose writers continued in this vein at the beginning of the 20th century, but it was Ciro Alegría (1909-1967) who gave major, fictional impetus to the racial question. Like Mariátegui, Alegría was politically committed, but to the APRA party, rather than Marxism. Of his first three novels, *La serpiente de oro* (1935), *Los perros hambrientos* (1938) and *El mundo es ancho y ajeno* (1941), the last named is his most famous.

Contemporary with Alegría was José María Arguedas (1911-1969), whose novels, stories and politics were also deeply rooted in the ethnic question. Arguedas, though not Indian, had a largely Quechua upbringing and tried to reconcile this with the hispanic world in which he worked. This inner conflict was one of the main causes of his suicide. His books include *Agua* (short stories, 1935), *Yawar fiesta* (1941), *Los ríos profundos* (1958) and *Todas las sangres* (1964). They portray different aspects of the confrontation of indigenous society with the changing outside world that impinges on it.

In the 1950s and 1960s, there was a move away from the predominantly rural and indigenist to an urban setting. At the forefront were, among others, Mario Vargas Llosa, Julio Ramón Ribeyro, Enrique Congrains Martín, Oswaldo Reynoso, Luis Loayza, Sebastián Salazar Bondy and Carlos E Zavaleta. Taking their cue from a phrase used by both poet César Mora and Salazar Bondy (in an essay of 1964), "Lima, la horrible", they explored all aspects of the city, including the influx of people from the sierra. These writers incorporated new narrative techniques in the urban novel, which presented a world where popular culture and speech were rich sources of literary material, despite the difficulty in transcribing them.

Many writers, such as Vargas Llosa (see box, page 558), broadened their horizons beyond the capital. His novels after *La ciudad y los perros* encompassed many different parts of the country. An additional factor was that several writers spent many years abroad, Vargas Llosa himself, for instance, and Ribeyro (1929-1994). The latter's short stories, though mostly set in Lima, embrace universal themes of delusion and frustration. The title story of *Los gallinazos sin pluma* (1955), a tale of squalor and greed amid the city's rubbish tips, has become a classic, even though it does not contain the irony, pathos and humour of many of his other stories or novels.

Other writers of this period include Manuel Scorza (1928-1983), who wrote a series of five novels under the general title of *La guerra silenciosa* (including *Redoble por Rancas*, *El jinete insomne*, *La tumba del relámpago*) which follow the tradition of the indigenist struggle, and also emphasize the need to defend indigenous society with growing militancy if necessary.

Alfredo Bryce Echenique (born 1939) has enjoyed much popularity following the success of *Un mundo para Julius* (1970), a brilliant satire on the upper and middle classes of Lima. His other novels include *Tantas veces Pedro* (1977), *La última mudanza de Felipe Carrillo* (1988), *No me esperen en abril* (1995), *Dos señoras conversan* (1990), *La amigdalitis de Tarzan* (2000) and *El huerto de mi amada*, which won the Premio Planeta (Barcelona) in 2002. Other contemporary writers of note are: Rodolfo Hinostroza (born 1941), novelist, playwright and poet, whose books include *Cuentos de Contranatura* (1972) and *Extremo occidente* (2002); Mario Bellatín (born 1960 in Mexico but educated in Peru), among whose works are the excellent short novels *Salón de belleza* (1994) and *Damas chinas* (1995); Jaime Bayly (born 1965), who is also a journalist and TV presenter. His novels include *Fue ayer y no me acuerdo*, *Los últimos días de la prensa*, *No se lo digas a nadie*, *La noche es virgen* and *Y de repente, un ángel*.

Recent trends for novelists include confronting the violence and the after-effects of the Sendero Lumnioso/MRTA and Fujimori/Montesinos period, with powerful, neorealist novels and stories. Among the best examples are Alonso Cueto (born 1954), *Grandes miradas* (2003), *La hora azul* (2005); and Santiago Roncagliolo (born 1975), see *Abril rojo* (2006). His newest book is *Tan cerca de la vida*, published in 2010. Another new voice is Daniel Alarcón, born in Lima in 1977 but brought up in Birmingham, Alabama, whose first collection of stories, *War by Candlelight* (*Guerra en la penumbra* – 2005) is set almost entirely in Lima but is written in English. His first novel, *Lost City Radio* (2007) tells the story of a radio presenter, whose most popular show unites people separated by civil war, and her relationship with a young boy who comes in person to deliver such a message. Another strand is writing about the reality of immigrant communities in Lima, such as Augusto Higa Oshiro's novel, *Final del porvenir* (1992), and Siu Kam Wen's stories in *El tramo final* (2009).

20th-century poetry

At the end of the 19th century, the term Modernism was introduced in Latin America by the Nicaraguan Rubén Darío, not to define a precise school of poetry, but to indicate a break with both Romanticism and Realism. In Peru one major exponent was José Santos Chocano (1875-1934), who labelled his poetry 'mundonovismo' (New Worldism), claiming for himself the role of Poet of South America. He won international fame (see, for example, *Alma América*, 1906), but his star soon waned.

A much less assuming character was José María Eguren (1874-1942) who, feeling alienated from the society around him, sought spiritual reality in the natural world (*Simbólicas*, 1911; *La canción de las figuras*, 1916; *Poesías*, 1929). It has been said that with Eguren the flourishing of Peruvian 20th century poetry began.

Without doubt, the most important poet in Peru, if not Latin America, in the first half of the 20th century, was César Vallejo. Born in 1892 in Santiago de Chuco (Libertad), Vallejo left Peru in 1923 after being framed and briefly jailed in Trujillo for a political crime. In 1928 he was a founder of the Peruvian Socialist Party, then he joined the Communist Party in 1931 in Madrid. From 1936 to his death in Paris in 1938 he opposed the fascist takeover in Spain. His first volume was *Los heraldos negros* in which the dominating theme of all his work, a sense of confusion and inadequacy in the face of the unpredictability of life, first surfaces. *Trilce* (1922), his second work, is unlike anything before it in the Spanish language. The poems contain (among other things) made-up words, distortions of syntax, their own internal logic and rhythm, graphic devices and innovative uses of sounds, clichés and alliterations. *Poemas humanos* and *España, aparta de mí este cáliz* (written as a result of Vallejo's experiences in the Spanish Civil War) were both published posthumously, in 1939.

In the 1960s writers began to reflect the broadening horizons of that increasingly liberal decade, politically and socially, which followed the Cuban Revolution. One poet who embraced the revolutionary fervour was Javier Heraud (born Miraflores 1942). His early volumes, *El río* (1960) and *El viaje* (1961) are apparently simple in conception and expression, but display a transition from embarking on the adventure of life (the river) to autumnal imagery of solitude. In 1961 he went to the

BACKGROUND
Mario Vargas Llosa

The best known of Peru's writers, Mario Vargas Llosa was born in 1936 in Arequipa and educated in Cochabamba (Bolivia), from where his family moved to Piura. After graduating from Lima's Universidad de San Marcos, he won a scholarship to Paris in 1958 and then, from 1959 to 1974, lived first in Paris then in London in voluntary exile. He was one of the leading figures in the so-called 'Boom' in Latin American writers in the 1960s and is regarded as an author of the highest international standing. In 2010, while teaching at Princeton University in the US, he was awarded the Nobel Prize for Literature, "for his cartography of structures of power and his trenchant images of the individual's resistance, revolt and defeat". At the time, he said "This Nobel goes to Latin American literature. It is a recognition of everything that surrounds me." Much has been written about his personal life, and his political opinions have been well documented, but it is for his novels that Vargas Llosa is best known.

The first three – *La ciudad y los perros* (1963), *La casa verde* (1966) and *Conversación en la Catedral* (1969) – with their techniques of flashback, multiple narrators and different interwoven stories, are an adventure for the reader. Meanwhile, the humorous books, like *Pantaleón y las visitadoras* (1973) and *La tía Julia y el escribidor* (1977) cannot be called lightweight. *La guerra del fin del mundo* (1981) marked a change to a more direct style and an intensification of Vargas Llosa's exploration of the role of fiction as a human necessity, extending also to political ideologies. *La fiesta del chivo* (2000) is another fictionalized account of historical events, this time the assassination of President Trujillo of the Dominican Republic in 1961 and the intrigue and fear surrounding his period in office. It is a gripping story, widely regarded as one of his best. More recently he has written *Travesuras de la niña mala* (2006; The Bad Girl), which the author called his first 'love story', and *El sueño del celta* (2010; The Dream of the Celt) about the Irishman Roger Casement.

Vargas Llosa has always maintained that in Peruvian society the writer is a privileged person who should be able to mix politics and literature as a normal part of life. This drive for authenticity led to his excursion into national politics. He stood as a presidential candidate in 1990, losing to Alberto Fujimori. He has since taken Spanish citizenship (2007) and has homes in Lima, Paris, Madrid and London.

In 2014 the Casa Museo Vargas Llosa opened at his birthblace in Arequipa (see page 266). Here, in innovative holographic displays, the writer himself tells about the highlights of his life and career.

USSR, Asia, Paris and Madrid, then in 1962 to Cuba to study cinema. He returned to Peru in 1963 and joined the Ejército de Liberación Nacional. On 15 May 1963 he was shot by government forces near Puerto Maldonado. Heraud's friend César Calvo, now living in Cuba, is a poet and essayist.

Other major poets born in the early 20th century are Emilio Adolfo Westphalen (1911) and Jorge Eduardo Eielson (see his book *Celebración*). Others who began to publish in the 1960s were Luis Hernández (1941-1977), Antonio Cisneros (born 1942) and Marco Martos (born 1942).

In the 1970s, during the social changes propelled by the Velasco regime (1968-1975), new voices arose, many from outside Lima, eg the Hora Zero group (1970-1973 – Enrique Verástegui, Jorge Pimentel, Juan Ramírez Ruiz), whose energetic poetry employed slang and obscenities and other means to challenge preconceptions. Other poets of the 1970s and after include José Watanabe (1946-2007), a film-maker as well as poet, with *Album de familia* (1971), *Historia natural* (1994) and the anthology *Elogio del Refrenamiento* (2004). Renato Cisneros (born 1976) is a poet (*Ritual de los prójimos*, 1998; *Maquina fantasma*, 2002), novelist (*Nunca confíes en mí*, 2010) and blogger (*Busco novia*, see www.renatocisneros.net).

Women poets and novelists In addition to Clorinda Matto de Turner (see above), modern writers worth checking out are: Blanca Varela (1926-2009), who was married to sculptor Fernando de Szyszlo (see below), published volumes of poetry from 1959 (*Ese puerto existe*) to her anthology *Como Dios en la nada* (covering 1949-1998). Her work was championed by the Mexican Octavio Paz, among others. Carmen Ollé (born 1947) introduced a style of writing that is regarded as feminist and confessional. Her best known poetry collection is *Noches de adrenalina* (1981), while her prose includes *Las dos caras del deseo* (1994) and *Una muchacha bajo su paraguas* (2002). Giovanna Pollarolo is a poet, short story writer and screenwriter (born 1952) whose collections include *Huerto de olivos*, 1982, *Entre mujeres solas*, 1996, *La ceremonia de adios*, 1997 and *Atado de nervios*, 1999. Rocio Silva Santiesteban (born 1967) has published short stories as well as the poetry collections *Asuntos circunstanciales* (1984), *Este oficio no me gusta* (1987) and *Mariposa negra* (1996). Laura Riesco's (1940-2008) novel *Ximena de dos caminos* (1994) is an episodic tale of a young girl growing up in the Sierra, experiencing the clash between the oral culture of the local people who look after her, the mining company her father works for, city people who visit and the life of the coast where she goes on holiday. Younger poets of note are: Ericka Ghersi (born 1972), *Zenobia y el anciano* (1994), *Contra la ausencia* (2002), Rosella di Paolo (born 1960), *Piel alzada* (1993), *Tablillas de San Lázaro* (2001) among other collections, and Marita Troiano, whose works include *Mortal in puribus* (1996) and *Secreto a veces* (2003). Novelists include Alina Gadea (born 1966), with *Otra vida para Doris Kaplan* (2009), and Giselle Klatic (born 1976), *Alguien que me quiera* (2010).

Fine art and sculpture

The Catholic church was the main patron of the arts during the colonial period. The churches and monasteries that sprang up in the newly conquered territories created a demand for paintings and sculptures, met initially by imports from Europe of both works of art and of skilled craftsmen, and later by home-grown products.

Colonial period

An essential requirement for the inauguration of any new church was an image for the altar and many churches in Lima preserve fine examples of sculptures imported from Seville during the 16th and 17th centuries. Not surprisingly, among the earliest of these are figures of the crucified Christ, such as those in the cathedral and the church of La Merced by Juan Martínez Montañés, one of the foremost Spanish sculptors of the day, and that in San Pedro, by his pupil Juan de Mesa of 1625. Statues of the Virgin and Child were also imported to Lima from an early date, and examples from the mid-16th century survive in the cathedral and in Santo Domingo by Roque de Balduque, also from Seville although Flemish by birth.

Sculptures were expensive and difficult to import, and as part of their policy of relative frugality the Franciscan monks tended to favour paintings. In Lima, the museum of San Francisco now houses an excellent collection of paintings imported from Europe, including a powerful series of saints by Zubarán, as well as other works from his studio, a series of paintings of the life of Christ from Ruben's workshop and works from the circles of Ribera and Murillo.

The Jesuits commissioned the Sevillian artist Juan de Valdés Leal to paint a series of the life of St Ignatius Loyola (1660s) which still hangs in San Pedro. The cathedral museum has a curious series from the Bassano workshop of Venice representing the labours of the monks and dating from the early 17th century. Another interesting artistic import from Europe that can still be seen in San Pedro (see Lima Churches) are the gloriously colourful painted tile decorations (*azulejos*) on the walls of Dominican monastery, produced to order by Sevillian workshops in 1586 and 1604.

Painters and sculptors soon made their way to Peru in search of lucrative commissions including several Italians who arrived during the later 16th century. The Jesuit Bernardo Bitti (1548-1610), for example, trained in Rome before working in Lima, Cuzco, Juli and Arequipa, where examples of his elegantly Mannerist paintings are preserved in the Jesuit church of the Compañia.

Another Italian, Mateo Pérez de Alesio worked in the Sistine Chapel in Rome before settling in Peru. In Lima the Sevillian sculptor Pedro de Noguera (1592-1655) won the contract for the choirstalls of the cathedral in 1623 and, together with other Spanish craftsmen, produced a set of cedar stalls decorated with vigorous figures of saints and Biblical characters, an outstanding work unmatched elsewhere in the Viceroyalty.

Native artists

European imports, however, could not keep up with demand and local workshops of Creole, mestizo and indigenous craftsmen flourished from the latter part of the 16th century. As the Viceregal capital and the point of arrival into Peru, the art of Lima was always strongly influenced by European, especially Spanish models, but the old Inca capital of Cuzco became the centre of a regional school of painting that developed its own characteristics.

A series of paintings of the 1660s, now hanging in the Museo de Arte Religioso in Lima (see page 37), commemorate the colourful Corpus Christi procession of statues of the local patron saints through the streets of Cuzco. These paintings document the appearance of the city and local populace, including Spanish and Inca nobility, priests and laity, rich and poor, Spaniard, Indian, African and mestizo. Many of the statues represented in this series are still venerated in the local parish churches. They are periodically painted and dressed in new robes, but underneath are the original sculptures, executed by native craftsmen. Some are of carved wood while others use the pre-conquest technique of maguey cactus covered in sized cloth.

A remarkable example of an indigenous Andean who acquired European skills was Felipe Guaman Poma de Ayala whose 1000-page letter to the King of Spain celebrating the Andean past and condemning the colonial present contained a visual history of colonial and precolonial life in the Andes.

One of the most successful native painters was Diego Quispe Tito (1611-1681) who claimed descent from the Inca nobility and whose large canvases, often based on Flemish engravings, demonstrate the wide range of European sources that were available to Andean artists in the 17th century. But the Cuzco School is best known for the anonymous devotional works where the painted contours of the figures are overlaid with flat patterns in gold, creating highly decorative images with an underlying tension between the two- and three-dimensional aspects of the work. The taste for richly decorated surfaces can also be seen in the 17th- and 18th-century frescoed interiors of many Andean churches, as in Chinchero, Andahuaylillas and Huaro, and in the ornate carving on altarpieces and pulpits throughout Peru.

Andean content creeps into colonial religious art in a number of ways, most simply by the inclusion of elements of indigenous flora and fauna, or, as in the case of the Corpus Christi paintings, by the use of a setting, with recognizable buildings and individuals.

Changes to traditional Christian iconography include the representation of one of the Magi as an Inca, as in the painting of the Adoration of the Magi in San Pedro in Juli. Another example is that to commemorate his miraculous intervention in the conquest of Cuzco in 1534, Santiago is often depicted triumphing over indigenous people instead of the more familiar Moors. Among the most remarkable 'inventions' of colonial art are the fantastically over-dressed archangels carrying muskets which were so popular in the 18th century. There is no direct European source for these archangels, but in the Andes they seem to have served as a painted guard of honour to the image of Christ or the Virgin on the high altar.

Independence and after

Political independence from Spain in 1824 had little immediate impact on the arts of Peru except to create a demand for portraits of the new national and continental heroes such as Simón Bolívar and San Martín, many of the best of them produced by the mulatto artist José Gil de Castro (died Lima 1841). Later in the century another mulatto, Pancho Fierro (1810-1879) mocked the rigidity and pretentiousness of Lima society in lively satirical watercolours, while Francisco Laso (1823-1860), an active campaigner for political reform, made the Andean people into respectable subjects for oil paintings.

It was not until the latter part of the 19th century that events from colonial history became popular. The Museo de Arte in Lima (see Lima page 37) has examples of grandiose paintings by Ignacio Merino (1817-1876) glorifying Columbus, as well as the gigantic romanticized 'Funeral of Atahualpa' by Luis Montero (1826-1869). A curious late flowering of this celebration of colonial history is the chapel commemorating Francisco Pizarro in Lima cathedral which was redecorated in 1928 with garish mosaic pictures of the conqueror's exploits.

Impressionism arrived late and had a limited impact in Peru. Teofilo Castillo (1857-1922), instead of using the technique to capture contemporary reality, created frothy visions of an idealized colonial past. Typical of his work is the large 'Funeral Procession of Santa Rosa' of 1918, with everything bathed in clouds of incense and rose petals, which hangs in the Museo de Arte, in Lima. Daniel Hernández (1856-1932), founder of Peru's first Art School, used a similar style for his portraits of Lima notables past and present.

20th century to today

During the first half of the 20th century, Peruvian art was dominated by figurative styles and local subject matter. Political theories of the 1920s recognized the importance of Andean indigenous culture to Peruvian identity and created a climate which encouraged a figurative indigenista school of painting, derived in part from the socialist realism of the Mexican muralists. The movement flourished after the founding of the Escuela de Bellas Artes in 1920. José Sabogal (1888-1956) is the best known exponent of the group which also included Mario Urteaga (1875-1957), Jorge Vinatea Reinoso (1900-1931), Enrique Camino Brent (1909-1960), Camilo Blas (1903-1984) and Alejandro González (1900-1984). Their work can be seen in the Museo de Arte and the Museo Banco Central de Reserva in Lima.

The Mexican muralist tradition persisted into the 1960s with Manuel Ugarte Eléspuru (1911) and Teodoro Núñez Ureta (1914), both of whom undertook large-scale commissions in public buildings in Lima. Examples of public sculpture in the indigenist mode can be seen in plazas and parks throughout Peru, but it was in photography that indigenism found its most powerful expression. From the beginning of the century photographic studios flourished even in smaller towns. Martín Chambi (1891-1973) is the best known of the early 20th-century Peruvian photographers but there were many others, including Miguel Chani (1860-1951) who maintained the grandly named Fotografía Universal studios in Cuzco, Puno and Arequipa.

From the middle of the century artists have experimented with a variety of predominantly abstract styles and the best known contemporary Peruvian painter, Fernando de Szyszlo (1925) has created a visual language of his own, borrowing from Abstract Expressionism on the one hand and from pre-Columbian iconography on the other. His strong images, which suggest rather than represent mythical beings and cosmic forces, have influenced a whole generation of younger Peruvian artists. Look for his monument, Intihuatana 2000, near the sea in Miraflores.

Viringo

If you go to a Peruvian museum at a coastal archaeological site, you may see an elegant dog with a long, thin nose and arched neck near the entrance. It might be a bit shy, and, if the weather is cold, it may be wearing a little woollen jacket. This is because the dog has no hair.

The Peruvian hairless, or viringo, is a rare breed today, but in Inca times was a companion animal whose main job was to warm his master s bed. The Chavín, Moche and Chimú cultures represented it on their ceramics, but its origins are unknown. The most likely theory is that it accompanied the first migrants to the Amercian continent from Asia. In its most common, hairless form, it has no fleas and no smell.

Breeders note that it needs protection against the sun and the cold, but there is also a coated variety (called 'powder puff' in the dog world).

In recognition of the importance of this dog in its history, the Peruvian government decreed in Law number 27537 that every site museum on the coast must have at least one viringo on the premises.

In 2006 archaeologists announced the discovery of over 40 mummified dogs at tombs of the Chiribaya people in the Ilo valley, dating from AD 900-1350. They weren't viringos, but a distinct breed, christened 'Chiribaya shepherds' because, it is supposed, they herded llamas.

Other leading figures whose work can be seen in public and commercial galleries in Lima include Venancio Shinki, Tilsa Tsuchiya, José Tola, Ricardo Weisse, Ramiro Llona and Leoncio Villanueva. Carlos Revilla, whose wife is his muse and principal subject of his painting, is clearly influenced by Hieronymous Bosch, while Bill Caro is an important exponent of hyperrealism. Víctor Delfín, a painter and sculptor (with beautiful work in iron) can be visited at his house in Barranco (Domeyko 366). His piece, The Kiss (El beso), is in the Parque del Amor in Lima. Pedro Azabache (from Trujillo) is a disciple of José Sabogal; his work is much broader in scope than the indigenism of his mentor. There are many other new artists whose work could be mentioned (Luz Letts, Eduardo Tokeshi, Carlos Enrique Polanco, Bruno Zepilli, Christian Bendayan – try to contact him in Iquitos, Flavia Gandolfo, Claudia Coca) and there are plenty of galleries in Lima with representative exhibitions. There is a museum of contemporary art in Barranco, Lima. One striking modern piece outside Lima is the mosaic mural at the Ciudad Universitaria UNT in Trujillo, which, at almost 1 km long, is the longest mosaic mural in the world.

Land & environment

Geography

Peru is the third largest South American country, the size of France, Spain and the United Kingdom combined, and presents formidable difficulties to human habitation. Virtually all of the 2250 km of its Pacific coast is desert. From the narrow coastal shelf the Andes rise steeply to a high plateau dominated by massive ranges of snow-capped peaks and gouged with deep canyons. The heavily forested and deeply ravined Andean slopes are more gradual to the east. Further east, towards Brazil and Colombia, begin the vast jungles of the Amazon Basin.

Geology

The geological structure of Peru is dominated by the Nazca Plate beneath the Pacific Ocean, which stretches from Colombia in the north southwards to mid Chile. Along the coastline, this Plate meets and dives below the mass of the South American Plate that has been moving westwards for much of the Earth's geological history. Prior to the middle of the Tertiary Period, say 40 million years ago, marine sediments suggest that the Amazon Basin drained west to the Pacific, but from that time to the present, tectonic forces have created the Andes range the length of the continent, forming the highest peaks outside the Himalayas. The process continues today as shown by the earthquakes and active volcanoes and, in spite of erosion, the mountains still grow higher.

Coast

The coastal region, a narrow ribbon of desert 2250 km long, takes up 11% of the country and holds 44% of the population. It is the economic heart of Peru, consuming most of the imports and supplying half of the exports. When irrigated, the river valleys are extremely fertile, creating oases that grow cotton throughout the country, sugar-cane, rice and asparagus in the north, and grapes, fruit and olives in the south. At the same time, the coastal current teems with fish, and Peru has on occasion had the largest catch in the world.

Not far beyond the border with Ecuador in the north, there are mangrove swamps and tropical rainforest, but southwards this quickly changes to drier and eventually desert conditions. South of Piura is the desert of Sechura, followed by the dry barren land or shifting sands to Chimbote. However, several rivers draining the high mountains to the east more or less reach the sea and water the highly productive 'oases' of Piura, Trujillo, Cajamarca and Chimbote.

South of Chimbote, the Andes reach the sea, and apart from a thin strip of coastland north of Lima, the coastal mountains continue to the Chilean border at Arica. This area receives less rain than the Sahara, but because of the high Andes inland, over 50 Peruvian rivers reach the sea, or would do naturally for at least part of the year. As in the north, there are oases in the south, but mostly inland at the foot of the mountains where the river flow is greatest and high sunshine levels ensure good crop production.

The climate of this region depends almost entirely on the ocean currents along the Pacific coast. Two bodies of water drift northwards, the one closest to the shore, known as the Humboldt Current, is the colder, following the deep sea trench along the edge of the Pacific Plate. The basic wind systems here are the South-East Trades crossing the continent from the Atlantic, but the strong tropical sun over the land draws air into Peru from the Pacific. Being cool, this air does no more than condense into mist (known as the *garúa*) over the coastal mountains. This is sufficient to provide moisture for some unusual flora but virtually never produces rain, hence the desert conditions. The mixing of the two cold ocean currents, and the cloud cover that protects the water from the strongest sunlight, creates the unique conditions favourable to fish, notably sardines and anchovy, giving Peru an enormous economic resource. In turn, the fish support vast numbers of seabirds whose deposits of guano have been another very successful export for the country. This is the normal situation; every few years, however, it is disrupted by the phenomenon known as 'El Niño'.

Highlands

The highlands, or la sierra, extend inland from the coastal strip some 250 km in the north, increasing to 400 km in the south. The average altitude is about 3000 m and 50% of Peruvians live there. Essentially it is a plateau dissected by dramatic canyons and dominated by some of the most spectacular mountain ranges in the world.

Mountains

The tallest peaks are in the Cordillera Blanca (Huascarán; 6768 m) and the neighbouring Cordillera Huayhuash (Yerupajá; 6634 m). Huascarán is often quoted as the second highest point in South America after Aconcagua, but this is not so; there are some five other peaks on or near the Argentina-Chile border over 6770 m. The snowline here, at nine degrees south, is between 4500 m and 5000 m, much lower than further south. For example, at 16 degrees south, permanent snow starts at 6000 m on Coropuna (6425 m). Peru has more tropical glaciers than any other country in South America, but in recent years scientists have recorded rapid shrinkage of snow and glaciers from Peruvian peaks. This loss is blamed on global warming.

The reasons for this anomaly can be traced again to the Humboldt current. The Cordillera Blanca is less than 100 km from the coast, and the cool air drawn in depresses temperatures at high altitudes. Precipitation comes also from the east and falls as snow. Constant high winds and temperatures well below freezing at night create an unusual microclimate and with it spectacular mountain scenery, making it a mecca for snow and ice mountaineers. Dangers are heightened by the quite frequent earthquakes causing avalanches and landslides which have brought heavy loss of life to the valleys of the region. In 1970, 20,000 people lost their lives when Yungay, immediately west of Huascarán, was overwhelmed.

Canyons

Equally dramatic are the deep canyons taking water from the high mountains to the Pacific. The Colca Canyon, about 100 km north of Arequipa, has been measured at 3200 m from the lower rim to the river, more than twice as deep as the Grand Canyon. At one point it is overlooked by the 5227 m Señal Yajirhua peak, a stupendous 4150 m above the water level. Deeper even than Colca is the Cotahuasi Canyon, also in Arequipa Department, whose deepest point is 3354 m. Other canyons have been found in this remote area yet to be measured and documented.

In spite of these ups and downs, which cause great communications difficulties, the presence of water and a more temperate climate on the plateau has attracted people throughout the ages. Present day important population centres in the Highlands include Cajamarca in the north, Huancayo in central Peru and Cuzco in the south, all at around 3000 m. Above this, at around 4000 m, is the 'high steppe' or puna, with constant winds and wide day/night temperature fluctuations. Nevertheless, fruit and potatoes (which originally came from the puna of Peru and Bolivia) are grown at this altitude and the meagre grasslands are home to the ubiquitous llama.

Volcanoes

Although hot springs and evidence of ancient volcanic activity can be seen almost anywhere in Peru, the southern part of the sierra is the only area where there are active volcanoes. These represent the northernmost of a line of volcanoes which stretch 1500 km south along the Chile-Bolivia border to Argentina. Sabancaya (5977 m), just south of the Colca canyon, is currently active, often with a dark plume downwind from the summit. Beyond the Colca canyon is the Valle de los Volcanes, with 80 cinder cones rising 50-250 m above a desolate floor of lava and ash. There are other dormant or recently active volcanoes near the western side of Lake Titicaca – for example Ubinas – but the most notable is El Misti (5822 m), which overlooks Arequipa. It is perfectly shaped, indicating its status as active in the recent geologic past. Some experts believe it is one of the most potentially dangerous volcanoes in South America. Certainly a major eruption would be a catastrophe for the nearby city.

Lake Titicaca

The southeastern border with Bolivia passes through Titicaca, with about half of the lake in each country. It is the largest lake in South America (ignoring Lake Maracaibo in Venezuela, which is linked to the sea) and at 3812 m, the highest navigable body of water in the world. It covers about 8300 sq km, running 190 km northwest to southeast, and is 80 km across. It lies in a 60,000 sq km basin between the coastal and eastern Andes that spread out southwards to their widest point at latitude 18 degrees south.

The average depth is over 100 m, with the deepest point recorded at 281 m. Twenty-five rivers, most from Peru, flow into the lake and a small outlet leaves the lake at Desaguadero on the Bolivia-Peru border. This takes no more than 5% of the inflow, the rest is lost through evaporation and hence the waters of the lake are slightly brackish, producing the totora reeds used to make the mats and balsa boats for which the lake dwellers are famed.

The lake is the remnant of a vast area of water formed in the Ice Age known as Lake Ballivián. This extended at least 600 km to the south into Bolivia and included what is now Lake Poopó and the Salar de Uyuni. Now the lake level fluctuates seasonally, normally rising from December to March and receding for the rest of the year but extremes of 5 m between high and low levels have been recorded. This can cause problems and high levels in the late 1980s disrupted transport links near the shoreline. The night temperature can fall as low as -25°C but high daytime temperatures ensure that the surface average is about 14°C.

Eastern Andes and Amazon Basin

Almost half of Peru is on the eastern side of the Andes and about 90% of the country's drainage is into the Amazon system. It is an area of heavy rainfall with cloudforest above 3500 m and tropical rainforest lower down. There is little savanna, or natural grasslands, characteristic of other parts of the Amazon Basin.

There is some dispute on the Amazon's source. Officially, the mighty river begins as the Marañón, whose longest tributary rises just east of the Cordillera Huayhuash. However, the longest journey for the proverbial raindrop, some 6400 km, probably starts in southern Peru, where the headwaters of the Apurímac (Ucayali) flow from the snows on the northern side of the Nevado Mismi, near Cailloma.

With much more rainfall on the eastern side of the Andes, rivers are turbulent and erosion dramatic. Although vertical drops are not as great – there is a whole continent to cross to the Atlantic – valleys are deep, ridges narrow and jagged and there is forest below 3000 m. At 1500 m the Amazon jungle begins and water is the only means of surface transport available, apart from three roads which reach Borja (on the Marañón), Yurimaguas (on the Huallaga) and Pucallpa (on the Ucayali), all at about 300 m above the Atlantic which is still 4000 km or so downstream. The vastness of the Amazon lowlands becomes apparent and it is here that Peru bulges 650 km northeast past Iquitos to the point where it meets Colombia and Brazil at Leticia. Oil and gas have recently been found in the Amazon, and new finds are made every year, which means that new pipelines and roads will eventually link more places to the Pacific coast.

Climate

Coast

On the coast summertime is from December to April, when temperatures range from 25° to 35°C and it is hot and dry. Wintertime is May to November, when the temperature drops a bit and it is cloudy.

The coastal climate is determined by the cold sea-water adjoining deserts. Prevailing inshore winds pick up so little moisture over the cold Humboldt current, which flows from Antarctica, that only from May to November does it condense. The resultant blanket of sea-mist (called *garúa*) extends from the south to about 200 km north of Lima. It is thickest to the south as far as Chincha and to the north as far as Huarmey, beyond which it thins and the sun can be expected to break through.

Sierra
From April-October is the dry season. It is hot and dry during the day, around 20°-25°C, and cold and dry at night, often below freezing. From November to April is the wet season, when it is dry and clear most mornings, with some rainfall in the afternoon. There is a small temperature drop (18°C) and not much difference at night (15°C).

Selva
April to October is the dry season, with temperatures up to 35°C. In the jungle areas of the south, a cold front can pass through at night. November to April is the wet season. It is humid and hot, with heavy rainfall at any time.

Flora and fauna

Peru is a country of great biological diversity. The fauna and flora are to a large extent determined by the influence of the Andes, the longest uninterrupted mountain chain in the world, and the mighty Amazon river, which has the largest volume of any river in the world. Of Earth's 32 known climate zones Peru has 28, and of the 117 recognized microclimates Peru has 84. Throughout the country there are 61 protected natural areas.

Natural history
This diversity arises not only from the wide range of habitats available, but also from the history of the continent. South America has essentially been an island for some 70 million years joined only by a narrow isthmus to Central and North America. Land passage played a significant role in the gradual colonization of South America by species from the north. When the land-link closed these colonists evolved to a wide variety of forms free from the competitive pressures that prevailed elsewhere. When the land-bridge was re-established some four million years ago a new invasion of species took place from North America, adding to the diversity but also leading to numerous extinctions. Comparative stability has ensued since then and has guaranteed the survival of many primitive groups like the opossums.

Coast
The coastal region of Peru is extremely arid, partly as a result of the cold Humboldt current (see Climate, above). The paucity of animal life in the area between the coast and the mountains is obviously due to this lack of rain, though in some areas intermittent lomas, which are areas of sparse scrubby vegetation caused by moisture in the sea mist. The plants which survive provide ideal living conditions for insects which attract insectivorous birds and humming birds to feed on their nectar. Cactuses are abundant in northern Peru and provide a wooded landscape of trees and shrubs including the huarango (*Prosopis juliflora*). Also common in the north is

the algorrobo tree – 250,000 ha were planted in 1997 to take advantage of the El Niño rains. Algorrobo forests (*algorrobales*), scrub thicket (*matorrales*) and coastal wetlands each provide habitat for some 30 species of birds. Mammals include foxes, three species of deer and six species of dogs from pre-Columbian times.

Andes

From the desert rise the steep Andean slopes. In the deeply incised valleys Andean fox and deer may occasionally be spotted. Herds of llamas and alpacas graze the steep hillsides. Mountain caracara and Andean lapwing are frequently observed soaring, and there is always the possibility of spotting flocks of mitred parrots or even the biggest species of hummingbird in the world (*Patagonia gigas*).

The Andean zone has many lakes and rivers and countless swamps. Exclusive to this area short-winged grebe and the torrent duck which feeds in the fast flowing rivers, and giant and horned coots. Chilean flamingo frequent the shallow soda lakes. The puna, a habitat characterized by tussock grass and pockets of stunted alpine flowers, gives way to relict elfin forest and tangled bamboo thicket in this inhospitable windswept and frost-prone region. Occasionally the dissected remains of a Puya plant can be found; the result of the nocturnal foraging of the rare spectacled bear. There are quite a number of endemic species of rodent including the viscacha, and it is the last stronghold of the chinchilla. Here pumas roam preying on the herbivores which frequent these mountain – pudu, a tiny Andean deer or guemal and the mountain tapir.

Tropical Andes

The elfin forest gradually grades into mist enshrouded cloudforest at about 3500 m. In the tropical zones of the Andes, the humidity in the cloudforests stimulates the growth of a vast variety of plants particularly mosses and lichens. The cloudforests are found in a narrow strip that runs along the eastern slopes of the spine of the Andes. It is these dense, often impenetrable, forests clothing the steep slopes that are important in protecting the headwaters of all the streams and rivers that cascade from the Andes to form the mighty Amazon as it begins its long journey to the sea. This is a verdant world of dripping epiphytic mosses, lichens, ferns and orchids that grow in profusion despite the plummeting overnight temperatures. The high humidity resulting from the 2 m of rain that can fall in a year is responsible for the maintenance of the forest and it accumulates in puddles and leaks from the ground in a constant trickle that combines to form myriad icy, crystal-clear streams that cascade over precipitous waterfalls. In secluded areas, orange Andean cock-of-the-rock give their spectacular display to females in the early morning mists. Woolly monkeys are also occasionally sighted as they descend the wooded slopes. Mixed flocks of colourful tanagers are commonly encountered as are the golden-headed quetzal and Amazon umbrella bird.

Amazon Basin

At about 1500 m there is a gradual transition to the vast lowland forests of the Amazon Basin, which are warmer and more equable than the cloudforests clothing the mountains above. The daily temperature varies little during the year with a high of 23-32°C falling slightly to 20-26°C overnight. This lowland region receives some 2 m of rainfall per year most of it falling from November to April. The rest of the year is sufficiently dry, at least in the lowland areas to inhibit the growth of epiphytes and orchids that are so characteristic of the highland areas. For a week or two in the rainy season the rivers flood the forest. The zone immediately surrounding this seasonally flooded forest is referred to as terre firme forest.

The vast river basin of the Amazon is home to an immense variety of species. The environment has largely dictated their lifestyle. Life in or around rivers, lakes, swamps and forests depend on the ability to swim and climb – amphibious and tree-dwelling animals are common. Once, the entire Amazon Basin was a great inland sea and the river still contains mammals more typical of the coast, eg manatees and dolphins.

Here in the relatively constant climatic conditions animal and plant life has evolved to an amazing diversity over the millennia. It has been estimated that 3.9 sq km of forest can harbour some 1200 vascular plants, 600 species of tree, and 120 woody plants. Here, in these relatively flat lands, a soaring canopy some 50 m overhead is the powerhouse of the forest. It is a habitat choked with strangling vines and philodendrons among which mixed troupes of squirrel monkeys and brown capuchins forage. In the high canopy small groups of spider monkeys perform their lazy aerial acrobatics, whilst lower down, cling to epiphyte-clad trunks and branches, groups of saddle-backed and emperor tamarins forage for blossom, fruit and the occasional insect prey.

The most accessible part of the jungle is on or near the many meandering rivers. At each bend of the river the forest is undermined by the currents during the seasonal floods at the rate of some 10-20 m per year leaving a sheer mud and clay bank, whilst on the opposite bend new land is laid down as broad beaches of fine sand and silt.

A succession of vegetation can be seen. The fast growing willow-like Tessaria first stabilizes the ground enabling the tall stands of caña brava Gynerium to become established. Within these dense almost impenetrable stands the seeds of rainforest trees germinate and over a few years thrust their way towards the light. The fastest growing is a species of Cercropia that forms a canopy 15-18 m over the caña but even this is relatively short-lived. The gap in the canopy is quickly filled by other species. Two types of mahogany outgrow the other trees forming a closed canopy at 40 m with a lush understory of shade tolerant Heliconia and ginger. Eventually even the long-lived trees die off to be replaced by others providing a forest of great diversity.

Jungle wildlife

The meandering course of the river provides many excellent opportunities to see herds of russet-brown capybara – a sheep-sized rodent – peccaries and brocket deer. Of considerable ecological interest are the presence of oxbow lakes, or cochas, since these provide an abundance of wildlife that can easily be seen around the lake margins. The best way to see the wildlife, however, is to get above the canopy. Ridges provide elevated view points. From here, it is possible to look across the lowland flood plain to the foothills of the Andes, some 200 km away. Flocks of parrots and macaws can be seen flying between fruiting trees and troupes of squirrel monkeys and brown capuchins come very close.

The lowland rainforest of Peru is particularly famous for its primates and giant otters. Giant otters were once widespread in Amazonia but came close to extinction in the 1960s owing to persecution by the fur trade. The giant otter population in Peru has since recovered and is now estimated to be at least several hundred. Jaguar and other predators are also much in evidence. Although rarely seen their paw marks are commonly found along the forest trails. Rare bird species are also much in evidence, including fasciated tiger-heron and primitive hoatzins.

The (very) early morning is the best time to see peccaries, brocket deer and tapir at mineral licks (collpa). Macaw and parrot licks are found along the banks of the river. Here at dawn a dazzling display arrives and clambers around in the branches overhanging the clay-lick. At its peak there may be 600 birds of up to six species (including red and green macaws, and blue-headed parrots) clamouring to begin their descent to the riverbank where they jostle for access to the mineral rich clay. A necessary addition to their diet that may also neutralize the toxins present in the leaf and seed diet. Rare game birds such as razor billed curassows and piping guans may also be seen.

A list of over 600 species has been compiled. Noteworthy are the black-faced cotinga, crested eagle, and the Harpy eagle, the world's most impressive raptor, easily capable of taking an adult monkey. Mixed species flocks are commonly observed containing from 25 to 100-plus birds of perhaps 30 species including blue dacnis, blue-tailed emerald, bananaquit, thick-billed euphoria and the paradise tanager. Each species occupies a slightly different niche, and since there are few individuals of each species in the flock, competition is avoided. Mixed flocks foraging in the canopy are often led by a white-winged shrike, whereas flocks in the understorey are often led by the bluish-slate antshrike.

Books

Culture and history

Bingham, Hiram *Lost City of the Incas (illustrated edition, with introduction by Hugh Thomson, Weidenfeld & Nicolson, London, 2002).*

Bowen, Sally *The Fujimori File. Peru and its President 1990-2000 (2000).* A very readable account of the last decade of the 20th century; it ends at the election of that year so the final momentous events of Fujimori's term happened after publication. Bowen has also written, with Jane Holligan, *The Imperfect Spy: the Many Lives of Vladimiro Montesinos* (2003), Peisa.

Hemming, John *The Conquest of the Incas (1970).* The one, invaluable book on the period of the conquest.

MacQuarrie, Kim *The Last Days of the Incas (2007, Piatkus).* A thrilling account of the events that led to the Incas' final resistance and of the explorers who have tried to uncover the secrets of their civilization.

Morrison, Tony *Qosqo. The Navel of the World (1997, Condor Books).* Cuzco's past and present with an extensive section of photographs of the city and its surroundings. *Pathways to the Gods: The Mystery of the Andes Lines* (1978), Michael Russell, obtainable in Lima; and *The Mystery of the Nasca Lines* (1987), nonesuch Expeditions, with an intro by Marie Reiche.

Mosely, Michael E *The Incas and their Ancestors: The Archaeology of Peru (2001, Thames and Hudson).*

Muscutt, Keith *Warriors of the Clouds: A Lost Civilization in the Upper Amazon of Peru (1998, New Mexico Press).* Excellent coffee table book and Chachapoyas memoir; also refer to its website (www.chachapoyas.com).

Starn, Orin, Carlos Iván Degregori, and Robin Kirk *The Peru Reader (2nd edition, 2005),* Duke Univeristy Press. A good collection on history, culture and politics.

Urton, Gary *The Social Life of Numbers (1997, University of Texas Press).* On the significance and philosophy of numbers in Andean society. Related to Urton's other studies on khipus and Inca mythology.

Capaq Ñan, the Royal Inca Road

Espinosa, Ricardo *La Gran Ruta Inca, The Great Inca Route (2002, Petróleos del Perú).* A photographic and textual record of Espinosa's walk the length of the Camino Real de los Incas, in Spanish and English. He has also walked the length of Peru's coast, described in *El Perú a toda Costa (1997 Editur).* The same company has published Zarzar, Omar, Por los Caminos del Perú en Bicicleta.

Muller, Karin *Along the Inca Road (2000, National Geographic).* A Woman's Journey into an Ancient Empire.

Portway, Christopher *Journey Along the Andes (1993, Impact Books).* An account of the Andean Inca road.

Non-Peruvian Fiction

Matthiessen, Peter *At Play in the Fields of the Lord (1965).*

Shakespeare, Nicholas *The Vision of Elena Silves (1989).*

Thubron, Colin *To the Last City (2002, Chatto & Windus).*

Vltchek, Andre *Point of No Return (2005, Mainstay Press).*

Wilder, Thornton *The Bridge of San Luis Rey (1941, Penguin).*

Travel

Murphy, Dervla *Eight Feet in the Andes (1983)*.

Parris, Matthew *Inca-Kola (1990)*.

Shah, Tahir *Trail of Feathers (2001)*.

Simpson, Joe *Touching the Void (1997, Vintage)*. A nail-biting account of Simpson's accident in the Cordillera Huayhuash.

Thomson, Hugh *The White Rock (2002 Phoenix)*. Describes Thomson's own travels in the Inca heartland, as well as the journeys of earlier explorers. *Cochineal Red: Travels through Ancient Peru (2006 Weidenfeld & Nicolson)*, explores pre-Inca civilizations.

Trekking and climbing

Biggar, John *The Andes. A Guide for Climbers (1999, Andes Publishing)*.

Gómez, Antonio, and Tomé, Juan José *La Cordillera Blanca de Los Andes (1998, Desnivel)*. Spanish only, climbing guide with some trekking and general information, available locally. Also *Escaladas en los Andes. Guía de la Cordillera Blanca (1999, Desnivel)*. (Spanish only), a climbing guide.

Ricker, John F *Yuraq Janka, Cordilleras Blanca and Rosko (1977, The Alpine Club of Canada, The American Alpine Club)*.

Sharman, David *Climbs of the Cordillera Blanca of Peru (1995, Whizzo)*. A climbing guide, available locally, from South **American Explorers**, as well as from **Cordee** in the UK and **Alpenbooks** in the USA.

Wildlife

Clements, James F and Shany, Noam *A Field Guide to the Birds of Peru (2001, Ibis)*.

Schulenberg, Thomas S, Stotz, Douglas F, et al *Birds of Peru (2007, Helm)*. A comprehensive field guide.

TReeS *(PO Box 33153, London, NW3 4DR, www.tambopata.org.uk)* publish *Tambopata – A Bird Checklist, Tambopata – Mammal, Amphibian & Reptile Checklist* and *Reporte Tambopata*; they also produce tapes and CDs of *Jungle Sounds* and *Birds of Southeast Peru* and distribute other books and merchandise.

Valqui, Thomas *Where to Watch Birds in Peru (2004)*. Describes 151 sites, how to get there and what to expect once there.

Walker, Barry, and Jon Fjeldsa *Birds of Machu Picchu*.

Practicalities
Peru

Getting there

From Europe

There are direct flights to **Lima** from Amsterdam (**KLM** via Bonaire), Madrid (**Iberia, Air Europa** and **LAN**) and Paris (**Air France**). From London, Frankfurt, Rome, Milan, Lisbon or other European cities, the best connections are made in Madrid, or via Brazilian or US gateways.

From North America

Miami is the main gateway to Peru, together with Atlanta, Dallas, Houston, Los Angeles and New York. There are flights, though not all are direct, with **American, Continental, Delta, LAN, Avianca/TACA, Copa** and **AeroMéxico**. Daily connections can be made from almost all major North American cities. From Toronto, **Air Canada** flies daily direct to Lima. From Vancouver, there are no direct flights or connections; fly via one of the gateways mentioned above.

From Australia, New Zealand and South Africa

There are no obvious connecting flights. One option would be to go to Buenos Aires from Sydney or Auckland (four flights a week with **Aerolíneas Argentinas**) and fly on from there (several daily flights). Alternatively, fly to Los Angeles and travel down. From Johannesburg, make connections in Buenos Aires or São Paulo.

From Latin America

There are regular, in many cases daily, flights to Peru from most South American countries. The **LAN** group has the most routes to Lima within the continent. The **Avianca/TACA** group also has extensive coverage, including to Central America and Mexico.

Prices and discounts

Peru is a popular destination served by many airlines and prices vary considerably. The following are examples of 2015 round-trip fares to Lima: from London via Miami, US$1200; from Madrid direct, US$1350; from Miami direct, US$700; all subject to change.

To find the best deals, you can either research online using discount flight websites, such as www.etn.nl/discount.htm, www.statravel.com and www.flightcentre.com, or check with a travel agent/tour operator specializing in South America (see page 599). Despite the convenience of using the internet to search independently, don't disregard the experience offered by a reputable agent. The best will not only find the most suitable flights for your itinerary, but also advise on documents, safety, routes, lodging and times of year to travel. A reputable agent will also be bonded to give you some protection if arrangements collapse while you are travelling.

TRAVEL TIP

Packing for Peru

A good principle is to take half the clothes and twice the money that you think you will need. As you pack for your trip to Peru, keep in mind the joy of travelling light and remember that many of the following articles are available locally. Always take out a good travel insurance policy to cover your belongings (see page 590).

Listed here are those items most often recommended by other travellers. These include strong shoes, waterproof clothing and waterproof treatment for leather footwear. An inflatable travel pillow and wax earplugs are vital for long bus trips and noisy hotels. Also important are flip-flops, which can be worn in showers to avoid both athlete's foot and electric shocks, and a sheet sleeping bag for use in cheap hotels.

Other useful things include: a clothes line, a nailbrush, a water bottle, a universal sink plug of the flanged type that will fit any waste-pipe, string, a pocket knife (don't carry it in your hand luggage when flying), an alarm clock, candles (for power cuts), a torch/ flashlight, pocket mirror, suitable chargers and adaptors for recharging all your electronic kit, a padlock for the doors of the cheapest hotels (or for the tent zip if camping), a small first-aid kit, sun hat, lip salve with sun protection, contraceptives, waterless soap, wipes and a small sewing kit. Always carry toilet paper, especially on long bus trips. The most security conscious may also wish to include a length of chain and padlock for securing luggage to a bed or bus seat. Contact lens wearers note that lens solution can be difficult to find in Peru; ask for it in a pharmacy, rather than an opticians.

Airport information

With the exception of a few regional connections between Arequipa, Cuzco and La Paz (Bolivia), all international flights arrive at **Jorge Chávez Airport** in Callao, 16 km from the centre of Lima, T01-511 6055, www.lap.com.pe. For details of facilities in the airport and onward transport, see page 35. Lima airport is very busy. Airlines recommend that you arrive up to three hours before international flights and 90 minutes before domestic flights. Check-in closes one hour before departure for international flights, 30 minutes for domestic flights, after which you may not be permitted to board. Look on your airline's website for current requirements.

The *aduana* (customs) process is relatively painless and efficient (a push-button, red light/green light system operates for customs baggage checks – see also Customs, page 586).

Baggage allowance

There is always a weight limit for your baggage, but this varies between airlines. You should therefore find out from the carrier exactly how much weight you are permitted. Some airlines allow only one piece of luggage, others two, usually with an additional charge for the second. In general the maximum weight of checked-in baggage will be 20 kg or 23 kg. You may find that allowances are different for each direction of your journey. Carry-on luggage is normally restricted by both size and weight. At busy times of the year it can be very difficult and expensive to bring items such as bikes and surfboards along. Airlines may let you pay a penalty for overweight baggage, but you should verify this in advance. Do not assume that you can bring extra luggage. The weight limit for internal flights is often 20 kg per person, but can be considerably less if the plane is small.

Airport taxes

Tax of US$31 is charged on international flight departures; US$9.40 on internal flights. There is also an 18% state tax. All these charges should be included in the price of flight tickets, not paid at the airport. When making a domestic connection in Lima, you don't have to pay airport tax; contact airport personnel to be escorted to your departure gate. Regional airports have lower departure taxes.

Road and river

Peru has land and river borders with neighbouring countries and they are heavily used, see Border crossings box, page 581. Taking an international bus is usually more expensive than travelling to and from the border on national buses.

Car

You must have an international driving licence and be over 21 to drive in Peru. If you bring your own vehicle into the country, you must provide proof of ownership. Officially you cannot enter Peru with a vehicle registered in someone else's name, but it may be possible with a notarized letter of authorization (at the discretion of the customs officer). There are two recognized documents for taking a vehicle into South America: a *carnet de passages* issued jointly by the **Fedération Internationale de l'Automobile** (FIA-Paris) and the **Alliance Internationale de Tourisme** (AIT-Geneva), and the *Libreta de Pasos por Aduana* issued by the **Federación Interamericana de Touring y Automóvil Clubs** (FITAC). Officially, Peru requires one or the other, but it is seldom asked for. Nevertheless, motorists seem to fare better with one than without it.

SOAT (*Seguro Obligatorio para Accidentes de Tránsito*) is a compulsory insurance that covers people injured in road accidents. Transit police regulary ask to see proof that you have it. It can be purchased at major border crossings but only during regular business hours, not weekends or holidays. Insurance for the vehicle against accident, damage or theft is best arranged in the country of origin, but it is difficult to find agencies who offer this service. The **Touring y Automóvil Club del Perú** ⓘ *Av Trinidad Morán 698, Lince, T01-614 9999, www.touringperu.com.pe*, offers help to tourists and particularly to members of the leading motoring associations in many countries.

Getting around

Air

If you only have a couple of weeks, travelling by air is the sensible option. It allows access to most major regions and means you can spend more time at your destination and less getting there. On the downside, you will see less of the country and will meet fewer people than if you travel overland.

Carriers serving the major cities are **Star Perú** ① *T01-705 9000, www.starperu. com*; **LAN** ① *T01-213 8200, www.lan.com*; **Avianca/TACA** ① *T01-511 8222, www.avianca.com*, and **Peruvian Airlines** ① *T01-716 6000, www.peruvianairlines.pe*. For destinations such as Andahuaylas, Ayacucho, Cajamarca, Jauja, Huánuco, Huaraz and Pisco, flights are offered by **LC Peru** ① *T01-204 1313, www.lcperu.pe*.

Flights from Lima to anywhere in the country start at about US$100 one-way, but prices vary greatly between airlines, with LAN being the most expensive for non-Peruvians. Prices often increase at holiday times (Semana Santa, May Day, Inti Raymi, 28-29 July, Christmas and New Year), and for elections. During these times and during the northern hemisphere summer, seats can be hard to come by, so book early. Flight schedules and departure times may change and delays are common. Always allow an extra day between national and international flights, especially in the rainy season, when some flights may be cancelled entirely. Be at the airport well ahead of your flight. Flights to jungle regions are particularly unreliable.

Rail

There are two lines of major interest to the traveller. The first is Cuzco–Machu Picchu, on which two companies operate services: **PerúRail** ① *www.perurail.com*, and **Inca Rail** ① *www.incarail.com*; the second is Puno–Cuzco, run by **PerúRail**. The other railway that carries passengers is the line from Lima to Huancayo, with a continuation to Huancavelica in the Central Highlands. The service runs on an irregular basis, so check www.fcca.com.pe for the latest schedule. Train schedules may be cut in the rainy season.

River

On almost any trip to the Amazon Basin, a boat journey will be required at some point, either to get you to a jungle lodge, or to go between river ports.

Motorized canoes

Motorized canoes with canopies usually take passengers to jungle lodges. They normally provide life jackets and have seats that aren't very comfortable on long journeys, so a cushion may come in handy. They are open to the elements, so take a waterproof to keep you dry and warm. The breeze can be a welcome relief from the heat and humidity in the daytime, but it can be cold in the early morning, and, if there is any rain about, it will blow into your face. You sit very close to the water and you soon learn to respect the driver's knowledge of the river.

Public river transport

There are various types of vessel: a *lancha* is a large riverboat; a *rápido* or *deslizador* is a speedboat (some are faster than others); a *yate* is a small to medium wooden colectivo, usually slow, and a *chalupa* is a small motor launch used to ferry passengers from the *lanchas* to shore. Standards are variable and generally not as high as in Brazil; always look at several vessels and talk to the staff before choosing. The best *lanchas* are on the Iquitos–Pucallpa and Iquitos–Yurimaguas routes. Not all *rápidos* are safe or reliable.

Practicalities Departure times are marked on a chalk-board on each vessel. All say '*sin falta*' ('without fail') but that does not necessarily mean the boat leaves at that time, nor even on that day. How long the trip takes depends on the water level, the weather, the size and state of the engine, the amount of cargo (boats go very loaded from Pucallpa to Iquitos), how long they wait at intermediate ports, and whether you're going upstream or downstream. Always allow extra time for your journey. A flexible attitude and an ability to speak Spanish are both essential.

Boats travel near shore upstream and in the middle of the river downstream. To flag down a boat at intermediate points along the river, use a white sheet during the day or strong light at night; sometimes they don't bother stopping even when they see you are calling. Pay the captain or *mestre* (manager) on the boat; avoid touts. On some boats, staff collect the fares in the middle of the first night, once passengers are all in their hammocks.

Sleeping and eating on board Accommodation on *lanchas* is either in a cabin for two or four passengers (on the best boats some cabins have a/c and private bath), which will be more expensive than slinging your hammock in the general hammock area. Some boats also have two classes of hammock space. It may be possible to sleep on board ahead of departure or if you arrive in the middle of the night. The quality of your experience depends largely on the level of crowding, especially if you're travelling hammock class.

Food on boats is of variable quality, often monotonous, and sometimes meagre; you need to take your own

> **Tip...**
> If you choose to sleep in a hammock, hang it away from lightbulbs, which aren't switched off at night and attract all sorts of strange insects, and away from the engines, which usually emit noxious fumes and, of course, noise. Another useful tip is not to sling your hammock near the bottom of the stairwell on double-decked river boats, as this is where the cook slaughters the livestock every morning. Do try to find somewhere sheltered from the cold, damp night breeze. Take a rope for hanging your hammock, plus string and sarongs for privacy. Use a double fabric (not string) hammock for warmth; you may need a blanket as well.

plate, cutlery and cup, plenty of drinking water (the silt in the rivers will clog filters; purifying tablets may not kill giardia), extra snacks and seasonings. Local produce can sometimes be purchased on route. There is usually (not always) a bar on board (often expensive) serving beer, soft drinks and a few snacks. Departures are after sunset and the first night's meal is not included.

You need to take a bag for your rubbish (rather than chucking it all overboard), toilet paper, mosquito repellent and long-sleeved shirts/long trousers for after dusk. DEET is the best mosquito repellent but it will be washed directly into the river and it is lethal to most fish. Thieves are a problem; do not leave any possessions out of your sight, not even your shoes under your hammock at night. Also take great care of your belongings when embarking and disembarking. Women travellers can expect the usual unwanted attention; it becomes more uncomfortable when you are confined to a small boat.

Road

Although Peru's geography is dominated by the Andes, one of the world's major mountain ranges, great steps have been taken to improve major roads and enlarge the paved network linking the Pacific coast with the highlands and jungle. The most important development has been the completion of the fully paved *Carretera Interoceánica*, which runs from the Pacific port of Ilo to Puerto Maldonado and on to the Brazilian border at Iñapari. Better roads mean more reliable bus services and improved conditions for drivers, but also more accidents caused by speeding. Regardless of road quality, travelling at night or in bad weather should be avoided whenever possible. Detailed accounts of major and minor road conditions are given in the travelling text.

It is always worth taking some time to plan an overland journey in advance, checking which roads are finished, which have roadworks and which will be affected by the weather. Most roads in the mountains are dirt, some good, some very bad, especially on the eastern slopes. The highland and jungle wet season, from mid-October to late March, can seriously hamper travel in these regions, with heavy rainfall and the ensuing landslides making many roads impassable. This makes for slow travel and frequent breakdowns, so allow extra time if planning to go overland at this time. You should check road conditions before you travel with locals (not with bus companies, who only want to sell tickets), as accidents are more common at these times. Finally, bear in mind that extended overland travel is not really an option if you only have a few weeks' holiday.

Major routes

Note that many paved roads in Peru charge tolls, which vary depending on the size of the vehicle. The Pan-American Highway runs north–south through the coastal desert and is mostly in good condition. Also paved and well-maintained is the direct road that branches off the Pan-American at Pativilca and runs up to Huaraz and on to Caraz. The northern route from Chiclayo through to Tarapoto and Yurimaguas is fully paved, as is the spur to Jaén. Cajamarca has a paved connection

Border crossings

The main entry points into Peru by land and river are as follows:

From Bolivia Desaguadero (the town has the same name on both sides of the border; see page 339) and Kasani–Yunguyo on the southeastern side of Lake Titicaca (see page 338). There is also an unpaved crossing on the north shore, from Puerto Acosta to Tilali (see page 339).

From Chile Arica–Tacna (see page 299).

From Ecuador At Huaquillas–Aguas Verdes (see page 187); Macará–La Tina (see page 178); La Balsa (Zumba)–Namballe (see page 229); and Nuevo Rocafuerte–Pantoja, a river crossing on the Río Napo (see page 499).

From Brazil The Assis Brasil–Iñapari crossing (see page 514) is part of the Interoceanic highway. There is also a river crossing in the Amazon from Tabatinga (Brazil) and Leticia (Colombia) to Santa Rosa in Peru (see page 490).

to the coast and the Central Highway from Lima to Huancayo is mostly paved. It continues (also mostly paved) to Pucallpa in the Amazon Basin. There is also a paved road from La Oroya to Tarma and Satipo. South of Lima, there's the paved 'Liberatores' highway from Pisco to Ayacucho. From Nazca to Abancay and on to Cuzco is paved. This is the main route from Lima to Cuzco. The main roads into the Sacred Valley from Cuzco are also paved. The Cuzco–Puno highway is fully paved and is a fast, comfortable journey. The paved road continues along the south shore of Lake Titicaca to Desaguadero on the Bolivian border. From there the paving runs down the western slope of the Andes to Moquegua and the coast; this is one of the best highways in the country. Also in the south, the road that runs into the sierra to Arequipa is in good condition. From Arequipa the road to Puno is paved. Roads from Arequipa to Mollendo and Matarani are also excellent.

Bus services

Services along the coast to the north and south as well as inland to Huancayo, Ayacucho and Huaraz are generally good, but on long-distance journeys it is advisable to pay a bit extra and travel with a reliable company. There are many different bus companies, but the larger ones are better organized, leave on time and do not wait until the bus is full. **Cruz del Sur**, **Móviltours**, **Oltursa**, **Flores** and **Ormeño** are among the better bus lines covering large parts of the country. **Cruz del Sur**, generally regarded as a class above the others, accepts Visa cards and gives 10% discount to ISIC and Under26 cardholders (you may have to insist). There are also many smaller but still excellent bus lines that run only to specific areas. An increasing number accept internet bookings and you may find good deals on their websites. For a centralized information and booking site, visit https://busportal. pe. Whatever the standard of service, accidents and hold-ups on buses do occur, especially at night; it is best to travel by day whenever possible, both for safety and to enjoy the outstanding views.

All major bus companies operate modern buses with two decks on interdepartmental routes. The first deck is called *bus cama*; the second, *semi cama*. Both have seats that recline, but *bus cama* seats go back further than *semi cama*. These buses usually run overnight and are more expensive than ordinary buses which tend to run earlier in the day. Many buses have toilets and show movies. Each company has a different

Tip...
Prices of bus tickets are raised by 60-100%, 2 or 3 days before Semana Santa, 28 Jul (Independence Day – Fiestas Patrias), Christmas and special local events. Tickets are sold out 2 or 3 days in advance at this time and transport is hard to come by.

name for its regular and *cama* or *ejecutivo* services. With the better companies you will get a receipt for your luggage, which will be locked under the bus. On local buses watch your luggage and never leave valuables on the luggage rack or floor, even when on the move. If your bus breaks down and you are transferred to another line and have to pay extra, keep your original ticket for a refund from the first company.

Most bus terminals charge a usage fee of about US$0.50 which you pay at a kiosk before boarding. Many also charge a small fee for use of the toilet. Take a blanket or warm jacket when travelling in the mountains. It is possible to buy food on the roadside at long-distance bus stops.

Light vehicles operate on many shorter routes, up to about four hours; these may be minibuses, modern vans, older combis, or cars. The latter are called colectivos or *autos* and are usually faster (sometimes too fast) and more expensive than the others. Luggage space is more limited than on buses, but these light vehicles make it possible, in many cases, just to turn up and travel within an hour or two. They leave only when full. They go almost anywhere in Peru; most firms have offices. Book a day in advance and they may pick you up at your hotel or in the main plaza.

Car
You must have an international driving licence and be over 21 to drive in Peru. For other rules on bringing a car into Peru, see page 577.

Fuel Prices fluctuate over time and are higher in remote areas; current prices are posted on www.facilito.gob.pe. In early 2015 84 octane petrol/gasoline cost approximately US$3.50/gallon; 90 octane, US$3.75; 95 octane, US$4.30; 98 octane, US$4.65. Diesel cost US$3.75. Unleaded fuel is available in large cities and along the Panamericana, but rarely in the highlands.

Car hire The minimum age for renting a car is 25. If renting a car, your home driving licence will be accepted for up to six months. Car hire companies are given in the text. Prices reflect high costs and accident rates. Hotels and tourist agencies will tell you where to find cheaper rates, but you will need to check that the car has such basics as spare wheel, toolkit and functioning lights, etc. A test drive is recommended before signing any contracts. It can be much cheaper to rent a car in a town in the Sierra for a few days than to drive from Lima; also note that companies don't have a collection service.

Hitchhiking

Hitchhiking in Peru is neither easy nor entirely risk-free. For obvious reasons, a female traveller should not hitch by herself. Besides, you are more likely to get a lift if you are with a partner, whether they are male or female. The best combination is a male and female together. Positioning is also key: try toll points, although these are often far from towns. You are usually expected to pay for a ride, so always check in advance.

Motorcycling and cycling

Motorcycling The motorbike should be off-road capable. Get to know the bike before you go; ask the dealers in your country what is likely to go wrong with it, and arrange a link whereby you can get parts flown out to you. Get the book for international dealer coverage from your manufacturer, but don't rely on it, since they frequently have few or no parts for modern, large machinery. An Abus D lock or chain will keep the bike secure and a cheap alarm will give you peace of mind if you have to leave the bike outside a hotel at night. Many hotels will allow you to bring the bike inside (see accommodation listings for details); look for hotels that have a courtyard or more secure parking. Never leave luggage on the bike overnight or while unattended. Passport, international driving licence and bike registration document are necessary. Riders fare much better with a *carnet de passages* than without it.

Cycling Unless you are planning a journey almost exclusively on paved roads – when a high-quality touring bike would suffice – a mountain bike is strongly recommended. The good-quality ones (and the cast-iron rule is **never** to skimp on quality) are incredibly tough and rugged, with low gear ratios for difficult terrain, wide tyres with plenty of tread, V brakes, sealed hubs and bottom bracket and a low centre of gravity for improved stability. A chrome-alloy frame is a desirable choice over aluminium as it can be welded if necessary. Although touring bikes, and to a lesser extent mountain bikes and spares, are available in the larger cities, remember that most locally manufactured goods are shoddy and rarely last. (Shimano parts are generally the easiest to find.) Buy everything you possibly can before you leave home.

Remember that you can always stick your bike on a bus, canoe or plane to get yourself nearer to where you want to go. This is especially useful when there are long stretches of major road ahead, where all that awaits you are hours of turbulence as the constant stream of heavy trucks and long-haul buses zoom by. It is possible to rent a bike for a few days, or join an organized tour for riding in the mountains. You should check, however, that the machine you are hiring is up to the conditions you will be encountering, and that the tour company is not a fly-by-night outfit without back-up, good bikes or maintenance.

South American Explorers (see page 56) have valuable cycling information that is continuously updated. Visit www.warmshowers.org for a hospitality exchange for touring cyclists. A related organization is Cyclo-Camping International ⓘ www.cci.asso.fr.

Taxi
Taxi prices in the mountain towns are fixed at about US$1-1.50 for journeys in the urban area. Fares are not fixed in Lima, although some drivers work for companies that do have standard fares. Ask locals what the price should be and always set the price beforehand; expect to pay US$3-5 in the capital. The main cities have radio taxis that can be hired by phone; these charge a little more, but are usually reliable and safe. Many taxi drivers work for commission from hotels. Choose your own hotel and get a driver who is willing to take you there. Taxis at airports are much more expensive; seek advice about the price in advance. In most places it is cheaper to walk out of the airport to the main road and flag down a cab; but this may not be safe, especially at night.

Another common form of public transport is the *mototaxi*, a three-wheel motorcycle with an awning covering the double-seat behind the driver. Fares are about US$1.

Maps

Lima 2000's *Mapa Vial del Perú* (1:2,200,000) is probably the best overall map of Peru, highly recommended even if you are not driving. It is sold by bookshops in Lima but is harder to find outside the capital. See Shopping tips, page 25, and www.lima2000.com.pe. Maps are available from the Instituto Geográfico Nacional in Lima (see page 73), the Ministerio de Transporte ⓘ Jr Zorritos 1203, Lima centre, T01-615 7800, www.mtc.gob.pe, and from the South American Explorers (see page 56).

A good tourist map of the Callejón de Huaylas and Cordillera Huayhuash, by Felipe Díaz, is available in many shops in Huaraz, including Casa de Guías. The Österreichischer Alpenverein ⓘ www.alpenverein.at, publishes three excellent trekking maps of the region: Cordillera Blanca Nord 0/3a and Cordillera Blanca Süd 0/3b at 1:100,000; Cordillera Huayhuash 0/3c at 1:50,000. All are usually available in Huaraz and Lima, but best bought outside Peru. The Cordillera Huayhuash map, 1:50,000 (second edition, 2004) by the Alpine Mapping Guild is also recommended and is available in Huaraz at Café Andino.

Essentials A-Z

Accidents and emergencies

Emergency medical attention (Cruz Roja) T115. **Fire** T116. **Police** (Policía Nacional del Perú) T105, www.pnp.gob. pe, for police emergencies nationwide. **Tourist Police** (Jr Moore 268, Magdalena, 38th block of Av Brasil, Lima, T01-460 1060/0844, daily 24 hrs), friendly, helpful and speak English.

Bargaining

Sooner or later almost everyone has to bargain in Peru. Only the rich and famous can afford to pay the prices quoted by taxi drivers, receptionists and self-proclaimed guides. Most Peruvians are honest and extremely hard-working, but their country is poor and often in turmoil, the future is uncertain and the overwhelming majority of people live below the poverty line. Foreigners are seen as rich, even if they are backpackers or students. In order to bring prices down, it is extremely helpful to speak at least some Spanish and/or to convince locals that you live, work or study in Peru and therefore know the real price.

You will not have to bargain in restaurants, department stores, expensive hotels or airline offices. However, prices almost everywhere else are negotiable. Almost all better-class hotels have 'corporate' rates; you can usually get a reduction by claiming that you work for some company, that you are a journalist (they never check ID) or you are a researcher. If you think a lower price is appropriate in a cheaper hotel, ask for *'una rebajita, por favor'* ('a discount, please'). You can negotiate the price of a tour booked through a travel agency, but not an aeroplane, bus or train ticket. In fact, you will probably get a better price directly from the airline ticket office.

Bargaining is expected when you are shopping for artwork, handicrafts, souvenirs, or even food in the market. Remember, though, that most of the handicrafts, including alpaca and woollen goods, are made by hand. Keep in mind, these people are making a living and the 50c you save by bargaining may buy the seller 2 loaves of bread. You want the fair price not the lowest one, so bargain only when you feel you are being ripped off. Remember that some Peruvians are so desperate that they will sell you their goods at any price, in order to survive. Please don't take advantage of this situation.

Children

Travel with children can bring you into closer contact with local families and, generally, presents no special problems – in fact the path may even be smoother for family groups. Officials are sometimes more amenable where children are concerned and they are pleased if your child knows a little Spanish. For more detailed advice, see *Travel with Kids* by William Gray (Footprint, 2012) and **www. babygoes2.com**.

Transport Remember that a lot of time can be spent waiting for planes and buses. You should take books and small games with you as they are difficult to find and expensive. Also look for the locally available comic strip *Condorito*, which is popular and a good way for older children to learn a bit of Spanish. On long-distance buses you pay for each seat, and there are no half fares. For shorter trips it is cheaper, if less comfortable, to seat small children on your knee. Sometimes there are spare seats which children can occupy after tickets have been collected. In city buses, small children generally do not pay a fare, but are not entitled to a seat when paying customers are standing. On most domestic flights, children under 12 pay less than adults, although the exact discounts vary. Make sure that children accompanying you are fully covered by your travel insurance policy.

Food This can be a problem if the children are not adaptable. It is easier to take food with you on longer trips than to rely on meal stops where the food may not be to taste. Stick to simple things like bread, bananas and tangerines while you are actually on the road. Avocados are also safe, readily available, easy to eat and nutritious; they can be fed to babies as young as 6 months. Biscuits, packaged junk food and bottled drinks abound. A small immersion heater and jug for making hot drinks is invaluable, but remember that electric current is 220 v in Peru. In restaurants, you can try to order a *media porción* (half portion), or divide a full-sized helping between 2 children.

Customs and duty free

On arrival Customs inspection is carried out at airports after you clear immigration. Such inspection is not usually carried out at land borders but there is often a customs post or spot check further inside Peru.

Visitors to Peru can bring in a limited amount of tobacco, alcohol and new articles for personal use or gifts valued at up to US$300. The VAT for items that are not considered duty-free but are still intended for personal use is generally 20%. Personal items such as laptops, cameras, bicycles, hiking and climbing equipment and anything else necessary for adventure sports are exempt from taxes and should be regarded as personal effects that will not be sold or left in Peru. Anything that looks like it's being brought in for resale, however, could cause you trouble at customs.

Goods shipped to you Customs duties must be paid on all goods (except for documents) shipped to Peru. It is better to bring anything you think you will need with you when you travel, rather than having it sent to you later on.

On departure All airline baggage is inspected by security personnel and sniffed by dogs for drugs. Never transport anything you have not packed yourself, as you will be held responsible for the contents. It is also prohibited to take any archaeological pieces or specimens of wild plants or animals out of the country without a permit.

Disabled travellers

As in most developing countries, facilities for the disabled traveller are sadly lacking. Wheelchair ramps are a rare luxury and getting a wheelchair into a bathroom or toilet is almost impossible, except in some of the more upmarket hotels. The entrance to many cheap hotels is up a narrow flight of stairs. Pavements are often in a poor state of repair (even fully able people need to look out for uncovered manholes and other unexpected traps). There are similarly few facilities and services for visually and hearing-impaired travellers, but experienced guides can often provide tours with individual attention. Disabled Peruvians obviously have to cope with these problems; they mainly rely on the help of others to get on and off public transport and generally move around.

Having said that, the Peruvian government has fostered accessible tourism during the past decade, and some travel companies (such as Apumayo in Cuzco; see page 376) now specialize in exciting holidays, tailor-made for individuals depending on their level of disability.

The **Global Access Disabled Travel Network** (www.globalaccessnews.com), is dedicated to providing information for 'disabled adventurers' and includes a number of reviews and tips from members of the public. Another informative site, www.sath.org, belongs to the **Society for Accessible Travel and Hospitality (SATH)**, and has lots of advice on how to travel with specific disabilities, plus listings and links. Also see **www.access-able.com**.

Drugs

Illegal drugs are the most common way for foreigners to get into serious trouble in Peru. Some people come specifically to consume or buy drugs and may have the false impression that the country is permissive in this regard. This is not the case. While drugs are easily available, anyone caught in possession will be assumed to be a trafficker. Drug use or purchase is punishable by up to 15 years' imprisonment and the number

of foreigners in Peruvian prisons on drug charges is increasing. If arrested on any charge, the wait for trial in prison can take up to a year and is particularly unpleasant. Be wary of anyone approaching you in a club and asking where they can score – the chances are they'll be a plain-clothes cop. Likewise, never respond to offers by anyone selling drugs on the street anywhere.

Tricks employed to get foreigners into trouble over drugs include slipping a packet of cocaine into the money you are exchanging, being invited to a party or somewhere involving a taxi ride, or simply being asked on the street if you want to buy cocaine. In all cases, a plain clothes 'policeman' will discover the planted cocaine — in your money, at your feet in the taxi — and will ask to see your passport and money. He will then return them, minus a large part of your cash. Do not get into a taxi in these circumstances, do not show your money and try not to be intimidated. Being in pairs is no guarantee of security, and single women may be particularly vulnerable. Beware also thieves dressed as policemen asking to see your passport and wanting to search for drugs; note that drug searches are only permitted if prior paperwork is done.

Many places in the Amazon and in Cuzco offer experiences using the psychoactive brew Ayahuasca or the San Pedro cactus, often in ceremonies with a shaman. Although these are legal, be sure to choose a reputable tour operator or shaman; do not go with the first person who offers you a trip. There are plenty of websites for starting your research. Single women should not take part. See under Iquitos, What to do, page 486.

In Cuzco many clubs and bars offer coupons for free entry and a free drink.

The drinks are made with the cheapest, least healthy alcohol; always watch your drink being made and never leave it unattended.

Electricity

220 volts AC, 60 cycles throughout the country, except Arequipa (50 cycles). Most 4- and 5-star hotels have 110 volts AC. Plugs are either American flat-pin or twin flat and round pin combined.

Embassies and consulates

For all Peru embassies and consulates abroad and for all foreign embassies and consulates in Peru, see http://embassy.goabroad.com.

Health

Before you travel
See your GP or travel clinic at least 6 weeks before departure for general advice on travel risks and vaccinations. Try phoning a specialist travel clinic if your own doctor is unfamiliar with health in the region. Make sure you have sufficient medical travel insurance, get a dental check, know your own blood group and, if you suffer a long-term condition such as diabetes or epilepsy, obtain a **Medic Alert** bracelet (www.medicalert.co.uk).

Vaccinations and anti-malarials
Confirm that your primary courses and boosters are up to date. It is advisable to vaccinate against polio, tetanus, typhoid, hepatitis A and, for more remote areas, rabies. Yellow fever vaccination is obligatory for tropical lowland areas but not for the Pacific coast or the highlands. Specialist advice should be taken on the best anti-malarials to take before you leave. The **International Health Department** at Jorge Chávez airport (Lima, T01-517 1845), is open 24 hrs daily for vaccinations.

Health risks
The major risks posed in the region are those caused by insect disease carriers such as mosquitoes and sandflies. The key parasitic and viral diseases are malaria, dengue fever, and in some areas South American trypanosomiasis (Chagas' disease). **Malaria** is a danger throughout the lowland tropics and coastal regions. **Dengue fever** is particularly hard to protect against as the mosquitoes can bite throughout the day as well as at night (unlike those that carry malaria). Try to wear clothes that cover arms and legs and also use effective mosquito repellent. Mosquito nets dipped in permethrin provide a good physical and chemical barrier at night. **Chagas' disease** is spread by the faeces of a bug called the *vinchuca* or *chirimacha* which occurs in the north-central highlands and, with a much greater prevalence, in southwestern Peru. Sandflies spread **leishmaniasis**, a serious skin disease; it is called *uta* in northern Peru.

Some form of **diarrhoea** or intestinal upset is almost inevitable, the standard advice is always to wash your hands before eating and to be careful with drinking water and ice. If you have any doubts about the water then boil it or filter and treat it. In a restaurant buy bottled water or ask where the water has come from. Food can also pose a problem. Be wary of salads if you don't know whether they have been washed or not, undercooked meat, reheated foods or food that has been left out in the sun having been cooked earlier in the day. There is a simple adage that says 'wash it, peel it, boil it or forget it'. The key treatment for diarrhoea is rehydration. Try to keep hydrated by taking the right mixture of salt and water. This is available as oral rehydration salts (ORS) in ready-made sachets, or can be made up by adding a teaspoon of sugar and half a teaspoon of salt to a litre of clean water. If diarrhoea persists for several days or you develop additional symptoms, see a doctor.

There is a constant threat of **tuberculosis** (TB) and although the BCG vaccine is available, it is still not guaranteed protection. It is best to avoid unpasteurized dairy products and try not to let people cough and splutter all over you. Another risk, especially to campers and small children, is that of the hanta virus, which is carried by some forest and riverine rodents. Symptoms are a flu-like illness which can lead to complications. Try as far as possible to avoid rodent-infested areas, especially close contact with rodent droppings.

One of the most common problems for travellers in the region is **altitude sickness**. Acute mountain sickness can strike from about 3000 m upwards and is more likely to affect those who ascend rapidly (for example by plane) and those who over-exert themselves. Smokers and those with underlying heart and lung disease are often hardest hit. The sickness presents with headache, lassitude, dizziness, loss of appetite, nausea and vomiting. Insomnia is common and often associated with a suffocating feeling when lying down in bed. If the symptoms are mild, the treatment is to rest from your trip, take it easy for the first few days and drink plenty of water. Should symptoms be severe and prolonged it is best to descend to a lower altitude immediately and re-ascend, if necessary, slowly and in stages.

It is essential to get acclimatized to the thin air of the Andes before undertaking long treks or arduous activities. No one should attempt to climb over 5000 m until they have spent at least a week at around 3000 m and then a couple of nights at 4000 m. Agencies who offer 2-day climbs without adequate acclimatization are not to be trusted.

The altitude of the Andes also means that strong **protection from the sun** is always needed, regardless of how cool it may feel. Always use sunblock and a hat. Mountaineers should use glasses that provide 100% UV protection. Infact a good pair of sunglasses and a high-factor sunscreen are recommended in all parts of Peru.

If you get sick

Make sure you have adequate insurance (see below). Contact your embassy or consulate for a list of recommended doctors and dentists who speak your language, or at least some English. Your hotel may also be able to recommend good local medical services. The following are in Lima:

Clínica Anglo Americano, Alfredo Salazar 350, San Isidro, a few blocks from Ovalo Gutiérrez, T01-616 8900, www.angloamericana.com.pe. Stocks Yellow Fever and Tetanus.
Clínica Good Hope, Malecón Balta 956, Miraflores, T01-610 7300, www.goodhope.org.pe. Has been recommended and will make visits to hotels; prices similar to US.
Clínica Internacional, Jr Washington 1471 y Paseo Colón (9 de Diciembre), downtown Lima, T01-619 6161, www.clinicainternacional.com.pe. Good, clean and professional, consultations up to US$35, no inoculations.

Instituto de Medicina Tropical, Av Honorio Delgado 430 near the Pan American Highway in the Cayetano Heredia Hospital, San Martín de Porres, T01-482 3903, www.upch.edu.pe/tropicales/. Good for check-ups after jungle travel.

Further information

Centres for Disease Control and Prevention (USA), www.cdc.gov.
Department of Health advice for travellers, www.gov.uk/foreign-travel-advice.
Fit for Travel (UK), www.fitfortravel.scot.nhs.uk, a site from Scotland providing a quick A-Z of vaccine and travel health advice requirements for each country.
National Travel Health Network and Centre (NaTHNaC), www.nathnac.org.
Prince Leopold Institute for Tropical Medicine, www.itg.be.
World Health Organisation, www.who.int.

Books

Dawood, R, editor, *Travellers' health*, 3rd ed, Oxford: Oxford University Press, 2002. Johnson, Chris, Sarah Anderson and others, *Oxford Handbook of Expedition and Wilderness Medicine*, OUP 2008. Wilson-Howarth, Jane. *Bugs, Bites and Bowels: the essential guide to travel health*, Cadogan 2009.

Insurance

We strongly recommend that you invest in a good insurance policy that covers you for theft or loss of possessions and money, the cost of medical and dental treatment, cancellation of flights, delays in travel arrangements, accidents, missed departures, lost baggage and lost passport. Be sure to check on inclusion of 'dangerous activities' if you plan on doing any. These generally include climbing, diving, skiing, horse riding, parachuting, even trekking. You should always read the small print carefully. Not all policies cover ambulance, helicopter rescue or emergency flights home.

There are a variety of policies to choose from, so it's best to shop around. Your travel agent can advise on the best deals available. Reputable student travel organizations often offer good-value policies. Travellers from North America can try the **International Student Insurance Service (ISIS)**, which is available through **STA**, T800-7814040, www.statravel.com. Companies worth trying in Britain include **Direct Line Insurance**, T0845-246 8704, www.directline.com, and the **Flexicover Group**, T0800-093 9495, www.flexicover.net. Some companies will not cover those over 65. The best policies for older travellers are through **Age UK**, T0845-600 3348, www.ageuk.org.uk.

Internet

You can find internet access almost anywhere in Peru. Access is generally quick in the main cities and towns. Free Wi-Fi is standard at even the most basic hotels in tourist areas and at better hotels everywhere. Some cafés and public areas also have connectivity. Internet cafés charge about US$0.35-0.70 per hr; try to use them in the morning when they are less crowded and watch your belongings at all times. Internet access is more expensive in hotel business centres and out-of-the-way places. Skype and similar services on Wi-Fi-enabled devices are the most economical form of international communication from Peru.

Language

The official language is **Spanish**. **Quechua**, an Andean language that predates the Incas, is spoken by millions of people in the *sierra* who have little or no knowledge of Spanish. Quechua has been given some official status and there is much pride in its use, but it is seldom taught in schools. Another highland indigenous language is **Aymara**, used in the area around Lake Titicaca. The jungle is home to a plethora of languages, but Spanish is spoken in all but the remotest areas. **English** is not spoken widely, except by those employed in the tourism industry (eg hotel, tour agency and airline staff).

Language schools can be found in major cities in Peru. Alternatively, contact one of the following international providers:

AmeriSpan, 1334 Walnut St, 6th floor, Philadelphia PA 19107, USA, T1-800-879 6640 (USA and Canada), T215-751 1100 (worldwide), SKYPE: amerispan, www.amerispan.com. Language programmes throughout Latin America and lots of information about travelling in the region. **Cactus**, T0845-130 4775, www.cactus language.com. UK-based company. **Languages Abroad.com**, 386 Ontario St, Toronto, Ontario, Canada, M5A 2V7, T1-800-219 9924, in UK T0800-404 7738, www.languagesabroad.com. Spanish and Portuguese programmes in most South American countries. Language immersion courses throughout the world. **Spanish Abroad**, 3219 East Camelback Rd No 806, Phoenix, AZ 85018, USA, T1-888-722 7623, or T602-778 6791 (UK T0800-028 7706), www.spanishabroad.com.

Lima language schools AC Spanish Classes (Luis Villanueva), Diez Canseco 497, Miraflores, T01-247 7054, www.acspanishclasses.com. Flexible, reliable, helpful teacher for private tuition. **Hispana**, San Martín 377, Miraflores, T01-446 3045, www.hispanaidiomas.com. 20- to 60-hr travellers' programmes and other courses, also salsa, surf and gastronomy. **Instituto de Idiomas (Pontífica Universidad Católica del Perú)**, Av Camino Real 1037, San Isidro, T01-626 6500, http://idiomas.pucp.edu.pe. Spanish for foreigners. **El Sol School of Languages**, Grimaldo del Solar 469, Miraflores, T01-242 7763, http://elsol.idiomasperu.com. Private and small group tuition, also homestays and volunteer programmes.

LGBT

Movimiento Homosexual de Lima (MHOL), C Mcal Miller 828, Jesús María, T01-433 5314, www.mhol.org.pe, is a great contact for the gay community in Lima. Online resources for gay travellers in Peru are http://lima.queercity.info/index.html (a good site in English, with lots of links and information) and www.gayperu.com. The latter also has a tour operator in Miraflores, T01-447 3366, www.gayperutravel.com.

There are also gay-friendly places in Cuzco, but the scene is not very active there. This does not mean, however, that there is hostility towards gay and lesbian travellers. As a major tourist centre that welcomes a huge variety of visitors, Cuzco is probably more open to gay travellers than anywhere in Peru.

Local customs and laws

Politeness – even a little ceremoniousness – is much appreciated in Peruvian society. Men greet each other with a handshake; women tend to kiss each other once on the cheek.

Once introduced, Peruvians will probably expect to greet visitors in the same way. Always say 'buenos días' (until midday) or 'buenas tardes' when you meet someone, and wait for a reply before proceeding further. When entering an office, it is polite to remove any headgear and say 'con permiso'.

When dealing with officials, always remember to be friendly and courteous no matter how trying the circumstances. Never be impatient and do not criticize situations in public; the officials may know more English than you think and they can certainly interpret gestures and facial expressions. In some situations, however, politeness can be a liability. Most Peruvians are disorderly queuers. In commercial transactions (buying a meal, goods in a shop, etc) politeness should be accompanied by firmness, and always ask the price first.

Politeness should also be extended to street traders. Saying 'no, gracias' with a smile is better than an arrogant dismissal. Whether you give money to beggars is a personal matter, but your decision should be influenced by whether a person is begging out of need or trying to cash in on the tourist trail; the reaction of locals may provide a clue. Giving money to children is more contentious. There are occasions where giving some healthy food may be appropriate, but first inform yourself of local practice.

In Peru it is common for locals to throw their rubbish, paper, wrappers and bottles into the street. This does not give you the right to apply the 'when in Rome' practice. There are usually rubbish bins in public areas, and tourists should use them.

Outside Lima and Arequipa, Peruvians dress informally, especially in the tropical lowlands. In the highlands, people are more conservative, though wearing shorts is acceptable on hiking trails. Men should not be seen bare-chested in populated areas. Nude bathing is not generally acceptable.

Media

Newspapers and magazines

Lima has several daily papers. The most informative are El Comercio, www.elcomercioperu.pe, and La República, www.larepublica.com.pe. Also with an online edition is Expreso, www.expreso.com.pe. Gestión, www.gestion.com.pe, is a business daily. Very popular are the sensationalist papers, written in raunchy slang and featuring acres of bare female flesh on their pages, alongside gory details of the latest crimes and road accidents. The main provincial cities have at least 1 newspaper each.

The most widely read magazine is the weekly news magazine Caretas, www.caretas.com.pe, which gives a very considered angle on current affairs and is often critical of government policy.

Radio

There are countless local and community radio stations that cover even the most far-flung places. It is common to see a farmer or herdsman miles from anywhere, carrying his faithful transistor radio. A popular station is Radioprogramas del Perú (www.rpp.com.pe), which features round-the-clock news.

TV

Peruvian television has little to recommend it. The usual assortment of Latin American telenovelas (soap operas) is accompanied by loud and mindless prime-time programmes featuring team competitions between scantily dressed participants. News reports are generally violent and sensationalist. In 2015 thousands of Peruvians staged a public protest against such *televisión basura* (trash TV). Plus TV (a private cable station) and the government-run Channel 7 offer a few redeeming programmes, including a travel series and features about Peruvian gastronomy. International satellite TV is available in the better hotels.

Money

→ *Exchange rates: £1 = S/4.94, US$1 = S/3.24, €1 = S/3.59 (May 2015).*

Currency

The *nuevo sol* (s/) is divided into 100 céntimos. Notes in circulation are: S/200, S/100, S/50, S/20 and S/10. Coins: S/5, S/2, S/1, S/0.50, S/0.20, S/0.10 and S/0.05 (being phased out). Some prices are quoted in dollars (US$) in more expensive establishments to avoid changes in the value of the sol. You can always pay in soles, however. Try to break down large notes whenever you can as there is a shortage of change in museums, post offices, even shops. S/50 and under are the most practical denominations. Taxi drivers are notorious for claiming they have no change; do not accept this excuse.

ATMs, traveller's cheques and credit cards

ATMs are by far the most popular and convenient way to obtain funds while travelling in Peru, but they are not cheap. Many add a service charge to whatever is charged by your home bank. ATMs also have a maximum withdrawal limit of between US$140 and US$200. It is safest

Tip...

Forged US$ notes and forged soles notes and coins are in circulation. Always check your money when you change it, even in a bank (including ATMs). Hold sol notes up to the light to inspect the watermark and that the colours change according to the light. The line down the side of the bill spelling out the bill's amount should appear green, blue and pink. Fake bills are only pink and have no hologram properties. There should also be tiny pieces of thread in the paper (not glued on). Forged 1-, 2- and 5-sol coins are slightly off-colour; the surface copper can be scratched off, and they tend to bear a recent date. Posters in public places explain what to look for in forged soles. See also www.bcrp. gob.pe, under **Billetes y Monedas**.

to use ATMs at bank branches during banking hours. At night and on Sun there is more chance of the transaction going wrong, or falling victim to a scam. Most ATMs allow you to request either soles or US$. The availability of ATMs decreases outside large towns, so always carry some cash soles in small notes.

Traveller's cheques can still be exchanged in a few places but they fetch poor rates and are generally not recommended.

Visa (by far the most widely accepted credit card in Peru), MasterCard, American Express and Diners Club are all valid. There is often an 8-12% commission for all credit card transactions. Note that not all businesses displaying credit card symbols will take foreign cards.

Banks and currency exchange

US$ and euros are the only currencies which should be brought into Peru from abroad (take some small bills). There are no restrictions on foreign exchange, but note that few banks change euros. All banks' exchange rates are considerably less favourable than those of *casas de cambio* (see below). Rates at airports and upmarket hotels are often the worst of all. Expect long queues and paperwork at banks; they may demand to see 2 documents with your signature before changing cash. Always count your money in the presence of the cashier.
As a rule, the following bank exchange policies apply (although these vary from town to town):

BCP (Mon-Fri 0900-1800, Sat 0900-1300) changes US$ cash to soles and offers cash advances on Visa in soles only. VíaBCP ATMs charge US$2 for Visa/Plus, MasterCard/Cirrus, Amex.

BBVA Continental changes US$ cash to soles, some branches also change TCs at US$12 commission. B24 ATMs charge US$5 for Visa/Plus.

Interbank (Mon-Fri 0900-1815, Sat 0900-1230) changes US$ cash and TCs to soles and TCs to US$ cash for US$5 per transaction up to US$500; branches have **Global Net** ATMs (see below).

Scotiabank (Mon-Fri 0915-1800, Sat 0915-1230) changes US$ cash to soles and offers cash advances on MasterCard. Charges US$3.50 per cheque to change TCs. ATMs accept Visa, MasterCard, Maestro and Cirrus. There are also **Global Net** and **Red Unicard** ATMs that accept Visa, Plus and MasterCard, Maestro and Cirrus.

Note No one, not even banks, will accept US$ bills that look 'old', damaged or torn. Be especially careful about any US$ you bring across the border from Ecuador, where they are notoriously tatty.

Casas de cambio

Changing US$ cash at *casas de cambio* will usually fetch the best rates. Ask around a few places before making your transaction. You can check the current exchange rate at www.elcomercio.pe, but remember that it will be little lower outside Lima. Soles can be exchanged back into US$ at the exchange desks at Lima airport (poor rates), and you can change soles for US$ at any border.

In Lima, there are many *casas de cambio* on and around Jr Ocoña off the Plaza San Martín. The following are recommended:

LAC Dolar, Jr Camaná 779, 1 block from Plaza San Martín, p 2, T01-428 8127, also at Av La Paz 211, Miraflores, T01-242 4069. Mon-Sat 1000-1800. Good rates, very helpful, safe, fast, reliable, 2% commission on cash and TCs, will come to your hotel if you're in a group.

Moneygram, Ocharan 260, Miraflores, T01-447 4044. Safe and reliable agency for sending and receiving money. Locations throughout Lima and the provinces. Exchanges most world currencies and TCs, but check rates and commission.

Virgen P Socorro, Jr Ocoña 184, T01-428 7748. Daily 0830-2000. Safe, reliable and friendly.

Street changers

In 2015 there was no real advantage in changing money on the street and there is a greater chance of getting counterfeit soles. If you choose to do so, use only official street changers, such as those around Parque Kennedy and down Av Larco in Miraflores (Lima). They carry ID cards and wear a green vest. Check your soles before handing over your US$ or euros, check their calculators, etc, and don't change money in crowded areas. If using their services, think about taking a taxi after the transaction to avoid being followed.

Cost of travelling

To travel around Peru fairly comfortably, the average budget is US$45-60 pp a day. Your budget will be higher the longer you stay in Lima and Cuzco and depending on how many internal flights you take. Rooms range from US$7-11 pp for the most basic *alojamiento* to US$20-40 for mid-range places, to over US$90 for more upmarket hotels (more in Lima or Cuzco). Living costs in the provinces are 20-50% below those in Lima and Cuzco.

Opening hours

Banks See under Money, above. Outside Lima and Cuzco banks may close 1200-1500 for lunch. **Government offices** Jan-Mar Mon-Fri 0830-1130; Apr-Dec Mon-Fri 0900-1230, 1500-1700, but these hours change frequently. **Offices** Mon-Fri 0900-1700. Most close on Sat. **Shops** 0900 or 1000-1230 and 1500 or 1600-2000. In the main cities, supermarkets do not close for lunch, some in Lima open 24 hrs. Some are closed on Sat and most on Sun.

Post

The central Lima post office is on Jr Camaná 195 near the Plaza de Armas. Mon-Fri 0730-1900, Sat 0730-1600. Poste Restante is in the same building but is considered unreliable. In Miraflores the main post office is on Av Petit Thouars 5201 (same hours). There are many small branches around Lima and in the rest of the country, but they may be less reliable.

Letters cost US$2.30 to South America, US$2.50 to North and Central America, US$2.70 to Europe and US$3.12 to Australia. Postcards cost US$1.90. You can also send registered letters at extra cost. Lima and Cuzco are both efficient for sending parcels, but this is expensive. Don't put tape on envelopes or packages; wait until you get to the post office and seal them there. For emergency or important documents, use Serpost's own **EMS** service (next to central post office in Lima, T01-533 2020), or **DHL** and **FedEx** in Lima and other major cities.

Try not to have articles sent by post to Peru as customs duties and taxes can be very high.

Safety

The greatest risk for travellers in Peru is the distressing frequency of road accidents; see page 580 for important advice on road and bus safety. Armed groups allied with drug traffickers operate in a very few remote areas of Peru, including the upper Huallaga Valley around Tingo María and the road from there to Tarapoto, among others. These areas change over time but are usually far from the popular tourist routes. If you visit remote areas, then be sure to enquire locally about the risks.

In terms of personal safety, the following notes should not overshadow the fact that most Peruvians are hospitable and helpful. Peru is not a particularly dangerous country to travel in, but it is by no means crime free. You can minimize the risks by being aware of possible problems and by using a mixture of common sense and vigilance. For up-to-date public safety information contact the **Tourist Police** (see Accident

& emergency), your embassy or consulate, fellow travellers or **South American Explorers** (Lima T01-444 2150, Cuzco T084-245484).

On the street
You need to take care everywhere but particularly in poor areas of cities, as this is where most theft takes place. Take local advice about being out at night, but do not assume that daytime is necessarily safer. You should also be on your guard during festivals, at markets and wherever there are crowds. Care should be taken at all times and in most parts of Lima.

A friendly attitude on your part, smiling even when you've thwarted a thief's attempt, can help you out of trouble. Be especially careful when using ATMs and when arriving at or leaving from bus and train stations, when you have a lot of important belongings with you. Do not set your bag down without putting your foot on it, even just to double check your tickets. Be wary of accepting food, drink, sweets or cigarettes from unknown people on buses or trains; they may be drugged. Also watch out for scammers who ask you to change dollars into (fake) soles and for strangers who offer you a leaflet or shake your hand, leaving a chemical that will knock you out. If someone spits, smears mustard or sprays paint or shampoo on to your clothes, walk on to a safe, private place before you clean yourself up. Similarly, ignore strangers' remarks like 'what's that on your shoulder?' or 'have you seen that dirt on your shoe?'. Furthermore, don't bend over to pick up money or other items in the street. These are all ploys intended to distract your attention and make it easy for an accomplice to rob you. If someone follows you when you're in the street, let him catch up with you and 'give him the eye'. Ruses involving 'plainclothes policemen' are infrequent, but it is worth knowing that the real police only have the right to see your passport (not your money, tickets or hotel room).

Personal belongings
Keep all documents secure and hide your main cash supply in different places or under your clothes. Keep cameras in bags, take spare spectacles and don't wear wristwatches or jewellery. If you wear a shoulder-bag, carry it in front of you. Backpacks can be covered with a sack (a plastic one will also keep out rain and dust). Make photocopies and scans of important documents to leave at home with family or friends and send yourself an email containing details of your documents, insurance, itinerary, tickets, addresses, etc, which you can access in an emergency. Where there is no safe or locker in your room, you should be able to leave valuables in the hotel's safe-deposit box, but keep a record of what you have deposited. If none of these options is available, lock everything in your pack and secure that in your room.

If you lose your valuables or have them stolen, always report it to the police and note details of the report for insurance purposes. Double check that all reports written by the police actually state your complaint. The **Tourist Police** in Lima are excellent so, if you can, report any incidents to them (see Accident and emergency, above).

Bribes
Do not offer a bribe unless the official suggests it, and never offer a bribe for anything illegal. A bribe should persuade

an official to do his job (or not), or to do it more quickly, or more slowly. You should not bribe anyone to do something which is against the law. If an official suggests that a bribe must be paid before you can proceed on your way, be patient and he may relent.

Public holidays

Most businesses such as banks, airline offices and tourist agencies close for the official holidays, while supermarkets and street markets may be open. Sometimes holidays that fall during mid-week will be moved to the following Mon to make a long weekend. If you are going to spend a holiday in a certain area, find out what the local customs and events are. Often there are parades, processions and special cuisine to mark the event. See also Festivals, page 18. The main public holidays are: 1 Jan **New Year,** 6 Jan **Bajada de Reyes,** 1 May **Labour Day,** 28-29 Jul **Independence** (Fiestas Patrias), 7 Oct **Battle of Angamos,** 24-25 Dec **Christmas** (Navidad).

Senior travellers

Those in good health should face no special difficulties travelling in Peru, but it is very important to know and respect your own limits and to give yourself sufficient time to acclimatize to altitude in the highlands. If you require a special diet or medications, these must be brought from home, as they may not be available locally. Senior discounts are not common in Peru, but there are usually preferential queues for golden agers (*personas de la tercera edad*) in banks and other offices. See also Health, page 588, and Insurance, page 590.

Smoking

Smoking is not permitted on buses and is not appropriate in restaurants. A few better hotels have non-smoking rooms or are entirely non-smoking.

Students travellers

Students can obtain very few reductions in Peru with an international students' card, except in and around Cuzco where such discounts are more common. To be any use in Peru, the card must bear the owner's photograph. An ISIC card can be obtained in Lima from **Intej**, Av San Martín 240, Barranco, T01-247 3230; they can also change flight itineraries bought with student cards. Other offices are at Portal de Panes 123, of 303, Cuzco, T084-256367, and Mercaderes 329, p 2, of 34, Arequipa, T054-284756; for other locations see www.intej.org and www.isic.org.

Taxes

Airport taxes should be included in the price of the ticket: US$31 on international flight departures; US$9.40 on internal flights (see page 577). VAT/IGV/IVA is 18%.

Telephone → *Country code +51.*

There are independent phone offices, *locutorios*, in Lima and other cities as well as coin-operated pay phones, but mobile (cellular) phones are by far the most common form of telecommunication. You can easily purchase a SIM card (*un chip*) for US$5.50 (much more at Lima airport) for either of the 2 main mobile carriers: **Claro** and **Movistar**. You must show your passport. The chips work with many foreign mobile phones, but enquire about your unit before purchasing. Mobile phone shops are everywhere; look for *chip* signs with the carrier's logo. You get a Peruvian mobile phone number and can purchase credit (*recarga*) anywhere for as much or as little as you like. Calls cost about US$0.20/min and only the caller pays. Mobile phone numbers (*celulares*) have 9 digits, landlines (*fijos*) have 7 digits in Lima, 6 elsewhere, plus an area code (eg 01 for Lima, 084 for Cuzco). When calling a landline from a mobile phone, you must include the area code.

Skype and similar services on Wi-Fi-enabled devices are the most economical form of international communication from Peru.

Time → *GMT-5.*

Peruvians, like most Latin Americans, have a fairly relaxed attitude towards time. They will think nothing of arriving an hour or so late on social occasions. If you expect to meet someone more or less at an exact time, you can tell them that you want to meet *en punto*.

Tipping

Restaurant service is included in the bill, but tips can be given directly to the waiter for exceptional service. It is not usual to tip taxi drivers; but you can bargain the price down, then pay extra for good service. If going on a trek or tour, it is customary to tip the guide, the cook and the porters.

Toilets

Most Peruvian toilets are adequate, but the further you go from main population and tourist centres, the poorer the facilities. In cheap hotels, the toilets may not have seats. Always carry extra toilet paper or tissues with you. Used toilet paper and feminine hygiene products should not be flushed down the pan, but placed in the receptacle provided. This applies even in quite expensive hotels; when in doubt ask.

Tourist information

Tourism is handled by **PromPerú**, Edif Minceतur, C Uno Oeste 50, p 13 y 14, urb Córpac, San Isidro, T01-616 7300, or Av República de Panamá 3647, San Isidro, T01-616 7400, www.prompero.gob.pe. See also www.peru.travel. PromPerú runs an information and assistance service, **iPerú**, T01-574 8000 (24 hrs). Main office: Jorge Basadre 610, San Isidro, Lima, T01-616 7300 or 7400, iperulima@promperu. gob.pe, Mon-Fri 0830-1830. There's also a 24-hr office at Jorge Chávez airport; and throughout the country. Service is generally excellent.

There are tourist offices of varying quality in most towns, either run by the municipality, or independently. Outside Peru, information can be obtained from Peruvian embassies/consulates.

Indecopi T01-224 7777 (in Lima), T0800-44040 (in the Provinces), www. indecopi.gob.pe, is the government-run consumer protection and tourist complaint bureau. They are friendly, professional and helpful.

Useful websites
www.leaplocal.org Recommends good quality guides, helping communities benefit from socially responsible tourism.
www.minam.gob.pe Ministerio del Ambiente (Spanish).
www.peruthisweek.com Informative guide and news service in English for people living in Peru.

www.peruviantimes.com The *Andean Air Mail & Peruvian Times* internet news magazine.
www.terra.com.pe TV, entertainment and news (in Spanish).

Tour operators

Peru-based operators are given in the text in the relevant chapter.

UK and Ireland
Contact the Latin American Travel Association (LATA), 46 Melbourne Rd, London SW19 3BA, www.lata.org, for useful country information and a list of all UK tour operators specializing in Latin America.

Adventure Peru Motorcycling, Coldharbour Barn, Battle Rd, Dallington, Nr Heathfield, East Sussex TN21 9LQ, T01424-838618, www.perumotorcycling. com. Based in Cajamarca, Peru, T+51 (0)76-366630. Motorcycling adventure tours from 10 days to 4 weeks throughout the country, bikes provided, full back-up team, run by experienced bikers.

Amazing Peru, 9 Alma Rd, Manchester M19 2FG, T0800-520 0309, T1-800-216 0831 (Canada), T1-800-704 2915 or 1-800-704 2949 (USA), www. amazingperu.com. Professional and well-organized tours to Peru, with knowledgeable guides.

Andean Trails, The Clockhouse, Bonnington Mill Business Centre, 72 Newhaven Rd, Edinburgh EH6 5QG, T0131-467 7086, www.andeantrails. co.uk. For mountain biking, trekking and other adventure tours.

Andes, 37a St Andrews St, Castle Douglas, Kirkcudbrightshire DG7 1EN, Scotland, T01556-503929, www.andes. org.uk. For climbing trips in Peru and all South America.

Audley Latin America, New Mill, New Mill Lane, Witney, Oxfordshire, OX29 0SX, T01993-838000, www.audleytravel.com.

Austral Tours, 20 Upper Tachbrook St, London SW1V 1SH, T020-7233 5384, www.latinamerica.co.uk. Tailor-made tours, flights and accommodation in Latin America.

Condor Journeys and Adventures, 2 Ferry Bank, Colintraive, Argyll PA22 3AR, T01700-841318. Eco and adventure tourism with specially designed tours to suit your requirements.

Discover South America Ltd, T01273-921655, www.discoversouthamerica. co.uk. British-Peruvian owned operator offering tailor-made and classic holidays in South America. Specialist in off-the-beaten-track locations in Peru. ATOL-protected flights and packages from the UK.

Dragoman, Camp Green, Debenham, Suffolk IP14 6LA, T01728-861133, www.dragoman.com. Overland camping and/or hotel journeys throughout South America.

Exodus Travels, Grange Mills, 9 Weir Rd, London SW12 0NE, T020-8675 5550, www.exodus.co.uk. Experienced in adventure travel, including cultural tours, trekking and biking holidays.

Explore, Nelson House, 55 Victoria Rd, Farnborough, Hampshire GU14 7PA, T0845-0131537, www.explore. co.uk. Highly respected operator. They offer 2- to 5-week tours in more than 90 countries worldwide, including Peru. Small groups. Well executed.

Galapagos Classic Cruises in conjunction with **Classic Cruises** and **World Adventures**, 6 Keyes Rd, London NW2 3XA, T020-8933 0613, www. galapagoscruises.co.uk, specialize in individual and group travel including cruises, scuba-diving and land-based tours to the Galapagos, Peru and Bolivia.

High Places, Globe Centre, Penistone Rd, Sheffield S6 3AE, T0845-257 7500, www.highplaces.co.uk. Trekking and mountaineering trips.

Journey Latin America, 401 King St, London W6 9NJ, T020-3432 5923, www.journeylatinamerica.co.uk. The world's leading tailor-made specialist for Latin America, running escorted tours throughout the region; they also offer a wide range of flight options.

KE Adventure Travel, 32 Lake Rd, Keswick, Cumbria CA12 5DQ, T017687-73966, www.keadventure.com. Specialist in adventure tours, including 3-week cycling trips in and around Cuzco.

Last Frontiers, The Mill, Quainton Rd, Waddesdon, Bucks HP18 0LP, T01296-653000, www.lastfrontiers.com. South American specialists offering tailor-made itineraries, plus family holidays and honeymoons.

Llama Travel, 55 Rochester Pl, London, NW1 9JU, T020-7263 3000, www. llamatravel.com. Promises high-quality holidays to Latin America at the lowest possible prices.

Naturetrek, Cheriton Mill, Cheriton, Alresford, Hampshire SO24 0NG, T01962-733051, www.naturetrek.co.uk. Birdwatching tours throughout the continent, also botany, natural history tours, treks and cruises.

Oasis Overland, The Marsh, Henstridge, Somerset BA8 0TF, T01963-363400, www.oasisoverland.com. Small group trips to Peru and overland tours throughout South America.

Reef and Rainforest Tours, Dart Marine Park, Steamer Quay, Totnes, Devon TQ9 5AL, T01803-866965,

www.reefandrainforest.co.uk. Specialists in tailor-made and group wildlife tours.

Select Latin America, 3.51 Canterbury Court, 1-3 Brixton Rd, Kennington Park Business Centre, London SW9 6DE, T020-7407 1478, www.selectlatinamerica.co.uk. Quality tailor-made holidays and small group tours.

South American Experience, Welby House, 96 Wilton Rd, Victoria, London SW1V 1DW, T0845-2773366, www.southamericanexperience.com. Flights and accommodation bookings as well as tailor-made trips.

STA Travel, T0871-230 0040, www.statravel.co.uk. 45 branches in the UK. Low-cost flights and tours, good for students.

Steppes Latin America, 51 Castle St, Cirencester, Glos GL7 1QD, T01285-880980, www.steppestravel.co.uk. Tailor-made itineraries for destinations throughout Latin America.

Sunvil Latin America, Sunvil House, Upper Sq, Old Isleworth, Middlesex TW7 7BJ, T020-8568 4499, www.sunvil.co.uk. Small groups or individual tours.

To Escape To, 8 Thames Reach, Purley on Thames, Reading RG8 8TE, T020-7060 6747, www.toescapeto.com. Adventurous tailor-made trips, specialists in family travel.

Trailfinders, 194 Kensington High St, London W8 7RG, T020-7938 3939, www.trailfinders.com. 22 branches throughout the UK.

Tribes Travel, 12 The Business Centre, Earl Soham, Woodbridge, Suffolk IP13 7SA, T01728-685971, www.tribes.co.uk. The associated charitable foundation aims to relieve poverty in indigenous communities.

Trips Worldwide, 14 Frederick Pl, Clifton, Bristol BS8 1AS, T0800-840 0850, www.tripsworldwide.co.uk. Tailor-made tours to South America.

North America

G Adventures, 19 Charlotte St, Toronto, M5V 2H5, Canada, T1-888-800-4100 (in North America), 40 Star St, London W2 1QB, T0870 999 0144, T1-416-260 0999 (outside North America and UK), www.gadventures.com.

Ladatco, 3006 Aviation, Suite 3A, Coconut Grove, FL 33133, USA, T1-800 327 6162, www.ladatco.com. 'Themed' explorer tours based around the Incas, mysticism, etc.

Myths and Mountains, 976 Tee Court, Incline Village, NV 89451, T775-832 5454, www.mythsandmountains.com.

Peru For Less, T1-877-269 0309 (USA toll free) T0203-002 0571 (UK),

www.peruforless.com. Customized tours to Peru and the rest of Latin America, price and service guaranteed. Based in Texas, offices in Lima and Cuzco.

Puchka Peru, www.puchkaperu.com. Specializes in textiles, folk art and market tours.

Tambo Tours, USA, T1-888-2-GO-PERU (246 7378), www.2GOPERU.com. Long-established adventure and tour specialist with offices in Peru and the US. Customized trips to the Amazon and archaeological sites of Peru, Bolivia and Ecuador.

Wildland Adventures, 3516 NE 155 St, Seattle, WA 98155-7412, USA, T206-365 0686, T800-345 4453, www.wildland. com. Specializes in cultural and natural history tours to the Andes and Amazon.

Australia

Adventure World, Level 20, 141 Walker St, North Sydney NSW, T02-8913 0755, and Level 9, 40 St Georges Terrace, Perth 6000, T08-9226 4524, www.adventure world.com.au. Escorted group tours, locally escorted tours and packages to Peru and all of Latin America.

Contours Travel, 287 Victoria St, Melbourne West VIC, T03-9328 8488, www.contourstravel.com.au. Tours to Peru and throughout South and Central America.

Vaccinations

Confirm that your primary courses and boosters are up to date. It is advisable to vaccinate against polio, tetanus, typhoid, hepatitis A and, for more remote areas, rabies. Yellow fever vaccination is obligatory for tropical lowland areas but not the Pacific coast, nor the highlands. Specialist advice should be taken on the best anti-malarials to take before you leave. See also Health, page 588.

Visas and immigration

ID

Keep ID, preferably a passport, on you at all times. You must present your passport when reserving travel tickets. To avoid having to show your passport, you can photocopy the important pages of your passport – including the immigration stamp, and have it legalized by a 'Notario público'. We have received no reports of travellers being asked for onward tickets at Lima airport, or the borders at Tacna, Aguas Verdes, La Tina, Yunguyo or Desaguadero.

Tourist cards

No visa is necessary for citizens of EU countries, most Asian countries, North and South America, and the Caribbean, or for citizens of Andorra, Belarus, Finland, Iceland, Israel, Liechtenstein, Macedonia, Moldova, Norway, Russian Federation, Serbia and Montenegro, Switzerland, Ukraine, Australia, New Zealand and South Africa. A Tourist Card (TAM – Tarjeta Andina de Migración) is free on flights arriving in Peru, or at border crossings for visits up to 183 days. The form is in duplicate, the original given up on arrival and the copy on departure. A new tourist card must be obtained for each re-entry. If your tourist card is stolen or lost, get a new one from **Migraciones**, Digemin, Av España 730, Breña, Lima, T01-200 1081, www.migraciones.gob. pe, Mon-Fri 0830-1300. There are also Migraciones offices in Cuzco (Av El Sol 612, T084-222741, Mon-Fri 0800-1600) and all departmental capitals.

Tourist visas
For citizens of countries not listed above (including Turkey), visas cost US$37.75 or equivalent, for which you require a valid passport, a departure ticket from Peru (or a letter of guarantee from a travel agency), 2 colour passport photos, 1 application form and proof of economic solvency. Tourist visas are valid for 183 days. In the first instance, visit the Migraciones website (as above) for visa forms.

Extensions
Once in Peru tourists may **not** extend their tourist card or visa under any circumstances. It's therefore important to insist on getting the full number of days to cover your visit on arrival (it's at the discretion of the border official). If you plan to return to Peru later in your trip, then only request the number of days you need, as the number of days you are granted (not the days you actually stay) is deducted from your 183-day limit. If you exceed your limit, you'll pay a US$1-per-day fine.

Business visas
If receiving money from Peruvian sources, visitors must have a business visa: requirements are a valid passport, 2 colour passport photos, return ticket and a letter from an employer or Chamber of Commerce stating the nature of business, length of stay and guarantee that any Peruvian taxes will be paid. The visa allows the holder to stay 183 days in the country. On arrival business visitors must register with the Dirección General de Contribuciones for tax purposes.

Student visas
These must be requested from Migraciones (address above) once you are in Peru. In addition to completing the general visa form you must have proof of adequate funds, affiliation to a Peruvian body, a letter of consent from parents or tutors if you are a minor. Full details are on the Migraciones website (in Spanish).

If you wish to change a tourist visa into another type of visa (business, student, resident, etc), you may do so without leaving Peru. Visit Migraciones and obtain the relevant forms.

Weights and measures
Metric.

Women travellers
Generally women travellers should find visiting Peru an enjoyable experience. However, machismo is alive and well here; you should be prepared for this and try not to overreact. When you set

out, err on the side of caution until your instincts have adjusted to the customs of a new culture.

It is easier for men to take the friendliness of locals at face value; women may be subject to much unwanted attention. To minimize this, do not wear suggestive clothing and do not flirt. By wearing a wedding ring, carrying a photograph of your 'husband' and 'children', and saying that your 'husband' is close at hand, you may dissuade an aspiring suitor. If politeness fails, do not feel bad about showing offence and departing. When accepting a social invitation, make sure that someone knows the address and the time you left. Ask if you can bring a friend (even if you do not intend to do so).

If, as a single woman, you can befriend a local woman, you will learn much more about Peru as well as finding out how best to deal with the barrage of suggestive comments, whistles and hisses that will invariably come your way.

Working and volunteering

Voluntourism

There are many opportunities for volunteer work in Peru (**South American Explorers** has an extensive database). Most volunteers do not need a visa for Peru, but you must check with a Peruvian consulate that this applies to you. The site www.trabajovoluntario.org helps volunteers and organizations to get in touch and browse for opportunities. Likewise, www.volunteersouthamerica. net, a continent-wide directory of low-cost to zero-cost programmes, offers several opportunities in Peru. In Cuzco,

Hope Foundation (at Marani Hotel, see page 360) and **Amauta Spanish School** (www.amautaspanish.com) accept volunteers. In Cajamarca, **I-Dev International**, Jr Amazonas 775, T01-992-705660, http://idevinternational.com, has a number of projects and development programmes. In Huaraz, **Seeds of Hope**, Jr Damaso Antunez 782, Huaraz, T043-396305, http://seedsofhope.pe, aims to get children away from work on the street or in the fields and into education. With a similar mission is **Luz de Esperanza**, Av Eternidad 316, Huancayo, T064-439913, www.peruluzdeesperanza. com. For information outside Peru on voluntary work and working abroad, try www.idealist.org for community organizations, volunteer opportunities and non-profit careers, or www. earthwatch.org for scientific and environmental projects.

There is some overlap between volunteering and gap-year or career-break tourism as many people who make this type of trip are going to do some form of work. The websites www. gapyear.com, www.lattitude.org.uk, www.thecareerbreaksite.com and www. yearoutgroup.org cater for that year away. For a range of other options, try www.i-to-i.com, www.handsupholidays.com for project vacations, www.madventurer. com, www.thepodsite.co.uk (Personal Overseas Development) and www. visionsserviceadventures.com, www. projects-abroad.co.uk, for teaching-based projects and other activities. The website www.amerispan.com is principally concerned with language learning and teaching but also has a comprehensive list of volunteer opportunities.

Footnotes
Peru

Basic Spanish for travellers

Learning Spanish is a useful part of the preparation for a trip to Latin America and no volumes of dictionaries, phrase books or word lists will provide the same enjoyment as being able to communicate directly with the people of the country you are visiting. It is a good idea to make an effort to grasp the basics before you go. As you travel you will pick up more of the language and the more you know, the more you will benefit from your stay.

General pronunciation

Whether you have been taught the 'Castilian' pronunciation (*z* and *c* followed by *i* or *e* are pronounced as the *th* in think) or the 'American' pronunciation (they are pronounced as *s*), you will encounter little difficulty in understanding either. Regional accents and usages vary, but the basic language is essentially the same everywhere.

Vowels

a as in English *cat*
e as in English *best*
i as the *ee* in English *feet*
o as in English *shop*
u as the *oo* in English *food*
ai as the *i* in English *ride*
ei as *ey* in English *they*
oi as *oy* in English *toy*

Consonants

Most consonants can be pronounced more or less as they are in English. The exceptions are:

g before *e* or *i* is the same as *j*
h is always silent (except in *ch* as in *chair*)
j as the *ch* in Scottish *loch*
ll as the *y* in *yellow*
ñ as the *ni* in English *onion*
rr trilled much more than in English
x depending on its location, pronounced *x*, *s*, *sh* or *j*

Spanish words and phrases

Greetings, courtesies

hello *hola*
good morning *buenos días*
good afternoon/evening/night *buenas tardes/noches*
goodbye *adiós/chao*
pleased to meet you *mucho gusto*
see you later *hasta luego*
how are you? *¿cómo está?/¿cómo estás?*
I'm fine, thanks *estoy muy bien, gracias*

I'm called... *me llamo...*
what is your name? *¿cómo se llama?/¿cómo te llamas?*
yes/no *sí/no*
please *por favor*
thank you (very much) *(muchas) gracias*
I speak Spanish *hablo español*
I don't speak Spanish *no hablo español*
do you speak English? *¿habla inglés?*

I don't understand *no entiendo/ no comprendo*
please speak slowly *hable despacio por favor*
I am very sorry *lo siento mucho/disculpe*
what do you want? *¿qué quiere?/ ¿qué quieres?*

I want *quiero*
I don't want it *no lo quiero*
good/bad *bueno/malo*
leave me alone *déjeme en paz/ no me moleste*

Questions and requests

Have you got a room for two people? *¿Tiene una habitación para dos personas?*
How do I get to_? *¿Cómo llego a_?*
How much does it cost? *¿Cuánto cuesta? ¿cuánto es?*
I'd like to make a long-distance phone call *Quisiera hacer una llamada de larga distancia*
Is service included? *¿Está incluido el servicio?*

Is tax included? *¿Están incluidos los impuestos?*
When does the bus leave (arrive)? *¿A qué hora sale (llega) el autobús?*
When? *¿cuándo?*
Where is_? *¿dónde está_?*
Where can I buy tickets? *¿Dónde puedo comprar boletos?*
Where is the nearest petrol station? *¿Dónde está la gasolinera más cercana?*
Why? *¿por qué?*

Basics

bank *el banco*
bathroom/toilet *el baño*
bill *la factura/la cuenta*
cash *el efectivo*
cheap *barato/a*
credit card *la tarjeta de crédito*
exchange house *la casa de cambio*
exchange rate *el tipo de cambio*

expensive *caro/a*
market *el mercado*
note/coin *le billete/la moneda*
police (policeman) *la policía (el policía)*
post office *el correo*
public telephone *el teléfono público*
supermarket *el supermercado*
ticket office *la taquilla*

Getting around

aeroplane *el avión*
airport *el aeropuerto*
arrival/departure *la llegada/salida*
avenue *la avenida*
block *la cuadra*
border *la frontera*
bus station *la terminal de autobuses/ camiones*
bus *el bus/el autobús/el camión*
collective/fixed-route taxi *el colectivo*
corner *la esquina*
customs *la aduana*
first/second class *primera/segunda clase*

left/right *izquierda/derecha*
ticket *el boleto*
empty/full *vacío/lleno*
highway, main road *la carretera*
immigration *la inmigración*
insurance *el seguro*
insured person *el/la asegurado/a*
to insure yourself against *asegurarse contra*
luggage *el equipaje*
motorway, freeway *el autopista/ la carretera*

north, south, east, west *norte, sur, este (oriente), oeste (occidente)*
oil *el aceite*
to park *estacionarse*
passport *el pasaporte*
petrol/gasoline *la gasolina*
puncture *el pinchazo/la ponchadura*

street *la calle*
that way *por allí/por allá*
this way *por aquí/por acá*
tourist card/visa *la tarjeta de turista*
tyre *la llanta*
unleaded *sin plomo*
to walk *caminar/andar*

Accommodation

air conditioning *el aire acondicionado*
all-inclusive *todo incluido*
bathroom, private *el baño privado*
bed, double/single *la cama matrimonial/ sencilla*
blankets *las cobijas/mantas*
to clean *limpiar*
dining room *el comedor*
guesthouse *la casa de huéspedes*
hotel *el hotel*
noisy *ruidoso*
pillows *las almohadas*

power cut *el apagón/corte*
restaurant *el restaurante*
room/bedroom *el cuarto/la habitación*
sheets *las sábanas*
shower *la ducha/regadera*
soap *el jabón*
toilet *el sanitario/excusado*
toilet paper *el papel higiénico*
towels, clean/dirty *las toallas limpias/ sucias*
water, hot/cold *el agua caliente/fría*

Health

aspirin *la aspirina*
blood *la sangre*
chemist *la farmacia*
condoms *los preservativos, los condones*
contact lenses *los lentes de contacto*
contraceptives *los anticonceptivos*
contraceptive pill *la píldora anti-conceptiva*
diarrhoea *la diarrea*

doctor *el médico*
fever/sweat *la fiebre/el sudor*
pain *el dolor*
head *la cabeza*
period/sanitary towels *la regla/las toallas femeninas*
stomach *el estómago*
altitude sickness *el soroche*

Family

family *la familia*
friend *el amigo/la amiga*
brother/sister *el hermano/la hermana*
daughter/son *la hija/el hijo*
father/mother *el padre/la madre*

husband/wife *el esposo (marido)/ la esposa*
boyfriend/girlfriend *el novio/la novia*
married *casado/a*
single/unmarried *soltero/a*

Months, days and time

January *enero*
February *febrero*
March *marzo*
April *abril*
May *mayo*
June *junio*
July *julio*
August *agosto*
September *septiembre*
October *octubre*
November *noviembre*
December *diciembre*

Monday *lunes*
Tuesday *martes*
Wednesday *miércoles*

Thursday *jueves*
Friday *viernes*
Saturday *sábado*
Sunday *domingo*

at one o'clock *a la una*
at half past two *a las dos y media*
at a quarter to three *a cuarto para las tres/a las tres menos quince*
it's one o'clock *es la una*
it's seven o'clock *son las siete*
it's six twenty *son las seis y veinte*
it's five to nine *son las nueve menos cinco*
in ten minutes *en diez minutos*
five hours *cinco horas*
does it take long? *¿tarda mucho?*

Numbers

one *uno/una*
two *dos*
three *tres*
four *cuatro*
five *cinco*
six *seis*
seven *siete*
eight *ocho*
nine *nueve*
ten *diez*
eleven *once*
twelve *doce*
thirteen *trece*
fourteen *catorce*
fifteen *quince*

sixteen *dieciséis*
seventeen *diecisiete*
eighteen *dieciocho*
nineteen *diecinueve*
twenty *veinte*
twenty-one *veintiuno*
thirty *treinta*
forty *cuarenta*
fifty *cincuenta*
sixty *sesenta*
seventy *setenta*
eighty *ochenta*
ninety *noventa*
hundred *cien/ciento*
thousand *mil*

Food

avocado *la palta*
baked *al horno*
bakery *la panadería*
banana *la banana*
beans *los frijoles/las habichuelas*
beef *la carne de res*
beef steak *el lomo*
boiled rice *el arroz blanco*
bread *el pan*

breakfast *el desayuno*
butter *la manteca*
cake *la torta*
chewing gum *el chicle*
chicken *el pollo*
chilli or green pepper *el ají/pimiento*
clear soup, stock *el caldo*
cooked *cocido*
dining room *el comedor*

egg el huevo
fish el pescado
fork el tenedor
fried frito
garlic el ajo
goat el chivo
grapefruit la toronja/el pomelo
grill la parrilla
grilled/griddled a la plancha
guava la guayaba
ham el jamón
hamburger la hamburguesa
hot, spicy picante
ice cream el helado
jam la mermelada
knife el cuchillo
lemon el limón
lobster la langosta
lunch el almuerzo/la comida
meal la comida
meat la carne
minced meat la carne picada
onion la cebolla
orange la naranja
pepper el pimiento

pasty, turnover la empanada/el pastelito
pork el cerdo
potato la papa
prawns los camarones
raw crudo
restaurant el restaurante
salad la ensalada
salt la sal
sandwich el bocadillo
sauce la salsa
sausage la longaniza/el chorizo
scrambled eggs los huevos revueltos
seafood los mariscos
soup la sopa
spoon la cuchara
squash la calabaza
squid los calamares
supper la cena
sweet dulce
to eat comer
toasted tostado
turkey el pavo
vegetables los legumbres/vegetales
without meat sin carne
yam el camote

Drink
beer la cerveza
boiled hervido/a
bottled en botella
camomile tea la manzanilla
canned en lata
coffee el café
coffee, white el café con leche
cold frío
cup la taza
drink la bebida
drunk borracho/a
firewater el aguardiente
fruit milkshake el batido/licuado
glass el vaso
hot caliente
ice/without ice el hielo/sin hielo

juice el jugo
lemonade la limonada
milk la leche
mint la menta
rum el ron
soft drink el refresco
sugar el azúcar
tea el té
to drink beber/tomar
water el agua
water, carbonated el agua mineral
  con gas
water, still mineral el agua mineral
  sin gas
wine, red el vino tinto
wine, white el vino blanco

Key verbs

to go	ir	to be	ser	estar
I go	voy	I am	soy	estoy
you go (familiar)	vas	you are	eres	estás
he, she, it goes,		he, she, it is,		
you (formal) go	va	you (formal) are	es	está
we go	vamos	we are	somos	estamos
they, you (plural) go	van	they, you (plural) are	son	están

(ser is used to denote a permanent state, whereas estar is used to denote a positional or temporary state.)

to have (possess)	tener
I have	tengo
you (familiar) have	tienes
he, she, it,	
you (formal) have	tiene
we have	tenemos
they, you (plural) have	tienen
there is/are	hay
there isn't/aren't	no hay

This section has been assembled on the basis of glossaries compiled by André de Mendonça and David Gilmour of South American Experience, London, and the Latin American Travel Advisor, No 9, March 1996.

TRAVEL TIP
Menu reader

Ají Hot pepper, found on every table as either a sauce or pepper slices, served with lemon wedges and meant for squeezing into the soup.
Ají de gallina Strips of chicken in a spicy cream sauce.
Almuerzo The midday meal. A set lunch is called *menú*, see below.
Anticuchos Kebabs of beef heart, popular street food.
Arroz Rice. White rice accompanies most dishes in Peru.
Cabrito Goat stew, typical of the north coast.
Caigua rellena A local vegetable stuffed with ground meat.
Cau cau Tripe.
Causa rellena Cold mashed potatoes with lemon juice, tuna or chicken salad and mayonnaise.
Cebada A non-alcoholic drink made from barley.
Cebiche (ceviche) The flagship of Peruvian cooking. Raw fish (*cebiche de pescado*) or fish and seafood (*cebiche mixto*) marinated in lemon juice, served mid-morning to lunchtime. It doesn't keep well and is best avoided in the evening.
Cena Supper or the equivalent of *menú* served in the evening, but usually less inspired.
Chicha morada Very popular non-alcoholic drink make from purple corn.
Desayuno Breakfast.
Escabeche de pescado o pollo Fried fish or chicken seasoned with pickled onions and hot peppers. May be served warm or cold.

Gaseosa Any soft drink.

Juanes Rice or manioc with bits of chicken, pork or fish, wrapped and steamed in *bijao* leaves, typical of the jungle.

Lomito saltado Strips of beef stir fired with potatoes, onions, tomatoes and hot peppers. Very popular with Peruvians and visitors alike.

Manjar blanco Spreadable soft toffee.

Mazamorra morada A purple corn-flour pudding served as a snack or light dessert.

Menú The set midday meal served at economical restaurants, not to be confused with the English word 'menu' which is *'la carta'* in Spanish.

Olluquito Strips of *olluco*, a small tuber related to the potato, cooked with ground meat.

Pallares Lima beans.

Palta rellena Avocado filled with tuna or chicken salad.

Papa a la huancaína Slices of cold boiled potato in a spicy creamy cheese sauce.

Papa rellena Mashed-potato fritters filled with ground meat.

Parihuela A hearty fish and seafood chowder.

Pastel de papas Potato and cheese casserole.

Pollo broster Deep-fried battered chicken.

Pollo a la brasa Barbeque chicken, a very popular evening meal.

Rocoto relleno Hot peppers stuffed with ground meat.

Salteado de vainitas Green beans and potatoes fried with eggs, a relatively common vegetarian option.

Sopa a la minuta Beef soup with thin noodles.

Sopa criolla A hearty beef soup.

Sudado de pecado Fish served in its broth.

Tallarín verde Spaghetti in a green herb sauce, usually served with beef or liver.

Tamales Ground corn with bits of pork or chicken, wrapped and steamed in banana leaves.

Index → Entries in bold refer to maps

Price codes

Where to stay

$$$$ over US$150
$$$ US$66-150
$$ US$30-65
$ under US$30

Price of a double room in high season, including taxes.

Restaurants

$$$ over US$12
$$ US$7-12
$ US$6 and under

Prices for a two-course meal for one person, excluding drinks or service charge.

FOOTPRINT

Features

Robert and Daisy Kunstaetter

In this edition Robert and Daisy have taken on co-authorship of the Peru Handbook for the first time but their experience with the country goes back over 25 years. Even so, it was not until they spent 12 months trekking and travelling in Peru between 2013 and 2014 that they began to really feel comfortable with it. Daisy hails from neighbouring Ecuador, Robert from Canada, and they had regularly travelled in Peru for work and play. But it was in both their natures as well as the nature of Peru that they had to walk the country in order to get a grip on it. Over the preceding years and miles, Robert and Daisy had become regular correspondents for Footprint, helping to update annual editions of the *South American Handbook*. Based in Ecuador since 1993, they have been closely involved with tourism there as well as in Peru and Bolivia. They are authors, co-authors, contributors to and cartographers for numerous Footprint guidebooks. They are also authors of a trekking guide to Ecuador and are currently writing one for Peru.

Ben Box

Author of the six previous editions of the Peru Handbook, Ben has been a freelance writer specializing in Iberian and Latin American affairs since 1980. He has contributed to newspapers, magazines and learned tomes, usually on the subject of travel. He has been editor of the *South American Handbook* since 1989. He has also been involved in Footprint Handbooks on *Central America & Mexico*, the *Caribbean Islands*, *Brazil*, *Peru*, *Cuzco & the Inca Heartland*, *Bolivia*, *Peru*, *Bolivia and Ecuador* and *Jamaica*. He is a graduate of the University of Southampton, UK, in Spanish, with Portuguese Studies, and has a PhD in the same subjects from the University of London. He has a strong interest in Latin American literature and speaks Spanish, Portuguese and French as well as English. In the British summer he plays cricket for his local village side and year round he attempts to achieve some level of self-sufficiency in fruit and veg in a rather unruly country garden in Suffolk.

Correspondents

Chris Benway

Originally from the USA, Chris has made his home in Huaraz since 1997, where he lives with wife Isabel and their two sons. He runs a popular café and provides logistic support for mountaineering groups and expeditions.

Rob Dover

Rob came to Peru from England in 1997. When not guiding tours, he divides his time between Chachapoyas and Chiclayo where he lives with his wife Sadie.

Ricardo Espinosa

Ricardo was born in Lima. His 1997 book, *El Perú a toda Costa*, describes his nearly 4000 km walk along the entire desert coast and earned him the nickname of El *Caminante*. *La Gran Ruta Inca* (2002) recounts another of Ricardo's epic journeys on foot, from Quito (Ecuador) to La Paz (Bolivia) along the great Inca road that traverses the highlands of Peru. He is also author of a guide to the natural protected areas of Peru and is active in environmental and cultural conservation. Ricardo lives in Caraz with his wife Analee and their son.

Analía Sarfaty

Analía is a Lima city-girl who, legend has it, fell into a *muyuna* (whirlpool) in Iquitos from which she has yet to emerge. Since 1999 she and her husband Percy have made the Amazon Jungle the focus of their life and work. Together they run a jungle lodge with the same affection as they devote to their teenage son.

Acknowledgements

When we (Robert and Daisy) first arrived in Lima in 1988 there was a strict curfew in force. Friends needed a special permit and had to fly a white flag from their car in order to pick us up at the airport. The peaceful, prosperous and heavily visited Peru described in this book is a far cry from those dark days and it is with much satisfaction that we have witnessed its evolution. At the same time, we are dismayed by the rising tide of unsustainable development in Peru and struck by the irony of so much narrowly focused mass tourism in a country perfectly suited to independent travel.

Peru is too complex to be seen exclusively through our eyes however, and we are grateful to our correspondents for their diverse points of view. This dedicated team of travel professionals and professional travellers has worked hard to share an intimate knowledge of their home. They are listed above and we thank them warmly.

Additional valuable contributions to this edition were made by Carola Behrendt, Richar Cáceres, Alberto & Aidé Cafferata, Cait Cambell, Paul Cripps, Jaime García-Heras, Christian Martínez, Keith Parkin, Gustavo Rondón, Mark Smith and Iris & Yvo Tettamanti. We would also like to thank all of the following for their assistance, including those readers who wrote about their experiences in Peru: Yashira Avalos, Baruch & Aviva Aziza, Catalina Borda, Otto Brun. Felipe Díaz, Yahira Echarri, Daniel Egger, Laura Ferradino, Peter & Rosi Frost, Kieron Heath, Michel Hediger, Al Hill, Julia Hofer, Lucho Hurtado, Edwin Junco, Craig Kolthoff, Carlos Manco, José Mestas, Diana Morris, Justo Motta, Kris Murphy, Grace & Marcelo Naranjo, Flavia RF Neves, Julio Porras, Hilary Prowse, Gustavo Reeves, Ronal Salvador, Anders Schou, Ella Smyth and Esther Vera. We likewise acknowledge the very kind and competent assistance of iPerú throughout the country.

For their help and hospitality in Lima, Ben Box would like to thank Siduith Ferrer and Rick Vecchio; Claudia Miranda (of GHL Hoteles and Sonesta Collection, Peru); Cecilia Kamiche; Miles Buesst; Mónica Moreno and staff at Posada del Parque; Carlos Jiménez of The Andean Experience Co; Maestro Máximo Laura and Sasha McInnes of Puchka Perú. He is also most grateful to a number of people for assistance with the text. Many have already been acknowledged in the *South American Handbook*. This edition of the *Peru Handbook* has also benefited from their generosity. Those not already mentioned above are: John Thirtle, Tony Morrison, Nicholas Asheshov, Richard Leonardi, John and Julia Forrest, Michael White, Eduardo Arambarú, Joaquín de la Piedra, Fiona Cameron and Armando Polanco, Heather MacBrayne and Aaron Zarate and Lic Arql Ignacio Alva Meneses.

This edition is built on the hard work of several generations of Footprint travel writers and editors. We thank the entire Footprint editorial and production team, in particular Sophie Jones and Felicity Laughton.

Credits

Footprint credits

Editor: Sophie Blacksell Jones
Production and layout: Emma Bryers
Maps: Robert Kunstaetter, Kevin Feeney
Colour section: Angus Dawson

Publisher: Patrick Dawson
Managing Editor: Felicity Laughton
Administration: Elizabeth Taylor
Advertising sales and marketing:
John Sadler, Kirsty Holmes,
Debbie Wylde

Photography credits
Front cover: Curioso/Shutterstock.com
Back cover: Top: Tony Waltham/
SuperStock. Bottom: Richard Cummins/
SuperStock

Colour section
Inside front cover: Robert Kunstaetter,
JeremyRichards/Shutterstock.com.
Page 1: Christian Vinces/Shutterstock.
com. **Page 2**: Dirk Ercken/Shutterstock.
com. **Page 4**: Christian Vinces/Shutterstock.
com, Minden Pictures/Superstock.
Page 5: Fotos593/Shutterstock.com, age
fotostock/Superstock, HUGHES Herv/
Superstock, Terry Carr/Dreamstime, John
Kershner/Shutterstock.com. **Page 6**: Elzbieta
Sekowska/Shutterstock.com, Rafal Cichawa/
Shutterstock.com, Elzbieta Sekowska/
Shutterstock.com. **Page 7**: Mint Images/
Superstock, Anton_Ivanov/Shutterstock.com,
Elzbieta Sekowska/Shutterstock.com, Robert
Kunstaetter. **Page 10**: Robert Kunstaetter.
Page 11: Neale Cousland/Shutterstock.
com. **Page 12**: Robert Kunstaetter, Mikadun/
Shutterstock.com. **Page 13**: Christian Vinces/
Shutterstock.com. **Page 14**: 3523studio/
Shutterstock.com, ostill/Shutterstock.com.
Page 15: Robert Kunstaetter, Mike Theiss/
Superstock, Michal Knitl/Shutterstock.com.
Page 16: Ksenia Ragozina/Shutterstock.com.

Printed in Spain by GraphyCems

Publishing information
Footprint Peru
9th edition
© Footprint Handbooks Ltd
July 2015

ISBN: 978 1 910120 31 6
CIP DATA: A catalogue record for this
book is available from the British Library

® Footprint Handbooks and the
Footprint mark are a registered
trademark of Footprint Handbooks Ltd

Published by Footprint
6 Riverside Court
Lower Bristol Road
Bath BA2 3DZ, UK
T +44 (0)1225 469141
F +44 (0)1225 469461
footprinttravelguides.com

Distributed in the USA by
National Book Network, Inc.

Every effort has been made to ensure
that the facts in this guidebook are
accurate. However, travellers should still
obtain advice from consulates, airlines,
etc about travel and visa requirements
before travelling. The authors and
publishers cannot accept responsibility
for any loss, injury or inconvenience
however caused.

Footprint Mini Atlas
Peru

Map 1

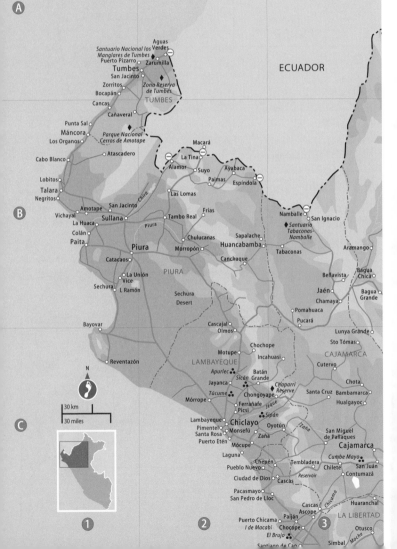

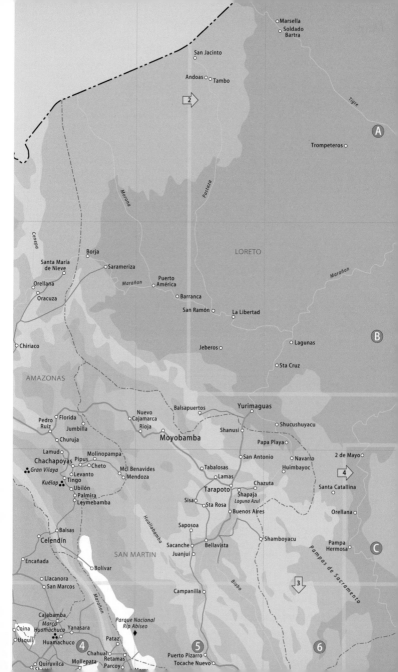

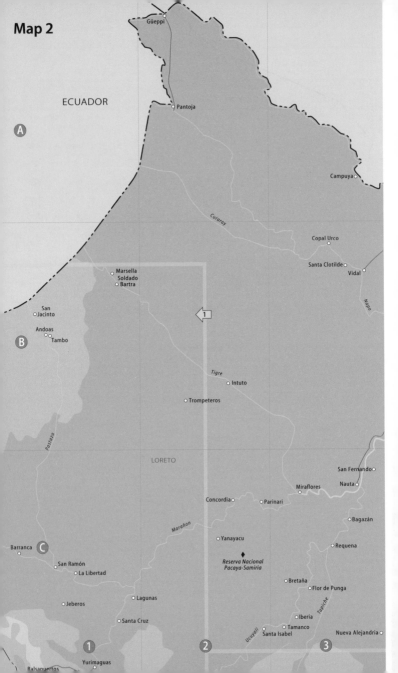

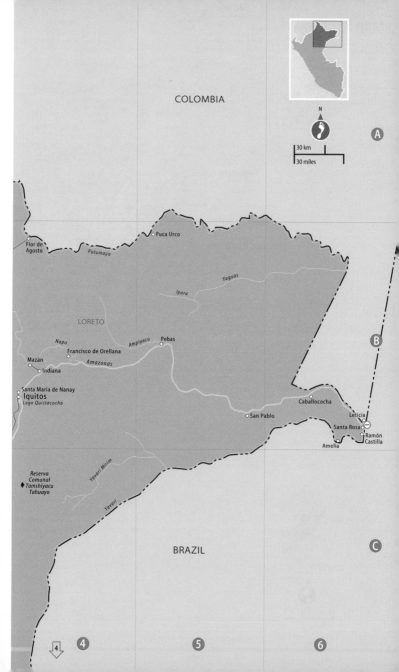

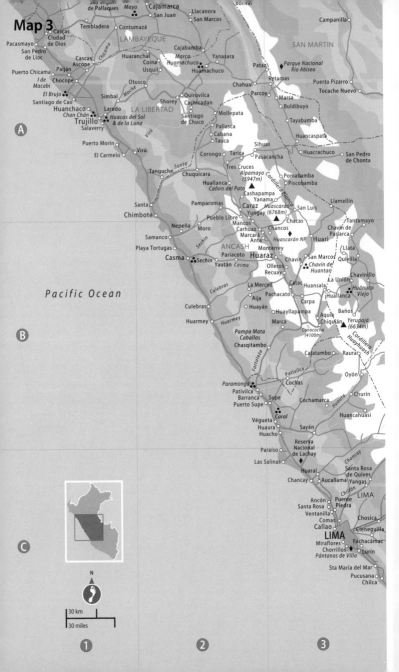

Map 3

Pacific Ocean

N

30 km
30 miles

A **B** **C**

1 **2** **3**

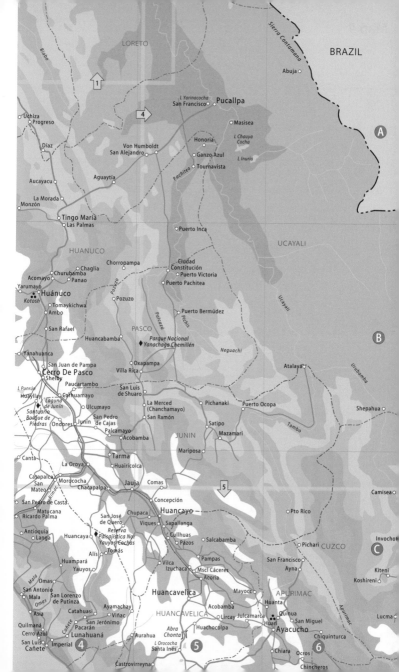

Map 4

LORETO

Orellana

Conamaná

Cerro do Canchyauya

Pampas de Sacramento

Sierra Contamana

Abuja

L Yarinacocha   Pucallpa

Masisea

Honoria   L Chauya Cocha

Von Humboldt
San Alejandro   Ganzo Azul

Pachitea   L Inuria

Tournavista

Aguaytía

HUANUCO

Puerto Inca

Chorropampa   Ciudad Constitución

UCAYALI

Puerto Victoria

Palcazú   Puerto Pachitea

Pozuzo

Curanja

Puerto Bermúdez

Huancabamba   **PASCO**

Neguachi

Oxapampa

Villa Rica   Atalaya   Ucayali

San Lus de Shuaro

La Merced (Chanchamayo)   Pichanaki   Puerto Ocopa

San Ramón   Shepahua

Palcamayo   Satipo

Acobamba   Mazamari   Tambo

JUNIN

Tarma   Mariposa   **CUZCO**

Huairicolca

Jauja   Comas

Chacapalpa   Concepción   Camisea

San José de Quero   Chupaca   Huancayo

Viques

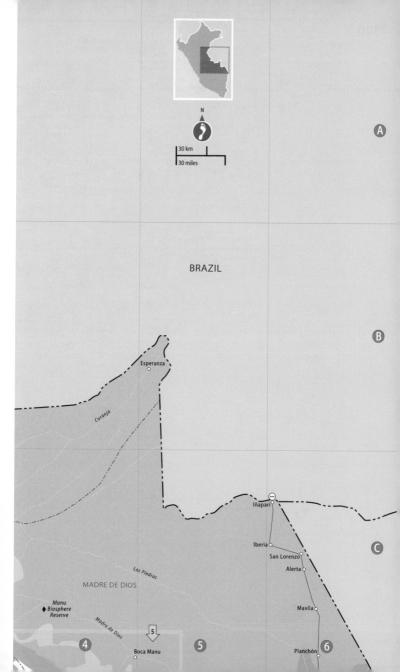

BRAZIL

Esperanza

Curanja

Iñapari

Iberia

San Lorenzo

Alerta

Las Piedras

MADRE DE DIOS

Manu
Biosphere
Reserve

Madre de Dios

Mavila

Boca Manu

Planchón

A

B

C

4

5

6

30 km
30 miles

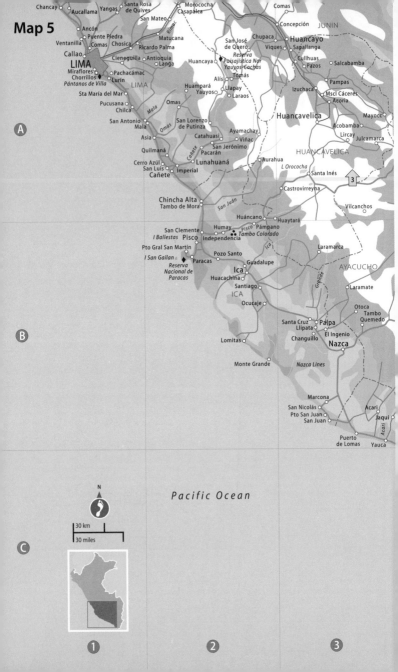

Map 5

Chancay · Aucallama · Yangas · Santa Rosa de Quives · Casapalca · Morococha · Comas

JUNIN

Concepción

Ancón · Puente Piedra · San Mateo · Río Rímac

Ventanilla · Comas · Chosica · Ricardo Palma · Matucana · San José de Quero · Chupaca · Huancayo

Callao · Cieneguilla · Antioquía · Huancaya · Viques · Sapallanga

LIMA · Miraflores · Pachacámac · Langa · Reserva Paisajística Nor Yauyos-Cochas · Cullhuas · Salcabamba

Chorrillos · Lurín · Pántanos de Villa · Huampará · Yauyos · Alis · Tomás · Pazos

Sta María del Mar · Omas · Llapay · Laraos · Izuchaca · Msci Cáceres

Pucusana · Chilca · San Lorenzo de Putinza · Acoria · Mayocc

San Antonio · Mala · Omas · Ayamachay · Huancavelica · Acobamba

Asia · Catahuasi · Viñac · HUANCAVELICA · Lircay · Julcamarca

Quilmaná · Pacarán · San Jerónimo · Aurahua · L Orococha

Cerro Azul · Lunahuaná · Santa Inés · **3**

San Luis · Imperial · Cañete · Castrovirreyna · Vilcanchos

Chincha Alta · Tambo de Mora · San Juán · Huáncano · Huaytará

Humay · Pámpano · Laramarca

San Clemente · Tambo Colorado · Pisco · Independencia · I Ballestas · AYACUCHO

Pto Gral San Martín · Pozo Santo

I San Gailán · Paracas · Guadalupe · Ica · Laramate

Reserva Nacional de Paracas · Huacachina · Santiago

Ocucaje · Otoca · Tambo Quemedo

Santa Cruz · Palpa · Llipata · El Ingenio

Lomitas · Changuillo · Nazca

Monte Grande · *Nazca Lines*

Marcona · Acarí · Jaqui

San Nicolás · Pto San Juan · San Juan · Puerto de Lomas · Yauca

Pacific Ocean

N

30 km
30 miles

A

B

C

1 · **2** · **3**

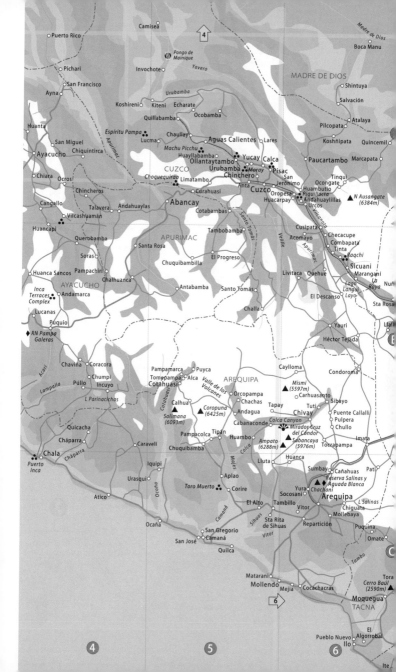

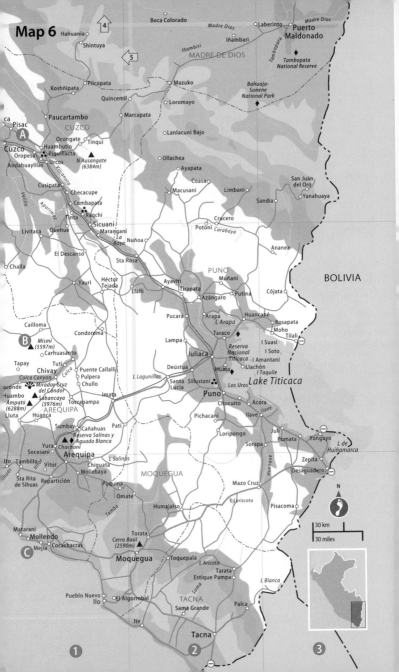

Distance chart

Distances in kilometres
1 kilometre = 0.62 miles

	Arequipa	Ayacucho	Cajamarca	Cuzco	Chachapoyas	Chiclayo	Huancayo	Huaraz	Ica	Lima	Piura	Puerto Maldonado	Puno	Tacna	Trujillo
Ayacucho	1078														
Cajamarca	1860	1394													
Cuzco	515	597	1957												
Chachapoyas	2195	1729	335	2292											
Chiclayo	1773	1307	260	1870	622										
Huancayo	1308	257	1150	854	1485	1063									
Huaraz	1417	951	857	1514	1192	770	707								
Ica	706	372	1154	803	1489	1067	602	711							
Lima	997	556	856	1153	1186	763	299	517	303						
Piura	1982	1516	496	2079	831	209	1272	979	1276	973					
Puerto Maldonado	1048	1130	2490	533	2825	2403	1387	2047	1336	1637	2612				
Puno	326	986	2186	389	2573	2099	1243	1743	1032	1542	2308	922			
Tacna	284	1306	2144	799	2479	2057	1592	1701	990	1293	2266	1332	610		
Trujillo	2022	1100	294	1663	629	207	856	563	860	557	416	2196	1892	1850	
Tumbes	2265	1799	750	2362	1114	492	1555	1262	1559	1299	283	2895	2591	2549	699

Index

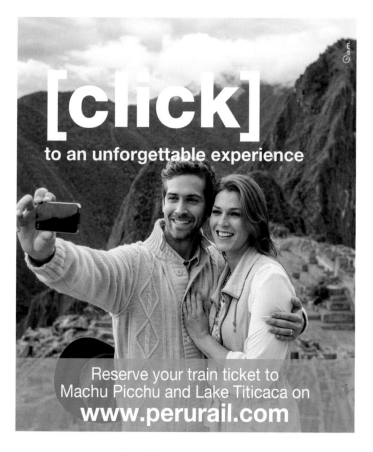